A Fatal Balancing Act

A FATAL BALANCING ACT

The Dilemma of the Reich Association of Jews in Germany, 1939–1945

Beate Meyer

Translated by William Templer

berghahn
NEW YORK · OXFORD
www.berghahnbooks.com

Published by
Berghahn Books
www.berghahnbooks.com

English-language edition
©2013, 2016 Berghahn Books
First paperback edition published in 2016

German-language edition
©2011 Wallstein Verlag GmbH
Tödliche Gratwanderung
By Beate Meyer

Library of Congress Cataloging-in-Publication Data

Meyer, Beate, 1952– author.
[Tödliche Gratwanderung. English]
A fatal balancing act : the dilemma of the Reich Association of Jews in Germany,
1939–1945 / Beate Meyer ; translated by William Templer. — First edition.
pages ; cm
Includes bibliographical references and index.
ISBN 978-1-78238-027-6 (hardback) — ISBN 978-1-78533-214-2 (paperback) —
ISBN 978-1-78238-028-3 (ebook)
1. Reichsvereinigung der Juden in Deutschland. 2. Jews—Germany—History—
1933–1945. 3. Holocaust, Jewish (1939–1945)—Germany. 4. Germany—Ethnic
relations. I. Title.
DS134.255M4913 2013
940.53'18—dc23

2013005560

British Library Cataloguing in Publication Data

A catalogue record for this book is available from the British Library

The translation was generously supported by the
Katharina & Gerhard Hoffmann Stiftung, Hamburg
and the Institut für die Geschichte der deutschen Juden, Hamburg

ISBN: 978-1 78238-027-6 hardback
ISBN: 978-1-78533-214-2 paperback
ISBN: 978-1-78238-028-3 ebook

Contents

TABLES

ACKNOWLEDGMENTS

I owe a debt of gratitude to many persons and institutions for their diverse support, helpful suggestions, and manifold assistance in completing this book. I would like to thank the German Research Foundation (DFG), which supported this project financially and also made it possible for me to present partial findings at international conferences. Prior to the actual work on the book, I was able to collect extensive material as a co-director of the exhibition project "Juden in Berlin 1933–1945" at the Foundation Neue Synagoge—Centrum Judaicum in Berlin. I had the good fortune of being able to carry out the first intensive archival studies at Yad Vashem in Jerusalem, thanks to a fellowship from the International Institute for Holocaust Research; I was then able to write most of the manuscript itself at the Institute for the History of the German Jews in Hamburg, and to complete it at the Center for Advanced Holocaust Studies at the United States Holocaust Memorial Museum (USHMM) in Washington. There I was privileged not only to use their extensive archives and superb library, but also profited from many discussions with interested and informed colleagues, whose findings and suggestions have also been utilized in this book.

Monika Richarz, when still director of the Institute for the History of the German Jews a decade ago, encouraged me to expand on this topic as a research project and to stick with the theme, and she was kind enough to read every essay I wrote on it with never-diminishing interest. I owe her special thanks. The encouragement from Israeli colleagues with whom I was able to discuss my project at Yad Vashem was extremely helpful, especially my talks with the late David Bankier, Dan Michman, Avraham Barkai, Walter Zvi Bacharach, and Otto Dov Kulka. They all welcomed my commitment in dealing with this sensitive topic, previously dealt with solely by Jewish historians.

I would like to express very special heartfelt thanks to Otto Dov Kulka for his generous support and encouragement, who himself chose work on the history of the Reich Representation and the Reich Association of the

Jews in Germany as a long-term project and published a large-scale volume of documentation on the Reich Representation.

I also wish to thank my two first readers, Frank Bajohr and Avraham Barkai. I could not have found better scholars for the task: they read each part of the book in its first draft, quickly sending me helpful feedback and numerous suggestions. Not only did they invest a great deal of time; of special value was their encouragement for me to continue with the study, and they responded in such a way that I felt they were eager to receive the next chapter. I also wish to express my sincere thanks to Stefanie Schüler-Springorum, Susanne Heim, and Jürgen Matthäus, who later intensively perused individual chapters or the entire manuscript with a critical eye, and gave me further very valuable suggestions.

In the course of archival research, evaluations, and the writing of the manuscript, I also received information and suggestions about literature and source materials, or answers to my questions from a number of dedicated archivists, whose names cannot all be mentioned here, but to whom I owe a great debt of gratitude; Barbara Welker from the Centrum Judaicum is representative as one among many. I was likewise assisted by numerous librarians, of whom I wish to mention Ron Coleman and Vincent Slatt of the USHMM as representative again of many, and by a number of colleagues who provided helpful input. Among them, I owe special thanks to Hermann Simon, Anna Hájková, the late Stefi Jersch-Wenzel and her late husband Thomas Jersch, Diana Schulle, Christiaan F. Rüter, Monica Kingreen, Gudrun Maierhof, and Beate Kosmala; I hope to have expressed my gratitude to all the others where relevant in a footnote, and that I have not forgotten anyone. Thanks to Benjamin Pavel Golubev and Niklas Wieczorek, who did excellent work in editing and arranging the material and corrections for the German and English edition. I wish to thank Hajo Gevers of the Wallstein Verlag for his constant careful attention to the original German manuscript.

For this English language edition, I extend my thanks to Marion Berghahn, Ann Przyzycki DeVita, Adam Capitanio, Elizabeth Berg, the very meticulous copyeditor Caitlin Mahon and their colleagues from Berghahn Books. I would like to thank Lina Bosbach for preparing the index. I am grateful to the Katharina and Gerhard Hoffmann Foundation, Hamburg, the Joseph-Carlebach-Arbeitskreis of the University of Hamburg, and the Institute for the History of German Jews, Hamburg, for financial support of the translation. Finally, I am most especially indebted to translator William Templer, who is based in Shumen in eastern Bulgaria. For many years he has accompanied my work by translating papers and articles into English, and I am grateful for his insightful and perceptive support.

Hamburg, June 2013

ABBREVIATIONS

AJDC	American Jewish Joint Distribution Committee
Altreu	Allgemeine Treuhandstelle für jüdische Auswanderung (General Trusteeship for Jewish Emigration)
BArch	Bundesarchiv (Federal Archive)
BBC	British Broadcasting Corporation
Bln.	Berlin
BStU	Die/der Bundesbeauftragte für die Unterlagen des Staatssicherheitsdienstes der ehemaligen Deutschen Demokratischen Republik (Federal Commissioner for the Stasi Archives, German Democratic Republic)
BZ	Bezirksstelle (district branch)
CJA	Centrum Judaicum, Archiv
CIC	Counter Intelligence Corps
Coll.	Collection
CSR	Tschechoslowakei (Czechoslovakia)
CV	Centralverein deutscher Staatsbürger jüdischen Glaubens (Central Association of German Citizens of the Jewish Faith)
DDP	Deutsche Demokratische Partei (German Democratic Party)
DDR	Deutsche Demokratische Republik (German Democratic Republic)
DFG	Deutsche Forschungsgemeinschaft (German Research Foundation)
DM	Deutsche Mark
DNVP	Deutschnationale Volkspartei (German National People's Party)
DP	displaced persons

FZH	Forschungsstelle für Zeitgeschichte (Research Center for Contemporary History)
Gestapo	Geheime Staatspolizei (Secret State Police)
Hess. HstA	Hessisches Hauptstaatsarchiv (Hesse Central Archive)
HJ	Hitlerjugend (Hitler Youth)
IGdJ	Institut für die Geschichte der deutschen Juden (Institute for the History of the German Jews)
JA	Jewish Agency for Palestine
JDC	see AJDC
JKV	Jüdische Kultusvereinigung (Jewish Religious Association = Jewish Community [Gemeinde])
JOINT	see AJDC
KG	Kultusgemeinde (jüdische) (Religious Community, Jewish = Jewish Community [Gemeinde])
KPD	Kommunistische Partei Deutschlands (German Communist Party)
KV	Kultusvereinigung (jüdische) (Religious Association, Jewish = Jewish Community)
KZ	Konzentrationslager (concentration camp)
LAB	Landesarchiv Berlin (State Archive Berlin)
LA NRW	Landesarchiv Nordrhein-Westfalen (State Archive North Rhine-Westphalia)
LBI, JMB	Leo Baeck Institute, Berlin branch, Jüdisches Museum Berlin (Jewish Museum Berlin)
LBI, NY	Leo Baeck Institute, New York
NSDAP	Nationalsozialistische Deutsche Arbeiterpartei (National Socialist German Workers Party)
NRW HStA	Nordrhein-Westfälisches Hauptstaatsarchiv (Main State Archive North Rhine-Westphalia)
ORT	Russian: Общество ремесленного и земледельческого труда среди евреев в России, ОРТ (Association for the Promotion of Handicrafts and Agriculture Among the Jews in Russia)
OT	Organisation Todt
pag.	page/pages, according to the German archival pagination system; in the notes, the abbreviation p/pp. is used for pagination in an individual document
Paltreu	Palästina-Treuhandstelle (Palestine Trust Office for Advice to German Jews)
RGBl.	Reichsgesetzblatt (Reich Legal Gazette)

RjF	Reichsbund jüdischer Frontsoldaten (Reich Association of Jewish Combat Veterans)
RM	Reichsmark
RSHA	Reichssicherheitshauptamt (Reich Security Main Office)
Rundschr.	Rundschreiben (circular letter)
RV	Reichsvereinigung der Juden in Deutschland (Reich Association of Jews in Germany) [abbreviation used in the text]
RVJD	Reichsvereinigung der Juden in Deutschland (Reich Association of Jews in Germany) [abbreviation used for the archival materials cited]
SA	Sturmabteilungen der NSDAP (storm troopers of the NSDAP)
SBZ	Sowjetisch besetzte Zone (Soviet zone of occupation)
SD	Sicherheitsdienst der SS (Security Service of the SS)
SED	Sozialistische Einheitspartei Deutschlands (Socialist Unity Party of Germany)
SMAD	Sowjetische Militäradministration in Deutschland (Soviet Military Administration in Germany)
SPD	Sozialdemokratische Partei Deutschlands (Social Democratic Party of Germany)
SS	Schutzstaffeln der NSDAP (Protective Squadrons of the NSDAP)
Sta München	Staatsarchiv München (State Archive Munich)
StaHH	Staatsarchiv Hamburg (State Archive Hamburg)
Stanw.	Staatsanwaltschaft (public prosecutor's office)
USHMM	United States Holocaust Memorial Museum
VdN	Verfolgter des Naziregimes (Victim of Nazi Persecution)
Verf.	Verfügung (directive)
Vern.	Vernehmung (interrogation)
VM	Vertrauensmann (intermediary functionary)
VO	Verordnung (decree)
VVN	Vereinigung der Verfolgten des Naziregimes (Association of those Persecuted by the Nazi Regime)
YV	Yad Vashem
WLL	Wiener Library, London
ZAGJD	Zentralarchiv zur Erforschung der Geschichte der Juden in Deutschland (Central Archive for Research on the History of the Jews in Germany)
ZVfD	Zionistische Vereinigung für Deutschland (Zionist Association of Germany)

INTRODUCTION

A study that deals with the behavior of German-Jewish functionaries in the Reich Association of Jews in Germany (Reichsvereinigung der Juden in Deutschland, RV) during the Holocaust risks receiving unwanted applause from the wrong side, that is, from those who wish to contend that the persecuted Jews participated in their own murder. It is my hope that my work does not in any way abet such mistaken assumptions, which serve to exculpate the German perpetrators. Rather, I have sought to determine what specific and ever-changing challenges and constraints the Jewish representatives faced in the years 1939 to 1945, and how they reacted to and grappled with these. Given the radicalization of the persecution of the Jews, intensified to the level of murder—evident from the rapid change in meaning that the concept of the so-called Final Solution was undergoing—they were repeatedly forced to attempt to fulfill what the National Socialist (NS) state demanded of them in a way that was not harmful to the Jewish population in the German Reich, but rather, if possible, was beneficial to the Jews remaining there. This was also the case when they were forced to participate directly in the preparations for the mass deportations. As we see more clearly in retrospect than the (Jewish) contemporaries were able to perceive at the time, such a delicate and dangerous balancing act was ultimately an impossible task. Nonetheless, over the span of some six years, they made the repeated attempt to achieve this aim.

Readers looking for simple answers will not find them here. Even if I focus on the attitudes, efforts, and ultimate unavoidable failure of the German-Jewish functionaries, it is important to be ever mindful of a central fact: they did not create the situation in which they were forced to act. If I endeavor to determine their latitude for action, this does not imply that they were in a position to exploit, refine, or expand that room to maneuver as they might desire. Moreover, even when they agreed to be included in (a small part of) the preparatory work leading to the murder of the Jews, and later did not refuse such entanglement, this does not mean that they were guilty of complicity in the Holocaust. That burden of culpability lies clearly with the perpetrators, their accomplices, and bystanders.[1]

At the outset of my investigation, I asked myself whether the Reich Association of Jews in Germany had been a kind of German *Judenrat* (pl. *Judenräte*), a Jewish council similar to those set up in the occupied territories.[2] The task of the Jewish councils in the ghettos or in a specific territory was to implement the measures ordered by the occupiers, to keep statistics, vacate apartments, provide forced laborers, hand over valuables and tribute payments, and assemble transports to the extermination camps based on corresponding instructions given to them. However, as a rule, they also tried to organize provision of food, care for the needy, delay execution of orders imposed on them or work out ways to mitigate their severity, and to these ends exploit the rivalries that existed among the various factions within the occupiers. In short, their efforts were aimed at "buying survival time" for the respective ghetto, or, later, for its inhabitants deemed still able to work.[3] As a rule, the German occupiers wanted the Jewish Communities (*Gemeinden*, sing. *Gemeinde*) to elect the Jewish councils themselves. These were to be headed by rabbis and influential individuals who were trustworthy and whom the ghetto residents would listen to and obey.

In the course of my own work on Jewish *Mischlinge* (i.e., "half Jews" and "quarter Jews," "mixed-blood" Jews, sing. *Mischling*) and mixed marriages, I had repeatedly encountered the Reich Association of Jews in Germany, often mentioned in very neutral terms in the memoirs of survivors, sometimes noted full of gratitude or vilified with undisguised hatred. But much more frequently, it was not mentioned at all, although the Jewish spouses in mixed marriages and their children had had contact with the organization in a whole ensemble of concerns.[4] By decree in 1939, all German or stateless Jews living in the German Reich had been forced to become members of the Reich Association.[5] Some joined it voluntarily, and even those who kept their distance from the organization were included in its files and received orders and instructions from it. Between 1939 and 1945, all "full Jews," according to the NS definition, who had not successfully concealed their Jewish origin had to deal with this organization in all matters of emigration, social welfare, relatives needy of support, children of school age, assignment to a *Judenhaus* ("Jews' house," pl. *Judenhäuser*), or for information of any kind. The members had to pay their dues, all Jews were obliged to report any change of residence or family status, and they were ordered to have any intended request or petition to a government office first checked by the Reich Association, to name but a few reasons for necessary contact. The Reich Association was directly subordinate to the Reich Security Main Office (RSHA), and was required to implement its orders or obtain permits for its activities and those of its district branches. Should the Reich Association be equated for these reasons with the *Judenräte* in the occupied territories?

The Jewish councils and the Reich Association had many similarities: the Jewish functionaries active on the boards of its predecessor organization, the Reich Representation of German Jews (Reichsvertretung der deutschen Juden), were placed in offices and leadership positions in the successor organization (at least those who were still in the country), at their head the respected rabbi Leo Baeck.[6] Like the Jewish councils, the Reich Association was also required to implement Nazi German policy on the Jews in the Jewish population, keep statistics, evacuate apartments, collect valuables, and prepare confiscations of property. However, the German Jews did not live in ghettos, although in many localities they were forced to reside in assigned residential areas, in *Judenhäuser* or in barracks camps. The Nazi state had largely taken over the organization of forced labor, but the Reich Association was forced to participate in the financial looting of the members and deportees. This money was deposited in blocked accounts to which the Jews had no access, and confiscation of property and assets upon deportation was to the benefit of the German Reich. Thus, there are certainly external similarities with the Jewish councils, but these should not mislead us to inappropriately equate these institutions: the Reich Association had been established primarily to promote mass emigration. Its other tasks did not gain central importance until later over the course of time, and in terms of the motivation of its leadership, it was perceived as the continuation of the predecessor organization, which had been formed freely in 1933 to serve as a mouthpiece and to represent the interests of the Jews vis-à-vis the Nazi German state. The term *Judenrat* is laden with certain further tacit suspicions: for one, it suggests that ultimately, the Jewish representatives on the council acted against the interests of their wards, finally delivering them into the hands of death. Second, it intimates that there had been a real alternative for action in the East. In the occupied territories, that concrete option was flight: to flee from the ghetto into the forest and join the armed resistance. However, the German Jews had no such option: they lived in the land of the perpetrators, surrounded by German *Volksgenossen* who profited more or less from the employment bans on Jews, their expulsion and plundering. The official anti-Jewish measures in the *Altreich* (Germany in its 1937 borders) had not been imposed by some foreign occupying power, but rather had been conceived, successively implemented, and intensified in the country where they were citizens and with whose culture they largely identified. German forests provided Jews no protection, and in most instances they were forbidden by new legislation from even entering these wooded areas. Partisan bands had not been formed in the *Altreich*; instead, a dictatorship had established itself that enjoyed broad support, and with which most *Volksgenossen* could accommodate quite well (at least until 1943). Ultimately, the German resistance movement did not begin to deal with the persecution of the Jews and their murder until 1943, when most Jews had already been killed.[7] In addition, the Jewish population in Germany that had not left the country by the time a prohibition on emigration was enacted in October 1941 was a group quite advanced in age, and with a high proportion of females. If they had remained leaderless, would they then have been able to rescue more people, as philosopher Hannah Arendt criticized the German-Jewish leadership in retrospect? Arendt called the role of the "Jewish leaders" "undoubtedly the darkest chapter of the whole dark story."[8] Yet she was mistaken if she sought to refer to the entire period from 1939 to 1945: yes, perhaps younger, more courageous Jews would have been able to flee across the border into neighboring countries up until the outbreak of the war. Maybe they would have succeeded in avoiding capture by the German troops. Nonetheless, these vague possibilities to flee the Reich were an option for only a very few, and only until September 1939. And these options evaporated in the autumn of 1941 with the beginning of the mass deportations. The majority of the German Jews, unorganized and leaderless (and here Arendt was right), would likely have lived in "chaos and plenty of misery."[9] And this majority, we must recall, was aged, often ill, or in need of care.

Most German historians who have dealt with the persecution of the Jews did not ask what possibilities and alternatives were open to the Jewish functionaries: for them, the Jews had been objects of action taken by the state and ultimately victims of the Holocaust, and as such they were devoid of any latitude for action, motives, or maxims.[10] By contrast, Jewish historians dealt intensively with these topics from the 1950s well into the 1970s.[11] Dan Diner gave important theoretical stimuli for analyzing the events.[12] Doron Rabinovici drew on Diner's ideas in his study of the Vienna Jewish Community, the "prototype" of a Jewish council,[13] and these ideas have also influenced the present study of the Reich Association. Thus, Diner stressed that the Jews (and Jewish councils) were acting in a historical situation in which, presumably or actually, no final decision on their fate had as yet been made by the Nazi leaders. Consequently, they proceeded on the assumption that they still had "socially viable time" available.[14] Confronted with real or apparent alternatives that might make their survival possible, they were forced "to anticipate the thinking of the National Socialists" and to develop a strategy to allow them to have a moderating influence on the thinking of their oppressors. They had to try to understand the logic of their adversaries rationally, and to attune themselves to this logic in order to be able to put forward proposals and suggestions that were in the interest of the National Socialists, but that always also served the aim of their own survival. For the Jewish councils in the ghettos, this was the exchange of work in order to buy time to survive.[15] This ultimately meant they had to sacrifice some in their community in order to save the others.[16] Yet unlike what the Jews assumed, the National Socialists, driven by a will to destruction, did not behave rationally; rather, as Diner terms it, they acted "counter-rationally." They negated all "anticipations of human behavior ordinarily deemed to be universally valid," instead bringing about the "rupture of civilization" (*Zivilisationsbruch*). Diner notes:

> At the phenomenon's center, the Jewish councils hovered between self-preservation and self-destruction; or put otherwise, at its center lay self-destruction by means of self-preservation. We face here a specific and terrible instance of a universally applicable borderline experience; it addresses basic assumptions about human nature and human behavior, bringing us to the fragile outer limits of reason and rationality.[17]

Caught up in the vortex of this "borderline experience," or what Diner terms a "boundary locus," this also means that the Jews were unable to fall back on any collective or individual experience in order to place in a familiar context what was happening to them and what they were reacting to; they were unable to apply again or modify any strategy that had been successful at some point in the past.[18] At the end of the process, they found themselves in a "trap for action": either they would contribute to the unobstructed course of destruction, or, by resisting, provoke mortal dangers for the community.[19] For that reason, the point of departure for all efforts by the Jewish functionaries was concern for the welfare of the Jewish community. Doron Rabinovici summarized his findings on the Vienna Jewish Community: "It was not because the Jewish councils betrayed the Jewish community but because they attempted to act in their interest that the Jewish functionaries were condemned to see things from the perspective of the authorities. They had to think like Nazis in the interest of the Jews. ... They followed the enemy's orders closely because they hoped that in return it would also keep to the system it had itself ordained."[20] The Jewish functionaries tried to get their persecutors to adhere to rules and ways of behavior that they themselves were also bound to. In order to achieve this, they sought to recognize what the (ostensible) material interests of their persecutors were, as well as disputes among them over competence, their likes and dislikes, and to then make optimum use of this knowledge for their own benefit.

Against this backdrop, I formulated my own research questions: What had motivated the Jewish functionaries to remain in the German Reich and to assume an official position in the Reich Association? How did they orient their behavior within their own institution, vis-à-vis their compulsory members and those in power? What rules did they wish to implement? How did they try to connect their own interests in escape and survival with the orders of the RSHA? Did the German-Jewish functionaries also put forward an imaginary "proposal" for cooperation with their rulers, and what did it entail? Did they study the intentions of their persecutors, and where was it presumably possible for them to build on and utilize these intentions? Did they achieve any success, and if yes, what did that consist of, and how long did it last?

The Jewish functionaries' "own interest" in the period 1939 to October 1941 lay primarily in assisting as many Jews as possible to flee from Germany. From 1941 to 1943, they sought to provide for those remaining in the Reich, while carrying out the orders for preparations for the deportations, seeking at the same time to postpone and mitigate the orders. They did this until, finally, the survival of the members and functionaries themselves was endangered. From 1943 to 1945, after the Reich Association was formally dissolved, Jewish intermediaries, so-called *Vertrauensmänner* (sing. *Vertrauensmann*), looked after the needs of Jews in mixed marriages. Central here too were provision of care and attempts to mitigate the situation as far as was possible, but they likewise were constrained to assist with preparations for the deportations. During all phases, the Jewish functionaries of the first and final hours always worked under strict control and overt or tacit threat of death. Thus, the question of how this impacted their activity and motivation runs like a dark thread through this entire study.

I examine these and further related questions in the five sections of this book: In chapter 1, the chaotic years from 1939 to 1941, after the establishment of the Reichsvereinigung, are explored. In chapter 2, my focus is on the work of their Berlin central office and the Jewish Community in Berlin, where by far most Jews in Germany lived. In chapter 3, the situation elsewhere in the Reich is examined, looking in particular at medium-sized cities where the regional branches of the Reich Association were active. I try to work out common features shared with the situation in Berlin, and also within the territory of the *Altreich*, as well as various differences. Chapter 4 investigates the working conditions of the Jewish intermediaries in the rump organization, the Rest-Reichsvereinigung, after the Reich Association was formally dissolved on 10 June 1943. Finally, chapter 5 looks at the postwar aftermath for the functionaries who had survived and stayed on in Germany, and the burdens and challenges they faced in starting a new life, concluding with a comprehensive summary of the entire study. In each of the five chapters, I also seek to shed light on the personal fate of the German-Jewish functionaries whose work I am examining. Since in contrast with the leading Berlin functionaries and heads of the regional branches, a larger proportion of the intermediaries survived, the final chapter of the study also explores their fate after the war. This look at the period after 1945 is intended to give an impression of the great burden of the past the small remaining German-Jewish community had to grapple with after liberation. The insidious functionalization of the Reich Association within the process of persecution had a lasting poisonous impact on relations within the Jewish Communities and between individuals. It brought the Allied occupying powers into the arena, who pursued a number of the few surviving Jewish functionaries as Gestapo collaborators, and ultimately also impacted on scientific inquiry of this topic.

To date, the history of the Reich Association of Jews in Germany, its leading functionaries, and its regional representatives has not been investigated in terms of the research questions formulated above. The research literature, which I confront critically in all sections of the present study, concentrated mainly on the fact that the Jewish community, even under the extreme conditions of National Socialist rule, preserved its concepts of humanity, its values and dignity.[21] It is the particular merit of Otto Dov Kulka and the late Esriel Hildesheimer to have explored the strands of continuity in the work of the Reich Representation and the Reich Association, which they identified in the spheres of education, vocational training, and social welfare. They concluded that the chief priority for the Jewish leadership in each and every phase of the persecution was to preserve and maintain the material and psychological/spiritual existence of the Jews. Later on, that became the desperate struggle for the survival of the Jews and the humane face of their community.[22] In this they agree with the surviving German-Jewish representatives.[23] Yet the Jewish community was not an isolated, untouched island within the National Socialist dictatorship: the Jewish representatives always worked under direct Nazi control, "whether they cooperated or attempted to sidestep official decrees," as Rabinovici noted regarding functionaries in Vienna.[24] The continuity in personnel stressed by Kulka and Hildesheimer undoubtedly existed, yet the democratic election of the leading functionaries of the

Reich Association lay up to six years in the past, when there were still a large number of Jewish groups operating in Germany. By 1939, most of their electors and colleagues had long since emigrated from the Reich. Nonetheless, the remaining Jewish representatives had actually almost all stayed on in Germany, principally in order to care for the needy. But the Reich Association was subordinated to the powerful RSHA, and the Jewish functionaries, who soon found themselves entrapped in the Reich, were walking down a dangerous path. They cooperated with their oppressors, yet an end to the process was nowhere in sight: in order to make mass emigration possible (especially from 1939 to October 1941) and to preserve the survival of the remaining community, they made decisions and accepted orders under duress that clashed fundamentally with their own identity and convictions. This practice served to turn their aspirations and claims into the very opposite of what they desired, and, with the slightest sign of protest, cost several of their most outstanding leaders, such as Otto Hirsch or Julius Seligsohn, their lives even before the beginning of the mass deportations. These representatives were forced to radically alter their ideas of social care and welfare, and ultimately had to sacrifice a part of the community in order—perhaps—to continue to care for the needs of those remaining and to be able to prevent even worse things. In short, their conceptions of humanity were subjected to an externally imposed rapid process of transformation, and they were in many instances stripped of their human dignity. In addition, from October 1941, they were constrained to participate in preparations for the mass deportations to the ghettos and concentration camps in the occupied Eastern territories. In this way, the focal point of their work successively shifted, until those dependent on protection and social care were likewise deported. To bracket out their part in preparations and organizing for the deportations—which became, step-by-step, in fact the main task of the Reich Association—means, at least at first glance, to concentrate solely on the non-problematic aspects of the history of the Reich Association. For Hildesheimer and Kulka, the history of the Reich Association ends with the deportation of the leading representatives in 1943, who had embodied the organization's continuity with the Reich Representation. However, the deported Jewish functionaries continued their work in the committees inside the Theresienstadt ghetto camp, and their successors in the *Altreich*, the intermediaries, headed up the New Reich Association (or rump organization, the *Rest-Reichsvereinigung*) until the war's end. Most of these final remaining Jewish functionaries had already worked earlier as legal "consultants" (*Konsulenten*, the Nazi term for Jewish lawyers) or "Jewish practitioners for the sick" (*Krankenbehandler*, the Nazi term for Jewish physicians)[25] for the Reich Association or its institutions.

They perhaps had little or no connection with Judaism as a religion, but they were not outsiders, and their activity is an integral component of the history of this organization. In the face of all the hostility they were subjected to by representatives of the Nazi regime or members of the Reich Association, they were the last Jewish officials who endeavored to protect the remaining not yet deported Jews.

In the 1960s, Otto Dov Kulka came across the extant though not complete files of the Reich Association in the Central State Archive in Potsdam in the German Democratic Republic (GDR),[26] now accessible in the Federal Archive (Bundesarchiv) Berlin and in copy form in other archives. Naturally, the official protocols of the association's board, memoranda, and correspondence of the board members and coworkers of the Reich Association had to be formulated in a neutralizing discourse under the Nazi regime. The memoranda in particular were presented to corresponding officials in the RSHA for approval. To express resistance and protest against these measures or fears about their effects in writing would have resulted in immediate arrest and internment in a concentration camp. Consequently, the existing documents seem almost like administrative instructions and orders, and thus strangely distant from the brutality of the persecution of the Jews of which they were nonetheless a part. In order to obtain a multiperspectival picture of how Jewish functionaries acted in the years 1939–1945, I utilized materials in Israeli, German, British, and American archives. These included posthumous papers, memoirs of survivors, letters or reports by later-murdered Jewish functionaries or their family members, and files on reparations. These reports, retrospective or written in the freedom of their country of emigration, constitute a necessary supplement to the central core of documentation of the Reich Association files: they enrich this material by adding the "unspeakable" and subjective perspectives on events, even if these sources were in part composed after the fact and with some cognizance of the Holocaust. Consequently, using these later-composed source materials harbors the danger that the judgment of a situation is distorted by knowledge acquired after the war. Frequently they also are tacitly imbued with the character of something written in order to justify and legitimate one's own past actions. This notwithstanding, I chose to make use of them because they can cast needed light on the accompanying circumstances under which an ostensibly "neutral" document of the Reich Association was composed, or they permit me to include events whose mention was assiduously avoided in the contemporary correspondence of the Jewish functionaries. For that reason, along with the subjunctive mood, the modal adverbs "apparently," "presumably," "possibly," "perhaps," "probably," and the qualifier "in retrospect" appear quite often in this study.

My investigation focuses on the history of the organization and its functionaries. But in order to make clear the different perspectives on events, I also always made selective use of source materials that provide a window into the perspective of the "ordinary members" and subordinate staff workers in the Reich Association, and that help to show how their attitude changed toward the activities of their representatives over time. I was able to locate such reports in the Yad Vashem Archive in Jerusalem, the US Holocaust Memorial Museum (USHMM) in Washington DC, the Leo Baeck Institutes in Jerusalem, New York, and Berlin, and the Wiener Library in London. Some of these subjective documents were composed in retrospect, immediately after emigration or in the postwar period, so that they involve the same set of problems described above.

The Jewish-German functionaries of the first hour were almost all murdered, and the few survivors left relatively few testimonies, at best some short statements, mostly in interrogation or testimony in court. This gives rise to the problem of finding it necessary to utilize by and large the extant "official" or organization-internal documents in order to illuminate their motivation, how they understood their work, and the possibilities and limits for action. These documents contain no expression of their doubts and despair, fears, aversion and reluctance, their reservations, the humiliations they suffered or maltreatment they endured. Rather, they were specifically drafted to consciously ensure that any such reference to this was eliminated. The files of the Jewish Communities that I used to sketch and reconstruct the work of the Reich Association branches have a similar self-censored character. The sources I employed to help reconstruct the work of the *Vertrauensmänner* after June 1943 provide a different picture: housed in the main state archives (or still within the files of the public prosecutors) are the files of a number of postwar legal proceedings against responsible Gestapo leaders or other perpetrators. In these proceedings, surviving Jewish representatives and Jews in mixed marriages testified as witnesses. If these legal proceedings were proximate in time to the actual persecution, then persecutors, family members of the victims, returnees from concentration camps, and intermediaries were among the witnesses summoned, that is, the entire spectrum of events was addressed. This encompassed knowledge and partial knowledge about the mass murder of the Jews, the constant threat of death associated with the office a person held, the concrete pressures connected with specific measures of the Gestapo and other institutions of persecution, the isolation from the non-Jewish-German surroundings and the indifference pervasive there, as well as the isolated position of the Jewish functionaries in their own environment.

These source materials differ from those on which chapter 2 is based. They enable us to develop greater empathy for the individual actors than the "neutral" memoranda or minutes from the Reich Association board in its central office tend to allow. In addition, in the American and Soviet occupation zones, the organs of the occupying power gathered evidence against Jewish functionaries who had been accused of collaboration, generally by their own membership. In the worst-case scenario, these persons were subsequently convicted of complicity in Gestapo crimes and imprisoned in the same concentration camps in which they had been interned in 1938 after the November pogrom. While persons so accused were in time rehabilitated in the American zone, in the Soviet zone it generally took years until they were released—if indeed they survived this second phase of persecution and did not perish in the special camps of the Soviet occupying power in Germany's east.

In this study, I have concentrated on the research questions outlined above, and have left out other thematic fields that likewise emerged as possible topics from work on the documentation of the Reich Association, such as the complex "Aryanization" of plots of land and buildings owned by the Reich Association and the educational efforts or work over years of the Jewish Kulturbund (Jewish Cultural Federation). I also have given only selective treatment to the various spheres of Jewish social welfare, in order to point to how their character changed over the course of the progressively worsening persecution, ultimately becoming part of the events of deportation.

This book deals with the leadership stratum of German Jewry from 1939 to 1945: the governing board of the Reich Association, Jewish functionaries in the Berlin central office, the key staff members and responsible officials in the branch offices across the Reich, and the heads of the Jewish Communities—that is, a limited circle of persons, yet one whose precise number is difficult to determine. They all had decided to remain in the German Reich, together with the members of their communities. As highly qualified legal experts, economists, or experts in other academic professions, they were accustomed to assuming the mantle of responsibility for others, to represent them and act on their behalf. They sought to build up a Jewish administration that implemented all orders and instructions from the Nazi rulers in such a manner that the latter would have no reason to carry out this work themselves. At the same time, this administration was structured so as to rule out any arbitrary action or corruption, in that it operated in accordance with the principles of adherence to a set of specified rules, transparent, working in accordance with fixed channels and assigned competencies and responsibilities. From the perspective of the Jewish representatives, their strategy of cooperation with the Nazi authorities was always bound up with their endeavor to decelerate events, and if possible to prevent the constant further radicalization of the National Socialist measures. That path proved to be a dangerous balancing act, a tightrope walk strung between their own desires, the massive external constraints, and an anticipatory obedience so as to avert further escalations. I also chose the concept of a "tightrope walk" (*Gratwanderung*, literally "walk along a ridge") in my first extensive study on the topic, when I sought to analyze the changes that transpired in the relation of the Jewish functionaries to their compulsory membership in the Reich Association, looking at their efforts while walking a thin line between responsibility and entanglement.[27] If the functionaries tried to extend their constantly shrinking latitude for action with respect to an (imagined) overall interest of their membership, then they themselves tended to curtail the individual latitude of the members for action by doing so. The members increasingly defended themselves against the control that the Reich Association exercised over them.[28] By means of the strategy of cooperation, the Jewish functionaries intended quite the opposite, but the National Socialist state used them in order to implement its panoply of ordinances against the Jews. For many of those impacted by these measures, the Nazi persecution of the Jews thus also bore the thumbprint and face of its Jewish representatives, then and in retrospect, whose supervision they endeavored to elude and escape.

Notes

1. See also Moshe Zimmermann, *Deutsche gegen Deutsche: Das Schicksal der Juden 1938–1945* (Berlin, 2008), 252–58.
2. See Dan Michman, "Reevaluating the Emergence, Function, and Form of the Jewish Councils Phenomenon," in *Ghettos 1939–1945: New Research and Perspectives on Definition, Daily Life, and Survival: Symposium Presentations*, ed. USHMM Center for Advanced Holocaust Studies (Washington DC, 2005), 67–83.
3. On the various tasks of the *Judenräte*, see Isaiah Trunk, *Judenrat: The Jewish Councils in Eastern Europe under Nazi Occupation* (New York and London, 1972).
4. See Beate Meyer, *"Jüdische Mischlinge": Rassenpolitik und Verfolgungserfahrung 1933–1945* (Hamburg, 1999).
5. This also held for mixed marriages if the Jewish spouse was the husband, or if the mixed marriage was not classified as "privileged" (10. VO zum Reichsbürgergesetz, RGBl. 1939, 1097). In addition, the Jewish Communities had to report the names of their members who had been included in the membership of the *Reichsvereinigung*.
6. On the Reich Representation, see chapter 1 of this book.
7. See Hans Mommsen, "The German Resistance Movement and the Holocaust," in *On Germans and Jews under the Nazi Regime: Essays by Three Generations of Historians: A Festschrift in Honor of Otto Dov Kulka*, ed. Moshe Zimmermann (Jerusalem, 2006), 239–58.

8. See Hannah Arendt, *Eichmann in Jerusalem: A Report on the Banality of Evil* (New York, 1977), 115.

9. Ibid., 125.

10. Günther Plum describes in a few pages the continuity between the Reich Representation and its successor, the Reich Association, and their tasks, but mentions only briefly the assistance given for organizing the deportations; see Günther Plum, "Deutsche Juden oder Juden in Deutschland?," in *Die Juden in Deutschland 1933–1945*, ed. Wolfgang Benz (Munich, 1988), 66–74.

11. On different views in the debate on the Jewish councils, see Trunk, *Judenrat*, 570–75; Aharon Weiss, "Jewish Leadership in Occupied Poland: Postures and Attitudes," in *Yad Vashem Studies* 12 (1977): 335–65; tabular overviews of Trunk's and Weiss's categorizations, reproduced in *Enzyklopädie des Holocaust: Die Verfolgung und Ermordung der europäischen Juden*, vol. 2, ed. Israel Gutman (Munich and Zurich, 1998), 695. Michman distinguishes between the concepts of "headship" (internally) and "leadership" (externally); see Dan Michman, "'Judenräte' und 'Judenvereinigungen' unter nationalsozialistischer Herrschaft: Aufbau und Anwendung eines verwaltungsmäßigen Konzepts," *Zeitschrift für Geschichtswissenschaft* 46, no. 4 (1998): 293–304. Saul Friedländer pointed out how the decisions were bound up with their specific context; see Saul Friedländer, *The Years Of Extermination: Nazi Germany and the Jews 1939–1945* (London, 2007), xxiv. On questions raised in recent research on the ghettos, see Christoph Dieckmann and Babette Quinkert, "Einleitung," in "Im Ghetto, 1939–1945: Neue Forschungen zu Alltag und Umfeld," ed. Christoph Dieckmann and Babette Quinkert, special issue, *Beiträge zur Geschichte des Nationalsozialismus* 25 (2009): 9–29.

12. Dan Diner, "Beyond the Conceivable: The Judenrat as Borderline Experience," in *Beyond the Conceivable: Studies on Germany, Nazism and the Holocaust* (Berkeley, 2000), 117–29. http://goo.gl/IKm1Q (accessed 30 July 2012).

13. Doron Rabinovici, *Eichmann's Jews: The Jewish Administration of Holocaust Vienna, 1938–1945*, trans. Nick Somers (Cambridge, 2011).

14. Dan Diner, "Historical Understanding and Counterrationality: The Judenrat as Epistemological Vantage," in *Beyond the Conceivable*, 133.

15. Ibid., 136.

16. Ibid.

17. Diner, "Beyond the Conceivable: The Judenrat," 128, 118; see also Diner, "The Limits of Reason: Max Horkheimer on Anti-Semitism and Extermination," in *Beyond the Conceivable*, 104.

18. Ibid., 133; Raul Hilberg, *The Destruction of the European Jews*, rev. ed., 3 vols. (New York. 1985), 1038–1039. Hilberg pointed out that to refrain from resistance had indeed been an old Jewish strategy to avoid pogroms. Later he was more differentiating, and recognized that the German-Jewish functionaries had tried with their limited possibilities to postpone the worst, to "retard the downward trend, to save at least some people," or through petition to achieve a period of grace or some modicum of mitigation; see Raul Hilberg, *Perpetrators, Victims, Bystanders: The Jewish Catastrophe, 1933–1945* (New York, 1992), 114–15.

19. Diner, "Beyond the Conceivable: The Judenrat," 129.

20. Rabinovici, *Eichmann's Jews*, 201.

21. Hans-Erich Fabian, "Die letzte Etappe," in *Festschrift zum 80: Geburtstag von Leo Baeck am 23. Mai 1953*, ed. Council for the Protection of the Rights and Interests of Jews from Germany (London, 1953), 85–97; see also Plum, "Deutsche Juden," 35–74.

22. On Otto Dov Kulka's debate with Hans Mommsen and Hannah Arendt, see Otto Dov Kulka, "Singularity and its Relativization: Changing Views in German Historiography on National Socialism and the 'Final Solution,'" *Yad Vashem Studies* 19 (1988): 177ff.

23. See Otto Dov Kulka, "The Reichsvereinigung and the Fate of the German Jews,1938/1939–1943: Continuity or Discontinuity in German-Jewish History in the Third Reich," in *Die Juden im nationalsozialistischen Deutschland*, ed. Arnold Paucker (Tübingen, 1986), 353–63; Esriel Hildesheimer, *Jüdische Selbstverwaltung unter dem NS-Regime* (Tübingen, 1994).

24. Rabinovici, *Eichmann's Jews*, 16.

25. On *Konsulenten* and *Krankenbehandler*, see Avraham Barkai, *From Boycott to Annihilation: The Economic Struggle of German Jews, 1933–1943*, trans. William Templer (Hanover, NH, 1989), 121–22, 156, 171.

26. Kulka, "Reichsvereinigung," 356; Otto Dov Kulka, *Deutsches Judentum unter dem Nationalsozialismus*, vol. 1, *Dokumente zur Geschichte der Reichsvertretung der deutschen Juden 1933–1939* (Tübingen, 1997).

27. Beate Meyer, "The Fine Line Between Responsible Action and Collaboration: The Reichsvereinigung der Juden in Deutschland and the Jewish Community in Berlin, 1938–45," in *Jews in Nazi Berlin: From Kristallnacht to Liberation*, ed. Beate Meyer, Hermann Simon, and Chana Schütz (Chicago, 2009), 310–62.

28. Beate Meyer, "Das unausweichliche Dilemma: Die Reichsvereinigung der Juden in Deutschland, die Deportationen und die untergetauchten Juden," in *Solidarität und Hilfe für Juden während der NS-Zeit*, vol. 5, *Überleben im Untergrund. Hilfe für Juden in Deutschland 1941–1945*, ed. Beate Kosmala and Claudia Schoppmann (Berlin, 2002), 273–96.

Chapter 1

From "Forced Emigration" to Assisting with the Deportations

Created in Chaos

Pogrom as Prelude: November 1938

When Benno Cohn arrived at the Palestine Office[1] on Meineckestrasse in Berlin on 10 November 1938, where he worked, a demolished building confronted him. Nonetheless, he was allowed to enter the ruined structure. Two hours later, all the telephone lines there had been cut. Paul Eppstein and Otto Hirsch from the Reich Representation of Jews in Germany (Reichsvertretung der Juden in Deutschland), whose office was located on Kantstrasse, did not even head for work first that day. Instead, they rushed immediately to the Reich Chancellery, hoping to be able to speak with State Secretary Lammers,[2] but that proved to no avail. In marked contrast, at the very same time, their associate Franz Meyer at the Zionist Association of Germany (ZVfD) was sitting down in his office, "in keeping with the false slogan we always adhered to: just go on as if everything was operating as per normal," he later noted in 1946.[3] Hans Reichmann experienced the pogrom that day in the main office of the Central Association of German Citizens of the Jewish Faith (Centralverein, CV) on Emserstrasse.[4]

Behind these Jewish functionaries lay a night of sheer violence: synagogues had burned, Jewish establishments, businesses, and institutions

both in Berlin and the provinces had been demolished, Jews had been attacked, robbed, manhandled, and mistreated, and more than ninety Jews
had lost their lives. In their organizations and beyond, the representatives feverishly discussed what should be done. Zionists and officials in the
Reich Representation and the Central Association ordered their offices
closed, although the CV decided to keep open an emergency service.[5]
Around noon, mass arrests commenced.[6] Some thirty thousand Jews, men
from all areas of the German Reich, were seized and sent off to the Sachsenhausen, Buchenwald, and Dachau concentration camps.[7] Not for the
first time, the functionaries of the Reich Representation and other Jewish
institutions were faced with a pressing existential question, but now in an
especially drastic form: should they elude their foreseeable fate by fleeing, or remain steadfast at their posts in order to forestall something even
worse? While some representatives such as Otto Hirsch (born 1885), in
the face of anticipated arrest, turned themselves in to the police,[8] younger
ones like Benno Cohn (born 1894) and Paul Eppstein (born 1902) chose
a kind of middle path. They went into hiding while the arrest roundup
was in progress, but kept in contact with other functionaries in order to
exchange information and consult with one another, preparing to be able
at the right moment to take action again. News was gathered and persons
met secretly in the apartment of Leo Baeck,[9] whom the Gestapo had put
under house arrest, and in several other private homes.[10] Without any
concrete, current picture of what was transpiring, they tried to put together a picture of events based on fragmentary news, and to assess the
possible consequences. As Franz Meyer recalled, Paul Eppstein, for example, wanted "in his characteristic way to find something systematic in
what was happening … By chance, among the Jews first arrested there
were three financial consultants of Jewish corporations. So he suspected
the ongoing operation targeted financial consultants."[11] Eppstein soon
had to revise that assumption.

Franz Meyer and Paul Meyerheim, the head of the finance department
of the Reich Representation, withdrew thousands of reichsmarks from an
off-the-books account; they then went out into the Berlin streets, this
money in their pocket, in an effort to provide some support to young men
in transit from the hachshara Zionist training centers, and others who were
penniless and trying to escape.[12]

Hans Reichmann and Alfred Hirschberg of the CV, who had simply
been sent home initially when their office was closed, were now taken into
custody. Later on, in comments on the November pogrom, Reichmann
said he had not been able at the time to "determine whether the people
around us are agitated. There's a wall between us and them. We have nothing more to do with each other. Perhaps we can still imagine what they may

be thinking. But how things appear to us, they have no inkling of that."[13] In the concentration camp, Reichmann and Paul Hirschfeld came across Otto Hirsch and Arthur Lilienthal, the secretary general of the Reich Representation, and other leaders of Jewish organizations interned there, while the personnel of the Zionist Association was largely spared any arrests.[14]

Reichmann of the CV spent seven weeks in internment until his release; Otto Hirsch and Arthur Lilienthal were set free after just two weeks in the Sachsenhausen concentration camp. This was because the Reich Representation, the Paltreu, the Hilfsverein (Aid Society for German Jews), and the Kulturbund were allowed to go on operating, while the other organizations were prohibited.[15] Their departments dealing with emigration would later be incorporated into the Reich Representation and permitted to continue their work there.

By contrast, the CV was liquidated and had to settle its affairs and assets. In this way, the Nazi state centralized the Jewish organizations, strengthened those concerned with emigration, and hence Zionist currents, while "assimilationists" were stripped of any possibilities for work. In this context, Franz Meyer of the ZVfD became one of the "six princes" who, according to Gestapo planning, were to lead the Reich Representation in transition until the establishment of a new structure and institution. But this plan was not realized and Meyer emigrated a short time later, correct in his assessment at the time that "whoever is put to work there will never ever make it out of Germany."[16] Hans Reichmann could have been able to work on in the Reich Representation, but likewise did not see a place for himself there. His clear-sighted final reckoning:

> Only a group of Jewish workers … is to remain: the leaders of the ghetto. The Gestapo is furthering a plan to unify all Jewish Communities and organizations in the "Reich Association of Jews in Germany." Only a small handful of the old knowledgeable Jewish representatives are still persevering … Whoever remains will sacrifice his years, perhaps his life, for a lost cause. Very few, scarcely a dozen make that sacrifice out of a sense of duty, internal compulsion or religious conviction. At the head of this captain's crew prepared to go down with the sinking ship are Leo Baeck, Otto Hirsch, Hannah Karminski, Cora Berliner, Arthur Lilienthal, Julius L. Seligsohn and Richard Joachim. Heinrich Stahl, aged over 70 and the head of the Berlin Jewish Community and [Alfred] Neumeyer, of the same age and judge at the Bavarian High Court in Munich, remain at the side of the German Jews.[17]

Hans and Eva Reichmann emigrated on 11 April 1939,[18] and they were followed over the next two years by many others.

The November 1938 pogrom constituted only the high point of three "operations" that followed one another that eventful year. It made clear to the Jews and their functionaries, publicly and violently, that in Germany not only those with a "criminal record" or "Eastern European Jews" were to be stripped of their civil rights and part of their property, made "fair game" and exposed to state and social persecution. Now precisely those Jews who formerly had thought they were integrated into German society, the wealthy and better educated, would also suffer a similar fate. With a dark premonition, Leo Baeck wrote to a friend who had emigrated: "And this year is going to be a hard one, the wheel is spinning ever faster. It will become a huge challenge to the nerves and the quiet of thought."[19]

Earlier that year, in June 1938, several thousand Jews with criminal records had been arrested during the operation "Work-shy Reich" (*Arbeitsscheu Reich*). In most cases, they had violated anti-Jewish legislation or were accused of minor offenses.[20] Along with this "June operation" (*Juni-Aktion*), there were boycott actions in Berlin the summer of 1938, in the course of which Jewish businesses were attacked and demolished, raids were organized, and Jews were openly abused and maltreated. Göring, responsible for the Four-Year Plan, whom the Jewish functionaries at this point still considered a possible contact person and interlocutor, no longer answered any petitions. In the Sachsenhausen concentration camp, the Jews were being mistreated and beaten to death; at the same time, the Berlin police chief cynically informed the Berlin Jewish Community that the number of the dead was not unusually high, in any case no more than in the jails or penitentiaries.[21]

In a consultation of all Jewish organizations, a serious conflict erupted, one that the Jewish representatives were not confronting for the first time, and would grapple with again: should they yield under external pressure and violence, and put their energies into fulfilling the demands placed upon them by the Nazi state, or should they refuse them? Should they remain silent vis-à-vis foreign organizations, or make the events in Germany public, even if at the cost of endangering the lives of the prisoners? The various organizations dealing with emigration had tried for years to help arrange for Jews to travel individually or in groups along secure routes to safe destinations. In the main, this was to destinations where, if possible, they might establish a new life for themselves based on their education or the qualifications needed in their new home. The mass internment in concentration camps in June 1938 left no further latitude for such a procedure: in the face of the massive wave of arrests, the Hilfsverein had applied for, implored, and purchased visas for those in custody in order to have them set free. Those who had met for consultation began to realize that Reinhard Heydrich, head of the SS Security Service (SD), the Gestapo and Political Police—and head of the Criminal Police, which was in charge in the *Juni-Aktion*—would feel more vindicated in his violent approach if the arrest and internment in a concentration camp served to accelerate departure of the Jews from Germany. However, not to react would mean dozens and even hundreds more might die. In addition, the functionaries feared negative effects on emigration as a whole if a large number of individuals with a "criminal record" were now to emigrate. As Reichmann later wrote:

> The conflict appears to have no solution. People then continued to try to obtain visas, and at the same time, at every opportunity, commented that the pressure for emigration was causing countries willing to take in emigrants now to close their borders. This pressure was pushing unsuitable persons toward countries that reject this form of immigration, but which would have welcomed competent skilled immigrants.[22]

Reichmann suggested a petition, which Baeck and Hirsch formulated in the name of the Reich Representation and then addressed to the Reich Chancellery, the Interior Ministry, and the Gestapo, with an attached list of those who had lost their lives during the first few weeks.[23]

However, even though not all those arrested in June had been released, in the next "operation" in October 1938, the Nazi state expelled seventeen thousand Jews of Polish descent across the border to Poland.[24] Thousands of these Jews vegetated for weeks in former stables in a no-man's-land, given provisional aid by the overstrained local Jewish Community there.[25]

In November 1938, the wave of arrests swept middle-class Jewish males in particular into the camps, no matter whether they were in mixed marriages or not, belonged to a Jewish Community or had converted to Christianity, or were "Eastern European Jews" or "Western Jews."

In the "fateful year 1938," the representatives had reason for concern not only in regard to the foreign policy that seemed headed for war but also domestic political developments and what they signaled.[26] Since 1935, they had found it increasingly difficult to find an open ear among ministry officials—most particularly in the case of Reich economy minister Hjalmar Schacht—and now they had come by duress to realize that their possibilities for intervention had shrunk even further.[27] From the now "annexed" Austria, unofficial emissaries were spreading "terrible" news, while the German-Jewish organizations had been strictly prohibited from engaging in any activity there.[28] "Vienna is accelerating our fall" is how Reichmann described developments.

Behind the scenes of these "operations" and the general political developments, the machinery of laws and ordinances against the Jews continued to churn out legislation. A law that at first glance seemed quite unspectacular had, in addition, seriously weakened the institution for representing their interests, the Reich Representation. On 28 March 1938, the Nazi state had changed the status of the Jewish Communities and thus also that of the Reich Representation as their umbrella organization (retroactive to 1 January 1938) by enactment of the Law on the Legal Status of Jewish Communities (*Gesetz über die Rechtsverhältnisse der jüdischen Kultusvereinigungen*): the Jewish Communities were now denied the status of statutory bodies under public law; they were to continue to exist as registered associations where members could join or leave the organization. Resolutions by the committees would in future require the approval of the "higher administrative agency," that is, the supervision of the Interior Ministry or the Gestapo.[29] Leo Baeck beseeched the members to be mindful that their obligations toward the Jewish Community continued, and it was their solemn duty to support the communities financially and to participate in their activities.[30] The representatives of the Jewish organizations also tried to work against this development by restructuring the Reich Representation. A renamed organization, based more strongly on the Jewish Communities, the Reich Federation of Jews in Germany (Reichsverband der Juden in Deutschland) was to be financed by the dues of the membership, that is, by the members of the Jewish Communities, which in this way might regain a portion of their former position of power. This restructuring was passed as a resolution on 27 July 1938, but represented only one more penultimate attempt to resolve the dilemma, and in the end was no longer a viable option.[31]

Looking Back at the History of the Reich Representation of German Jews, 1932–1938

Already in 1932, the leadership of the large Jewish organizations such as the CV or the Zionist Association, as well as the Jewish Communities, were convinced that some kind of umbrella organization would be necessary in order to confront the looming persecution associated with the rise of National Socialism, and to implement the interests of the Jews living in Germany. From these first deliberations, the Reich Representation of Jews in Germany developed over several stages during the course of 1933. Elected to its board were the liberal rabbi Leo Baeck as president, Otto Hirsch, a leading CV member, as executive director, along with three representatives of the Zionist Association, two from the Association for Liberal Judaism, a further member of the CV and a representative of the Reich Association of Jewish Combat Veterans (Reichsbund jüdischer Frontsoldaten, RjF). In this way, power relations were carefully balanced, and only a few smaller Jewish groups rejected creation of the organization. Historian Otto Dov Kulka points out that at this juncture, there were three alternative paths: first, subjugation to the National Socialist terror, which would serve to atomize the Jewish community and would have forced individuals to grapple on their own with the new situation; second, application of the strong-man "Führer" principle within the Jewish community, which was demanded by the Jewish minority who were German-nationalist in outlook; and third, the chosen path of continuity in the democratic-pluralistic tradition within a new framework.[32]

Many of the participating organizations, such as the Jewish Communities or the Hilfsverein der deutschen Juden, retained their autonomy; others, such as the Central Committee for Relief and Rehabilitation (Zentralausschuss für Hilfe und Aufbau), were incorporated into the Reich Representation as the years passed. The Central Committee provided economic assistance and social support; the Hilfsverein, with financial support from international Jewish relief organizations, was active in the sphere of general emigration; the Palestine Office, under the aegis of the Zionist Association, took over emigration to Eretz Israel. Along with concrete assistance in economic distress or for emigration, the triple focus of efforts continued to be as it had been before 1938: seeking to confront state and social discrimination, both materially and by other means; strengthening Jewish identity, which in the process of assimilation had to some extent been lost; and countering exclusion by creating Jewish schools, sports and cultural associations.

By writing the concrete revocation of civil rights for Jews into the law, the Nuremberg Laws and their implementation ordinances constituted a turning point. A declaration of protest signed by Leo Baeck and Otto Hirsch, which has gone into the literature as the "Prayer," was not permitted to be read aloud in the synagogues. Instead, Baeck and Hirsch were taken for a short time into custody.[33] While the Nuremberg legislation triggered an emigration wave of thousands, the hope spread among Jews who felt they were German that on the basis of this legally codified exclusion, they would be able to continue leading a Jewish life in Germany at a reduced level. For that reason, the organizations associated with the Reich Representation sought to further strengthen internal Jewish life by means of education and training, albeit without neglecting the promotion of emigration. Now the Zionists in particular attracted great interest, with their preparation for emigration oriented to Palestine. Youth and young adults specifically regarded this as a realistic alternative to the options offered by "assimilationist" circles, which called for self-restraint, sticking to a program of long-term vocational retraining. From the perspective of the younger generation, they were accommodating in this way to the existing situation, and did not offer a conception with a promising future. After the Zionists also managed to garner significant gains in voting in the elections for officers in the Jewish Communities, the composition of the leading bodies in the Reich Representation was adjusted to reflect these changes: the board was composed on a parity basis, that is, half were from the Zionist camp, and their functionaries Siegfried Moses and Franz Meyer were appointed vice president and Hirsch's deputy, respectively.[34] A further council consisting of twenty-three members exercised legislative powers and oversight, supervising the Reich Representation and its committees. They thus succeeded, relying on older democratic structures, in overcoming for a time internal Jewish antagonisms.[35] Nonetheless, the efforts to achieve hegemony by the large Berlin Jewish Community plunged the Reich Representation in 1937 into the greatest crisis in its history. The representatives of the large urban Jewish Communities, especially Berlin, Frankfurt am Main, and Breslau, had already preferred another option during the first deliberations on establishing the Reich Representation: namely, a union on the basis of the Communities. They did not wish to see activists of the "political parties" at the head of a federation, and believed they could better represent the interests of the Jewish community as a whole and promote emigration more actively.[36] The former chair of the Berlin Jewish Community and founder of the Jewish People's Party, the bankrupt banker and exponent of a Zionist state, Georg Kareski,[37] entered into a pact with the former head of the Community, Heinrich Stahl. At the end of May 1937, they issued a vehement demand that the Reich Representation should be reduced to the level of a financial "transit office." The previous representatives were to be dismissed; only Leo Baeck would be allowed to stay on the job, supported by Stahl and Lilienthal. The opposition brought the Gestapo into the conflict, and it in turn put pressure on the Jewish organizations.[38] The Gestapo, which initially supported Kareski's ideas, evidently soon became aware of the danger that a forcible implementation of Kareski's conception of restructuring entailed; it could endanger support from the financially strong foreign aid and relief organizations. These organizations intervened in the conflict in favor of maintaining the existing Reich Representation.[39] In print and orally, Kareski defamed the "red Meineckestrasse" and the Palestine Office there as a refuge where Marxism was still alive and well,[40] and he appears to likewise have denounced certain persons to the authorities.[41] Hedwig Eppstein, the wife of Paul Eppstein and since 1933 active in the Jewish Youth Aid/Youth Aliyah, reported on these events in uncensored letters written while on a trip to London:

Our situation has changed fundamentally, because the Secret Police has ordered a number of co-workers, including Paul to stop working within 6 months, and to employ other gentlemen for the job. The reason is earlier

Marxist activity. Happily, the affair is based on denunciations to the authorities by our dear racial comrades. ... In Paul's case, it proved possible to negotiate, since he never was a member of the SPD. It's quite possible that the order will be retracted for him.[42]

When the Gestapo then decided to replace Hirsch with Kareski, Baeck brought his authority to bear and sought to prevent this personal encroachment on the "autonomy" of the Reich Representation by threatening that in that case, he would no longer be available for any further work.[43] Eppstein was also able to stay on. In actual fact, until the summer of 1943, the Gestapo avoided any further attempt to place representatives whom the Gestapo favored in leadership positions in the Reich Representation or later the Reich Association, although in the district branches it certainly did appoint or dismiss directors. Kareski's "State Zionist Organization" was dissolved on 31 August 1938.[44]

Thus, the Jewish representatives had gone through a turbulent period. On the one hand, networks had crystallized that overarched the various currents, and that were grounded on trust, commitment, reliability, and discretion toward third parties, especially exponents of the Nazi state. On the other, dividing lines had also deepened and reservations had strengthened. This was because the adversaries inside the organization mutually distrusted one another: they feared some were not acting openly, by functionalizing the foreign relief organizations or bringing in the Gestapo. In other times, these differences might perhaps have been nothing but "normal" disputes regarding whose opinion would emerge dominant and the struggle over positions of power in a highly ramified, financially powerful association. However, under the external pressure of Nazi terror, the conflicts were exacerbated, often developing into a threat for individuals if the Gestapo intervened.

Between Reich Representation and Reich Association: Adaptation under Duress

The Zionist Ernst-Ephraim Frank later recalled:

After November 1938, there was no longer any independent creativity. People lived in a world of shadows. Everywhere you could see the shaven heads of those who had returned from the camps. Life consisted solely of hunting for a visa. ... It was a situation of rapid dissolution, everything was provisional.[45]

Nonetheless, already on 29 November, under orders from the Gestapo, the Reich Representation resumed its work.[46] There was more than enough to do, especially in regard to emigration. In particular, the Zionists from Hechalutz sent more than one thousand confirmations for (alleged) openings in *hachshara* training in Great Britain, Sweden, or Holland in order to have their members released from the concentration camps.[47] In 1938, according to the Reich Association, some thirty-three thousand Jews had left Germany, nearly thirteen thousand in the fourth quarter.[48] The figure of forty thousand emigrants for this period arrived at by historian Herbert A. Strauss indicates that, presumably, seven thousand persons had fled without utilizing assistance from the Reich Association.

The forced centralization that the Reich Representation was ordered at the same time to implement eliminated all the consultative committees as well as the autonomy of the Jewish Communities.[49] It constituted a move anticipating future structural changes that the leading representatives had already tried to achieve earlier on, even if under completely different circumstances.

In parallel, Jewish functionaries and representatives of the Nazi state were working on plans for a new organization. On 16 December 1938, the Reich Representation handed the Gestapo a proposal on how the financing of the future Reich Association might look after 1 January 1939.[50] For its part, the Nazi state needed a central agency for implementing its policies of "forced emigration," which was now taking on a visible form. Thus, at a conference of the Reich Interior Ministry on the "Jewish Question," it was noted:

> The Jews are being consolidated in a single unified organization. All Jewish institutions, foundations, institutes, schools, Jewish social welfare, etc. are to be incorporated into this organization. The organization will have its main office in Berlin. The intention is to restructure the previous Reich Representation of the Jews in Germany, which has proved itself suitable for this purpose. Plans are for the Jewish religious associations [Jewish Communities] to serve as local sub-formations. This question has not as yet been finally resolved. The sole purpose of the organization and its incorporated institutions is to prepare Jews for emigration. Thus, the principle will be upheld that to a substantial degree, the emigration of the Jews is to be left to the Jews themselves to organize. The organization shall function under strict state supervision.[51]

In its report for the first quarter 1939, the Security Service Main Office stated:

> In the course of the establishment of the "Reich Association in Germany," numerous Jewish organizations on the territory of the Reich have disbanded. With the exception of the Palestine Fund and Palestine Office, which will be incorporated as a whole, this will create an amalgamation of all Jewish

organizations, and in this way achieve a concentration of all forces and cut costs. The "Reich Association" will encompass the Jewish organizations in the "Altreich," including the Sudetengau, while the Jewish Community Vienna shall have sole competence for the Ostmark.[52]

At the same time, Conrad Cohn and Hannah Karminski sent out an internal circular letter about the downside of "forced emigration," expressing concern for the destitute individuals remaining behind:

> The Reich Association of the Jews in Germany has now been created as the comprehensive organization of all Jews in the German Reich, with the exception of the Ostmark. One of its principal tasks is care and support for the Jews. The Jewish Communities remain in existence as the local offices of the Reich Association.[53]

A set of draft model statutes stipulated the rights of the Communities and the Reich Association.[54]

The new structure was somewhat controversial on the Jewish side, even if leading representatives described it as a "further development" (Otto Hirsch) or "only a legal restructuring, not a real one."[55] The external pressures increasingly blurred the political differences between the groups, highlighting instead the necessity for joint action. Nonetheless, the claims to hegemony by the large Jewish Community in Berlin remained an issue. In the middle of creating the comprehensive organization, Heinrich Stahl once more formulated his claim to leadership in a memorandum he sent likewise to the Gestapo.[56] Contacted as an arbitrator, the Gestapo left it up to Eppstein, Hirsch, and Stahl to put together the personnel of executive committees of the Berlin Jewish Community and the future Reich Association. In other matters, it instructed the Jewish organizations to clarify differences, including personal ones, but wished to have a report back on this.[57] Baeck is said to have described Stahl's letter to the Gestapo as a denunciation and intended for that reason to end cooperation,[58] but in the face of the necessity to act united, the dispute was (temporarily) settled. Ultimately, Stahl resigned in February 1940 from the board of the Reich Association and the Berlin Jewish Community.[59] According to later statements by his wife, his successor, Moritz Henschel, is believed to have been forced by the "agency" (i.e., the Gestapo) to succeed Stahl in his post.[60]

In early 1939, at a time when the Reich Association had not yet been officially established, Adolf Eichmann summoned Eppstein and Lilienthal from the Reich Representation, Cohn from the Palestine Office, and Stahl and Philipp Kozower from the Berlin Jewish Community. The SS-*Untersturmführer* had achieved recent "success": he had been sent by the

Security Service Main Office to Vienna, and had set up a Central Office for Jewish Emigration (*Zentralstelle für jüdische Auswanderung*) there and later in Prague. He proceeded to brief the German-Jewish representatives he had summoned about the resolution of the conference in the Aviation Ministry on 12 November 1938 chaired by Hermann Göring: it stated that based on the example of the Vienna Central Office for Jewish Emigration, a similar office was now also to be established for the emigration of German Jews.[61] The Vienna office, which Eichmann had created, had put forward binding emigration quotas and had forced wealthier Jews to provide for the emigration of their less fortunate fellow Jews. By means of pressure and extortion, it had achieved a situation in which the emigrants, after deduction of all taxes and levies, were compelled to leave their homeland reduced to destitution.[62] Eichmann was proud of this system; it had proved his "success," boasting a total of some fifty thousand emigrants from Vienna, contrasted with nineteen thousand from Germany, in the second half of 1938. He announced that a similar office was to be set up for Germany.[63] Stahl, Kozower, and Meyer were ordered to proceed to Vienna to look at the procedures, and "the impression was horrible."[64] These procedures were to be institutionalized in Berlin as well under the direction of Reinhard Heydrich.

Initially a scandal flared in the run-up to the creation of this office, because in spite of a strict prohibition on such talks, the representatives of the Reich Representation had engaged in discussions on the depressing situation with the Vienna Jewish Community, and had also defended their right to do so. Eichmann was furious, and is reported to have cursed Stahl as a "miserable wretch" and "old shithead" who had not been kept in concentration camp for a long time.[65] Noteworthy is Eppstein's response to Eichmann regarding his insult of Stahl; it serves as an example pointing to how the leading Jewish functionaries in the spring of 1939 reacted to verbal injuries and confinement in a concentration camp, despite their internal differences:

> The gentlemen who are sitting here before you are representatives of German Jewry, not of the Gestapo. And they regard themselves as persons elected by the German Jews and not mere recipients of orders handed down from the German Reich. You, gentlemen, find yourselves in a historical situation of the German people. Our Jewish people is also in a historical if tragic situation. We are accountable to our people for our behavior. If you speak to us in this manner, we cannot work together with you. You can order to have us sent at any time to a concentration camp and can deal with us as you please. But as long as we are still free, you must respect our human dignity and treat us correspondingly.[66]

Even if Benno Cohn, who quoted this twenty years later, probably recalled more the tenor of Eppstein's remarks than the actual verbatim, it is none-theless clear that Eppstein, although in a dangerous situation here, was courageous in standing up for the dignity of the Jewish representatives.[67] It is true that Stahl had to concede to the Jewish Community in Vienna that the Central Office there was a "quite practical facility" that was signif-icantly speeding up the formalities of emigration. He also emphasized that he "was in no position to criticize" the Viennese system.[68] Yet there were no further negative consequences, largely because Eichmann and his supe-riors were interested in ensuring that the planned Reich Central Office for Jewish Emigration could commence operations only four days later.

The Jewish representatives were confronted once again with a dilemma. They were enjoined to accept a guarantee that they would meet the emi-gration quotas prescribed by the German authorities, although this was dependent on the readiness of the countries of possible emigration to ac-cept emigrants, and not on them. There was huge pressure for emigra-tion; the formalities for the applicants necessitated much time and energy, so that centralizing these procedures appeared to be desirable. However, they did not want to agree to the humiliating implications that were part of the everyday procedures associated with emigration in Vienna. Thus, in a statement Eppstein submitted the following day, they stressed that

> we are interested in the establishing of a central office for emigrants, and regard this as a normalization of emigration. As we understand this, it will mean that the expulsions across the border shall cease, and that we cannot assume guarantees for numbers. And we repeat that we have our mandate solely from the Jewish side.[69]

As important as this clarification may have been for how the Jewish rep-resentatives viewed their own role, it had no subsequent impact on the later practices of the Reich Central Office for Jewish Emigration. Upon its opening, they were already required to present a total of two hundred emigrants, "and from that point on, the heads of the Jewish associations had only one concern, namely how they could furnish this apparatus with sufficient 'material.'"[70] In view of more strict entry requirements in the countries of destination and increased levies and taxes, the Reich Central Office was quite unable to fulfill the hopes initially harbored for a rapid rise in the number of emigrants. In a report by the Security Service Main Office, there is mention "only of 6,187" Jews who had arranged their emi-gration through the new office in April/May 1939; this was due in part to the "lack of adequate organization in the structure of the Reich Central Office and the planned Jewish 'Reich Association,'" and in part to the "increasing tendency for all countries of immigration to impose ever more restrictions on immigration."[71] Thus, the creation of the Reich Central Office accelerated the formal genesis of the Reich Association. Eichmann stated that with this new organization, a "Reich Association of all Jewish Communities" would come into being.[72] In the meantime, by the spring of 1939, the daily routine in the work of the Reich Representation had been reestablished. Kurt Goldmann later recalled:

> Eppstein led a normal financial administration run on a rigorous and strict basis. We were epigones and tried optimistically to normalize everything once again. Unfortunately, at the same time Jewish life was being intensified, namely Jewish public life. … The internal antagonisms were intermixing, both in the Zionist camp and in general.[73]

For the Reich Representation, it was high time to find a new form of organization, because it had to organize the emigration of thousands of Jews while operating in a financial vacuum. In May 1939, there were still 213,930 Jews living in the *Altreich*. By establishing the Reich Association, the Jewish functionaries hoped they could finally obtain control over levies imposed on the Jewish members; they were already planning increases in membership dues,[74] and wanted permission to access the blocked reichsmark (RM) accounts of those who had emigrated.[75]

When the Reich Association was formally created by the 10th Implementation Ordinance to the Reich Citizenship Law on 4 July 1939, it emphatically saw its place within the continuity of the "7th year of activity of the central Jewish organization in the Altreich."[76] Heading up the new organization were the familiar representatives of the Reich Representation: Leo Baeck, Otto Hirsch, Julius Seligsohn, Paul Eppstein, and others. On the level below them, as department heads, several women were also appointed, including Cora Berliner, Hannah Karminski, and Paula Fürst.[77] Most of these functionaries were university graduates, often holding doctorates. Many had worked earlier as legal or economic experts in government administration and had been dismissed from their posts for "racial reasons." Some had relocated to Berlin because the Reich Representation had offered them a new sphere of activity. They continued that work in the Reich Association. For their work, they made use of the old offices of the Reich Representation, and even utilized the stationery of the former Reich Representation. However, this externally similar surface image masked a rapid process of transformation, which intensified in subsequent years. Unlike the predecessor organization, the Reich Association was placed directly subordinate to the Reich Security Main Office (RSHA), set up in September 1939, or to its regional offices, the Gestapo branches, as "supervisory agencies" (*Aufsichtsbehörden*, or superior authorities). The members of the Reich Association were no longer Jewish Communities and associations, but rather individual persons classified as Jews according to the "racial" definition of the Nazi regime. Membership was obligatory for them. The new organization was responsible for the concerns of all "Jews who were members of the state and stateless Jews" as well as the "non-Aryan Christians" and dissidents (a self-designation by Jews who had formally left the Community but had not converted to Christianity); these persons were now direct members of the Reich Association, an organization they could leave only by their death or emigration.[78] Excluded from this regulation were only individuals in mixed marriages. Foundations, societies, and associations, as well as the smaller Jewish Communities, were incorporated into the Reich Association, aside from a small number of exceptions. They thus lost their independence and most particularly their assets, which the National Socialist state then wished to have centralized access to. After the war's end, the Jewish successor organizations discovered that the Reich Association had a balance of more than sixty-seven million RM, stemming from the expropriated assets of Jewish Communities, foundations, and single persons.[79]

The principal spheres of activity left for the Reich Association were assistance for emigration, along with education, professional training, and welfare.[80] Erich Simon, statistician of the Reich Association, summed up the situation with a touch of sarcasm: "In 1939, German Jewry in its entirety was made a legal person, an almost autonomous body within the German population, with shared responsibility, obligations, but seemingly also with some rights."[81]

Even if it became increasingly difficult for the responsible staff in the Reich Association to fulfill their duties, until the autumn of 1941, the interests of the National Socialist state and those of the Jewish organization nonetheless still coincided in a central point: efforts to spur mass emigration. Indeed, the Jewish functionaries were even proceeding on the assumption that the creation of the Reich Association meant that the moderate National Socialists had prevailed over those in the party top echelon who already in 1939 had wanted to confine the Jews in ghettos.[82] While the Nazi regime plundered, harassed, arrested, and tormented the Jews in concentration camps, the Jewish representatives were feverishly looking for any still practicable legal ways (and seen from the perspective of immigration regulations for Palestine, illegal ways as well) to get Jews out of Germany. They appealed to wealthier emigrants to cover the costs for less fortunate emigrants; they appealed to those who had already emigrated to make contributions from their blocked RM accounts in Germany; they turned to foreign aid and relief organizations, asking them to cover the costs for steamship tickets. And in the *Jüdisches Nachrichtenblatt*, they extolled the last remaining possibilities for refuge in South America, the Caribbean, and Shanghai, when the preferred countries of destination refused to admit any more German-Jewish refugees. Thus, those who left Germany were mainly younger, better-situated individuals, with a knowledge of foreign languages, persons with professional skills in demand, and persons with family or other connections abroad. Along with those who did not emigrate for political or emotional reasons—including many women who chose not to leave their older family members—it was largely the elderly, the sick, and those unable to work who stayed behind. Caring for their needs absorbed a substantial proportion of the Reich Association's resources.[83] Financial expert Hans-Erich Fabian estimates that from 1939 to 1943, a total of more than three thousand Jewish organizations, institutions, and Communities were incorporated into the Reich Association.[84] The Jewish Communities still in existence functioned as local branches of the Reich Association, and in addition cared for the religious needs of their members. If a Jewish Community shrank to less than one thousand members, it was dissolved as a separate institution and then incorporated into a district or branch office of the Reich Association. At the end of 1939, there were a total of forty district or branch offices; these were subordinate to both their central office and to the local Gestapo.[85]

In this difficult process of establishing the Reich Association, all the problems with which the organization would subsequently grapple over the next two years were already evident. They could no longer rely on contacts to the non-Jewish population and non-Jewish officials, who until 1938 had often been helpful. From 1939, the Jewish community stood largely isolated. The right to life and physical integrity of the Jews and their functionaries could no longer be regarded as guaranteed. Although external pressures increasingly blurred the internal Jewish lines of conflict, the fundamental conflict still remained, namely, whether the power to decide rested with the Jewish Communities or the umbrella organization. This, for example, had a palpable impact on cooperation with foreign aid and relief organizations. The Berlin Jewish Community and other *Gemeinden* endeavored to conduct separate negotiations with these organizations abroad, while the Reich Association insisted this was not a matter of regional concerns; rather, such relief assistance affected all Jews in Germany, and as such was under the purview of the central institution of German Jewry, the Reich Association.[86]

"Forced Emigration"

The Jews fled in three waves from Germany: after the National Socialist takeover of power in 1933 (1933–1935: 112,500), after promulgation of the Nuremberg Laws in the autumn of 1935 (1936–1938: 101,400), and after the events surrounding the November 1938 pogrom (1939: 68,000).[87] Heydrich had made the release of Jewish men arrested during the November pogrom from the concentration camps dependent on valid papers to emigrate; this was bound up with an oral threat of life imprisonment in a concentration camp should they not leave the country after release.[88] As a result of this threat and against the background of the new anti-Jewish measures that followed the *Kristallnacht* pogrom in 1939/1940, emigration figures soared.

Administratively under the National Socialist regime, the Reich Migration Office in the Interior Ministry was the unit that traditionally dealt with emigration. The Hilfsverein, the Jewish organization that handled emigration to European countries and overseas, had a good working relationship with this agency until 1938. Both sides agreed that only legal departures that were in strict accordance with the immigration regulations of the countries of destination would be permitted. The emigrants were to be persons of good repute, young, healthy, prepared in terms of the language and culture of the target destination, equipped with qualifications in line with the needs in the labor market there; if possible, they should also have some personal funds. In the course of 1938 and the following years, that changed fundamentally, as the Gestapo increasingly intervened in emigration policy and practice. While the Jewish functionaries prudently sounded out the possibilities for group settlement in several countries, and subsequently rejected the idea, aside from a few small projects,[89] the Gestapo preferred mass resettlement by expulsion, a practice that proved a total failure. At the same time, the Propaganda Ministry and National Socialist organizations abroad were blocking potential paths as a result of their anti-Jewish propaganda.[90]

Orderly Emigration or Flight at Any Cost?

Already before the November 1938 pogrom, the Jewish Communities, the Reichsvertretung, and several other organizations had regarded promotion of emigration as their principal task. However, when it came to details, their ideas differed substantially, and various conceptions existed side-by-side within the different political currents as well. Some of the larger Jewish Communities believed they would be able to work more efficiently through their own negotiations and through systems of financing they constructed themselves. They imposed levies on wealthier emigrants, financing the emigration of poorer Jews in this way. Working on their own, they not only collected funds but also acquired visas, Roman Catholic baptismal certificates, or forged certificates of professional qualification by means of black money or bribery, as in the case of the later head of the

Northwest Germany branch of the RV, the Hamburg-based functionary Max Plaut.[91] Often this was with the approval of the local Gestapo. By contrast, the Reichsvertretung was seeking to centralize procedures, and tried hard to avoid risking the good will of the countries of destination by engaging in any illegal practices.[92] At the Evian conference in the summer of 1938, attended by the representatives of the German-Jewish organizations with great hopes (while the German government cancelled its participation), they presented a multi-annual plan for structuring Jewish emigration over an extended period and in harmony with the interests of the countries of destination. Yet Evian fell far short of expectations, and it was not until November 1938 that events in Germany roused the participating countries of destination to take action. Now the Netherlands accepted seventeen hundred, Belgium several hundred, and Great Britain some ten thousand German-Jewish children in the so-called *Kindertransporte*.[93] However, along with the German and Austrian Jews, some ten to twelve thousand Polish Jews and twenty to twenty-five thousand stateless Jews also wished to emigrate; these Jews were often in a precarious situation and were grappling with even greater difficulties.[94]

In 1939, more and more countries closed their doors to Jewish refugees, some already before the outbreak of the war, others only after 1 September 1939. Nonetheless, another thirty thousand persons emigrated in 1939 to European countries, and equally as many overseas (without including Palestine). Now South American countries and Shanghai emerged as destinations over the previously more preferred countries of immigration. More and more frequently, the maxims of "'every man for himself' and … 'necessity knows no law' supplanted emigration policy and preparation."[95] The often quite complicated and time-consuming formalities for emigration now were replaced by an array of stratagems: tourist and transit visas for illegal stay or in-transit further travel, forged papers or documents with partially incorrect data, bogus purchases of land, or passports obtained by bribery. The staff of the RV were also unable to avoid these practices. Eppstein was the only one who adhered to legalism even where the boundaries of legal work had long since been overstepped. Thus, he demanded to see the visas for the Latin American countries given as destination, and only after he had personally inspected them did he cover the expenses, while the organizers required the money beforehand for securing the visas or paying bribes. In order to set his conscience at ease, his associate organizers ultimately presented Eppstein with forged visas that he mistakenly believed were genuine.[96] He also did not want to pay contributions for illegal emigration to Palestine until the emigrant had successfully arrived in the country of destination, a condition that neither the ship owners nor the suppliers of provisions (food, oil, sails, bedding, etc.) for the ships accepted. In actual fact, the boom in migration had brought speculators and swindlers into the picture; they promoted highly adventurous emigration projects, either on their own initiative or encouraged by the Gestapo, and were able to find an interested ear among desperate Jews. However, Paul Eppstein's possibilities to protect emigrants from such machinations proved to be very limited. This was because during the course of the journey, changes and surprises repeatedly occurred in regard to the route, travel times, or other matters. Since he signed vis-à-vis the RSHA for responsibility to cover the costs of such projects, every project that proved abortive, was overpriced, or backfired also endangered him personally.

World public opinion became more attentive to the plight of the Jewish refugees after Cuban authorities failed to permit the more than nine hundred passengers on the SS *St. Louis* to wait for their US visas, as had been promised. The ship was forced to wander from harbor to harbor without permission to dock, until it finally returned to Europe, where its refugees were set ashore in Antwerp. The JOINT,[97] alarmed by the dramatic emergency it itself had not caused, moved swiftly to initiate negotiations with diverse governments. The JOINT was able to arrange for refugees to be accepted in the Netherlands, Belgium, France, and the UK in order to at least prevent their repatriation to Germany.[98] In the meanwhile, Paul Eppstein reportedly insisted that the best option was for the SS *St. Louis* to return to Germany; this would serve as proof to the Gestapo that such a forced emigration was not a practicable option. The risk to the passengers resulted in another decision.[99] However, many of them later became victims of persecution in France, the Netherlands, or Belgium when the occupying German troops poured into these countries.

The fallout from the odyssey of the *St. Louis*—though not the only refugee ship, then the best known that had been denied permission to dock—was that the leading representatives of the Jewish relief organizations met in London to discuss whether visas would best be issued exclusively through their offices. But this could not be implemented in view of the large number of papers that had been obtained privately, or had been purchased or acquired by a bribe. Consequently, these organizations restricted themselves simply to requesting the countries of destination in writing not to change their entry regulations without informing the relief organizations. It was also decided at this meeting not to lend any support to illegal emigration to Palestine, neither financially nor by providing aid to participants left stranded in abortive projects.[100]

Shanghai, for which no entry visa was required appeared as a new destination on the agenda. In 1939, six to seven thousand German Jews emigrated there. Here too the Jewish functionaries, necessarily aware of any alternative option for emigration, nonetheless tried to organize this in an orderly and inconspicuous manner, while the Gestapo remained relentless in its pressure for forced departure. Thus, travel bureaus, acting on Gestapo instructions, hired steamships to transport Jewish welfare recipients in particular to Shanghai, financed by the Jewish Communities or through a special levy on wealthier Jews. The Jewish functionaries attempted to prevent this, fearing that the arrival of "special Jewish ships" in Shanghai would lead to a clampdown there, immediately slamming the door shut on this last possibility for escape and refuge that they were compelled by circumstance to continue to utilize.[101]

Once the war erupted, emigration faltered. Hirsch telegraphed the JOINT: "Emigration of the Jews from Germany now as before unlimited STOP Expansion and acceleration of possibilities for immigration hence of decisive importance."[102] However, German Jews were no longer permitted to emigrate to what were classified as "hostile countries abroad." Transit countries denied travelers legal transit, and it remained very unclear whether ships could, for example, apply to dock at neutral ports. In addition, passage costs on the Dutch, Swedish, and Norwegian steamship lines had increased by 40 to 100 percent, as they demanded a "war surcharge."[103] Until the United States entered the war, North and South America, China, and Palestine still remained open as countries of possible refuge.[104] However, that itself was only on a conditional basis, since the extension of the war in the West and the entry of Italy into the conflict had shut the door on departures from Dutch, Belgian, and Italian ports, and Spain was denying Jewish emigrants a transit visa to Portugal.[105]

This notwithstanding, in the first half of 1940, 9,227 Jews left Germany; of these, 4,347 went to the United States, 1,259 to other European countries, 830 to Shanghai, 670 to Bolivia, 459 to Brazil, and 268 to Argentina. More than half were supported by the migration department of the RV.[106] The Far East and Shanghai could now only be reached overland, which entailed difficult, time-consuming negotiations in order to obtain the long string of transit visas necessary. Organizers and emigrants hoped that from there they could then make arrangements to travel on to other destinations overseas. Until the end of 1941, a total of more than twenty thousand Jews from Germany and Austria fled to Shanghai, where they found neither proper accommodations nor possibilities for work.[107] After the outbreak of the war, the Nazi state began to wonder if, "given the exigencies of state security, should a Jewish emigration, in itself quite insignificant, be in any way promoted?"[108]

Legal or Illegal? Emigration to Palestine (*Aliyah*)

The "natural" destination for Zionist emigration was Palestine. The British mandatory power issued entry visas for so-called capitalists, who could present 1,000 Palestinian pounds (on par with the pound sterling) in their possession; for self-employed professionals, who were able to enter with at least 400 pounds; and for craft artisans, required to have at least 250 pounds. They also issued visas for pensioners with a secure pension, individuals with professional skills in high demand, orphans, blue-collar workers, parents of immigrants, and a few other special groups. In addition, Recha Freier[109] and others had built up an organization for aiding the emigration of children and youth, the Youth Aliyah, which also was granted certificates. The number of "capitalist certificates" was unlimited. But the middle class, which was in a material position to profit from this arrangement, tended to prefer countries such as Great Britain or the United States as a new home. At any rate, legal immigration under the British mandatory power was halted in 1939 in response to Arab pressure, so that this option, specifically in the final phase of the wave of flight from Germany, was no longer available.[110]

Along with such official immigration to Palestine, Zionist circles also operated an illegal immigration, termed "Aliyah Bet" or "Special *Hachshara*." Before the November pogrom, entry to Palestine not accepted as legal by the mandatory power had still been a highly controversial matter among German-Jewish functionaries. According to his own statement, Benno Cohn had endorsed this non-legal migration since the spring of 1938, and Hans Friedenthal had negotiated regarding this several times in London with Chaim Weizmann and David Ben-Gurion. They represented the interests of the Jews of Palestine and Jews desirous of emigration there on behalf of the Jewish Agency[111] vis-à-vis Great Britain. However, prior to November 1938, Weizmann and Ben-Gurion were both opposed to illegal immigration, as were the leading German Zionists, and they changed their position on this only in the wake of the pogrom.[112] Hence, the German Zionists initially concentrated their efforts on legal possibilities for emigration to Palestine, while the "Revisionists" in Vienna and Prague were engaged in arranging illegal immigration by private firms right from the start. Their contractual partners acted mainly on motives of profit, dealing principally with wealthier Jews. The ships they provided were often poorly equipped, and took the largest possible number of passengers on board, which constituted a threat to safety. The German Zionists did not want to accept the associated risks.

The principal concern for the Gestapo was that as many Jews should leave the country as soon as possible. The Nazi regime had already expelled Polish Jews[113] and had no scruples about chasing German Jews over the border to Belgium or promoting and supporting illegal emigration. At the same time, however, on a number of occasions the Gestapo had torpedoed such illegal attempts. The Jewish functionaries were thus acting in a treacherous space where law did not apply, and one and the same act could be accepted as appropriate or treated as a crime. Cohn later recalled: "Eppstein, who acted as liaison with the Gestapo, always came back from discussions there drenched in sweat. Eppstein pursued the tack of legality, he was a legalist in a positive sense, seeking to utilize this for our work."[114]

In connection with emigration to Palestine, the Zionist functionaries instituted their own system of selection among the graduates of the retraining and *hachshara* centers, who had gone through professional, political, and physical training there as preparation for emigration. A transport was supposed to consist of at least 70 percent youths and young adults aged seventeen to twenty-eight. They embodied the largely male "new man," who would be willing and able to cope successfully with the difficulties of the transports often over weeks and months, and enlist his strength and energy in the building of Eretz Israel and serve in the Haganah, the Jewish defense force in Palestine. After the November pogrom, this selection system proved hard to maintain, since an (illegal) Palestine certificate, which the Reichsvertretung/Reichsvereinigung could itself issue, was sufficient for gaining the release of a concentration camp prisoner. In view of the torture and maltreatment in the concentration camps, it was often a matter of life and death. For that reason, it was evidently out of the question to insist on examining the physical condition and other capacities of the prisoners in order to decide about their rescue. In addition, the relatives of the internees stormed the consultation offices in desperation: "The question then was: Zionism or humanity."[115] Interim camps in Great Britain, Holland, and Denmark constituted a compromise solution. Concentration camp inmates, released with the help of *aliyah* permits, were sent to these camps, and after a fitness examination, emigrated either to Palestine or to other countries.[116]

Faced with the threatening overall situation, individuals who had gained some recognition for their contributions to the Zionist movement, but were beyond the stipulated age limit, now started to press for a place in the transports. For example, the representatives of the "movement of the older pioneers" in the Hechalutz, the nonreligious Zionist youth leagues, had the task of selecting six hundred persons who satisfied their criteria from a total of fourteen hundred applicants for a transport.[117]

The Palestine Office, which was later merged with the migration department in the RV together with its staff[118]—and the Hechalutz, as "Occupational Training," was likewise active as a department inside the RV—were permitted in 1939/1940 to open new training farms and *hachshara* camps to handle the huge influx of applicants. The international organization ORT not only created new places abroad, but also opened up its training courses in Berlin to "adults in need of occupational retraining and willing to emigrate" in order to help cope with the dilemma.[119] At the end of

1939, the department of occupational training in the RV listed a total of 28 *hachshara* centers for agriculture, forestry, horticulture, and soil cultivation, with some 1,800 trainees.[120] The Reichsvereinigung was at a point where it might no longer be able to keep track of the number of places for trainees available and the number of certificates already issued.[121] At this juncture, a total of more than 3,400 persons were waiting to emigrate.[122] Yet only 117 German Jews had entered Palestine with proper papers, and 627 without passports.[123]

The RSHA promoted the expansion of the centers over the short term, especially since it had insisted the Reichsvereinigung include "Christian non-Aryans" and Soviet Jews in these programs. But despite expansion of capacity, the number of slots for trainees was insufficient to absorb the youth and adults who now applied. In the spring of 1941, the RSHA shifted to a new tack, severely limiting the number of courses and training possibilities "in favor of labor deployment," that is, the trainees were placed in forced labor groups and most of the workshops were closed down.[124] The Berlin ORT school was allowed to continue operating under the condition that it would cover its expenses by "productive work."[125] Some of the training farms were transferred to non-Jewish leaseholders, but the farms Neuendorf and Steckelsdorf, the Horticulture School Ahlem, the Gehringshof training farm, and the Occupational Retraining Camp Wannsee continued to function.[126]

When emigration was prohibited with the beginning of deportations, more young people, along with most of the leaders of Zionist groups still in Germany, flocked to the last centers, where they believed they would be protected. The leaders Herbert Growald, Kutti Salinger, and Alfred Selbiger from Hechalutz had certainly been in a position to emigrate in the summer of 1940 to Palestine, but out of a sense of responsibility, they had remained.[127] In the late autumn of 1941 only a small number of Jews were debating whether to go underground, an option that did not emerge as a seriously contemplated prospect until the following year.[128] But then the situation became difficult specifically for younger men, who otherwise had good physical and other prerequisites for surviving underground, to go into illegality: they now had to fear the danger of frequent checks of young men by the military police looking for presumed conscripts. The *hachshara* camps seemed good places of refuge.[129]

Subordinated to the Gestapo and transformed into forced labor camps,[130] the centers at least continued to offer the possibility of an internal Zionist educational training, and to organize life together as kibbutzim, even if the young inmates were deployed in part in work gangs beyond the camp in road construction or forestry. Kurt Goldmann reported that the Zionist functionaries intended to continue their work even after the outbreak of war. The youth they trained would prove themselves useful "deployed on the civilian front" in the labor camps, and would in this way survive the war.[131] The internal freedom to shape things deceived the directors, and most certainly the young trainees in particular, about the real seriousness of the situation: it was their illusive hope to be able in this way to outlast the war, and then construct kibbutzim, if not in the "Promised Land," then in the "*Judenreservat* Lublin," on Madagascar, or in the Dominican Republic.[132] On 29 October 1941, just after the beginning of systematic deportations from the *Altreich*, the RV suggested to Martin Gerson that he send the youth from the *hachshara* camps as construction gangs to Eastern Europe, where they could prepare possible accommodations of some kind for the more elderly German Jews in the Lublin district in Poland. Gerson declared in writing his readiness if his conditions were accepted: it would have to be made clear

> that it is the agency's intention for the Jews to shape their own lives by themselves under the supervision of the German agency. And that they can count on the support of the German authorities for receiving their most elementary needs, namely work and food. It would have to be made clear that … the German authorities would also safeguard their lives. … I proceed on the assumption that it must be the duty of Jewish youth … to do everything they can in order to support the resettlement planned by the authorities in such a manner that the absorption of the Jews in the localities of destination will occur without difficulties.[133]

Reportedly, he reiterated his readiness a year later to provide construction services, without his plan being implemented or utilized by the RSHA, as a pretext for deporting this group.[134] Herbert Growald of Hechalutz was deported to Auschwitz together with the last young people from the *Hachshara* Center Neuendorf on 20 April 1943,[135] where he survived. Gerson, as last director of the *Hachshara* Center Neuendorf, was deported via Theresienstadt to Auschwitz, where he was murdered.[136]

However, in 1939, the Zionist leaders, who had set aside their internal differences in the course of cooperation,[137] were unable to anticipate this development. By contrast, they were quite aware that their efforts to promote illegal immigration had contributed to a halt imposed by the mandatory authorities on legal migration to Palestine from October 1939 to April 1940 as a penalty. Its victims were other immigrants, mainly older Jews who had "capitalist" certificates or other papers. Only illegal entry to Palestine was now possible, which in the meantime was also being promoted by the Reich Central Office for Jewish Emigration.[138]

After the war began, the Nazi state initially did not seek to hinder emigration to Palestine. Jewish functionaries explained this as a kind of "routine" and "part of the legalistic thinking of the Germans," since Palestine was "only" a British mandate territory, and thus technically not at war with the German Reich.[139] Of the seven transports of the Special *Hachshara* for which the Gestapo issued exit permits, three left before and four after the war's outbreak.[140] These initiatives were "illegal" in respect to the specified points of departure located outside Germany and in regard to Palestine, where they were in violation of the existing regulations on immigration.

In the first transport in March 1939, the participants went by rail to a Yugoslav port and then sailed on to Palestine. In the second transport, mid-July to mid-August 1939, they had to cross into Belgium illegally and then sail from Antwerp. The third transport, planned by ship from Hamburg, was aborted due to the outbreak of the war. The fourth transport sailed down the Danube in October 1939 and then into the Mediterranean, arriving in Palestine in January 1940. The fifth sailed in November 1939, likewise down the Danube, but was stopped in Yugoslavia, where in 1941 most of the participants were seized and murdered by German troops; a small number managed to flee on to Palestine. The sixth, in May 1940, the paddle steamer *Pentcho*, traveled down the Danube and into the Mediterranean, where the boat capsized. Italian ships rescued the five hundred shipwrecked passengers, and they survived the war in an Italian internment camp. In the seventh transport, twelve hundred German and Austrian Jews reached Haifa after going down the Danube.[141] It is reported that for this last transport, there were thirty thousand applications, some of which were only for the purpose of gaining a certification they could present to the Gestapo, but most in order to actually leave for Palestine.[142]

In retrospect, German Zionist leaders assessed their long adherence to the "pure doctrine," that is, the criteria of strict selection, as having been mistaken from the "standpoint of pure and simple rescue," even if there had also been swindlers involved among the private providers.[143]

In July 1940, the RV informed the JOINT that emigration to Palestine "was almost at a standstill." Only 237 persons, who had been in possession of certificates issued before the war's outbreak, had been able to immigrate, and despite great efforts, it had been impossible to implement further illegal special transports.[144] The war had forced the Zionist leaders Weizmann, Ben-Gurion, and others to come to the side of the British mandatory power. At the end of 1940/early 1941, "there was a danger that Aliyah Bet could be at odds with the ultimate goal of Zionist policy, since it was principally oriented to short-term successes at the expense of the long-terms goals. The Zionist leaders had concluded that such a risk was no longer justified."[145] Aliyah Bet dropped in the list of priorities, declining right to the bottom. The last ship organized by Aliyah Bet arrived on 19 March 1941, and over the next twenty months, no additional illegal transports were organized. Groups of refugees waiting in the Balkans for further transport and Jews in Germany or the occupied countries were now on their own. Emigration to Palestine—whether infused with great political hopes, considered only as a kind of backup solution because other countries had closed their doors, or because it remained the last risky option for escape—did not fulfill the lofty expectations. The country was unable to become a home for the German Jews who were still trying to exit Germany. The Zionist organizations had a well-developed network of facilities for preparing Jews for immigration into Palestine, but these had been conceived for select groups and not large-scale Jewish migration, and were most certainly not equipped for mass flight from Germany. The British mandatory power was not furthering immigration to Palestine in any way; rather, it sought to regulate it, halting immigration when Arab revolts erupted. Even for the leadership in the Jewish Agency for Palestine, the plight of the German and Austrian Jews was only one political factor among other more weighty ones that ultimately influenced their actions.

To Emigrate or Stay On? Functionaries between Duty, Responsibility, and Self-Overestimation

The Gestapo "promoted" and at the same time hindered the emigration of the members of the Reichsvereinigung. Yet how did it deal with the emigration of its leading functionaries, and what was the attitude of these leaders toward leaving Germany? We know that Baeck, according to his own statements, had received six invitations for appointments to positions abroad, but "did not wish to desert."[146] After the war broke out, he wrote to a friend: "We are busy at work, and it shows a different face all the time, sometimes a kind of Medusa. But we are trying hard to achieve what we can, and to give people the feeling that what is possible for them is happening."[147] Moritz Henschel's daughter later reported that aside from his sense of responsibility, what had kept her father, then almost sixty years old, from emigrating was the insight that he would be unable to create a new life for himself anywhere but in Germany: "so I'm staying here, and I'll send my children out at the last moment."[148]

The couple Hedwig and Paul Eppstein were living with the idea of future emigration, but repeatedly rejected plans: already at the end of 1937, during the Kareski crisis, Hedwig had written to relatives that they were determined to leave soon.[149] But for Paul Eppstein, his work was more than just a job to earn a living: "For him [Paul Eppstein], work has to be in some bigger context, and that this is the case here in our situation is very clear. After all, the difficulty of a task doesn't diminish the experience of its value."[150] And in December 1938: "We want to try to go to England in January or February and then wait there. It's still uncertain whether that will work out. … At the moment, leaving is out of the question. For a few weeks, we have to do here what basic responsibility demands. Now is no time to think about one's paltry self."[151] And a short time later: "It's not exactly clear when P. can disentangle himself from work. In any case, he can't suddenly stop working and won't. Ultimately, and this is perfectly clear, the most valuable years of our lives are coming to an end. I am certain that for P., responsibility is more important than his own security."[152] Shortly thereafter, the couple received an entry visa for the United Kingdom, valid for twelve months, where Eppstein had an offer of an academic post to teach. An acquaintance stated that Eppstein had asked Hirsch for advice, who replied that if Eppstein or Lilienthal were to leave, Hirsch likewise would no longer feel obligated to stay. Eppstein interpreted this as "moral pressure," though in some way, Hirsch's answer might have been welcome to him as a pretense for staying. While Hedwig Eppstein emphasized the great importance that this work and responsibility had for her husband, the Zionist Moritz Spitzer, who knew Eppstein, also had some suspicion that there was a certain portion of egotism involved on Eppstein's part: "Maybe he accepted the danger because he didn't want to give up his powerful position. Along with all his good qualities, he was egotistical. Staying on certainly seemed to him personally to be a sacrifice. His wife wanted very much for him to leave Germany."[153] Given the plight of the Jews in Germany, the prospect of an academic position did not seem to be much of a temptation for Eppstein.[154] Paul and Hedwig Eppstein were childless and had only small assets, amounting to 4,100 RM in securities. Along with the entry visa for England, they had put their names on the waiting list for a visa to the United States.[155] Paul's brother Lothar had emigrated to France in 1933 and later on fled to the United States, while his mother survived in unoccupied southern France. The possibility of simply remaining abroad without going through the emigration formalities was prohibited by the RSHA: "Paul and Hedwig were never both issued an exit permit at the same time. One passport was always retained. One was always a hostage for the other," wrote Paul Eppstein's sister-in-law later on, aptly describing the situation not just of the Eppsteins but of many functionaries who had remained on in Germany.[156]

When the Reich Central Office for Jewish Emigration was set up, the Jewish representatives had to leave their passports, which they needed in order to travel abroad to negotiate with foreign relief organizations, in a depository, and then apply for the passport to be handed over to them when traveling abroad.[157] In the interest of "continuity of work," the Gestapo later demanded that every member of the Reichsvereinigung board had to supply his or her personal data, data on family and assets, as well as information on the state of any preparations for emigration.[158]

This questionnaire shed light on the personal situation of the board members and the senior personnel in the RV. Thus, the wife and children of Julius Seligsohn were living in the Netherlands, and he himself was on the waiting list for entry to the United States; Arthur Lilienthal and his wife had an affidavit for the United States and were waiting for a visa. Heinrich Stahl's son was in Belgium and Stahl wanted to join him there, and others as well, such as Leo Baeck, assumed that his departure was imminent.[159] Moritz and Hildegard Henschel had sent a daughter to England, another to Palestine, and hoped to receive a "permit" for family members from one of these countries. Two daughters of the Hirsch couple lived in England and their son was an "agricultural worker" in the United States, where they had also applied for entry; Paul Meyerheim, whose daughter was in Copenhagen, wished to travel on from there to the United States. Cora Berliner had applied for a US visa; Conrad Cohn, Paula Fürst, and Philipp Kozower and his wife and two young daughters (aged five and seven) had applied for a Palestine certificate. But Victor Löwenstein could see no possibility for obtaining an entry permit anywhere for himself, his wife, his two children, and his seventy-nine-year-old father-in-law, who lived with them.[160]

Immediately after he resigned from the Reichsvereinigung, Heinrich Stahl tried to realize his plans for emigration. The RSHA prohibited that, using the hypocritical pretext that Eichmann wished to call a discussion with the entire old board of the RV.[161] In August 1939, the "supervisory agency" in Germany issued a directive stipulating that the replacement for a functionary should be regulated some two months before his departure and in consultation with the agency. Eppstein stressed "that we ourselves have an interest in the uninterrupted continuation of the work of the RV, and as a result have to resolve the question of the emigration of staff and replacement from the standpoint of the demands of the job."[162] At this point in time, his own departure, set for 30 September 1939, was imminent, and the permit for packing was to expire two weeks before that.

The war's outbreak foiled these plans. Several functionaries were at this time at the Zionist congress in Geneva. The executive of the Jewish Agency for Palestine in Geneva decided who from the German delegation should return to Germany and who should emigrate to Palestine. Fritz Berger later explained:

[T]he decisive aspect was whether the type of activity carried out in Germany was still possible and meaningful. It was thus decided that Eppstein (liaison with the Gestapo) and Conrad Cohn (social welfare), and Jacoby [Jacobi] (head of the Palestine Office) should return to Germany, while I, for example, should remain outside. This was because all Polish citizens had been sent to concentration camps the day the war began, and my area of work (rescue of Poles) had thus lost its function. … Arthur Lilienthal, who as a non-Zionist was not attending the congress but happened to be in Paris at the time, returned on his own to Germany.[163]

So Eppstein did not emigrate, even though his application was still active and was being dealt with by the "supervisory agency" as though his departure was always imminent, and that all that was necessary was just to clarify a few outstanding formalities. Thus, for example, in January 1940, he was asked to explain in writing what he could do for emigration if he were to be located abroad.[164] With procedures for him months later still in stagnation, in June 1940 the JOINT did a follow-up,[165] but this failed to change anything in Eppstein's situation.

On 15 August 1940, Eppstein was arrested, charged with having opposed orders by the Central Office for Emigration. In actual fact, Eppstein and the Palestine Office had hesitated to send off five hundred illegal emigrants to Palestine, whose departure had been organized down to the smallest details, when it was suddenly decided that the ship was not authorized to fly the Greek flag. The Gestapo insisted the ship had to sail.[166] In vain, Eppstein emphasized how much he always endeavored to satisfy all orders and instructions "thoroughly and with no consideration for his own person and that of his co-workers."[167] Concerned, foreign relief organizations demanded that Eppstein specifically should be sent to engage in negotiations, this in order to achieve his release.[168] But he remained behind bars.[169] In the meantime, representatives of the RSHA pressed for administrative procedures in the migration department to be simplified; in addition, they recommended that there should be more use of voluntary nonpaid staff and salaries should be reduced.[170]

During the entire four months of his arrest, the Gestapo did not consider it necessary to give Eppstein a reason for why he had been taken into custody. Instead, he was constantly subjected to maltreatment throughout this period in jail, and later needed months to recuperate.[171] After his release, Walter Jagusch[172] informed him that the charges were "serious."[173] It involved how he had managed the *Nachrichtenblatt*: it was alleged that Eppstein had delayed obeying orders, and without the RSHA having been informed, he had contacted "other offices." This last point was evidently not true in regard to Eppstein's activities, but is nonetheless noteworthy: it indicates that the RSHA was still unable to claim it was the sole final authority and arbiter in matters of policy on the Jews. It thus tried to eliminate troublesome competition by seeking to intimidate key representatives of the RV.

Along with the "other offices," this was aimed especially at the Propaganda Ministry, which had supervisory control of the *Jüdisches Nachrichtenblatt*. In future, Eppstein was not allowed to deal with technical matters pertaining to emigration, and was instructed to concentrate on occupational training, legal questions pertaining to assets, and communication with agencies.[174] It would appear that these four months of incarceration had significantly weakened his power to resist. Yet why did he not try to flee, instead continuing to work on? Later his former colleague Berthold Simonsohn explained this in the following words:

> It was Eppstein's aim to maintain the autonomy of the Jewish administration as long as possible, and where feasible to prevent the worst from transpiring. But that could only be achieved if the orders were carried out in such a manner that the Gestapo found no pretext to take over their implementation itself.[175]

To ensure that, he had to carry out orders against his fellow coworkers at least as good or better than the Gestapo, quicker or more smoothly. Indeed, he had to think them through, pondering details and consequences that the RSHA had perhaps not taken into account yet at all. Eppstein considered this a special ability only he and a small group of others possessed. He thus vacillated for four years between a desire to emigrate, the impossibility of leaving his important position, and the external compulsion to stay on.

In February 1941, the RSHA issued a prohibition on emigration by RV board members.[176] Probably for that reason, six days later Paul Meyerheim urgently requested that the JOINT, in an emergency case, should arrange visas for the male leadership echelon of Leo Baeck, Otto Hirsch, Paul Eppstein, Meyerheim himself, Julius Seligsohn, Arthur Lilienthal, and Victor Löwenstein. Once these were obtained, in no case were the beneficiaries to be notified directly, but rather only be informed via confidential coded messages of the JOINT office in Lisbon.[177]

In August 1941, a directive was issued stating that all members of the board and senior staff of the Reichsvereinigung, the Jewish Communities, and the local branches could only emigrate if they had a special permit from the supervisory agency; this should be announced by a circular letter.[178] A short time later, those affected learned that with the beginning of the deportations, there was a total ban on emigration, although this would not apply to them as functionaries. All senior staff of the RV main office had to swear in writing that they would keep the information on the beginning process of deportations confidential. However, the RSHA probably never intended to keep this promise.[179]

Viewed as a whole, most of the representatives and senior staff members of the Reichsvereinigung remained on in Germany out of a sense of responsibility and a feeling that they were indispensable to the organization. The emergency situation of the German Jews led to a dramatic reassessment of activity for the association: it was not a matter of professional work as such or a source of income, but rather the securing of the social and physical existence of those German Jews who could not help themselves. Despite the quite dangerous situation they faced in their high-profile positions, the functionaries could have no doubt about the importance of their work. Even if Paul Eppstein (and most certainly some others as well) were able to gain something from their important function in the organization, since their supposed or actual position of power satisfied their personal need for recognition, they underestimated their own endangered situation. Deceived by promises of the RSHA and evidently operating under a kind of group compulsion among those who had stayed on, they postponed their own emigration for a long time. The fact that by 1939/1940 they were already trapped and those in power did not want to let them leave was something they noticed only if they were arrested under some pretext. Because now the National Socialist state did not even permit persons who had their full emigration papers ready in hand to exit the country. The visas arranged in a lightning operation through the JOINT arrived too late; they could no longer rescue the leadership of the German Jews.

"Losing sight of the big picture for the sake of something smaller": The Conflict over Rescuing the Polish Jews 1939/1940

As mentioned, the National Socialist state had, on 28 October 1938, deported the Jews in Germany of Polish origin to Poland or expelled them into a no-man's-land on the Polish border. Later groups that arrived in the localities along the border, such as those transported from Augsburg, were sent back to their point of departure.[180] But this expulsion operation scarcely encompassed the seizure and expulsion of all Jewish "Poles" living in Germany at the time. In addition, some of those affected were allowed for a limited time to return in order to take care of and settle matters pertaining to their assets and property. Thus, after the German attack on Poland, there were still more than 11,500 Polish Jews in Germany.[181] On 8 September 1939, some 2,000 men were arrested,[182] including around 1,000 in Berlin. This also impacted the functionaries of the Association of Polish Jews over the shorter term, including its director, Moshe Ortner. However, he was soon released so as to be able to look after the relatives of prisoners.

Although the RV had tried to obtain a time extension in June 1939 for the Polish Jews resident in Germany, it remains unclear whether this organization was the responsible body for the interests of this group of

Jews.[183] Nonetheless, Eppstein had requested the Association of Polish Jews to voluntarily disband as an independent organization, and to merge into the Reichsvereinigung. So he evidently regarded the Reichsvereinigung as their representative body. He repeated his request on 1 September 1939.[184] But Ortner received permission from the head of the Office for Foreigners (*Fremdenamt*) to continue work, and the RV then initially broke off relations. On the basis of an inquiry by Eppstein (at least Ortner and Recha Freier believed that was the factor behind this[185]), the Gestapo issued a decree on 19 September dissolving the Association of Polish Jews. Ortner turned to the Swedish embassy for assistance, but in vain; the officials there regarded Sweden as being heavily dependent economically and politically on the German Reich, and so did not wish to represent the interest of the Polish Jews who were incarcerated. Consequently, now there was no longer any organization providing care for the concentration camp prisoners and their relatives, who for the most part received neither information nor material support. In the meantime, the wives were receiving daily reports of prisoner deaths; ultimately fifty (according to Freier) or one hundred (according to Ortner) of these wives gathered in their distress at the building of the Berlin Jewish Community on Rosenstrasse and asked, though in vain, to speak with a responsible official. Two days later, the women disturbed Sukkot services at the synagogue, which had to be interrupted, with shouts of "Help our husbands!" and one woman informed foreign journalists. The Hilfsverein now offered Ortner a consultation room in its premises. On 1 October, five hundred women gathered in the courtyard of the New Synagogue on Oranienburger Strasse, demanding information about what steps had been taken. It is impossible to determine whether Recha Freier, the founder and director of the Youth Aliyah, had in the meantime been approached by the Polish Jewish women, whether she had received instructions from Ortner or the Jewish Community to take action to assist the women, or had decided on her own to act. In any case, she accepted the mandate, and Heinrich Stahl agreed to provide financial help and a consultation room on the premises of the Berlin Jewish Community.

In the subsequent period, Freier actually received cash on a weekly basis from the Jüdische Winterhilfe (Jewish Winter Relief Aid), though from her perspective, this was not sufficient to alleviate the acute distress of the women. Recha Freier repeatedly exceeded the amounts of money allocated as she deemed necessary, in this way obtaining a successive increase in the contributions. However, the conflict between the Palestine Office and the Hilfsverein as well as the RV intensified during the months of her work to assist these women. It reached a point where, in April 1940, the Berlin Jewish Community decided to halt all cooperation with her on this initiative. The spurious reason they gave was that the Jewish Winter Relief was now coming to an end, Freier's work was no longer needed, and the Welfare and Youth Welfare Office would now take her place.[186]

The conflict erupted over the issuance of immigration certificates for Palestine. As mentioned, certificates from the Palestine Office had already helped several German prisoners in concentration camps to obtain their release after the November pogrom. Since an Aliyah Bet group had been readied for 20 November, Recha Freier demanded that the imprisoned Polish Jews be allocated the certificates for this. But the Palestine Office and the RV stated that there were no funds for such an initiative; foreign currency was not available to cover the travel expenses of what Eppstein dubbed the "Polish cases." Freier proceeded to negotiate with the Zionist Abraham Silberschein in Geneva, who set up a trustee office. She then arranged for relatives of the prisoners who had already emigrated to deposit US$200 per prisoner there. If two hundred relatives were to put up this money, Freier calculated that this would be enough to cover the travel expenses of five hundred individuals. In fact, after several weeks a total of US$25,000 was on deposit. This was less than what Freier had calculated, but enough for three hundred persons to leave. Nonetheless, the responsible functionaries in the RV and the Palestine Office were still hesitating. Freier's single-handed efforts to obtain the foreign currency earmarked for this specific purpose were not to their liking, nor did they welcome the prospect that they would have to deviate from Zionist selection criteria for issuing the certificates. In the meantime, further daily reports of prisoner deaths in the camps were received. At the same time, the representatives of the Palestine Office were discussing "to what extent certificates regarding inclusion in special transports could be issued for the purpose of obtaining the temporary release of those imprisoned."[187] They rejected the idea of certificates with deadline dates for departure, since they were afraid that they as functionaries would be held responsible for compliance with those specified dates. By contrast, they did not want to make a decision yet about open-ended certificates, because the functionaries regarded them as hopeless under the circumstances. They did not wish to implement the alternative of issuing confirmations on accommodation in occupational retraining camps after release from confinement; in any case, they were unwilling to consider this option until they had an exact picture of the absorption capacities of the camps. In fact, there was no longer accurate information on the actual occupancy of the camps as a result of emigration, accommodation of German Jews released from concentration camps, and the acceptance of Jews from areas to which deportations had already occurred. By contrast, Freier assumed that it was not the Jewish functionaries who would bear responsibility and liability for the departure, but the individuals who were leaving. And she suggested that overcrowded professional retraining camps could be quickly emptied again by the preferred emigration of "her category," the Polish prisoners.

Ultimately, Freier managed to obtain the first thirteen papers by "surprise tactics" and arranged another thirty through her persistent pressure.[188] However, most of those affected were no longer able to take part in the November *aliyah*. The Reichsvereinigung dragged out the procedure; sessions of the committees making the decision were scheduled but then decided they had no authority to decide and were adjourned. In December, the decision-making body authorized the issuance of seventy-five certificates for the Youth Aliyah under Freier, fifty from the quota of the Palestine Office and twenty-five from the Hilfsverein.[189] Erich Frank, Kurt Silberpfennig, and Alfred Selbiger immediately insisted that these seventy-five certificates should be exclusively on the basis of the non-*hachshara* (i.e. non-Zionist) quota, and that the Zionist selection criteria could not be suspended in any case.[190] Kurt Goldmann succeeded in putting forward a compromise amendment accepted by both sides, that reduced Freier's certificates to just fifty. Eppstein himself, according to Freier, had rejected her proposals with the argument that "he had his own policy vis-à-vis the Gestapo, and could not deviate from that … since, if a larger number of Polish Jews were to emigrate, the camps could be filled up with German Jews in order in this way also to force their emigration."[191] If Eppstein was in any case extremely reluctant to support the concerns of the Polish Jews, his negotiations with the RSHA were made even more difficult by the fact that not only was there no clarity about who bore competence within the RV, it was also unclear who was responsible at the RSHA.[192] Finally, Eppstein asked the RSHA whether Poles of an age liable for military service could be allowed to travel to Palestine at all, since it was British mandate territory (and the British armed forces might then benefit from this by their conscription). Based on (as Freier saw it) this "leading question," the RSHA issued a prohibition on this group for traveling to Palestine, and stated that any vacant places in transports should be assigned to German Jews.[193] Now it was important for the Polish prisoners to find possibilities to emigrate somewhere overseas, but at this juncture such options scarcely existed.[194]

Yet Eppstein's thinking ran in another direction. With the backing of his colleagues on the board, he made a proposal to the RSHA to transfer the Polish concentration camp inmates to occupied Poland, that is the *Generalgouvernement*.[195] This deportation of the prisoners to Lublin in Poland was actually scheduled for the end of March/early April 1940.[196] In the meantime, some one hundred men had been released. Of these, twenty-five who were to travel via Pressburg (Bratislava) to Palestine were able after pressing for this to begin their journey.[197] In Pressburg there was a transit camp supervised by local Jewish organizations. The confrontation escalated between the Reichsvereinigung/Palestine Office and Freier. She could hardly tolerate a situation where decisions in the committees were not being taken immediately and in the interest of the prisoners, endangered by imminent possible death. By contrast, the decision makers in the Jewish organizations wanted to ensure that all aspects would be taken into account and discussed. Freier's (sole) supporter in the Palestine Office, Rudolf Pick, faced with continually incoming reports of prisoner deaths, simply decided to issue the certificates secretly, according to Freier some two hundred.[198] However, since the Palestine Office (when asked) informed the Gestapo that it would not accept any guarantee for the departure of those in possession of certificates, the Gestapo did not release these prisoners.[199] Although the long-established governmental Consultation Office for Emigration declared its readiness to accept a period of departure valid for several months, the Jewish functionaries refused to grant priority to the incarcerated Polish Jews for illegal transports, instead giving such priority to the German Jews who were not behind bars. Once again, in a single week in January, reports arrived of twenty-four deaths among Polish prisoners in the camps. In the meantime, the Palestine Office Commission rejected even voting on certificates because at that juncture, they had no idea whether these would even be recognized. Thus, Freier and Pick issued thirteen more certificates at a meeting that had no authority for making decisions, and these were later not recognized by the absentee members. Pick ultimately resigned from his position on the Palestine Office Commission,[200] and on 9 February 1940 the director of the Palestine Office suspended Recha Freier as director of the Youth Aliyah (termed within the RV, Jüdische Jugendhilfe, Jewish Youth Aid), an initiative that she had established herself. In actual fact, the conflict over the Polish camp prisoners had nothing to do with the successful work of this organization. Her removal was intended as a prophylactic measure to prevent her from continuing to have a post within the RV from which she could act with apparent legitimacy.

The Reichsvereinigung was striving for a step-by-step agreement: Recha Freier was requested to expressly acknowledge the "institutional discipline of the Jewish organizations," and then her suspension from office would be revoked. She was then to resign from the chair of the Youth Aliyah and would receive a special assignment to arrange foreign currency for special transports to Palestine. Freier rejected this proposal. She said she was unwilling to justify her actions before a body that, for its part, did not account for its decisions to the Jewish public, and she launched a counterattack. She criticized the rapid change by Erich Frank from an advocate of legal entry into Palestine to the leader of the Special *Hachshara*. She pointed out that she had personally checked the prisoners regarding their qualifications for Palestine, and she appealed to religion and Zionism to clarify the legitimacy of her concerns, which involved matters of life and death. "Most certainly," she conceded, "you bear the responsibility for everything that is happening, and people cannot demand that you should lose sight of the big picture for the sake of something smaller."[201] Nonetheless, "because of petty formalities and competencies," the rescue of the concentration camp inmates was not accelerated. In addition, she was adamant in demanding to see the minutes of the Youth Aliyah committee meeting regarding her removal from office. Ultimately, one representative who had participated in the meeting, Lyon, had to admit that there had been no vote but only "questioning of certain individuals."[202] Thus, the "attempt to resolve the matter" had rather aggravated the conflict even further; Freier lost not only her mandate for the Polish Jews but was also stripped of her position as head of the youth organization. Its executive board did not declare solidarity with her; on the contrary, the board later confirmed her removal from office.[203] Eppstein followed suit, stating that her behavior had "seriously shaken … his previous trust in her as a person and in her work."[204]

Not until after Freier was suspended from her tasks did the RV finally intervene on 28 February 1940 with the RSHA regarding the "Polish cases," this after Eppstein a week before had obtained permission to submit a memorandum.[205] In his memo, he pointed out that more than 10 percent of those incarcerated in Berlin had died, and he asked for the release of those who could emigrate overseas, those born after 1900, who were to go to Palestine, and those who could be brought to Russia. Those over the age of sixty were to be sent to a home for the elderly.[206] In September/October 1939 this intervention might have had some success, but now it came too late for the dead, and without any success for the living. The RSHA instructed Eppstein to retain the trustee account in Switzerland and, if possible, to use the money to support the emigration of German Jews or to obtain payments for them.[207]

Recha Freier's personal situation worsened after she was summoned to Eichmann because, contrary to regulations, she had not immediately returned her passport after an official trip abroad.[208] She reported later that an official warned her: "Frau Freier, you know what your colleagues did, they had their suspicions and reported you! You have to leave here as soon as possible."[209] Supposedly, colleagues from the Reichsvereinigung had accused her of anti-Nazi propaganda. Recha Freier fled in July 1940 with her daughter to Vienna, and with the help of smugglers went on to Yugoslavia. After arrival in Zagreb, she organized a meeting of the Jewish organizations there and persuaded them to engage the smugglers to rescue the children of the Polish Jews detained in concentration camps as well. Although the foreign organizations agreed to this project, the Reichsvereinigung refused to hand over the children. Freier then claimed that 100 certificates for entry to Palestine were ready in Zagreb, and threatened to inform the international public if the RV allowed these certificates to expire unused. In the end, the Reichsvereinigung gave in and agreed, and the smugglers, according to Freier, brought 120 children across the border.

Freier encountered problems similar to those she had come up against in Germany when she notified Henriette Szold, director of the Youth Aliyah in Palestine, about the children. Szold did not want to take in any children who had left Germany during the war. If they were to enter mandate territory, they would be violating British law. This notwithstanding, Freier arranged to have ninety children brought to Palestine without a formal safeguard. Those who remained behind managed with great difficulty to elude the invading German troops, and finally made it via Italy to Switzerland. Freier and her daughter traveled by land through Turkey and Syria to Palestine, where Henriette Szold then informed her she no longer had any place in the Youth Aliyah. Recha Freier had to look for another field of activity.

From 1933 to 1938, the results of the inner-Jewish elections had determined the power relations inside the Jewish Communities and shaped the committees of the Reichsvertretung. Under conditions that did not allow for further democratic elections, this internal Jewish power structure was carried forward in the RV and perpetuated in a frozen form. Those making the decisions in 1939/1940 had for many years no longer had any democratic legitimation from the German Jews, and naturally they could no longer give an account of their actions to them. Instead they were subordinate to the RSHA, required to report to them and bound by the agency's orders. Nonetheless, they attempted to maintain internal transparency in the organization and coordination. They safeguarded their decisions through internal discussion in the committees and consulations with one another. Under the conditions of National Socialism, what other option for action did they have, especially since no end to the war was in sight? The outsider Recha Freier, with her radical commitment to the cause of the Polish Jews, interrupted the carefully balanced power relations in the Palestine Office, the commissions, and the RV, calling it into question. Impetuous and full of ideas, she sought to assist "her category," angering in this way other functionaries, whose structures, built up over years of work (*hachshara* camps, Aliyah Bet), she endeavored to utilize. In view of the threat to the lives of the Polish camp inmates, Recha Freier categorically rejected rules and regulations, voting procedures, and consideration for other particular interests or even personal orientations. The Zionist decision makers had never objected to Freier's activity in the Youth Aliyah, because that did not impinge on their spheres of responsibility; rather, it supplemented these quite well.[210] But now they reacted with hesitation, even delaying tactics, in a petty and destructive manner; indeed, they repeatedly violated their own procedural rules, which they were so adamant about. Traditional reservations against the Polish Jews as *Ostjuden* may well have strengthened this attitude, although there are no explicit references to that except for the somewhat derogatory expression "Polish cases" (*Polen-Fälle*) employed by Eppstein. Probably predominant among the organizational representatives was a defensive stance against encroachment upon their spheres of competency and responsibility.

Most particularly, they did not want to surrender their right to select the qualified emigrants. Even much later, after almost two decades, Kurt Goldmann, for example, stuck adamantly to his view back in 1939/1940: unlike the legalist Eppstein, who acted in a positive way for the Jewish side, he stated that Recha Freier had been engaged "solely for 'partisan struggle,'" and that she espoused the thesis: 'Eppstein is selling the Jews.' But she was always one-sided, and never contemplated the consequences of her proposals and actions."[211] It was only Rudolf Pick, who worked together with Freier, who later commented that the committee for special transports was always intent on "preserving its competencies and shielding all events from the eyes of the controlling authorities."[212] He conceded that the opponents of Freier represented justified valid interests, but argued that at that juncture, it had been a mistake to jealously reject new ideas such as self-financing and to seek to counter the rising interest in illegal migration to Palestine. Historian Yfaat Weiss, who investigated relations between Polish and German Jews in the 1930s, comments on the behavior of the Zionists in this situation: "It is unclear why the Zionists failed to comprehend the urgency of assistance for the Polish Jews in Germany and why they thought there was no longer any possibility for assistance."[213] Pick's summary largely answers her question: they were fighting for their right of determination over their own achievements, or to put it in more everyday discourse, to protect the claim they had staked out as their own preserve of decision making.

In addition, Eppstein's attitude in each and every situation of decision was fundamentally shaped by his interest in determining in what way this decision could impact on the ostensible overall general interest of the German Jews, and that he could be held personally responsible for the failure of a project or its unintended consequences. He thus tried to take into consideration all possible objections, all adversities and dangers that might arise, all reproaches that could be directed against him, and tried preemptively to counter them. It is very likely that he was actually afraid—as already earlier on during the "June operation," which targeted Jews with a "previous criminal record"—that the Gestapo could make use of the rescue efforts by the Reichsvereinigung for the group incarcerated as a precedent to expel the other remaining Jews in the *Altreich* via arrest and internment in a concentration camp. Organizing the emigration of the Jews from Germany was a daunting enough task in any case for the RV—as well as for the potential emigrants—especially since all doors were gradually closing. Eppstein's inquiry to the RSHA about whether those of an age liable for possible military service could be permitted to leave for Palestine proves to what extent he had already internalized the thinking of his persecutors. Indirectly in this way, he warned the RSHA not to permit something that perhaps later on would turn out to clash with National Socialist or German interests. In addition, that could have negative consequences for Eppstein himself, should the RSHA representative accuse him of having tricked them and "foisted" something on them—that is, that Eppstein had made proposals that went against German interests and were thus damaging. At no time were Recha Freier's actions characterized by the presence of such scruples. With a feeling of being morally in the right and relegitimated by every new report of another prisoner's death, she acted in a bid to ward off acute danger, irrespective of the conceivable implications for the German Jews as a whole or for the Jewish functionaries. The more the conflict escalated, the more desperate (as she saw it) or more polemical (from the vantage of the others) did her actions become. One such example was when, at a meeting, she demanded the same number of certificates equal to the total number of death reports from the camps the week before. Mercilessly, in her attempt to keep misery and death at bay, Recha Freier tore down the walls behind which the functionaries had entrenched themselves, and she ignored their rules of procedure—bureaucratic structures with which the functionaries sought to persuade themselves that they had some modicum of latitude and freedom of action.

At the end of 1939 and in early 1940, the RSHA was quite willing to approve travel visas for functionaries, especially when the purpose was to acquire foreign currency for paying the passage of emigrants, and such visas could be applied for at the designated office. When functionaries traveled to such negotiations abroad, the hopes and desires of the others (and even the good will of the regime) went with them. The fact that Eppstein did not even consider going on the trip to Geneva arranged by Recha Freier, and did not even try to apply for a visa for her and himself, points to how fundamentally reluctant he was to make use of the connections of this unpopular activist, and to appear elsewhere accompanying her as a representative of the RV. The purpose of the trip, namely, to secure foreign currency for emigrants who were barred from going to Palestine because they were in an age bracket liable for possible military service, was deemed less important.

Expulsion of the Polish prisoners to Poland, which Eppstein supposedly proposed to the RSHA, may have appeared to him a suitable solution to the crisis. After all, there were Nazi plans to construct a "Jewish reservation" in Poland in which millions of Jews from the German Reich, Poland, and elsewhere would be concentrated. And it should be kept in mind that at this juncture, Eppstein still probably had not received any alarming reports on the living conditions in Lublin, where Polish Jews were being squeezed together in ghettos and the first transport from the *Altreich*, consisting of Jews from Stettin, had just arrived.

Vis-à-vis the RSHA, Eppstein explicitly distanced himself from Freier.[214] But it is not evident from the files whether he, another functionary in the Reichsvereinigung, or Leo Baeck—who in Freier's view bore overall responsibility, as Reichsvereinigung president—had denounced her to the authorities because of alleged anti-Nazi propaganda activities, as she stated on several occasions after the war's end.

Perhaps the Polish concentration camp prisoners could have been rescued at the last minute; it is possible more German concentration camp inmates could have been released on the basis of Palestine certificates or supposedly guaranteed places in *hachshara* camps. Perhaps criminals like Freier's smugglers would have brought them across international borders. But despite the disputes in Berlin over legal versus nonlegal immigration to Palestine and the controversy over the possible rescue of Polish or German prisoners, in the spring of 1940, the Aliyah Bet faltered. It was precisely the wave of refugees from occupied Poland that put the Balkan countries on the alert. They tightened regulations for entry and transit, so that the last remaining pathway to freedom, sailing down the Danube, tended to be closed at points, and had become more unpredictable, more costly, and more fraught with danger. In addition, the outbreak of the war plunged Palestine into economic crisis, so that Aliyah Bet could no longer be continued as had been planned. Decisions about its continuation or termination were not made by the German Jews and their functionaries; they and the Jews in the occupied territories had no real influence on these decisions.

The "Territorial Solution": "Reservations for Jews" and Early Deportations

The renewed efforts by the Reichsvereinigung in 1939/1940 to implement the demands of "forced emigration" were because of the pressure of time: the plans of those in power now were moving forward to resettle the Jews from the *Altreich* together with those in the occupied territories in "reservations" or colonies on the periphery of the German Reich. This initiative, by no means a new idea among the schemes bandied about by anti-Semites, marked the transition after the outbreak of the war from mass or individual expulsion to a "territorial solution of the Jewish Question." It meshed with plans for huge removals and shifts of population in line with the "racial restructuring" of Europe. Browning correctly notes that "the *Endlösung* in this period meant the expulsion of the Jews to the furthest extremity of the German sphere of influence, first Lublin and then Madagascar."[215] But at this point in time, anti-Jewish policy did not play a central role in the plans for massive demographic restructuring and a new order.

While ideas were being developed and debated among the top echelon of the National Socialist state, and individual *Gauleiters* (district leaders of the Nazi Party) seized the opportunity to deport "their" Jews, the representatives of the RV evidently received no official message regarding the Lublin plan, even if the documentary sources indicate that they were aware of the rumors in rife circulation.[216] When this plan for reservations was replaced by the vague notions of a Madagascar plan, the Jewish representatives were brought into the planning process, ordered to draft at short notice potential possibilities for concrete implementation. However, they were only provided with a rough idea of the project the National Socialists had in mind, and were not informed about the actual destination area.

Although the Jewish representatives were not made privy to the ideas under discussion, they were repeatedly confronted by surprise with problems that preliminary discussions on the new "territorial solutions" generated, such as when the Jews in individual regions were suddenly evacuated—without any forewarning and with no information about rationale or destination. Only in the small number of cases where the RV happened to learn earlier about planned "resettlements," and there were divergent interests at play between local actors and the RSHA, was it possible to prevent the deportation of the Jews. Otherwise, Reichsvereinigung officials sought with great difficulty to gather information about those deported, to improvise care for the Jews remaining behind, to clarify questions of property law, and if possible to prevent any future deportations. Yet despite all their efforts, they were unable to have any substantial influence on events, nor could they even obtain the right to advance information or the right to act. I wish to illustrate this as exemplified in the "*Reichsghetto* Lublin" and, in a more brief form, in the "Madagascar Plan" (since the latter is extensively documented in the literature), and in the deportations ordered in anticipation of these vague options.

A Jewish Reservation in Lublin

After the attack on Poland, some 2 million more Jews came under German control, added to the approximately 346,000 Jews then under National Socialist rule in the German Reich (including the Sudeten area and the Saar). To render the German Reich "free of Jews" thus demanded increasingly extensive planning. Over the short term, the decision makers were evidently contemplating the idea of deporting some 2 million Jews to the Soviet Union, which had already taken in 200,000 Polish Jewish refugees. Birobidjan or western Ukraine were the settlement areas being considered. However, the Soviet Union showed no interest in such a plan.[217] In the phase of "relative euphoria of victory, massive use of force and destructuring in Poland,"[218] at the end of September 1939 the area around Lublin loomed central in thinking about the creation of a *Judenreservat* or *Reichsghetto*,[219] about which Hitler had often spoken. Adolf Eichmann found himself at this juncture in a professional dead end due to the faltering of Jewish emigration. According to Browning, he used the opportunity that the new possibilities (still to be worked out) offered him. After conferring with Gestapo chief Müller, he informed his coworkers in Prague that Jewish construction gangs were initially to build barracks camps in the area in question. He thought that the participation of the Jews themselves was "necessary in the interest of preserving a certain 'voluntary character' and also to arrange a departure of the transport as unobtrusive as was possible."[220] Plans were for some three hundred thousand Jews from the *Altreich* and the *Ostmark* to be resettled and concentrated in Lublin. In October 1939, the first Jews were deported from Eastern Upper Silesia and Vienna to the areas bordering on Nisko on the San, but this test case met with failure right at the outset. The operation turned out to be a fiasco for the Jewish construction gang that the head of the Vienna Jewish Community, Josef Löwenherz, had put together on a volunteer basis. A contemporary report, assembled for the Zionist Organisation of America from "trustworthy reports," states that an area of some eight hundred to one thousand square kilometers had been set aside for constructing a "reservation totally separated from the surrounding environs and under the most heavy guard."[221] In "Judaea," as it was to be called, it was anticipated that the elderly, women, and children would die a slow death from starvation. The reporter noted that the German Jews had concluded from the fact that the RSHA had just presented its Three-Year Plan that there were no plans for immediate evacuation, even if the activity of the

Jewish institutions had become "extremely precarious." But "the Jewish leaders were fighting like true heroes in a battle which they knew was lost."[222] The Lublin operation was terminated, although not because it had failed or even because Jewish functionaries could have prevented its realization. Rather, this was probably because the planned resettlement of the Baltic Germans was given priority, although only after several additional smaller transports had been carried out.[223]

In the *Altreich*, where the *Gauleiters* and mayors were endeavoring to remove the Jews from their respective spheres of competence, the plans for deportation hardly remained confidential. Thus, for example, the SD district office in Bad Kissingen reported in November 1939 that there was

> animated discussion about the problem of the former Polish territories. The story was being circulated that the Jews, the whole lot of them, are being resettled in the territory between the San and Bug rivers around Lublin. The area is reportedly about 300 km² in size. Jews from Austria and the Czech state are already reported to have arrived there. [...] At the same time, people say that all Gypsies and vagabonds living in Poland are being deported and relocated to this area, and that there is no possibility for return, unless the residents of this settlement area are attempting to emigrate to Russia. These measures have been welcomed by members of the Party and a large proportion of the *Volksgenossen*, and proposals have been advanced that the Jews who still live within Germany should likewise begin to relocate to this area.[224]

The mayor of a town in Rhine-Hesse hoped that the migration of the Jews to the East would be clarified by some "higher authority."[225] Jews potentially affected, the RSHA reported, were trying to relocate to the large cities of Berlin, Breslau, and Leipzig, which might not be included in the deportations.[226]

Hans Frank, the Governor General in the *Generalgouvernement* (occupied Polish territories), initially interpreted the halt to transports to the Lublin district as Göring giving Frank the power to veto any undesired deportation into his territory. He now also assumed that later on, there would be far fewer persons than planned who would be deported to the *Generalgouvernement*, including "a still to be determined number of Jews from the Reich."[227] Some eighty thousand Poles and Jews had been resettled there up to January 1940, and another thirty thousand had been "shoved into the General Government 'illegally.'"[228] When the Jews from Stettin arrived in February, he complained to Göring.

This expulsion from Stettin sparked an international furor.[229] The press in the United States and Great Britain reported on the removal, and the small German-language paper of the Palestine immigrants, *Yedioth*

Hayom, also carried articles.[230] Just three days after the deportation, the paper wrote (with exaggerated figures): "New Transports to Lublin. Amsterdam: In the past few days, numerous Jews were for the first time sent from Germany to the Lublin District, a total of some 8,000 ... Previously only Jews from the CSR and Austria have been sent to Lublin."[231] And the same issue noted: "The German Free Radio reports that the Nazis have begun deporting Jews from the districts of Cologne and Aachen."[232] Three days later: "The 'Times' in Rotterdam has reported that the transfer of Jews to Lublin from Danzig, Luebeck, Rostock, Stettin and other cities on the Baltic coast has now started ... 1,057 Juden who were expelled from Stettin have been transported to Piaskow, east of Lublin."[233] Apparently the anonymous writer of this article suspected, like others at the time, that Jews were being forcibly resettled from the towns on the Baltic coast for military reasons. But the resettlements were being carried out in Danzig and Stettin, not Lübeck or Rostock.

How did the deportation of the Jews from Stettin, which caused such an international uproar, unfold? The order on 12 February 1940 stating that Stettin Jews had seven hours to pack came as a total surprise to them, although they had been waiting for days in anticipation of some analogous kind of operation.[234] On 1 January 1940, the *Gauleiter* Franz Schwede-Coburg, notorious as a fanatic anti-Semite, and the local mayor informed Jews in Stettin and elsewlere in Pomerania in writing that they would be concentrated within two weeks in an empty department store.[235] Privy to these plans and probably also involved in their organizing on the Jewish side was Paul Hirschfeld, a member of the board of the Stettin Jewish Community, and, in the words of Berthold Simonsohn, "a man devoid of any scruples." Hirschfeld had acquired a certain position of power when it became evident that Levy, the older head of the Community, was unable to resolve the problems that had arisen when a large number of Austrian Jews had attempted to depart to Finland via Stettin.[236] Hirschfeld then organized emigration for Austrian Jews using dubious arrangements, and with the backing of the Gestapo.

He did not inform the central office of the RV in Berlin about the "relocation" of the Jews affected in Stettin. It learned about this from members of the Community and intervened successfully with the RSHA. In general, the RSHA tried to prevent so-called individual operations (*Einzelaktionen*), which it was not officially in charge of. The appointed trustee for the building in which the Jews had been housed and the Stettin public health authorities now put forward their objections, so that the whole plan came under fire and had to be cancelled in mid-January. But the Jews involved were fearful, and correctly so, that the Nazi Party officials would not acquiesce in this. And indeed, four weeks later, police, together with the SS and SA, launched a roundup operation, arresting Jews young and old, men and women, religious Jews, "dissidents" who had left the Jewish Community, and Jews who had been baptized as Christians; only those in mixed marriages were left behind. After a few hours, Jews arrived in Stettin from Stralsund, and the train departed toward Schneidemühl in the direction of Lublin, where the prisoners were then transported to Piaski and Belczek. The elderly remained in Glusk, and some two hundred are believed to have soon perished there. There were numerous deaths already during the transport, and it is reported that 30 percent died in the harsh conditions at the destination during the first six months after arrival, while "the others struggle to barely survive on contributions coming in from everywhere in the world."[237]

The RSHA prohibited the RV from providing any direct assistance at their destination in the Lublin district to those transported.[238] Nonetheless, staff workers at the central office in Berlin and members of the Munich and other Jewish Communities sent aid parcels, using a false return address, as long as that was possible.[239]

When the Reichsvereinigung central office was finally permitted to dispatch an accredited representative to Stettin, Max Plaut, head of the Northwest Germany district branch, his task was solely to implement the liquidation of the Jewish Community. He found only a few sick Jews who had remained behind, orphans and the elderly, and organized care for them. He reported later that he was successful in buying back ninety thousand RM in movable goods (furniture, clothing, etc.) from the trustee of the expropriated property and was able to send this on to the deportees. He noted that postal correspondence and sending of cash remittances and parcels to the Lublin district was still possible.[240] But the assets of the deportees and the proceeds from their furniture that had been auctioned, etc., were placed in a closed trustee account to which neither Plaut nor the Jews deported from Stettin had access. The only possible payment transfers were to Jews in the Reich who had a claim to maintenance by a Stettin Jew. Supposedly the emigration of Stettin Jews from the Lublin district was permitted, but it was impossible to arrange due to the large amount of foreign currency necessary, or was restricted solely to persons who were already in the possession of valid emigration papers.[241] Rabbi Max Nussbaum in Berlin reported on an attempt by the RV "to arrange a group emigration for the German Jews in Piaski, but we failed."[242]

Only on one occasion was the Reichsvereinigung officially able to assist the deportees: on 17 April 1942, Jews formerly from Stettin contacted the association after they had been ordered to wear the German *Judenstern*, the yellow star (not the Polish one), which was obligatory for them in the Lublin district. Walter Skomlinski wrote urgently:

> We have no chance to purchase anything, we have no yellow cloth, etc. Is the *Reichsvereinigung* in a position to help us with procurement <u>as quickly as possible</u>, which seems so important? We are still 225 people, and hope to remain at that number, and are happy to comply with the regulations for identification.... It is extremely important for us. 1,000 thanks from our people in advance.[243]

With this coded formulation, he intimated cryptically that once there had indeed been one thousand Jews there.

Not only the Jewish contemporaries were in the dark about the reasons for this early deportation of the Stettin Jews; their deportation continues to give rise to speculation. Was it an individual operation ordered by the *Gauleiters* or other leading local Nazis, was it perhaps an act of revenge, did it have military reasons, or was it centrally planned?[244] Paul Meyerheim and other contemporary German-Jewish functionaries suspected an act of revenge by local persons in power in Stettin or Pomerania, while the other resettlement operations (East Frisia, Baden, the Palatinate) had had strategic reasons, not anti-Semitic ones.[245] The historian Wolf Gruner, referring to an announcement by Heydrich at the end of January 1940 to deport the Stettin Jews, stresses the active role of the Gestapo in Stettin as the implementing body, suggesting that the RSHA had initiated the operation.[246] By contrast, it is clear from the memos on the summons orders to Jewish representatives in Berlin that the lower-ranking representatives of the RSHA knew nothing about the plans or concrete events or the involvement of the Gestapo offices (or perhaps only pretended to know nothing in order to deceive the Jewish representatives, although that appears unlikely). Eichmann declared three days after the deportation that it had been carried out for special reasons that he did not explain, and had not been due to his own order.[247] Max Nussbaum, who emigrated in August 1940, was instructed by the RV to provide the JOINT in the United States with a full and genuine oral report on these events. Nussbaum informed the representatives of the Jewish relief organization that the Reichsvereinigung had only learned about events in Stettin from one Jew there who had managed through a visa to the United States to avoid deportation. He stated that the RSHA had not been informed and had only been able to establish after several phone calls that this was an "individual operation by the regional governor of Pomerania."[248] It is also evident from Eppstein's memos about the operation in Stettin and Schneidemühl that Walter Jagusch, responsible in the RSHA for "Jewish Affairs,"[249] had not been informed. Eppstein complained that

> such a deportation seriously jeopardizes our work. State assessor Jagusch replies that his agency was against such deportations for the "Altreich,"

and that Stettin constituted a special case for particular reasons, but that further deportations would probably not occur. Then the report on the announcement of the deportation of the Jews from the Schneidemühl District is submitted. Assessor Jagusch now explains that this measure had not been ordered by the central agency, and that he would contact the state police in Schneidemühl regarding this ... Replying [to Eppstein's statement] that we feel obliged to inform the ministries who are signatories to the 10th Implementation Ordinance on the Reich Citizenship Law about the situation, Assessor Jagusch states that in his view this is not necessary, because the practice still in force remains the same; in accordance with previous declarations of the agency, if there are no special reasons, there should be no deportations from the Altreich.[250]

During this summons meeting, Eppstein protested with two helpless gestures against the procedure: first, he stated that he wished to inform the ministries that were dealing with the persecution of the Jews about events in Stettin. That implied that the RV assumed (probably correctly) that these ministries were not informed about the deportations and would perhaps intervene if they were aware of events. However, at this point the ministry officials were no longer allies of the German Jews. They probably might have raised an objection in order to demonstrate their involvement in Nazi Jewish policy, but it is doubtful whether this would have had a retarding rather than an energizing effect on the whole process. Eppstein's second gesture was when he announced: "You can probably understand that under these conditions, we find ourselves unable to go ahead with the performance of the Kultur-Bund scheduled for 16 February."[251] The RSHA did not care about this form of protest by means of cancellation of a scheduled event.

On the basis of the documents cited, it is reasonable to suspect that the regional deportation operations came as a surprise to the RSHA, which then stepped onto the scene.[252] The RSHA was unable to cancel the Stettin operation, but it at least intervened in respect to the deportation of the Jews from Schneidemühl[253] so that only a portion of the Jews there were deported. Evidently, not all Jews in Schneidemühl were deported to the Lublin district as planned, but "only" 165 persons.[254] Later, contrary to the facts, Eichmann claimed that they had been sent only as far as Poznan and had been brought back and resettled in the Altreich, though not in Schneidemühl itself.[255]

The RSHA "generously" permitted the RV to temporarily accommodate the other Jews from Schneidemühl in hachshara centers and to assign them to other localities. Later they were also allowed to prepare assembly camps and emergency accommodations for Jews from Stettin and Schneidemühl who had been absent from the area when the deportations took place, for scattered Jews from Danzig, or for other "resettled" Jews from "evacuated areas."[256]

In relation then to Stettin, all the Reichsvereinigung could do was to sweep up the broken pieces. It transferred competency for the Stettin area to the Northwest Germany district branch, and competency for the previous branch office of Köslin to the branch office of Brandenburg. Under Plaut's supervision, the controversial board member in Stettin, Paul Hirschfeld, completed several special tasks, after he had initially threatened Plaut with having the Gestapo arrest him.[257] Since Plaut was acting at the behest of the RV and with the approval of the RSHA, and in addition knew the head of the Gestapo office in Stettin personally from his previous activity in Hamburg, he was able to carry out his assigned task undisturbed. Later, the Jews deported from Stettin gave the RV powers of attorney for their property. The RV central office then relieved Hirschfeld of his post as director of the district office.[258]

Paul Meyerheim secretly informed representatives of the JOINT that the Jews from the small towns in Pomerania had been treated like those from Stettin. After arrival at their destination, they had been crowded together in two halls. But now, in May 1940, the deportations to Lublin had finally been halted. According to Meyerheim, some eleven hundred persons had been deported there (a figure probably too low), and the Reichsvereinigung had been unable in any way to intervene on their behalf.[259]

The plan that soon followed to resettle the Jews from East Frisia was likewise not authored by the RSHA. The RSHA apparently disapproved of the initiative of the Gestapo office in Wilhelmshaven, which it had not authorized, as well as the rescue operation that the Northwest Germany branch and the Reichsvereinigung central office had initiated together with the Jewish Communities affected and the local Gestapo.

By way of exception, the Reichsvereinigung this time had received advanced knowledge that the Gestapo was planning to relocate Jews from the districts of Wilhelmshaven, Jever, and Aurich, since the region was slated to be a "closed military deployment zone."[260] It is clear from documents that mayors and Nazi Party offices here had taken the initiative already before the deportation of the Jews from Stettin. They utilized the pretext that they needed to prevent spying in the border region and on the coast, and wished to vacate living quarters that were in urgent demand.[261] The Gestapo had summarily designated the son of the head of the Jewish Community in Aurich, Wolf Wolffs, as his father's successor, and ordered him to resettle all Jews by 1 April 1940. Two weeks later, the Gestapo threatened him with arrest and internment in a concentration camp, since the Jews were still in Aurich.[262] Impressed by the events in Stettin, the Gestapo radically altered its conception and now wished to deport the Jews to the Lublin district. Max Plaut, head of the RV North-west Germany branch that was responsible for the area, and the leaders of the Jewish Community, then arranged an agreement with the local Ge-stapo "Jewish specialist" (*Judendezernent*) to "relieve" the Gestapo "of the task" and to relocate the Jews within three weeks, sending some to Berlin, Hanover, and Hamburg, and some to live with relatives elsewhere.[263] Ac-cording to the final report of the Gestapo office in Wilhelmshaven, this involved 843 Jews who were relocated between January and March 1940, while some 160 elderly Jews remained behind in homes for the aged.[264]

The RSHA, not privy to these plans, criticized the RV, saying it had no authority to carry out resettlement inside the Reich.[265] The RSHA itself had been intending since the end of 1939 to dissolve the smallest Jewish Communities in the *Altreich* and to relocate the Jews affected to new quarters. It evidently feared that regional offices and the Reichsver-einigung might launch unauthorized operations on their own before the RSHA acted. It therefore announced a meeting with Jewish representa-tives where it would "possibly" be decided in future only to allow Gestapo offices to participate in relocation.[266]

In the Jewish Communities, people were puzzled about the significance of the Stettin deportation. The contemporary Breslau Jewish historian Willi Cohn suspected it was a "preliminary operation to a large-scale operation in Scandinavia."[267] This arbitrary action proved upsetting for many weeks to those who remained behind; they read it as an ominous "sign of a storm on the horizon."[268] Max Nussbaum informed his discus-sion partners in the United States that the "evacuation" of the Jews from Stettin and environs had increased fears among the German Jews that "general wartime measures" were going to be imposed on them.[269]

Eichmann exploited these fears to put pressure on the German-Jew-ish functionaries regarding the question of emigration and to break their resistance to the idea of illegal transports. Erich Frank, responsible in the Reichsvereinigung for these "special transports," noted a clear change in Eichmann's behavior when the Jewish representatives from Berlin, Vi-enna, and Prague presented their memoranda on this. Eichmann threat-ened that if they did not meet the emigration quotas (especially for illegal emigration), "we will initiate resettlement, and that is our order at the highest level!"[270] Against the backdrop of the transports from Stettin, the Jewish functionaries knew immediately what was meant.

In this sense, the RSHA profited from the dynamic impact emanating from the Stettin deportation, and pressured the Jewish organizations into compliance, although the plan of setting up a *Judenreservat* was initially not pursued any further. On the contrary, in March 1940, Hitler stated that a reservation in Lublin would not solve the "Jewish Question." Nothing more was done beyond the one deportation from the *Altreich*.[271] In early April the project was (temporarily) frozen.[272]

The planning and implementation of the early deportations suggest that *Gauleiters*, regional persons in power, and others did not necessarily cooperate with the RSHA when it was a question of expelling the Jews from the areas under their competence. These initiatives "from below" proved to be fraught with danger, precarious both for the RSHA and the Reichsvereinigung. The RSHA recognized that its leading role in "Jewish policy" had not yet been consolidated, and sought to instrumentalize events in terms of its interest and conception. The RV, which after all was supposed to be the main institution to which this Jewish policy was addressed, was ignored on a regular basis. If by exception it learned ahead of time about the plans and then made an agreement with the local authorities, it came under pressure from the RSHA. But if the Jews targeted had already been deported, it was not allowed to play any role at the destinations, and at no time was there any possibility for a return of those Jews who had been transported elsewhere.

The Madagascar Plan

In May 1940, the victory over France induced high-ranking National Socialist politicians to develop new ideas about a mass resettlement of the Jews: the island of Madagascar, part of overseas French colonial territory, appeared soon to be within the German sphere of domination.

Foreign minister Joachim von Ribbentrop saw this as an opportunity to ensure his ministry a central role in Jewish policy, and he commissioned his "Jewish expert" Franz Rademacher to work out a "Madagascar plan."[273] Since the turn of the century, Madagascar as a "colony for Jews" had repeatedly inspired the imagination of anti-Semites.[274] Rademacher's plan envisioned holding Western European Jews in particular on Madagascar as hostages vis-à-vis the United States, while Eastern European Jews were to be sent off in freight trains to Lublin or the Soviet Union.[275] Rademacher assumed that Madagascar could absorb 4.9 million European Jews and 1.6 million from other parts of the world.[276] Alarmed, Heydrich insisted that he was the one who had been put in charge of a solution to the "Jewish Question." After the failure of emigration, he was now thinking "of a territorial solution." Under his orders, Eichmann was working then on his own Madagascar plan for some four million Eastern European and Western European Jews. To this end, one million Jews per year were to be transported there.[277] In anticipation of this initiative, Hitler had promised Governor General Frank that he would no longer need to accept any further Jews into the territory of the *Generalgouvernement*. In a draft plan completed in mid-August, Eichmann sketched a similar procedure as in emigration: local offices were to handle registration, processing of departure documents, transfer of assets, and assembling of the transports, and two ships per day would depart, each with fifteen hundred emigrants on board, initially with "advance parties" for constructing the infrastructure, and then with the great mass of Jews for resettlement.[278] If Rademacher's plans envisioned an autonomous Jewish administration, under a police governor, Eichmann's Madagascar was to be a "police state." Evident already in Eichmann's Madagascar Plan was a tendency that was "genocidal in its implications,"[279] because the demographic engineers were openly reckoning with a "decimation" of the Jews deported to the tropical island. Both the RSHA and the Foreign Ministry stopped work on the plan when victory over England was in December 1940 still uncertain, and the planners realized that a fleet with which the Jews could be shipped by sea would not be available even in the future.

But Eichmann apparently was not informed about the sole concrete effect that his Madagascar Plan generated, namely, the deportation of the Jews from Baden and Saarpfalz in October 1940 in anticipation of that plan, a deportation operation discussed below. In this regard, two *Gauleiters* had obtained Himmler's permission to move a large proportion of the Jewish population into France, still unoccupied, where Eichmann then had to act on the ground as a kind of "fire department" for the train route.

The German-Jewish and Austrian-Jewish representatives now accommodated to the planning for Madagascar. In June 1940, Jagusch had already summoned Eppstein to inform him that a basic solution to the "Jewish Question" in the form of a Jewish reservation was on the drawing boards: the Reichsvereinigung should deal with this "thoughtfully, so that if so ordered they could present plans."[280] On 3 June 1940, Eichmann then informed Jakob Edelstein and Franz Weidmann, summoned from Prague, Josef Löwenherz from Vienna, and Paul Eppstein, summoned from Berlin, that plans were afoot for a "comprehensive solution to the European Jewish Question" after the war's end for some four million Jews.[281] This solution would involve a span of some three to four years for completion. The Jewish representatives should put forward suggestions on how such a plan could be smoothly implemented. Eichmann mentioned no specific destination, and in their written response those summoned were demonstrative in relating the conception to Palestine, and explicitly rejected destinations like Madagascar and Guiana due to the tropical climate and the fact that these places were very hard to reach. Along with Palestine, the Jewish functionaries suggested "underpopulated areas" in Alaska, Australia, Brazil, New Zealand, and Rhodesia as possible destinations for consideration. Moreover, the Jewish community could not finance such a gigantic undertaking alone; state assistance would be necessary. Settlement would have to be carried out in stages: younger men for construction, then emigration according to professions in demand, and finally children and the elderly.[282] Likewise, in a discussion with Eichmann's deputy Dannecker, they stressed that Palestine could absorb about three million persons. Dannecker then explicitly rejected Palestine as a possible destination.

A version evidently based on insider knowledge, but that appears to have less validity, was published in the paper *Yedioth Hayom* in May 1941 entitled "Das Nein der deutschen Juden: Hinter den Kulissen des Madagaskar-Planes."[283] It stated that after the victory over France and with the apparent victory over England on the near horizon, Hirsch and Eppstein had been informed that the war would be over in the autumn of 1940. Europe was to be liberated of its Jews. To this end, the RV was being offered "an opportunity that National Socialism had not yet given to any Jewish institution. It was to take matters into its own hands, though of course under the full supervision of the German government."[284] The RSHA had demanded a draft plan from the Reichsvereinigung sketching the basic outlines of a scheme for implementation, and given the Jewish representatives forty-eight hours as a deadline. The RV board and several members of its advisory council had convened a special meeting; it lasted for almost the entire forty-eight hours that had been allowed them. For reasons of preserving self-esteem, and numerous other concrete factors, the Jewish functionaries did not wish to cooperate in realizing this initiative. No one among those present had any doubts about the "will to destroy" of those in power. The only important matter for discussion was the form of their rejection. Leo Baeck warned they should reject the project, with the explanation that the RV had been created to preserve the Jewish community, not to destroy it. This was in his view a dignified response, albeit fraught with danger. Given the uncertainties of the war situation, he recommended a halt to such planning. Eppstein and Hirsch, who from experience were doubtful that the RSHA would accept such a response, recommended that they should stress that it was impossible to gather material for the report demanded, given the wartime situation, or to declare that they had no competency in this matter.

Baeck rejected that approach. Finally, the participants of a meeting of Jewish representatives had (according to the article in *Yedioth Hayom*) declared that if they were to assist the authorities in "removing" 7.5 million European Jews, it would be necessary to facilitate an opportunity to inspect conditions on the spot, to visit the occupied territories and the neutral countries. They would also need to contact the large Jewish organizations in the United States in regard to questions of financing, to the extent that finances were not to be made available from the Reich. The paper stated that the RSHA regarded this argument by the Jewish representatives as a delaying tactic. The representative of the RSHA had pointed to a file labeled "Madagascar," and suggested that the Jews from Palestine would also be brought there after the war's end. He said the RSHA thought the "Jewish millionaires in the United States" ought to finance the undertaking, and for that reason the Reichsvereinigung would be permitted to contact them. The paper noted that Baeck had later asked Rabbi Max Nussbaum, who, as mentioned, had emigrated in August 1940, to function as an intermediary and to inform the representatives in the United States: "The German Jews respond with a clear and resolute 'no!' to this new attack by the Nazis." They were insisting on the settlement destination of Palestine, but they did not see this as an alternative to Madagascar. According to the paper's report, the German Jews said they were leaving it to the Jewish organizations in the United States to reject the project from the start or, under protest, to address the matter of possible financing. The paper *Yedioth Hayom* concluded the report by stating that further developments in the war had prevented such plans from becoming more concrete, and that the Gestapo "had seen itself compelled to indefinitely postpone its project of destruction." [285]

In actuality, however, Nussbaum had sent a memo to Hans Morgenthau immediately after emigrating to the states, requesting that they think through the financial aspects of resettlement just in case, so that perhaps within the span of ten years Jews aged twenty to forty could be transported by ship.[286] This would have to be done very quietly, because

> this plan at the moment is absolutely secret, and it is possible to refer only to one single item in this connection without exposing the Jewish institutions in Germany to huge danger: namely an article in the official Italian paper *Stampa* of 18 July, [where] ... this program ... in principle ... is discussed and presented as a *fait accompli*.[287]

It is clear from the sources that both Arthur Spier and Paul Eppstein, acting in 1940 on orders from the Gestapo, carried on discussions with Jewish organizations in the United States regarding cooperation with and financing of the Madagascar Plan.[288] But no one treated the underlying intentions as confidential: the American-Jewish press reported on the plan (generally negatively), and high-ranking National Socialists and the Nazi press mentioned the plan repeatedly, even when its realization in 1942/1943 was no longer considered an option and had been reduced to a purely propagandistic concept.[289]

By contrast, another initiative remained largely unknown: Baeck, Eppstein, and Hirsch approached the pope via the secretary general of the Roman Catholic Raphael Association, Alexander Menningen. They articulated their fear that the Jews would be in an "intolerable situation in the unsuitable climatic conditions on Madagascar, and were hopeful that the Pope could assist in opening up the path for mass Jewish immigration in southern Alaska."[290] Like many other attempts, this bid for assistance also proved abortive.

Two aspects should be kept clearly in mind here. First, the German-Jewish functionaries recognized the genocidal character of Nazi planning, which had not yet become a feature of the deportations across the border into Poland, Russia, or Belgium. Second, they became aware just how important (and at risk) Palestine was as a land of refuge for Jews if the National Socialist leadership were to continue its triumphal chain of victories. This is why they stressed the place of Palestine as a future destination on other occasions as well: "The decline in individual emigration has placed an ever increasing obligation on the Reich Association of the Jews in Germany to make preparations for group and mass emigration."[291] In their view, educational work had to be intensified in order to "awaken and fortify ... the consciousness of a close bond of identity with the people."[292] Every Jew was to have access to religion and instruction in Hebrew. "The tasks of mass settlement demand education for life in a social community within society," and the place to realize this was, in their view, Palestine.

During deliberations on the Madagascar Plan, Jewish functionaries noted that there was a marked change in the attitude of the German authorities toward emigration. They reported that in June/July 1940, the Gestapo had declared "again and again, clearly alluding to Madagascar," that it was no longer interested in individual emigration, but rather looked to the "mass emigration of all Jews in Europe." "It is only natural that this threat weighs upon the Jews of Germany like a heavy shadow, and their sole hope is that the end of the war will not allow for this plan to be realized."[293] Nussbaum observed:

> [F]rom a specific day in July on, the German authorities appeared to have lost all interest in the policy of emigration that the *Reichsvereinigung* of the German Jews had pursued over a number of years. One fine day the Gestapo told the responsible Jewish institutions that all this could continue in this same way. It stated that the emigration was much too slow and that the entire Jewish problem could not be solved in this manner. This all the more so, because now it was not at all (!) just a question of the German Jews. It also involved the Jews of Poland, Belgium, France, Holland, Denmark, and as they believed, tomorrow likewise the Jews of England.[294]

The Deportation of the Jews from Baden and the Saarpfalz

The Jews in the regions bordering on France had in any case been living in a state of constant fear of possible resettlement for military reasons, and after the war erupted many left their homes. In 1939, hundreds of Jews had been forced by the local authorities to relocate; some were accommodated and cared for with the help of the Munich Jewish Community. After several months, they were able temporarily to return.[295] It is clear from a report by the regional governor of Franconia in October 1939 that Jews from the "Evacuation Zone West," that is, Rhine-Palatinate and Baden, had arrived in Nuremberg and were being cared for there by the Jewish Community.[296] Immediately after victory over France, the *Gau* administrative authorities and Gestapo offices in the former border area began to deliberate on how to expel the Jews. Such rumors were in circulation in Mannheim, for example, and later proved true.[297] The local Gestapo in Kehl tried on its own initiative to deport the local Jews across the Rhine into Alsatia, but their plan was halted because the High Council of the Jews in Baden had informed the Reichsvereinigung in Berlin, and they in turn had informed the RSHA.[298] Nonetheless, these Jews were in fact only granted what turned out to be a short postponement. Heydrich, chief of the Security Police and the SD, wrote to the Foreign Ministry:

> The Führer has ordered the expulsion of the Jews from Baden via Alsatia, and Jews from the Pfalz [Palatinate] via Lorraine. Regarding implementation of the operation, I can inform you that on 22 and 23 October 1940, 7 transport trains from Baden, and on 22 October 1940, 2 transport trains from the Pfalz ... brought 6,504 Jews, in agreement with the local command posts of the Wehrmacht, and without the prior knowledge of the French authorities, into the unoccupied region of France. ... The operation itself, as it unfolded, was barely noted by the population.[299]

Reports by survivors from the regions or individual cities are available in the source documentation, and research has investigated these.[300] In the following, I therefore limit my comments to the reactions of those Jews involved and the (im)possibility for the RV to intervene in the process, to alleviate it, or at the very least to engage in an open sign of protest against the operation.

News about the deportation spread immediately, and like the expulsion of the Stettin Jews to Lublin, it greatly alarmed the German Jews, as reflected in the following extract from a report:

> It is impossible to describe how depressing the news was of the evacuation of the Jews in Baden and the Pfalz. A paralyzing sense of fear weighed down

upon all. In Berlin, news spread by word of mouth that the same fate had befallen our brothers and sisters in Wuerttemberg, Hesse, Frankfurt and the Rhineland, and that Jews everywhere had to make ready to be prepared to leave their hearth and homes.[301]

The RSHA had neither informed the Reichsvereinigung about the measures nor did it receive its representatives or accept their reports.[302] Eppstein, whose mother-in-law and sister-in-law were among the deportees, was behind bars at the time. Otto Hirsch, a legal expert and former high-ranking regional government official in Württemberg, cofounder of the Reich Representation, and a member of the RV board, sought in vain to be admitted to speak with the Gestapo. Hirsch, who still exuded some of the authority of his former high post, was in any case reportedly considered by the Gestapo a "persona non grata." Four days after the operation, he was then informed by Jagusch that the "removal of the Jews from Baden, Pfalz [the Palatinate] and the Saar area was a regular and proper emigration. The RV would be informed about the matter and brought in at the end of the next week. No information could be given about the whereabouts of the individuals and whether further evacuations were planned."[303] It was stated that the Reichsvereinigung, like after the Stettin operation, should have the deportees sign powers of attorney in order to be able later on to deal properly with questions of assets and property. For the moment, everything else remained unclear.

In view of the threatening situation for the Jews affected and the ban on their taking any action, the Jewish functionaries decided to engage in actions to openly protest what was happening. Hirsch informed the RSHA that the RV had asked the Kulturbund to cancel all performances for one week, because "what has now occurred strikes at the very heart of the *Reichsvereinigung*."[304] In addition, the members and all RV staff as well as the representatives and staff of the Jewish Communities were to hold a fast day on 31 October 1940 "in memory of those evacuated" and to announce this at the upcoming Sabbath religious services.[305]

The Propaganda Ministry responded by forbidding the Kulturbund to cancel any performances, and the RSHA prohibited the announcement in the Communities and their synagogues of a fast day. It played down the threat, saying that a continuation of the operation was not planned, and this "was a one-time event."[306]

In early November, the members of the RV board learned that some of the deportees had been sent to a camp in Gurs. The instruction from the RSHA was that in the official statistics, they should be listed as "emigrated, initially to France." The Karlsruhe RV district branch office was allowed to settle the affairs of the deportees "in liquidation." Postal communication and remittances of cash were not possible, and the notes on summons in the following weeks were filled with questions about the confiscation of property by the *Gau*,[307] which the RSHA disapproved of, the auction of their movable property, which the deportees urgently needed, and other questions. Julius Seligsohn, the initiator and organizer of the idea of "fasting as a protest," was arrested shortly thereafter. Hirsch, in "honest naivete," had apparently mentioned the name of Seligsohn as organizer to the RSHA after it had inquired, even though he added that the operation had been supported by all.[308] Hirsch pointed out, although in vain, that Seligsohn had voluntarily returned to Germany in the autumn of 1939, that he was working on a volunteer basis for the Reichsvereinigung, and that he headed the important US section in the Department of Migration there. Hirsch also stressed that for Jews, fasting was the "traditional religious expression of mourning."[309] His efforts to intercede proved a failure. Seligsohn remained under arrest, and in the following daily summons sessions, Hirsch spoke now about the "case of protective custody for Seligsohn" along with the "case of protective custody for Eppstein." The RSHA decided to set an example: "anyone who resists orders will be treated in the same way as Dr. Seligsohn," noted Eppstein after his release in February 1941 in reference to his colleague still behind bars.[310] Soon Eppstein had to discuss the "protective custody cases" of two colleagues in parallel at the RSHA, Seligsohn and Otto Hirsch; in the meantime, Fritz Woehrn[311] was now responsible for the Reichsvereinigung matters there, replacing Jagusch, who had been promoted.[312] Hirsch was now likewise under arrest,[313] supposedly because he had tried to smuggle news about the situation of those deported to Gurs to the outside world.[314] In the cases of both Seligsohn and Hirsch, Eppstein cited urgent matters of work for which these two colleagues were absolutely necessary as a reason for release, in particular when there were upcoming negotiations with international Jewish organizations on the agenda. When the RSHA stated that further activity by the two men for the RV was out of the question, Eppstein requested that they be allowed to emigrate, but this too was in vain. Both "prisoners in protective custody" were never released. Seligsohn died on 28 February 1942 in the Sachsenhausen concentration camp,[315] Hirsch on 19 June 1941 in the Mauthausen concentration camp.[316]

The Madagascar Plan was not practicable, since the French government raised objections, and, most especially, the sea routes were not open. It thus was scuttled. As Browning noted: "Like a spectacular meteor, the Madagascar Plan blazed across the sky of Nazi Jewish policy, only to burn out abruptly."[317] But its first and last victims, the Jews deported "initially to France" from Baden lay vegetating in the Gurs internment camp, and would never be sent on to Madagascar.

When in March 1941 the RSHA cautioned the RV that it should endeavor to be more economical, because "substantial amounts of money were necessary for the total emigration of Jews fit for settlement," the destination was not mentioned.[318] A short time later, the RSHA kept its word: although there were more and more signs that plans for deportation were still being explored and pursued, and regional officials continued to press increasingly vociferously for the deportation of "their" Jews, for the duration of an entire year no further German Jews were deported. However, the Jewish functionaries could hardly feel any sense of relief: in February 1941, five thousand Jews from Vienna were deported to the Lublin district. In the meantime, reports had appeared from this region about the living conditions and the mass suffering pervasive there, and the German-Jewish representatives knew that those "relocated" were living in terrible misery and were dying. Moreover, in view of the resumption of deportations, they were able to understand that their members would, at some time in the future, also be swept up in this vortex.

Welfare

Our previous focus was on the efforts of Jewish representatives grappling with emigration. Their "second most important duty" was in coping with the "social question,"[319] which was also a reason for the Jews in positions of responsibility to stay on and persevere in Germany, motivated by their concern for the impoverished, the needy, and the helpless among the remaining Jews in the country. For most, this task was the deep moral motive underlying their continued activities in the RV. In December 1940, Leo Baeck put it this way: "Our work goes its usual way; it becomes more necessary by the month—despite each and everything it is constructive in its destruction and destructive in its construction [*Aufbau im Abbau, Abbau zum Aufbau*]. But often it's not easy to stand fast; still we stand together."[320] In May 1939, Hedwig Eppstein expressed the feelings of every Jewish functionary active in the sphere of social work and assistance: "Do you really understand what I mean when I say that everything we did before, and I mean everything, was just child's play compared to what is happening now? Nonetheless, it is totally impossible to imagine leaving!"[321] Otto Hirsch is quoted as saying: "But not everyone can leave, someone has got to care for the elderly."[322]

Until the end of 1938, it was the state's task to care for welfare and the task of the Jewish Communities to provide additional benefits. Only after that did foundations, associations, and the RV enter the picture. However, it was precisely the smaller Jewish Communities that, under the pressure of their strapped financial situations, saw themselves increasingly unable to meet their growing obligations. Those tasks demanded ever-larger expenditures, and as a result of their spatial fragmentation, were more and more difficult to deal with. In October 1939, there were Jews still living in some twenty-six localities in Germany, the greater majority in small groups of less than fifty persons.[323] For this reason, the RV was promoting the relocation of their (involuntary) members into towns with larger Jewish Communities, so that care and provisioning could be centralized, thus rendering it more effective and economical. However, it was necessary beforehand to eliminate the resistance of the larger cities to this undesired influx from the countryside and smaller towns. Adler-Rudel commented: "Naturally, the *Reichsvereinigung* could not suspect just how much they were, unsuspectingly, supporting the plans of the Nazis aimed at deportation and 'Final solution' … through this concentration."[324] However, the leading National Socialists in 1939/1940 were still not pursuing the aim of systematic deportation and murder of all Jews living in Germany, as is evident from the Nazi Jewish policy previously sketched here, and clearly substantiated by the present-day state of research. Consequently, Adler-Rudel's conclusion goes too far here. Ultimately, any spatial concentration served to protect the Jews involved; it enabled them to continue to live, practice their religion, and sometimes also to find employment in the context of the Jewish environment. At the same time, it rendered them potentially vulnerable, because the Gestapo and the authorities could exercise control all the more easier over larger Jewish residential and administrative complexes, and could also direct or harass these Jews more readily. On the other hand, Jews living scattered in the countryside or in smaller towns found themselves repeatedly exposed to attack, defenseless, so that many were quite happy to utilize options for a change and relocation.

Prior to the regime's revoking of state welfare provision for Jews, several cities and towns had already decided to shirk their responsibility, and had taken action to allocate lower benefits to their Jewish welfare recipients than to their "Aryan" clients.[325] In the wake of the November 1938 pogrom, the Nazi state abruptly saddled the newly created Reichsvereinigung with full responsibility for all Jewish welfare, effective January 1939.[326] The German-Jewish representatives traditionally viewed welfare (and education, which will not be further explored here) as "a way of guaranteeing the most dignified material and cultural existence possible under the deteriorating conditions," as Otto Dov Kulka describes the intention of the Jewish leadership.[327] Rivka Elkin, who examined the continuities and changes in German-Jewish welfare work from WWI to the period after National Socialist rule,[328] emphasizes the growing importance that welfare assumed for the impoverished and aged group in the population:

As the situation progressively worsened, the Jewish leadership recognized that social concern and care constituted the last reflection of Jewish community life of the past and the only factor enabling continued existence of such life for the time being. This goaded the Jewish public leaders to unite all their forces in organizing self-help and preserving the moral foundations of Jewish society even at a time of atrocious hardship.[329]

Until the end of 1938, the numerous associations, foundations, and Jewish Communities had thus stepped in and provided support and assistance when government benefits proved insufficient. After its creation, Jewish Communities with less than one thousand members and the other organizations—and their assets, which the National Socialist state later wished to have central access to—were incorporated into the RV. This initially led to a huge expansion of those assets. Likewise, the necessary bureaucratic effort associated with administering this property and other assets also increased. The individual departments and the Reichsvereinigung board were now able to draw up budget plans, including utilization for social purposes of revenues obtained from leasing, rental, and sale of property, income from membership dues, and levies imposed on emigrants. However, every budgetary draft had to be approved by the RSHA, which as a "superior authority" was restrictive in its approach, slashing funds and ordering evictions and cuts in personnel.

At the same time, after government benefits had generally been eliminated, income declined and problems mounted: in 1935/1936, the collections of the Jewish Winter Relief (Jüdische Winterhilfe) had provided assistance to some eighty-five thousand needy Jews; in 1936/1937, that figure dropped to around eighty-two thousand, and in the following period of 1938/1939, it fell to some seventy-one thousand, plummeting in 1939/1940 to about fifty thousand. Of the funds collected, 20 percent was allotted to the budget of the RV.[330] During the summer collection drive called "Jewish Duty" (Jüdische Pflicht), 8 percent of the wage tax of Jewish employed persons was directly transferred to the Reichsvereinigung, without the explicit prior agreement of these employees.[331]

Concomitantly, fewer and fewer individual contributions were coming in from wealthier Jews, because most of the contributors had in the meantime emigrated or had lost the right of access to their accounts. Meanwhile, almost all Jews had been "eliminated from economic life"[332] by the "Aryanization" of Jewish firms, and there were no replacement jobs available in the Jewish economic sector. Thus, the process of destitution was rapidly intensifying and was not absorbed by the obligation of conscript labor imposed by the state, with its rock-bottom minimal wages. It was mainly younger Jews who had emigrated. Those remaining were the elderly, the ill, the handicapped, and the frail, whose families were no longer on hand to take care of them, and who were now unable to provide for themselves. The financial means of the associations and foundations incorporated into the RV, donations from foreign organizations, and contributions—as among the non-Jewish population, contributing now became an obligation—were insufficient. They could not cover the huge expenses the Jewish leaders had to grapple with.[333] For example, at the end of 1939, some 52,000 Jews (26 percent of the remaining German-Jewish population) were already receiving welfare benefits, and their number was on the rise.[334] In addition, 70,682 Jews were being supported by the Jewish Winter Relief, with a total expenditure of 2.4 million reichsmarks.[335]

Faced with increasingly restrictive laws, ordinances, and new local regulations, the functionaries in the RV initially sought to create and maintain institutions in which orphans, the sick and infirm, and mentally and physically handicapped Jews could lead a tolerable life and be appropriately cared for. All still available care facilities and existing nursing homes were full to capacity and beyond, and as a matter of principle, the only option was to create new facilities to accommodate these groups of individuals in need of care. There was a lack of suitable buildings, and at the same time, the RSHA was exerting pressure to sell the properties that had been owned by the incorporated foundations and associations, and cancel the leases for social institutions housed on rented premises.[336]

In 1940, the RV put together an overview of the number and occupancy of the care facilities and nursing homes it had established or taken over, as in table 1.[337]

Table 1. RV Care Facilities and Nursing Homes, 1940

	1933		1940		Occupancy in Berlin
	Homes	Occupancy	Homes	Occupancy	
Homes for the aged and infirm	64	2,677	122	7,101	2,428
Homes for children and youth	55	2,157	30	1,601	377
Special homes	8	431	6	5 50	239
Hospital facilities	14	1,777	14	1,657	470
Convalescence homes	45	2,889	1	26	

The RV trained some of the personnel for the new homes and facilities itself. For this reason, for example, up until the spring of 1942, kindergarten teachers were able to complete a recognized training course,[338] while other training courses had long since been closed to Jews.

The budget for the first six months of 1940 amounted to a total of 11.3 million RM; for the second half of 1940, the Jewish functionaries assumed a reduced amount of 10.4 million RM.[339] These expenses had to be financed by membership dues (1940: 8 million RM) and levies on the emigrants, who paid these more or less voluntarily to the Reichsvereinigung. In the second half of 1939, these revenues amounted to some 18 million RM.[340] The organization would have liked to take between 30 and 60 percent of the remaining assets of the emigrants. Yet this would have entailed a serious risk: while being able to finance the sphere of welfare, it might have massively hindered emigration, since only destitute immigrants would have been available to propose to the few remaining countries of possible destination. For that reason, the Jewish functionaries agreed to an emigration levy of between 1 and 10 percent, depending on the amount of the total assets of the respective emigrant. For the years 1940–1942, they projected expenditures of 125 million; of this, 71 million was to be financed through retroactive and future levies on emigration.[341]

Although the RV had to cut personnel from nursing homes and schools, increase occupancy in such homes and other institutions, expand school fees, and reduce the wages of employees, the RSHA was still dissatisfied: it considered the costs too high. In the spring of 1941, the RV was forced for the first time to establish a set of priorities in its range of task areas, whereas previously all necessities had been recognized and included. These priorities were: (1) emigration, (2) welfare and elementary education, (3) vocational training (which in given cases came before welfare and basic education), and (4) expenses for cultural and religious affairs.[342] Thus, religious concerns were relegated to the lowest priority, at least in terms of financing. Month after month, Woehrn now reduced even further the appropriations for schooling, welfare, and culture, while the outlays for emigration, administration, taxes, and property were deemed acceptable.[343]

One year after this setting of priorities, emigration had been eliminated, culture and religion had become insignificant, and more cuts were necessary in the area of welfare. Since the number of needy Jews was steadily on the rise, the budget for welfare in the summer of 1941 was still 1.5 million RM per month.[344] Woehrn declared that in future, the RV would be allowed to set the budget for this amount.[345]

The RV had now expanded nursing home occupancy to the highest level possible, increased the amount of participation in expenses covered by the clients or their families, and repeatedly made cuts in personnel. In April 1941, the RV board decided to institute an entry fee of two thousand RM for homes for the aged and the infirm, and in the special homes for the blind, the deaf and dumb, or "feeble-minded children," fees for care were once again increased.[346] Nonetheless, even that same month they were unable to raise the required sum and were forced, as in subsequent months, to rely on revenue from the anticipated contributions to the collection drives of the Jewish Winter Relief and Jewish Duty. In the meantime, these drives had been extended to last the entire year.[347]

Conrad Cohn, a member of the board of the Berlin Jewish Community, and from May 1940 also on the board of the RV, was the responsible functionary for the entire sphere of welfare, while Hannah Karminski bore responsibility for general welfare and Walter Lustig for medical welfare. Numerous documents and recurrent passages in the minutes of the RV board meetings testify to their continued efforts to secure at least the basic necessities in care for the needy, and to take some of the sting out of the ever-increasing demands imposed by the authorities. Those demands could never be averted on a general basis, but only in their specific details. Often enough, the savings measures ordered by the RSHA led not only to restrictions for the clientele affected in the welfare facilities but also sparked conflicts within the organization, as when the level of personnel in Berlin was retained and savings were made at the expense of the regional offices. Commenting on the situation faced by the functionaries, strung between the best of intentions, external pressures, general hopelessness, and the hopes they nonetheless continued to harbor, Leo Baeck noted: "Work is very demanding, in terms of human and material efforts, and has to be done. Helping one person helps to get over many things, and you have the right to be hopeful if you do your duty."[348] Welfare work in the tradition of Jewish social welfare as the Jewish functionaries had envisioned, and which would have been possible to realize given the assets and property of the RV, soon foundered on the rocks of intervention by the National Socialist state.

All the investments and efforts by the Jewish representatives and those active in the various spheres of social welfare proved to no avail where the decisions by those in power not only involved cost cutting or change of location, but engineered another fate for a group badly in need of welfare, like the Jewish mentally ill. The latter were among the groups whose care was part of the array of tasks of the Jewish functionaries. However, they were unable to save them: before the mass deportations, they fell victim to the program of murder that was euphemistically termed the "Euthanasia Operation" and code-named T-4.

The general hereditary biological measures of the National Socialists and the "euthanasia measures" from 1939 to 1941 (and the subsequent continuation of the murder of patients, which was kept secret) are well-known.[349] The historian Henry Friedlander regards the murder of the sick patients in gas vans and gas chambers in the newly constructed killing centers in Meseritz-Obrawalde, Tiegenhof, Grafeneck, Brandenburg,

Hartheim, and Sonnenstein as a preliminary exercise for the Holocaust, and correctly so in retrospect: this operation used poison gas vans and gas chambers for the first time; here the personnel later deployed in the extermination camps gathered their fundamental experience with the mass murder of persons, the great majority of whom were not Jews.

What was the situation of mentally ill Jews? According to RV estimates, they numbered between twenty-five hundred and three thousand individuals in 1939.[350] Most had remained on in Germany when their families emigrated, either because the country of destination generally did not grant entry to the sick, or because accommodation and care for them was not guaranteed there.[351] They were largely in institutions run by the church or the state. In most cases, the emigrated families had tried hard and done as much as possible to at the very least financially ensure their provision with basic necessities. If this had not succeeded, they were then "fed and cared for," that is, supported by the RV.

In the course of diverse anti-Semitic measures, the Nazi state informed the church-connected nursing homes and asylums that they would forfeit their tax-free status as charitable nonprofit institutions if they did not relocate their Jewish patients elsewhere. Although the threat was not implemented, many directors of these homes used the threat as an occasion for transferring their Jewish residents to state-run facilities.[352]

From June 1938 on, those who had remained in church-run or state-run institutions had to be housed and tended to separately from non-Jewish patients, ostensibly to prevent "race defilement" (so-called *Rassenschande*) through sexual encounter. This was a senseless measure, since men and women in any case were housed in different sections.[353] This regulation, which demanded a reorganization of the structure for care of nursing home residents, was also utilized by the direction of several homes as an occasion to press ahead with transferring their Jewish residents to Jewish homes, and since the latter barely had any available capacity for new patients, then on to state-run homes and asylums. A number of individual *Gau* administrations now ordered that Jews should no longer be dispersed and accommodated among a number of facilities; rather, they should be cared for centrally in their area of competence in the respective *Gau*.

Only a very small number of Jewish patients were housed in homes under Jewish sponsorship. At the end of 1939, the RV leased the Jacoby Hospital and Nursing Home, a facility in Sayn near Koblenz, for the Jewish "mentally ill." It offered places for 190 patients.

A small number of patients were additionally housed in other Jewish institutions, such as in Lorch or Berlin-Weissensee. The RV was unable to establish any more closed institutions of this type due to "insurmountable difficulties," so that the majority of Jewish mental patients had to remain in state facilities, where they were exposed, basically defenseless, to state intervention.[354]

Friedlander assumes that a portion of the Jewish patients still living in mixed facilities were murdered along with their non-Jewish fellow patients already before the middle of 1940, even if according to official proclamation the Jews actually were not supposed to be granted the "blessing of a mercy killing."[355] The decision to kill all Jewish patients was presumably not made until March or April 1940.[356]

Unlike in the case of Christian patients, the fitness for work of the Jewish patients played no role here. They were seized as "Jewish patients," transferred to collection centers, and were transported from there to the liquidation centers between June 1940 and February 1941.[357] In June 1940, two hundred Jewish children and adults from Berlin were murdered by poison gas in the former Brandenburg prison. Further victims were murdered in other liquidation facilities. The "Cholm Insane Asylum, Post Office Lublin," a nonexistent institution, was the purported destination of the transports. A fictitious registration office certified the death of the patients, which was later sent in writing to the relatives, the district offices of the RV, or the Jewish Communities.

The clandestine operation was partially leaked when the Hamburg Jewish functionary Max Plaut, with permission from the local "Jewish expert" of the Gestapo, asked the Jewish elder in Lublin and Cholm (Chelm in Polish spelling) to pay a visit to the patients from northern Germany there and to make efforts, should that be necessary, to provide them with supplementary care at the expense of the Hamburg branch of the RV. The unambiguous reply stated that there was no such institution, neither in the Lublin area nor anywhere in occupied Poland.[358] When the RV central office inquired about the deported Jews sent to the mental asylum Pflegeanstalt Cholm, the evasive answer was that they had been brought to Warsaw and Kraków. The senior staff member of the Kultusvereinigung für Württemberg und Hohenzollern, the regional association of Jewish Communities in Württemberg, Theodor Hirsch, received news of some deaths from the liaison officer of the Jewish Community in Heilbronn. The latter had been asked to take possession of urns containing the ashes of Jewish patients from Grafeneck, one of the killing centers. With a permit from the Security Service in hand, one of the local Jewish functionaries then traveled to the former hunting lodge. He obtained no further information there, but heard about nocturnal transports and "terrible screams." The functionaries in the Württemberg regional association concluded from this that while the patients had previously always been murdered in their respective facilities, now they were being gathered together in centers and liquidated there.[359]

However, the Nazi regime did not stop with the clandestine murder of the patients; it went on to make a veritable business of this. From March 1941 on, a number of Jewish Communities and district branches of the RV received bills for expenses for the accommodation, care, and cremation of patients. This was because "a substantial proportion of them have in the meantime died." Plaut compared nineteen reports of death received the same day regarding Hamburg patients for whom he had already paid forty thousand RM in expenses: the identical text, dated the same day, contained the same information, namely, that the patient had died of dysentery. He recalled later that "the entire text including the date was pre-printed, only the names had been typed in."[360] Yet most particularly, in this case there was also a death notice for a patient whom Plaut had brought to his relatives shortly before being sent off by transport, and who thus had been protected. In retrospect, Plaut stated that "we," that is, the Hamburg and probably also the Berlin representatives in the RV, with whom he was in close contact, had at this point understood the direction developments on the ground were heading toward; namely, "that the solution of the Jewish Question, the cardinal point in Hitler's party program, was moving toward the total annihilation of all Jews in the territory under his control."[361] Today it is impossible to determine the actual extent of this recognition at the time, and the "Euthanasia Operation" did not primarily target Jews.

Nonetheless, it must be clearly noted: in 1940, the Jewish functionaries, for whom a major reason for staying on in Germany had been their work in welfare, understood that a portion of their clientele in need of protection had simply been removed: transported to destinations unknown, where they perished. In what way they had died was not necessarily known to them, yet these events made clear to the Jewish representatives what narrow limits had been put in place for their permitted sphere of action.

Contrary to Plaut's statement, it is not clear from the documentation of the RV that they were aware of the fact that these mentally ill patients had been murdered. Definite is only one thing: the Jewish functionaries were astonished and enraged about the overly high bills they had received. However, their attempts to avoid paying them proved to be in vain. In May 1941, Conrad Cohn was cunning in arguing that the RSHA had after all strictly stipulated that the RV was only permitted to care for the needs of Jews *inside* the country. Now he wondered: was the RV actually the correct addressee for these bills? After all, it had been ordered that "our area of competence extends only to the Altreich, and persons whose residence ... is no longer in our sphere of competence are, from the point in time of their transfer, no longer our members."[362] Yet in this instance, the RSHA insisted that the RV should pay the bills as demanded, and should also make an advance payment for private "caregivers," information they passed on in a circular letter to the regional branch offices and Jewish Communities.[363] At the beginning of October 1941, the costs amounted to some 479,000 RM for 1,100 patients who had been sent off in transports, of whom 1,050 had been reported to have died. Henry Friedlander terms these efforts to raise funds for support long after the death of those murdered a "completely amateurish" deception.[364]

When the systematic deportations of the German Jews began, most of the Jewish mental patients had already been murdered. Those who had not been liquidated in the framework of the "Euthanasia Operation" were now accommodated in the asylum in Bendorf-Sayn run by the RV.[365]

In the meantime, the RV had cancelled the customary multiclass system for admission and treatment in hospital, and had substantially hiked fees for care in order to finance the home in Bendorf-Sayn.[366] Between the spring and November of 1942 (see chapter 2), the Jewish mental patients there, and also in the Jewish Hospital in Berlin, were seized and included in the mass deportations and murdered in the death camps.[367]

Interim Summary

The official establishment of the Reichsvereinigung der Juden in Deutschland by law in the 10th Ordinance to the Reich Citizenship Law (*Reichsbürgergesetz*) on 4 July 1939 was the result of a long and difficult process of development and adaptation of Jewish organizations to conform with the dictates of National Socialist policy on the Jews, a policy whose supervision was taken over after the November 1938 pogrom by the SD and later the RSHA.[368] But the RV should also be seen as a way out of the continuing shock under which the Jewish representatives labored after the events of the "fateful year 1938." In 1938, they were forced to witness, initially and then in increasingly violent form, that their latitude for action on behalf of the Jews living in Germany, as well as their own very individual options for taking action under the National Socialist system, was beginning to be reduced to zero. At the end of this process stood the reorganizing of the now (almost) sole and only German-Jewish organization, geared to the primary aim of emigration. Under the heavy impress of the surveillance of the Gestapo and from September 1939 on the RSHA, an oversight implemented in minute detail, the mouthpiece and former structure for representation of the interests of the German Jews was transmogrified into a hybrid, whose chief function, imposed from above, was the merciless plunder and expulsion of the Jews. In the meantime, the remaining representatives still sought to halt this headlong fateful development, or at least to cushion and attenuate its crushing impact. And in

connection with all activities and actions against its members, these functionaries endeavored, despite everything and against all odds, to preserve
the members' dignity and to struggle for justice and solidarity.

The German-Jewish organizations in existence before the creation of
the RV had been unable to act or had been destroyed. Many of their active members and functionaries had left Germany. Open violence against
Jews was on the daily agenda. The Jewish representatives of the RV, who
for the most part remained on in Germany despite their own options for
emigration, found themselves confronted with ever-increasing problems
that conventional strategies could not solve, and for which the past offered no paradigms. Internal conflicts between the Jewish Communities
and the Reich Representation/Reich Association, and intraorganizational
struggles between the various camps and currents within the umbrella
body, had a negative impact on joint action. Increasingly, legal, transparent, or even "democratically" decided actions and initiatives were forced
to yield to illegal practices that promised rapid rescue for individuals in
life-threatening situations. Functionaries who insisted on another procedure, intensive, thorough preparations, and the examination of various
options soon appeared out of touch with reality, rigid in their approach;
indeed, their legalistic stance seemed ultimately to be leading to the failure
of rescue and escape for the RV members. Paul Eppstein, Otto Hirsch, and
others were still fixated on such action over the longer term. They sought
to maintain their conception of an orderly emigration even when the
external circumstances had long since changed for the worse. Faced with
the threat of incarceration in concentration camps, their colleagues in
Berlin or the regional representatives of the RV, who used every chance to
achieve short-term gains, had long since begun to utilize bribes or, where
deemed necessary, accept forged visas or the paid assistance of hired criminals. However, as a next step, they then also had to deceive their more
legalistically minded fellow representatives and colleagues in order to locate funds to finance their plans. From their perspective, hesitation cost
lives, especially in the case of prisoners in concentration camps, while
the "Eppstein faction" feared that by rescuing prisoners in this way, ultimately one unintended consequence would be the abandonment of the
many others desiring to emigrate. This was because these actions could
generate an impression in the countries of immigration that the crucial
interests of those rescued were being given priority over the demands and
regulations for immigrants in these countries. Eppstein also feared that
at the same time, the Gestapo would feel confirmed in its approach: it
would then order further arrest operations, assuming that the number of
those emigrating would automatically increase. For their part, the Zionist
functionaries, at a relative advantage after the November pogrom by dint

of their retraining centers and international organization, sought to make sure that *aliyah* to Palestine did not deteriorate into one mere possibility for rescue among others. In the conflict surrounding the Polish Jews expelled from Germany, the Zionist demand that they determine, according to their own criteria, who were suitable immigrants for the construction of Eretz Israel fused with the legalistic stance that no certificate would be issued unless the recipients were "covered" by concrete possibilities for accommodation and emigration. Once again, fears mounted that the interests of the Jews as a whole might be sacrificed for the interests of a small minority, and a little-loved group of Eastern European Jews at that.

In this phase, when the RSHA took control of Jewish policy, in practice it fought for that control of *Judenpolitik* on a daily basis against competing National Socialist institutions. There were repeated parallel or overlapping violent "operations" organized by different authorities, such as Nazi Party *Gau* district head offices, town mayors, local Gestapo branches, and the like. If already before the November pogrom the representatives of Jewish organizations had understood that they no longer had any available interlocutors on the other side, that is, contact persons for possible discussion in the ministries and government agencies, the RSHA now used this transition phase to intimidate the German-Jewish functionaries to the point that they would no longer even dare to contact other institutions of persecution. In addition, any protest by the Jewish representatives was nipped in the bud, and punished by arresting the functionaries responsible.

The RSHA thus tethered the Jewish functionaries to an exclusive orientation that was geared to its plans and desires. The RV representatives were cut off from all information except what they could gather piecemeal by themselves. However, if it became known that they had learned about something, no matter in what way, they were punished. They experienced in a drastic form a stark reality: that they had no right to any say in decision making, and were unable to protect their members from incarceration in concentration camps, deportation, or plunder by the state, nor were they themselves safe from physical or psychological violence. When the policy of "forced emigration" shifted into the policy of a "territorial solution," the problems multiplied. If the German-Jewish representatives initially were mistrustful of the Central Office for Jewish Emigration as a result of the violent practices of its prototype set up by Eichmann in Vienna, they ultimately felt constrained to accept it, because the pressure was too great not to make use of such a possibility, even if it was at best a bad option. At the end of 1938, they still had a skeptical view of illegal immigration to Palestine, due to the physical hardships, dangerous routes, and uncertain future it entailed. Yet in a short time, that option became one of the very last resorts that definitely had to be utilized. Although the

Jewish representatives recognized the genocidal core of the "territorial solutions" discussed in 1940, they secretly hoped to be able to play a role in forging plans for a Jewish settlement area somewhere, in order to ensure the survival of the community, even if at a lower material level of daily existence. However, the sudden deportations from Stettin/Schneidemühl, Baden, and the Palatinate, and the further turn of the screw in the radicalizing of anti-Jewish policy, brought them to the simultaneous realization of their own utter powerlessness. As Erich Simon noted, "The dream of autonomous administration of Jewish concerns within Germany came to an end already in 1940, and there was a horrible awakening."[369]

The Jewish functionaries had similar experiences in other areas of work that had been a significant motive for their remaining on in Germany, particularly in the sphere of welfare for children, the aged, and the ill. Nonetheless, it was still possible to provide that assistance, even if it demanded all their strength and resources, financial and in terms of personnel, and the provision of care was fraught with change as a result of the new and increasing regulations imposed by the RSHA on the safekeeping of their "wards." By contrast, in the case of the mentally ill, the National Socialist state realized its murderous aims early on. The Jewish functionaries were not necessarily able to recognize the mass murder that was taking place, but they were subjected here to a repeated lesson: namely, that narrow limits were set on their scope of activity, and that they were unable to rescue groups in need of protection once their deportation was on the agenda of the Nazi state.

The painful insights regarding the strict limits of their own possibilities for helping the needy members of their community were compounded by the awareness of their own personal peril. The rulers had set a chilling example with the arrests of Eppstein, Hirsch, and Seligsohn, incarcerations that cost Hirsch and Seligsohn their lives and left deep existential scars in the case of Eppstein. Against this backdrop, it is not surprising that the German-Jewish representatives in October 1941 accepted the "offer" of participating in the systematic deportations, in the fond hope for an orderly, transparent procedure, and, most particularly, one that they would also have a concrete hand in shaping.

Notes

1. The Palestine Office, operated by the German Zionists, was a branch of the Jewish Agency for Palestine. It dealt with organizing and implementing *aliyah* (immigration) to Palestine, and in particular issued the certificates necessary for immigration.

The main office was located in Berlin. The Palestine Office was able to operate until April 1941 as an independent institution, and was then integrated into the Reich Association. On the activity of the aid organizations, see also Herbert Strauss, "Jewish Emigration from Germany: Nazi Policies and Jewish Responses (II)," *LBI Yearbook* 26 (1981): 396ff.

2. See Hans Reichmann, *Deutscher Bürger und verfolgter Jude: Novemberpogrom und KZ Sachsenhausen 1937 bis 1939* (Munich, 1998), 116.

3. Yad Vashem (hereafter YV), 01/13, Franz Meyer (sometimes also Meier in the sources), November 1938, p. 2; on the November pogrom and its aftermath, see, inter alia, Kurt Jakob Ball-Kaduri, *Vor der Katastrophe: Juden in Deutschland 1934–1939* (Tel Aviv, 1967), 158–74; Barkai, *Boycott*, 133–38; Walter H. Pehle, *November 1938: From "Reichskristallnacht" to Genocide*, trans. William Templer (New York, 1991); Eliyahu Kutti Salinger, *"Nächstes Jahr im Kibbuz": Die jüdisch-chaluzische Jugendbewegung in Deutschland zwischen 1933 und 1943* (Paderborn, 1998), 88–106.

4. See Reichmann, *Bürger*, 114–15. The Central Association of German Citizens of the Jewish Faith (Centralverein deutscher Staatsbürger jüdischen Glaubens, CV), established in 1893 with the aim of combating anti-Semitism, sought full equal civil rights for the Jews in Germany and the overcoming of anti-Semitic prejudice within the non-Jewish population. It concentrated in its work on political and legal discussion and debate. It had a membership of some fifty to sixty thousand Jews. While a majority of the functionaries emigrated, others remained in Germany, including Cora Berliner, Otto Hirsch, Hanna Karminski, Julius Seligsohn, and Heinrich Stahl.

5. YV, 02/546, Erich Cohn, "Before and after the November Pogrom 1938," p. 6.

6. YV, 01/5, Benno Cohn, November 1938, 1; on events in Berlin elsewhere, see also the reports composed shortly after the events that the American Jewish Joint Distribution Committee (hereafter AJDC) passed on and today are housed in its archive: JDC Coll. 33/44, File 632, documentation on correspondence from AJDC to Joseph C. Hyman, 2 December 1938.

7. The order stated that twenty to thirty thousand "wealthy Jews in particular" were to be arrested. See BArch, R 58/276, RSHA, confidential telegram Müller to all Gestapo offices, 9 November 1938 (copy from the files of the Gestapo office Würzburg); see also Hans-Jürgen Döscher, *"Reichskristallnacht": Die November-Pogrome 1938* (Frankfurt am Main and Berlin, 1988), 109–112.

8. See, inter alia, YV, 01/212, Moritz Spitzer, "In Berlin als Leiter des Schockenverlages, Verbindung mit der Überwachungsstelle für jüdische Kultur im Propagandaministerium" [In Berlin as director of the Schocken publishing house, connection with the surveillance office for Jewish culture in the Propaganda Ministry], 26 November 1957, p. 3.

9. YV, 02/340, Hubert Pollack, "Captain Foley and other Reports," p. 12.

10. YV, 01/13, Franz Meyer, "November 1938," p. 2.

11. Ibid., p. 1.

12. Ibid., p. 3.

13. Reichmann, *Bürger*, 116.

14. Ibid., 135. The Zionist Association for Germany (Zionistische Vereinigung für Deutschland, ZVfD), established in 1897, was the German national affiliate of the World Zionist Organization. It saw the "Jewish Question" largely as a political and national issue that could be resolved by the creation of a homeland in Palestine. After 1933, its membership ranks swelled; on the organization, see Jehuda Reinharz, "Ideology and Structure in German Zionism, 1882–1933," in *Essential Papers on Zionism*, ed. Jehuda Reinharz and Anita Shapira (New York, 1996), 268–97.

15. Paltreu is an abbreviation of Palästina Treuhandstelle, the Palestine Trustee Office. This office, for clearing and consultation, was set up in 1933, when the Reich Economy Ministry signed the Ha'avara Agreement with the ZVfD and the Anglo-Palestine Bank, on the basis of which German Jews were able to transfer assets to Palestine. In 1937, the Altreu (Allgemeine Treuhandstelle für jüdische Auswanderung, General Trustee Office for Jewish Emigration) was created, a counterpart institution via which Jews could transfer assets to other countries insofar as that was possible. The Hilfsverein der deutschen Juden (Relief Organization of German Jews), founded in 1901, was initially set up to assist the Jewish victims of pogroms and wartime catastrophes, Eastern European Jews, and emigrants. During the Nazi period, it became, within the framework of the Central Committee for Relief and Rehabilitation (Zentralausschuss für Hilfe und Aufbau), the main organization for dealing with emigration to countries other than Palestine. It maintained eighteen branch consultation offices. Like other organizations, it later had to change its name to Hilfsverein der Juden in Deutschland (Relief Organization of Jews in Germany). In 1939, it was merged into the migration department within the Reich Association. The Kulturbund deutscher Juden (Cultural Federation of the German Jews), founded in 1933, made it possible for Jewish artists, who in general were not permitted to belong to the Reich Chamber of Culture, to continue their activities. The Kulturbund was under the supervision of the Reich Propaganda Ministry (under the office of Hans Hinkel, Reich culture governor); it maintained its own theaters and a periodical, and its local groups were active in most of the larger cities in Germany. In 1939, reorganized under a changed name (Jüdischer Kulturbund in Deutschland), it was able to continue its work independently from the Reich Association until September 1941, and after that within the framework of the Reich Association. Its newspaper, *Jüdisches Nachrichtenblatt,* was from 1939 to 1943 the only Jewish paper that the Reich Association could use to disseminate information.

16. YV, 01/13, Franz Meyer, "November 1938," p. 4.

17. Reichmann, *Bürger,* 264. Neumeyer served as head of the Munich Jewish Community in until he emigrated to Argentina in January 1941; see chapter 3.

18. Michael Wildt, "Introduction," in Reichmann, *Bürger,* 35.

19. USHMM, Washington, Brodnitz Collection, Acc. 2008.189.1, letter Baeck to Friedrich Brodnitz, 29.4.1938 (Letter 4). I wish to thank Jürgen Matthäus for pointing out to me the letters he has in the meantime edited in their full length; see Jürgen Matthäus, "'You have the right to be hopeful if you do your duty': Ten Letters by Leo Baeck to Friedrich Brodnitz, 1937–1941," *LBI Yearbook* 54 (2009): 344–45.

20. On the "June operation," see Wolfgang Ayass, *"Asoziale" im Nationalsozialismus* (Stuttgart, 1995); Wolfgang Ayass, "Ein Gebot der nationalsozialistischen Arbeitsdisziplin: Die Aktion 'Arbeitsscheu Reich,'" *Beiträge zur nationalsozialistischen Gesundheits- und Sozialpolitik* 6 (1988): 43–74; Christian Dirks, "The *Juni-Aktion* (June Operation) in Berlin," in *Jews in Nazi Berlin: From Kristallnacht to Liberation,* ed. Beate Meyer, Hermann Simon, and Chana Schütz (Chicago, 2009), 22–35.

21. Reichmann, *Bürger,* 87–88.

22. Ibid., 89.

23. Ibid.

24. See Trude Maurer, "The Background for Kristallnacht: The Expulsion of Polish Jews," in *November 1938,* ed. Walter H. Pehle (New York, 1991), 44–72; see also S. Adler-Rudel, *Ostjuden in Deutschland 1880–1940* (Tübingen, 1959), 152–55.

25. See the report by Franz Meyer, who was asked by Hirsch to go to Beuthen and look into the events that had transpired there. In addition, the Reichsbahn had demanded

that the Upper Silesian Jewish Association should cover the expenses incurred for transporting the "Polish" Jews to the border; see YV, 01/13, Franz Meyer, "November 1938," p. 1.

26. Reichmann, *Bürger*, 47. The expression "fateful year 1938" (*Schicksalsjahr 1938*) derives from a working report of the Reich Representation for 1938 that stated, "The year 1938 signifies a historical turning point in the fate of the Jews" and a Reich Foreign Ministry report on "The Jewish Question as a Factor in Foreign Policy in 1938," which began: "It is probably no coincidence that the fateful year 1938 has brought the Jewish Question closer to a solution with the realization of the conception of a Greater Germany"; see Avraham Barkai, "The Fateful Year 1938: The Continuation and Acceleration of Plunder," in Pehle, *November 1938*, 95; see also Barkai, *Boycott*, 110–51.

27. Ibid., 52ff.; see also Jacob Boas, "German-Jewish Internal Politics under Hitler 1933–1938," *LBI Yearbook* 29 (1984): 5.

28. See Rabinovici, *Eichmann's Jews*, 44–45; see also Doron Rabinovici, *Instanzen der Ohnmacht: Wien 1938–1945: Der Weg zum Judenrat* (Frankfurt am Main, 2000), 89–90; see also YV, 01/215, Benno Cohn, "Vorladung von Vertretern des deutschen Judentums im März 1939 (Eichmann)" [Summons of representatives of the German Jews in March 1939 (Eichmann)], 2 April 1958, p. 2.

29. RGBl. 1938 I, 338.

30. BArch, R 8150/21, *Informationsblätter*, ed. Reichsvertretung der Juden in Deutschland, V, Nos. 1 and 2, Berlin, January/February 1938 (n.p.): 5.

31. See Otto Dov Kulka, *Deutsches Judentum, Dokumente*, 27–28 and 410ff.; from the perspective of the SD, see "Lagebericht der Abteilung II 112 für das Jahr 1938," reproduced in *Die Judenpolitik des SD von 1935 bis 1938: Eine Dokumentation*, ed. Michael Wildt (Munich, 1995), 197.

32. Kulka, *Deutsches Judentum, Dokumente*, 14; on the Reich Representation, see also Strauss, "Jewish Emigration," 389–404.

33. Kulka, *Deutsches Judentum, Dokumente*, 18 and 244ff.

34. Ibid., 285ff.

35. Ibid., 20–21, 293ff., and 517–18.

36. On this in detail, see LBI, NY, AR 221, Folder B 30/3/5, Bruno Blau (Coll. 57), "Zur Geschichte der Reichsvertretung," pp. 10ff.

37. The State Zionist Organization in Germany was part of the radical right-wing Revisionist Party founded by Jabotinsky in 1925, which then departed from the World Zionist Organization in 1935. It was separate from the broader Zionist Association of Germany (ZVfD). One of its representatives was Georg Kareski. Although the National Socialist leaders for a time promoted this group, it was forcibly disbanded in 1938. On earlier conflicts of the Reich Representation with Kareski, see YV, 01/6, Benno Cohn, stenographic copy, "Vortrag über den Kampf um die Leitung des jüdischen Kulturbundes in Deutschland—ein Kapitel des Kampfes um jüdische Autonomie nach 1933" [Lecture on struggle and management of the Jewish Cultural Federation in Germany—a chapter in the struggle for Jewish autonomy after 1933]; in detail and with further literature, see Francis Nicosia, "Revisionist Zionism in Germany (II): Georg Kareski and the Staatszionistische Organisation, 1933–1938," *LBI Yearbook* 32 (1987): 231–67; see also Francis Nicosia, *Zionism and Anti-Semitism in Nazi Germany* (New York, 2008), 181–206.

38. LBI, JMB, MF8, letter Adler-Rudel to Georg Landauer, 10 June 1937, pp. 1–4.

39. Ibid., p. 5.

40. Benno Cohn, in YV, 01/245, "Begleitbericht zum Protokoll VI, Sitzung des Arbeitskreises von Zionisten aus Deutschland" [Accompanying report on minutes VI,

meeting, working group of Zionists from Germany], 5 March 1959, pp. 4–5. Kareski believed some of the Zionists were close to the SPD or other Marxists; see also Nicosia, *Zionism*, 194, 204.

41. YV, 01/243, Protokoll VI, Sitzung des Arbeitskreises von Zionisten aus Deutschland (Benno Cohn u.a.) [Minutes VI, meeting, working group of Zionists from Germany (Benno Cohn et al.)], 5 March 1959, Franz Meyer, p. 8.

42. Municipal Archive Mannheim, Posthumous Papers Eppstein, 31, excerpt from letter Hedwig Eppstein to [sister-in-law and brother-in-law] Paula and Lothar Eppstein, n.d. (1937), mixed lot Miriam Warburg, II.

43. YV, 01/245, "Begleitbericht zum Protokoll VI, Sitzung des Arbeitskreises von Zionisten aus Deutschland," 5 March 1959, Ball-Kaduri, p. 7.

44. See "Lagebericht der Abteilung II 112 für das Jahr 1938" [Situation report, Dept. II 112 for 1938], reproduced in Wildt, *Judenpolitik*, 198; see also Nicosia, "Revisionist Zionism," 266ff.; Nicosia, *Zionism*, 206.

45. Ephraim Frank, in YV, 1/216, "Die jüdische Situation in Berlin in der Zeit von Ende November 1938 bis zum März 1939 (und teilweise bis August 1940)" [The Jewish situation in Berlin from November 1938 to March 1939]. Reports by Benno Cohn and others in the meeting of the working group of Zionists from Germany, 2 April 1958, in the apartment of Dr. Ball-Kaduri in Tel Aviv, p. 3.

46. See LBI, Jerusalem, 555/4, "Arbeitsbericht der Reichsvertretung der Juden in Deutschland für das Jahr 1938" [Working report, Reich Representation of the Jews in Germany for 1938], p. 2.

47. YV, 01/294, Kurt Goldmann (Reuven Golan), "Hechaluz und Jugendaliyah in Deutschland von 1936 bis Ende 1939," p. 4. Hechalutz, a leftist Zionist organization, prepared young Jews in *hachshara* centers for life in Palestine, especially in kibbutzim. Founded in 1921 in Warsaw, the German section was created in 1922, and there was a great surge in interest after 1933. Hechalutz was disbanded as an independent organization after the November 1938 pogrom.

48. LBI, Jerusalem, 555/4, "Arbeitsbericht der Reichsvertretung der Juden in Deutschland für das Jahr 1938," p. 5; Herbert A. Strauss proceeds on the assumption of forty thousand for 1938 and seventy-eight thousand for 1939; see Strauss, "Jewish Emigration," 326.

49. Franz Meyer, in YV, 1/216, "Die jüdische Situation in Berlin in der Zeit von Ende November 1938 bis zum März 1939," pp. 4–5.

50. CJA, 2 B 1/1, memo (Eppstein, Hirsch, Stahl), 16 December 1938, point 2.

51. BArch, R 58, "Tagung zur 'Judenfrage'" [Conference on the "Jewish Question"], 16 December 1938, pp. 299ff.; later, the German-language periodical *Yedioth Hayom* also reported on this plan, "Juden und Flüchtlinge, Einzelheiten des neuen Judenerlasses in Deutschland," 21 May 1939.

52. Otto Dov Kulka and Eberhard Jäckel, eds., *Die Juden in den geheimen NS-Stimmungsberichten 1933–1945* (Düsseldorf, 2004), CD-ROM, 2851, SD-Hauptamt II, Bericht für Januar, Februar und März 1938 [Report for Jan./Feb./March 1938], p. 2. The designation *Ostmark* refers to Austria after annexation.

53. LBI, Jerusalem, 556/1, RVJD, Dept. Social Welfare, circular letter No. 453, 2 February 1939.

54. LBI, Jerusalem, 556/1, RVJD, Dept. Social Welfare, letter RVJD to Communities with more than 500 souls, 14 February 1939; LBI, Jerusalem, 556/1, RVJD, Dept. Social Welfare, Mustersatzung für Kultusvereinigungen (Ortsvereinigungen der Reichsvereinigung der Juden in Deutschland e.V.) [Exemplary bylaws for Communities (local associations of the Reichsvereinigung)].

55. See Hans-Erich Fabian, "Zur Entstehung der 'Reichsvereinigung der Juden in Deutschland,'" in *Gegenwart im Rückblick: Festgabe für die Jüdische Gemeinde zu Berlin 25 Jahre nach dem Neubeginn*, ed. Herbert. A. Strauss and Kurt R. Grossmann (Heidelberg, 1970), 171.

56. LBI, Jerusalem, 556/1, "Die Konzentration der jüdischen Arbeit in Deutschland durch Schaffung einer Reichsvereinigung" [Concentration of Jewish labor in Germany by creation of a Reich Association], pp. 11–12.

57. CJA, 2 B 1/1, memo, summons to Gestapo office (Lischka), 18 April 1939, p. 4.

58. YV, 01/204, Kurt Goldmann, "Hechaluz," enclosure, letter Kurt Goldmann to Josephstal et al., May 1939.

59. BArch, R 8150/1.1, minutes, meeting of the board, 12 February 1940, p. 1. Actually, the Reich Association had named Carl Fuchs as successor, and Stahl agreed explicitly to this, but the Gestapo/RSHA evidently did not accept this; see *Heinrich Stahl (13. April 1868–4. November 1942)*, ed. Neue Synagoge—Centrum Judaicum (Berlin, 1993), 30–31.

60. YV, 01/156, letter Hildegard Henschel to Ball-Kaduri, 5 December 1968. The supposed reason was that Henschel was "not a lodge brother."

61. See Döscher, *"Reichskristallnacht,"* 112–17.

62. On the Vienna Central Office, see Gabriele Anderl and Dirk Rupnow, *Die Zentralstelle für jüdische Auswanderung als Beraubungsinstitution* (Vienna, 2004); see also Dirk Rupnow, "'Zur Förderung und beschleunigten Regelung der Auswanderung': Die Zentralstelle für jüdische Auswanderung Wien," in *Ausgeschlossen und entrechtet. Raub und Rückgabe: Österreich von 1938 bis heute*, ed. V. Pawlowsky and H. Wendelin (Vienna, 2006), 13–31.

63. LBI, JMB, MF 546, Joseph Löwenherz Coll. (AR 25055), memo on conversation Löwenherz with Eichmann, 23 February 1939.

64. YV, 01/013, Franz Meyer, "November 1938," p. 4.

65. YV, 01/215, Benno Cohn, "Vorladung von Vertretern des deutschen Judentums im März 1939 (Eichmann)," 2 April 1958, p. 3.

66. Ibid.

67. Esriel Hildesheimer also arrived at this assessment; see Esriel Hildesheimer, *Jüdische Selbstverwaltung unter dem NS-Regime* (Tübingen, 1994), 88.

68. YV, Tr3-1129, T/142, Bo6-1129, letter Stahl to Jewish Community Vienna and Palestine Office, 1 March 1949. I am grateful to Bettina Stangneth for referring me to this document.

69. YV, 01/215, Benno Cohn, "Vorladung von Vertretern des deutschen Judentums im März 1939 (Eichmann)," 2 April 1958, p. 5.

70. In a travel report of a staff member of the JOINT, there is mention of four thousand persons per month (JDC, Coll. 33/44, File 642, Notes on Visit to Germany 17 v. 19.2.1939); already on 26 April 1939, a memorandum notes that a "large number" of individuals designated to appear by the Jewish Community had not shown up at the Central Office (CJA, 2 B 1/1, memo, 26 April 1939, p. 1); Adler-Rudel refers to a secret report by the RSHA of 15 June 1939, stating that in April/May only 6,187 individuals had submitted applications for emigration (S. Adler-Rudel, *Jüdische Selbsthilfe unter dem Naziregime 1933–1939* [Tübingen, 1974], 112); in the minutes of a board meeting, there is a note that from March 1940 on, fifty persons a day had to be assigned, which was only possible if emigrants were included already before a visa was issued or before they reported for special *hachshara* (BArch, R 8150/1, minutes of board meeting, 4 March 1940, p. 2 [pag. 187]) (in this notation and hereafter, pag. refers to the supplementary page numbering system used by the archive, whereas p.

indicates the actual page number in the document); Nussbaum reports that the daily quota was raised from twenty-five to fifty, seventy, and one hundred (YV, 01/232, Document No. 3, German MS of an article by Rabbi Dr. Max Nussbaum, in the *Contemporary Jewish Record*, November/December 1940, 12); by targeted publicity in the city neighborhoods and more local course offerings, in April 1940 once again four hundred persons were to be registered (BArch, R 8150/1.1, minutes of board meeting, 5 April 1940, pp. 1–2); on the creation of the Central Office, see also E.L., "Begegnungen mit Eichmann," *Yedioth Hayom*, 6 April 1956.

71. See Kulka and Jäckel, *Juden*, 2914, SD-Hauptamt II 112, 15 June 1940; see also Otto Dov Kulka and Eberhard Jäckel, *The Jews in the Secret Nazi Reports on Popular Opinion in Germany, 1933–1945*, trans. William Templer (New Haven, CT, 2010), 454.

72. LBI, JMB, MF 546, Joseph Löwenherz Coll. (AR 25055), memo discussion Löwenherz with Eichmann, 10 February 1939.

73. Kurt Goldmann, in YV, 1/216, "Die jüdische Situation in Berlin in der Zeit von Ende November 1938 bis zum März 1939," p. 5.

74. CJA, 2 B 1/1, memo, summons to Gestapo office (Lischka), 5 May 1939, p. 5.

75. BArch, R 8150/1, minutes of board meeting, 3 July 1939, p. 2.

76. LBI, Jerusalem, 556/1, "Arbeitsbericht der der Juden in Deutschland für das Jahr 1939," p. 1.

77. See Gudrun Maierhof, *Selbstbehauptung im Chaos: Frauen in der Jüdischen Selbsthilfe 1933–1943* (Frankfurt am Main, 2002).

78. According to Otto Hirsch, *Jüdisches Nachrichtenblatt*, 11 July 1939.

79. See Ernest H. Weismann, "Die Nachfolge-Organisationen," in *Die Wiedergutmachung nationalsozialistischen Unrechts durch die Bundesrepublik Deutschland*, vol. 2, *Das Rückerstattungsgesetz*, ed. Bundesminister der Finanzen (Munich, 1981), 776ff.

80. The Jewish newspaper *Aufbau* wrote in an article entitled "Jewish Unified Organization in Germany: A New Nazi Ordinance" with great concern: "Anyone can imagine what it portends, given the plundering of the Jews in Germany that has already occurred, when half a million human beings, 80 percent of whom are reduced to the destitute status of a *lumpenproletariat*, are supposed to maintain themselves without any possibility for earning a living." "Jüdische Einheitsorganisation in Deutschland: Eine neue Nazi-Verordnung," *Aufbau*, 15 July 1939, 4.

81. YV, 02/772 (Wiener Library P.III.h. [Theresienstadt] No. 894), Erich Simon, "Theresienstadt als autarkes Stadtwesen" [Theresienstadt as a self-contained municipal entity], pp. 1–2.

82. Ibid., p. 2.

83. See Maierhof, *Selbstbehauptung*; Wolf Gruner, "Poverty and Persecution: The Reichsvereinigung, the Jewish Population, and Anti-Jewish Policy in the Nazi State, 1939-1945," *Yad Vashem Studies* 27 (1999): 23–60.

84. See Fabian, "Entstehung der 'Reichsvereinigung,'" 172.

85. BArch, R 8150/1, RVJD, "Entwurf Beitragsordnung für die Erhebung eines außerordentlichen Beitrages" [Draft rules for levying an exceptional contribution], pp. 4–5, pag. 10–11.

86. CJA, 2 B 1/1, memo 5 May 1939, p. 1, point 2 (Hamburg), memo 26 June 1939, pp. 2–3, points II and III.

87. Figures according to LBI, Jerusalem, 556/1, "Arbeitsbericht der Reichsvereinigung der Juden in Deutschland für das Jahr 1939" [Working report Reichsvereinigung 1939], p. 11. According to a later report of the Reich Association, which contained figures for each year until the prohibition on emigration, a total of 352,696 Jews emigrated from the *Altreich*; see BArch, R 8150/31, "Auswanderung von Juden aus dem

Altreich 1933 bis 1941," pag. 218. Strauss gives other figures: 1933–1935, 81,000; 1936–1938, 88,000; 1939–October 1941, 101,000; see Strauss, "Jewish Emigration," 326.

88. Juliane Wetzel, "Auswanderung aus Deutschland," in *Die Juden in Deutschland 1933–1945: Leben unter nationalsozialistischer Herrschaft*, ed. Wolfgang Benz (Munich, 1988), 420. There is still a need for a systematic in-depth study of Jewish emigration from Germany and the occupied countries.

89. See LBI, Jerusalem, 555/4, "Arbeitsbericht der Reichsvereinigung der Juden in Deutschland für das Jahr 1938," 10–11; on the Dominican Republic, see JDC, Coll. 33/44, File 632, letter from RVJD to AJDC, New York, 24 July 1940, pp. 12–13; on Jewish group settlements, see Marion Kaplan, *Dominican Haven: The Jewish Refugee Settlement in Sosúa, 1940–1945* (New York, 2008); Susanne Heim and Hans Ulrich Dillmann, *Jüdische Emigranten in der Dominikanischen Republik* (Berlin, 2009); Bonnie M. Harris, "Refugee Rescue in the Philippines, 1937–1941," in *"Wer bleibt, opfert seine Jahre, vielleicht sein Leben": Deutsche Juden 1938–1941*, ed. Susanne Heim, Beate Meyer, and Francis R. Nicosia (Göttingen, 2010), 265–80.

90. YV, 01/18, Artur Prinz (member of the Exec. Comm. of the Hilfsverein der Deutschen Juden), September 1945, "Die Gestapo als Feind und Förderer jüdischer Auswanderung," pp. 1–5; on the Reich Office for Emigration, see also LBI, JMB, MM 131, Coll. Fritz Schwarzschild, Hermann von Freeden, "Ein Beitrag zur Geschichte der Judenauswanderung aus Deutschland," December 1945.

91. Forschungsstelle für Zeitgeschichte (hereafter FZH), Judenverfolgung/Berichte, "Interview H. Schottelius mit Max Plaut," 25 January 1954, transcript, pp. 6–7.

92. These differing views and criticisms become clear, for example, in LBI, NY, AR 7171, letter (confidential) from Leo Löwenstein to Ernst Noah, Martin Salomonski, Heinrich Stahl, and Hermann Stern, 26 February 1940.

93. See Wetzel, "Auswanderung," 423ff.; on the children's transports, see also Gudrun Maierhof, Chana Schütz, and Hermann Simon, eds., *Aus Kindern wurden Briefe: Die Rettung jüdischer Kinder aus Nazi-Deutschland* (Berlin, 2004).

94. JDC, Coll. 33/44, File 666, (Confidential) Notes on Status of Jewish Refugees from Germany and former Austria in various Countries of Europe based on reports on file in the New York Office of the Joint Distribution Committee, 5 July 1939 (Katzki).

95. YV, 01/18, Artur Prinz (member, Exec. Comm., Hilfsverein der Deutschen Juden), September 1945, "Die Gestapo als Feind und Förderer jüdischer Auswanderung," pp. 7–8.

96. YV, 01/320, K. J. Ball, "Illegale Alya [sic] 1939/1940 aus Hitler-Deutschland," p. 32.

97. The American Jewish Joint Distribution Committee was established in 1914 as the relief organization of American Jewry for their fellow Jews abroad, especially in Eastern Europe. After the National Socialists took power, it also helped finance the social welfare work of the German Jews and promoted plans for emigration. Until 1941, it also supported Jews in the territories occupied by the German Reich. See Yehuda Bauer, *American Jewry and the Holocaust: The American Jewish Joint Distribution Committee, 1939–1945* (Detroit, 1981).

98. JDC, Coll. 33/44, File 666, "A Statement of Policy by the American Jewish Joint Distribution Committee (Hyman)," January 1939; on the voyage of the SS *St. Louis*, see Gordon Thomas and Max Morgen Witts, *Voyage of the Damned* (New York, 1974).

99. YV, 01/263, Max Zimels, "In Berlin von Ende Dezember 1938 bis Anfang September 1939 als Scheliach des Hechaluz," 20 October 1960, supplemented January/February 1961, p. 8.

100. JDC, Coll. 33/44, File 666, Letter from AJDC to the Officers, 10 August 1939, "Memorandum on Illegal Emigration to Palestine," 24 July 1939, and "Note on the Meeting with Sir Herbert Emerson held on the 25th July 1939." On the internal Jewish discussion, see also Yehuda Bauer, *Jews for Sale? Nazi-Jewish Negotiations, 1933–1945* (New Haven, CT, 1994), 44–54.

101. See Adler-Rudel, *Selbsthilfe*, 16–17; see also Moshe Ayalon, "'Gegenwaertige Situation': Report on the Living Conditions of the Jews in Germany: A Document and Commentary," *LBI Yearbook* 43 (1998): 280–81; Avraham Altman and Irene Eber, "Flight to Shanghai, 1938–1940: the Larger Setting," *Yad Vashem Studies* 38 (2000): 51–86. For interviews with Shanghai Jewish refugees and an overview of the migration of refugees to Shanghai, see http://goo.gl/lO6cQ (accessed 25 July 2012).

102. JDC, Coll. 658, telegram from Hirsch, 3 October 1939.

103. Kulka and Jäckel, *Juden*, 2997, SD-Abschnitt Leipzig, 13 October 1939; see also Kulka and Jäckel, *The Jews*, 479.

104. Kulka and Jäckel, *Juden*, 3057, "District president Upper and Central Franconia, report for January 1940," 6 February 1940.

105. Ibid., 3133, "Office for Advising Emigrants Cologne, report for April, May June 1940," n.d., p. 3.

106. JDC, Coll. 33/44, File 642, Letter, RVJD to AJDC, 24 July 1940.

107. Adler-Rudel, *Selbsthilfe*, 117; see also "Memorandum Nathaniel Peffer, Columbia University," in JDC, Coll. 33/44, File 666, appendix to letter by Chamberlain to Hyman, 5 April 1939.

108. "Memorandum Nathaniel Peffer, Columbia University," in JDC, Coll. 33/44, File 666, appendix to letter by Chamberlain to Hyman, 5 April 1939.

109. Recha Freier, born in 1892 in Norden/East Frisia, died in 1984 in Jerusalem; she was a teacher and folktale researcher, and had lived with her husband Rabbi Moritz Freier in Berlin since 1925. The couple had three sons and one daughter. In 1932, Recha Freier established the association Jewish Youth Aid (Jüdische Jugendhilfe) or Youth Aliyah, which made it possible for thousands of young Jews to emigrate to Palestine. Although in the Nazi period her husband emigrated together with their sons, she continued her work, fleeing in 1941 with her daughter to Palestine, where, for the children of poor families, she built up an Agricultural Training Centre for Israeli Children. On Freier in the late 1950s and the controversy over her book *Let the Children Come* (London, 1961), see the section "Aftermath" in chapter 5.

110. See Dalia Ofer, "Die illegale Einwanderung nach Palästina: Politische, nationale und personliche Aspekte (1939–1941)," in "Flüchtlingspolitik und Fluchthilfe," special issue, *Beiträge zur nationalsozialistischen Gesundheits- und Sozialpolitik* 15 (1999): 9–38; see also Wetzel, "Auswanderung," 451ff.

111. The Jewish Agency for Palestine (JA) was the representative organization for the Jews recognized by the British mandatory power in Palestine; it worked together with the British mandatory authorities, advising them, and its aim was to safeguard the interests of the Jews and those who wished to immigrate into the country. Until the establishment of the state of Israel, the JA represented the Jews in Palestine politically. From 1929, Weizmann was at times its president, and Ben-Gurion served as head of its executive committee until the state of Israel was established.

112. YV, 01/226, Benno Cohn et al., "Verschiedene Informationen über die jüdische Situation in Berlin in den Jahren von 1933 bis 1940," meeting, working group of Zionists from Germany, 20 May 1958, here Benno Cohn and Hans Friedenthal, p. 3.

113. YV, 01/4, Fritz Berger, "Polenaktion 1938," 6 September 1948, p. 2.

114. YV, 01/204, Kurt Goldmann (Reuwen Golan), "Hechaluz und Jugendaliyah in Deutschland von 1936 bis Ende 1939," February 1958, p. 6; on illegal emigration, see also Maierhof, *Selbstbehauptung*, 215–33.

115. YV, 01/226, Benno Cohn et al., "Verschiedene Informationen über die jüdische Situation in Berlin in den Jahren von 1933 bis 1940," meeting, working group of Zionists from Germany, 20 May 1958, Benno Cohn, p. 5.

116. Ibid., 5; see also YV, 01/204, Kurt Goldmann (Reuwen Golan), "Hechaluz und Jugendaliyah in Deutschland von 1936 bis Ende 1939," February 1958, p. 4.

117. Salinger, *"Nächstes Jahr im Kibbuz,"* 116.

118. BArch, R 8150/4, letter RVJD to Labor Office Berlin, 31 March 1941; at the same time, the staff of the Jewish Seminar for Kindergarten and Daycare Teachers was taken over; BArch, R 8150/4, letter RVJD to Labor Office, 1 April 1941.

119. BArch, R 8150/1/1, letter ORT (Simon) to Oberfinanzpräsident [regional finance director] Berlin, 3 August 1939, pag. 94.

120. Salinger, *"Nächstes Jahr im Kibbuz,"* 149; see also JDC, Coll. 33/44, File 632, letter RVJD to AJDC, New York, 24 July 1940, pp. 17–18; on the *hachshara*, see also Barkai, *Boycott*, 87–92.

121. BArch R 8150/1, minutes, meeting of board, 11 December 1939, p. 1; after taking stock, the board ruled that only seventy-five certificates could be issued, fifty by the Palestine Office.

122. Salinger, *"Nächstes Jahr im Kibbuz,"* 127.

123. JDC, 678, *Palcor Bulletin*, 9 October 1939. Amounting to 3,362 persons, the number of stateless immigrants was the largest.

124. CJA, 2 B 1/2, memo, No. 59, consultation in RSHA, 24 April 1941, p. 7, point 11, and CJA, 2 B 1/2, memo, No. 59, consultation in RSHA, 26 April 1941, p. 3, point 13.

125. CJA, 2 B 1/2, memo, No. 83, consultation in RSHA, 27 May 1941, p. 3, point 9c.

126. CJA, 2 B 1/2, memo, No. 89/Z 81, consultation in RSHA, 12 June 1941, p. 4, point 16; it notes here the handing over of the Winkel training farm and the transfer of its director Martin Gerson to the Neuendorf farm; CJA, 2 B 1/2, memo, No. 109/B 19, telephone call from RSHA, 16 July 1941, pp. 1–2, points 2a–f.

127. YV, 01/241, Herbert (Ehud) Growald, "Hachscharah und Hachscharahzentren in Deutschland von 1940–1943," meeting of Zionists from Germany, 23 June 1958, p. 2.

128. See Beate Kosmala, "Zwischen Ahnen und Wissen: Flucht vor der Deportation (1941–1943)," in "Die Deportation der Juden aus Deutschland: Pläne-Praxis-Reaktionen," ed. Birthe Kundrus and Beate Meyer, special issue, *Beiträge zur Geschichte des Nationalsozialismus* 20 (2004): 142ff.

129. YV, 01/241, Herbert (Ehud) Growald, "Hachscharah und Hachscharahzentren in Deutschland von 1940–1943," meeting of Zionists from Germany, 23 June 1958, p. 1.

130. See Wolf Gruner, "Terra Incognita? Die Lager für den 'jüdischen Arbeitseinsatz' (1938–1943) und die deutsche Bevölkerung," in *Die Deutschen und die Judenverfolgung im Dritten Reich*, ed. Ursula Büttner (Hamburg, 1992), 131–60; see also Salinger, *"Nächstes Jahr im Kibbuz,"* 156–57.

131. YV, 01/204, Kurt Goldmann (Reuwen Golan), "Hechaluz und Jugendaliyah in Deutschland von 1936 bis Ende 1939," February 1958, p. 7.

132. Salinger, *"Nächstes Jahr im Kibbuz,"* 153; LBI, NY, AR 25033, Rischowsky Coll., MF 537, memo, 13 March 1940, p. 2, point 7.

133. Archive of the Family Schocken in the Schocken Publishing House, Jerusalem, file 921/141/761, letter Martin Gerson to RVJD, Eppstein, 29 October 1941.

134. See YV, 01/204, Kurt Goldmann (Reuwen Golan), "Hechaluz und Jugendaliyah in Deutschland von 1936 bis Ende 1939," February 1958, p. 3; Salinger, *"Nächstes Jahr im Kibbuz,"* 162.

135. YV, 01/241, Herbert (Ehud) Growald, "Hachscharah und Hachscharahzentren in Deutschland von 1940–1943," meeting, Zionists from Germany, 23 June 1958, p. 5; see also the report by Anneliese-Ora Borinski, *Erinnerungen 1940–1943* (Nördlingen, 1970).

136. Salinger, *"Nächstes Jahr im Kibbuz,"* 163; on Martin Gerson, see Salinger, *"Nächstes Jahr im Kibbuz,"* 165–78; he was deported on 16 June 1943 to Theresienstadt, and on 1 October 1944 to Auschwitz and murdered there. See Gedenkbuch, "The Memorial Book of the Federal Archives for the Victims of the Persecution of Jews in Germany (1933–1945)," www.bundesarchiv.de/gedenkbuch/index.html.en (accessed 26 July 2012).

137. Growald thus reports that the directors of the Hechalutz had later worked together well with Martin Gerson, who "in terms of youth policy had always been our opponent," see YV, 01/241, Herbert (Ehud) Growald, "Hachscharah und Hachscharahzentren in Deutschland von 1940–1943," meeting, Zionists from Germany, 23 June 1958, p. 2.

138. Kulka and Jäckel, *Juden*, 3090, "Auswandererberatungsstelle Köln, Bericht für Januar, Februar und März 1940," n.d., p. 3.

139. YV, 01/220, Benno Cohn et al., 3, meeting, Zionists from Germany, 23 June 1958, p. 2.

140. Salinger, *"Nächstes Jahr im Kibbuz,"* 118.

141. YV, 01/320, K. J. Ball, "Illegale Alya [sic] 1939/40 aus Hitler-Deutschland," pp. 10–11; YV, 02 /1063, Emma Israel, "I was on the 'Patria,'" April 1960; on the ill-fated *Pentcho*, see John T. Bierman, *Odyssey* (New York, 1984).

142. YV, 02/283, Michael Meyer, "Emigration to Palestine during the War: Eine Wanderung nach Erez-Israel im Jahre 1940," lecture, 21 August 1941, transcript, p. 8.

143. YV, 01/226, Benno Cohn et al., "Verschiedene Informationen über die jüdische Situation in Berlin in den Jahren von 1933 bis 1940," meeting, Zionists from Germany, 20 May 1958, pp. 4, 6.

144. JDC, Coll. 33/44, File 632, letter RVJD to AJDC New York, 24 July 1940, p. 14.

145. Ofer, "Illegale Einwanderung," 34.

146. See Willy Cohn, *Kein Recht, nirgends: Tagebuch vom Untergang des Breslauer Judentums 1933–1941,* vol. 2 (Cologne, Weimar, and Vienna, 2006), 846.

147. USHMM, Washington, Brodnitz Collection, Acc. 2008.189.1, letter Baeck to Friedrich Brodnitz, 12 September 1939 (Letter 5), reproduced in its entirety in Matthäus, "'You have the right to be hopeful'" 346–47.

148. CJA, Sammlung Ausstellung Juden in Berlin 1938–1945, Interview with Marianne Givol née Henschel, conducted by Alexandra von Pfuhlstein, 6 October 1999, transcript, p. 2.

149. Municipal Archive Mannheim, posthumous papers Eppstein, 31, bundle Miriam Warburg, p. III, excerpt letter Hedwig Eppstein to Paula and Lothar Eppstein, n.d. (1937).

150. Municipal Archive Mannheim, posthumous papers Eppstein, 31, bundle Miriam Warburg, p. IV, excerpt letter, Hedwig Eppstein to Paula and Lothar Eppstein, 21 September 1938.

151. Municipal Archive Mannheim, posthumous papers Eppstein, 31, bundle Miriam Warburg, p. VI, excerpt letter, Hedwig Eppstein to Paula and Lothar Eppstein, 3 December 1938.

152. Municipal Archive Mannheim, posthumous papers Eppstein, 31, bundle Miriam Warburg, p. II, excerpt of letter, Hedwig Eppstein to Paula and Lothar Eppstein, 31 December 1938.
153. YV, 01/212, Moritz Spitzer, "In Berlin als Leiter des Schockenverlages, Verbindung mit der Überwachungsstelle für jüdische Kultur im Propagandaministerium," 26 November 1957, p. 9.
154. Municipal Archive Mannheim, posthumous papers Eppstein, 31, bundle Miriam Warburg, p. VII, excerpt letter Hedwig Eppstein to Paula and Lothar Eppstein, 27 January 1939 and 16 February 1939.
155. BArch, R 8150/1, questionnaires Eppstein, pag. 232.
156. Municipal Archive Mannheim, posthumous papers Eppstein, 27/2002/7, Paula Eppstein, 1 July 1994, p. 9.
157. CJA, 2 B 1/1, memo, 26 June 1939, p. 2, points VI–VII f.
158. BArch, R 8150, minutes of board, letter from RVJD to all board members, 18 August 1939.
159. See the postscript of a letter to Brodnitz, 28 January 1940: "Heinrich Stahl is leaving Berlin this week to move to Brussels where his son is" (USHMM, Brodnitz Collection, Acc. 2008.189.1, Letter 6, reproduced in full in Matthäus, "'You have the right to be hopeful,'" 347–48); Paul Meyerheim at the Reichsvereinigung still assumed in May 1940 that at the time, Stahl's emigration was still prohibited by the authorities, but that he would soon be able to emigrate to Belgium (JDC, Coll. 33/44, File, 631/2-f2, conversation between Dr. X (Paul Meyerheim), Mr. Katzki, Miss Emanuel, and Mr. Asch in Brussels, 6 May 1940, Annex, Confidential, p. 4, point 13); see also Aufbau, "Heinrich Stahl darf nicht auswandern," 19 April 1940, 1.
160. BArch, R 8150/1, questionnaires of those mentioned, pag. 238–43. Löwenstein, who was ill for a long time, and his spouse remained in Berlin and were killed in the ruins of their home during a bombing raid. Their daughters were deported in 1943: Sophie with Transport 37, Rose with Osttransport 31. See LBI, JMB, 111, Sammlung Kreutzberger, Bericht A. Gutfeld, "Erinnerungen an die Arbeit im Hilfsverein," p. 3; see also data on Sophie, Rose, and Victor Löwenstein, data bank, Berlin Gedenkbuch.
161. CJA, 2 B 1/1, memo, summons to Gestapo office, 19 February 1940, p. 2, point 3.
162. CJA, 2 B 1/1, memo, 15 August 1939, pp. 2–3, point 5.
163. YV, 1151/92, Fritz Berger, "Sprecherlaubnis in der Strafanstalt Tegel im Winter 1938–1939: Polenaktion 1938 und Fremdenamt Berlin," 7 June 1958, pp. 5–6; see also YV, 01/263, Max Meir Zimels, "In Berlin von Ende Dezember 1938 bis Anfang September 1939," p. 8.
164. CJA, 2 B 1/1, memo, 30 January 1940, p. 5, point 12.
165. LBI, JMB, MF 488/2, letter Morrissey to Warburg, 10 June 1940.
166. YV, 02/283, Michael Meyer, "Emigration to Palestine during the War," p. 10. In a report to the JOINT in June 1939, there is already mention of the fact that Jewish persons and organizations who expressed objections to illegal emigration were being arrested as saboteurs and imprisoned in concentration camps, JDC, Coll. 33/44, File 678, B. K., report, 15 June 1939, p. 3. Erich Frank gave another reason for arrest: Eppstein had changed an article in the Jüdisches Nachrichtenblatt on emigration after the article had been cleared for publication, see YV, 01/227, supplement to testimony of E. Frank on "summons of representatives of Jewish umbrella organizations in Berlin, Vienna and Prague to Gestapo in Berlin (Eichmann), March 1940," p. 2. Yet given this reason, the order from the RSHA that he should no longer deal with questions pertaining to the technicalities of emigration seems meaningless.

167. BArch, R 8150, 112/45/2, memo, 20 August 1940, p. 1, (pag. 153), point 3; BArch, R 8150, 112/45/2, memo, 24 August 1940, p. 1 (pag. 152), point 1; BArch, R 8150, 112/45/2, memo, 27 August 1940, p. 1 (pag. 149), point 1.

168. LBI, JMB, MF 488/2, memo, telegram, 9 September 1940, Kahn to Hirsch; LBI, JMB, MF 488/2, Kahn to Leavitt, 6 September 1940; LBI, JMB, MF 488/2, telegram, 20 December 1940, Troper to Joint. The first telegram, which still spoke about arrest, overlapped with his release.

169. CJA, 2 B 1/1, memo, 11 November 1940, p. 1, point 1; CJA, 2 B 1/1,, memo, 26 November 1940, p. 1 (pag. 118), point 2; CJA, 2 B 1/1, memo, 4 December 1940, p. 1 (pag. 169), point 1; CJA, 2 B 1/1, memo, 16 December 1940, p. 1 (pag. 102), point 5.

170. On summons to Theodor Dannecker, see LBI, NY, AR 25033, MF 537, Rischowsky Coll., memo, Kozower, 17 August 1940; on Dannecker himself, see Claudia Steur, *Theodor Dannecker: Ein Funktionär der "Endlösung"* (Essen, 1997).

171. Entschädigungsamt Berlin, 253555, enclosure to questionnaire A, pag. A 1a.

172. Walter Jagusch, with a doctorate in law, headed from February 1939 the section "Emigration" in the Gestapo, which he continued to head until after the RSHA was established. From February 1940, he was the official responsible for "Jewish affairs (incl. *Reichsvereinigung*)," until he left the RSHA at the end of 1940. Shortly after the above-mentioned summons, this sphere of activity was finally placed under Eichmann's special section, Department IV B 4. See Michael Wildt, *An Uncompromising Generation: The Nazi Leadership of the Reich Security Main Office* (Madison, WI, 2010), 189, 249.

173. BArch, R 8150/45, memo, 20 December 1940, p. 2, point 2 (no pag.).

174. CJA, 2 B 1/1, memo, 20 December 1940, p. 1 (pag. 100), point 1; this prohibition was in effect for about six months, and then it was informally revoked; see LBI, NY, AR 25033, MF 537, Rischowsky Coll., memo, No. Z 84, 24 June 1941, pp. 1–2, point 3.

175. LBI, Jerusalem, 643, offprint, 18 September 1959, "Gedenkblatt für Dr. Paul Eppstein," Berthold Simonsohn, pp. 1–2.

176. BArch, R 8150/45, memo, No. 8a/41, 20 February 1941, p. 1, pag. 74, point 2.

177. JDC, Coll. 33/44, File, 631/2 of 2, memo, 26 February 1941, Schargo to Troper, re: Request from Dr. Meyerheim. According to Bauer, most of the visas were approved but never used; see Bauer, *American Jewry*, 62. All those named (with the exception of Baeck, who survived in Theresienstadt, and Victor Löwenstein, who perished in a bombing raid) were murdered in concentration camps or ghettos between 1941 and 1945.

178. CJA, 2 B 1/2, memo, No. 129, 9 August 1941, p. 5.

179. LBI, NY, AR 25033 Rischkowsky Coll., memo, 24 October 1941, consultation Eppstein/Storfer with Eichmann. Berliner, Sänger, Meyerheim, Braun, Henschel, Kozower, Wolffsky, Cohn, Lilienthal, and Kreindler signed the pledge to maintain confidentiality.

180. See YV, 01/26, Albert Dann, "Erinnerungen an die Augsburger Gemeinde," 8 August 1944, p. 7.

181. Yfaat Weiss, *Deutsche und polnische Juden vor dem Holocaust: Jüdische Identität zwischen Staatsbürgerschaft und Ethnizität 1933–1940*, Schriftenreihe der Vierteljahrshefte für Zeitgeschichte 81 (Munich, 2000), 211.

182. YV, P1/5, list Freier, 22 February 1940, pag. 139; a short description of the conflict can be found in Recha Freier, *Let the Children Come* (London, 1961), 64–74; see also Weiss, *Deutsche und polnische Juden*, 211–17; Maierhof, *Selbstbehauptung*, 221–33.

183. Weiss, *Deutsche und polnische Juden*, 212.

184. YV, P1/10, Recha Freier, "Interview, Baruch Zwi Ophir and Shaul Esh with Moshe Ortner," n.d., pp. 8, 12.

185. YV, P1/10, Recha Freier, "Interview, Baruch Zwi Ophir and Shaul Esh with Moshe Ortner," n.d, p. 15; YV, 033/85, Recha Freier, "Die zwangsweise Abschiebung der polnischen Juden," pp. 3–4.

186. YV, P1/5, board Berlin Jewish Community to Freier, 1 April 1940, pag. 176. Although it initially was stated that the Reichsvereinigung had no authority to provide support benefits to the Polish Jews from its budget, the RV later concluded an agreement with the Main Trustee Office for the East (Haupttreuhandstelle Ost), which had confiscated all the assets of the formerly Polish Jews. This office paid out an annual sum of 12,500 RM to support 300–600 cases "for welfare of the Poles in the Altreich" (except the areas for which the Vienna Jewish Community or the Prague Jewish Community were responsible); see BArch, R 81501/6, memo consultation with head, Main Trustee Office for the East, 31 July 1941, pag. 65; BArch, R 81501/6, memo, no heading, signed Cohn and Meyerheim, pag. 84.

187. YV, P 1/3, Recha Freie, minutes of meeting, 1 December 1939, Lyon; Conrad Cohn was initially given the task of finding out exactly what possibilities there were for accommodating the Jews released, and until that was established, no certificate was to be issued; see BArch, R 8150 1.1, minutes board meeting RVJD, 11 December 1939, p. 1, point 3.

188. YV, P1/3, "Note of protest, message to Special hachshara Confirmation Comm., for Mr. Schönfeld," 15 January 1940, pag. 164.

189. YV, P1/3, minutes, meeting, Palestine Office Commission, 14 December 1939, pag. 38; YV, P1/3, memo, Freier, 10 January 1940, pag. 84; see also BArch, R 8150/1.1, minutes board meeting RVJD, 21 December 1939, pag. 196, point 5.

190. YV, P1/3, appendix 2, minutes, meeting, Palestine Office Commission, 13 December 1939.

191. YV, 033/85, Recha Freier, "Die zwangsweise Abschiebung der polnischen Juden," p. 10.

192. CJA, 2 B 1/1, memo, 30 January 1940, pp. 1–2, point 2.

193. LBI, NY, AR 25033, MF 537, Rischowsky Coll., memo, No. 7, 11 March 1940, p. 1, point 1.

194. YV, P1/3, memo, "Only for Poles and stateless Poles," 9 March 1940, pag. 162–63.

195. BArch, R 8150/1.1, minutes board meeting RVJD, 22 January 1940, point 5, p. 2, pag. 193. The *Generalgouvernement* was the largest administrative unit in German-occupied Poland, including the cities of Warsaw, Kraków and Lvov.

196. YV, 033/85, Recha Freier, "Die zwangsweise Abschiebung der polnischen Juden," p. 11.

197. YV, P1/3, letter delegation (6 signatories) to Lyon, Palestine Office, 13 March 1940, pag. 168; YV, 01/15, Anne Nieder, "Polen-Aktion, Bericht v. August 1944," p. 3. According to Nieder, the transport left on 2 May 1940 from Pressburg (Bratislava) and capsized near Rhodes, from where the passengers were sent to a camp in southern Italy, and later went to Palestine, arriving on 3 June 1944; see also Bierman, *Odyssey*.

198. YV, 033/85, Freier, "Die zwangsweise Abschiebung der polnischen Juden," p. 14. Max Nussbaum also mentions that two hundred certificates were issued, but in his report, he leaves out any comment on the disputes raging within the Jewish committees; see YV, 01/232, Document No. 3, German MS of an article by Rabbi Dr. Max Nussbaum, *Contemporary Jewish Record*, November/December 1940, 4–5.

199. YV, 033/85, Freier, "Die zwangsweise Abschiebung der polnischen Juden," p. 15; see also YV, 01/15, Anne Nieder, "Polen-Aktion, Bericht v. August 1944," p. 3.

200. Extracts from his letters; see YV, 033/85, Freier, "Die zwangsweise Abschiebung der polnischen Juden," p. 18.

201. YV, P1/4, "memo on a detailed discussion," n.d. (probably 23 March 1940), "Erklärung Freier," pag. 57.

202. YV, P1/4, letter Lyon, 1 March 1940, pag. 62.

203. YV, P1/4, minutes of meeting, n.d., n. auth., n. pag.

204. YV, P1/4, letter Eppstein to Freier, n.d., pag. 65.

205. CJA, 2 B 1/1, memo, 19 February 1940, p. 5, point 13.

206. YV, P1/15, Recha Freier, "RVJD to Main Office Security Police," 28 February 1940, pag. 53.

207. LBI, NY, AR 25033, MF 537, Rischowsky Coll., memo, 13 March 1940, p. 4, point 12.

208. YV, P1/15, Recha Freier, letter Recha Freier to RVJD, Eppstein, 26 February 1940, pag. 140; YV, P 1/3, accompanying letter RVJD, Eppstein, Lilienthal to Gestapo, 27 February 1940, pag. 83.

209. YV, 03/3455, Testimony by Recha Freier, n.d., p. 13; see also LBI, Jerusalem, 364, Radio Freies Berlin, "Recha Freier, die Gründung der Jugend-Aliyah und das Portrait einer außergewöhnlichen Frau," p. 32.

210. For an assessment of this activity (with a somewhat sugar-coated ending), see Tom Segev, *The Seventh Million: The Israelis and the Holocaust* (New York, 1994), 165–67.

211. YV, 01/204, Kurt Goldmann (Reuwen Golan), "Hechaluz und Jugendaliyah in Deutschland von 1936 bis Ende 1939," 29 December 1957, p. 6.

212. YV, P 1/5, Recha Freier, copy of letter, Rudolf Pick to Lyon, 22 May 1940, pag. 171a.

213. Weiss, *Deutsche und polnische Juden*, 214.

214. This is clear, for example, from LBI, NY, AR 25033, MF 537, Rischowsky Coll., memo, 8 February 1940, p. 4, point 9.

215. Christopher Browning, "Nazi Resettlement Policy and the Search for a Solution to the Jewish Question, 1939–1941," in *The Path to Genocide: Essays on Launching the Final Solution* (Cambridge, 1995), 24.

216. On the Lublin planning, see H. G. Adler, *Der verwaltete Mensch: Studien zur Deportation der Juden aus Deutschland* (Tübingen, 1974), 125ff. Rabinovici reports that the representatives of the Vienna Jewish Community were summoned to Eichmann in Mährisch-Ostrau regarding the construction gangs, but no mention is made of representatives from the Reichsvereinigung; see Rabinovici, *Eichmann's Jews*, 89. Philipp Friedman is the only one who points out that shortly after the German attack on Poland, Eichmann summoned the Jewish representatives from Berlin, Vienna, Prague, and other cities (possibly also from Upper Silesia), and informed them that an autonomous territory for Jews was to be set up in the Lublin district; he also asked for volunteers, which Löwenherz then arranged. However, my own inspection of the three sources mentioned by Friedman found no reference to a summons by Eichmann for this purpose; instead, there is mention of possibilities for emigration or general criticisms directed to Otto Hirsch, who had assumed responsibility and blame; see Philipp Friedman, "The Lublin Reservation and the Madagascar Plan: Two Aspects of Nazi Jewish Policy during the Second World War," *YIVO Annual of Jewish Social Science* 8 (1953): 154–55.

217. See Hans Mommsen, "Der Wendepunkt zur "Endlösung": Die Eskalation der nationalsozialistischen Judenverfolgung," in *Zur Geschichte Deutschlands im 20. Jahrhundert: Demokratie, Diktatur, Widerstand* (Munich, 2010), 218–19; *Die Jüdische*

Allgemeine, "Abschiebung zu Stalin," 23 June 2005; and, Tobias Kaufmann, "Eine Vorstufe zu Madagaskar. Pavel Polian über NS-Pläne, Juden in die Sowjetunion zu deportieren," interview, *Die Jüdische Allgemeine*, 23 June 2005, 1; Polian found references to such plans.

218. Dieter Pohl, *Von der "Judenpolitik" zum Judenmord: Der Distrikt Lublin des Generalgouvernements 1939–1941*, Münchner Studien zur neueren und neuesten Geschichte 3 (Frankfurt am Main, 1993), 54.

219. Ibid., 48.

220. Memo, Dannecker, 11 October 1939, YV, A, 0-53/93/194-197, quoted in Christopher Browning, *The Origins of the "Final Solution": The Evolution of Nazi Jewish Policy, September 1939–March 1942* (Lincoln, NE, 2004), 39.

221. Central Zionist Archives, Jerusalem, Zionist Organisation of America 1918–1976, "Bericht über die politische Lage in Deutschland, dem Protektorat Boehmen-Maehren, der Slowakei und Polen. Unter besonderer Beruecksichtigung der Juden in diesen Gebieten," pp. 7ff.

222. Ibid., p. 11.

223. See Rabinovici, *Eichmann's Jews*, 92; Browning, *Origins*, 42ff.

224. SD Außenstelle Bad Kissingen, report, 27 November 1939, in Kulka and Jäckel, *The Jews*, No. 3025, 483.

225. Mayor, town in Rhine-Hesse, report, 8 December 1939, Kulka and Jäckel, *Juden*, 3050.

226. RSHA, Amt III (SD), report (*Meldungen aus dem Reich*, no. 75), 10 April 1940, in Kulka and Jäckel, *The Jews*, No. 3094, 495.

227. Quoted in Browning, "Nazi Resettlement," 14.

228. See Browning, *Origins*, 57.

229. Pohl, *"Judenpolitik,"* 52; see also Browning, *Origins*, 64ff.

230. *Yedioth Hayom*, a German-language paper published in Palestine from 1936, edited by Friedrich Reichenstein. Until the outbreak of war, some articles were based on insider information, and later news reports from the press of neutral countries was evaluated and utilized.

231. *Yedioth Hayom*, "Neue Verschickungen nach Lublin," 15 February 1940.

232. Ibid.

233. *Yedioth Hayom*, "Aus der Golah," 18 March 1940.

234. For a photocopy of the "Staatspolizeiliche Verfügung" [Gestapo order], 12 February 1940, see www.ghwk.de/2006-neu/stettin.jpg (accessed 9 August 2012).

235. Wiener Library, London (hereafter WLL), P. III.c.No. 622, "Evakuierung der Juden aus Stettin," 1 September 1941; if not otherwise indicated, this and the following data are based on this report.

236. YV, 01/200, Ball-Kaduri papers, "Bericht und Ergänzung Berthold Simonsohn," quoted in Wilma Aden-Grossmann, *Berthold Simonsohn: Biographie des jüdischen Sozialpädagogen und Juristen (1912–1978)* (Frankfurt am Main, 2007), 89ff.

237. WLL, P. III.c.No. 622, "Evakuierung der Juden aus Stettin," 1 September 1941, p. 2; on the living conditions there, see also Robert Kuwalek, "Das kurze Leben 'im Osten': Jüdische Deutsche im Distrikt Lublin aus polnisch-jüdischer Sicht," in Kundrus and Meyer, *Deportation*, 112–19.

238. BArch, R 8150/1, minutes of board meeting, 29 February 1940.

239. See Else Behrend-Rosenfeld and Gertrud Luckner, eds., *Lebenszeichen aus Piaski: Briefe Deportierter aus dem Distrikt Lublin 1940–1943* (Munich, 1968), 20–21.

240. YV, 01/53, Max Plaut, "Die Juden in Deutschland von 1939 bis 1941," pp. 6–7; see also YV, 01/232, Document No. 3, German MS of an article by Rabbi Dr. Max

Nußbaum, "Life in Wartime Germany," *Contemporary Jewish Record* 3 (November/December 1940): 9.

241. WLL, P. III.c.No. 622, "Evakuierung der Juden aus Stettin," 1 September 1941, p. 3; JDC, Coll. 33/44, File, 631/2-f2, "Conversation between Dr. X (Paul Meyerheim), Mr. Katzki, Miss Emanuel and Mr. Asch in Brussels," 6 May 1940, p. 5.

242. YV, 01/232, Document No. 3, German MS of an article by Rabbi Dr. Max Nußbaum, "Life in Wartime Germany," *Contemporary Jewish Record* (November/December 1940): 10; see also Behrend-Rosenfeld and Luckner, *Lebenszeichen*, 21.

243. BArch, R 8150/18, letter Skomlinski to RVJD, 17 April 1942, pag. 156; Governor Zörner had issued this order on 1 April 1942 for the Jews evacuated from the Reich, and the district governors were instructed to pass this on to the Jewish councils; see BArch, R 8150/18, R 8150/18. Copy, "Anordnung betreffend Kennzeichnung" [Order regarding special identification badge], 1 April 1942, pag. 151. The deportees who managed to survive until the early summer of 1942 were transported to the extermination camps; see YV, 01/65, Erich Mosbach, circular letter, 1 January 1946.

244. See Hildesheimer, *Selbstverwaltung*, 181–82.

245. JDC, Coll. 33/44, File 631/2-f2, "Conversation between Dr. X (Paul Meyerheim), Mr. Katzki, Miss Emanuel and Mr. Asch in Brussels," 6 May 1940, p. 5.

246. See Wolf Gruner, "Von der Kollektivausweisung zur Deportation der Juden aus Deutschland (1938–1945)," in Kundrus and Meyer, *Deportation*, 37.

247. LBI, NY, AR 25033, MF 537, Rischowsky Coll., memo, 15 February 1940, p. 1, point 2.

248. YV, 01/232, Document No. 3, German MS of an article by Rabbi Dr. Max Nußbaum, "Life in Wartime Germany," *Contemporary Jewish Record* 3 (November/December 1940): 9.

249. On Walter Jagusch, see Wildt, *An Uncompromising Generation*, pp. 189, 249.

250. CJA, 2 B 1/1, memo, 19 February 1940, pp. 3–4, point 10.

251. Ibid.

252. At the meeting to which Eppstein was summoned on 13 March 1940, Eichmann told Eppstein that he would have known about the deportation of 160 persons from Schneidemühl to Poland, if it had taken place; see LBI, NY, AR 25033, MF 537, Rischowsky Coll., memo, 13 March 1940, p. 2, point 3.

253. BArch, R 8150/45, memo, summons, 26 October 1940, pag. 132, p. 1; Hirsch wrote: "At Schneidemühl and Breisach, there was immediate assistance from the central authorities."

254. Jagusch promised Eppstein that "the Jews in the Schneidemühl District can stay where they are. There will be no deportation," CJA, 2 B 1/1, memo, 19 February 1940, appendix: "phone call Jagusch, 7 p.m.," p. 5. On 19 August 1940, the "last remaining 29 Jews in a camp in Schneidemühl" were sent to stay in three residence homes in Berlin and with relatives; see BArch, R 8150/1.2, minutes board meeting, 19 August 1940, pag. 91, point 5.

255. See Browning, *Origins*, 65.

256. JDC, Coll. 33/44, File 642, RVJD to JOINT, 24 July 1940, "Übersicht über die Entwicklung des 1. Halbjahres 1940" [Overview of developments, Jan.–June 1940], p. 21.

257. BArch, R 8150/1.1, minutes board meeting, 29 February 1940, pag. 187, point 3; , BArch, R 8150/1.1, minutes board meeting, 9 April 1940, p. 2, pag. 199, point 2; FZH, Judenverfolgung/Berichte, "Unterredung Schottelius Plaut" [discussion Schottelius/Plaut], 11 July 1953, p. 4.

258. BArch, R 8150/1.1, minutes board meeting, 1 May 1940, pag. 183, point 3; the board left it up to the Community Department to announce the decision, which it did in

mid-May; see BArch, R 8150/1.1,, minutes board meeting, 15 May 1940, pag. 178, point 2.

259. JDC, Coll. 33/44, File, 631/2-f2, "Conversation between Dr. X (Paul Meyerheim), Mr. Katzki, Miss Emanuel und Mr. Asch in Brussels," 6 May 1940, p. 5. Elsewhere he gave a figure of 1,500 Jews; see YV, 01/232, Document No. 3, German MS of an article by Rabbi Dr. Max Nußbaum, "Life in Wartime Germany," *Contemporary Jewish Record* 3 (November/December 1940): 9.

260. FZH, Judenverfolgung/Berichte, "Unterredung Schottelius Plaut," 11 July 1953, p. 4.

261. The urban historian Herbert Reyer evaluated the files of the head of the regional government in Aurich (Regierungspräsident) and published the most important documents; there are also further references to relevant literature there. See Herbert Reyer, "Die Vertreibung der Juden aus Ostfriesland und Oldenburg im Frühjahr 1940," in *Collectanea Frisica: Beiträge zur historischen Landeskunde Ostfrieslands: Walter Deeters zum 65. Geburtstag*, ed. H. van Lengen, Abhandlungen und Vorträge zur Geschichte Ostfrieslands 74 (Aurich 1995), 363–90.

262. YV, 033/102, Wolf Wolffs, "Kurze Schilderung der Evakuierung der Juden Ostfrieslands im März 1940" [Short description of the evacuation of the Jews of East Frisia, March 1940], 11 September 1960.

263. YV, 01/53, Max Plaut, "Die Juden in Deutschland von 1939 bis 1941," p. 8.

264. See Reyer, "Vertreibung," 375.

265. CJA, 2 B 1/1, memo, 25 June 1940.

266. CJA, 2 B 1/1, memo, 19 February 1940, p. 3, point 9.

267. See Cohn, *Kein Recht*, 757; see also 760–65.

268. YV, 033/99, Alfred Neumeyer, "Tätigkeit als Gemeindevorsitzender," p. 234.

269. YV, 01/232, Document No. 3, German MS of an article by Rabbi Dr. Max Nußbaum, "Life in Wartime Germany," *Contemporary Jewish Record* 3 (November/December 1940): 9.

270. YV, 01/227, "Nachtrag Erich Frank über "Vorladung der Repräsentanten jüdischer Dachorganisationen in Berlin, Wien und Prag vor die Gestapo Berlin (Eichmann) 1940" [Supplement, Erich Frank to "Summons of the representatives of Jewish umbrella organizations in Berlin, Vienna and Prague to the Gestapo in Berlin (Eichmann) 1940"], December 1958, p. 2.

271. Pohl, *"Judenpolitik,"* 52; see also Browning, *Origins*, 66ff.

272. Pohl, *"Judenpolitik,"* 51.

273. See Browning, *Origins*, 81–88; Hildesheimer, *Selbstbehauptung*, 185–92.

274. On its prehistory, see Magnus Brechtken, *"Madagaskar für die Juden": Antisemitische Idee und politische Praxis 1885–1945* (Munich, 1997); Hans Jansen, *Der Madagaskar-Plan: Die beabsichtigte Deportation der europäischen Juden nach Madagaskar* (Munich, 1997). The French and Polish governments had also discussed a plan to create a Jewish reservation there; see Kurt Düwell, *Die Rheingebiete in der Judenpolitik des Nationalsozialismus vor 1942: Beitrag zu einer vergleichenden zeitgeschichtlichen Landeskunde* (Bonn, 1968), 251; see also detailed video in English with Magnus Brechtken at http://goo.gl/mQEHP (accessed 9 August 2012). In late April 1941, the Jewish press in New York reported that the new anti-Semitic Hungarian Premier Ladislas Bardossy had expressed fresh interest in the Madagascar plan as a possible destination for Hungarian Jewry, and there were press reports into late March 1942 about Madagascar as a Jewish reservation assisted by Japanese military involvement; see Jewish Telegraphic Agency: 27 April 1941, http://goo.gl/ZF8rB; 30 April 1941, http://goo.gl/zzZJg; 3 August 1941, http://goo.gl/gqmPw; 22 March 1942, http://goo.gl/l8GXX (accessed 27 July 2012).

275. See Browning, *Origins*, 81ff.
276. Ibid., 86.
277. Ibid., 87; David Cesarani, *Adolf Eichmann: His Life and Crimes* (London, 2004), 84-5.
278. Cesarani, *Eichmann*, 86.
279. See Browning, *Origins*, 87–88.
280. BArch, R 8150/45, memo, 25 June 1940, pag. 178, point 2.
281. Memo on consultation with the RSHA, quoted in Browning, *Origins*, 87, see also Cesarani, *Eichmann*, 364-65; Hildesheimer, *Selbstbehauptung*, 187; see Doron Rabinovici on the "Löwenherz-Bericht," in which the matter is described along similar lines, but the non-Austrian Jewish functionaries are not mentioned: Rabinovici, *Eichmann's Jews*, 99.
282. LBI, JMB, MF 546, Joseph Löwenherz Coll. (AR 25055), memo 44, "Rücksprache Edelstein, Weidmann, Löwenherz und Eppstein im RSHA," 3 April 1940; "Stellungnahme 'Ansiedlung von Juden aus europäischen Ländern in zur Verfügung gestellten Siedlungsraum ausserhalb Europas'" [Position on "settlement of European Jews in the settlement area made available outside Europe"], pp. 1–2.
283. *Yedioth Hayom*, "Das Nein der deutschen Juden: Hinter den Kulissen des Madagaskar-Planes," 2 May 1941, 11–12.
284. Ibid.
285. Ibid.
286. YV, 01/26, "Denkschrift von Rabbiner Dr. Max Nussbaum, geschrieben für Mr. Morgenthau oder Stephan Wise sofort nach seiner Einwanderung in U.S.A. (August 1940)" [Rabbi Dr. Max Nußbaum, intended for Mr. Morgenthau or Stephan Wise immediately after his immigration to the U.S. (August 1940)], p. 18.
287. YV, 02/411 (No. 625), Anonymous, "Die politische Situation in Deutschland und in den Nachbarstaaten unter besonderer Berücksichtigung der Judenfrage" [The political situation in Germany and neighboring states with special consideration of the Jewish Question, written before Sept. 1941], p. 12 (same as YV, 01/26, Max Nussbaum). In an article in the autumn of 1940, Nussbaum warned that Germany was proceeding on the assumption of obtaining financing for the transports. Otherwise, the Jewish Agency for Palestine, after a victory by the Axis, when Palestine would fall under Italian control, would have to provide the funding for transports from there to Madagascar; see Jansen, *Madagaskar-Plan*, 405ff., 486.
288. YV, 01/256, data from Prof. Dr. Leschnitzer (unfortunately no details), 25 June 1959; LAB, B Rep 58, 1 Js 9/65, Box 66, Interrogation Franz Rademacher in Bonn, 11 June 1970, pp. 2–3.
289. See Friedman, "Lublin Reservation," 174–75.
290. Brechtken, *Madagaskar*, 236–37.
291. BArch, R 8150/1.2, minutes board meeting, 30 December 1940, pag. 70, points 1.1–5.
292. Ibid.
293. YV, 01/232, Document No. 3, German MS of an article by Rabbi Dr. Max Nußbaum, "Life in Wartime Germany," *Contemporary Jewish Record* 3 (November/December 1940): 13.
294. YV, 02/411 (No. 625), Anonymous, "Die politische Situation in Deutschland und in den Nachbarstaaten unter besonderer Berücksichtigung der Judenfrage" [written before Sept. 1941], p. 11. Also available as YV, 01/26, memo, Rabbi Dr. Max Nußbaum, intended for Mr. Morgenthau or Stephan Wise immediately after his immigration to the U.S. (August 1940).

295. See Baruch Z. Ophir and Falk Wiesemann, *Die jüdischen Gemeinden in Bayern 1918–1945* (Munich and Vienna, 1979), 54; on the deportations from the Upper Rhine, see Düwell, *Rheingebiete*, 253–62.

296. "Regierungspräsident Ober- u. Mittelfranken, Bericht für Monat Oktober 1939," 7 November 1939, in Kulka and Jäckel, *The Jews*, No. 3010, 482. Later on, these Jews were not permitted to return to their home area; see "Regierungspräsident Ober- u. Mittelfranken, Bericht für Monat September 1940, 6.10.1940" (District governor Upper and Central Franconia, report Sept. 1940, 6 October 1940], in Kulka and Jäckel, *The Jews*, No. 3165, 505–6.

297. YV, E/210 (129/56), Dr. Neter, Camp de Gurs, September 1943.

298. YV, 01/28, Jüdische Gemeinde Karlsruhe/Baden, 27 December 1945, and Jüdische Gemeinde Karlsruhe/Baden, from an article, E.K., last secretary, Jewish Community Karlsruhe.

299. Letter, chief, Security Police and SD, to Foreign Ministry, 24 October 1940 (emphasis in original), reproduced in Tuviah Friedmann, *Die verantwortlichen SS-Führer für die Durchführung der Endlösung der Judenfrage in Europa* (Haifa, 1993).

300. See, for example, with additional literature, Gerhard J. Teschner, *Die Deportation der badischen und saarpfälzischen Juden am 22. Oktober 1940: Vorgeschichte und Durchführung der Deportation und das weitere Schicksal der Deportierten bis zum Kriegsende im Kontext der deutschen und französischen Judenpolitik* (Frankfurt am Main, 2002).

301. YV, 02/421, Anonymous report, "Autumn and Winter 1940 in Germany," 25 February 1941, p. 20.

302. BArch, R 8150/45, memo, 26 October 1940, pag. 132, point 1.

303. BArch, R 8150/1.2, minutes board meeting, 27 October 1940, pag. 81, point 1. The Reichsvereinigung had learned that they had been sent to "southern France."

304. BArch, R 8150/45, memo, 26 October 1940, p. 1, pag. 132, point 1.

305. BArch, R 8150/1.2, minutes board meeting, 25 October 1940, pag. 82, point 2.

306. BArch, R 8150/45, memo, 31 October 1940, p. 1, pag. 128, point 1.

307. BArch, R 8150/1.2, minutes board meeting, 4 November 1940, pag. 79, point 1.

308. BArch, R 8150/45, memo, 26 November 1940, pp. 4–5, pag. 115–16, point 13.

309. BArch, R 8150/45, memo, 26 November 1940, p. 5, pag. 116, point 13; on Seligsohn, see also Ayalon, "'Gegenwaertige Situation,'" 276ff.

310. BArch, R 8150/45, memo, 20 February 1941, p. 1, pag. 74, point 1.

311. Fritz Woehrn, born 12 March 1905, in charge of handling "individual cases," "general matters," and matters of personnel in the Reichsvereinigung in the RSHA *Judenreferat* Department IV B 4, had the rank of a senior government official and was later an *SS-Hauptsturmführer* (captain). He was sentenced in 1969 to twelve years in prison, of which five years were a suspended sentence. He died on 18 December 1979.

312. BArch, R 8150/45, memo, No. 21, 11 March 1941, p. 4, pag. 72, points 12 and 13.

313. *Aufbau*, 21 March 1941, reported in an article entitled "Verhaftungen in Berlin" about Hirsch's arrest (p. 7).

314. See Hildesheimer, *Selbstbehauptung*, 201.

315. Extract, Berlin Memorial Book, database Julius Seligsohn; the paper *Aufbau* published an obituary formulated by Max M. Warburg on 1 May 1942 entitled "In Memoriam Julius Seligsohn" (*Aufbau*, 8 May 1942, 13), expressing the hope that after the war's end there would "also be monuments for men like Julius Seligsohn" (*Aufbau*, 8 May 1942, 1). His wife, children, and some four hundred German-Jewish emigrants took part in the funeral services in New York (*Aufbau*, 19 June 1942, 24); Hildesheimer, *Selbstbehauptung*, 202.

316. CJA, 2 B 1/2, memo, No. 141, 3 July 1941, p. 2, point 7. According to this memo, the news about him came to the Reichsvereinigung from Hirsch's wife. Hirsch had been arrested on 16 February 1941 and transferred on 23 May to the Mauthausen concentration camp. He was given prisoner no. 559 (List of nationalities of prisoners who died, Y/39); in the death registry (Y/46), "colitis ulcerosa," an intestinal disease, was recorded as cause of death (according to information from the archive, Mauthausen Concentration Camp Memorial Site, 8 October 2008). In typical cynical fashion, five days after the death of her husband, Hirsch's wife was given permission, subsequent to intervention by the Reichsvereinigung, to submit a clemency plea (CJA, 2 B 1/2, memo No. 91, 24 June 1941). Hirsch's brother reported that during his time of imprisonment, visas for the United States arrived, but neither the prisoner nor his wife was able to make use of them (YV, 01/285, testimony, Theodore Hirsch, "Die letzten Tage von Otto Hirsch," transcribed by Ball-Kaduri, 12 May 1960, p. 2). The paper *Aufbau* reported in an article entitled "Dr. Otto Hirsch gestorben" (1 July 1941, 1) about his death and published several obituaries on 18 July 1941.

317. Browning, *Origins*, 88; Düwell, *Rheingebiete*, 257–58.

318. CJA, 2 B 1/2, memo, 17.3.1941, p. 1, point 1.

319. See Leo Kreindler, *Jüdisches Nachrichtenblatt*, 9 December 1939, 1.

320. USHMM Archive, Washington, Brodnitz Collection, Acc. 2008.189.1, letter Baeck to Brodnitz, 18 December 1940, reproduced in full in Matthäus, "You have the right to be hopeful," 352–53.

321. LBI, NY, AR 1619, Coll. Neter, Letter, Hedwig Strauss-Eppstein to Mia and Eugen Neter, 2 May 1939.

322. YV, 01/267, "Zur Gedenkfeier für Dr. Otto Hirsch" [Otto Hirsch memorial], in *Schawe Zion*, July 1941 (no author), p. 3.

323. LBI, Jerusalem, "Arbeitsbericht der Reichsvereinigung 1939," p. 38.

324. Adler-Rudel, *Selbsthilfe*, 158.

325. Ibid., 160.

326. See Wolf Gruner, *Öffentliche Wohlfahrt und Judenverfolgung: Wechselwirkung lokaler und zentraler Politik im NS-Staat (1933–1942)* (Munich, 2002); on the first phase, 1939–1941, see pp. 157–234. Gruner shows just how difficult this shift in competence was in terms of practical implementation, since many Jewish Communities and district branches of the RV were completely unable to take on this responsibility, which was not only financial; the local municipalities, still continuing to resist, were in part called upon for assistance. This problem was particularly pronounced in Berlin, where one-third of the German Jews lived. However, at the end of 1939, as noted in the working report for that year, responsibility was largely on the shoulders of the RV (LBI, Jerusalem, 556/1 (239) AB, p. 34).

327. Kulka, *Deutsches Judentum*, 31.

328. Rivka Elkin, "Some Remarks in the Wake of My Book The Heart Beats On," in Guy Miron, Jacob Borut, and Rivka Elkin, eds., *Aspects of Jewish Welfare in Nazi Germany*, Search and Research: Lectures and Papers 7 Yad Vashem (Jerusalem, 2006), 47. The doctoral dissertation and book *Halmut ha-lev* [The heart beats on], is only available in the Hebrew original, published by Yad Vashem in 2004.

329. Elkin, "Remarks," 51; see also Gruner, "Poverty," 39–40.

330. BArch, R 58/1501/1, "Bericht über die Jüdische Winterhilfe 1939/1940," pp. 1, 3, pag. 335, 337.

331. See BArch, R 58/1015, letter, RSHA to Sec. V, Reich Interior Ministry, 13 June 1942, pag. 407, with the note that in previous years, this had been dealt with in this manner.

332. LBI, Jerusalem 555/4, "Arbeitsbericht der Reichsvertretung der Juden in Deutschland für das Jahr 1938 (244)," p. 14.

333. For this reason, several cities were unable to halt their welfare support for Jews ad hoc. In Berlin in particular, Jews received support from municipal welfare offices until the beginning of 1941. See Gruner, "Armut," 39–40; Maierhof, *Selbstbehauptung*, 174–75.

334. See Adler-Rudel, *Selbsthilfe*, 161.

335. LBI, Jerusalem 555/6, "Arbeitsbericht der Reichsvertretung der Juden in Deutschland für das Jahr 1939," p. 35.

336. See, for example, CJA, 2 B 1/2, memo, No. 64, 2 May 1941, pp. 2–3.

337. BArch, R 8150/1/2, pag. 175, Number of Homes (H) and Places (Occup.), 1937, omitted here, since little data is available.

338. See Maierhof, *Selbstbehauptung*, 253.

339. BArch, R 8150/1/2, pag. 146, "Kostenvoranschlag 2. Halbjahr 1940" [Cost estimate 2nd half year 1940].

340. LBI, JMB, MF 546, "Bericht Löwenherz über die am 16./17.1.1940 im Auftrage Eichmanns vorgenommene Besichtigung der Einrichtungen der Reichsvereinigung der Juden in Deutschland, der Jüdischen Gemeinde in Berlin und des Palästinamtes Berlin" [Report by Löwenherz on the inspection on 16/17 Jan. 1940 by order of Eichmann of the facilities of the Reichsvereinigung, the Berlin Jewish Community and the Palestine Office Berlin], p. 2.

341. BArch, R 8150/1, "Voranschlag der RVJD für das erste Halbjahr 1940," pag. 3; BArch, R 8150/1, "Entwurf Beitragsordnung für die Erhebung eines außerordentlichen Beitrages" [Draft contribution regulations for an exceptional contribution], pag. 7, 22ff.; and BArch, R 8150/1, memo Seligsohn, 30 October 1939, pag. 38–39; BArch, R 8150/1, "Haushaltsplan für 1940, Vorbemerkung" [Budget for 1940, prefatory remark], p. IV, pag. 44.

342. BArch, R 8150/2, minutes of board meeting, 24 March 1941, pp. 2–3.

343. CJA, 2 B 1/2, memo, No. 89/Z 81, consultation in RSHA, 12 June 1941, p. 5, point 19.

344. Ibid.

345. Ibid., p. 6.

346. BArch, R 8150/2, minutes of board meeting, 28 April 1941, p. 2.

347. CJA, 2 B 1/2, memo, 129, 9 August 1941, p. 3, memo 133; CJA, 2 B 1/2, memo, 129, 16 August 1941, p. 1.

348. USHMM Archive, Washington, Brodnitz Collection, Acc. 2008.189.1, letter by Baeck to Brodnitz, 21 May 1941, reproduced in its entirety in Matthäus, "You have the right to be hopeful," 352–53.

349. For an overview, see Ernst Klee, *"Euthanasie" im NS-Staat: Die "Vernichtung lebensunwerten Lebens"* (Frankfurt am Main, 2004); Henry Friedlander, *The Origins of Nazi Genocide: From Euthanasia to the Final Solution* (Chapel Hill, NC, 1997); Robert J. Lifton, *The Nazi Doctors: Medical Killing and the Psychology of Genocide* (New York, 1986), www.holocaust-history.org/lifton/ (accessed 28 July 2012); Winfried Süss, *Der "Volkskörper" im Krieg: Gesundheitspolitik, Gesundheitsverhältnisse und Krankenmord im nationalsozialistischen Deutschland 1939–1945* (Munich, 2003). In the meantime, there are now individual studies on most of the killing centers; the court judgments from the Federal Republic of Germany (FRG) and the GDR to punish this crime have been published in Dick de Mildt, ed., *Tatkomplex: NS-Euthanasie*, 2 vols. (Amsterdam, 2009); see also Dick de Mildt, *In the Name of the People: Perpetrators of Genocide in the Reflection of Their Post-War Prosecution in West Germany: the "Euthanasia" and "Aktion Reinhard" Trial Cases* (Leiden, 1996).

350. LBI, Jerusalem, 556/1, AB 1939, p. 38. Friedlander proceeds on the basis of a higher figure, within which, however, unlike the RV, he also includes the Austrian and German Jews in mixed marriages, and the so-called *Mischlinge* or "mixed-blood" Jews. Friedlander assumes that between four and five thousand Jewish patients were victims of the "euthanasia" murders; see Friedlander, *Origins*, 271.

351. Friedlander, *Origins*, 265.

352. Ibid., 267ff.

353. Ibid., 268.

354. Ibid., 263; see also USHMM, RG-14.035M, reel 10, Jewish Community of Leipzig records (2001.150), "letter RVJD to district branches and Jewish Communities, re: accommodating mentally ill Jewish patients," 29 January 1941.

355. See Karl Friedrich Kaul, *Nazi-Mordaktion T 4: Ein Bericht über die erste industriemäßig durchgeführte Mordaktion des Naziregimes* (Berlin, 1973), 97.

356. Friedlander, *Origins*, 413.

357. Ibid., 272, 282; transfer to "several collection centers" is also noted in the minutes of the board meeting, BArch, R 8150/2, minutes of board meeting, 23 September 1940, p. 2.

358. YV, 01/53, Max Plaut, "Die Juden in Deutschland 1939 bis 1941," p. 21; on the Cholm Insane Asylum, see Lifton, *Nazi Doctors*, 78.

359. YV, 01/285, Eyewitness report, Theodore Hirsch, "Die letzten Tage von Otto Hirsch" [Hirsch's last days], recorded by Dr. Ball-Kaduri, 12 May 1960, pp. 3–4.

360. YV, 01/53, Max Plaut, "Die Juden in Deutschland 1939 bis 1941," pp. 21–22.

361. Ibid., p. 22.

362. BArch, R 8150/4, internal letter by Cohn, 6 May 1941, pag. 76.

363. USHMM, RG-14.035M, reel 10, Jewish Community of Leipzig records (2001.150), letter RVJD to district branches and Jewish Communities, 27 March 1941; BArch, R 8150/7, RVJD to district branches and Jewish Communities, 13 August 1941, pag. 222; BArch, R 8150/7, memo by Cohn to Eppstein, 2 November 1941, pag. 221.

364. Friedlander, *Origins*, 280–81.

365. On the facility, see http://goo.gl/kelyl (accessed 27 July 2012).

366. BArch, R 8150/1, minutes of board meeting, 19 April 1940, p. 1.

367. Klee, *"Euthanasie,"* 261.

368. On this, see also Günter Plum, "Deutsche Juden oder Juden in Deutschland?," in *Die Juden in Deutschland 1933–1945*, ed. Wolfgang Benz (Munich, 1988), 35–74; Uwe Dietrich Adam, *Judenpolitik im Dritten Reich* (Düsseldorf, 1972; Königstein im Taunus, 1979), 214ff.; Wildt, *Judenpolitik*, 62–63.

369. YV, 02/772, WL P. III.h. (Theresienstadt) No. 894, Erich Simon, lecture, 13 April 1946: "Theresienstadt als autarkes Stadtwesen" [Theresienstadt as a self-contained municipality], p. 2.

Chapter 2

WALKING ON A THIN LINE

The Participation of the Reichsvereinigung and the Berlin Jewish Community during the Deportations

The process of Nazi decision making on deporting all Jews from the *Altreich*, by no means linear, had more or less come to a conclusion after the German attack on the Soviet Union in the summer of 1941.[1] It was not only Hitler and Heydrich who were pushing ahead with the deportations, but also individual *Gauleiters* as well. In particular, Joseph Goebbels in Berlin, as well as others such as Karl Kaufmann in Hamburg, pressed more and more vociferously for finally rendering their areas "Jew-free." The plan envisioned deporting the German, Austrian, and Czechoslovakian Jews to ghettos in occupied Poland as a temporary "way station" and then transporting them on into occupied Soviet territory. At the time this decision was being finalized, the local Jews in the occupied territories were already being murdered in mass shootings and other liquidation operations. Around mid-September 1941, Hitler probably decided to go ahead with mass transports from the *Altreich*.

Meanwhile, the Jews in Germany were being deployed as forced conscript laborers under humiliating conditions. Now impoverished, those remaining had largely been excluded from all spheres of life. Their Jewish Communities and the RV district branch offices had been assigned the task of informing them about the various prohibitions, ordinances, or new restrictions as they were imposed. The ordinance issued on 1 September 1941 ordering the wearing of an identifying badge, the "yellow star," was intended to intensify the isolation from the non-Jewish population of the Jews already concentrated in so-called *Judenhäuser* (Jews' houses, segregated Jewish apartment blocks) or barracks settlements in some parts of the Reich. This was a prerequisite for the deportations now on the near horizon. The rulers planned "partial operations," in which sixty thousand Jews from the larger cities would be transported "from West to East," initially to the Lódz ghetto. After the Wartheland *Gauleiter* Arthur Greiser lodged a protest, that target figure was reduced to twenty thousand Jews and five thousand "Gypsies."

In September 1941, the *Judenreferenten* or "Jewish specialists" in the Gestapo offices in the *Altreich* gathered together in Berlin to discuss the practical problems arising from the planned transports.[2] The RSHA told the Gestapo offices they could, if they so chose, make use of the local RV branches or Jewish Communities in preparations for the deportations. Most Gestapo local headquarters then implemented this immediately or soon thereafter, ordering the Jewish offices to assist with various tasks in preparing the deportations and helping to ease the process of their organization and implementation.

In retrospect, one aspect seems quite striking in the procedure the RSHA adopted prior to launching the deportations: it did not first inform the RV central office, and then instruct the Berlin office to inform its own district branch. Instead, it was the individual local Gestapo office from whose area of competence Jews were to be deported that contacted the local Jewish Communities or RV district branches, assigning them various tasks. The sources provide no explanation for that behavior. Using this approach, perhaps the RSHA wished to forestall any protests by the leading Jewish functionaries, even if it had acted swiftly to forcibly prevent earlier attempts by Jewish representatives to protest, and it did not encounter any sustained resistance in response. Or maybe it viewed the RV solely as an administrative office whose main job was to handle finances. In any event, the National Socialist state demonstrated no readiness to negotiate in advance with the Jewish central organization it had itself created regarding the modalities of *Abwanderung*—"migration," literally "moving away from a place," a misleading euphemistic term that was increasingly used for deportation, along with "evacuation," "relocation," and "resettlement"—as the deportation transports soon came to be designated in official Nazi parlance. Importantly, the formal term for "emigration" in German, *Auswanderung*, disappeared both from discourse and concrete practice.

In fact, however, as addressee of the regime's anti-Jewish policy, the RV had already undertaken some preliminary spadework: it had been ordered in a large-scale operation to disseminate the "stars of David" to all Jews aged six and older, who were instructed to wear the star in a visible place on their clothing. At the same time, Jews were prohibited from leaving their locality of residence without a permit. In the "star operation," the RV was ordered to distribute the rolls of cloth with the printed badges (for a charge of ten pfennigs per badge), and to pass on the instructions for their use. They also had to pay the bill from the manufacturer, Geitel & Co. At the same time, the Kulturbund was dissolved as an independent organization. Its book distribution and the *Jüdisches Nachrichtenblatt* were permitted to continue under the framework of the Reichsvereinigung, but its artistic activity was halted.[3]

In order to organize the marking of the Jews in the German area of influence and control, Eppstein and Löwenherz (in Vienna) were given the unusual order to become active outside their own actual territory, otherwise a form of action strictly forbidden to them. The RV took on the function of intermediary in the Litzmannstadt (Lódz) ghetto and sent on the badges to the occupied Eastern territories that had been incorporated into the German Reich.[4] It furnished the Council of Elders in Sosnowitz with rolls of cloth containing 104,000 stars, which the council then distributed in the territory of "Southeastern Prussia" (i.e., including the occupied Polish areas). The *Ostmark* (Austria) received 88,000 stars from the RV, Eastern Upper Silesia was given 80,000, Danzig-West Prussia received 1,800, and Luxembourg 2,700 stars.[5] Every German Jew in labor deployment was initially provided with two stars. Later the badges for family members and persons not working were handed out. The stars, made of poor-quality cloth, were to be sewn tightly to the respective garment. Their number was strictly limited, so that the badges had to be removed and sewn on again if other clothing was used.

Individual Jews signed a receipt for the RV so the organization could put together a list of the "star bearers," *Sterntröger* in Nazi officialese. In the subsequent period, the RV was allowed to order additional rolls of cloth with printed badges so that all Jews living in the *Altreich* would be able to comply with the order, and it had to present the RSHA with a plan for distribution.[6] In a number of localities, the Jewish offices ran up against difficulties, because the towns or even individual firms had designed their own badges and were insisting that these had to be worn there. Then the RV passed the problem on to the RSHA, which had commanded that there be a uniform procedure.[7] Within half a year, the RV distributed 950,000 stars.[8]

Especially (but not only) among the voluntary members, the "obligation of the star" spawned a desire to leave the forced community of the Reichsvereinigung as quickly as possible. The RSHA issued an order stipulating that the RV and its district branches should, as a matter of principle, refuse approval of any such requests to formally resign from the organization if they had been submitted after 1 September 1941.[9] In Berlin, 1,767 persons refused to wear the badge. Some 700 reminder letters from the RV were returned marked "undeliverable" or "receipt declined."[10]

At this juncture during the preparatory measures for deportation, there was already a visible gap between the functionaries and the obligatory membership of the RV. The members—who up to now had more or less willingly followed "their" organization in regard to matters of emigration or welfare, and had trusted their leaders—realized, perhaps for the first time, that the orders the functionaries were obligated to implement were to their detriment. Even if they did not call into question the necessity for the RV to operate schools, nursing homes, or hospitals for children, the needy, or the sick, these Jews nonetheless attempted to evade stigmatizing measures imposed by the authorities, such as the order to wear the star or the constantly mounting financial demands being made by the RV.

Decisions Based on a Basic Principle: Avoid Hardship, Participate in "Partial Operations"

The RV board learned about the beginning of deportations in a round-about way: the Gestapo Main Office (Stapoleitstelle) in Berlin informed three key functionaries, the chair of the Berlin Jewish Community, Moritz Henschel, its board member, Philipp Kozower, who was the contact person for the Gestapo, and Martha Mosse, director of the accommodation advice center in the RV, who was supposed to prepare the transport. At this juncture, the Berlin Jewish Community (now redesignated Jüdische Kultusvereinigung, JKV) was, as a section of the RV, responsible for almost one-third of all Jews in Germany.

Martha Mosse was characterized by contemporaries as a "woman whose nerves were made of mooring ropes; experienced in police work, with years of training, she knew how to put up with surprises and expressions of sentiment unfazed, remaining cool, externally unimpressed."[11] She reported after the war that they had been allowed to discuss the plan solely with a few board members of the RV.[12]

> It was on October 1 or 2, 1941 ... when two board members and myself, as head of the accommodation advice center, received a phone call summoning us to the Gestapo ... There Detective Sergeant Prüfer put it on record that we would be immediately taken to a concentration camp if we discussed what he was about to say with any third parties.... Mr. Prüfer then told us that the "resettlement" of the Berlin Jews was now starting and that the Jewish Community had to participate in it. Or otherwise it would

be carried out by the SA and SS—and "you know what that would be like." Several thousand Jews were initially to be summoned. The instrument for this was the Jewish Community *Kataster* [tax registry], and Community officials would go over questionnaires with them provided by the Gestapo. The completed questionnaires then had to be submitted to the Gestapo. … The Jewish population was to be led to believe that this was an eviction operation. The Gestapo would then … put together a transport of around 1,000 people, which would go to Lódz.[13]

Department head Mosse had to select and summon three thousand Jewish Community members prior to the first deportation. Her coworkers helped them fill out the questionnaires (called "lists" by the Jews summoned), which were then sent on to the Gestapo.[14] The Gestapo then wrote the transport numbers on these papers and sent back the portion that the undersigned had determined they were to be included in the first deportation. Based on this, Mosse's department proceeded to put together the transport list. The Gestapo retained the remaining papers as a reserve for future deportations. Mosse recalled that the Berlin Gestapo had always demanded "at least double the number of questionnaires necessary for a transport" in order to compensate for any "shortfall" in numbers.[15]

However, the information that the "resettlement" was to begin probably did not come as a surprise for the functionaries, since several deportation transports had left Vienna in the spring of 1941. The regime had still not completely abandoned the policy of expulsion: in 1941, there were deportations of Jews from Vienna to the Lublin district conjunct with forced emigration. Some six thousand Jews in Vienna were still able to emigrate, while another five thousand had already been deported to the East.[16] Even if there was a ban on official contacts between Jewish leaders in Berlin and Vienna, these events were impossible to conceal. The participation of the central Jewish organization in Vienna, the Vienna Jewish Community, had already been put to the test in the "annexed territory" of Austria: it had to inform the deportees, set up assembly camps, and provide for their food and basic necessities. The Central Office for Jewish Emigration in Vienna had put together the deportation list itself, immediately including a number of Jewish Community staff workers on the list. After submitting complaints, the Jewish Community was then at least allowed to reclaim the services of those staff workers who were deemed indispensable for handling the transports. When alarming news and reports of deaths were received from the deportees, Josef Löwenherz tried to secure permission to repatriate them, but this was denied. In the summer of 1941, the transports were temporarily halted. In early September, rumors circulated in the Jewish Community that they would soon be resumed, which Eichmann told the Jewish functionaries was not true. Yet on 30 September 1941, Eichmann informed Löwenherz that Jews from Vienna, along with Jews from Germany and the "Protectorate," were to be deported to Łódz.[17] This then came to pass: beginning 15 October, deportation trains departed in rapid succession from Vienna, Prague, Luxembourg, Berlin, Frankfurt am Main, Cologne, Hamburg, and Düsseldorf.[18]

No one was surprised that the first transport of Jews from the Reich involved Jews from Berlin, because in the summer of 1941, there were still some seventy-four thousand living in Berlin who had been classified as Jews by the Nazi regime. The greater proportion of them, forced conscript laborers in the armaments industry, were (still) considered indispensable for the German economy. In addition, the regime had been less successful in Berlin than elsewhere in strictly separating the Jewish from the non-Jewish population. Until the outbreak of the war, the presence of foreign journalists and diplomats had a moderating effect on the visible public persecution of the Jews. But these factors, which after the November 1938 pogrom led to a rise in the numbers of German Jews relocating to the capital, were also accompanied by other developments that made the life of the Jews in Berlin far more difficult. For years, the rabid anti-Semite Joseph Goebbels had as *Gauleiter* been propagating the goal of a "Jew-free" capital; Berlin housed the main offices of the Reich authorities dealing with the plunder and persecution of the Jews. The head of police was Wolf Heinrich Graf von Helldorf; particularly in the summer of 1938, months before the November pogrom, he had instituted violent operations against Jews. Moreover, Hitler's general construction inspector, Albert Speer, had been moving ahead with plans for realizing a gigantic redesign of Berlin as the National Socialist metropolis "Germania." Operating on a huge scale, he planned to hand over the homes and apartments of the Jews to former "Aryan" tenants from the districts of the city slated for demolition.[19] The Gestapo apparently thought it wouldn't seem suspicious to initially present the first large-scale deportation as an eviction operation, since two similar such extensive operations had already taken place.[20] In Berlin as elsewhere, existing problems in accommodations for the non-Jewish population were put forward as a pretext in internal documentation for justifying the deportation of the Jews. But to conclude from this, as historian Susanne Willems suggests in the case of Berlin, that the Jews were deported primarily in order to forcibly gain access to their housing—or, as the local Nazi Party officials argued as the war progressed, to be able to utilize replacement housing for those who had been bombed out, and seize their possessions as disposable property for use in social policy—is mistaken. It ignores the primacy of racist thinking within the National Socialist leadership. Right from the outset, they had envisioned and planned the removal of the Jews from German society as a logical consequence of their anti-Semitic worldview, waiting for the right moment to implement this plan. In any case, they categorized the property and possessions of the Jews as stolen public property, which it was necessary to reappropriate. For that reason, government offices, organizations, and individuals, such as Albert Speer, subsequently profited in many places—rapidly, ruthlessly, and often shrewdly planned—from the resources that had become "freely" disposable as a result of the deportations. Like Speer, all these officials and their institutions pressed more and more energetically for deportation of the Jews from Berlin.

Nonetheless, the Jewish functionaries still hoped that they would be able to influence further developments in ways favorable for the Jews. After all, as an exception, they had in fact learned about the plans for deportations in advance, even though not directly. After the Gestapo had informed Henschel, Kozower, and Mosse, the boards of the RV and the Berlin Jewish Community met together that same evening. They decided, "despite grave misgivings" (Henschel) and "with a heavy heart" (Mosse), to adhere to the strategy of cooperation with the authorities. However, the plan to participate in the "resettlement" confronted them with an entirely new situation. Although they understood that this was a decisive turning point, nevertheless they interpreted it against the backdrop of the previous two years as a continuation of their former activity, which had not been totally hopeless. In particular, they harbored the hope to be able to intervene and shape the direction events might take. In addition, they believed it was better for the Jews to accept the assigned tasks, "since in this way, it seemed possible to avoid even greater hardships."[21] In view of the relations of power they faced, Leo Baeck also agreed with this position, since the Jewish marshals would be "more gentle and helpful than the Gestapo and make the ordeal easier," especially given the fact that the Jewish functionaries were unable to defy the orders of the German authorities.[22]

The Jewish functionaries who met in consultation interpreted the Nazi discourse of these so-called partial operations (Teilaktionen) as a "partial evacuation" of the Jews, which would not encompass all of Jewry. Then, they believed, after that they would once again be able to devote themselves to their main task, namely, provision of care for the remaining Jewish community in Germany.[23] Moreover, they actually had no real alternative: they were not granted a transition period, as in "annexed" Austria, where emigration and deportation ran parallel. Once systematic deportations commenced, the RSHA banned Jewish emigration, although, as mentioned, this did not apply in the case of the Jewish leadership echelon.[24] The functionaries likewise were sworn to secrecy regarding this misleading information.

In the meeting mentioned at the beginning of October, the Berlin Gestapo official had made three points extremely clear to Henschel, Kozower, and Mosse. First, he obligated the Jewish functionaries to secrecy, coupled with the threat of incarceration and death. Second, he obligated them to deceive the Jewish Community members: the planned operation was to be passed off as an "eviction operation," in line with housing policy. Third, he made it absolutely clear that the "resettlement" would take place in any case, quite apart from any decision by the Jewish representatives.

The absolute secrecy regarding everything connected with the deportations was an obligation repeatedly demanded from the Jewish functionaries in the subsequent period, especially prior to large-scale deportations,[25] and was always closely welded to the ominous threat of "measures" that would be taken if this order was violated.[26]

Although later the reports from the district branch offices on the dates of the transports, their extent, and their cost were routinely sent on to the central office,[27] and the Jewish representatives were thus always precisely informed about events in the *Altreich*, frequently in advance, in the board meetings practice differed. There they treated the deportations as an agenda item that was best not mentioned in any detail in the minutes of their meetings. Vis-à-vis coworkers, RV members, and most especially non-Jews (aside from a few exceptions), they maintained strict silence about these events. Board members and subordinate staff involved in the process adhered to this obligation of secrecy, and the latter were also repeatedly reminded of the secrecy order. Thus, "Urgent Guidelines for the Levetzowstrasse Helpers" stated: "Once again, we point out with great urgency the following: 1. Each person must observe the strictest secrecy regarding everything that occurs in the Levetzowstrasse assembly camp!"[28] A directive that each and every coworker had to sign carried the warning: "Any violation of the duty to secrecy will be subject to severe punishment."[29]

The Jewish functionaries also agreed to deceive the scheduled deportees. However, they actually knew very little about what awaited the deportees in the ghettos (information coming from the Stettin Jews or the Polish Jews), aside from the fact that a return was not planned. Some individuals may have suspected the genocidal core inherent in the contemporary measures, but the coming "Final Solution," the murder of the European Jews in their entirety, had not yet crystallized. The victims were thus not aware of it. Yet even later on, the Jewish functionaries were never officially informed about events in the ghettos and death camps; they depended on bits of news and conjecture that were unofficial, and had to draw conclusions on the basis of that. Their sole involvement was always limited strictly to the transport operations, and never encompassed what occurred after arrival of the deportees at their destination. On the other hand, at times one of their appointed tasks was to pass on death notices from the concentration camps, and from 1942/1943 on, rumors began to reach the Jewish representatives about massive fatalities at most of the deportation destinations. Gradually they became aware, at least in basic outline, of the murderous events unfolding in the East. Nonetheless, they chose to adhere to the neutral term "resettlement" (*Umsiedlung*) and continued with their participation in organizing the deportation transports. In so doing, the representatives of the Reichsvereinigung stepped out unawares onto a taut tightrope, walking on a thin line between responsible action and collaboration, upon which they later lost their footing.

Clinging to a Lost Life

The few sources that provide a window onto the private life of the Jewish representatives during this period indicate that they tried to preserve some remnants of middle class life and tidy domesticity in smaller circles. In short, they sought to create spaces of refuge into which their oppressive realities would not manage to penetrate. Their joint work, formidable and difficult to execute, brought board members, department heads, and staff employees together outside the office in their free time as well, and thus tended to separate them from the members of their organizations. After the war, Inge Deutschkron, who stemmed from a Social Democratic family background, noted: "At the time, most Jews living in Berlin envied the functionaries of the Jewish Community and the Reichsvereinigung, because they appeared to have so much more power. But that was a deceptive illusion, which these Jewish functionaries also consciously sought initially to maintain." Deutschkron worked as a lady's helper in the Conrad Cohn family, and gazed in amazement at their solid middle class style of life and home décor, and their continued attempts to cultivate sociability in the circle of their Jewish colleagues: the Henschels, who lived downstairs, and the Lilienthals. The Lilienthals had not emigrated in 1939 because they believed it was "necessary to stick it out," the recurrent motif among the Jewish leadership echelon for staying on in Germany. These families belonged to different age groups, but all stemmed from circles of university graduates, the Jewish *Bildungsbürgertum*; they were trained lawyers who had placed their skills at the service of the broader Jewish community. Now and then, their group also included Hanna Karminski, Paula Fürst, and Franz-Eugen Fuchs. They too had remained on in Germany, convinced they "were still needed in Berlin." It is likely that when they met, meals were not particularly sumptuous, but the discussions at their table were on a high level, dealing with the works of Heinrich Heine and Johann Wolfgang Goethe.[30]

Thus, the Jewish functionaries created a private and highly educated bourgeois counterpoint to the general brutalization, social decline, and unreasonable demands and challenges they were being forced to confront. In her study on the leading women in the RV, Gudrun Maierhof shows that these women, some on closer terms as a result of their earlier work together in the League of Jewish Women (Jüdischer Frauenbund), likewise spent their leisure time largely together. Cora Berliner, Hildegard Böhme, Paula Fürst, and Hannah Karminski referred to themselves as the "quartet." The latter two lived together as life partners. The single women spent vacations together, to the extent still possible, or attended synagogue services together, especially if Leo Baeck was also present. They also felt a close personal bond with Rabbi Baeck. Gudrun Maierhof advances the thesis that there was a fundamental difference between the female networks and the male functionaries, who were oriented in their free time more to their families. In my view, networks existed of both genders, as well as mixed gender networks, which fulfilled different needs: they preserved a "better" counterworld, but also created spaces where people could speak openly about their fears, their sense of sadness and loss, as in the walks and conversations with Leo Baeck that Maierhof describes. The male and female networks were not clearly separated one from the other. We know that Paul Eppstein, alone or with others, found consolation in music, often while still at the office after hours. An observer at the time noted: "Right down to the final days, we would sit many an evening and on into the night in a room at the R.V. office and listen to Dr, Eppstein playing the piano, generally assisted by a female coworker. They thus created a kind of counterweight to the frustrating day-to-day round of work, and allowed others to participate."[31]

Straying from the Path or "Legal Work in the Underground"?[32] Preparatory Tasks Executed by the RV

Changes in Tasks and Structures (1941–1943)

Once the ban on emigration was imposed in October 1941, along with the order to participate instead in organizing the deportations, the RV was confronted with new tasks and problems. These impacted on its internal structure. The first change in structure was the separation between the RV and the Berlin Jewish Community: Eppstein proposed to the RSHA that the boards of *both* the RV and the Berlin Jewish Community should be headed by the same persons "in the interest of a further concentration of administration and responsibility." Perhaps he had more general fears that he might lose his role as a contact person for the RSHA as a result of the deportations, with the chain of command shifting instead from the Gestapo to the district branches of the RV and the local Jewish Communities. Most certainly he also wished to prevent a renewed split between the Berlin Jewish Community and the RV central office when the transports from the *Altreich* started. Now Baeck was to function as overall chairman, assisted by five individuals who up until now had belonged to the boards of the Berlin Jewish Community or the RV: Cohn, Eppstein, Henschel, Kozower, and Lilienthal. The RSHA approved this proposal.[33] After the Kulturbund was liquidated, Leo Kreindler also joined the board, which in this composition guided the fate of the RV until the summer of 1942.[34] Then, on 23 June 1942, Conrad Cohn and Arthur Lilienthal were forced to resign from the board subsequent to "orders from the supervisory authority"[35]—they were already confined in concentration camps and were later murdered.

As a result of the ban on emigration, problems with finance also arose for the RV: previously it had depended on revenues from the levy on emigrants to cover expenses for its social tasks. That is why Eppstein hesitated in announcing the ban on emigration, so as to not be obliged to return remittances for levies already paid in the organization's books. In actuality, the RSHA permitted the RV to retain costs for passage to Palestine already remitted, as well as costs for burial or fees for services that after the deportation of the payee could no longer be provided, calling them "exceptional contributions."[36] At the same time, Eppstein explored with the RSHA whether new compulsory levies on members, designated by another name, might be able to close the gap in finances.[37] Even before this had been regulated, the RV was ordered to set up a "special account W" ("W" for *Wanderung*, migration), which would be used in future to settle and deduct costs for deportations with the district branch offices.[38]

During the first wave of deportations from the *Altreich*, problems mounted around the financing of the transports. Thus, the Gestapo in Hamburg ordered the head of the RV Northwest Germany district branch, Max Plaut, to withdraw ninety thousand RM from the local account, and then to raise seventy thousand RM to cover this from assets of the "individuals resettled." The RV, drawn into liability for payment by its district branches, requested the RSHA to order the local Gestapo offices to consult first with the RV central office before initiating such local actions (which in turn would have to contact the RSHA for clarification).[39] Instead, the RSHA decided that the RV should cover expenditures by funds from the "special account W," and then demand reimbursement from the district branches.[40] In connection with another transport, the Hamburg Gestapo confiscated the entire assets of those slated to be deported without further ado, and did not release any funds for the local district branch.

This district branch again approached the central office; it in turn contacted the RSHA.[41]

Despite the clear and unambiguous decision by the RSHA, in many localities the Gestapo offices demanded payment in cash for transport expenses. These funds had not been approved by the RV or could not be handled by transfer from the "special account W." In any event, the participants had to cover the transport costs, or the district branches were obliged to cover the expenses in the case of the needy. No funds from the RV were permitted for this purpose.[42] For this reason, the former head of the Berlin Jewish Community, Heinrich Stahl, acquired coverage from wealthy Jews for the two hundred thousand RM the Jewish Community had spent for the first deportation transports.[43] The JOINT also transferred ninety thousand RM to the RV for equipment (in ways not known) for the first deportations.[44]

Some Gestapo offices, such as that in Breslau, simply phoned up the central office of the RV and ordered them to provide funds. They operated on the assumption that a Jew would immediately obey any Gestapo order without hesitation.

These events point to a fundamental problem: the Gestapo officials believed that automatically by virtue of their office, they were able to give orders to "their" local Jewish functionaries, and those at the RV central office in Berlin. But to complete any payment, the district branch heads had to obtain authorization from the RV main office, and the RV main office was also required in turn to obtain authorization from the RSHA. The source materials do not allow us to answer the question as to why the RSHA did not issue clear directives on this directly to the Gestapo offices, thus clarifying matters and solving the problems within its own chain of command structures.

Instead, certain basic constellations reoccurred again and again: the Gestapo officials regarded the deportations as a welcome source for personal enrichment or the material benefit of their office, and thus helped themselves to items they fancied from the deportees' baggage, confiscated permitted or illegal sums of money in the possession of the deportees, and demanded reimbursement of expenses. The RSHA sought to ensure that the funds of the Reichsvereinigung were not "lost" in this way, disappearing into the pockets of the Gestapo. These funds were earmarked to flow into the coffers of the Nazi state. On the other hand, the RSHA carefully avoided compromising and exposing the Gestapo personnel in front of the Jewish functionaries via any decision to overturn and vitiate Gestapo orders. Thus, in the above-mentioned case of the Breslau Gestapo, it "permitted" the RV to release the thirty thousand RM demanded, but only with restricting instructions.[45] Such orders annoyed the local Gestapo personnel in Breslau (and not only there), and they let the Jewish functionaries and the Jews summoned for deportation sense their anger very clearly.

To name but a few further examples: the Gestapo in Bayreuth demanded seven hundred RM per person for deportees in a transport as "reimbursement of expenses." Although the RSHA thought this was still barely inside the bounds of what was "legal," they considered the amount excessive. For that reason, the RV was ordered to request from the Gestapo a specification of their actual expenses.[46]

Some district branches of the RV, such as in Magdeburg, were unable to provide deportees with warm clothing, dishes, soap and towels, blankets, or food. If the central office stepped into the breach, according to RSHA instructions, the central office had to request reimbursement of the equivalent amount from the local Gestapo office or the head of the regional finance office (*Oberfinanzpräsident*), which had confiscated the deportees' assets.[47]

These examples can suffice to point to the multitude of different financial problems that the Jewish functionaries had to grapple with as a result of their participation in the deportations. They were in a triple bind of sorts, forced to respond and react to demands from the Gestapo offices, their own district branches, and the RSHA. In part, these problems arose because there were no previous regulations people could operate under; but also because the Gestapo offices and individual officials saw the deportations as a new source for their own unregulated self-enrichment, before the victims boarded the trains for their journey with no return.

Thus, in December 1941 the Reich Audit Office (Reichsrechnungshof) noted that in connection with the deportation transports, the Berlin Gestapo had "neither submitted a bill or kept a cash account record. In addition, sums of money, valuables and bank books were not properly accounted for, receipts were incomplete or completely lacking."[48] The Audit Office also stated that the Berlin Gestapo office had deposited 541,601 RM in the "special account W" instead of the 880,805 RM actually received by the RV, so that some 340,000 RM had apparently "vanished." Irregularities were also noted in deposits and withdrawals during the first ten deportations.[49] However, the Audit Office, at the time a weak institution with little authority, was unable to halt this process. Barely a year later, the Berlin corruption affair assumed such proportions that the RSHA felt obliged to intervene: the staff workers in the Jewish Department (*Judenreferat*) in the Berlin Gestapo were suspended. Alois Brunner arrived with his retinue from Vienna, took over operations there for several months, and reorganized the course of deportations in line with the Vienna paradigm. Ten Gestapo officials were arrested, and some were later convicted, and others acquitted, before internal SS courts. The head of the *Judenreferat*, Franz Prüfer, committed suicide. Otto Bovensiepen, Gestapo office chief, received a disciplinary transfer and was rebuked for not having been more careful in selecting his coworkers.[50]

But let us return to the financial distress of the RV that sprang from the shift in Nazi policy from forced emigration to mass deportation. A levy on "migrants" (*Abwandererabgabe*, i.e., a tax on deportees under forced *Abwanderung*, or migration) paid by RV members was in future to relieve financial emergencies. It was calculated so that beyond covering the transport costs, it would also generate a surplus for financing the work of the RV, thus enabling the organization to continue on with welfare assistance.[51] A short time later the RSHA issued a directive that the RV was permitted to demand 25 percent of the liquid assets of a transport participant as a "voluntary contribution" and then deposit this in the "special account W." The amount per transport was not to exceed five hundred thousand RM in toto.[52] The (compulsory) members of the RV were to be called upon "in a suitable way" to provide these "contributions." Later it was spelled out more clearly: they were to be called upon "in all seriousness" to make a contribution, and if they refused, there loomed the threat of being reported to the Gestapo.[53] The RSHA expected that those slated for deportation would contribute their "entire remaining cash assets."[54]

The Jewish functionaries were not apprised of the rationale behind this order, but the RSHA informed the Gestapo offices that the "special account W" was at its disposal "after it now no longer had access to the assets of the Jews." The reasons for this somewhat barbed formulation lay in rivalries between the Finance Ministry and the RSHA over *Judenvermögen* (Jewish wealth).[55]

As already mentioned in connection with the order on the wearing of the yellow star, it is evident that here too, now in regard to questions of finance, the gulf between the RV and its compulsory membership was deepening. The earlier emigration levy (*Auswandererabgabe*) benefited destitute emigrants and facilitated the work of the competent Jewish offices involved with emigration. Thus, those paying the levy profited directly or indirectly from this "contribution." When the deportations began and new levies for *Abwanderung* were to be paid, the future deportees could figure out that this would be of no benefit to them at their destination, since the spatial competence of the RV was restricted to the *Altreich*. It is true that there had been a directive issued that was intended to set the RV representatives somewhat at ease, but most certainly was unknown to the membership: namely, to appoint six German-Jewish men to supervise Jewish autonomous administration in the Łódz ghetto. However, in October 1941, the RSHA revoked the order.[56] If there reportedly were ideas broached about linking the activity of the RV with that of the Jewish councils in the ghettos, such conceptions were in any case not implemented. There was likewise no financial support. In November 1941, Paul Meyerheim submitted a request to the JOINT through a Swedish intermediary: he suggested they should try to bring in an international non-Jewish organization like the International Red Cross to provide care and assistance for the approximately twenty thousand Jews deported to Poland in the autumn of 1941, since no measures had been been taken for accommodation.[57] Even when Jewish Social Self-Assistance in Kraków requested a grant from the RV via the Jewish council in Lublin "giving consideration to the migration transports from the Altreich into the Generalgouvernement," the RSHA rejected this. They argued that in regard to their "integration at the point of destination, another financial arrangement had been decided on," and this was valid should similar requests be made by other Jewish councils.[58] In short, once deported, the Jews were no longer regarded as Germans, not even second-class Germans. They lost their citizenship, and their membership in the RV also expired.

If anything, a "migration" levy could only help those remaining behind, not the deportees. In the eyes of the slated deportees, the Reichsvereinigung now most likely joined the ranks of those who endeavored to gain access to their assets, which in any case were no longer at their disposal.[59] In the meantime, the National Socialist state had placed all assets of five thousand RM and more under security orders, thus blocking these funds from their owners. While the owners had to seek special approval for access to any amount in excess of the permitted monthly sum, state institutions were permitted to debit the account for taxes and levies. Likewise, the RV district branch offices could deduct fees owed to them directly from these accounts. After the deportation of the owner of an account, the state then confiscated his or her remaining assets on the basis of the 11th Ordinance to the Reich Citizenship Law issued on 25 November 1941.[60] Any debts owed by a deportee could be claimed by submitting a request to the head of the regional finance office.

While the Nazi state proceeded on the basis of the notion that Jewish property was in truth (illegally acquired) "property of the people," so-called *Volkseigentum*, that the German Reich had to reappropriate and secure for the state, the RV also treated the assets blocked from their rightful owner as funds available to the association. The RV could, in the name of the German Jews, claim a portion of these funds in order to finance the spheres of social welfare and education for the Jews remaining in the German Reich. From the perspective of the RV board, their motives, oriented to the general well-being of the remaining Jews, justified this action.

In any case, the Reichsvereinigung had no other alternatives for solving their financial dilemma, because it was not permitted to make use of its own assets in the form of real estate and land in order to finance social concerns. In the minds of the Jewish functionaries and their conception of their role, it was out of the question that they should halt their activities in the area of education and training, and most especially their work in social welfare. Ultimately, they had stayed on in Germany specifically for that purpose, and with each additional deportation, the importance of their work for the sick and aged increased, since they remained behind without any care or provisions, and were dependent on aid.

Surviving functionaries later sometimes explained the great care with which they had put together and maintained their accounts on debits and credits as action grounded on a secret hope: that they would later able to demand reimbursement on the basis of this record keeping, "once the Nazis had been overthrown."[61] But such explanations are doubtless a product of the postwar perspective on the past, such as that cited here, given in 1957 in Berlin by Siegmund Weltlinger, a Jewish functionary who had dealt with emigration and deportation levies.[62]

Initially, another change in the ensemble of activities of the leading Jewish functionaries was barely noticeable: there are hardly any traces in the files of activity by the chair, Leo Baeck, during the time of the deportations. Although the RSHA sought to ensure that the respected rabbi, who had headed the former Reich Representation, should also become head of the Reich Association, it is difficult from the existing contemporaneous documentation or reports written later on to establish what positions Baeck actually espoused in the organization at the time of the deportations. His biographers are also largely silent on this question.[63] From Baeck's tenure as head of the Reich Representation, we know that "the cardinal," as he was dubbed, actively led the meetings, broached topics, and ensured that all views on some matter could be expressed and discussed. He would then sum matters up with a kind of synthesis (which, in terms of conception, in general he himself had purportedly anticipated).[64] That apparently became more uncommon once deportations had commenced: in both categories of documentary materials, contemporaneous and later reports, Baeck's actions within the RV fade from view. The extant memos were written by Eppstein. Eppstein was the functionary the RSHA gave orders to; he had to report on their implementation or inquire whether the RV was permitted to realize its own ideas. Only on special occasions, when Eichmann, rather than a subordinate in the RSHA, personally summoned the Jewish functionaries, was Baeck also among the participants. For example, in connection with the summons following the arson attack on the propaganda exhibition "The Soviet Paradise" in Berlin, it was reported that after the functionaries had been forced to stand for hours facing the wall, Baeck was the only one allowed to sit down for a short time on a chair.

It is clear from the minutes of the RV board, which in 1942 became increasingly brief in any event, that Baeck participated in almost all meetings. However, others in charge of various task areas gave reports on the diverse fields of activity or upcoming tasks and challenges. Contemporaries stated that Baeck had inwardly withdrawn from the work of the RV, which increasingly had become preparatory work in organizing the deportations. It is said that he objected to the extent of Eppstein's cooperation with the authorities: "Dr. Baeck bore responsibility for actions that depressed him, but whose implementation by his no. 1 man [Eppstein] he could not act to prevent."[65] Herbert (Ehud) Growald remained just as vague when he later wrote that Baeck only dealt "with the very big things," but that in doing so, he "always was a fighter. Yet otherwise, Eppstein did everything."[66]

Baeck had cultivated a close relationship with the murdered functionary Otto Hirsch, whom he held in high regard. But he tended to keep a certain distance from Eppstein, although he rarely commented on the reasons why (even later on). Baeck apparently saw his real professional role in his activity as a rabbi and scholar, or as long as that was still possible. He gave sermons where religious services were permitted, taught in the seminars of the Hochschule für die Wissenschaft des Judentums, and in the General Lectures series, open to the interested Jewish public,[67] until the Hochschule was shut down in the summer of 1942 in the course of the liquidation of all Jewish educational institutions.

In 1942, on orders from the RSHA, Baeck also wrote an extensive scholarly work on the "Legal Status of the Jews in Europe."[68] After the war, on the one hand he stated that this had sprung from stimulus by an official in the Interior Ministry in 1941.[69] On the other hand, he also commented that the manuscript had come into being between 1938 and 1941 on behalf of the German resistance. To complete it, he noted that he had worked regularly, arising before 4:00 AM. Whether one of these versions is true cannot be examined here. The fact remains, and Hermann Simon has pointed this out,[70] that in March 1942, Baeck was ordered by the RSHA to compose this work, and given very specific instructions. As Baeck had already been dealing since 1933 with the legal status of Jews in Germany and other European countries, it may well be that he was able to make use of a manuscript written earlier; with the help of Leopold Lukas and Hilde Ottenheimer, perhaps he was able to revise this within seven months (initially he was granted three months, then six) along the lines that Friedrich Suhr of the RSHA had demanded. Suhr instructed

Baeck to utilize as few Jewish authors as possible, and to specifically identify these authors as Jews. Instead, he stipulated that Baeck must utilize
works by "Aryan researchers on the Jews," which should then be evaluated. Baeck was told he should especially underscore the active role the
Jews themselves had played in gaining their legal status, and insisted this
should be placed in the context of broader developments in the history
of ideas. Whether under external constraint or based on his own wishes,
Baeck gained the possibility in this way to do research in his most familiar field of personal interest. Thus, it may have been more a matter of
accommodation by the RSHA and less one of coercion to allow the RV
chairman to engage in scholarly work based on a "special assignment"
(Suhr) or "intellectual conscript forced labor."[71] He was permitted to order newer literature in libraries (something otherwise forbidden to Jews),
thus providing him with a recognized and secure position, as called for
by Eppstein, Mosse, Kozower, and others, far removed from the sad and
hectic activities of the organization. They still needed Baeck at the helm
of the RV, because a large proportion of the membership trusted and followed the highly respected rabbi.

It is clear that Baeck himself greatly valued his lengthy manuscript,
some sixteen hundred pages. That is evident solely from the measures he
took to preserve it: he smuggled the manuscript to Theresienstadt disguised as toilet paper, carefully protected it there, and then took it along
to England after liberation.[72] Apart from how long and intensively Baeck
maintained relations with the conservative German resistance, the pastoral care, teaching, and scholarship he engaged in during 1942 enabled
him to find some inward distance from the swirl of daily events.

The large-scale deportations that commenced in the autumn of 1941
diminished the number of remaining Jews and thus also the number of administrative positions necessary. At the end of 1941, there were still seventeen Jewish Communities (each with more than one thousand members)
and fourteen district branch offices of the RV. Given the reduced number
of members, the RSHA pressed for stepping up conversion of the Jewish
Communties into RV district branches, along with mergers and closures.
In March 1942, their number was to be reduced to thirteen branch offices
and five Communities.[73] Yet in June of that year, there were still nine mid-
dle-sized Jewish Communities left (Beuthen, Dortmund, Dresden, Essen,
Cologne, Leipzig, Mainz, Munich, Nuremberg); of these, seven were to be
maintained, while the others would be integrated into the twelve existing
RV district branches.[74] These were the branches in Bavaria, Brandenburg-
East Prussia, Central Germany, including the Sudeten, Northwest Germany, Rhineland-Westphalia, Silesia, and Southwest Germany, including
Baden-Palatinate, Hesse, Hesse-Nassau, and Württemberg.[75]

The RV and the Jewish Communties were still responsible for a total of 60,400 Jews.[76] In June 1942, the RSHA issued a directive that all Jewish Communities must be incorporated into the district branches within six months, with the exception of Berlin, Breslau, Frankfurt am Main, and Hamburg.[77] In the autumn of 1942, these, aside from the Berlin Jewish Community, were also absorbed into the district branches.[78]

In November 1942, the administrations of the RV central office and the Berlin Jewish Community were merged.[79] In December, the RV board, evidently pressured by the RSHA, accepted Walter Lustig as an additional board member,[80] as well as Kurt Levy, on 27 January 1943. He replaced Paul Eppstein, deported a few days later to Theresienstadt. Lustig, who enjoyed the confidence of the RSHA, was to head the RV until the end of the National Socialist regime.

In May 1943, the institutions and departments in the RV central office and Berlin Jewish Community were downsized, and for the last time, the number of district branches in the *Altreich* shrank. The activities of the previous district branch of Brandenburg-East Prusssia were now to be handled from Berlin,[81] the branch office in East Prussia was to be absorbed by the Jewish Community in Königsberg,[82] and the district branch in Hanover-Kassel was ordered to transfer its tasks to the Northwest Germany branch office, based in Hamburg, and the Saxony-Thuringia district branch in Leipzig.[83] One month later, the Reichsvereinigung in its existing form was dissolved: with the continuing implementation of its tasks assisting in the deportations, it had become successively more superfluous in the eyes of the Nazi authorities, until it was finally disbanded.

A residual RV, the so-called Rest-Reichsvereinigung, also called the New Reich Association, run by Jews in mixed marriages, was to care for the concerns of those in mixed marriages and fulfill the demands of the RSHA and the Gestapo offices. This rump organization existed until the autumn of 1945.

The RV central office was able to inform its membership of new directives via the district branch offices or the newspaper *Jüdisches Nachrichtenblatt,* which was published from November 1938 to June 1943 as the sole permitted Jewish periodical.[84] Since the paper belonged to the Kulturbund, it was subject on the one hand to censorship by the Propaganda Ministry, and on the other by the RSHA as "superior authority." As a consequence, the chief editor, Leo Kreindler, came increasingly under fire in disputes over competence between the Hinkel Office in Goebbel's Propaganda Ministry and the RSHA, until in the fall of 1941 the latter assumed sole supervision. When the paper was launched it appeared twice a week with a print run of sixty to seventy thousand copies, but the number of copies and the size of the paper shrank steadily once deportations had begun. Local columns informed readers about the times of distribution for ration cards, the time and place of religious services, and gave the names of physicians approved as *Krankenbehandler* (practitioners for the sick) or lawyers approved as *Konsulenten* (legal counsels). Occasionally the paper also contained short articles on the significance of religious festivals or wise sayings from the Talmud. This editorial feature shrank successively. Until the autumn of 1942, the paper also carried private classified ads, ads for sale, and marriage announcements that mirrored the decline, hopes, and everyday life of the Jews in Germany, supplemented by special wartime recipes based on the restricted access to various foods. In May 1943, the paper was to appear solely as a biweekly for publishing laws and ordinances, but then it was shut down completely in June 1943 with the liquidation of the Reichsvereinigung, and it was not continued as a press organ of the Residual RV.

A New Task: The Compilation of Personal Data and Card File Systems

One of the most important functions assigned to the RV and its district branch offices by the regime was the compilation of personal data on Jews and their listing in card file systems.

The Israeli historian Esriel Hildesheimer, who treats only cursorily the entanglement of the RV in the policies of the so-called Final Solution,[85] suspects that for the Gestapo, the *Judenkarteien* (card file systems on Jews) compiled by the RV and the Jewish Communities in order to implement the deportations "were in reality unnecessary."[86] He is doubtless correct in that assessment. A number of state and party institutions in Nazi Germany maintained corresponding "lists of Jews," although these generally only contained the names of a certain proportion of the total number of Jews: owners of land, business establishments, pharmacies, etc. Naturally the Gestapo would have been able to determine the names and addresses of future deportees from the local residents' registration office (*Einwohnermeldeamt*) in all German localities. The 1939 census had, for the first time, also listed data for those considered Jews by Nazi racial criteria who had formally left the Jewish Community, had been baptized, or called themselves (religious) "dissidents." But the evaluation of these mass data stretched on for years, and some of those included in the count had, in their own interest, probably supplied false or incomplete information on their origin—or indeed none at all, thus generating a "dark figure" of unreported cases.[87]

Whether these were the reasons or simply for convenience, the Gestapo offices did not rely on state data compilations. Instead, it looked to the data gathered by the RV and its branch offices, making duplicates of this for its *Judenreferate*.

In particular, the extensive Berlin registry, maintained over many years, contained important personal data for the large-scale deportations. It dated back to 1933, when the Jewish Community had compiled a card file of members on the basis of the tax lists of the revenue offices. In 1934, there was a statistical compilation of data through questionnaires sent to all Jewish households. Between 1933 and 1938, the Berlin Jewish Community received a carbon copy of all registered changes of address from the tax offices; this practice was rendered obsolete by the Law on the Legal Status of the Jewish Communities of 28 March 1938. In addition, in 1936/1937, the Berlin Jewish Community—whether voluntarily or under coercion cannot be determined from the documentation—compiled a card file of Jews who had formally left the Community.

With the genesis of the Reichsvereinigung, all Jews who were German subjects and stateless Jews living in the territory of the Reich (residents) became compulsory members of the organization, including Jews in "non-privileged" mixed marriages; those in "privileged" mixed marriages were excluded.[88] In May 1941, the RV was ordered to compile a card file of its membership.[89] At this juncture, it was already at work on a "central card file," slated to be completed in June 1941.[90] The two card files, which have been lost, differed according to whether or not they included the Jews in "privileged" mixed marriages, their offspring, and baptized Jews. The RSHA hypocritically stressed that it was integral to the "efficiency of the Reichsvereinigung" that it should be able at all times to provide an exact overview of the number of members and their personal data.[91] In addition, the RV compiled an "emigrants' card file," containing 260,000 "slips" stored in 130 boxes.[92] In order to compile the exact data demanded for the emigrants, a team of 50 persons worked in the RV central office, in several shifts a day; this did not include the personnel providing data from the district branch offices, who as a precaution were required to forward duplicate regional card files by registered mail to the RV statistical department in Berlin.[93] However, since not all emigrations had been arranged via the Jewish Communities and relief organizations, in many cases the RV personnel could only obtain precise data from the government offices. But to inquire there was soon prohibited to them. Nonetheless, the already-contacted state institutions complained to the RSHA, and Eppstein, who had always sought to anticipate and prepare for all coming demands, had to face sharp criticism. Initially, *Sturmbannführer* Günther accused Eppstein specifically of responsibility for a situation where the RV was performing at a minimum level of what had been demanded of it, and was even inadequate in that. He stated that if further deficiencies were noted, the "functionaries responsible would be arrested … and not in the form of protective custody, but incarcerated in concentration camps."[94]

Adolf Eichmann then ordered Eppstein to immediately fire all staff members who could not effectively handle their jobs, and threatened him with a further reduction in the number of district branches "if the Reichsvereinigung could not prove itself capable and efficient."[95]

In September 1941, Eppstein reported to the RSHA that data on the members of the RV had now been compiled, although not on the "non-Mosaic Jews." Their papers had to be obtained from the authorities. However, the RSHA immediately refused the request, without citing any reasons.[96] The RV was enjoined from establishing any direct contacts with offices and government agencies.

In October 1941, Eppstein noted that now the *Rassejuden* (Jews by race) had been registered "to the greatest extent possible without involving the authorities." Those registered were not informed about this.[97] In a letter to a lawyer who had filed a protest against this for his client, the RV spelled out its practice:

> As a matter of course, the membership lists of the Reichsvereinigung contain only those persons who belong as members to the organization. Regardless of this fact, we are required by the supervisory authority ... to register in the central card file of the Jews in Germany all Jews in the sense of the Nuremberg Laws, without taking into consideration whether or not they are Reichsvereinigung members. Of course, in the case of individuals who are not members of the Reichsvereinigung, this is noted immediately and exactly on the file card.[98]

Such a note was useful for a person who wished to refuse to pay membership dues, but it was of no help whatsoever in regard to an order for deportation.

The Jewish Communities and district branch offices of the RV regularly had to provide the central card file with all changes in personal data. Extant in part are their announcements on "internal migration," death notices, and "counting cards for the foreigner card file."[99] If the district branch office had received a death notice from a concentration camp, the responsible staff worker recorded, for example, under "previous address of the household" the entry "Dachau concentration camp" or wrote in by hand "died in detention," "died in Ravensbrück," or, beginning in 1943, "died in Auschwitz concentration camp."[100] When the mass deportations commenced, the staff in the district branches were instructed to submit lists of the deportees using the keyword "resettlement" (*Aussiedlung*).[101]

The large Berlin Jewish Community likewise maintained extensive card files in all its areas of activity. Thus, for example, in the sphere of education, more than 8,400 registration cards for Jewish pupils in Berlin are still extant.[102] In 1941, in Berlin the accommodation advice center of the Jewish Community became the sole responsible unit for changes in the registry, which was manifested externally in the newly created "subsection for card files."[103] Receipts for the "Jewish stars" had made it possible to register precisely the "star wearers," who from 1 September 1941 received questionnaires and were included in the registry. The subsection for card files soon filled more than one room. After the names of those to be deported were removed from the card file of the Berlin Jewish Community in October/November 1941, the Gestapo subsequently relied on a duplicate of this card file, a *Judenkartei* or "card file of Jews," with special Gestapo labels to mark specific groups in order to determine participants in the transports.[104]

When the Berlin Jewish Community had to prepare operations under the pressure of a deadline, it brought in volunteers in order to check through and select the questionnaires according to specific criteria.[105] Depending on instructions, and evidently also at times acting in advance, the section selected, for example, those in the bracket of sixty-five to sixty-eight years old, or fifty-two to fifty-four years old, from the registry. These then were broken down into further groups, depending on whether they had families or not, and corresponding lists were prepared.[106]

In order to prevent manipulations, no outsider was allowed onto the premises, as Martha Mosse noted in witness testimony in a trial in August 1942. In addition, for purposes of security, the card file system was divided into three spheres of work: one staff worker was responsible for the area of acceptance of questionnaires and the need to check whether all those included in the lists of the Gestapo had filled out the questionnaires. In the registry, under different supervision, were the actual card file and the file sheets of those temporarily exempted or deferred. Finally, still another staff worker put together the transport lists from the available material. It was also his job to ensure that "the persons would be collected … in an orderly and timely fashion if that was not handled immediately by the agency [the Gestapo]."[107]

The card file in Berlin, repeatedly brought up to date, and its counterparts in the district branches, comprised the foundation for the deportation of the Jews, in keeping with the respective preferences of the Gestapo. This fact is not changed, even in light of the postwar reports by some Berlin Jews, who noted that in some individual cases, staff employees in the department or the department head Bertha Mendelsohn herself had caused cards in the file to "disappear," or that they had recorded a false date of death or the note "emigrated" on a card, and thus arranged a postponement for these persons, enabling them to survive disguised or in hiding.

In her trial testimony mentioned earlier, Martha Mosse also explained certain details about the participation of her department in preparations for the deportations from Berlin:

> Data on the Jews in question are gathered on the basis of lists, which in most cases are sent by the Gestapo in Berlin for this purpose. But in addition, the Jewish Community also put together and revised several lists for the registration of specific age groups, based on its card file ... The Jewish Community does not defer individuals. The state police is the sole body responsible for all such decisions.[108]

Mosse did not mention that in her capacity as section head, she could request that a person be temporarily exempted, namely, in cases when the Gestapo did not adhere to its own regulations.[109]

Mosse also described in detail the "transports of the aged" to Theresienstadt that commenced from the summer of 1942:

> The process is as follows: already administered questionnaires of individuals who because of their age were not included in migration, are selected, compared with the registry and card file in respect to change of address, case of death, etc. and then sent on to the Gestapo office. After transport numbers are issued there, the declarations on assets are brought to the individuals' domiciles by staff workers, since to send by post is too uncertain and time-consuming. The declarations on assets are then picked up after two days. Transport lists are assembled for the individual transports of the aged, migration notifications are written, and once again distributed to the individuals involved by staff workers. Declarations on assets are processed later by our coworkers on Grosse Hamburger Strasse [assembly camp for deportees], and collection of levies (Winter Relief, contributions department, W-Stock) is likewise first handled by our coworkers on Grosse Hamburger Strasse and collected. ... Once a transport has departed, our temporary transport list is then compared with the final list of the state police office. Through inquiries on the spot, our coworkers determine who among the migrants was a main tenant, who a subtenant, and whether the apartments were in Aryan or Jewish ownership. The apartments are ... carefully registered, and then reported to the State Police Office and the Economic Group for purposes of unsealing and clearance.[110]

In the case of transports to the East, Mosse's personnel had summoned four to five hundred persons per day and completed the formalities; now it was only able to "process" about eighty per day, since these Jews, mostly elderly, had to be visited in their homes. For purposes of a smoothly functioning process, as had in the meantime been worked out, the "lists department" had to put together comparison lists for the card file and the contributions department—this in addition to the transport lists—and work out the sequence in which the marshals were to pick up the deportees (departures list).

The rehousing and eviction operations, closing of homes, mass deportations, and attempts by the Jews to elude these led generally, and particularly in Berlin, to a situation where the file system, by the end of the summer if not earlier, did not reflect the actual current situation. The RV "requested" permission from the RSHA to be allowed to bring the files up to date by means of a basic survey (*Urerhebung*).[111] The plan was delayed until the end of 1942; then, as the *Jüdisches Nachrichtenblatt* announced, members were required at short notice to submit registration slips.[112] Of particular importance was the need to determine the precise number of Jews not deployed in forced labor.

> It is planned that after processing the registration slips with this perspective in mind, the files will be relocated to the rooms of the registry of the Jewish Community Berlin, and stored there under lock and key. A comparison between the files and the registry should be undertaken as soon as feasible, in order to determine for which persons there are cards in the Community registry, but no registration slips in the card file. This should be done additionally so as to be able to include those individuals who did not submit registration slips.[113]

However, the responsible functionaries had evidently underestimated the problems involved in comparing the huge card file system and bringing it up to date. To that end, the coworkers had to consult the registration slips, the household passes of the food offices, the ID card file, and other lists, plus the "cases to be clarified," that is, the pending applications to be exempted from the obligation to wear the star.[114] The "Factory Operation" (*Fabrik-Aktion*) on 27–28 February 1943, which Mosse later noted had been staged without any bureaucracy, took the idea of putting together an up-to-date registry of the Jews once again ad absurdum, even though this could not be publicly admitted. Mosse commented later: "From this point in time on, neither the Gestapo nor the Community knew who from the Jewish Community was still in Berlin, and who wasn't."[115] Yet for the period prior to that, it was doubtless true what a court of honor determined after the war: in the Berlin Jewish Community, the registry had been maintained for many years so conscientiously, and with such zeal, that it proved "ultimately harmful" for those registered.[116]

A New Imposed Challenge: Setting Up and Maintaining Assembly Camps for Deportations

Along with registering the Jews in a card file system, the tasks of the RV and its district branch offices also included the setting up and maintenance of assembly camps for the deportations.[117] The Jews summoned for deportation were concentrated there under conditions of internment. In the camps, the tax and Gestapo officials took care of final formalities before the large-scale transports were put together for departure. In order to render a large metropolis such as Berlin "Jew-free," the Gestapo required facilities with a large capacity, unlike the situation in the smaller towns, where halls, restaurants and inns, bowling alleys, or other large buildings could be utilized for a short term when needed: in Berlin, assembly camps available on a permanent basis were needed.

The Jewish Community there was initially ordered to convert the synagogue on Levetzowstrasse into central emergency housing with a capacity for one thousand persons, who were then to depart from the city in a train transport. When those summoned arrived at the appointed time, they first were required to wait in the courtyard until their turn for processing in the foyer. There they were ordered to hand over money, jewelry, and any food in their possession. The Gestapo then inspected their luggage in another room. As a rule, the Jews summoned to the camp then stayed there for one to two days. Mattresses were available only for the elderly and the frail; the others had to make do with the benches and chairs in the synagogue. In the first deportations, the children were kept in the camp but separated from their parents.[118]

The Jewish Community fed the inmates in canteen kitchens; it provided marshals, medical personnel, and a kindergarten teacher. Prior to the first deportations, Philipp Kozower called together the department heads and informed them that some of the staff employees would soon be deployed in special service as marshals. He threatened consequences for those who wished to "shirk" from this duty.[119] Once the marshals had been appointed, he briefed them on their work, stressing that the Jewish Community regarded it as a service of honor to ease the fate of their emigrating fellow Jews by means of a personal effort.[120] This auxiliary personnel—at a personal risk to themselves—was in fact often able to provide some relief or prohibited emergency services to those interned, such as notifying their relatives, smuggling medication into the camp, etc. But they did not have any possibility to assist them in any attempt to escape, because the Gestapo itself had taken over camp surveillance and security, the searching and "sifting through" of baggage, the stamping of ID cards, and transport to the railroad station;[121] Jewish Community employees only assisted.

A physician summoned for deportation, Dr. Edmund Hadra, did not think that Mosse's coworkers, the marshals, and Kozower, who supervised operations inside the synagogue, showed much empathy. On the contrary, they had looked on at what was happening to their fellow Jews, seemingly unmoved, and Kozower had "quite callously" rebuffed him.[122] It probably can be doubted that there was such a general level of indifference. Yet perhaps specifically in these first deportations, the Jewish assistants "steeled themselves" against requests and appeals, which in any event they were enjoined from acceding to. Nevertheless, Edmund Hadra commended the quality of the food being provided, and the former banker Karl Loewenstein, deported in November 1941 to Minsk, remarked on a positive note that all deportees were given cooking utensils as a gift from the Jewish Community.[123] Both individuals and their baggage were given transport numbers in the assembly camp, and their passports were marked with an evacuation stamp. Coworkers of the Jewish Community staff checked their declarations of assets,[124] on the basis of which the head of regional finance later confiscated the assets of the deportees for the benefit of the German Reich.

Over the course of a year, recipients of deportation orders proceeded to the synagogue assembly camp on Levetzowstrasse. When, later, they no longer obeyed orders to report so willingly and trustingly, as in the case of the initial deportations, they were brought to the camp under escort. Although the duration of stay at the camp at the start averaged one to three days, Jews interned there later on sometimes had to wait for weeks or even months for a deportation transport. Additional smaller camps fulfilled special purposes: for example, one was for "prisoners in protective custody," who as former combat veterans or members of mixed marriages were able to claim Theresienstadt as deportation destination; other camps served Jewish forced laborers as internment facilities from which they went to their places of assigned work until their deportation. Thus, Jewish Community facilities on Gerlachstrasse, Auguststrasse, Gormannstrasse, Johannisstrasse, and Kleine Hamburger Strasse were for a time converted into assembly camps for Berlin Jews.

In October 1942, the Gestapo ordered the Jewish Community to convert and equip the synagogue on Levetzowstrasse and the home for the aged on Grosse Hamburger Strasse to accommodate twelve hundred to fifteen hundred persons each. Subsequently, the assembly camp on Grosse Hamburger Strasse, now expanded into a prisonlike facility, replaced the synagogue on Levetzowstrasse as the central assembly camp in Berlin. It also accommodated a Gestapo office on the premises. Up to the spring of 1944, Jews were interned at this facility until deportation.[125]

From the summer of 1943, after all "full Jews" had been deported except for so-called *Geltungsjuden* and Jews in mixed marriages, a central assembly camp was set up on Schulstrasse, located in a section of the Jewish Hospital. The hospital was directly under the control of the RSHA. The assembly camp on Schulstrasse would remain in existence until liberation in May 1945.[126]

Another New Task: "Collecting Deportees"

But let us return to the events in the autumn and winter of 1941: the greater majority of Berlin Jews initially obeyed the written instructions from their representatives to report to the assembly camp with a pre-scribed limited amount of travel baggage. An instruction sheet from the Jewish Community informed them about "suitable travel clothing," the correct prescribed manner of fastening the "Jewish star" on this apparel, baggage permitted and prohibited, and about possibilities to deposit personal documents with the Community.[127]

The Gestapo soon changed the procedure in the transports. Gestapo officials, accompanied by assistants working for the Jewish Community, now picked up and escorted the Jews to the assembly camp. The Community employees helped them to pack and then transport the baggage. Siegmund Weltlinger—who, influenced by Heinrich Stahl, had chosen to stay on in Germany although he had the possibility to emigrate to the United States via Great Britain[128]—later reported that opinions on this "were divided. The predominant view was that it was better for the Jews to be picked up by their own people, because they allowed more time, and an opportunity to conceal some belongings."[129] Weltlinger personally declined to participate in such operations, and went underground in 1943, when Moritz Henschel attempted to order him to take part in the "Factory Operation" and purportedly threatened to report him to the Gestapo if he refused. Among the functionaries, Weltlinger's behavior remained an isolated exception, first because in connection with the larger-scale "operations" (arrests after the arson attack on the exhibition "the Soviet Paradise," the "Community Operation" in 1942, the "Factory Operation" in 1943), no staff member of the Jewish Community could refuse to participate in these special obligatory duties. Second, unlike members of the RV, the functionaries generally did not flee into hiding and go underground; most remained at their post until they themselves were deported.

In the autumn of 1942, that is, one year after the beginning of the mass deportations, the system of Jewish marshals was fundamentally re-structured: Alois Brunner, head of the Vienna Central Office for Jewish Emigration, was sent with his team, as mentioned, to replace the Gestapo personnel in Berlin entangled in a corruption affair, and likewise to ac-celerate the deportations according to his Vienna model. He had the as-sembly camps restructured into prisons. A new Jewish camp commander, the former principal of the Jewish Boys' School, Max Reschke, ruled with an iron fist, especially if escape attempts were involved.[130] Contempo-raries stressed his "exemplary order" and "quasi-military" bearing, such as when he had the marshals assemble in formation after many hours on the job.[131]

Now the Jewish Community was only able to exercise a slight influence on how Jews were collected from their homes and the internal organization of the assembly camps; it was only permitted to set up a new medical service, and had to cover the expenses for everything. The assistants mutated into "collectors" (*Abholer*).[132] One of them, Hermann Samter, who had been "released" from his job at the *Jüdisches Nachrichtenblatt* and actually had to consider himself lucky to still be allowed to remain on the staff of the Jewish Community as an *Abholer*, described this activity as "the worst thing ... you could imagine. ... It is awful, even if you tell yourself that you can still help the people a bit as soon as the (Gestapo) official has left."[133] Between forty and one hundred "strong and capable men" were now deployed in the assembly camps along with the "regular marshals."[134] They had to accompany the Gestapo personnel, but often were required to "process" entire apartment buildings, doing this on their own "without officials."[135]

Not all deportees considered it positive or helpful to be collected by fellow Jews. For example, a Berlin Jew characterized the "collectors" as a "Jewish Gestapo, i.e. hired Jewish scum, despised by all Jews," and accused them of picking up and escorting their own "racial comrades" from their homes in order to elude the prospect of "certain death" in Poland.[136]

Two Jewish guards (*Wachhabende*, in effect "senior marshals") divided up and assigned the marshals and "collectors" for duty, while in terms of command chain, they were subordinate to the Gestapo. All were considered liable for any infractions: "it is necessary by all means to prevent people from going underground, and the functionaries are personally liable for this."[137] Plans for escape were to be reported to the "supervisory authority."[138] What originally had been conceived as a form of assistance for the "better and more gentle" implementation of Gestapo orders, namely, the use of Jewish Community assistants, had now developed into an effective tool of the Gestapo. The "collectors" were, along with the camp personnel, generally the last Jewish "office holders" the deportees had any contact with, and whom they remembered as representatives of the RV, if they survived.

These "collectors" were now given daily lists of buildings or streets with the names of Jews, and after a day's work had to report the "actual number" collected and the "head count" or target number for the day. "In the event of failure" to meet their daily quota, they faced possible incarceration in a concentration camp. If units of officials and marshals did not find their victims, the Jewish marshals were required later to "check the apartments at intervals of one to three days during the evening hours. This control measure should be taken independently by the collection service and a report submitted."[139] In other cases, they were instructed to wait in darkness in the apartment until the residents came back home. Occasionally they were also ordered to assist the manhunt units, the notorious Jewish *Greifer* (snatchers).[140]

The fourteen-day reports of the "collectors" indicate that more and more Jews tried to elude deportation. One illustrative example: the report of 16 December 1942–2 January 1943 notes that 1,339 persons had been "processed." Of these, the "collectors" had only found 807 at the premises where they were registered. The report states that 362 were "not located," and 70 were listed as "moved to an unknown address," 56 with "false address," and 44 were declared to have "disappeared."[141] The 532 missing persons were grouped under different categories. In this way, the fact that they had eluded seizure was given a patina of something temporary, and the number of those who were reported as having "disappeared" appeared to be smaller. The "collectors" evidently endeavored to avoid creating the impression in the eyes of the Gestapo that they had indeed "failed" in their appointed task. The "collectors" had already been included in the "basic survey" mentioned above, because 1,607 Jews had not submitted a registration slip and the marshals now had to investigate their whereabouts.[142]

Jewish contemporary witnesses report both about marshals who despite being personally at risk assisted them to escape, as well as marshals they described as "scum," who added a bit of nastiness to their sad duty so as to relish a fleeting moment of power in the face of their general impotence.[143]

Other Supplementary Assistance: Postal Services

In addition to their tasks as described above, the RV district branch offices and Jewish Communities were ordered to specify a Jewish transport supervisory team for the individual deportations; it was responsible for the orderly step-by-step implementation of the process of deportation. In each carriage of the train, a marshal, wearing a special armband, was charged with maintaining "law and order" during the journey, and to ensure that the compartments were cleaned after arrival. A doctor or paramedic was also assigned to this transport team.[144]

The first two deportations from Berlin left the assembly camp headed for Łódz. For several months, postal correspondence was still received from there. The RV was permitted by circular letter to announce how relatives and friends remaining in Berlin could obtain the addresses of the deportees, and what regulations were binding for remittances of money and the sending of gift parcels.[145] But in February 1942, the RSHA ordered a prohibition on postal correspondence, referring to the excessively large number of letters that had been previously sent as a reason for the ban. However, the sending of money and gift parcels was permitted to continue and would be provided with receipts.

By contrast, there were no signs of life from the subsequent deportation destinations of Minsk, Kovno, and Riga, except for those instances when individual deportees were able to find a possibility to send clandestine news back home via soldiers, policemen, or employees of the civil administrations. Attempts by those remaining in Germany to write to these areas also proved abortive: letters were officially not sent on, because the army postal service was not to be burdened with this task. The RV, which also was not permitted to maintain contact with the ghettos, was instructed to convince its members to halt any contact through correspondence, although this ultimately was not in the power of the RV to regulate.[146] Remittances of money and gift parcels to (forced) "migrants" (*Abgewanderte*) in these destination areas were also prohibited.[147]

Social Work as Exemplified in Care for Children

After her liberation from Theresienstadt in 1945, Martha Mosse reported that the Jewish functionaries in 1941/1942 could not agree on whether they should try in particular to protect the elderly or the very young from deportation.[148] They did not succeed with either group, yet representatives in the RV and those active on the ground made great efforts to care for both these categories, and most especially for the very young. As already underscored, caring for groups in need of special protection was a central motive for the Jewish functionaries to stay on in Germany. Nonetheless, under the conditions of Nazi rule, even such necessary work tended to act against the interests of those who were to be protected. This will be illustrated here in a little-known instance: provision of care external to school for Jewish children who after the November 1938 pogrom were no longer allowed to attend state schools and nurseries.

In the 1930s, in view of the mounting exclusion of the Jews, the Jewish functionaries in the Reichsvertretung had placed great value specifically on the education of Jewish children. They had a binary approach to this: on the one hand, they sought to send as many children as possible into safety abroad. But as long as the children lived in Germany, they were to be educated so as to be "secure" in their Jewish identity, and despite all deprivations, they should develop a sense of pride in being Jews. They were to be prepared to "engage in and successfully cope" with the anticipated and particularly difficult struggle of life.[149] Ultimately, after all, children symbolized the future of the Jewish people.

At the beginning of the 1940s, the Jewish functionaries (now in the Reichsvereinigung) had not in any way abandoned these aims, yet already before the beginning of systematic deportations, they had to step back in their efforts as the Nazi state imposed ever-increasing demands and constraints on the organization. The number of children attending the institutions of the RV mounted steadily. On the one hand, the Jewish leaders had to create options for their care; yet on the other hand, the RV was being forced, depending on orders, to steadily reduce the size or close down day care centers and nurseries, to economize on expenditures and personnel, and to vacate buildings.

In Berlin, the problems fused in magnified intensity. In 1939, the aging Jewish population in Germany still had some 15,000 children up to the age of 15, of which approximately 10,000 were of compulsory school age.[150] When the systematic deportations began in October 1941, 2,446 children were attending Jewish schools.[151] A large proportion of them spent the afternoon in nurseries, and more than 1,000 still not of compulsory school age were attended to in day care centers. Some 300 children lived in foster homes and more than 600 in children's homes.[152]

One of the reasons why children who before had spent the afternoon at home were now being supervised, cared for, and fed in institutional facilities was because the German Jews (males aged fourteen to sixty years, females aged sixteen to fifty) from May 1940 on were required to perform forced labor. The average number of conscripted working hours for men was fifty to sixty per week, for women and youth forty-five to fifty-five. The RV was ordered to provide care for the children during the hours that their parents were absent.[153] The Berlin Jewish Community, like the Jewish Communities elsewhere on a smaller scale, had to accommodate and provide care for the children of school age from noon on in nurseries and care centers, and take care of youngsters not yet of school age for the entire day in day care centers. To cope with this, it expanded the capacity of its institutions to the extent feasible; however, in 1940, facilities were already filled. Meanwhile, the need continued to steadily mount as the workloads for their parents were increased.[154] In addition, the day care centers and nurseries had to extend their operating hours during the week in the winter 1940/1941, because the schools had begun teaching in shifts due to a lack of coal for heating. The nurseries and care centers now opened their doors early in the morning, and then also six days a week, due to the required labor deployment of the parents on Saturdays as well.[155] Soon enough, the functionaries in the Berlin Jewish Community were faced with the necessity for developing new admission criteria for vacancies in facilities, and the need to reduce expenditures and locate other options for financing. In this process, they were simply not permitted to revise and restructure their budget. Rather, they had to seek approval from the RSHA via the channel of the RV for each and every individual item on the budget. The RSHA obligated them to provide care, yet reduced the financial means that could be allotted for this. Thus, as an emergency measure in April 1941, the day care centers, nurseries, and other care centers initially released all children who had only one parent deployed at forced labor. This was followed by hikes in fees and cuts in personnel.[156] Initially, there had been one trained kindergarten teacher for every twenty-five children under care; now unpaid and unskilled personnel replaced the educators.[157]

At the same time, the care provided to the children changed fundamentally. Many tasks that the parents had previously taken on were now impossible to handle due to time restrictions, for example, if their start of shift clashed with the opening and closing times of the facilities. Along with their deployment in conscript labor (mainly in the armaments industry), the parents also had to adhere to very brief prescribed hours for shopping allotted to the Jews. It is clear from reports that for this reason, "teenage helpers" picked up most of the children at home, where they first helped to get them dressed and prepared their breakfast. In the evening they brought the children back home. In the case of children at day care nurseries, they oversaw the daily homework and ensured that their passing on to the next grade was not endangered. The "teenage helpers" accompanied children to individual medical examinations, arranged orthopedic gymnastics groups when necessary, and made sure that the children were able to get outside into the fresh air. If possible, they accompanied them to the children's film presentations of the Kulturbund

If, due to measures of economy or expropriations of buildings, facilities were dissolved or merged, in most cases this resulted in longer travel distances for the children. If they arrived unaccompanied, they were defenseless, and subjected to insults, abuse, and physical attacks, especially after the obligation to wear the "Jewish star" for all Jews age six and above had been introduced in September 1941.[158]

In addition, in the years 1939 to 1941, the composition of the children's groups was constantly changing as a result of restructuring in the facilities and emigration, which until October 1941 was still possible. This depressed the children and increased their anxieties, since they repeatedly had to bid farewell to close friends, teachers, and other individuals they trusted. The separations, losses, and the resultant fears and insecurity rendered teaching and learning all the more difficult.

The kindergartens and nurseries themselves were hardly protective spaces for the children, because the Gestapo would burst in and check these facilities on a regular basis. The former kindergarten teacher Lieselotte Pereles reported after the war that she had been repeatedly summoned and questioned about the books she gave the children to read, the songs she taught them, and what topics were discussed at the evening meetings with parents.[159] Pereles worked in a day care facility with an attached nursery housed in adjoining rooms of the synagogue on Thielschufer (to-day Fraenkelufer) in Kreuzberg; the synagogue had in the meantime been shut down as a place of worship. In 1941, the Gestapo seized rooms in this building for a branch office. In addition, the RV had to store valuables in the synagogue: furs, electric appliances, bicycles, and other items that Jews had been forced to hand over. The storeroom was frequently inspected and looted by Gestapo personnel working in the branch office and personnel from other offices. Pereles noted that on such occasions, four or five SS men in uniform also liked to inspect the rooms of the day care facility.[160] They checked adults and children to see if they were wearing the "Jewish star" sewn properly on their clothing, the hygiene in the toilets, and whether certain foods prohibited to Jews were being secretly kept in storage cupboards.

The "question of the star" generally arose in the facilities. Especially in summertime, when the children were playing in the schoolyard without any outer garments, there was a danger that the Gestapo could suddenly arrive and complain about the lack of the star on a child's clothing in the playground. One director of a day care facility then filed a request with the Gestapo to allow the stars to be sewn on the left trouser leg, but this was declined. The kindergarten teacher Edith Königsberger arranged a code word with the children to warn them if an inspection was imminent.[161] This procedure entailed the risk that the children, if interrogated, might answer truthfully and reveal that they had been warned in advance.

This work was demanding for the educators for other reasons as well. In the years before, "suddenly, from one week to the next, a basic structure of [the children's] experience collapsed—and collapsed for them alone," as the American historian Deborah Dwork formulated in her study *Children with a Star*.[162] Jewish children had experienced being thrown out of school, non-Jewish friends had turned away from them; not only could their parents no longer provide them any protection, but they themselves were in need of much more of it. Even if mothers and fathers, the Jewish Community, and teachers and educators now offered them Jewish lifeworlds as a replacement, this "trauma of ostracism and expulsion" lay behind them, psychologically unprocessed, while the new Jewish world of experience repeatedly proved to be fraught with danger and unstable.[163] In her work as an educator, Edith Königsberger was confronted on a daily basis with the effects of this fundamental state of insecurity: "Each child showed himself or herself from their most difficult side. The [general] discomposure and nervousness were automatically communicated to the children." The children did not only react anxiously or especially in need of affection; they also had psychosomatic problems, and some were aggressive. The caregivers constantly had to expect that the children would live out their needs to let off steam by making noise, to defend themselves, or to be destructive, contrary to the constant warnings given them. This was understandable yet also dangerous for the Jewish institutions and their devoted personnel. In particular between October 1941, when the mass deportations began, and June 1942, when the Jewish school system was liquidated, there were frequent cases of refusal to attend school. The senselessness of striving for good grades, working for a diploma that was no longer possible to obtain, was obvious to all. Edith Königsberger recalls that the children often cut classes and did not do their homework. When she confronted an eleven-year-old boy, he only asked, justifiably: "What for?"[164]

From October 1941 on, there were significant changes in the makeup of the children's groups as a result of the deportation transports. To be sure, the Gestapo initially still tried to deport families together in the large-scale deportations, and in the beginning often left aside several persons from a family if one member was deemed unfit for transport. But beginning in 1942, Gestapo personnel repeatedly showed up at institutions for children when transports were imminent. Lieselotte Pereles later testified in court:

> It reached the point where they [the Gestapo] selected children of any age to fill up the transport lists, in particular orphans and children in foster homes, or did a selection based on a list of specific children whose parents had already been collected for transport ... Every time the SS men appeared, the children had to stand up and remain silent. Almost nothing was said on these occasions, [the SS was] only pointing and gesturing.[165]

The day care centers and nurseries had thus finally lost their function as a space of protection.

Children who had been baptized—but who were still considered Jewish in terms of the "racial" ideology of the National Socialists—were confronted with more serious problems of identity. A number stemmed from families that were second-generation Protestants or Roman Catholics and had no connection with Judaism. Others came from Jewish families that had arranged to be baptized as a measure of protection against persecution (some Christian clergy had violated prohibitions on conducting these baptisms).

If these children had been classified as "full Jews" or *Geltungsjuden*, they would have been required after 1938 at the latest to attend Jewish schools and corresponding nurseries. Initially, one possible solution was the four-grade Family School for Non-Aryan Christians that the pastoral office of the Protestant pastor Heinrich Grüber had established in 1939 in Berlin.[166] Conceived for 90 children, initially some 50 were admitted, and later 120 children of compulsory school age were taken in. The RV, which had been given responsibility for the schooling of Jewish children, bore half the expenses, while the other half was financed by the parents or by scholarships. Pastor Grüber's office provided the teachers; the RV had no influence on their selection, nor on the religious instruction imparted there. In addition, the school director, Margarete Draeger,[167] was connected with the Swedish Mission to the Jews, a circumstance Moritz Henschel criticized.[168] Due to a deteriorating financial situation in the spring of 1941, the RV in any case was unable to continue financing the school. Eichmann decided that the pupils had to transfer to a Jewish school, but could be instructed there in special classes. Thus, beginning in October 1941, the 98 remaining pupils attended the Jewish Boys' School as a "tolerated minority within a persecuted minority,"[169] until that school was dissolved.

Let us leave aside the question as to whether the Christian churches should have had to continue to organize support for the "Christian non-Aryans" and cover its financing, and whether they were not perhaps creating new conflicts for the pupils, who were only baptized as a pretense, by their decidedly Christian education. It is arguable that the Family School nonetheless provided these children—who felt ostracized and emotionally distraught, both in other social spheres *and* inside the Jewish community—with a stable framework, within which they were able to establish relations and friendships with their peers. One illustrative example was the experience of Horst Gessner, born in 1928. He attended the Family School from 1940 to 1942. His Christian father had converted to Judaism in 1926 when he married Horst's Jewish mother, and Horst was later also a member of the Jewish Community. In 1938, both the father and son formally resigned from the Community in order to avoid measures of persecution. Horst was baptized as a Protestant on 15 May 1938. But neither his formal resignation from the Community nor baptism changed his "racial status" as *Geltungsjude*. Moreover, not only the regime regarded him as a Jew; his mother likewise insisted that her son accompany her to the synagogue, that he wear a skullcap, etc. Like in numerous mixed-marriage families, the dividing line also split the relatives in the family: the majority of Christian relatives broke off contact, and the Jewish relatives had in any case frowned on the marriage of his mother to a Christian convert to Judaism. Gathered together in the Family School were pupils who all had a similar background. In an interview conducted some sixty years later, Horst Gessner could barely remember any details of the instruction there, and recalled only a bit about his teachers. But he stressed how important for him throughout his subsequent life the stable relations that he was able to establish with peers during his two years at the school were: "because we certainly were welded together, not only by our age, but through the common experiences we shared."[170]

In June 1942, there were still 1,601 pupils in Berlin attending Jewish schools (i.e., 773 had already been deported) when the RV was ordered to shut down the schools.[171] In a circular letter, it instructed the Jewish Communities and the RV district branches about how they should proceed: children over fourteen years were to be registered for forced labor, younger children should be deployed at unskilled labor in Jewish institutions, for example, as messengers, picking weeds in cemeteries, helping in households and canteen kitchens, taking care of other children, assisting in cleaning children's homes and nurseries, or helping with sewing and needlework. The now dismissed teachers would be permitted to continue to supervise them, but were not allowed to teach them. Children between the ages of six and eleven were to continue to be cared for in Jewish institutions, and a fee should be paid for this. Attempts by Protestants and Catholics to accommodate the children from special classes in their own institutions so that they did not "return" to Judaism proved abortive from the start.[172]

In general, parents remained responsible for the education of their children, but the staff workers of the Jewish Community were to check on the presence of the children. "Unexcused absences" would result in the "necessary conclusions."[173] In Berlin, 625 pupils had to be accommodated in day care centers, 372 of them for the entire day.[174]

There as elsewhere, the Jewish cemetery offered to occupy the children at smaller kinds of tasks and thus make it possible for them to be active out in the fresh air, since for years they had been banned from entry to sports grounds and playgrounds. In retrospect, the children and youth who survived the Nazi period had very different views of their deployment on the cemetery grounds. While some stressed the depressing direct contact with death there (they also were put to work digging the graves for Jews who had committed suicide),[175] others enjoyed the work out in the open, tending to flowers in the cemetery nursery garden, and the fact that the Gestapo generally kept its distance from this particular facility.[176]

The "Factory Operation" in February 1943, when the Jewish forced labors and their families, previously exempted from the transports, were deported, forcibly thinned out the ranks of the "youthful helpers": of sixty, only three remained on deployed at the cemetery. Together with Rabbi Martin Riesenburger, they maintained the cemetery grounds, and the young Jews followed the coffins at funerals in the procession of mourners, often the sole persons to pay their final respects to the deceased. Liselotte C., one of the helpers, reported in retrospect, still with a sense of great pride, that they had been allowed to assist in concealing and thus rescuing a truck filled with Torah scrolls in the foyer of the waiting hall.[177]

After the schools were liquidated, the younger Jewish children were sent to day care centers. In September 1942, there were still ten such facilities in Berlin, with approximately 1,100 children.[178] Yet already in October 1942, in the course of the "Community Operation" involving more than 800 coworkers of the Jewish Community staff and their families, a large proportion of the kindergarten teachers and day care providers were deported to the East. The head of the welfare department of the Berlin Jewish Community, Dora Silbermann, had refused to name coworkers who were nonessential, and offered instead to join the transport herself, but that proposal was rejected. After the schools had been dissolved, the regime pushed on with liquidating the institutions for provision of care to children. Kindergarten teachers and their superiors were put on the deportation lists. Hannah Karminski, a teacher trained in Froebel pedagogy, and director of the department of general welfare in the RV, was also among them. Gertrud Staewen, a Protestant caregiver and member of the Confessing Church, passed on a story about Hannah Karminski. It is one of the rare indications that the Jewish functionaries were still secretly seeking to give the children consolation and confidence based on religion. As Staewen narrated, the afternoon before her deportation, Hannah discussed and "interpreted" the story of God speaking to Abram, talking with children who were likewise slated for deportation. She read the words, "Get thee out of thy country, and from thy kindred, and from thy father's house, unto the land that I will show thee" (Genesis 12:1), explaining this to her young wards in the sense of the line from Job (36:16): and God "allured thee out of distress into a broad place, where there is no straitness,"[179] thus stressing the prospect, in biblical discourse, that they were going to a spacious place free from restriction.

Only a very few went to their deaths consoled in such a way with a prospect for return to God and divine care. The head of the children's day care center on Greifswalder Strasse, who was in the assembly camp together with the remaining children of her day care facility, the adjoining children's home, and the children from the Auerbach orphanage, smuggled a desperate secret letter out to a friend shortly before their transport to the East: "Dear R., it's crazy and bewildering. The children (orphans, already more than 100), are already perishing here.... We're starving, sleepless, and without any dreams."[180] In December 1942, most of the still remaining open institutions for children were liquidated.

However, the educators were not only providing care for children in the kindergartens and day care centers; some were also drawn on into active involvement in the organizing of the deportations.

When the large-scale deportations began in October 1941, and the Gestapo had established the former synagogue on Levetzowstrasse as the central assembly point, the Jewish Community set up separate canteens for children and adults. Small children were housed in the synagogue in a separate room under the care of kindergarten teachers.[181] Out of necessity, the trained kindergarten teacher Edith Königsberger took over this difficult task in connection with twelve transports, since the Gestapo insisted that only a trained and licensed kindergarten teacher was permitted to do this work.[182] She was given the white armband of a marshal and allowed to move freely throughout the building. Edith recalls:

> The official sent me to the "children's room" in the synagogue's former marriage hall. Now it was full of field cots piled with straw mattresses, and a few tables and benches in the middle. … The air in the room was fetid and hard to bear. The small room had a capacity for 20 children at the most, but now there were more than seventy. On top of it, the Gestapo had crammed in all of the elderly and frail people as well. It was forbidden to open the windows. … We tried to keep the children busy. A dreadful future awaited them, and some of them already guessed this. But what would have been the use to tell them the truth? … The older ones wanted to be left alone. They thought about these new things they could not explain. The smaller ones were crying for their mothers, from whom they had been cruelly separated in the same building.[183]

Mothers were reunited with their children only shortly before the transport was to depart.[184] Fearing spies and informers, marshals like Edith Königsberger dared only to help the prisoners whom they knew personally.[185] Later on, when the assembly camp was made secure along prison lines, they had to desist even from these small attempts to ease the deportees' misery.[186]

In 1942/1943, inclusion in the process of deportation went a step further: kindergarten teachers and nurses were made "collectors" and ordered to bring the children to the assembly camp. Thus, a nurse who had just turned twenty reported that in August 1942, she and her colleagues had been instructed to pick up foster children from their families for an imminent transport of orphans. Since the number of children from children's homes did not meet the quota figure for the deportation transport, the Gestapo had decided to include children from foster families. The young women were ordered to proceed in pairs to collect these children from their unsuspecting families. The arrival of these women triggered dramatic scenes, which they found almost unbearable.[187]

During the "Factory Operation," the Jewish Community instructed all staff workers in the welfare department, kindergarten teachers and nurses, to collect those children who had been left alone in the apartments of Jews who had been taken into custody for deportation, or who had remained behind with neighbors. They were then brought to their parents in the assembly camps and deported together with them. These efforts to care for the children were in a tragic sense "successful": as Hildegard Henschel later summed up with some satisfaction, there had been "no case where parents had not been reunited with their children."[188]

While for persons over sixty-five there was a special regulation for "transports of the elderly" to Theresienstadt, pregnancy and the need to care for children were not a valid reason to be exempted from deportation. Only if the time of birth coincided with the scheduled time for transport did the RSHA give mother and infant six weeks until their names were put on the next deportation list.[189] By the summer of 1943, all children deemed "full Jews" had been deported with their parents, or taken from foster homes and children's homes and transported "to the East," and the care facilities had been liquidated.

For two further years, there was a so-called *Kinderunterkunft* or "children's shelter" in the Jewish Hospital in Berlin.[190] Hilde Kahan, then on staff in the hospital, noted later:

> Those remaining were only the children, the *Mischlinge* or those whose data of descent had not been clarified. And we struggled on behalf of these people. In the main, they were children born out of wedlock. We did research on the Christian parent. ... Our welfare department procured all marriage and baptismal certificates. And armed with "proof of Aryan descent" of the Christian parents to the third generation, we fought at the RSHA for the continued right of survival of our half-Jewish children.[191]

Two sections in the Jewish Hospital, dubbed among Jews "children's mini-concentration camps" (*Kinderkazettchen*), cared for the "cases needing clarification" from the liquidated children's homes or the assembly camps, on average some eighty to one hundred children, who lived there sometimes for weeks or up to a year. Those aged fourteen and older had to perform forced labor externally, while the younger children were put to work helping around the hospital. The hospital's welfare department tried to motivate "Aryan" parents or relatives to take in the children at their homes, and thus to remove them from this zone of danger. Perils lurked because the last central deportation assembly camp, Schulstrasse, was also housed in the Jewish Hospital, and the Gestapo conducted surveillance checks of the hospital and the extensive hospital grounds regularly. For the welfare department, as the historian Stefanie Schüler-Springorum has noted, "the degree of kinship or sex of the 'rescuing' parent or relatives was immaterial."[192] Occasionally the efforts of the staff members resulted in success, but often the non-Jewish relatives shied away from taking in a "child with a star," and in this way coming to the attention of the Gestapo. Efforts by the Jewish caregivers to rescue the children were "always within the limits of the law," as emphasized by historian Rivka Elkin.[193] Only if the Jewish functionaries were able to prove that the children did *not* belong to them did the children have a chance of avoiding deportation. Still, when the soldiers of the Red Army occupied the hospital, they found ninety-four children there who had survived in the precarious protection of the *Kinderunterkunft*.

It is clear from RV documents, and also from the minute books of the Berlin police, that even under these deplorable and frightening living conditions, the children rebelled and sought to create a certain free space for themselves.[194] While some engaged in sexual contact early on (similar to adult behavior in the assembly camps),[195] the younger ones sought to break free: some registered against the will of their caregivers for labor deployment in order to get hold of a few more pennies than the meager pocket money they were allotted. And they undertook forbidden excursions into the city, where some, not wearing a star, were then stopped and apprehended by the police.[196] The adult supervisory personnel always had to bear ultimate responsibility for any youthful attempts to flee from the premises.

Thus, the extraordinarily great efforts by the female caregivers were ultimately not able to save the young from deportation. All they could do was try to make the situation somewhat more bearable and create small spaces of latitude in which children could live out their needs. Ultimately they even had to actively help to hand over children directly to the Gestapo, and to keep them quiet in the assembly venues. Only in "cases to be clarified"—in Nazi parlance, *Geltungsjuden* and "mixed-blood" *Mischlinge*—whose degree of "Jewishness" was still a matter of dispute, did the possibility exist of protecting them from deportation, and this likewise only if the indisputable proof had been brought that these children did *not* belong to the Jewish community.

The Limited Possibilities of the Reichsvereinigung to Influence the Deportations

Possibilities for the RV to exert some influence on the process of deportation proved from the start to be very limited. The Jewish functionaries were unable to have any influence whatsoever on the size and timing of the transports, and events after arrival in the ghettos. For a time, it was possible to have some impact on the practice of collection of the deportees and their stay in the assembly camps. Otherwise, they were able to intervene in individual cases if (1) guidelines had not been adhered to, (2) a potential deportee came under criteria for being sent to Theresienstadt, or (3) it could be convincingly shown that the person was unfit for transport. They could also turn to (4) bribery, and encourage relatives or attempt themselves to bribe Gestapo officials.

(1) From the first deportation on, the RSHA issued guidelines for every transport, without consulting with the RV, regarding which Jews were to be exempted from deportation in that transit.[197] It thus indirectly also specified the categories of those to be included. During the deportations of 1941/1942, those deferred from deportation were Jews in mixed marriages, foreign nationals (but not stateless Jews or Jews who had had Polish or Luxembourg citizenship), forced laborers in the armaments industry who had not been released for deportation by the Labor Office or the Armaments Inspectorate and their family members, and (initially) Jewish invalids aged fifty-five and older, Jews aged sixty-five and older, and World War I combat veterans. In November 1941, Reinhard Heydrich announced his desire to use the Theresienstadt ghetto—planned for the Jews of the "Protectorate Bohemia and Moravia" and to be constructed by them—simultaneously as an "old age ghetto" for German Jews. At the Wannsee Conference, this function was expanded to include a "preferred camp" for Jewish war veterans and Jews decorated in World War I.[198] Nonetheless, secret agreements were made between the RSHA and the Gestapo offices that stipulated that quite apart from the guidelines, the "biggest troublemakers" were to be included in the initial transports; moreover, no consideration would be given to Jews with wartime decorations and, "up to a certain percentage," members of the protected groups (such as the disabled, Jews sixty-five years or older, war veterans, Geltungsjuden and forced laborers) were also to be deported. The only Jews to be deferred were those with protection from superior Reich offices, so as to avoid protests.[199]

Martha Mosse was able to exploit this contradiction between openly announced guidelines given to the RV and secret supplements: if the Gestapo officials did not act in accordance with the RSHA guidelines for deportation, she was often able to arrange temporary deferments if she presented reasons in keeping with the instructions as to why a certain individual (and his or her family as well) should not be included in the transport. After the war, she pointed to the double-sided character of most of the Gestapo officials: on the one hand, they were "loyal bureaucrats"; on the other hand, they were "yet often amenable to the human side of things. So you could talk with them."[200] When Mosse put forward "objective reasons" (i.e., reasons as mentioned in the guidelines) against the deportation of specific individuals, she was generally listened to, although this became more difficult over the course of time.[201] What she did not openly state was that in each of these cases, another had to take the place of the person deferred. Thus, successful interventions did not lead to a reduction in the number of deportees in a transport—that is, for every "rescued" individual, there was someone who was deported earlier than planned. For some, such a temporary exemption provided them with time to go underground, while for others, it took such time away.

Mosse herself later pointed out that most of the deferments were only temporary, but were able to give those deferred some glimmer of hope, since they still assumed that the transports would "soon be halted." Nonetheless, despite authorized deferments, the Gestapo men included some of these Jews in the transports. For that reason, Mosse sent the notifications of deferment in writing to those exempted. She noted that the Gestapo respected such letters. In addition, she stated that there had been instructions "from higher level offices, such as the RSHA, senior ministerial officials or high-level party functionaries, to protect certain individuals," as, for example, in the instance of the former Weimar Republic minister Eugen Schiffer, born in a Jewish family converted to Protestantism, after minister Franz Schlegelberger and Johannes Popitz intervened. Some of these deferments, according to Mosse, actually proved permanent; others did not.[202] In addition, a list (now lost) deposited in the assembly camp, issued by Göring, protected some two hundred Jews, who today are not known by name, from deportation. The Gestapo was obliged to honor this protection. If it failed to do so, interventions also led to their release.

(2) The second possibility, namely, to exert influence on the deportation destination, did not yet exist at the time of the first large-scale transports. It is not known whether the Jewish functionaries had learned about the planned "old age ghetto" prior to a discussion arranged by Eichmann on 19 February 1942. Ten Jewish representatives from Berlin, Vienna, and Prague took part in this meeting, where Eichmann (according to Löwenherz in an annual report) informed them about the total deportation of Jews from "Greater Germany," and stressed Theresienstadt as deportation destination for Jews sixty-five and older, disabled war veterans, and Jews decorated for service in WWI.[203] It is also not known whether this differentiation for certain categories was due to the efforts of the Jewish leaders. In any event, Berthold Simonsohn considered it a great success for himself and his colleagues

> when we managed to achieve a decree that Jews over the age of 65, and certain privileged groups, such as disabled war veterans, mixed-blood *Mischlinge* and "persons with close Aryan kin" [*arisch Versippte*], along with their family members, would not have to embark on the journey to the East and Auschwitz, but rather would be taken to Theresienstadt, regionally and climatically a more favorable location.[204]

Hildegard Henschel later commented that this soon was regarded as "the dream of everyone threatened by evacuation," and Paul Eppstein saw Theresienstadt as "a possibility to save human lives over time."[205] Other functionaries were also relieved by the prospect of being able to send the more elderly and weaker Jews to this ghetto, where they would be taken care of. This then came about beginning in June 1942.[206] However, this differentiation, seen from today's vantage in any event, likewise proved to be ambivalent: it led the Jewish functionaries to believe that some social viewpoints could be taken into account; at the same time, when the mass deportations to Theresienstadt commenced, it finally shattered the hope that the deportations were "partial operations."

(3) The "examinations for transport fitness" introduced in the Jewish Hospital in Berlin and for bedridden patients at home had a certain calming effect on the Jewish functionaries and both the Jewish and non-Jewish population (insofar as the latter was in any way perturbed by thoughts about deportation). Jewish doctors decided whether a person summoned for deportation was physically fit for the journey or should be deferred for several months for reasons of health. The decision on whether the medical recommendation would be followed ultimately lay in the hands of the Gestapo,[207] although the opinion of Walter Lustig, later the hospital director, definitely also carried some weight. The Jewish physicians were under heavy pressure, as the doctor Lucie Adelsberger later described: she classified a man as being unfit for transport whom a younger doctor had thoroughly examined and declared able-bodied for deportation. Asked about the reasons for his decision, this doctor justified himself by saying that he had already been reprimanded for having deferred too many sick patients, and said that it was "me or him."[208]

These medical exams for fitness were carried out for about one year. Then the Gestapo halted this procedure, which from its perspective was in any case superfluous.

The Jewish functionaries were also unable to have any say when it came to the deportation of the sick from institutions and nursing homes. After Jewish mental patients had been murdered even before the large-scale deportations (see chapter 1), those not included in that operation were concentrated in the Jacoby Hospital and Nursing Home (Jacoby'sche Heil- und Pflegeanstalt) in Bendorf-Sayn under the trusteeship of the RV. This plan was only implemented in part; in the first half of 1942, there were still some 160 patients in other institutions when the RSHA began deporting mentally ill Jews from the hospital in Bendorf-Sayn. In February 1942, there were 167 male and 255 female patients there. They were attended to by 40 percent fewer medical staff than in comparable state institutions. In addition, the Jacoby Hospital, due to the closing of several infirmaries, had also been required to admit patients suffering from "dementia" and in need of particularly great care; in the closed ward, there were 368 seriously "disturbed" patients to attend to. In any case, the institution could only admit the most pressing and serious cases. At this juncture, Walter Lustig was still the representative responsible for health service in the RV, and on a number of occasions he had criticized the existing shortage of staff. Beginning in February 1942, the patients appeared on the Koblenz deportation lists. Lustig repeatedly pressed at the RSHA, both directly and via Paul Eppstein, to have doctors brought in on selection procedures for the potential deportees; after all, more than one hundred of these patients were classified as "dangerous and violent," and fifty were bedridden; over seventy patients, who otherwise were housed in a closed ward, required constant supervision. In the opinion of the doctors, only about fifty were fit for transport, and that only if any cause for excitement was carefully avoided. These objections were of no concern to the RSHA and the local Gestapo. Lustig's proposal for the RV to concentrate patients unfit for transport in one of the buildings, "based on the application of strict medical criteria," and to continue to care for them there was brushed aside. Without any medical examination and consultation—indeed, after the participation by doctors had been expressly denied—on 24 March 1942, 100 patients were included on one of the transports of 1,000 Jews each that had been ordered, sent to the Izbica ghetto. On 30 April, another 100 were transported to Krasniczyn, and on 19 June 1942 a train with 250 "stretcher patients" and some 80 doctors and nurses left Koblenz headed for Sobibor. The mental patients were crowded together, as Walter Lustig noted, "without regard for their mental and physical condition," with the personnel in nine freight cars that had been coupled behind onto the coaches with the other deportees; only 21 patients of foreign nationality or from mixed marriages were deferred and remained at the hospital. Eight patients were sent on 29 November 1942 directly to Auschwitz and murdered.[209] A total of 573 Jewish men, women, and children from Bendorf-Sayn are believed to have become victims of the Nazi death machine. The RV functionaries were powerless to ease their fate, postpone their deportation, or save them from murder.

Over the following two years, the usable buildings of the Bendorf-Sayn hospital remained empty. They were designated to be used as an alternative emergency facility if the Koblenz hospital was damaged or destroyed in the war.[210]

(4) One further precarious possibility to influence the deportation of individual Jews was bribery. In actuality, through bribes to Gestapo officials, it was possible to gain partial forms of relief, extending even to being included in a transport to Theresienstadt. The Gestapo itself conducted

investigations against "emigrant consultants" providing dubious services at the time of the deportations: they offered deferments or specification of a preferred destination in return for a bribe to Nazi officials.[211]

This kind of intervention came to an initial abrupt halt when Alois Brunner and his subordinate Gestapo staff arrived in October 1942 in order to replace the members of the Berlin Gestapo *Judenreferat* suspected of corruption, and to accelerate the process of deportation. Now there was a tendency to revoke the existing guidelines, allowing only conditional protection. Brunner was rarely amenable to interventions, and attempts at bribery also became pointless during the months he was there.

The Reichsvereinigung as Employer and a Protective Space for Functionaries and Staff

On 1 September 1941, there were some six thousand Jews working across the Reich in institutions of the Reichsvereinigung, including unpaid helpers and assistants.[212]

The leading Jewish functionaries had presumably operated on the assumption that they themselves, involved in the organization of the deportations, would remain protected from deportation. However, already during the first wave of deportations, the Gestapo office heads and directors of the *Judenreferate* demonstrated that they had no intention whatsoever to guarantee that this group of individuals could stay on in safety in the RV district branch offices or the Jewish Communities. When Eppstein informed the RSHA of this, it issued an order that the individual RV district branch offices should submit applications for exemptions to the RSHA via "their" Gestapo branch office.[213] The RSHA thus carried the farce to the extreme in that now those who had specifically selected the Jews to be deported were given the responsibility for deciding on their later possible deferment. Here the RV initially encountered no good will on the part of the authorities.

In March 1942, Eppstein complained again: he noted that several RV district branch offices had reported that a substantial number of their staff employees were on the lists for "migration."[214] Three days later he reported that coworkers from Frankfurt am Main, Halberstadt, Magdeburg, Munich, and Nuremberg were on the transport lists. The RSHA representative, Gutwasser, replied that although there had to be cuts in personnel, work as a whole must not be impaired. For that reason, Eppstein should inform *Obersturmführer* Nowak in connection with any doubtful cases.[215] Thus, Eppstein reported that Altmann (Königsberg), Hechinger (Munich), and Angerthal (Karlsruhe) were on the lists. He stressed that as a consequence, the "maintenance of the orderly administration of the

RV appeared to be at risk."[216] Two weeks later, senior staff in Essen and Düsseldorf discovered their names on the deportation lists. The RSHA then intervened and removed the names of Altmann, Hechinger, and Angerthal.[217] In April 1942, the RSHA dispatched a telegram of warning to the Gestapo branch offices:

> There are ever more cases where individual Gestapo branch offices are including virtually the entire office staff of the district branches of the *Reichsvereinigung der Juden in Deutschland* and the Jewish Communities in the ongoing evacuation operations. As a consequence of the loss of this personnel, the smoothly functioning continuation of the tasks assigned to the Jewish organizations and the appropriate liquidation [of the branch offices] are put at risk. Of course, Jewish functionaries should be evacuated in a corresponding relation to the number of the Jews initially deferred on the basis of the regulations on exceptions and the limitations in transport. But in most instances it is expedient, in your own interest!, for the present to exclude a number of suitable Jewish functionaries from the evacuation, until further notice, and/or to include these functionaries only in the final evacuation transport. This is appropriate in order to relieve the strain of the individual Gestapo branch offices and the staff members in dealing with the tasks assigned to the Jewish organizations, the smooth implementation of which is considered important. In cases of doubt, I request submission of a list, for my decision, of the functionaries included in evacuation and/or initially to be deferred from evacuation. (signed) Eichmann.[218]

However, this warning did not mean that the Jewish functionaries could now feel secure, because at the same time, several board members were arrested in Leipzig and Ludwigshafen.[219] In addition, in parallel with the transports, the RSHA also specified the respective cuts in personnel that became possible in the eyes of the RSHA as a result of the concomitant reduction in necessary effort and expenditures for administration and supplies.[220] It then was the task of the RV or the individual departments to report the nonessential "dispensable" staff who, if they were not transferred to another department, were included in the next lists for deportation.

The RV continued to employ the "Jewish officials" in its district branches and in the Jewish Communities, who already before 1939 had constituted the administration. The apparatus expanded on the level of the department heads and in the attached "enterprises" by addition of highly qualified personnel, individuals who had lost their position as civil servants in the wake of the Law on the Restoration of the Professional Civil Service of 7 April 1933. The RV offered them the possibility of continuing to perform qualified work in their former area of activity or in a new sphere. But over and beyond this, the RV saw itself as an organization that in its highly ramified apparatus could offer jobs for Jews who were deemed unsuitable for forced labor in armaments factories because of their age, state of health, or other reasons. In affiliated homes for the aged and the disabled, hospitals and infirmaries, cemeteries, kindergartens, and schools and canteens there were jobs for both skilled and unskilled personnel. The RV also sought to provide university graduates who had been banned from their professions the possibility of a post in the administration. As an employer, the Reichsvereinigung offered a regular salary, relatively acceptable working conditions, and protection from deportation for male and female employees and their families.

When the mass deportations commenced, the Berlin Jewish Community alone had a staff of some sixteen hundred employees.[221] The functionaries, that is, the board members and department heads in the RV, the Berlin Jewish Community, and the district branches, amounted to one hundred persons.[222] Additional employees worked in the institutions subordinate to the district branches and the Jewish Communities.

From the autumn of 1941, the new main task of the RV, namely, to take over diverse preparatory and organizational tasks in the deportations, went hand in hand with the liquidation of those departments that the RSHA now regarded as superfluous. Thus, the staff of the Kulturbund and those who had dealt with emigration in the broadest sense were now threatened with deportation. For that reason, the leading functionaries in the RV and the Berlin Jewish Community sought to incorporate these employees into jobs in departments that were expanding in conjunction with the deportation operations. It was then possible to designate them as indispensable for the smooth course of registration and rehousing, or for operations in the assembly camp.

In Martha Mosse's accomodation advice center, converted into a "migration" center (Abwanderungsstelle), employees of the liquidated Kulturbund, for example, were employed to clear apartments,[223] or teachers who had been dismissed because of the declining number of Jewish pupils were taken on by the center as staff. But now their salaries were paid via the newly created "special account W."[224] There was plenty of work: sequences of administration had to be documented, special tasks had to be taken care of, and, again and again, they had to comply with the orders of the Gestapo and the RSHA to provide statistics and graphic representations under extreme time pressure. Hildegard Henschel later spoke of a "well-organized madhouse."[225]

The strategy of maintaining the size of the staff and even expanding it if possible protected these employees from deportation, and provided them with paid employment (even if the RSHA ordered salaries to be steadily lowered). It also protected them from forced labor in armaments factories or plants vital to the war effort. In addition, this strategy confirmed the existential justification of the Jewish functionaries, who were directing a large, personnel-intensive institution dealing with the most diversified tasks and consequently in need of a knowledgeable management.

In the initial phase of deportation, it did not seem necessary to provide this proof. On the contrary: the Nazi state "privileged" the five leading Jewish functionaries. Their personal accounts were exempted from the security ordinance,[226] that is, they could freely dispose of their assets and current salary (in the framework of other restrictions). In addition, the RSHA held out the prospect for Eppstein of a raise in salary of three hundred RM. But he rejected that "in the interest of uniformity." Eppstein was not amenable to bribery. Instead, he obtained permission to deposit the money in a "'special fund E" ("E" for Eppstein) in order to provide remuneration to low-paid fellow workers for special tasks assigned and completed. In fact, he was able to dispose of cash in this fund according to his own discretion until he was forced to relocate to Theresienstadt, or rather was deported there, in January 1943.[227]

Even if employees on staff or in an executive post in the RV or the Berlin Jewish Community were offered a form of protection from numerous measures of coercion and immediate deportation, the everyday rounds of life under persecution often looked quite different. During checks in public transport or raids on the street or in apartment blocks, for example, to refer to one's employment at the RV did not prevent harassment or even possible arrest by the Gestapo. For that reason, corresponding ID cards were issued to the executives and employees of the RV and the Berlin Jewish Community.

The repeated instructions from the RSHA to reduce personnel confronted the RV with the problem of dismissing employees it had hired for social reasons, "yet whose work basically had no real value,"[228] as Martha Mosse later expressed it. Or, as an alternative, it had to grapple with the problem of sifting through and potentially reducing the ranks of senior personnel that the organization needed in order to maintain its structures for administration and provision of welfare. If the RSHA demanded a general reduction in personnel, but left it to the Jewish functionaries to implement this concretely, quite naturally, the management of every branch office and department tried to fend off these unreasonable demands. Martha Mosse was especially stubborn and successful in her struggle to maintain her personnel. Moreover, against the backdrop of the ongoing deportations, her arguments against losing members of her staff made sense. For example, in the summer of 1942, she refused any reduction in the size of her staff of ninety-five employees. She painstakingly enumerated their workloads.[229] Arthur Lilienthal, board member of the united board of the RV and the Berlin Jewish Community, angrily noted that the Berliners were demanding special treatment both for the "special account W" and for the budget of the RV: "The offices outside the capital are faced more or less with precisely the same problems as in Berlin (for example, Munich!), and Berlin must simply also learn to get along on less, because there's no alternative."[230] Compromises, as, for example, employing those coworkers dismissed from one department in a temporary job in another, but without hiring them on as regular personnel, helped to postpone their deportation (and that of their family members) only for a brief period.[231] After several cuts in personnel, which were conjoint with the ordered closing of certain social facilities and schools, and the ongoing deportations, in January 1943 the Berlin Jewish Community reported a staff of 838 employees.[232]

Thus, the protection a work contract with the RV had provided for a certain time now proved to be a double-edged sword: unlike an armaments plant, which was able to use the argument of its importance for the war economy in claiming a continued need for "its" Jews (until the spring of 1943, at least), employees of the RV were bereft of protection, and at the same time exposed as individuals when their spheres of work had shrunk, supposedly or in reality, and the RSHA called for cuts in personnel.

"Day after Day, Terrifying News": The Year 1942

In a very short time, under the pressure of the RSHA and the Berlin Gestapo, the character of registration, deportee collection, the organization of the assembly camps, and welfare work had changed, swiftly and radically. As early as the summer of 1942, only nine months after the deportations had begun, efforts by the Jewish functionaries to avoid worse developments and to offer some modicum of protective space proved largely abortive. The forced membership of the RV, its staff, and ultimately also its leaders were all endangered. Departments and entire areas of organizational work were now being successively dissolved and eliminated. In most cases, that liquidation was prefaced by the seizure and deportation of the respective department heads. After less than a year and a half, in January 1943, the RSHA in effect decapitated the RV by deporting its leading functionaries; it was then only a matter of a few short months until a decree in June 1943 ordered the formal liquidation of the Reichsvereinigung, in any event in its original form as established in 1939. All delaying tactics had proved useless, and through the deportation of its members, the organization itself had become superfluous in the eyes of the RSHA.

The "draft plan" of the Nazi leaders to have the deported Jews from the Reich "spend the winter" in the ghettos in the East had already taken into positive account the prospect that a substantial proportion of these Jews would perish under the harsh living conditions there, especially since few or no measures had been taken for their housing, food provisions, and basic needs. Thus, a portion of the deportees "resettled" there as *Eingesiedelte* actually did soon meet their death, victims of starvation, cold, disease, arbitrary punitive actions, or attacks by the local population. Probably in December 1941, a basic decision to also include the Jews from the German Reich in the mass murder was taken, sometime after the United States declared war on Germany on December 11. Prior to that, a Berlin transport to Riga with one thousand Jews had already been summarily liquidated on November 30 shortly after arrival, and a further five thousand Jews from Berlin, Munich, Frankfurt am Main, Vienna, and Breslau, initially sent to Riga, had been rerouted to Kovno (Kaunas), where they were shot by an SS *Einsatzkommando*. While the circumstances of these first mass executions of six thousand German Jews are known, the underlying reasons remain largely unexplained.[233]

That was because mass shootings were still the exception rather than the rule. When the postponed Wannsee conference finally took place on 20 January 1942, deportations were already in high gear. In Christian Gerlach's view, the significance of this conference lay less in decision making on the deportations and more in the intention accepted by participants to include the Western European Jews, especially the "Reich Jews," in the program of mass murder, along with deliberation on the future fate of the Jews in mixed marriages and the "mixed-blood" Jews (*Mischlinge*) in the Reich. In Gerlach's view, in the wake of the Wannsee conference, there was general consensus on inclusion of the German and Central European Jews in the systematic program of murder.[234]

The first deportation wave of twenty-four transports to the Litzmannstadt/Lódz ghetto was followed, until the end of February 1942, by a second comprising thirty-three transports to Riga, Kovno, and Minsk.[235] A total of some sixty thousand Jews were deported. In the process, the RSHA, the Reich Finance Ministry, the Transport Ministry, the Gestapo offices, the Reichsbahn (railway), and the local administrations developed their organizing schemes from concrete practice, as did the RV: it presented conceptions on organizing deportations to the RSHA in January 1942. In a tone of reassurance, Eppstein informed his "supervisory authority": "It is evident from the reports received from the Jewish Communities and district branches that after initial important differences in the organizing of the migration transports, now the only differences are largely local."[236]

The initial chaos in transport financing and other ambiguities had now largely been eliminated. What tasks the RV central offices, its individual departments, and district branches had to take over was now firmly established in the practice of deportations. Likewise, largely clarified were the questions regarding what funds for what "services" were transferred via specific accounts, who was responsible for what aspects of the process, and when Eppstein (or Kozower and Mosse in the case of Berlin) could or could not intervene. The aged and frail Jews, in most cases, were deferred for "residential relocation" to Theresienstadt. The Jews responsible for the retraining and *hachshara* centers, now subordinated to the system of forced labor deployment, endeavored to continue their Zionist work with youth under the altered conditions. Alfred Selbiger, who came from the Zionist organization Hechalutz but was now responsible for all training centers, did not express any despairing sense of resignation regarding his sphere of activity, but rather proclaimed "more work," that is, stepping up the effort.[237] But despite tireless exertions by the dedicated, 1942 brought no reassurance and calm; instead, "day after day, terrifying news."[238] There were far-reaching serious consequences following the measures against the RV functionaries and members after the arson attack by the Baum Group on the propaganda exhibition "The Soviet Paradise" in Berlin. In particular, this entailed the arrest of leading functionaries, the liquidation of schools and educational work, reductions in welfare work, and acceleration of deportations by Alois Brunner and his henchmen. This tightening of the screw peaked in the "Community Operation," involving the deportation of a large proportion of Berlin Jewish Community staff workers.

Repercussions of the Arson Attack on the Nazi Propaganda Exhibition "The Soviet Paradise"

On 18 May 1942, the communist-oriented resistance circle surrounding the young Jew Herbert Baum in Berlin engaged in an arson attack on the anti-Soviet propaganda exhibition "The Soviet Paradise" in the Berliner Lustgarten.[239] Twenty-two resistance fighters and their helpers, among them seven Jews and Jewish *Mischlinge*, were soon arrested and tortured. In several court proceedings, they were sentenced to death or committed suicide. The arrests of further group members dragged on into 1943.[240] Aside from two exceptions, none of the Baum group had had any contact with the Berlin Jewish Community or the RV. While the actual damage caused to the exhibition was minimal, the attempt had disastrous consequences for the Jews in Berlin and beyond: propaganda minister and NSDAP *Gauleiter* Goebbels took the attack as a pretext for obtaining permission from Hitler to arrest five hundred Jewish hostages and received the go-ahead to respond with executions if there were any new such incidents. In Berlin, Goebbels ordered the Gestapo to put together a "hostage list," which, inter alia, also included Jews with a previous "criminal" record. Shortly thereafter, on 27 May 1942, two Czechs dispatched by the Czechoslovak government in exile carried out an assassination attempt in Prague on Reinhard Heydrich, the Reich Protector of Bohemia and Moravia, to which he succumbed a week later. Although there was no causal link between these events, Goebbels ordered the prepared arrests of hostages that same day. While apparently some inmates were released from the assembly camp on Levetzowstrasse, 154 of those seized were sent to the Sachsenhausen concentration camp, where they were shot the following day. A total of 96 Jews, mainly of Polish origin, already incarcerated in the camp, were selected during the evening assembly formation and shot. Their relatives were summoned for deportation shortly thereafter.[241] A further 250 Berlin Jews were arrested on 29 and 30 May 1942 and sent to the Sachsenhausen camp. Of these "reprisal Jews," who were treated with particular brutality, more than half died there, and those remaining were murdered in Auschwitz in October 1942.[242]

While the Jews on the prepared lists were being shot, the RSHA took further hostages, mainly from the boards of the RV and the Vienna and Prague Jewish Communities. Baeck, Eppstein, Kozower, Kreindler, and Lilienthal from Berlin, Murmelstein and Löwenherz from Vienna, and Weidmann and Friedmann from Prague were forced to stand, their faces to the wall, waiting for hours for an explanation. They were finally told that for each of the five Jews involved in the arson attack, fifty hostages were shot. Should further events of this nature occur, a corresponding or even multiple number of Jews would be executed.[243] The Jewish representatives were ordered to inform their memberships in a suitable form.

On 30 May 1942, Eichmann told Eppstein he would soon provide him with the names of the 250 Jews shot. It was then left up to the RV to notify the relatives, soon themselves to be deported. That was to be done "best in the following manner: the transport head of the transport leaving on 5 June to Theresienstadt should be given the list of names of the relatives in a sealed envelope, so that notification can be carried out at the destination." Eichmann stressed that care should be taken to prevent suicides. In the following days, Eichmann and his subordinates revoked their instructions several times regarding various related matters: notification of the bereaved relatives, the exact wording of a circular letter to the district branches, and an article of admonition in the *Jüdisches Nachrichtenblatt* entitled "Verantwortlichkeit für die Gemeinschaft" (Responsibility for the Community).[244]

Eppstein actually received the first 154 names that very same day, and instructed the responsible district branch offices to pass on the names, along with the following text: "We hereby fulfill the sad duty of informing you of the passing of your relative on 29 May 1942."[245] In contrast with

Goebbels's first order to spread word of the shootings, the ultimately authorized text contained no reference to the cause of death.

In addition, the RV was ordered to check whether the arrested resistance fighters had had any contact with their organization. Eppstein's inquiries revealed that a kindergarten teacher arrested had been employed by the RV. He had her superior questioned a number of times, until she finally gave detailed information, stating that a roommate of the woman in question had burned certain papers belonging to her and her husband in the evening. Eppstein wrote a report for the RSHA. "OSTBF Eichmann takes note of this and has issued an order of strict secrecy regarding the entire report."[246]

In retrospect, it cannot be clearly determined whether these were sham activities designed to set the RSHA at ease or whether Eppstein had allowed himself to become a lackey of Eichmann under the extreme pressure in those days and the dangers threatening the Jewish community. In view of the young communists involved, the inquiries may have been somewhat easier for him than if an RV board member had been the focus of investigation. In general, the leaders in the RV, strict in their adherence to notions of legality, took a dim view of symbolic actions such as an arson attack.

In order to prevent a repetition of the situation, Leo Baeck sent Norbert Wollheim to speak with the resistance fighters. As a result of this discussion, there are two slightly differing statements in existence. According to Avraham Barkai, one participant in the talk, Richard Holzer, one of the communist resistance members who survived, rejected the appeal as pointless, since the group had after all already been destroyed. By contrast, Wollheim himself reported that the communists had no interest in what the Jewish leadership thought.[247] Barkai agrees with the view of Konrad Kwiet and Helmut Eschwege that given the mass shootings and their own experience as hostages during the murder operation, Baeck and the other RV functionaries were trying to prevent any further actions that might endanger the Jewish community.[248]

Arnold Paucker noted that the operation, "given its Jewish-communist connection, was not exactly a heroic deed."[249] In addition, he sees here a conflict of generations, or more precisely, the continuation of such a conflict that had stirred murky waters in the relations between assimilated and middle-class Germans of the parents' generation and their youthful and young adult offspring in the early years of the Nazi regime, from 1933 to 1938. At the time, their children had not wished to acquiesce to the status of second-class human beings, with no prospects for the future.

The overall impression that remained with the Jewish leaders, even if they were not directly implicated, was one of unmitigated horror: extremely repressive structures were part of their everyday life, but this incursion of open violence targeting hundreds of Jews was for them something new. Not just the board members, but their subordinate employees as well felt that at this dark juncture, a new and ominous quality to the persecution was emerging, as is expressed in texts written later on.

Two can serve as illustrative examples. Thus, a nurse noted that she had been unable to account for the arrests she had observed in the streets, but had huddled together with her colleagues terrified, and had trembled at every ring of the bell until the reason had finally seeped through: it was "the punishment for our !!! attack on the Soviet exhibition."[250] The exclamation points preserve their continuing sense of rage in the face of this collective wave of arrests. Alfred Selbiger, mentioned earlier, the last secretary of the Zionist Hechalutz in Germany and a department head of the RV, was reportedly hardly able to speak about the events that day, because "the monstrous thing was incomprehensible." Nonetheless, he pulled himself together and regained inner courage to continue the daily struggle for survival, girded by the slogan "just stay strong."[251]

Socially Acceptable Deportations? Destination Theresienstadt

In the heated atmosphere of those days in May 1942, Eichmann also sent the Vienna representative Löwenherz the news (after the announcement in February about the total deportation of Jews from "Greater Germany," no longer surprising) that the "total evacuation of the Jews from the Altreich, the Ostmark and the Protectorate" was now imminent.[252] In the meantime, the Czechoslovakian residents of Theresienstadt had vacated the small town, so that now the entire built-up area was available. The city was to be administered by a Jewish Council of Elders, and would be financed jointly by the RV and the Vienna and Prague Jewish Communities.[253] At this juncture, the hope that previous evacuations were "partial operations" was finally pronounced dead, if the Jewish functionaries had not long since laid the notion to rest. Instead, the RV was facing new practical work, namely, to draft home purchase contracts and to provide for equipping the town of Theresienstadt for its new functions.[254] In the Berlin assembly camp, separate "East rooms" and "Theresienstadt rooms" were set up.[255]

The accommodation advice center of the Jewish Community Berlin informed the future residents of Theresienstadt that they now had to vacate their present accommodations, notify the landlord, and relocate to an old people's home. They would be allowed to put their household effects at the disposal of the "home for the aged in the Protectorate," and it would be collected from their domicile without charge.[256] But the RSHA was particularly interested in accelerating the financial arrangement procedures in order for a person's assets to be transferred before relocation to Theresienstadt.[257] The whole process, in terms of particulars and time schedule, had to be coordinated and agreed upon with the individual Gestapo offices, the regional head of finance, and the banks.[258] The persons involved initially had "only" to remit payments in advance for support from their assets, based on anticipated life expectancy; but in August 1942, the RSHA issued a decree that their "entire movable assets" had to be transferred.[259] In Berlin, Martha Mosse's employees worked with this contract; then, to implement matters, Siegmund Weltinger and the lawyers on his staff were also called in.

In August 1942, the payments into the newly created "special account H" ("H" = *Heimeinkaufsverträge*, home purchase contracts) already amounted to 3.4 million RM, and by the end of that month, Eppstein calculated the total sum at 5 million. RSHA representative Friedrich Suhr held out the prospect of a rapid transfer of the funds to the Jewish Council of Elders.[260] The plan envisioned transfer from the "special account H" of 70 million RM in monthly installments of 8 million; in October 1942, 13 million RM had already been transferred.[261] Later the goal was raised to 90 million, and it was planned to "transfer the entire fluid assets of the RV for Theresienstadt."[262] But this did not occur. The RV financial expert Hans-Erich Fabian calculated in 1946 that some 109 million RM (elsewhere the figure mentioned is 107 million RM[263]) was transferred to Prague for the maintenance of Theresienstadt. Of this, after the end of the war, the Czechoslovakian government found 80 million still in the account, and confiscated it.[264]

The RV and its district branches sought to equip the ghetto by having bed frames, mattresses, tools, stocks from clothing storerooms, and equipment from the former training workshops sent on to Theresienstadt.[265] Although the RSHA had refused the Łódz ghetto permission to purchase the sewing machines of deported Jews that had been handed over to the authorities,[266] it was generous in regard to Theresienstadt when it came to the transport of goods. The costs for this were to be charged by the RV to the Prague Jewish Community, covered by the "Emigration Fund for Bohemia and Moravia."[267] It remains questionable whether all the goods actually reached the ghetto, for which lists had to be laboriously put together noting the value of the used articles. Some of the transports took months on end; many actual receipts of articles were never confirmed. To name but one example, the district branch in Nuremberg complained that in April 1942, on orders from the Berlin central office, it had sent a boxcar to Berlin full of machines, tools, and raw materials for Theresienstadt. This had been followed in December 1942 by a shipment of 498 kilos of clothes and linen, and in January 1943, 656 kilos of typewriters and duplicator machines. But it had never received confirmation that the shipments had indeed arrived.[268] Other ghettos were not permitted to be given provisions in this way.[269]

Beginning on 2 June 1942, hundreds of larger and smaller transports containing Jews who had previously been temporarily deferred were rolling toward Bohemia.[270] The RV as well as other participating offices were required, at substantial expense, to prepare and implement group transports containing fifty persons each. Perhaps this was the reason why only a portion of the Jews deemed eligible for this transport destination actually arrived there. Maybe the Gestapo offices simply made use of the fact that there was now a designated deportation destination—namely, Theresienstadt—to transport the elderly to other destinations in greater numbers than in the winter of 1941. In any event, of the approximately 13,400 Berlin Jews from the generation born between 1860 and 1877, some 5,000 persons, that is, in excess of one-third of this demographic, lined up silently to be included in transports heading to the East.[271]

Later, the RSHA increased the number of participants in the transports to Theresienstadt to one hundred, and scheduled large-scale transports from several cities in order to speed up the removal of the older Jews under intensive care. More and more, the directives targeted individuals who had to be cared for in nursing homes, so that the buildings could be "Aryanized" after their deportation. Hannah Karminski wrote a friend: "This work is no longer a source of any satisfaction: it now has hardly anything in common with what we used to understand as welfare work, and where it is a matter of human beings, and not real estate or money, liquidation is especially difficult."[272] It was not just the liquidation of the homes that proved heartbreaking, given that most of their residents were helpless and in need of protection. There was also the grim certainty that employees "laid off" were to be put on the transport list; now, for the first time, some were headed for the "preferential camp" (*Vorzugslager*) Theresienstadt.

Until September 1942, some thirty-eight thousand German and Austrian Jews arrived in Theresienstadt, deceived and deluded by the fraudulent character of the home purchase contracts they had signed; most were elderly and badly in need of care. At the same time, the RSHA repeatedly ordered transports from Theresienstadt to the extermination camps, and after a short time German Jews were also included in these transports. Initially, the RV learned nothing about this. When, from the summer of 1942 on, more and more Jews from the *Altreich* began arriving in Theresienstadt, the Council of Elders in the ghetto was restructured in October of that year. Six Czechs left and four Germans and two Austrians were named in their stead.[273] Among the first Jews deported to Theresienstadt was the former chair of the Berlin Jewish Community, Heinrich Stahl,[274] who was appointed by the SS as the deputy of Jakob Edelstein, the head of the Jewish Council of Elders. This news in turn reassured Jews not yet deported, as is reflected in correspondence. However, if Adolf Eichmann and Rolf Günther had been hoping to spark continual conflict in the Council of Elders by naming Stahl as a deputy head, that intention quickly evaporated, because on 4 November 1942, Stahl died, only a month after his appointment.[275]

There was a ban in effect on postal service for Theresienstadt from June to September 1942. When this was lifted, the RV central office in Berlin was ordered to function as the point of censorship and postal address for postcards from anywhere in Germany, along with postal replies from Theresienstadt. From the summer of 1943 on, mail from there, designated "from the camps," went on to the RSHA, which collected, sorted, and stamped these items. Mail to Theresienstadt was channeled by the RV to the RSHA. It is almost superfluous to mention that the RV had to cover the costs for postcards and stamps.[276]

The Daily Round of Work under the Threat of Arrest

Since the large-scale deportations over the course of 1941/1942 had drastically decimated the number of Jews remaining in Berlin and the *Altreich*, the RSHA ordered repeated new cuts in personnel and slashes in finances. The important area of welfare was forced to downsize personnel by dismissing 340 employees, "putting aside the previous guiding perspectives on welfare." In April 1942, after measures to cut costs, the Jewish Hospital fell far beneath the official level for proper staffing as specified in the public guidelines (instead of a ratio 1:4, it was now 1:5.5). The Jewish representatives were able to ward off additional dismissals of personnel by conjuring up the threat of possible epidemics, one of the few arguments the RSHA was receptive to. However, this resulted in orders to dismiss staff in the health sector in the district branches.[277] The report for the RSHA contains a list of the economy measures in Berlin: personnel for food provision and in children's day care centers were cut, children's homes were merged, some special homes were shut down, and the permanent asylum for the mentally ill was dissolved and its residents transferred to the Jacoby Hospital and Nursing Home in Bendorf-Sayn. According to the new regulations, there was to be one employee for every twenty-two residents in homes for the aged, and one employee for every twenty patients in nursing homes for the frail.

Despite mergers of facilities and liquidations, in Berlin alone in May 1942 there were still 15 homes for the aged and 3 asylums, with a total of 1,829 residents and a staff of 82. Three hospitals with 620 patients had a staff of 31 working in administration and 37 in patient care. After repeated cuts in personnel, the RV fell below the prescribed number of staff.[278] The situation differed in the district branches: even when the administrative directors applied the reduced Berlin patient/staff ratio, they reported a shortage of 50 employees, because they had taken in a number of patients from private nursing homes, and their staffing situation was significantly worse than in Berlin.[279]

The "Aryanization" of the real estate formerly owned by Jewish organizations and Communities and then transferred to the RV progressed at a steady pace in Berlin and elsewhere. According to regulations, and supervised by the RSHA, plots of land and buildings of large value changed ownership. Without going into this in any further detail, it should be noted that Jewish lawyers were engaged in working on these matters under extreme pressure in the corresponding departments of the district branches and the Berlin central office. On 27 November 1942, the director of the finance department in Berlin provided the "supervisory authority" with a brief overview. This furnishes a picture of the value of assets that the RV "owned,"[280] while at the same time grappling with a situation of mounting austerity: it was ordered to reduce its social work on a continual basis, its members were pressed into forced labor at the wages of unskilled laborers, or were dependent on insufficient support payments, and the ghetto residents in Theresienstadt were on the brink of starvation. Yet the central office had some 62 million RM in cash, securities, and bonds valued at approximately 47 million RM, plus transferred mortgages for home purchase contracts with a value of around 1.1 million RM. The district branches had more than 10 million RM on their books, along with some 2,300 properties to be sold with an estimated value of 36 million RM. Thus, the assets formally belonging to the RV totaled some 157 million RM. Nonetheless, it was not permitted to freely dispose of these assets in any way.

The RV was steadily losing members by "migration" (*Abwanderung*), while at the same time, the level and scope of its liability for the behavior of those remaining were repeatedly increased. Already in December 1941, it had been required to set up so-called petition departments in the district branch offices. Every matter of concern addressed by a Jew to a state office had in future to first be clarified with the RV. In the initial 2 months, 3,722 petitions and requests were received, of which 2,550 were presented to the relevant Gestapo offices. The latter approved 1,613, agreed to another 166 with some restrictions, and rejected 85.[281] These figures indicate that as a precaution, the RV had itself initially rejected about one-third of these requests, and had approved two-thirds, of which the Gestapo offices then on average recognized approximately two-thirds as justified.

Yet not all of the (compulsory) members of the RV followed this procedure, perhaps due to ignorance of the rules, perhaps because they hoped they could better represent their concerns themselves or through their "legal consultant." "State police measures" were introduced to penalize such Jews.[282] Using the pages of the *Jüdisches Nachrichtenblatt*, the RV repeatedly had to remind its members that it was necessary for any request to be initially presented to the RV or its district branch; it had to be reviewed there, and if it appeared admissible, it would then be sent on.[283] It also instructed the Jewish "legal consultants" to avoid lodging an appeal even if it seemed justified on the basis of the "substantive legal" circumstances. Of importance was only the "admissibility of an appeal in the sense of the state police regulations." The RV petition unit had the right to reject a request. If it approved a request, then the supervisory authority reserved the power of final decision.[284] Once again, the RV threatened Jews who failed to comply and directly contacted the authorities with "measures by the state police."[285]

The RV staff employees themselves were now obligated not only to sign letters of the RV or the Jewish Community to offices and agencies, giving their name as the person responsible, but to add their personal ID number as well.[286] In connection with every document, this reminded them that both the content of their work and their personal security were under constant scrutiny.

The Jewish organization was forced to inform Berlin Jews about the ban on using public parks and main streets in the city center "in a suitable manner, by word of mouth," rather than through a circular letter. Now the Jews were banned from entering the area around the Brandenburg Gate, the Tiergarten, the Kurfürstendamm, Tauentzienstrasse, Hardenbergstrasse, and Wilhelmsplatz.[287] A similar form of harassment was a regulation forbidding Jews from smoking in Grunewald, the large wooded area in Berlin's west; or a regulation on the movement of visitors to the Jewish cemetery Weissensee: they were required to cross to the other side of the street straight, not at an angle. If they crossed diagonally, they walked directly into a police trap. The Jewish Community had only one alternative in such cases: to spread news of the measures by word of mouth, and if they received permission, to mount a warning sign, as at the cemetery entrance in Weissensee.[288]

In view of the increasingly threatening situation, a fairly substantial number of Jews sought to formally leave the obligatory community and resign as RV members. But through a retroactive ordinance, the Interior Ministry endeavored to block this move.[289] The "voluntary" members of the RV remained in fact compulsory members of the organization. Given this ordinance, there was no use in protesting now against a fait accompli, that their respective Jewish Community had transferred them as members to the new compulsory organization some two years earlier when the RV was created.[290]

Others continued tenaciously to refuse to wear the "yellow star."[291] Still others decided such "legal means" were hopeless and sought other options. Illegality beckoned. When news from the deportees failed to arrive, death notices were received, and rumors began to circulate about mass shootings, persons handed the "lists" for deportation reacted: in ever-mounting numbers from the summer and autumn of 1942, they chose to go into hiding.[292] In such cases, the RV staff tried to convince RV members to adhere to proper behavior if they learned about such plans or suspected them; if the staff employees failed in this effort, they were under orders to inform their functionaries about the matter, who in turn passed a report on to the Gestapo.

While the RV board still tenaciously negotiated in a bid to prevent reductions in personnel, making use of statistics and numerous arguments, the Gestapo proceeded to slash, without further ado, the number of Jewish staff workers through arrests and raids euphemistically termed "inspection visits." During such a *Kontrollbesuch* on 12 March 1942, for example, they arrested Conrad Cohn, head of the welfare section.[293] Cohn, born in 1901 and board member of both the RV and the Berlin Jewish Community, was responsible for the areas of welfare and evacuation of properties. The ostensible reason for his arrest and that of the director of the children's home Wörthstrasse in Weissensee was that a quantity of prewar soap stored in the home had not been properly entered in the books. For over a month, the RSHA left Cohn's family and the RV in the dark about his fate. After five weeks in detention, it turned out that he would not be released, even though the RV had in the meantime appointed a commission for the regular inspection of its homes.[294] Cohn's wife, who up until then had been required to work on staff as a stenographer (unpaid, like other wives of functionaries), was now provided with a regular salary: this so that the family might at least avoid material hardship.[295] On 22 April, Eppstein requested in her name that the family be allowed to "migrate" (*abwandern*) together.[296] Even this was refused. In June, the RSHA ordered that Cohn be removed from the two boards he served on, and that they be merged.[297] That same day, he was incarcerated in the Sachsenhausen concentration camp, and transferred from there on 8 August 1942 to the Mauthausen camp. In this "category three camp," with among the fiercest conditions of incarceration in any concentration camp, he died one week later.[298] According to Simonsohn, Cohn, a key RV functionary in Hamburg, later a close associate of Eppstein and confined in Theresienstadt himself, had been hounded to his death.[299] All his colleagues at the RV could do was to gather in mournful prayer and say the Kaddish for him.[300] His wife Leonore and their daughter Marianne, who had just turned eleven years old, were deported on 24 / 26 June 1942 to Minsk, and probably murdered in Maly Trostinez.[301] The Breslau Jewish Community, where Cohn had been a coworker for many years, requested to be allowed to bury his urn. The RSHA informed Eppstein that such a request was not permissible.[302]

The transport that Cohn's family was included in, *Osttransport* No. 16, was classified by the RV as a "penal transport." A number of other functionaries of the RV and the Berlin Jewish Community were also forced to "migrate" to the East in this transport: at 8:00 AM sharp on 19 June 1942, Gestapo men arrived by surprise and occupied the rooms of the RV. Based on a person's appearance, they then proceeded to single out "superfluous employees." Anyone arriving a minute too late was duly noted,[303] amounting to a total of forty-eight staff personnel seized, including board member Arthur Lilienthal, eleven staff specialists in different areas, sixteen stenographers, and six bookkeepers. Eppstein sought in vain to have a number of them released: at the very least, Lilienthal, head of the finance and administration department, Cora Berliner, staff specialist for housing and food provision, statistics, registry, and the unit for petitions and applications, Selma Gerson, specialist in the card file on plots of land, Paula Fürst, specialist for child welfare and the previous head of the education department, and two secretaries (Meta Ehrenhaus and Rita Klein). Cora Berliner and Paula Fürst also were members of the RV home inspection unit, newly created after Conrad Cohn's arrest, which was intended as a prophylactic to prevent any future such punishment operations. Eppstein's arguments on how urgently these staff members were needed were summarily brushed aside by the representative of the RSHA, Friedrich Suhr. He stated that Eppstein should just simplify the steps in processing matters within the RV.[304] In a subsequent "control visit," seventeen "legal consultants" were selected on the spot to be deported,[305] and later a number of staff and temporary staff were selected as well.[306] The Gestapo issued an ultimatum to the Berlin Jewish Community on the premises demanding the dismissal of one hundred and fifty employees, especially in its welfare facilities.[307]

Simultaneous with the arrest of the director of the education department, Paula Fürst, the RV was ordered on 30 June 1942 to liquidate all Jewish schools across the *Altreich*.[308] This time, the dismissed teachers could not be employed at alternative posts in other departments. The RV central office was forced once again to fire staff,[309] and Leo Kreindler, who had succeeded Cohn, was given orders to have institutions and homes vacated and their residents sent to Theresienstadt.[310] For residents in nursing homes for the frail, contracts were signed similar to those for home purchase.[311]

The approximately twenty-seven thousand Jewish forced laborers in Berlin and their family members were still protected in 1942, since at that point in time they could not be replaced. To offset this, there was increased deportation of persons not employed as conscript laborers or receiving some form of support,[312] that is, the helpless, aged, and weak. In short, those in need of welfare aid in the broadest sense were now targeted by the planners in the RSHA.

In this context, the summer of 1942 proved to be the low point in the previous work of the Jewish functionaries. The influence they had hoped to exert on the process of deportation had turned out to be nothing but detailed supplementary preparatory work, with minimal options for exercising any influence, and even these options had soon evaporated into thin air. Leo Baeck lamented:

> It has become much lonelier around me, Otto [Hirsch] and Julius [Seligsohn] are no more, some close to me have departed. It's often difficult to be alone. But I try to be available for those entrusted to me, to do and give as much as I'm able. And all around me there is great devotion to duty and dedication.[313]

In daily practice, there was now a rapidly rising flood tide of prohibitions and new regulations, work was under the iron impress of massive financial restrictions and cuts in personnel, and the Gestapo was omnipresent.

The "Community Operation" in October 1942

The stubborn struggle of the RV to retain its personnel had apparently lasted too long for the RSHA. In particular, the RSHA directed that the personnel of the Berlin Jewish Community, in the autumn of 1942 still numbering more than fifteen hundred employees (not including the unsalaried working wives of RV staff, other unsalaried coworkers, and young helpers) was to be drastically reduced. In keeping with this crackdown, Franz Prüfer, *Judenreferent* of the Berlin Gestapo, ordered Moritz Henschel on 19 October 1942 to arrange a mass roll call at 7:00 AM the following morning for more than one thousand employees at the main office of the Berlin Jewish Community on Oranienburger Strasse.[314] Indispensable emergency services, such as in the Jewish Hospital, were reduced to a minimum. Subsequent to a very hastily arranged plan, the departments crowded into the packed rooms and halls allotted for this roll call.[315] After waiting for several hours, *SS-Sturmführer* Rolf Günther and *Hauptsturmführer* Fritz Woehrn from the RSHA appeared, along with several Gestapo officials under the direction of Franz Prüfer. Rolf Günther informed those present that the department heads were now ordered to select five hundred "nonessential" employees for dismissal. While some dealt with the procedure in an orderly fashion, others intentionally delayed it, arrived at lower figures, or sought to negotiate in order to retain their staff. Then the Gestapo suddenly changed its tack, deciding to itself determine who from the staff would be affected. Moritz Henschel and Walter Lustig managed to protect the jobs of some employees, such as the head of the payroll office of the Community.[316] A total of 533 employees, with 328 further relatives dependent on their employment, were thus singled out and ordered to "migrate," and were sent to the RV accommodation advice center to fill out the necessary forms. This grand total of 861 persons were ordered to report on 22 October 1942 to the assembly camp on Grosse Hamburger Strasse, to be included there in a transport either to the East or to Theresienstadt, depending on their age and "racial status."

However, in the fall of 1942, rumors had long been circulating. According to them, deportation to the East meant certain death. Hundreds of Jews had already gone "illegal" and disappeared into hiding. There were no high-ranking Jewish functionaries among them, but there were some who worked at poorly paid jobs in institutions run by the RV. For that reason, Günther had threatened the Jewish Community staff that he would shoot a leading member of the RV or the Berlin Jewish Community for any person who did not arrive punctually for deportation. In actual fact, twenty persons summoned did not appear. The Jewish Community made extensive inquiries in order to prevent a large-scale arrest and execution operation.[317] Some who had fled were apprehended; others turned themselves in. Notwithstanding this, the Gestapo seized twenty hostages. Four or five among these, including Adolf Wolffsky, who headed the application section in the Community, were released. However, seven (other sources speak of eight) of those arrested were shot on 20 November in the Sachsenhausen concentration camp (reported dates of their deaths are 1 December and 3 December 1942), and their family members were subsequently deported.[318]

In 1960, the state prosecutor's office determined that the persons involved were Dr. Fritz Lamm (welfare department), Dr. Bruno Mendelsohn (head of central administration), Alfred Selbiger (former head of the Palestine Office, later active in personnel administration in the RV), Dr. Julius Blumenthal (legal department), Dr. Goldstein (arbitration board and consultation office), Arnold Looser (Community staff worker) and Dr. Adler (audit department).[319] The day after the "Community Operation," Moritz Henschel was ordered to draw up a new draft plan of organization for the Berlin Jewish Community.[320]

The "Jewish policy" in the Nazi state had clearly been exacerbated. In 1942, the RSHA had deported more than sixteen thousand Jews from

Berlin, compounded by the shooting of hostages in May and the "Community Operation" in October.[321] The Jewish functionaries, themselves arrested as hostages, were ordered to designate openly in the organization fellow employees who were to be deported, and on two occasions had directly experienced hostage executions. But this was not enough: in late October/early November, new calamity befell the Berlin Jews.

The "Time of Brunner"

The corruption affair in the Berlin Gestapo previously mentioned led to the temporary suspension of the *Judenreferat* there. Instead, Alois Brunner, Rolf Günther, and other Gestapo officers were transferred to Berlin. Up until then, they had been extremely successful in organizing the deportations from Vienna, from the perspective of the regime. Now Brunner moved to restructure the process of deportations from Berlin.

He ordered that the synagogue on Levetzowstrasse be expanded and the capacity of the assembly camp for Theresienstadt transports, the former home for the aged on Grosse Hamburger Strasse, be multipled to accommodate ten times the number of persons, structured along the lines of a prison: the windows were barred, the grounds surrounded by a palisade, the building illuminated at night. Twenty-five to thirty police officers stationed there were instructed to open fire immediately in the case of attempts to escape. The card file of the Berlin Jewish Community had to be relocated to this building. Jail cells were constructed downstairs in the cellar rooms. Employees of the Jewish Community were instructed that it was forbidden, under threat of "severe penalty and collective imprisonment," to convey any news inside or out or to distribute information about the assembly camps and their inmates.[322] While up to that point marshals had been individually threatened with concentration camp if regulations were violated (or they had created the impression of an infraction), now all marshals were collectively declared as hostages for any persons who would dare to do this.

Brunner and his henchmen, including *Jupos* (Jewish police) from Vienna, whom the RV was obligated to remunerate,[323] basically overhauled and restructured the system of "collectors." The "collectors" and marshals were put under heavy pressure. Both they and the Jewish functionaries, in whose sphere of work they were active, were threatened with arrest and concentration camp if they should "fail" to perform as deemed requisite at their job.[324] In view of this threat, it was not only the Gestapo that tightened the screw; the Jewish Community also endeavored to prevent conflicts by instructing the "collectors" to behave toward the Jews they were sent to escort to the assembly camp in a harsh manner, as if they were their persecutors. Hildegard Henschel later summed this up: "The more brutal the methods of Brunner and comrades became, the more the marshals were told to proceed in an authoritative manner, for the benefit of those being escorted, should the deportees refuse to obey Brunner's men."[325] The marshals thus threatened the Jews ostensibly "for their benefit," in order to avoid bloody confrontations with the Gestapo. As a consequence, "the unpopularity of the marshals increased from week to week … and their comportment became ever more like that of the police." But in retrospect, Hildegard Henschel also thought that "all kinds of terrible things" had indeed been prevented by this approach, the marshals acting "in a rough but never cruel manner."[326]

If the Berlin Gestapo had already gone over to "inspection visits" for the purpose of reducing personnel, Brunner expanded this approach: for example, on 19 November 1942, at 1:45 PM he issued an order for some 200 employees in the welfare department to appear for a roll call at 3:30 PM. From among the 132 who came, he selected half for deportation. During this procedure, the functionary Leo Kreindler, an RV board member, suffered a heart attack and died on the spot.[327]

Generally, one of Brunner's common practices was to issue orders at extremely short notice: one morning he ordered Kozower, responsible for deportation matters at the Berlin Jewish Community, to provide him within one hour with a list of all orphans housed in children's homes. Then he gave the order to bring those orphans from two larger homes to the assembly camp for deportation by 8:00 PM. The personnel in these homes as well as four doctors, as well as their families and all the auxiliary medical staff, were also ordered to report there for transport.[328]

In the meantime, in the grip of the increasingly violent repression of the Gestapo, the moral principles of the Jewish leaders had evidently also changed. Although the RV had tried at the beginning of the deportations to protect the sick and have them deferred, this priority was no longer operative: Martha Mosse later testified that at the end of 1942, sick Jews from the Jewish Hospital were included in every transport. Walter Lustig, appointed director of the Jewish Hospital in October 1942 and to the RV board later that year, is quoted as observing: "They're candidates for death in any case."[329]

In rapid succession, Brunner put groups of orphans, the blind, the frail, and welfare recipients on the deportation lists. In his view, the remaining Jews required but a small number of doctors and dentists, and he ordered the families of these professionals deported, as well as more than a thousand other Jews who were not deployed as forced laborers.[330] In November and December 1942 and January 1943, transports of one thousand Jews again departed from Berlin, now with a new, direct destination: Auschwitz.

Brunner and his staff filled the transports indiscriminately so as to meet the target quota for the number of deportees. If there were no residents in homes and asylums available, he simply ordered raids in apartment blocks where a larger number of Jews were registered as tenants.[331] From January 1943 on, accepted policy now stated that there were no misgivings about including Jewish forced laborers in the transports as well. Up until that point, they, together with their family members, had been exempted from deportation.[332]

Under the impact of the three-month tenure of Brunner in Berlin, the small residue of influence that the Jewish leaders had still been able to previously exercise evaporated. Even worse, the Jewish functionaries now saw themselves forced to act toward their (nonvoluntary) RV membership in a form similar to that of the Gestapo. At least, they repeatedly threatened members that they would be reported to the Gestapo and face "state police measures" should they not obey the orders and attempt in any way to resist. And the leadership instructed subordinate staff to behave likewise in this strict manner when they were deployed as "collectors" or ordered to serve as marshals.

More and more Jews in Berlin came to the same and sole conclusion left to them if they wanted to avoid deportation: they went into hiding. In view of what likely awaited them "in the East," they preferred to hazard the consequences of degrading conditions in a hiding place, separation from their children or spouses, the loss of their last salvaged possessions, or even sexual exploitation. The RV functionaries reacted to this as always: no one issued the slogan "every man for himself!" On the contrary, Eppstein managed to obtain permission for a fundamental revision and overhaul of the card file by means of a new "basic survey" or *Urerhebung*,[333] since due to the mass deportations, the "filling up to target quota" of the transports, and increasing numbers of Jews fleeing into hiding, the card file no longer reflected the actual situation on the ground.

The Stepwise Liquidation of the Reichsvereinigung (1943)

Deportation of the Leading Functionaries

While no reports were officially received from the other deportation destinations, or came in through informal channels only rarely, the RV Jewish functionaries were provided with updates on the construction and development of the Theresienstadt ghetto. The Czechoslovakian Jews were unenthusiastic about the newly assigned function of their "settlement area" as an "old age ghetto" and "preferential camp" for German Jews. But Edelstein, head of the Jewish Council of Elders, acquiesced to the inevitable, and in December 1942 sent "Dear Dr. Eppstein" a four-page letter. In it he once more underscored the accomplishments of Czech Jewry and described their relation to the German deportees:

> It's only all too understandable that initially there were some misunderstandings and difficulties. The different special character, different manners and customs … necessarily must cause some disagreements. But very soon, it proved possible to get over these "childhood diseases." Today the Jewish Council of Elders consists half of Jews from the Reich, and half of Jews from the Protectorate Bohemia and Moravia. They all have equally important functions and are working together in harmony. The awareness of the experience of a shared fate created the basis for substantial understanding, and we are sincerely very pleased with that.[334]

In his reply of 2 January 1943, Eppstein enumerated what his organization had accomplished for Theresienstadt. But when Edelstein was instructed some three weeks later to share the function as head of the Jewish Council of Elders with Paul Eppstein (and Benjamin Murmelstein), the mutual sense of satisfaction rapidly dissipated. What had happened? On 26 January 1943, in anticipation of the planned liquidation of the RV, the RSHA deported its leading functionaries from Berlin.

Although the RSHA had still been warning the Gestapo offices in 1942 not to put the Jewish representatives, so useful for supplementary tasks, on the deportation lists, now it appeared that the time was ripe to remove them too: the transports had largely been completed, aside from the still unresolved problems of the forced workers in the armaments industry and Jews in mixed marriages. The functionaries were now promised a place in the "preferential camp" Theresienstadt as a "reward for the cooperation that went so smoothly" (Erich Simon),[335] while subordinate staff workers were only sent there if they met the necessary criteria.[336] Once again those in power decided on a cleverly devised maneuver of deception: parallel with his job as head of the RV central office in Berlin, Paul Eppstein was given the double task of director in Theresienstadt as well.[337] He was to remain on the board as a "non-local absentee member," registered with the police with a dual residence; he would be permitted to travel to Berlin for important meetings.[338] Eppstein informed the heads of the district branches of this new dual function:

> Since I still bear responsibility for the Reichsvereinigung, I shall be able to remain in contact on a constant basis with the RV central office and thus also in touch with you. I'm certain that you'll continue to carry out the delegated tasks we share in common … and do so with the same exacting level of correctness, precision and punctuality as before.[339]

Yet Eppstein never returned to Berlin, even though this fiction was kept alive for a time.[340] For him, like for Leo Baeck, who upon transport to Theresienstadt had left the RV board, the strict regulations on baggage were eased. Eppstein was permitted to have his piano shipped into the ghetto, a decision on his part later much criticized.[341] The RSHA instructed the RV to cover the moving expenses so as to complete the farce that this was a professional relocation, even a promotion.

Leo Baeck had been assured he would be spared deportation; in any event, that is what he later told Robert Weltsch. Nonetheless, early one morning, police appeared suddenly at his door to take him away; he was allowed but ninety minutes to get ready.[342] Baeck was not spared from internment in the assembly camp; he was forced to conclude a home purchase contract, in which he handed over his movable assets of 15,400 RM and stipulated the sum of 200 RM for "care in the home for the aged."[343] Along with Baeck and Eppstein, other functionaries were also relocated, including Philipp Kozower,[344] Friedrich Meyer,[345] and Alice Myrants.[346] Their families accompanied them, as in the case of Gisela Kozower, with her two daughters, aged ten and eight, and her two-month-old infant son.

Only the day after all had reached the ghetto did the Theresienstadt camp commandant, *SS-Hauptsturmführer* Seidl, inform Jakob Edelstein, head of the Council of Elders, and his deputy Zucker that the "most important functionaries from Berlin, Vienna and Prague" were arriving in Theresienstadt and that his time as head of the ghetto was now at an end.[347] In future, Eppstein, Löwenherz, and Edelstein were to take over camp management functioning as a leadership troika. They could make proposals regarding the extent to which their coworkers from Berlin, Vienna, and Prague should be brought on into the process of autonomous organization of ghetto affairs. It was stated that Edelstein, along with his staff, might possibly be able later on to take over direction of another ghetto to be newly established. Eppstein objected, saying that "he was left with a very awkward feeling if the man who had done the initial difficult work was expected to suddenly step down."[348] Even though Edelstein's demotion was embellished with some words of recognition, Seidl made it quite clear the following day that "should disagreements arise under the members of the triumvirate, he himself would take severe drastic measures."[349] When the RSHA decided that Löwenherz should remain in Vienna and continue to work as Elder of the Jews there, his substitute Benjamin Murmelstein, a former rabbi, was appointed to the position in the troika: Eppstein on top, then Edelstein, and Murmelstein third.[350] H. G. Adler, who published the corresponding memos, stresses in his commentary the "patronizing role of the camp commandant" that he had evidently assumed "vis-à-vis the main Jewish functionaries from Berlin,

Vienna and Prague, who were behaving like ambitious, jealous and immature children, among whom it was necessary to take steps so as to ensure good discipline."[351] At the same time, the RSHA transported seven thousand ghetto inmates to Auschwitz, where they were murdered; this is only mentioned marginally in the memo.

The "Great Inferno": The "Factory Operation"

The day after Eppstein was deported, Moritz Henschel in Berlin had to submit a plan to the RSHA for the reorganizing of the RV. He, Kurt Levy, Paul Meyerheim, and Walter Lustig were now at the helm of the Reichsvereinigung and the Berlin Jewish Community, directing the fate of both, because the Community had been stripped of its autonomous status on 29 January 1943. In the minutes of board meetings, Henschel and his associates were meticulous in noting directives to slash personnel, merge nursery and children's homes, and introduce changes in organization, but the next harrowing event was not even mentioned (or was not allowed to be): namely, the brutal large-scale raid and roundup that has gone down in history as the *Fabrik-Aktion* or "Factory Operation" and was described by eyewitness Rabbi Martin Riesenburger as the "great inferno."[352] This operation involved some 15,100 Berliners and more than 5,000 Jewish forced laborers in other cities in the *Altreich*. It had long been on the planning boards. However, from the winter of 1942 the number of foreign forced laborers did not suffice to replace the Jewish conscript workers, and the situation was compounded by a ban on transport due to the war effort, effective from mid-December 1942 to mid-January 1943, so the day for the operation was postponed. After an announcement in early December 1942, the armaments firms were aware that the special protection for Jewish forced laborers would soon come to an end, at the latest by the end of March 1943. After the German defeat at Stalingrad and the propagandistic declaration of "total war" on 18 February 1943 in his speech at the Berlin Sportpalast, Goebbels pressed Hitler anew to implement the long contemplated plan. Ten days prior to the operation, now scheduled for 27/28 February 1943, Goebbels noted that the seizure of Jews was to be "sudden," and that they should be deported in transports of two thousand persons each from the provisional assembly camps.[353] This was what transpired. The operation in Berlin itself lasted for one full week. The employees of the RV were given a "yellow certificate" in advance signed by an RV board member, containing their names, the names of their protected family members, their age, and their place of work. This was to be affixed to the apartment door in order to prevent these persons from being deported,[354] even if it was clear that this meant only temporary protection. On 26 February 1943, Moritz Henschel, after being forced to wait for hours during the night, was ordered by the Gestapo to make available the furnishings and equipment of five or six offices, along with the office and medical personnel, and to set up first aid posts. He apparently was not given any explanation about the planned operation.

In the early morning hours, armed SS men cordoned off the grounds of the Berlin factories where Jews worked, rounded up Jewish forced laborers, and herded them onto waiting trucks. They were taken to provisional collection points to await deportation. The Jews were held in a large garage in the Hermann Göring barracks, stables in the barracks on Rathenower Strasse, the administration building of the Jewish Community on Rosenstrasse, the auditorium of the Clou Concert Hall, the synagogue on Levetzowstrasse, and smaller assembly camp facilities.[355] The sheer brutality of actions in Berlin (in other parts of the *Altreich*, the operation was carried out more discretely[356]) induced some surviving eyewitnesses to these events to later attribute the operation to Alois Brunner, but at this juncture he had already left Berlin. Raids in the factories were followed by roundups in apartment blocks, on the streets, in front of the food distribution points, and the labor office for Jews. The Jewish staff employees registered the name of those arrested, while those classified as with "close Aryan kin" (*arisch Versippte*) or "Jewish kin" (*jüdisch Versippte*)—it depended on the point of view—were taken to the building of the Jewish Community on Rosenstrasse and housed there. The following morning, the RV was "permitted" to feed some nine thousand detainees. On 1 March, deportations to Auschwitz of a total of some eleven thousand Jews commenced, two-thirds from Berlin. The SS proceeded with extreme brutality, whipping and beating the detainees, some of whom were transported in open cattle trucks. Since this operation had been long expected and announced, a fairly large number of Jews were able to flee in advance. The *arisch Versippte* in the Rosenstrasse camp were registered and released, but ordered to not work any longer in armaments factories.

If they were classified as prospective future Reichsvereinigung employees, they received a red armband that they were obliged to wear along with the "Jewish star."[357] Whoever was spotted not wearing the armband had to reckon with immediate arrest. On 7 March 1943, the operation was considered finished, and the temporary function of the protective "yellow certificates" and red armbands expired.

The "Factory Operation" had an equally violent sequel: on 10 March 1943, the Gestapo arrived at the Jewish Hospital, equipped with trucks to round up and deport staff and patients. The hospital director, Walter Lustig, managed to prevent the immediate liquidation of the hospital by refusing to allow seizure of personnel and patients by the Gestapo, referring to the fact that the hospital was under the direct control of the RSHA. The Gestapo, "unauthorized," had encroached on the sphere of competence of the RSHA, and the RSHA's responsible official, Fritz Woehrn, prevented the Gestapo from carrying out this arrest operation, although he himself went ahead and immediately ordered the deportation of three hundred hospital employees.[358] Lustig had thus at the last minute prevented the hospital's closing—showing great courage in doing so, because it was difficult to estimate the sheer explosive dynamism of a situation where a hospital was being occupied—but for this, the people there paid a high price.

During these days, Jews had been hunted down and seized at their places of work, in apartment blocks, and on the streets; yet quite a few, some four thousand, had nonetheless managed to elude arrest.[359] On the one hand, at this tumultuous point, the lives of Jews who had fled, gone into hiding, or been deferred from deportation were at risk, as were the lives of all others in Berlin as a result of the heavy bombing raids. On the other hand, the chaos of destroyed buildings and blocked streets provided them with options for escape, to find shelter as "bombed-out residents" in the ruins or in allotment garden areas; possibly, by giving a false name, they might even manage to get hold of new identification papers or ration cards. But in these efforts, they could not hope for any assistance from the RV. On the contrary, the organization was under heavy pressure from the authorities to ferret out their new addresses.

During this "great inferno," the Jewish leaders experienced a form of helplessness they had never seen before. Ultimately, they had not been able to do anything for the deportees except to provide them with a few items of clothing from the RV storeroom and a plate of soup. If they wished to at least save their organization, they had to take on and train the dismissed "persons with Aryan kin," that is, Jews living in mixed marriages and the *Geltungsjuden*, before the last unprotected "full Jew" had been deported. It was a race against the clock. After the "Factory Operation," 320 persons classified as "with Jewish kin" (*jüdisch Versippte*) were sent from Rosenstrasse to Oranienburger Strasse in order to be screened regarding their suitability as replacement personnel for the deported staff employees of the RV. Fritz Woehrn from the RSHA instructed Kurt Levy to hire a maximum of 225, but to make sure there were none among those selected who could be deported. The relatives of the newly hired employees were to work unpaid, and those who were unable to perform well would be assigned "hard manual labor." Woehrn held out the prospect to those former employees now to be deported that he might be able to cancel restrictions regarding baggage. He also wanted to inquire whether "experienced coworkers" might be considered for deportation to Theresienstadt.[360] ID cards were issued for the new personnel (seventy plus seven persons in the district branch Brandenburg-East Prussia) and for Jews already working in "special deployment."[361] Yet evidently not all workers had at this point been exchanged, because in April 1943, the RV board deliberated once more on how "coworkers who have no Aryan kin" could be exchanged for workers classified as *arisch Versippte*. "Henschel states that a card file is now being assembled at the supervisory authority containing the data of Jews registered, including those in mixed marriages [illegible] also containing professional data, and which perhaps could be utilized to locate [suitable] exchange personnel."[362] Both the RSHA and the RV board members now recognized the necessity to immediately train the Jews in mixed marriages so they could learn the ropes on the job, in order that "even if full Jews were to totally disappear, the machinery would continue running smoothly." And the RV board members at this point found themselves in the role of the last unprotected "full Jews" whose reprieve had not yet expired—this thanks only to the office they held in the organization.[363]

The "Factory Operation" marked a further clear decisive turning point in the activity of the Jewish leaders, the associated functionaries, and their organization: they had assisted in the deportation of their last members, thus largely losing the clientele they felt responsible for. They had also forfeited their function as protective employer. Yet, in the meantime, they had apparently come to see the continued existence of the RV as a value in itself: the "machinery" still had to continue running even if its purpose was no longer evident. The Jewish staff members were deported on 12 and 17 March 1943, 941 to Auschwitz and around 1,300 to Theresienstadt. But in the Jewish administrations on Oranienburger Strasse (the Berlin Jewish Community, which had now turned into a district branch of the RV) and Kantstrasse (the RV), work had to continue; there was no interruption.

(Temporary) Closure of the Business Offices

In May 1943, the RSHA continued the stepwise liquidation of the Reichs-vereinigung. Ernst Kaltenbrunner, since January 1943 head of the RSHA, informed the Gestapo offices by telegram that the remaining Jews, including the sick and frail, would have to be removed from the territory of the Reich by 30 June 1943. This directive also applied to forced laborers, except for those interned in labor camps. Residents of the *hachshara* camps were transported in closed groups to Auschwitz-Buna, where a small number managed to survive.[364]

> Likewise, the Jews still employed at the RVJD or its district branches or in Jewish Communities are to be registered according to guidelines for transport. As a result, these institutions will, for all practical purposes, be liquidated. In their place, in so far as this is required for implementation of

official orders pertaining to the Jews still remaining, an "association of Jewish spouses in mixed marriage" is to be established, with its main office in Berlin; its personnel will consist exclusively of spouses in mixed marriages who have remained behind.[365]

And precisely this came to pass: first, hundreds more employees from Berlin were deported, at the same time as a large proportion of their last clientele: frail and bedridden patients along with medical personnel.

Hildegard Henschel described the departure of the Jewish functionaries who had served from 1939 to 1943:

> And thus no one was astonished when at 10:00 AM on 10 June 1943, the Gestapo announced in the main office of the Jewish Community at Oranienburgerstrasse 29 that all employees who had no Aryan kin should regard themselves as under arrest. The same thing was happening over on Kantstrasse. People were arrested, taken to the assembly camp on Grosse Hamburgerstr., taken care of there until 16 June by remaining colleagues who had Aryan relatives, with much devotion and kindness on their part. And at noon on Wednesday 16 June, the furniture truck that was already a familiar sight on the Berlin streets brought us to the Puttlitzerstrasse railway station.[366]

In the eyes of historians Esriel Hildesheimer and Otto Dov Kulka, the history of the Reichsvereinigung der Juden in Deutschland comes to an end with this deportation and the order by the RSHA for its liquidation. However, I think such a view does not go quite far enough: on the one hand, the organization continued to exist in a residual form; on the other hand, the Jewish functionaries certainly proceeded with their work in another place, and with no less dedication. Thus, at this juncture the history of the Reichsvereinigung split into two parallel developments, continuing on until May 1945: while the Jews in mixed marriages took over the offices in the now extremely shrunken apparatus of the Residual or New Reichsvereinigung in the *Altreich* as *Vertrauensmänner* or intermediaries, the Jewish representatives "there from the beginning" (if 1939 can be so designated) who were still alive pressed on with their work as functionaries in the Theresienstadt ghetto.

Theresienstadt as a New Field of Activity for the German-Jewish Functionaries

A Veritable Army of Officials

The reality of Theresienstadt quickly unmasked the deceptive legend of a "preferential camp."[367] However, the German-Jewish functionaries were not so helplessly exposed to the situation as other new arrivals: they were able to communicate in German with those in power; in addition, they had experience, over many years, with trying to accommodate to and deal with their mentality and worldview. Eppstein was immediately accorded the status of a prominent inmate entitled to two rooms and double rations, while Leo Baeck had to wait for weeks for better accommodation. Eppstein was also able to arrange privileges for other functionaries from Berlin who now assumed functions in the autonomous administration of the ghetto. Five months later, in May and June 1943, Paul Meyerheim, Kurt Levy,[368] and Moritz Henschel arrived with their families, as well as the heads of the liquidated district branches; they likewise took over certain tasks in the Jewish administrative apparatus.

All these new arrivals brought with them the will and competence to grapple with misery and chaos, organizing and shaping this reality, utilizing the sparse means available. They could rely on each other because they were well acquainted from years of working together. They were a "community sworn to a bond of comradeship in life and death, in which each was the brother and friend of the other," as the Hamburg functionary Max Plaut had once pointedly characterized the Jewish representatives.[369]

The special privileges ordered by the RSHA were reserved for the top echelon of the Jewish functionaries:

> The category Prominent A included all members of the Council of Elders and those declared as prominent by the Berlin Gestapo [probably rather by the RSHA], such as Kurt Levy, Eppstein's successor as head of the Reichs-vereinigung. These persons had special apartments, extra food rations, special privileges in case of illness (free choice of doctor), all benefits for laundry, fuel and work. And most importantly, the ghetto administration could only give them orders with prior authorization from the SS. The second category was Prominent B. On Eppstein's suggestion, all department heads of the Reichsvereinigung and provincial heads were granted Prominent B status, i.e. they were given better apartments, more passes for bathing, and later the assurance by the SS head Hauptsturmführer Moes … not to be transported from Theresienstadt to anywhere else.[370]

In addition to those mentioned, Jacob Jacobsohn, "specialization: Jewish genealogy and family research," and Martha Mosse, "detective bureau," and, from May 1944, head of the "central registry" in Theresienstadt,[371] belonged to the specially privileged group of "Prominent A." As already had been the practice in Berlin, the canopy of protection Eppstein offered here covered the respective individuals and their families.[372] Thus, for example, Hans-Erich Fabian was granted "Prominent B" status likewise for his wife Ruth Hanna, his sons Fabian Joel and Fabian Judis, and his daughter Reha, who most certainly otherwise would not have survived. In the case of Fritz Grunsfeld, head of the district branch for Central Germany, protection extended to his sister Hildegard, father Iwan, and mother Meta; family protection for Ludwig Merzbach, who worked in Theresienstadt in the central administration, also covered his wife Margarethe and daughter Uta.

Eppstein and the other Jewish functionaries evidently did not ask themselves whether or not they should try to elude the responsibilities they had been assigned. After their first rude awakening, Theresienstadt became for them a field of action where they were able to press on with their previous longstanding activities, and indeed they felt had to continue in terms of their own identity, and in the vital interest of those entrusted to them. They wished to make some contribution to ensuring the community's survival, and their own.

The German-Jewish leaders not only held important positions in the "autonomous administration," they also created regional networks. In these networks, information was passed on about events in the ghetto or bits of news from the hometowns of the ghetto residents, and the local bonds of cohesion between compatriots from the same town or region were strengthened.[373]

However, Eppstein and the heads of the various departments, working within a commission of thirty to forty members, were now making decisions that they originally would never have wanted to be confronted with: they had to determine who would be deported elsewhere.

> The readying of a transport was done on orders from the SS commandant to the Jewish autonomous administration. The number of persons to be included in a transport was a set figure, and this was supplemented by various directives stipulating who should be included and who should not, what age categories, "mixed-blood" *Mischlinge,* persons from mixed marriages, disabled war veterans, veterans with special medals from their World War I service, the mentally ill, sick Jews, laborers in agriculture, specialists, etc. These instructions varied from case to case. In addition, the SS commandant office also passed on a list with the names of those who necessarily had to be included in the transports, the "directives."[374]

If the German-Jewish functionaries in their hometowns had done preparatory work for implementing the deportations (such as keeping a card file, listing specific categories of persons, submitting requests for deferment of deportation), now they—although under orders and with special instructions—were directly involved in putting together lists with the names of persons to be deported. They were the officials these Jews on the deportation list appealed to at the last minute, they were the ones who ticked off the names before the transport deported. Eppstein, according to his successor Murmelstein, devised complicated precautionary measures so as to avoid mistakes and arbitrary actions. Yet this did not change the system of the transports. And on occasion, Eppstein himself went beyond these measures. In a later interview, the survivor Trude Simonsohn stated that Eppstein had, at her request, removed her mother from a transport. She and probably her mother as well understood what this implicated: "another person would go instead, and so I had dirtied my hands with this. But, look, I didn't make these inhuman laws, and nobody should tell me that it's possible to get through such a time with hands still clean. . . . Yet I wasn't able to save her, later on she went as well."[375]

It is reported that Moritz Henschel had a different attitude: he refused to remove close associates from a transport because he did not want to do some good for someone he knew—and thus unavoidably cause harm to a stranger: "so he did nothing and was much more despised … People did not respect this neutrality on his part."[376]

Trude Simonsohn knew from her friend Hedwig Eppstein that her introverted husband Paul had been working nonstop, to the point of exhaustion, with no regard for his physical condition. Paul Eppstein compensated for the pressures, almost impossible to bear, by sitting down to play the piano after he came back from the SS, or he "tore all the books from the shelves"; he was "under unbelievable pressure."[377]

The German new arrivals assumed important functions in the structure of the autonomous administration of the ghetto:

> There had to be a German and a Czech as head or deputy head for every office, i.e., the directorates were supplemented. Our man Merzbach,[378] from the economy office Berlin, joined the housing office, in welfare, Peyser,[379] from Cologne, and David Braun.[380] Into the labor department, Werner Simon,[381] Berlin; into the youth office; Simonsohn, Hamburg; into the detective bureau … Rosenthal, Berlin. Metz,[382] Berlin, into the health office … , into the postal service Kozover [sic], Berlin, etc.[383]

The individual leaders benefited (to the degree any "benefit" was possible in Theresienstadt) from the posts they occupied. Kozower, for example, was given a furnished room with cooking facilities for himself and family, a luxury in the ghetto. As head of postal services, he was also permitted to send over two hundred postcards and nine letters to his relatives in Berlin alone over the course of eighteen months, not including correspondence to other persons, from whom the family received food parcels.[384] But this was probably a welcome secondary benefit, not the motive for working in the Jewish administration of the ghetto.

Eppstein's involuntary acceptance of the position of director and his "covey of personal coworkers"[385] were understandably viewed with some dislike by the Czech functionaries and the "long-established" ghetto residents. In letters and postwar reports, they spoke of the "arrogant and provocative behavior" of the Berlin functionaries,[386] complained about the "vitamin P" (for protection) that the Berlin Jews enjoyed; they had been active previously in the Community and had now "once again arranged comfortable jobs" for themselves.[387] Jakob Jakobsohn spoke in a neutral way about a "temporarily heavily bloated administration," which later was simplified.[388] Others mockingly commented on the "host of officials":

> It required a certain flair of genius here in stacking up one post on top of another. The amount of paper consumed for a trifle or technicality soon bulged to the point of enormity, and when a person looked at these hundreds of kilos of manuscripts and scraps of paper heaped up when things came to an end with liberation, you felt a mild shiver creeping slowly up your back. ... Each official regarded himself as terribly important and indispensable.[389]

Several examples can serve to illustrate what "paper consumed for a trifle or technicality" actually meant: it is well-known that Theresienstadt had its own currency, not valid outside the ghetto; it likewise had no buying power or practical use inside the ghetto, since there was nothing to buy (although it came to enjoy some popularity among collectors). The ghetto residents who worked were paid in this currency. They were classified into no less than forty different wage categories. The elderly and those in need of special care received a support payment in Theresienstadt money. Wages and benefits were paid out half in worthless bills, half in credits deposited in forty-five thousand newly established closed accounts, for which savings books were issued. A guardian received the money for patients in the psychiatric clinic; the inheritance of those deceased was collected in a special account. Ghetto resident Else Dormitzer, who in October 1944 "found employment" with the postal service, later reported that twenty-six "officials" were employed there under the official direction of Henschel and his deputy, thirteen from Germany, five from Holland, two from Austria, and one each from Czechoslovakia and Denmark, along with at least ten mail carriers.[390] The "flow of capital" just of the Theresienstadt paper money occupied dozens of staff. The Council of Elders also had a highly complex codex written for labor laws, as well as regulations for administrative officials, a code of legal rules for a youth court, and organizational norms for the internal guard duty.

The Czechoslovakian Egon Redlich wrote: "The Germans have sent various 'leaders' [*Führer*] here, with the sole intention to cause arguments and chaos."[391] However, in actual fact the German Jews were trying to achieve precisely the opposite, namely, to bring the chaos under control by introducing regulations. Yet even the most "bloated apparatus of officials" was unable to improve the situation: in August, September, and October 1942, more than 10,300 Jews had died, of these 56.2 percent German Jews. Even later, when the general mortality rate decreased, the German mortality was higher than that of any other nation in the ghetto. According to Kárný, a total of some 42,000 German Jews were sent to Theresienstadt, of whom more than 20,000 perished (48.5 percent), and just under 16,000 were deported elsewhere.[392]

Despite postal censorship, Theresienstadt was not an island, and news about those deported made its way through various channels to the hometowns and the intermediaries there. This information also included the news that "it is certain … residents there were sent further east, presumably to Riga."[393] This means that the transports from Theresienstadt were known despite the cloak of secrecy, and alarmed the successors back in the hometowns of those already deported. They endeavored to construct further networks for obtaining information and for support of the ghetto residents. The head of the district branch of Northwest Germany, Max Plaut, deserves special merit for his work in these efforts. He himself, his coworkers, and later his successor maintained contacts with those deported to Theresienstadt (and with others), and send parcels to the Hamburg Jews as well as to colleagues from the RV central office, for which Paul and Hedwig Eppstein, for example, expressed their "exceptional delight" on a number of occasions. Expressions of gratitude came from Leo Baeck, who emphasized being "satisfied with his own activity" in Theresienstadt; from Jacob Jacobsohn, who was able to continue his "histories of personal biography" in Theresienstadt; from Berthold Simonsohn, who wrote that he was working in the head office for youth welfare, and his sister was employed with the postal service; and from Philipp Kozower, unceasingly active "day and night," who as head of the postal services praised the Hamburg Jewish Community for its "quite exemplary work in caring for its friends here."[394]

The Bitter End of Activity by Functionaries in Theresienstadt

The continuation of functionary activity in autonomous administration in the Theresienstadt ghetto came to an end with the deportation of almost all functionaries in the autumn of 1944. The survivor Jacob Jacobsohn wrote later that Eppstein's position had become increasingly difficult. It is likely that he foresaw "a blow" coming, and "the circle of the former employees of the Reichsvereinigung der Juden in Deutschland were entangled in his fall."[395]

On 23 October, the blow struck Walter Fackenheim,[396] the former chief cashier of the Berlin Jewish Community. He survived Auschwitz and reported after the war:

Dr. Braun (head of the finance department of the Jewish Community) and his family followed us, as well as Martin Gerson[397] (head of agriculture, director of many agricultural retraining camps), with his family, the attorney Kozower (board member) and the staff coworkers Alice Herzog,[398] Else Juda,[399] Salomon Schlome[400] and his wife, Dr. Käte Joachimsohn,[401] Gottfried Salomon[402] and many others.[403]

Eppstein himself was arrested on 27 September 1944, taken to the separate section of Theresienstadt known as the Small Fortress, and shot there on 28 September, as reported in testimony after the war. With his death, protection through special status as a prominent person was finally eliminated. Between 28 September and 28 October 1944, eighteen thousand Jews were sent to their death,[404] including almost all previous employees of the RV central office and the district branches: ordered by special instructions to appear for transport, brought separated from the others into the awaiting carriages and separately removed from them, and many of them murdered immediately.[405] Others, like Paul Meyerheim, began an odyssey through a series of forced labor camps, an ordeal they did not survive.[406]

Meanwhile, through an exchange, Max Plaut was probably the only one of the German-Jewish functionaries to escape from Europe in the summer of 1944 to Palestine. In the winter of 1944, he sent a petition from there to the Foreign Office in London seeking to gain the release of prisoners.[407] At the very top of his list were Paul and Hedwig Eppstein, followed by other familiar names from the RV central office, coworkers in Hamburg, as well as the former heads of the district branches of Westphalia, Hanover, Frankfurt am Main, Saxony, Leipzig, and others.[408] However, most of those listed had at that juncture already been murdered.[409]

In his magisterial work on Theresienstadt, H. G. Adler sketched a now widespread picture of Paul Eppstein that was hardly complimentary. He described him as

a poser, theatrical, soft and vain. His glance contained a look of shy anxiousness and mournful sadness. He always stood bent over a bit, like a man who hardly feels the equal of the huge burden upon his shoulders. People had the impression he represented the concerns of the Jews with the SS in a weak manner and without putting up any opposition. He accepted the orders and implemented them. Eppstein certainly was no monster, his bent-over bearing alone was testimony to that. But it was not possible to attribute any warmth or kindness to him.

He was an "admirer of power," even in its "National Socialist form," and had "long since departed from the path of a strictly law-abiding individual."[410] Eppstein's companion Ernst Simon, by contrast, stressed Eppstein's qualities as an intellectual in the tradition of Max Weber, with a penchant for conceptual analysis, sharp and precise formulation, and meticulous observation. He considered Adler's assessment of him to be a false judgment. At another time, Eppstein would hardly have occupied a post of senior "leadership," yet an inner disposition and the external pressures had in Simon's view brought him into a situation whose "claims for accomplishing something and presenting a certain bearing" exceeded Eppstein's "inner native strengths and capacities," or had pushed him in the wrong direction. In Simon's eyes, Eppstein ended tragically, and not guilty.[411]

Eppstein, based on experience in Berlin accustomed to appear for a summons from the RSHA by himself, insisted likewise in Theresienstadt on such an approach and his concomitant monopoly on information and its interpretation. As a result, according to Adler, he created a certain problem for the ghetto residents: it was difficult for them to distinguish between instructions coming directly from the ghetto commandant and Eppstein's passing on of those same instructions (along with an unnecessary pecking order in relation to Edelstein). Eppstein's close associates Jacob Jacobsohn and Berthold Simonsohn rejected this characterization, putting forward persuasive arguments. Based likewise on my own research into Eppstein as head of the Reichsvereinigung, the picture Adler sketched seems to lack consistency. Ultimately, Eppstein's four-month incarceration during his tenure in Berlin, with no explanation or date of release given, doubtless left deep wounds. It is known that he was subjected to maltreatment and abuse, and it becomes clear from the source materials that thereafter he behaved more moderately toward the SS. In any case, his strategy of dealing with the SS involved a kind of anticipatory form of obedience: he calculated the future intentions of the rulers, adjusted to their likelihood, and sought arrangements that took into account the interests of the Jews. This approach also prevented him from being held personally liable for imprudent instructions. In this conflict situation, it probably seemed less dangerous to him to proceed unaccompanied to the representative of the RSHA or to the commandant rather than to have to argue with other Jewish functionaries about interpretations and implementation. He preferred to seek out avenues to avoid conflicts. Under certain circumstances he may perhaps have rendered orders more harsh himself so as to prevent possible objections, or suggested to his interlocutor certain solutions that were in keeping with both interests, those of the RSHA and Eppstein's (as in the case of the Polish inmates in concentration camps described in chapter 1). Courageous demonstrations of his own superiority, as is reported in the case of Edelstein, and which Eppstein had also been somewhat prone to himself in 1939, were later on just as alien to him as were the tactics employed by his successor Murmelstein. On the other hand, shortly before his arrest, he gave a relatively open and for him potentially very dangerous speech, in which he warned about any premature joy over the approaching end of the war. Adler quotes its gist:

> We are as it were of a ship outside a port but not allowed entry because a heavy barrier of mines is preventing that. Only the ship's command knows the narrow route leading to safe land. It must pay no heed to deceptive signs and signals coming from land. The ship must remain outside and await instructions. People have to trust its command; it is doing everything humanly possible in order to guarantee the security of our existence.[412]

A fellow prisoner, Rabbi Richard Feder, cites Eppstein's speech from memory in his report, first published in Czech in 1947, where he underscores more strongly the urgent appeal Eppstein directed to the prisoners:

> You don't know the true situation, don't comprehend it, but you loudly accuse me and the other members of the Council of Elders. Your judgment about us is totally mistaken. I don't hold that against you, maybe we'd behave the same way if in your place. But we fervently request of you one thing: have trust in us! Believe us that we have only your well-being in mind. The situation doesn't permit me to speak openly.[413]

Feder then gives the passages that Adler also mentions, and notes that Eppstein ended his speech with the words, "Rely upon us! Have patience, we shall lead you all into a new era," finishing with the prayer, "Our father! Our King! Inscribe us in the Book of Good Life."[414] Baeck is said to have urgently warned Eppstein not to make such imprudent statements.[415] Most probably his warning involved not mentioning so clearly the imminent defeat in the war.

In my view, this speech clashes with a characterization of Eppstein as "lacking in courage." On the contrary, here we can sense the attitude of the "old" Eppstein flaring up again. That stance had once shown to Eichmann when he established the Central Office for Jewish Emigration in Vienna that the power of the Nazi state (still) had its limits, despite all the brute force directed against the Jews. But above all else, the speech indicates how Eppstein saw himself—and this self-image differs little from the leader Eppstein in the 1930s: he acted as the only one, or one of a select few, to whom the path and truth were known, a leader who demands trust—but does not in any case divulge his knowledge in return, and does not consult jointly with others and take action only after that. Murmelstein described this behavior as the mistrust characteristic of the

Judenältester, the chief elder "who could only be at rest if he did everything himself,"[416] even if he was for that reason subjected to maltreatment behind closed doors.[417]

The historian Wolfgang Benz believes that Eppstein's "tragedy" "lay in the simple fact that, whatever he undertook, he had only the methods of a middle-class academic at his disposal. He had had no other training. It was his dilemma that his existence in Theresienstadt was by definition two-faced; he could be an aid to the Jews only by attempting to gain the confidence of their torturers."[418] Benz asks posterity to judge Eppstein—who had accepted responsibilities from the National Socialists, "for whatever personal reasons"—as a representative of German Jewry "in the search for justice." I can only agree with him. But Eppstein's behavior in the years 1939–1944 was not due simply to his middle-class academic background: given the absence of any alternatives, and in the face of the constant erosion of the institutions of the bourgeois democratic state during National Socialism, he sought to counter the increasingly radicalized racial anti-Semitism by building up a traditional bureaucracy, combined with an authoritarian style of management (his own) at the top. Eppstein's contemporary Klara Caro also referred to this aspect when she later noted that Eppstein, who never discarded the habitus of the unapproachable "superior" even in the ghetto, personified the "pedantry, for better or worse, of so-called Prussian character."[419] Benjamin Murmelstein classified him as a follower of Hegel's notion that "the state is the realization of the moral idea," even if under Nazism the authoritarian state had become the very personification of evil.[420] This ultimate faith in an institution and in authority became for Eppstein his doom, because the Nazi state had no respect for any sense of duty and responsibility; it honored no loyalty or meritorious service.

After Eppstein's death, the RSHA simplified the administration of Theresienstadt: Benjamin Murmelstein functioned as Elder of the Jews, and Leo Baeck became his deputy and chair of the Council of Elders.[421] Baeck had not pressed for an office, but rather had kept his distance from everyday work in the Jewish administration, as he had during the time of deportations from Berlin. Although classified as a "prominent" (probably category A), he did strenuous menial labor in his first few weeks in Theresienstadt: he dragged around a garbage cart, until with his seventieth birthday he was released from labor for pastoral work in the ghetto.[422] He sought in Theresienstadt to promote "peace between religions," participated in Czechoslovakian-Jewish religious services and also gave lectures on the history of religions or philosophical topics to Roman Catholic inmates and others.[423] Ernst Simon stated that he possessed a "quiet effectiveness," less when religious concerns were involved and more when he reached hundreds with his lectures, strengthening them spiritually.[424] According to H. G. Adler, Baeck embodied "the conscience of the camp, and was at the center of a moral resistance movement against the corruption and abject wretchedness of the Jewish leadership,"[425] which says less about Baeck's merits and more about Adler's misgivings vis-à-vis Eppstein. Baeck is said to have warned Eppstein a number of times, but about what? Regarding corruption among his closest associates, or personal complicity in the murder of Jews? The documentary sources say nothing about this, and the accusations remain speculative. In any event, out of necessity Baeck took over welfare work after the autumn transports, a sphere he had in any case already dedicated himself to in some of his pastoral work.[426] Baeck's accomplishments in office were later criticized as well-meaning promises that could not be kept given the resources available. For example, Rolf Grabower, who was active in the Theresienstadt justice system, often conferred with Baeck about legal-ethical problems in connection with his decisions. But Grabower accused Baeck of making promises to everyone for the sake of friendliness—promises it was impossible to keep. The upshot was that Grabower, who valued Baeck's advice, ultimately came to regard him as unreliable.[427] On the whole, Baeck's eminent contribution—over many years, under increasingly oppressive conditions—lay in his ability to make the fate of hundreds if not thousands of Jews easier, by listening to them individually in their distress, and offering them consolation and hope.

Eppstein's execution by the SS rang in a new chapter in the sad history of the Theresienstadt ghetto. The autumn transports followed. A sense of resignation and despair spread. Erich Simon later summed up the mood among those still remaining: "The old Jewish administration had vanished; the remainder worked without any pleasure.... We ... had been proud to create a substitute home for the inmates. But the transports taught us another lesson."[428] When thousands of Jews from evacuated camps began arriving in Theresienstadt from 20 April 1945, news of the gas chambers in Auschwitz started to spread.[429] In retrospect, this cast a renewed pall over the efforts of the functionaries, questioning these efforts as both a deception and simultaneous self-deception.

On 5 May 1945, the SS withdrew from Theresienstadt. Eppstein, Kozower, and many other German-Jewish functionaries and their families were dead. Only very few of those deported, like Ludwig Löffler and Berthold Simonsohn, had survived Auschwitz and the subsequent camps. Others, such as Leo Baeck, Martha Mosse, or Ludwig Merzbach were liberated in Theresienstadt. Most went to the Deggendorf displaced persons (DP) camp, but forty of the "thoroughly meritorious employees of the Jewish organizations in Germany or the local Jewish autonomous administration"[430] wished to stay on working in Hamburg until the emigration they aspired to could be realized, presumably because they still had contacts with the local district branch there. For this purpose, the Theresienstadt survivors issued testimonials for one another in which their activity in autonomous administration was now listed as part of a professional qualification. Thus, Ludwig Merzbach obtained a certificate regarding his organizational work over many years in the economy department, whose director he had become in October 1944. There he had dealt with the provisioning of "45,000-30,000-11,000, 18,000-31,000 persons with goods of all kinds, including foodstuffs and their distribution, and finally liquidation of the camp and repatriation of individuals, especially from the German Reich."[431] The figures here refer to the respective occupancy of Theresienstadt; the differences reflect the murder of thousands of ghetto residents: from 45,000 down to 30,000, and then 11,000, and then the influx into the camp of new deportees (from 18,000 to 31,000) and, later, the arrivals from Auschwitz.

Karl Basch had a certificate issued that stated he had been active "in a high-ranking post" in "the card file, statistics and central registry."[432] Martha Mosse's certificate, not intended for Hamburg, confirmed she had

> worked … as an investigator initially in the detective bureau and later in the court of autonomous Jewish administration. In May of this year, [1945] Dr. Mosse assumed a post as director of the central registry … Over the entire period of her activity in Theresienstadt, Dr. Mosse demonstrated she was an exceptionally conscientious official and showed extensive interest in and understanding of the needs of the community … The autonomous administration of the former Theresienstadt concentration camp expresses its gratitude to Dr. Mosse for her work in service on behalf of the community in Theresienstadt and wishes her all the best for the future … signed Josef Vogel.[433]

It is not known whether the last surviving functionaries engaged in reflection in their respective private circles about their involuntary role in the total process of the deportations, or whether they sought to reach some understanding among themselves. The extant written sources contain no indication of this. At most, there were brief intimations of dismay when Erich Simon mentioned the inclusion of Jewish functionaries as a short parenthetical insertion in a lecture he gave in April 1946: "Awful when we recall today, but seen from the perspective then, it was being done in the interest of our people; we believed that through our cooperation we had helped to bring them in an orderly way to a place abroad."[434] In tacit agreement, the surviving functionaries kept the horror at an emotional distance. Instead, the sources indicate the sense of pride among the surviving functionaries to have successfully coped with and managed the chaos, at least in organizational terms—this along with the fact that they believed it was self-evident their participation in autonomous administration should be acknowledged as an accomplishment.

Knowledge among the German-Jewish Functionaries about the Murder of the Jews

After the war, the Theresienstadt survivor Hans-Erich Fabian sketched the conceptions of the Jewish functionaries regarding the deportation destinations. He stressed that in their minds, although Theresienstadt was not an ideal place to live, they thought it was considerably better than it actually turned out to be. In his view, people had suspected nothing when it came to further transports, but had rather proceeded on the assumption of "comparative security." They imagined the conditions in the ghettos in Riga and Lódz were terrible, and that the Lublin district was a particularly bad destination area. In the case of Auschwitz, it was, Fabian noted, soon clear that there was little chance of survival there, although nothing had been known about gas chambers and mass shootings.[435] Martha Mosse summed matters up later in a similar vein: people put the ghettos of Minsk, Lódz, and "the camp Auschwitz with Birkenau" together in a series along with the concentration camps Oranienburg and Dachau, "where a hard life was to be expected, but no systematic murder." In Mosse's assessment, Theresienstadt had had a better reputation.[436]

Inside Theresienstadt itself, all residents were aware of the further transports to extermination camps. The Jewish functionaries belonging to the responsible commission most probably suspected that a call to report for such a transport meant certain death for most deportees. Nevertheless, after the war the few survivors among them claimed they had known about the transports but nothing about the systematic mass murder. Leo Baeck, who heard rumors in Theresienstadt about the gassings in Auschwitz, and according to his own statements was given specific information about this in August 1943 by a Czechoslovakian engineer named Grünberg, decided not to pass this on to the Council of Elders. In retrospect, he stated: "If the Council of Elders were informed the whole camp would know within a few hours. Living in the expectation of death by gassing would only be harder. And this death was not certain for all: there was a selection for slave labor; perhaps not all transports went to Auschwitz. So I came to the grave decision to tell no one."[437] Eppstein's confidant in the Berlin years, Herbert Growald, suspects that Eppstein "probably was aware of the extermination, perhaps had precise news, but he always denied that to us. The more I think about the situation now afterwards, the more I think that he knew everything but wanted to keep our morale up."[438] Eppstein would not have been far from Baeck's position if this supposition by Growald is accurate. Moritz Henschel and Hans-Erich Fabian disclaimed after the war to have had final knowledge of the mass murder of the Jews during their tenure in office in the Reichsvereinigung and also later in Theresienstadt.[439] Fabian, who (as mentioned) returned to Berlin during his internment in Theresienstadt to settle the financial affairs of the RV, evidently likewise concealed from third parties there and the functionaries of the Residual RV the fact that further transports from Theresienstadt were taking place.[440]

It was a similar situation in regard to knowledge had by the heads of RV district branches: the extant archival sources and personal testimonials indicate that they were collecting information from the camps and ghettos, such as Piaski, Minsk, Lódz, some isolated reports from Riga, and large numbers of reports from Theresienstadt on the living conditions there. They had gathered isolated reports about the murder of Jews, such as in Sobibor, and a number of individuals also had some idea of the dangers in the camps as far as this was known to them. But even if one or another of them had put these fragments of information from the ghettos and camps together into a composite comprehensive picture, the fact remains: the process was unstoppable, and the Jewish functionaries were unable to end their participation in it. That move would have spelled the more rapid and brutal deportation of the elderly and weak, and also their own death.

Subordinate staff workers in the Reichsvereinigung likewise had extensive but fragmentary knowledge of the mass murder of the Jews, as, for example, is evident from extant letters written by Hermann Samter, employed with the *Jüdisches Nachrichtenblatt* and a (forced) member in the Reichsvereinigung. He showed himself to be precisely informed about what was happening in each phase of the deportations, and was certainly in a position to relate these facts to his own possible fate. Yet, like the Jewish functionaries, he was unable to put together an overall picture from these pieces of the puzzle.

On 24 October 1941, after the third deportation transport had left Berlin, he wrote: "This is the situation: 20,000 Jews are being sent off in the 1st operation (to the beginning of November), including five or six thousand from Berlin. Whether and when things continue, nobody knows. But one can assume it won't remain with just the 20,000. However, it can stretch on for over a year until all have been included [in transports]."[441] Five weeks later, Samter figured his own deportation would come in the spring of 1942. He knew about postcards from Lódz that "all have the same content: 'utter destitution. Send money!'"[442] Four weeks later he reported that the limit on age in the transports had been revoked (which was not true according to the guidelines still in force, but was often handled in that way in practice); the only criterion now was whether the person was fit for transport. A month later he mentioned rumors he had heard that there was an epidemic of typhus in Lódz, and that participants in a transport of one thousand deportees to Kovno "were shot on the way or murdered in some other way."[443] In May 1942, Samter enumerated the available knowledge about the deportation destinations: nothing had been heard from the deportees to Minsk, Kovno, and Riga, but "the general belief is that treatment in Riga is decent." From Lódz only hand-signed printed cards were arriving confirming receipt of money, no other mail. The deportees from Berlin to Warsaw appeared to be in acceptable accommodations. It was reported that the Jews from Stettin were transported from Piaski, near Lublin, to an unknown destination, where it is very dirty and there is "terrible distress"; the elderly and sick had died of starvation.[444] In August 1942, he was aware that seventy thousand persons had been deported in the meantime, and he anticipated he would be among those deported by the end of the year.[445] In actual fact, he was taken on by the RV as a "collector,"[446] a final postponement, until he too was deported to Auschwitz and murdered there.

In the case of the non-Jewish German *Volksgenossen*, Frank Bajohr has established a "broad current of information about murder operations" flowing into the *Altreich* via soldiers and employees in the civil administrations of the occupation.[447] The historian Dieter Pohl notes that from July 1942 on, the Western press and BBC carried reports "every few days" on the murder of the Jews, and after the first liberation of a German concentration camp, Lublin-Majdanek, on 22 July 1944, there was extensive and continuous reporting on this.[448]

The German-language newspaper of the Jews who had emigrated to Palestine, *Yedioth Hayom*, reported on 30 October 1941 that a third large-scale transport of Jews had left Berlin heading eastward on 21 October. *Yedioth Hayom* had taken information on evacuation of apartments and conditions in the assembly camp from the Swedish paper *Tidningen*.[449] By contrast, the areas of destination appeared to have been only vaguely known, as the paper reported the following day in an article entitled "Vernichtung des deutschen Judentums" (Destruction of German Jewry). It reported that it was not known whether the transport was going to the "already overcrowded Lublin reservation" or to the Rokitno swamps in the Pinsk district. The article concluded:

> If it should now prove true that the entire elderly Jewish population is to be deported to Poland, this would be tantamount to a total destruction of the Jewish community in Germany and Austria, given the age structure of

the Jews in Germany. If it is doubtful how many of those younger will survive the hard drudgery of forced labor in Germany until the war's end, the chances for older persons—torn from their in any case familiar surroundings and forced into menial hard labor under the most unfavorable climatic and spatial conditions imaginable, in surroundings alien to them—must be deemed equivalent to zero.[450]

Just under two years later, the newspaper referred to reports from Switzerland, according to which there were "no longer any Jews already for several months now" in Berlin.[451] And in 1944, based on reports in the Swedish press, it wrote that in 1943 alone, some 3.4 million Jews had been murdered, and enumerated how few Jews were still living in Germany and the occupied European countries.[452] Rumors were circulating on transports from Theresienstadt "to Poland."[453]

Interim Summary

Like Hermann Samter, many Jews were cognizant of details about the deportations, and this knowledge caused them, like Samter, to fear for their own fate. Yet they had no conception that all German and European Jews were doomed to mass murder. In this they scarcely differed from the Jewish functionaries, who likewise did not actually have "knowledge" of the catastrophe, in any event in the sense that from their abundance of information, they were able to piece together a picture of a general murder of the Jews. In addition, there was no contemporary concept such as Holocaust or Shoah to bring events together and thus, at least in an approximate way, to grasp their sheer enormity. What historian Dan Diner has termed the "rupture of civilization" (*Zivilisationsbruch*) was inconceivable for those affected, impossible to imagine. It thus appears that the German Jews and their representatives, if they were not directly warned by soldiers or contacts abroad,[454] had a more limited knowledge at their disposal than German *Volksgenossen* or attentive newspaper readers among the German-Jewish emigrants. Even in Theresienstadt, the Jewish representatives retained their former approach: not to accept the worst, to concentrate on obvious practical tasks, and to endeavor to act as effectively as possible in the sense of the German authorities, simply for the sake of maintaining the organization, while at the same time working in the interest of their members.

From October 1941 on, the German-Jewish functionaries carried out the supplementary tasks demanded to the best of their knowledge and judgment. Nonetheless, between the autumn of 1941 and the end of 1942, every single sphere of work changed that had been designed to guarantee a smooth operation—and, insofar as possible, to likewise ensure acceptable conditions for the RV members before or during deportation, precisely because of their participation in these procedures. This complex of work turned into a sophisticated instrument of coercion, rendering it easier for the Gestapo to locate the last remaining Jews in Germany, and then to seize, plunder, and deport them. This was also true of social work, as the example regarding care for children showed. At the same time, the possibilities to exert some influence, in any event quite limited, evaporated. Even in its function as employer, the Reichsvereinigung was soon no longer able to shield its employees from deportation. With their continued cooperation, already after several months now based increasingly on coercion, the Jewish functionaries also transposed their moral dilemma to all the subordinate staff workers in the organization. They were the employees charged with implementing the decisions, the danger of their own deportation constantly looming before their eyes. To ensure a smooth operation, they were instructed to treat their fellow Jews along harsh lines, similar to the behavior of the Gestapo. And they were not even held out the promise of the "preferential camp Theresienstadt."

Once deportations had begun, a gulf opened up between the organization and its functionaries on the one side and the (compulsory) membership on the other, and that chasm quickly deepened.

In short, the work—performed with great dedication, under adverse conditions, and with the best of intentions—in effect boomeranged, turning against the members (and the nonmembers administered by the organization), then against the staff workers, and finally against the leading RV functionaries themselves. This was because the Nazi regime did not follow rules or keep assurances or promises made. The RSHA, no matter if represented by Jagusch, Eichmann, Dannecker, or another official, never felt in any way obligated to the Jewish organization. It utilized the RV as long as it needed to, laying upon its shoulders a perfidious collective liability, and deported and murdered its representatives, staff employees, members, and nonmembers all the same. What still appeared to the Jewish leaders in the autumn of 1941 as a continuation of their previous work turned out, as shocking news came in on a daily basis over the course of 1942, to be a "rupture of civilization."

The Jewish functionaries endeavored to slow down the dynamics of Nazi policy on the Jews, countering where they could by engaging in their style of Prussian bureaucratic behavior, and recording in the minutes any agreements or small concessions, creating transparency and sticking to official channels. Even after they themselves had been deported to Theresienstadt, they firmly adhered to this strategy, although their forced participation in autonomous administration included more extensive participation and complicity in the deportations than their earlier limited assistance had entailed in the *Altreich*. And it was to cost almost all the Jewish functionaries their lives.

Notes

1. Some of the representative key literature on this topic: Browning, *Origins*, 309–29; Peter Longerich, *Holocaust: The Nazi Persecution and Murder of the Jews* (New York, 2010), 259–71; Saul Friedländer, *The Years of Extermination: Nazi Germany and the Jews 1939–1945* (New York, 2007), 197ff.; see also Christian Gerlach, "Die Wannsee-Konferenz, das Schicksal der deutschen Juden und Hitlers politische Grundsatzentscheidung, alle Juden Europas zu ermorden," *WerkstattGeschichte* 18 (1997): 7–44; Cesarani, *Eichmann*, 91ff.; for further literature, see the bibliographies in these studies.

2. Unfortunately, there is no extant documentation on the content of this and further discussions. Only the later statements by former Gestapo officials indicate that these talks actually took place. On these discussions, see also Browning, *Origins*, 379.

3. CJA, 2 B 1/2, memo, 149, phone call in RSHA, 13 September 1941; BArch, R 8150/2, RVJD, minutes of board meeting, 16 September 1941.

4. CJA, 2 B 1/2, memo, summons to RSHA, 8 September 1941, p. 1, point 2.

5. CJA, 2 B 1/4, memo, K 12, 24 December 1941, pp. 1–2.

6. CJA, 2 B 1/4, memo, R 9, 18 May 1942; BArch, R 8150/18, "Plan Reichsvereinigung, badge distribution," n.d., pag. 19.

7. Thus, for example, in Coburg in Upper Franconia, CJA, 2 B 1/4, letter, RVJD to RSHA, 29 September 1941, pag. 203.

8. CJA, 2 B 1/4, memo, K 39, 5/7 March 1942, p. 1.

9. CJA, 2 B 1/3, memo, K 6, consultation in RSHA, 17 September 1941, p. 3, point 4; CJA, K 9, 19 September 1941, p. 1, point 4; later it instituted a two-year period that voluntary members had to adhere to when canceling their membership, BArch, R 8150/17, Reichsvereinigung announcement, changing of §4 in the statutes of the Reichsvereinigung, n.d., pag. 12–13.

10. CJA, 2 B 1/3, memo, K 46, consultation in RSHA, 21 May 1942, p. 1, point 1; BArch, R 8150/18, Auerbach report, 6 October 1941, pag. 187–91; BArch, R 8150/17, letter, Jewish Community Berlin to Reichsvereinigung, 24 June 1941, pag. 55; see also explanations, pag. 59–165, and reports from the district offices on resignations from the RV, pag. 177–91.

11. This is how her contemporary Lucie Adelsberger described her; see Lucie Adelsberger, *Auschwitz: Ein Tatsachenbericht* (Berlin, 1960), 13.

12. Landesarchiv Berlin (LAB), B Rep 058, 1 Js 9/65 (Stapoleit) P. 32, Gohlke, Interrogation Martha Mosse, 11 July 1967, p. 2; on Martha Mosse, see also Elisabeth Kraus, *Die Familie Mosse: Deutsch-jüdisches Bürgertum im 19. und 20. Jahrhundert* (Munich, 1999), 570–95; Peter Reinicke, "Erster 'Polizeirat' in Preußen und Arbeit in der jüdischen Gemeinde unter Aufsicht der Gestapo: Martha Mosse (1884–1977)," in *Jüdische Wohlfahrt im Spiegel von Biographien*, ed. Sabine Hering (Frankfurt am Main, 2006), 296–304.

13. LAB, Rep. 235-07, MF 4170-4171, Martha Mosse, Memoirs: appendix: "Die Jüdische Gemeinde zu Berlin 1934-1943," report, 23/24 July 1958, p. 2. The term in the original German for "eviction operation" is *Wohnungsräumungsaktion*.
14. LAB, B Rep 058, 1 Js 9/65 (Stapoleit.) P. 32, Interrogation Martha Mosse, 11 July 1967, pag. 120ff., p. 2.
15. Ibid., p. 4.
16. See Rabinovici, *Eichmann's Jews*, 102–3.
17. LBI, JMB, MF 546, Joseph Löwenherz Coll., memo, meeting, Löwenherz with Eichmann, 30 September 1941.
18. See transports in the calendar year 1941, in Alfred Gottwaldt and Diana Schulle, *Die "Judendeportationen" aus dem Deutschen Reich 1941–1945* (Wiesbaden, 2005), 444.
19. On this, see Susanne Willems, *Der entsiedelte Jude, Albert Speers Wohnungsmarktpolitik für den Berliner Hauptstadtbau* (Berlin, 2000).
20. Ibid., 277ff.
21. LAB, B Rep 058, 1 Js 9/65 (Stapoleit.) P. 32, Interrogation Martha Mosse, 11 July 1967, pag. 120ff., p. 3; YV, 01/51, Moritz Henschel, lecture, "Die letzten Jahre der Jüdischen Gemeinde Berlin," Tel Aviv, 13 September 1946, transcript, p. 3.
22. Leo Baeck, "A People Stands before Its God," in *We Survived: Fourteen Histories of the Hidden and Hunted in Nazi Germany*, 2nd rev. ed., edited by Erich H. Boehm (Boulder, CO, 2003), 288.
23. YV, 01/51, Moritz Henschel, "Die letzten Jahre der Jüdischen Gemeinde Berlin," lecture, 13 September 1946, transcript, p. 3.
24. See chapter 1.
25. See, for example, minutes of the board meeting, No. 8, 30 July 1942 (BArch, R 8150/1), pag. 15: "Kozower reports on the disclosed dates for three further emigration transports from Berlin, ... which will be carried out in August in addition to the five transports every week to Theresienstadt.... This information must be kept in strict secrecy."
26. See Beate Meyer, "Das unausweichliche Dilemma: Die Reichsvereinigung der Juden in Deutschland, die Deportationen und die untergetauchten Juden," in *Solidarität und Hilfe für Juden während der NS-Zeit*, vol. 5, *Überleben im Untergrund: Hilfe für Juden in Deutschland 1941–1945*, ed. Beate Kosmala and Claudia Schoppmann (Berlin, 2002), 280–81.
27. See, for example, BArch, R 8150/1, minutes No. 19, 28 September 1942, p. 2; BArch, R 8150/1, minutes, No. 8, 30 July 1942.
28. For a facsimile of these instructions (*Merkblatt*), see Christian Dirks, "Sad Experiences in the Hell of Nazi Germany: The Scheurenberg Family," in Meyer, Simon, and Schütz, *Jews*, 219.
29. CJA, Sammlung Ausstellung Juden in Berlin (private copy), Ordinance No. 10/43 of the RVJD, District Office Berlin, 19 March 1943.
30. Inge Deutschkron, *Ich trug den gelben Stern* (Cologne, 1978), 70.
31. YV, 033/69 (probably Schwersenz), "Zum 16. Mai 1945, Alfred Selbiger," p. 4.
32. Baeck also commented that work was done "legally," but clandestinely; see AJR Information, May 1953, p. 9, Leo Baeck, "Bewaehrung des Deutschen Judentums," speech at the AJR rally, 1 April 1953.
33. CJA, 2 B 1/3, memo, K 20, 5 November 1941, p. 3, point 6.
34. BArch, R 8150/3, memo, 1 March 1942.
35. BArch, R 8150/3, letter, RVJD to board Jewish Community, 23 June 1942.
36. CJA, 2 B 1/4, memo, R 38, consultation in RSHA, 27 November 1942, p. 4.
37. CJA, 2 B 1/3, memo, K 20, consultation in RSHA, 9 November 1941, p. 2, point 2.

38. CJA, 2 B 1/3, memo, K 20, consultation in RSHA, 5 November 1941, p. 2, point 3.
39. Ibid.
40. BArch, R 8150/46, memo, F 28, consultation in RSHA, 21 November 1941, p. 3, pag. 150, point 3i.
41. CJA, 2 B 1/4, memo, K 27, 1 December 1941, p. 1, point 2.
42. CJA, 2 B 1/4, memo, K 21, 8 November 1941, pp. 1–2. The RV also informed the Jewish Communities and district branches about this; see USHMM, RG-14.035M, reel 10, Jewish Community of Leipzig records (2001.150), letter, RVJD to district branches and Communities, Re: evacuations, 30 October 1941; letter, RVJD to same, re: evacuations III, 12 November 1941.
43. CJA, 2 B 1/4, memo, K 22, 12 November 1941, pp. 1–2, point 4.
44. JDC, NY, Coll. 33/44, File 664, letter, AJDC Lisbon to AJDC New York, memo Conversation with Mr. Schwartz, 5 November 1941, p. 2.
45. CJA, 2 B 1/4, memo, K 25, 24 November 1941, pp. 1–2, point 4.
46. BArch, R 8150/46, memo, F 48, consultation in RSHA, 7 February 1942, p. 2, point 1e, n. pag.
47. BArch, R 8150/69, memo, F 69, consultation in RSHA, 15 April 1942, p. 2, point 1g, n. pag.
48. I would like to thank Frank Bajohr for the document "Erinnerungen des Prüfungsgebietes VI 6 aus dem letzten Jahre, die sich gegen Eigennutz, Verschwendung usw. Richten," BArch, R 2301/2073/2, fol. 99; see also Frank Bajohr, *Parvenüs und Profiteure in der NS-Zeit* (Frankfurt am Main, 2001), 122.
49. BArch, R 2301/2073/2, fol. 101, p. 20.
50. See Beate Meyer, "The Fine Line Between Responsible Action and Collaboration: The Reichsvereinigung der Juden in Deutschland and the Jewish Community in Berlin, 1938–1945," in Meyer, Simon, and Schütz, *Jews*, 328.
51. BArch, R 8150/46, memo, F 28, consultation in RSHA, 21 November 1941, p. 3, pag. 150, point 3i.
52. CJA, 2 B 1/4, memo, K 26, 28 November 1941, p. 2. The RSHA informed the "evacuation offices" accordingly in a letter dated 3 December 1941; see NRW Staatsarchiv Münster, 45 Js 29/78, doc. 004, appendix IV, pag. 45ff. Later the RV applied for an increase of 50 percent, with which deportees to the East would then have financed the transports to Theresienstadt. But the RSHA rejected this, stating that these funds should best be withdrawn ahead of time from the "special account H" ("H" = *Heimeinkaufsverträge,* home purchase contracts).
53. LBI, NY, AR 2038, Reichsvereinigung BZ Baden-Pfalz in liquidation, circular letter, Re: preparation of the emigration transport, 16 August 1942, p. 2.
54. LBI, NY, AR 2038, Reichsvereinigung BZ Baden-Pfalz in liquidation, circular letter, Re: emigration, 20 September 1942, p. 2.
55. LAB, B Rep 058, 1 Js 9/65, Düsseldorf, report on discussion in RSHA, 6 March 1942, p. 2.
56. LBI, NY, AR 25033, MF 537, Rischowsky Coll., memo, 59/23, 12 March 1941, p. 1, as well as annex, lists of names of the men proposed; memo, 24 October 1941, consultation Eichmann with Eppstein and Storfer, p. 2.
57. JDC, NY, Coll. 33/44, File 664, AJDC Lisbon to AJDC New York, memo, conversation with Mr. Schwartz, 5 November 1941, p. 2.
58. CJA, 2 B 1/4, memo, K 42, 15 April 1942, p. 3, point 4.
59. JDC, NY, Coll. 33/44, file 631/2, unknown author, Jews in Germany—October 1941, report, 17 March 1942, p. 6.

60. 11. VO zum Reichsbürgergesetz, 25 November 1941, RGBl. I, p. 1146 (revoked 20 September 1945 by Law No. 1, Allied Control Council).

61. YV, 01/192, Ball-Kaduri: discussion with Mr. Siegmund Weltlinger in Berlin late May 1957, "Activity for the Berlin Jewish Community, 1939–1943," p. 1.

62. This interpretation after the fact is understandable, given that in the postwar period, Weltlinger was very active in helping to reorganize Jewish life in Berlin, and struggled for years to regain the lost property of the Berlin Jewish Community; see Philipp J. Nielsen, "'I've never regretted being a German Jew': Siegmund Weltlinger and the Re-establishment of the Jewish Community in Berlin," *LBI Yearbook* LIV (2009): 3–24.

63. See, for example, Albert H. Friedlander, *Leo Baeck: Leben und Lehre* (Stuttgart, 1973), 55ff.; on Baeck's withdrawal from practical work, see also Avraham Barkai, "Von Berlin nach Theresienstadt: Zur politischen Biographie Leo Baecks 1933–1945," in *Hoffnung und Untergang: Studien zur deutsch-jüdischen Geschichte des 19. und 20. Jahrhunderts* (Hamburg, 1998), 155–56; Gerd Stecklina, "'Was wir am Mitmenschen tun, ist Gottesdienst': Leo Baeck (1873–1946)," in Hering, *Jüdische Wohlfahrt*, 66–73.

64. See Friedlander, *Leo Baeck*, 54–55.

65. See Leonard Baker, *Hirt der Verfolgten: Leo Baeck im Dritten Reich* (Stuttgart, 1982), 363.

66. YV, 01/241, Herbert (Ehud) Growald, "Hachscharah und Hachscharahzentren in Deutschland von 1940–1943," 23 June 1958, p. 3.

67. See also his pupils Herbert Strauss and Ernst Ludwig Ehrlich, who studied there until the Hochschule was closed down by the Gestapo: Ernst Ludwig Ehrlich, "Erinnerungen an Leo Baeck," in *Leo Baeck 1873–1956: Aus dem Stamme von Rabbinern*, ed. Georg Heuberger and Fritz Backhaus (Frankfurt am Main, 2001), 188–91; Herbert A. Strauss, "Erinnerungen an Leo Baeck," in Heuberger and Backhaus, *Leo Baeck*, 191–94; see also Herbert A. Strauss, *In The Eye of The Storm: Growing Up Jewish in Germany, 1918–1943* (New York, 1999), 133–56.

68. Baeck himself sketched his relation to the resistance and the genesis of the manuscript in a conversation with Robert Weltsch; see Robert Weltsch, "Aufzeichnung über eine Unterredung," in *Worte des Gedenkens für Leo Baeck*, ed. Eva Reichmann (Heidelberg, 1959), 238–39; see also Barkai, "Von Berlin nach Theresienstadt," 158ff. In 2001, controversy erupted regarding Baeck's manuscript; Hermann Simon, based on memos by Paul Eppstein, pointed to contradictions in Baeck's own statements, who claimed he had written the manuscript between 1938 and 1941 for Carl Goerdeler and the German resistance. On this controversy, see Hermann Simon, "Bislang unbekannte Quellen zur Entstehungsgeschichte des Werkes 'Die Entwicklung der Rechtsstellung der Juden in Europa, vornehmlich in Deutschland,'" in Heuberger and Backhaus, *Leo Baeck*, 103–110; see also Fritz Backhaus and Martin Liepach, "Leo Baecks Manuskript über die 'Rechtsstellung der Juden in Europa': Neue Funde und ungeklärte Fragen," *Zeitschrift für Geschichtswissenschaft* 50, no. 1 (2002): 55–70; see also diverse articles in the (daily) press, including *Frankfurter Allgemeine* (FAZ), *Frankfurter Rundschau* (FR), *Aufbau*, *Die Welt*.

69. Baeck, "A People Stands before Its God," 289.

70. Simon, "Unbekannte Quellen," 103–110.

71. Fritz Backhaus and Martin Liepach, "Ein Schatten im Leben des hoch angesehenen Rabbiners: Über die Rolle Leo Baecks im Nationalsozialismus: Neue Funde, Spurensuche und ungeklärte Fragen (Dokumentation)," *Frankfurter Rundschau*, 1 October 2001.

72. Weltsch, "Aufzeichnung über eine Unterredung," 239.

73. BArch, R 8150/46, memo, F 65, consultation in RSHA, 30 March 1942, p. 4, point 2, n. pag.
74. BArch, R 8150/3, minutes of the meeting of the board and committee, 24 June 1942.
75. BArch, R 8150/2, Reichsvereinigung der Juden in Deutschland, minutes No. 18, board meeting, 23 September 1942.
76. BArch, R 8150/2, Reichsvereinigung der Juden in Deutschland, minutes, board meeting, 28 August 1942.
77. CJA, 2 B 1/3, memo, K 52, consultation in RSHA, 2 July 1942, p. 1, point 1.
78. BArch, R 8150/3, minutes No. 18, 23 September 1942, p. 2. (1) Bavaria, (2) Brandenburg- East Prussia, (3) Central Germany, including the Sudeten, (4) Northwest Germany, (5) Rhineland-Westphalia, (6) Saxony, and (7) Southwest Germany, including Baden-Palatinate, Hesse, Hesse-Nassau, and Württemberg.
79. BArch, R 8150/3, minutes No. 26, 18 November 1942.
80. BArch, R 8150/3, minutes No. 31, 12 December 1942.
81. BArch, R 8150/3, minutes No. 10/43, 19 May 1943.
82. BArch, R 8150/3, memo, committee meeting, 12 March 1942.
83. BArch, R 8150/3, memo 11, committee meeting, 28 May 1942.
84. On this, see Clemens Maier, "Das Jüdische Nachrichtenblatt (1938–1943): Ein jüdisches Presseerzeugnis im Kontext nationalsozialistischer Verfolgung" (MA thesis, Free University Berlin, 2001); Clemens Maier, "The Jüdisches Nachrichtenblatt 1938–43," in Meyer, Simon, and Schütz, Jews, 100–20; Reiner Burger, Von Goebbels Gnaden: "Jüdisches Nachrichtenblatt" (1938–1943) (Münster, Hamburg, and London, 2001) (with some errors, such as the consistently incorrect spelling of the chief editor's name as "Kreidler").
85. Hildesheimer, Selbstverwaltung, 202ff.
86. Ibid., 209.
87. See Jutta Wietog, Volkszählung unter dem Nationalsozialismus: Eine Dokumentation zur Bevölkerungsstatistik im Dritten Reich (Berlin, 2001), 170–71; Beate Meyer, "Jüdische Mischlinge": Rassenpolitik und Verfolgungserfahrung 1933–1945 (Hamburg, 1999), 162. "Dissidents" was the designation for those Jews who had by formal declaration left the Jewish Community but did not convert to another religion.
88. BArch, R 8150/32, Ernst Rosenthal, "Die katastermäßige Erfassung der Juden in Berlin," 23 December 1942, pag. 7–10.
89. BArch, R 8150/2, Reichsvereinigung der Juden in Deutschland, minutes, board meeting, 9 June 1941.
90. CJA, 2 B 1/2, memo, No. 64, consultation in RSHA, 2 May 1941, p. 2, point 6; see also StaHH, 522-1 Jüdische Gemeinden, section 1993, file 20, letter, RVJD to district branches and Jewish Communities, 17 June 1941, re: card file of the Jews in Germany, central card file.
91. LBI, NY, AR 25033, MF 537, Rischowsky Coll., memo, Z 76, 5 June 1941.
92. As a remainder of this card file, extant are the registration slips of 1,430 Jews, which the "Jewish Communities Germany" sent on 28 July 1947 to the International Tracing Service Bad Arolsen. Today they are part of a card file composed of several postwar receipts of documentation; see Reichsvereinigung der Juden (Kartei), Bestand 1.2.4.1.
93. USHMM, RG-14.035M; Acc.2001.150, Reel 11, Jewish Community of Leipzig, RVJD, circular letter to district branches and Jewish Communities, 18 March 1941.
94. LBI, NY, AR 25033, MF 537, Rischowsky Coll., memo, Z 76, 4 June 1941, p. 1; LBI, NY, AR 25033, MF 537, Rischowsky Coll., memo, No. 59/23, Eppstein summoned by Eichmann, pp. 1–2, point 2.

95. Ibid.
96. CJA, 2 B 1/2, memo, No. 141, consultation in RSHA, 23 August 1941, pp. 5–6, point 10.
97. BArch, R 8150/46, memo, F 14, consultation in RSHA, 8 October 1941, p. 6, point 17.
98. BArch, R 8150/17, letter, RVJD to Landgerichtsrat Neukamp, ret., Bielefeld, 1 October 1941, pag. 2.
99. The registration cards of some nineteen thousand Jews, which the Jewish Cultural Committee Germany handed over in 1949/1950 to the International Tracing Service Bad Arolsen, are today part of a card file composed of several postwar receipts of documentation; see "Reichsvereinigung der Juden (Kartei)," Bestand 1.2.4.1.
100. In the order of the examples mentioned: Kurt Bibo, Hamburg, pag. 01005, Alice Bloch, pag. 01273, Regina Dombrowski, pag. 04118, Ernst Ehrenfeld, pag. 01480, ITS Arolsen, 1.2.4.1, Reichsvereinigung der Juden.
101. LAB, B Rep 058, 1 Js 9/65, Box 66, letter, RVJD to Jewish Communities and district branches, 30 October 1941, re: evacuation.
102. These are registration cards of Berlin pupils that were provided to the International Tracing Service Bad Arolsen from an unknown source. Today they are also part of the Reichsvereinigung der Juden (Kartei), Bestand 1.2.4.1.
103. See Meyer, "Fine Line," 317.
104. See Klaus Dettmer, "Die Deportationen aus Berlin," in Buch der Erinnerung: Die ins Baltikum deportierten deutschen, österreichischen und tschechoslowakischen Juden, vol. 1, ed. Wolfgang Scheffler and Diana Schulle (Munich, 2003), 194.
105. CJA, Sammlung Ausstellung Juden in Berlin 1938–1945, Interview by Beate Meyer with Herbert A. Strauss, 4 November 1999, transcript, p. 5. Strauss reports that he as well as other students at the Hochschule had, at Leo Baeck's request, assisted in a questionnaire initiative, under the direction of Mosse and/or Bertha Mendelsohn (card file department).
106. BArch, R 8150/3, memo 3, committee meeting, 17 March 1942.
107. LAB, B Rep. 057-01, proceedings against J. Baumann, R 34/1, interrogation Martha Mosse, 19 August 1942, p. 3, pag. 100–1.
108. LAB, B Rep. 057-01, proceedings against J. Baumann, R 34/1, interrogation Martha Mosse, 19 August 1942, pp. 1–2, pag. 98–99.
109. LAB, Rep. 235-07, MF 4170-4171, Martha Mosse, "Memoirs," pp. 2–3.
110. BArch, R 8150/50, Martha Mosse, "Bericht zu der Frage der früheren Mitarbeiter des Kulturbundes," 8 June 1942, pag. 19–20.
111. BArch, R 8150/2, RVJD, minutes, No. 14, board meeting, 7 September 1942; BArch, R 8150/3, minutes, No. 13, 3 September 1942, Statistik der Juden in Berlin; BArch, R 8150/3, minutes, No. 15, board meeting, 9 September 1942; BArch, R 8150/3, minutes, No. 13, 3 September 1942, Statistik der Juden in Berlin; BArch, R 8150/3, minutes, No. 15, board meeting, 9 September 1942, Jewish Community board meeting.
112. BArch, R 8150/3, minutes, No. 27, board meeting, 22 November 1942, p. 2.
113. BArch, R 8150/3, minutes, No. 30, board meeting, 7 December 1942.
114. BArch, R 8150/3, minutes, No. 1/43, 4 January 1943.
115. LAB, B Rep 058, 1 Js 9/65 (Stapoleit) P. 32, Gohlke, Interrogation Martha Mosse, 11 July 1967, p. 7.
116. LAB, Rep. 20, Nr. 4860-4861, judgment in case before court of honor, Martha Raphael, 7 May 1947, p. 2.
117. On the individual Berlin assembly camps, see Meyer, "Fine Line," 319ff., 328ff., 330ff.

118. Edith Dietz, *Den Nazis entronnen: Die Flucht eines jüdischen Mädchens in die Schweiz: Autobiografischer Bericht 1933–1942* (Frankfurt am Main, 1990), 36.
119. LAB, B Rep 058, 1 Js, 9/65, Interrogation Hermann Blumenthal, 9 March 1970, p. 5.
120. LAB, B Rep 058, 1 Js, 9/65, Interrogation Abrahamson, 1 November 1946, by city police Braunschweig.
121. See Dietz, *Den Nazis entronnen*, 36–37.
122. See LBI, NY, AR 1249, Edmund Hadra, MS "Theresienstadt," Part I, p. 8; I wish to thank Anna Hájková for pointing out this source to me. On Hadra, see also http://archive.org/details/edmundhadra (accessed 5 June 2012).
123. Karl Loewenstein, "Minsk: Im Lager der deutschen Juden," in "*Aus Politik und Zeitgeschichte,*" supplement, *Das Parlament*, B XXXXV/56, 7 November 1956: 707.
124. See Siegmund Weltlinger, *Hast Du es schon vergessen? Erlebnisbericht aus der Zeit der Verfolgung, herausgegeben von der Berliner Gesellschaft für jüdisch- christliche Zusammenarbeit* (Berlin, 1954), 27.
125. For the assembly camp on Grosse Hamburger Strasse, see Akim Jah, "Vom Altenheim zum Sammellager: Die Große Hamburger Straße 26, die Deportation der Berliner Juden und das Personal der Stapoleitstelle Berlin," *Theresienstädter Studien und Dokumente* 14 (2007): 176–219.
126. See Meyer, "Fine Line," 334–39. The term *Geltungsjude* (literally "person considered a Jew") covered individuals deemed Jews by a supplementary decree to the Nuremberg Laws (14 November 1935): (1) offspring of a mixed marriage when both partners had formally belonged to the Jewish Community at the time of the child's birth; (2) offspring of a mixed marriage born after 1935 when the partners were not married; (3) the illegitimate child of a Jewish woman born after 1935; (4) 'half-Jews' who belonged to the Jewish Community.
127. See "Merkblatt für die Teilnehmer an Abwanderungstransporten," quoted in Inge Hartwig-Scharnberg and Jan Maruhn, "Das kann doch nicht lange dauern," unpublished MS, appendix. Numerous personal papers deposited with the Jewish Community testify to the fact that the deportees hoped to be able to return to a normal life, where they might need their school transcripts or documents on pensions, or even don their medals and badges of honor at a memorial day celebration.
128. YV, 01/192, Ball-Kaduri, discussion with Mr. Siegmund Weltlinger in Berlin in late May 1957, activity for the Berlin Jewish Community, 1939–1943, p. 2.
129. Ibid.
130. LAB, B Rep 058, 1 Js 9/65, Beistück 30, Report, Harry Schnapp II, report on the "Brunner period," pp. 3ff., pag. 151ff..
131. LAB, B Rep 058, 1 Js 9/65, Box 78, No. 73, "Ehrengerichtsakten der Jüdischen Gemeinde zu Berlin betreffend div. Personen" [Files, court of honor, Berlin Jewish Community, on diverse individuals]; Max Reschke, here; minutes of the court of honor, session, 5 April 1956, p. 2.
132. The "collectors" (*Abholer*) were organized in keeping with the model of the Vienna "lifters" (*Ausheber*), which Alois Brunner had set up there in November 1941. Josef Löwenherz, the responsible head of the Vienna Jewish Community, had initially refused to comply with participation in such escorts on the part of the Community. In response, a Jewish Gestapo informer, on Brunner's instructions, organized an especially brutal Jewish troop of some forty men, likewise acting under orders: "Primitive, frightened and brutal men were selected and they treated the victims harshly and roughly" (Rabinovici, *Eichmann's Jews*, 129). When reports reached the Community, with complaints charging theft, blackmail, bribery, and even rape, Löwen-

herz backed down; he agreed to cooperate and made some Community staff workers available (Rabinovici, *Eichmann's Jews*, 130). Presumably, the functionaries in Berlin were aware of these events.

133. YV, 02/30, Hermann Samter: Letters, Sept. 1940–7 Feb. 1943 to Hannah Kobilinski et al., here; letter, 7 February 1943. Samter's letters have since been published on behalf of Yad Vashem; see Hermann Samter, *Worte können das ja kaum verständlich machen": Briefe 1939–1943*, ed. Daniel Fraenkel (Göttingen, 2009).

134. CJA, 2 B 1/5, memo, 17 December 1942.

135. CJA, 2 A 1, memo on consultation with Dobberke/Gestapo, 2 February 1943.

136. YV, 033/988, memoirs, M. Strassburger, p. 16.

137. CJA, 2 B 1/5, memo, 14 November 1942 (Henschel).

138. CJA, 2 B 1/5, memo, 14 November 1942, point 15 (Kozower).

139. CJA, 2 A 1, memo on consultation with Scharführer Zit(t)a, 15 January 1943. The memo includes the notable term "collection service" (*Abholedienst*).

140. The *Greifer* will not be discussed here because the RV had no influence on their creation and activities. See, inter alia, Christian Dirks, "Snatchers: The Berlin Gestapo's Jewish Informants," in Meyer, Simon, and Schütz, eds., *Jews*, 248–74.

141. CJA, 2 B 1/5, 2 A 1, report "re: collection service," 4 January 1943.

142. CJA, 2 B 1/5, 2 A 1, Statistics of the N-lists for the period 18 December 1942 to 4 January 1943. The "N-lists" probably involved Jews who could not be located. On the *Urhebung* or "basic survey," see also fn. 111 above.

143. Yet my sample check on the data concerning sixty-five marshals showed that exceeding the "target number" (daily assigned quota) ultimately did not protect these "collectors": sixty were eventually deported, four went into hiding; one (Max Plaut) managed to make his way to safety with the Palestine exchange of German citizens living in Palestine (mostly from the German Protestant sect of the Templers) and Jews still living in Germany, but who had obtained one of the very few certificates from the British government to enter Palestine.

144. "Richtlinien," 4 June 1942, reproduced in Gottwaldt and Schulle, *"Judendeportationen,"* 174.

145. CJA, 2 B 1/4, memo, K 30, 19 December 1941, p. 3, point 8.

146. LBI, NY, AR 25033, Rischowsky Coll., memo, Z 116, p. 1.

147. CJA, 2 B 1/4, memo, R 19, 7 July 1942, p. 32.

148. YV, 02/769, Martha Mosse, "resettlement" of the Berlin Jews, report, 23–24 July 1958, recorded by Dr. Wolfgang Scheffler, "Ergänzungen zu meinem Bericht vom 23./24.7.1958" [Supplement to my report of 23/24 July 1958], p. 1.

149. Teaching aims, quoted in Adler-Rudel, *Selbsthilfe*, 38.

150. Dieter Maier, *Arbeitseinsatz und Deportationen: Die Mitwirkung der Arbeitsverwaltung bei der nationalsozialistischen Judenverfolgung in den Jahren 1938–1945* (Berlin, 1994), 49.

151. See Wolf Gruner, "Die Reichshauptstadt Berlin und die Verfolgung der Berliner Juden 1933–1945," in *Jüdische Geschichte in Berlin*, ed. Reinhard Rürup (Berlin, 1995), 257.

152. LBI, Jerusalem, 427, "Berlin und die Juden, Bericht über die Verhältnisse der Juden in Berlin 1933–1941," n.p., see chap. "Monatliche Fürsorgeleistungen im Durchschnitt des 1. Halbjahres 1941" [Average monthly expenses for welfare, first six months 1941]. For details on school meals, number of day homes for children, and number of children in care there, as well as in secure residential homes (residents not allowed to leave), see Central Archives for the History of the Jewish People, Jerusalem, D/Be 4/329A, "Juedische Kultusvereinigung zu Berlin e.V., Wohlfahrts- und Jugendpflegestelle, Tätigkeitsbericht v. 1.1.1941-31.3.1941," pp. 1–7.

153. See Maier, *Arbeitseinsatz*, 73; see also Wolf Gruner, *Der Geschlossene Arbeitseinsatz deutscher Juden: Zur Zwangsarbeit als Element der Verfolgung 1938–1943* (Berlin, 1997), 116–51.

154. Maier, *Arbeitseinsatz*, 73.

155. LBI, Jerusalem, 427, "Berlin und die Juden, Bericht über die Verhältnisse der Juden in Berlin 1933–1941," n.p., see chap. "Monatliche Fürsorgeleistungen im Durchschnitt des 1. Halbjahres 1941."

156. Ibid.

157. The training seminar for Jewish nursery teachers and kindergarten teachers in Berlin was in existence until the spring of 1942; see Maierhof, *Selbstbehauptung*, 253.

158. Dietz, *Den Nazis entronnen*, 33.

159. LAB, B Rep 058, 1 Js 9/65, ZH 105, Interrogation Lieselotte Pereles, 18 October 1966, p. 3.

160. Ibid.

161. Dietz, *Den Nazis entronnen*, 64.

162. Deborah Dwork, *Children with a Star: Jewish Youth in Nazi Europe* (New Haven, CT, 1993), 15.

163. Ibid.

164. Dietz, *Den Nazis entronnen*, 59.

165. LAB, B Rep 058, 1 Js 9/65, ZH 105, Interrogation Lieselotte Pereles, 18 October 1966, p. 4.

166. On this, see Jana Leichsenring, *Die katholische Kirche und "ihre Juden": Das "Hilfswerk beim Bischöflichen Ordinariat Berlin" 1938–1945* (Berlin, 2007), 160ff., with further literature given there; see also Hartmut Ludwig, "'So gehe hin und tue desgleichen!': Zur Geschichte des 'Büros Pfarrer Grüber' 1938–1940," in *Bevollmächtigt zum Brükkenbau: Heinrich Grüber: Judenfreund und Trümmerprobst: Erinnerungen, Predigten, Berichte, Briefe*, ed. Jörg Hildebrandt (Leipzig, 1991), 38; Heinrich Grüber, "An der Stechbahn: Erlebnisse und Berichte aus dem Büro Grüber in den Jahren der Verfolgung," in Hildebrandt, *Bevollmächtigt zum Brückenbau*, 64.

167. Margarete Draeger, née Lubowski, born 30 August 1895 in Essen, directed the Family School in 1941/1942, until it was dissolved on 30 June 1942. She went underground at the end of 1942, was later arrested, and then deported on 10 August 1944 to Auschwitz, where she was murdered; see www.bundesarchiv.de/gedenkbuch/index.html.en (accessed 26 July 2012). In May 2011, a Margarete-Draeger-Haus was dedicated in Tempelhof in Berlin in her memory; see http://goo.gl/jrp79 (accessed 5 June 2012).

168. BArch, R 8150/1.1.1./7/4, memo, Fürst, 22 May 1941; BArch, R 8150/1.1.1./7/4, memo, Henschel, 18 April 1941; BArch, R 8150/1.1.1./7/4, memo, Fürst, 24 April 1941; BArch, R 8150/1.1.1./7/4, memo, Henschel, 25 July 1941.

169. As stated by Heinrich Herzberg, quoted in Leichsenring, *Die katholische Kirche*, 174.

170. CJA, Sammlung Ausstellung "Juden in Berlin 1938–1945," Interview with Horst Gessner (audio recording), by Beate Meyer, 15 October 1999, transcript, p. 8. Cohesion among them proved to be lasting. Despite being dismissed from school in 1942, the war, the building of the GDR wall, and very different patterns of postwar socialization in the two Germanies, East and West, the former classmates from the Family School remained in contact and had reunions at regular intervals until the 1990s.

171. See Rita Meyhöfer, *Gäste in Berlin: Jüdisches Schülerleben in der Weimarer Republik und im Nationalsozialismus* (Hamburg, 1996), 219.

172. Leichsenring, *Katholische Kirche*, 176–77.

173. BArch, R 8150/7, circular letter, re: liquidation of the Jewish school system, p. 2.

174. According to Hanna Karminski; see BArch, R 8150/2, minutes, board meeting, 29 June 1941, p. 1.

175. CJA, Berlin, Sammlung Ausstellung "Juden in Berlin 1938–1945," letter, E.A. to Dr. Munk, 25 November 1947.

176. CJA, Berlin, Sammlung Ausstellung "Juden in Berlin 1938–1945," Liselotte C., "Dennoch. Ein Leben am Rande" (typescript), p. 41.

177. See Arthur Brass, "Die Rückkehr der Torarollen," *Berliner Allgemeine*, 9 March 1984; Liselotte C., letter to the editor, *Berliner Allgemeine*, 18 March 1984.

178. See also Stefanie Schüler-Springorum, "Fear and Misery in the Third Reich: From the Files of the Collective Guardianship Office of the Berlin Jewish Community," *Yad Vashem Studies* 27 (1999): 94; see also Shoah Resource Center, Yad Vashem, http://goo.gl/2qAfX (accessed 30 July 2012).

179. YV, 02/560, Gertrud Staewen, "Efforts by Members of the 'Bekenntniskirche' to help Jews," p. 4; for Bible text, see Jewish Publication Society of America, *The Holy Scriptures According to the Masoretic Text: A New Translation* (Philadelphia 1917 [5677 Hebrew calendar]), http://goo.gl/2eEmL (accessed 4 June 2012).

180. Quoted in Regina Scheer, "Eine Treppe ins Nichts: Josepha Gutmann, Kinderheim Greifswalder Str. 138/9," in *Leben mit der Erinnerung: Jüdische Geschichte am Prenzlauer Berg*, ed. Kulturamt Prenzlauer Berg (Berlin, 1997), 102.

181. Hildegard Henschel, "Aus der Arbeit der Jüdischen Gemeinde Berlin während der Jahre 1941–1943: Gemeindearbeit und Evakuierung von Berlin (16. Oktober 1941–16. Juni 1943)," *Zeitschrift für die Geschichte des Judentums* 9, nos. 1/2 (1972): 35.

182. Dietz, *Den Nazis entronnen*, 34–35.

183. Ibid., 36; see also Beate Meyer, "Fine Line," 320–21.

184. Dietz, *Den Nazis entronnen*, 38.

185. Ibid.

186. See Meyer, "Fine Line," 328–29.

187. "Das Ende einer Gemeinde: Eine Krankenschwester berichtet," in *Zeugen sagen aus: Berichte und Dokumente über die Judenverfolgung im "Dritten Reich"* ed. Mira Schoenberner and Gerhard Schoenberner (Berlin, 1988), 324.

188. Henschel, "Aus der Arbeit," 47–48.

189. Ibid.

190. Rivka Elkin, "Kinder zur Auf bewahrung im Jüdischen Krankenhaus zu Berlin in den Jahren 1943–1945," *Tel Aviver Jahrbuch für deutsche Geschichte* 23 (1994): 247–74; on the "children's accommodation section," see also Schüler-Springorum, "Fear and Misery," 100ff.; Daniel B. Silver, *Refuge in Hell: How Berlin's Jewish Hospital Outlasted the Nazis* (New York, 2003), xix, 28, 55–56.

191. LBI, Jerusalem, 207, Hilde Kahan, "Chronik deutscher Juden 1939–1945," pp. 33–34.

192. Schüler-Springorum, "Fear and Misery," 102.

193. Elkin, "Kinder," 273.

194. See also Schüler-Springorum, "Fear and Misery," 99.

195. Cordelia Edvardson, *Burned Child Seeks the Fire*, trans. Joel Agee (New York, 1997), 54–56; see also Silver, *Refuge*, xix.

196. Ulla Jung, "'Ich werde mich wehren': Werner Jacobowitz, ein Überlebender des Auerbach'schen Waisenhauses, Schönhauser Allee 162," in Kulturamt, Prenzlauer, and Berg, *Leben*, 53.

197. The still extant guidelines pertaining to the respective transports are reproduced in Gottwaldt and Schulle, *"Judendeportationen."*

198. The editors of the book *Der Dienstkalender Heinrich Himmlers 1941/42* point out that on 23 October 1941, Eichmann had already ordered the deferment of those sixty-five and older in the deportation guidelines, and that since October 1941, a transit camp had been planned for specific Jews from the Reich, and Jews from Bohemia were also to be sent there. The preparations for Theresienstadt began on 24 November 1941; Peter Witte, Michael Wildt, Martina Voigt, Dieter Pohl, Peter Klein, Christian Gerlach, Christoph Dieckmann, and Andrej Angrick, eds., *Der Dienstkalender Heinrich Himmlers 1941/42* (Hamburg, 1999), 251; Goebbels noted Heydrich's plan for an "old age ghetto" in a diary entry dated 18 November 1941, where he wrote: "Likewise, a number of elderly Jews can no longer be expelled to the East; for them, a Jewish ghetto is to be set up in a small city in the Protectorate"; see Elke Fröhlich, ed., *Die Tagebücher von Josef Goebbels, Teil II, Diktate 1941–1945*, vol. 2, *Oktober- Dezember 1941* (Munich, 1996), 309; see also Miroslav Kárný, "Theresienstadt 1941–1945," in *Theresienstädter Gedenkbuch: Die Opfer der Judentransporte aus Deutschland nach Theresienstadt 1942–1945*, ed. Institut Theresienstädter Initiative (Prague, 2000), 15–16.

199. Staatliches Zentralarchiv in Prag, Innenministerium, Z-845-1, Mapy zprav zpracovanych Studijnum ustaven, Notes on the discussion on 10 October 1941 on the solution of Jewish questions (participants: Heydrich, Frank, Böhm, Maurer, v. Gregory, Eichmann, Günther, Wolfram), p. 2.

200. LAB, B Rep 058, 1 Js 9/65 (Stapoleit.) P. 32, Interrogation Martha Mosse, 11 July 1967, pag. 120ff., p. 2.

201. Ibid., p. 3.

202. Ibid., p. 4–5. Popitz was later active in conservative resistance circles against the Nazi regime, and was executed in February 1945.

203. Report, reproduced in part in H. G. Adler, *Die verheimlichte Wahrheit: Theresienstädter Dokumente* (Tübingen, 1958), 11.

204. Berthold Simonsohn, "Gedenkblatt für Paul Eppstein," *Jüdische Sozialarbeit* 4, nos. 3/4 (18 September 1959), offprint.

205. Henschel, *Aus der Arbeit*, 41; Simonsohn, "Gedenkblatt für Paul Eppstein," *Jüdische Sozialarbeit* 4, nos. 3/4.

206. Starting in May 1942, references to "Theresienstadt" appear in the minutes of the RV board.

207. LAB, B Rep. 058, 1 Js 9/65 (Stapoleit.), Box 48, Interrogation Hilda H. Kahan, 30 October 1968, p. 3; see also Rivka Elkin, *Das Jüdische Krankenhaus in Berlin zwischen 1938 und 1945* (Berlin, 1993), 45ff.; Dagmar Hartung-von Doetinchem and Rolf Winau, eds., *Zerstörte Fortschritte: Das Jüdische Krankenhaus in Berlin (1756-1861-1914-1989)* (Berlin, 1989), 182ff.

208. See Adelsberger, *Auschwitz*, 13.

209. BArch, R 8150, memo by Lustig for Eppstein," 22 February 1942, pag. 255; memo by Karminski to Eppstein/Lustig, 6 June 1942, pag. 243; memo by Lustig, 8 June 1942, pag. 249; memo by Lustig to Eppstein, 10 June 1942, pag. 244; letter, RVJD Lustig to RSHA, 10 June 1942, pag. 241; memo by Karminski to Eppstein, 9 June 1942, pag. 241; Gottwaldt and Schulle, *"Judendeportationen,"* 185, 204, 217, 399.

210. See www.bendorf-geschichte.de/bdf-0155.htm (accessed 5 June 2012).

211. See Beate Kosmala, "Missglückte Hilfe und ihre Folgen: Die Ahndung der 'Judenbegünstigung' durch NS-Verfolgungsbehörden," in *Solidarität und Hilfe für Juden während der NS-Zeit*, vol. 5, *Überleben im Untergrund, Hilfe für Juden in Deutschland 1941–1945*, ed. Beate Kosmala and Claudia Schoppmann (Berlin, 2002), 205–22.

212. I wish to thank Barbara Welker, CJA, for this information, provided on 9 December 2010. On the basis of the list of staff employees dated 1 September 1941, she calculated a total number of 5,524 coworkers. Board members or district office heads should be added to this figure, and the small number of "Aryan" employees deducted. In addition, there were an undetermined number of unpaid helpers.

213. BArch, R 8150/46, memo, F 25, consultation in RSHA, 7 November 1941, pp. 1–2, pag. 161–162, point 4b; in this case, an RV board member in Essen and two ranking members of staff in the Stuttgart RV branch office were to be deported.

214. BArch, R 8150/46, memo, F 63, consultation in RSHA, 18 March 1942, p. 3, pag. 36, point 2a.

215. BArch, R 8150/46, memo, F 64, consultation in RSHA, 21 March 1942, p. 3, pag. 30, point 2c; correct spelling: Novak.

216. BArch, R 8150/46, memo, F 65, consultation in RSHA, 30 March 1942, pp. 4–5, pag. 26, point 3e; on Hechinger and Angerthal, see chapter 3.

217. BArch, R 8150/46, memo, F 69, consultation in RSHA, 15 April 1942, p. 4, point 3b; BArch, R 8150/46, memo, F 70, consultation in RSHA, 20 April 1942, p. 5, point 6.

218. LAB, B Rep. 058, 1 Js 9/65, telegram from Eichmann to Gestapo Düsseldorf and other Gestapo offices, 22 April 1942, pag. 62; see also Bundesarchiv, Außenstelle Ludwigsburg, Zentrale Stelle der Landesjustizverwaltungen, documentation "Judendeportationen aus dem Reichsgebiet."

219. BArch, R 8150/46, memo, F 70, consultation in RSHA, 20 April 1942, p. 6, point 6i and k, n. pag.

220. USHMM, RG-14.035M, reel 10, Jewish Community of Leipzig records (2001.150), letter, RVJD to district offices and Jewish Communities, re: adapting the administrative apparatus to the no. of members reduced by evacuation, 25 November 1941.

221. CJA, 2 B 1/2, memo, Nr. 1291, consultation in RSHA, 9 August 1941, p. 41, point 11; Berlin Jewish Community, p. 9, point 21; see also BArch, R 8150/46, memo, F 10, consultation in RSHA, 24 September 1941, p. 1, point 4.

222. BArch, R 8150/50, Reichsvereinigung der Juden in Deutschland, list by name of the "leading staff members," 24 May 1942, pp. 1–5 (pag. 7–12).

223. CJA, 2 B 1/4, memo, K 29, 17 December 1941, p. 3, point V; BArch, R 8150/46, memo, F 21, consultation in RSHA, 29 November 1941, p. 6, point 4b.

224. BArch, R 8150/46, memo, F 24, consultation in RSHA, 6 November 1941, p. 2, point 5; BArch, R 8150/46, memo, F 29, consultation in RSHA, 28 November 1941, p. 6, point 8–9, n. pag.

225. YV, 01/156, Ball-Kaduri, discussion with Hildegard Henschel, p. 1.

226. CJA, 2 B 1/4, memo, K 30, 19 December 1941, p. 3; see also LBI, JMB MF 456, RV certificate for Leo Baeck, 15 December 1941, and Conrad Cohn, 15 December 1941 (for their accounts, there were no restrictions on access and disposal), and Cohn's confirmation (22 December 1941, LBI, JMB MF 456,) that the supervisory agency had issued a directive that he was nonetheless permitted "to dispose of funds solely up to a limited and absolutely necessary amount."

227. CJA, 2 B 1/4, memo, K 24, 20/21 November 1941, p. 3; CJA, 2 B 1/4, memo, R 44, 25 January 1943, p. 4.

228. YV, 02/769, "'Resettlement' of the Berlin Jews," report by Dr. Martha Mosse, recorded 23/24 July 1958 by Dr. Wolfgang Scheffler, p. 5.

229. BArch, R 8150/50, Martha Mosse, Report on the question of the former staff members of the Kulturbund, 8 June 1942, pag. 19–20.

230. BArch, R 8150/50, letter, Lilienthal to Eppstein, 9 June 1942, pag. 21.

231. BArch, R 8150/50, report, Lilienthal, brief application to RSHA, 9 June 1942, pag. 22; BArch, R 8150/50,, letter, RVJD to Gestapo HQ Berlin, 21 August 1942, pag. 24.

232. BArch, R 8150/51, letter, Berlin Jewish Community to RV, 8 January 1943, pag. 62. Of these, 136 were deployed in the assembly camps at Grosse Hamburger Strasse, Gerlachstrasse, and Auguststrasse, at the canteen on Gormannstrasse, and in construction gangs for the Gestapo and the RSHA. Another 156 were employed at jobs in administration, 334 worked in welfare, and 212 in health services, while 120 were men who served as "collectors" in shift work.

233. For a description of events, see Wolfgang Scheffler, "Massenmord in Kowno," in *Buch der Erinnerung: Die ins Baltikum deportierten deutschen, österreichischen und tschechoslowakischen Juden*, vol. 1, ed. Wolfgang Scheffler and Diana Schulle (Munich, 2003), 1–43 (murder of the Jews on the Berlin transport, 4 ff.); Wolfgang Scheffler, "Das Schicksal der in die baltischen Staaten deportierten deutschen, österreichischen und tschechoslowakischen Juden 1941–1956," in *Buch der Erinnerung: Die ins Baltikum deportierten deutschen, österreichischen und tschechoslowakischen Juden*, vol. 1, ed. Wolfgang Scheffler and Diana Schulle (Munich, 2003), 83–87; Browning, *Origins*, 393ff.; Andrej Angrick and Peter Klein, *The "Final Solution" in Riga: Exploitation and Annihilation, 1941–1944* (New York, 2009), 147.

234. See Gerlach, "Wannsee-Konferenz," 7–44.

235. See Longerich, *Holocaust*, 286ff.

236. CJA, 2 B 1/4, memo, K 31, 13 January 1942, p. 3.

237. YV, 033/69, "Zum 16. Mai 1945," Alfred Selbiger (probably written by Jizchak Schwersenz), p. 2.

238. Ibid., p. 3.

239. On this, see Wolfgang Scheffler, "Der Brandanschlag im Berliner Lustgarten im Mai 1942 und seine Folgen: Eine quellenkritische Betrachtung," in *Berlin in Geschichte und Gegenwart: Jahrbuch des Landesarchivs Berlin, 1984*, ed. Hans J. Reichard (Berlin, 1984), 91–118.

240. Ibid., pp. 93, 95–96; on the individuals involved and their subsequent fate, see Regina Scheer, *Im Schatten der Sterne: Eine jüdische Widerstandsgruppe* (Berlin, 2004).

241. According to Scheffler, the arrests occurred on 4 June, the deportation on 5 June 1942; see Scheffler, "Brandanschlag," 110.

242. Ibid.

243. BArch, R 8150/1.1.1./8.2., memo, 29 May 1942; LBI, JMB, MF 456, Coll. Löwenherz, memo, 1 June 1942, p. 1; see also Fröhlich, *Tagebücher*, 432; the figure of "five" later led to some confusion: Moritz Henschel reported after the war that "five Germans" had been killed during the arson attack (see YV, 01/51, Henschel, lecture, p. 4); Baeck's biographer Baker spoke of "five Nazis" killed (Baker, *Hirt*, 366), whereas in actuality it presumably involved five Jews involved in the operation.

244. BArch, R 8150/1.1.1./8.2., memo, 30 May 1942 and memo, 4 June 1942; BArch, R 8150/1.1.1./8.2., draft of a publication in the *Jüdisches Nachrichtenblatt*.

245. BArch, R 8150/1.1.1./8.2., draft of "confidential" letter, 10 June 1942.

246. BArch, R 8150/1.1.1./8.2., memo, 1 June 1942 (the transcriber of the minutes added: "I have also been sworn to secrecy as a scribe for this memo"); BArch, R 8150/1.1.1./8.2., report, 1 June 1942.

247. See Barkai, "Von Berlin nach Theresienstadt," 161. For a description of the circle by Holzer's later wife, herself a member of the Baum circle, see Charlotte Holzer, "Bericht über die 'Herbert-Baum-Gruppe,'" in *Erinnerungen deutsch-jüdischer Frauen, 1900–1990*, ed. Andreas Lixl (Leipzig, 1992), 333–36.

248. See Konrad Kwiet and Helmut Eschwege, *Selbstbehauptung und Widerstand: Deutsche Juden in Kampf um Existenz und Menschenwürde* (Hamburg, 1984), 129.

249. Arnold Paucker, *Deutsche Juden im Kampf um Recht und Freiheit: Studien zu Abwehr, Selbstbehauptung und Widerstand der deutschen Juden seit dem Ende des 19. Jahrhunderts*, 2nd ed. (Teetz, 2004), 239.

250. YV, 033/987 (E/987), anonymous, "Das Leben der Juden in Berlin 1940 bis 1943," p. 4.

251. YV, 033/69, anonymous (probably Jizchak Schwersenz), "Alfred Selbiger, zum 16. Mai 1945," pp. 8–9.

252. LBI, JMB, MF 456, Coll. Löwenherz, memo, 1 June 1942, p. 1.

253. Ibid., pp. 1–2.

254. BArch, R 8150, minutes of board meetings, 11 May and 9 June 1942.

255. YV, 02/373, WL P. III 432, Jakob Jakobsohn, "From Berlin to Theresienstadt," pp. 1–2; see Beate Meyer, "Fine Line," 330: from the summer of 1942, the former home for the elderly at 26 Grosse Hamburger Strasse was converted into an assembly point for transports to Theresienstadt, and in the autumn of 1942 was expanded into the general assembly camp, where the rooms were divided into three sections: Theresienstadt rooms, East rooms, and accommodation rooms for those persons whose destination and departure dates had yet to be determined.

256. See form sheet from the Jewish Community (Formblatt der Jüdischen Kultusvereinigung), 24 August 1942, reproduced in Adler, *Verheimlichte Wahrheit*, 38–39.

257. CJA, 2 B 1/3, memo, K 56, consultation in RSHA, 22 August 1942, p. 1, point 1.

258. Ibid.

259. BArch, R 8150/2, Reichsvereinigung der Juden in Deutschland, minutes of board meeting, 24 August 1942; see also BArch, R 8150/9, internal letter, Königsberger to Lustig, 3 September 1944, p. 1 (pag. 164). These home purchase contracts stipulated that the deportees to Theresienstadt had to transfer their entire liquid assets to the RV, including outstanding debts and life insurance claims. "In return, the Reichsvereinigung 'obliged itself' to support the 'contract partner' for the rest of his or her life, supplying everything needed"; see Barkai, *Boycott*, 181. For the text of the home purchase contract (*Heimeinkaufsvertrag*), in German and with an English translation, see www.kfkronenberg.com/reich.htm (accessed 31 July 2012), i.e., private papers (Kronenberg).

260. CJA, 2 B 1/3, memo, K 56, consultation in RSHA, 22 August 1942, p. 1, point 1.

261. BArch, R 8150/2, Reichsvereinigung der Juden in Deutschland, minutes, No. 21, board meeting, 12 October 1942.

262. CJA, 2 B 1/3, memo, K 61, consultation in RSHA, 2 October 1942 and 7 October 1942.

263. Weismann, "Nachfolge-Organisationen," 777–78.

264. CJA, Z 1997/47, Hans-Erich Fabian, memo, Development of Jewish property in Germany, to Mr. Wise, Finance Division, Property Control Branch, p. 2; Adler also mentions 109 million RM; see Adler, *Verheimlichte Wahrheit*, 51.

265. CJA, 2 B 1/3, memo, K 62, consultation in RSHA, 7 October 1942, p. 5, point 10 and 11.

266. Peter Klein mentions that the ghetto administration Litzmannstadt had contacted Paul Eppstein on 13 November 1941 in order to purchase en bloc the sewing machines left behind. Eppstein agreed, but had to decline after receiving instructions from the RSHA; see Peter Klein, *Die "Ghettoverwaltung Litzmannstadt" 1940 bis 1944: Eine Dienststelle im Spannungsfeld von Kommunalbürokratie und staatlicher Verfolgungspolitik* (Hamburg, 2009), 521.

267. BArch, R 8150/480/2, letter, RV to Prague Jewish Community, 7 September 1942 and 15 October 1942.
268. BArch, R 8150/480/2, letter, RVJD to clothing storeroom Berlin Jewish Community, 12 February 1943.
269. Thus, a request by the Jewish Council Izbica came to naught; it had been ordered to take in two hundred Jews from Würzburg and environs, a number unfit for work. The council had hoped that the Würzburg Jewish Community would be able to assist with money, linen, and food, but it in turn was not permitted to do this without an express authorization from the RV central office (and they could not authorize this without prior approval by the RSHA); see letter, Jewish Council Izbica, District Krastnystaw to Würzburg Jewish Community, 29 March 1942, reproduced in Adler, *Verheimlichte Wahrheit*, 69–70.
270. Richtlinien [Guidelines], reproduced in Gottwaldt and Schulle, "*Judendeportationen*," 268–75.
271. See ibid., 276, with reference to Rita Meyhöfer.
272. Quoted in Maierhof, *Selbstbehauptung*, 195.
273. See H. G. Adler, *Theresienstadt 1941–1945*, 2nd ed. (Tübingen, 1960), 115.
274. On the eve before his deportation to Theresienstadt, Stahl bitterly criticized the RV board in a farewell letter; from his point of view, all of them "careerists and bootlickers," none of whom assisted him, and who had "Julemann" (Julius Seligsohn) on their consciences. The letter of 10 June 1942 is reproduced in Neue Synagoge—Centrum Judaicum, *Heinrich Stahl*, 34–35; on Stahl, see also his papers, http://findingaids.cjh .org/?pID=121492 (accessed 5 June 2012).
275. Heinrich Stahl, born 13 April 1868, was deported at the age of seventy-four to Theresienstadt on 12 June 1942, where he died of pneumonia and heart failure on 4 November 1942; his wife Jenny survived. Information from Anna Hájková, 20 September 2010, National Archive Prague, Institute Theresienstadt Initiative, death notice, Heinrich Stahl.
276. BArch, R 8150/9, memo, 23 June 1943, pag. 782. For a postcard from a prisoner in Theresienstadt, see http://goo.gl/JZ7Cw (accessed 30 July 2012).
277. BArch, R 8150/46, memo, F 66, consultation in RSHA, 2 April 1942, p. 3, pag. 12, point 2.
278. BArch, R 8150/50, report, Reichsvereinigung to RSHA, 6 May 1942, pag. 3–4.
279. Ibid., pp. 1–3 (pag. 5ff).
280. BArch, R 8150/2.2.1/480/3, List Meyerheim, re: Jewish assets, for Reich interior ministry, RSHA, 27 November 1942.
281. CJA, 2 B 1/4, memo, K 39, 5/7 March 1942, p. 2. The remainder had not yet been processed when this report was completed.
282. LBI, NY, AR 25033, Rischowsky Coll., memo, K 46, 21 May 1942, p. 1.
283. *Jüdisches Nachrichtenblatt* 22 (29 May 1942); see also Joseph Walk, *Das Sonderrecht für die Juden im NS-Staat* (Heidelberg, 1996), 373.
284. BArch, R 8150/39, extract from circular sent to the "legal counselors," 27 July 1942, pag. 2.
285. Ibid., pag. 3.
286. BArch, R 8150/6, letter, RVJD to Jewish Communities and district branches, 17 August 1942, pag. 262.
287. BArch, R 8150/18, letter, Berlin Jewish Community to RVJD, RSHA and Gestapo office Berlin, 8 May 1942, pag. 10.
288. See a photograph of this sign reproduced in Meyer, Simon, and Schütz, *Jews*, 5. The sign reads in German: "Attention! Cemetery visitors! It is forbidden at the intersec-

tion Lothringenstrasse-Berliner Allee to walk along the streetcar track to the island for the streetcar stop. **Adhere in your own interest to traffic discipline.** Proceed at the corner **straight** across the street to the opposite sidewalk." (Words in bold here marked in red in the original).

289. The Third Decree on Implementation of the Law on the Legal Situation of the Jewish Communities, 25 March 1942 (RGBl. I, p. 161), was declared effective from 1 September 1941.

290. Thus, for example, USHMM, RG-14.035M, reel 10, Jewish Community of Leipzig records (2001.150), letter, Friedrich Joseph to Leipzig Jewish Community, 27 August 1942; there you can find further correspondence between the Leipzig Jewish Community and the RV and its members. However, the Gestapo regularly permitted converted "Aryan" members to resign from the organization.

291. BArch, R 8150/1.1.2/17/1, letter, Berlin Jewish Community to Reichsvereinigung, 23 June 1942 (plus list).

292. See Beate Kosmala, "Zwischen Ahnen und Wissen: Flucht vor der Deportation (1941–1943)," in Kundrus and Meyer, *Deportation*, 140–41.

293. CJA, 2 B 1/4, memo, K 40, 12 March 1942, p. 5.

294. CJA, 2 B 1/4, memo, K 41, 11 April 1942, p. 3.

295. BArch, R 8150/55, letter, RVJD to Labor Office Berlin, Central Office for Jews, 21 April 1942.

296. CJA, 2 B 1/4, memo, K 43, 22 April 1942, p. 3.

297. CJA, 2 B 1/4, memo, K 50, 20 June 1942 and R 18, 27 June 1942.

298. See www.bundesarchiv.de/gedenkbuch/index.html.en (accessed 26 July 2012). In the Mauthausen camp, Cohn received the prisoner number 12106 and was housed in Block 5. As cause of death, the register of death of the SS garrison doctor (Y/46) listed "suicide by high voltage current" (according to information from the Archive, Concentration Camp Memorial Mauthausen, 8 October 2008).

299. Simonsohn, "Gedenkblatt für Paul Eppstein."

300. See Maierhof, *Selbstbehauptung*, 214.

301. Date of deaths in *Gedenkbuch*, vol. 1, ed. Bundesarchiv (Koblenz, 2006), 497, 517, 520; see also Deutschkron, *Gelber Stern*, 101–2; on young Marianne Cohn, see also Meyer, Simon, and Schütz, *Jews*, 235.

302. BArch, R 8150/113/50/1, letter, Breslau Jewish Community to Eppstein, 29 September 1942; BArch, R 8150/113/50/1, certificate Breslau Jewish Community, 29 September 1942; BArch, R 8150/113/50/1, letter, Eppstein to Jewish Community, 6 October 1942.

303. YV, 01/50, letter, Hans-Erich Fabian to Kurt J. Ball, 6 July 1947, p. 1.

304. CJA, 2 B 1/4, memo, K 50, 20 June 1942, p. 2.

305. BArch, R 8150/2, minutes of board meeting, 6 August 1942, p. 1.

306. Ibid., p. 2.

307. BArch, R 8150/2, minutes of board meeting, 18 August 1942.

308. BArch, R 8150/7, draft, circular letter to Jewish Communities, district branches and Jewish school directors, pag. 105; see also pag. 99–107.

309. BArch, R 8150/7, minutes of board meeting, 24 August 1942, p. 2. A total of 105 salaried, 10 unsalaried, as well as some cleaning personnel and conscript compulsory laborers remained; most of those fired were registered for deportation to the East, a small number (nine persons) to Theresienstadt.

310. BArch, R 8150/7, minutes of board meeting, 15 July 1942, p. 1.

311. BArch, R 8150/7, minutes of board meeting, 6 August 1942.

312. See Gruner, "Reichshauptstadt," 250.

313. YV, 033/99, Alfred Neumeyer, "Tätigkeit als Gemeindevorsitzender," p. 259: letter, Baeck, 18 November 1942.
314. See Hildegard Henschel, Statement in Eichmann trial, published in State of Israel, Ministry of Justice, *The Trial of Adolf Eichmann: Record of Proceedings in the District Court of Jerusalem*, vol. 2 (Jerusalem, 1992), 672–73.
315. See Meyer, "Fine Line," 323–27, for greater detail.
316. LAB, B Rep 057-01, 1 Ks 1/69, R 11/20, Interrogation Selmar Neumann, 11 August 1968, p. 2; Henschel, "Aus der Arbeit," 42.
317. CJA, I 75a Be 2, No. 14, inquiries.
318. See www.bundesarchiv.de/gedenkbuch/index.html.en (accessed 26 July 2012).
319. LAB, B Rep 057-1, 1 Ks 1/69, R 11/18, memo, 27 March 1968, pag. 79; see also YV, 01/197 Georg Glückstein, report, "In Berlin 1933–1945," p. 5.
320. BArch, R 8150/2, minutes of the board meeting, 21 October 1942.
321. Hildegard Henschel testified about this operation in detail in the Eichmann trial in Jerusalem; see State of Israel, *Trial of Adolf Eichmann*, 667–74.
322. CJA, 2 B 1/5, memo, Henschel, 17 December 1942.
323. CJA, 2 B 1/5, memo, summons of Eppstein to Brunner, 3 January 1943.
324. CJA, 2 B 1/5, memo, 14 November 1942.
325. YV, 01/52, letter, Hildegard Henschel to Ball-Kaduri, 30 October 1953.
326. Ibid.
327. CJA, 2 B 1/5, memo, 19 November 1942; see also Maierhof, *Selbstbehauptung*, 176. Immediately after the fatal heart attack, Brunner reportedly commented cynically: "Schafft's den Juden da weg, damit er net so kalt liegt" [Carry that Jew over there out of here. He'll be less cold someplace else]; see Hans Safrian, *Eichmann's Men*, trans. U. Stargardt (Cambridge 2010), 119.
328. CJA, 2 B 1/5, memo, 20 November 1942.
329. LAB, B Rep 058, 1 Js 9/65, T IIa, Interrogation Martha Mosse, 6 May 1970, p. 3; on the deportation of the sick, see also Elkin, *Jüdisches Krankenhaus*, 51–52.
330. CJA, 2 B 1/5, memo, Kozower, 21 November 1942; CJA, 2 B 1/5, memo, Rockmann, 24 November 1942; CJA, 2 B 1/5, memo, Eppstein, summons to RSHA, 6 December 1942. On the deportation of Jewish welfare recipients, see Wolf Gruner, *Öffentliche Wohlfahrt und Judenverfolgung: Wechselwirkungen lokaler und zentraler Politik im NS-Staat* (Munich, 2002), 301–2.
331. CJA, 2 B 1/5, memo, summons, Eppstein, Henschel, Kozower and Lustig to RSHA, 13 December 1942.
332. CJA, 2 B 1/5, memo, summons Eppstein to Gerbing, 4 January 1943.
333. CJA, 2 B 1/5, memo, summons Eppstein to RSHA (Brunner), 10 December 1942.
334. BArch, R 8150/2.2.1/480/1, letter, Edelstein to Eppstein, 8 December 1942; on this, see also Miroslav Kárný, "Jakob Edelsteins letzte Briefe," *Theresienstaedter Studien und Dokumente* 4 (1997): 218–19.
335. YV, 02/772 (WL, P. III.h. Theresienstadt), No. 894, Dr. Erich Simon, "Theresienstadt als autarkes Stadtwesen," lecture, 13 April 1946, p. 3.
336. See Henschel, "Aus der Arbeit," 50, 52.
337. See Simonsohn, "Gedenkblatt für Paul Eppstein."
338. CJA, 2 B 1/5, memos, 25 January 1943, p. 4; 27 January 1943, p. 1; 24 January 1943, p. 2.
339. YV, 01/199, letter, Eppstein to Max Plaut, District Branch Center Northwest Germany, 25 January 1943.
340. Thus, it was stated in March: "his coming to Berlin is planned, but not yet decided on"; see YV, 01/199, letter, RVJD to Plaut, 21 March 1943.

341. Max Plaut later testified that vaccines for thirty thousand persons had been smuggled into the ghetto hidden inside Eppstein's piano; see Research Center for Contemporary History (FZH), Judenverfolgung/Berichte, minutes, Schottelius, discussion with Dr. Max Plaut, 25 January 1954, p. 1.

342. Weltsch, "Aufzeichnung über eine Unterredung," 240; on his deportation, Leo Baeck also reported to Boehm; see Baeck, "A People Stands before Its God," 290.

343. CJA, 2 B 1/4, memo, 27 January 1943; BArch, R 8150, 581/1, Home purchase contract Baeck, 27 January 1943; ibid., correspondence 1940–1943 on Baeck's assets; ibid., letter RVJD to Deutsche Bank, 10 November 1943, re: confiscation of assets.

344. Philipp Kozower, his wife, and three children, Alice, Eva, and Uri, were arrested on 27 January 1943 (USHMM, 2010.200, Klaus Zwilsky Coll., Notice "Cousins remembered," n.d.), deported on 28 January to Theresienstadt, and transported on 12 October 1944 to Auschwitz, where they were murdered; see www.bundesarchiv.de/gedenkbuch/index.html.en (accessed 9 August 2012); see also Meyer, Simon, and Schütz, *Jews*, 353.

345. Friedrich Meyer was deported on 26 January 1943 to Theresienstadt and on 16 October 1944 to Auschwitz, where he was murdered; see www.bundesarchiv.de/gedenkbuch/index.html.en (accessed 9 August 2012).

346. Alice Myrants was deported on 26 January 1943 to Theresienstadt and on 28 October 1944 to Auschwitz, where she was murdered; see www.bundesarchiv.de/gedenkbuch/index.html.en (accessed 9 August 2012).

347. Memo Edelstein, 27 January 1943, reproduced in Adler, *Die verheimlichte Wahrheit*, 131.

348. Ibid., 131–32.

349. Ibid., 133.

350. Ibid., 135. It is striking that the jointly issued memos are nonetheless signed in alphabetical order, not by rank: Edelstein, Eppstein.

351. Ibid., 136. In particular see the commentary on the memo by Edelstein, 30 January 1943.

352. See Wolf Gruner, *Widerstand in der Rosenstraße: Die Fabrik-Aktion und die Verfolgung der "Mischehen" 1943* (Frankfurt am Main, 2005); Martin Riesenburger, *Das Licht verlöschte nicht. Ein Zeugnis aus der Nacht des Faschismus* (Berlin, 1960), 18; see also Wolf Gruner, "The Factory Action and the Events at the Rosenstrasse in Berlin: Facts and Fictions about 27 February 1943—Sixty Years Later," *Central European History* 36, no. 2 (2003): 179–208; Wolf Gruner, "Rosenstrasse Protest," H-Holocaust, 23 November 2003, http://goo.gl/vW4cZ (accessed 9 August 2012); Beate Meyer, "Geschichte im Film: Judenverfolgung, Mischehen und der Protest in der Rosenstraße 1943," *Zeitschrift für Geschichtswissenschaft* 52 (2004): 23–36. This operation is also termed "Factory Action" or "Factory Raid" in English.

353. Fröhlich, *Tagebücher von Joseph Goebbels*, vol. 7 (January/March 1943), entry, 18 February 1943, 369.

354. See Henschel, "Aus der Arbeit," 45.

355. See Gruner, *Rosenstraße*, 65–66.

356. See Meyer, *"Jüdische Mischlinge,"* 57ff.

357. Henschel, "Aus der Arbeit," 49.

358. Hartung-von Doetinchem/Winau, *Zerstörte Fortschritte*, 191ff.; Elkin, *Jüdisches Krankenhaus*, 57ff.

359. Fröhlich, *Tagebücher von Joseph Goebbels*, vol. 7 (January/March 1943), entry, 11 March 1943, 528.

360. BArch, R 8150/50, memo, No. 243, consultation in RSHA, 9 March 1943, pp. 1–2, pag. 417–18) (Theresienstadt: p. 2); see also Gruner, *Rosenstraße*, 9.

361. BArch, R 8150/50, Reichsvereinigung der Juden in Deutschland, list of employee ID cards issued on 12 March 1943, pp. 1–3 (pag. 419–21).

362. BArch, R 8150/3, minutes, No. 8/43, 5 April 1943.

363. Henschel, "Aus der Arbeit," 50.

364. See the report by Anneliese-Ora Borinski, who survived in Auschwitz; Anneliese-Ora Borinski, *Erinnerungen 1940–1943* (Nördlingen, 1970), 36ff.; see also YV, 01/241, Herbert (Ehud) Growald, "Hachscharah und Hachscharahzentren in Deutschland von 1940–1943," 23 June 1958, p. 5.

365. Hess. HStA Wiesbaden, 461/30983/29, telegram Kaltenbrunner to all Gestapo offices et al., 22 May 1943, pag. 337.

366. Henschel, "Aus der Arbeit," 52.

367. See, in greater detail, Beate Meyer, "'Altersghetto', 'Vorzugslager' und Tätigkeitsfeld: Die Repräsentanten der Reichsvereinigung in Deutschland und Theresienstadt," *Theresienstaedter Studien und Dokumente* 12 (2006): 125–51.

368. Paul Meyerheim, deported on 19 May 1943 to Theresienstadt and on 19 October 1944 to Auschwitz, was selected for forced labor, and on 27 January 1945 was sent from the Dachau concentration camp to the external camp Leitmeritz of the Flossenbürg concentration camp in a transport with 855 others, where he died on 6 February 1945; he was declared officially dead on 20 February 1952 (USHMM/ITS, Central Name Index, GCC 5/IC, Vol. III, Pg. 695, death certificate, registry office Arolsen, 20 February 1952); Kurt Levy was deported on 16 June 1943 to Theresienstadt, and sent on 28 October 1944 to Auschwitz and murdered there; see www.bundesarchiv.de/gedenkbuch/index.html.en (accessed 8 June 2012).

369. Institute for the History of the German Jews, 14.001.1, Plaut, "Aufzeichnungen," p. 20.

370. Municipal Archive Mannheim, Posthumous papers Eppstein, report with no named author (on Eric Warburg), Das Leben in Theresienstadt, Part II, p. 7.

371. Martha Mosse's father had distinguished himself in connection with the building up of the Japanese administration, and Germany's ally sought to reward him for his work: the embassy counselor in Berlin intervened with the SS, requesting that Mosse's daughter not be deported. As her transport nonetheless became imminent, the Japanese embassy intervened once more, in an effort mediated by the widow of the former German ambassador to Japan, Wilhelm Solf (1920–1928), and was able to arrange a change in the deportation destination. The SS assured her that Mosse would be "taken care of in a good home for the aged" in Theresienstadt, LBI, NY, AR 7183, box 7, folder 6, MM reels 121, sworn statement by Hanna Solf, 28 November 1947.

372. Information, Institute Theresienstadt Initiative, Dr. Jaroslava Milotowa, 10 April 2006.

373. LAB, B Rep 058, 1 Js 5/65, addendum No. 30, Manfred Fackenheim, report (LBI), fol. 131.

374. Miroslav Kárný, "Die Theresienstädter Herbsttransporte 1944," *Theresienstaedter Studien und Dokumente* 2 (1995): 9.

375. Private papers, interview with Trude Simonsohn, conducted by Beate Meyer, March 2003, transcript, p. 10.

376. Ibid., p. 13.

377. Ibid., p. 11.

378. Ludwig Merzbach survived.
379. Ernst Peiser, from Cologne, was deported on 19 June 1943 to Theresienstadt and on 28 October 1944 to Auschwitz, where he was murdered; see www.bundesarchiv.de/gedenkbuch/index.html.en (accessed 9 August 2012); on Peiser, see also http://goo.gl/gauhT (accessed 10 June 2012).
380. David Braun was deported on 18 May 1943 to Theresienstadt and on 23 October 1944 to Auschwitz, where he was murdered; see www.bundesarchiv.de/gedenkbuch/index.html.en (accessed 9 August 2012).
381. Werner Simon was deported on 17 June 1943 to Theresienstadt and on 23 October 1944 to Auschwitz, where he was murdered; see www.bundesarchiv.de/gedenkbuch/index.html.en (accessed 9 August 2012).
382. Adolf Metz was deported on 30 June 1943 to Theresienstadt and on 28 October 1944 to Auschwitz, where he was murdered; see www.bundesarchiv.de/gedenkbuch/index.html.en (accessed 9 August 2012).
383. Municipal Archive Mannheim, Posthumous papers Eppstein, "Das Leben in Theresienstadt," p. 8.
384. USHMM, 2010.200, Klaus Zwilsky Coll., Cousins Remembered, n.d., p. 3, correspondence from Theresienstadt, p. 1.
385. Adler, *Theresienstadt*, 115.
386. YV, 01/286 (02/244), Klara Caro, Paul Eppstein in Theresienstadt, 10 October 1961, p. 1.
387. YV, 02/241, WL P. III 405 (Theresienstadt), letter, Hedwig Ems, 16 July 1947, p. 10; Erna Goldschmidt describes the living conditions of Kurt Levy and his family in YV, 033/76, letter, Erna Goldschmidt to Ilse Redlich (Kurt Levy's sister), 13 December 1945, pp. 1–5.
388. YV, 02/373, WL P. III 432 (Theresienstadt), Jacob Jacobsohn, "From Berlin to Theresienstadt," pp. 7–8.
389. YV, 033/998, M. Straßburger, report, p. 18.
390. YV, 02/53, Else Dormitzer, "Experiences in Nuremberg, Holland, Theresienstadt," p. 5.
391. Quoted in Kárný, "Theresienstadt," 38.
392. That is, some 86 percent of the German Jews deported to Theresienstadt died there or were deported onward to extermination camps; Kárný, "Theresienstadt," 39–40.
393. Central Archive for Research on the History of the Jews in Germany (Zentralarchiv zur Erforschung der Geschichte der Juden in Deutschland, hereafter ZAGJD), Heidelberg, file 1/19, No. 333, letter, Jewish Community Württemberg to administrative office, RVJD, Karlsruhe, 5 February 1943. The destination is probably incorrect, and likely involved transports to Treblinka or Auschwitz.
394. StaHH, 552-1, section 1993, Jüdische Gemeinde, file 15, div. postcards. Plaut himself reported after the war that for a time, some three hundred parcels per week were being sent under the name of various addressors from different post offices on the perimeters of Hamburg. The contents of these parcels could not be covered by the Reichsvereinigung; rather, this involved allotted foodstuffs or food obtained on the black market, which was stored in cabinets sealed by the regional head of finance as "emigrant goods" that the Gestapo had left aside during house searches. See Research Center for Contemporary History (FZH), Persecution of the Jews/reports, report by Schottelius, 25 January 1954, p. 1.
395. YV, 02/373, WL 432, Jacob Jacobsohn, "From Berlin to Theresienstadt," p. 7.
396. Manfred Fackenheim was deported to Theresienstadt on 19 M/ay 1943 and to Auschwitz on 23 October 1944, and survived.

397. See chapter 1, "Legal or Illegal? Emigration to Palestine (Aliyah)."

398. Alice Herzog, from Stuttgart, was deported to Theresienstadt on 17 February 1945 and liberated there; she apparently was erroneously included in the listing here.

399. Else Juda, from Cologne, was deported on 16 June 1942 to Theresienstadt and on 19 October 1944 to Auschwitz, where she was murdered; see www.bundesarchiv.de/gedenkbuch/index.html.en (accessed 9 August 2012).

400. Salomon Schlome, from Berlin, was deported on 17 May 1943 to Theresienstadt and on 18 December 1943 to Auschwitz, where he was murdered; see www.bundesarchiv.de/gedenkbuch/index.html.en (accessed 9 August 2012).

401. Dr. Käthe Joachimsohn, from Berlin, was deported on 17 June 1943 to Theresienstadt and on 23 October 1944 to Auschwitz, where she was murdered; see www.bundesarchiv.de/gedenkbuch/index.html.en (accessed 9 August 2012).

402. Gottfried Salomon was deported on 17 May 1943 to Theresienstadt and on 29 September 1944 to Auschwitz, where he was murdered; see www.bundesarchiv.de/gedenkbuch/index.html.en (accessed 9 August 2012).

403. LAB, B Rep 058, 1 Js 5/65, addendum 30, report Manfred Fackenheim, fol. 131.

404. Kárný, "Theresienstädter Herbsttransporte," 12, 13; LAB, B Rep 058, 1 Js 5/65, addendum 30, report Fackenheim, fol. 131.

405. On this, see, inter alia, Municipal Archive Mannheim, posthumous papers Eppstein, report, n.a., pp. 8, 11; YV, 01/50, letter, Hans-Erich Fabian to Kurt J. Ball, 6 July 1947; YV, 033/76, letter, Erna Goldschmidt to Ilse Redlich (Kurt Levy's sister), 13 December 1945, p. 5. See also Kárný, "Theresienstädter Herbsttransporte," 18; Livia Rothkirchen, "Die Repräsentanten der Theresienstädter Selbstverwaltung," *Theresienstaedter Studien und Dokumente* 3 (1996): 114-126, 12 f.

406. See fn. 368, chapter 2.

407. On Max Plaut's emigration, see chapter 3 (Hamburg).

408. LBI, NY, Plaut, posthumous papers, AR 7094, list Plaut, n.d. From other correspondence it is clear that Plaut sent the list in the winter of 1944. The files contain no reply.

409. Whether there is a possible connection here with inquiries made by the International Red Cross looking for certain persons from October 1944 on has not been established. In her above-cited letter to Ilse Redlich, Erna Goldschmidt reports on lists from the International Red Cross that had been received in Theresienstadt, and which she accidentally had been able to inspect. These lists had contained the names of persons whose release from Theresienstadt had been requested (by whomever), and such requests were later repeated; see YV, 033/76, letter, Goldschmidt to Redlich, 26 July 1946, pp. 2–3.

410. Adler, *Theresienstadt*, 116–17.

411. Ernst Simon, *Aufbau im Untergang: Jüdische Erwachsenenbildung im nationalsozialistischen Deutschland als geistiger Widerstand* (Tübingen, 1959), 93.

412. Adler, *Theresienstadt*, 191.

413. Richard Feder, *Jüdische Tragödie—letzter Akt. Theresienstadt 1941–1945: Bericht eines Rabbiners* (Potsdam, 2004), 91.

414. Ibid. The prayer line is similar to that said in prayer during Rosh Hashanah and Yom Kippur.

415. Adler, *Theresienstadt*, 192.

416. Benjamin Murmelstein, *Il Ghetto Modello di Eichmann* (Bologna, 1961), 97.

417. Murmelstein mentions that Rahm had given Eppstein a black eye; ibid., 108.

418. Wolfgang Benz, *The Holocaust: A German Historian Examines the Genocide* (New York, 1999), 116.

419. YV, 01/286 (02/244), Klara Caro, Paul Eppstein in Theresienstadt, 10 October 1961, p. 1.
420. Murmelstein, *Il Ghetto Modello*, 80.
421. Státnú ústredni archiv v Praze, URP-109, 109-4-985, memo L 557, 13 January 1945 (appointment of Baeck).
422. See Fritz Backhaus, "'Ein Experiment des Willens zum Bösen': Überleben in Theresienstadt," in Heuberger and Backhaus, *Leo Baeck*, 115.
423. See Ernst Simon, "Epilog: Theresienstadt und Jerusalem," in *Aufbau*, 96–97.
424. Ibid., 96. On the extensive program of lectures in Theresienstadt, see Elena Makarova, Sergei Makarov, and Victor Kuperman, *University Over The Abyss: The Story Behind 520 Lecturers and 2,430 Lectures in KZ Theresienstadt 1942–1944* (Jerusalem, 2004); see also http://makarovainit.com/first.htm (accessed 4 July 2012) for a list of lecturers there and other data.
425. Adler, *Theresienstadt*, 254.
426. See Barkai, "Von Berlin nach Theresienstadt," 162–63.
427. Rolf Grabower, "Tagesberichte," reproduced in *Lesebuch und Materialband Grabower: Wenn im Amte, arbeite, wenn entlassen, verbirg dich*, ed. Werner Nigbur, Bundesfinanzakademie im Bundesministerium der Finanzen (Brühl, 2010), 127.
428. YV, 02/772, WL, P. III.h. Theresienstadt, No. 894, Erich Simon, "Theresienstadt als autarkes Stadtwesen," p. 9; others, such as the Munich doctor Julius Spanier, who were not deported elsewhere, explained that they had been able to remain in Theresienstadt because they had refused to accept special privileges and had lived there as simple ghetto residents (see YV, 02/772, WL, P. III.h. Theresienstadt, No. 1106, "In Memoriam Dr. Julius Spanier," speech given at the memorial in Munich on 5 March 1959 by Gerty Spieß, p. 6). In view of the mass deportations in the autumn of 1944, this reason says perhaps more about the need of the survivors to explain their fate than about the special orders. Other ghetto residents appeared not to have even taken note of the deportation of the functionaries; see YV, 02/74, WL 306, Richard A. Ehrlich, "Ghettobriefe, Erinnerungen."
429. YV, 02/443, WL P. III Theresienstadt, No. 545, Willy Goerner, "KZ-Ghetto Theresienstadt," dated 1 August 1949, p. 20.
430. StaHH, 522-2, 58, Jüdische Gemeinde, correspondence Heinemann, letter, Simonsohn to Aid Community, 25 July 1945. Simonsohn notes in this letter: "These still, among others, were Dr. Merzbach and family, Mr. Moritz Henschel—head of the Berlin Jewish Community, Dr. Jakobsohn [*sic*], comprehensive archive, Dr. Gutfeld—Reichsvereinigung, statistics dept., thus a small remainder of the surviving former staff."
431. StaHH, 522-2, 58, Jüdische Gemeinde, biography Dr. rer. pol. Ludwig Merzbach, economist.
432. StaHH, 522-2, 58, Jüdische Gemeinde, testimony Karl Basch.
433. Compensation Office Berlin, file 11659, testimonial from the autonomous administration of the former concentration camp Theresienstadt-city, 3 July 1945. The name of the signer, "Jiri," was falsely translated in the document as "Josef" instead of "Georg."
434. YV, 02/772, WL, P. III.h. Theresienstadt, No. 894, Erich Simon, lecture, 13 April 1946: "Theresienstadt als autarkes Stadtwesen," p. 3. In the manuscript of the lecture, this passage is set in brackets.
435. LAB, B Rep 058, 1 Js 9/65, Interrogation Hans-Erich Fabian, 28/29 October 1968, pp. 9–10. See also LAB, B Rep 058, 1 Js 9/65, stenographic transcript of a radio broadcast Sender Freies Berlin, 7 June 1968 (16 pp.). Hermann Krebs and Hans-Erich Fabian were ordered to return to Berlin from Theresienstadt to settle the finan-

cial affairs of the Reichsvereinigung. Krebs returned in January 1944 to his family in Theresienstadt at his own wish, and was deported on 28 October 1944 to Auschwitz; see www.bundesarchiv.de/gedenkbuch/index.html.en (accessed 9 August 2012). After completing his work in Berlin in December 1944, Fabian was sent a second time to Theresienstadt, where he survived.

436. LAB, B Rep 058, 1 Js 9/65, Interrogation Martha Mosse, 11 July 1967, p. 8, pag. 120ff..

437. Baeck, "A People Stands Before Its God," 293. In her forthcoming dissertation at the University of Toronto on the Terezin ghetto, "The Inmate Society of Theresienstadt: A Laboratory of the Middle Class? Social History of the Theresienstadt Transit Ghetto," Anna Hàjkovà provides some new perspectives relating to Baeck's attitude concerning the gas chambers; see http://utoronto.academia.edu/AnnaHajkova (accessed 1 August 2012).

438. YV, 01/241, Herbert (Ehud) Growald, "Hachscharah und Hachscharahzentren in Deutschland von 1940–1943," 23 June 1958, p. 4.

439. LAB, B Rep 058, 1 Js 9/65, Interrogation Hans-Erich Fabian, 28/29 October 1968, p. 7; YV, 01/51, Henschel, "Die letzten Jahre," transcript, p. 4; on Leo Baeck, see Baker, *Hirt*, 360–65; Baeck, "A People Stands before Its God," 293.

440. LAB, B Rep 058, 1 Js 9/65, Interrogation Hans-Erich Fabian, 28/29 October 1968, p. 7. However, the controversial intermediary of the Residual Reichsvereinigung, Walter Lustig, had learned in October/November 1944 from correspondence between the Fabian couple that "Hedwig and Paul [Dr. Paul Eppstein and his wife] were no longer there and had gone the same way as Otto Hirsch"—because of this information, Lustig evidently denounced Fabian to the RSHA; ibid., p. 10.

441. YV, 02/30, Hermann Samter: Letters, Sept. 1940–7 February 1943 to Hannah Kobilinski et al., letter, 24 October 1941. Hermann Samter, born 5 December 1909, was deported 12 March 1943 to Auschwitz and murdered there; see www.bundesarchiv.de/gedenkbuch/index.html.en (accessed 9 August 2012).

442. YV, 02/30, Hermann Samter: Letters, Sept. 1940–7 February 1943 to Hannah Kobilinski et al., letter, 30 November 1941, p. 2.; see also "Letters of Hermann Samter from Berlin," Shoah Resource Center, Yad Vashem, p. 3, http://goo.gl/LZbVs (accessed 1 August 2012).

443. YV, 02/30, Hermann Samter: Letters, Sept. 1940–7 February 1943 to Hannah Kobilinski et al., letter, 26 January 1942; "Letters of Hermann Samter," p. 5.

444. YV, 02/30, Hermann Samter: Letters, Sept. 1940–7 February 1943 to Hannah Kobilinski et al., letter, 11 May 1942; "Letters of Hermann Samter," pp. 5–6.

445. YV, 02/30, Hermann Samter: Letters, Sept. 1940–7 February 1943 to Hannah Kobilinski et al., letter, 10 August 1942.

446. YV, 02/30, Hermann Samter: Letters, Sept. 1940–7 February 1943 to Hannah Kobilinski et al., letter, 7 February 1943.

447. See Frank Bajohr, "Vom antijüdischen Konsens zum schlechten Gewissen: Die deutsche Gesellschaft und die Judenverfolgung 1933–1945," in *Der Holocaust als offenes Geheimnis: Die Deutschen, die NS-Führung und die Alliierten*, ed. Frank Bajohr and Dieter Pohl (Munich, 2006), 59–60.

448. Dieter Pohl, "Das NS-Regime und das internationale Bekanntwerden seiner Verbrechen," in Bajohr and Pohl, *Der Holocaust als offenes Geheimnis*, 95–96, 119. See also Richard Breitman, *Official Secrets: What the Nazis Planned, What the British and Americans Knew* (New York, 1998), 155ff.

449. *Yedioth Hayom*, 30 October 1941. The Jewish Telegraphic Agency also relied on reports in the paper *Tidningen* in a news report it published on 27 October 1941

(vol. 3, no. 263) dealing with the deportations from Berlin entitled "800 More Jews Deported from Berlin to Poland; Jewish Emigration Office Closed"; see http://goo.gl/zzkeo (accessed 12 June 2012).
450. *Yedioth Hayom*, 31 October 1941.
451. Ibid., 24 June 1943.
452. Ibid., 8 August 1944.
453. Ibid., 1 September 1944.
454. For examples of this, see Kosmala, "Ahnen und Wissen," 151–52; on "rupture of civilization," see Diner, "The Limits of Reason: Max Horkheimer on Anti-Semitism and Extermination," in *Beyond the Conceivable: Studies on Germany, Nazism and the Holocaust* (Berkeley, 2000), 104, http://goo.gl/IKm1Q (accessed 30 July 2012).

Chapter 3

THE "PSYCHOLOGICAL ENVIRONMENT" IN THE COUNTRYSIDE

Latitude for Action by Jewish Functionaries in the District Branches

In the capital of Berlin, where the government, its ministries, and the RSHA had their main offices, the Reichsvereinigung central office, the large Berlin Jewish Community, and its members were under the constant attention and surveillance of the organs of persecution. Just under two-thirds of the around 320,000 Jews remaining in Germany in 1938/1939 lived in Berlin. The remainder was distributed across the country, concentrated primarily in the larger and medium-sized cities. What unreasonable demands did the heads of the district branches and the Jewish Communities there have to grapple with? What possibilities and latitude for maneuver were they able to make use of to mitigate the severity of the anti-Jewish measures? What limits did they run up against? In retrospect, what did the efforts of the RV out in the "provinces" actually look like, aimed at countering the "fighting administration" of the RSHA by means of a traditional administration seeking at least to dampen the dynamic of the Nazi policy on the Jews, if not halt it? When did conflicts within the organization and with the "supervisory authority" flare up? Why did they occur? What strategies did the heads of the district branches develop in dealing with the Gestapo and other organs of persecution?

Individual ministries, the RSHA, Gestapo offices, municipal authorities, and the *Gau* directorates of the Nazi Party, with their special departments or specialist staff for Jews, sought to exercise an influence not just in the capital. They also tried to directly influence the RV district branch offices, which took care locally of their membership and were obliged to implement the anti-Jewish measures. Until the November pogrom, the cities and municipalities had undertaken diverse and multifaceted initiatives designed to make life difficult for the Jews. Some of those initiatives remained regionally limited; others were coordinated by the German Council of Municipalities (Deutscher Gemeindetag) or other institutions and unified on a national scale.[1] After the pogrom, the RSHA took over the official reins of Jewish policy and its implementation. However, in the period 1939–1941, the RSHA was frequently obliged to follow the measures of the respective regional pacesetters in Jewish persecution (especially the *Gau* directorates, sometimes individual district chief executives [*Landräte*] or town mayors). It endeavored to adopt these measures as its own, seeking to shape anti-Jewish policy in the Nazi state in such a way so as to ensure that the "egoistic" interests of individual *Gau* districts, cities, municipalities, or large-scale organizations did not hinder a uniform approach. Their desire for personal enrichment should not end up being at the expense of the German Reich as a whole. Wolf Gruner provides a striking illustration for this: the exclusion of the Jews from state social welfare. This decision placed the financial consequences squarely on the shoulders of the RV. That released pressure on the budgets of the municipalities; these in turn soon raised new demands, calling for the RV to also assume responsibility in caring for Jews in mixed marriages and "mixed-blood" *Mischlinge*. But the RSHA now stepped in and set a limit on these local demands, because otherwise the Reichsvereinigung would not have been able to complete its other assigned tasks, given the financial means at its disposal.[2]

Under instructions from the Berlin central office (and the local Gestapo), the district branches were responsible for implementing all orders and prohibitions, and like the organization as a whole, their most urgent task now was to promote emigration. In addition, they kept extensive card files on their membership, regularly reported changes to the RV central office in Berlin and generally also to the local Gestapo, and met all demands for statistical material. Since the Reichsvereinigung had become the official provider for all Jewish institutions, the district branches and boards of Jewish Communities were responsible for hospitals, homes for the aged, kindergartens, schools, and other institutions, as well as public welfare, religious services, and burials. As a result of the radical exclusion of the Jews from all state services and social spheres, especially after the outbreak of the war, the district branches and/or Jewish Communities developed into "small, self-administered states of their own inside the large

German Reich," as Else Behrend-Rosenfeld, a former social worker in Munich, later aptly formulated it,[3] although bracketing out in her perspective the dominant power of the ever-present "supervisory authority."

Several heads of district branches had already been involved with the early deportations in 1940/1941 from their territory of competence. They had been confronted with the painful experience of being powerless when face-to-face with the power of the state. Their petitions and objections got nowhere, and their central office in Berlin could achieve nothing more than obtaining permission to care for the basic daily needs of the few Jews remaining outside Berlin and take over settlement of the questions of property and assets. From the autumn of 1941, all leading functionaries in the district branches were also busy with preparatory measures for organizing the transports. They assisted with preparing the deportation lists, organized collection points, food and medical care, and transport for baggage. Later they attempted to obtain information on the deportees and passed on any reports of death received. As a rule, the staff of the district offices were asked to assist in preparing the declarations of assets of the future deportees for the regional finance office, so that the state could then confiscate their possessions after deportation. In the course of 1940, they had to liquidate nursing homes and other institutions and send residents and personnel toward an unknown future. They were ordered to sell off the properties of the Reichsvereinigung at ridiculously low prices, while the members awaiting transport were forcibly housed in unsuitable crowded quarters, such as *Judenhäuser* ("Jews' houses"), converted barracks, or remote buildings outside the cities.

Earlier research on the deportations of the Jews from Germany concentrated on the central process directed from above, creating the impression that everything took place exclusively according to orders from the RSHA, and was everywhere a similar process. But a close look at realities clearly shows that early on, in the years after establishment of the Reichsvereinigung, different forms of (forced) cooperation developed between the RV central office and district branches and the local persecution authorities, and these diverse modes of working together extended on into the period of the mass transports. The concrete configuration of this cooperation under duress was highly dependent on the respective local nexus and ensemble of power formed by the *Gau* directorate, the district chief executives, town mayors, Gestapo offices, finance and labor offices, and other agencies. Their interaction determined what practical working structure emerged from the orders dictated "from above," in what atmosphere the Jewish functionaries worked, and how the Jews in their territory of competence were to spend their final years, months, or days in their hometown. It is true that from October 1941, the RSHA issued specific orders for the respective "migrations." The local actors were unable to have any influence on the period of time in which an area was to be rendered "Jew-free," or on the scope of the "evacuations." These deportations ultimately included all "full Jews," except for those protected by mixed marriages. Nonetheless, as Raul Hilberg correctly pointed out, "each city had its own deportation history, and each history reveals a great deal about the mechanics of the deportations and the psychological environment in which they took place."[4]

The District Branches

Structure and Motivation of the Jewish Functionaries

The RV central office maintained a department for "finances and administration," within which there was a subdepartment for "branch and district offices." The latter was responsible for the regional bureaus. Initially this subdepartment was headed by Arthur Lilienthal, and after his arrest and murder, Kurt Levy succeeded him. Both functioned as contact persons if problems arose, but also oversaw the work of the district offices. Several employees assisted the departmental heads. The card file for land plots and the audit unit for district offices formed their own subdepartments.[5]

Initially there were seventeen district offices and fourteen Jewish Communities equal to them in rank. The RSHA reduced this number successively, in parallel with the deportations. In 1942, the still existing large Jewish Communities were incorporated into the district branches, so that by 1943, the number of institutions still operating had been reduced by half, down to fifteen.

Subordinate to the district offices were branch offices, administrative offices, external or consultation bureaus, and a number of one-man (and more rarely one-woman) offices staffed by so-called intermediaries (*Vertrauensmänner*). There is no extant documentation on lists of personnel for staffing or liquidating these smaller offices. They become visible briefly only in connection with conflicts with the Gestapo or the central office. The Jewish representatives worked mainly as "legal consultants" on a volunteer basis out of their apartments or offices. Their positions were short-lived and were dissolved when they were relocated, or were deported together with the Jews they were assisting.

As a rule, heads of district branches were proposed by the Jewish side, and then reviewed and confirmed by the RV central office, its supervisory agency (RSHA), and the local Gestapo. The heads of the larger Jewish Communities, which were permitted to continue as branches of the RV, generally remained at their post initially. These Jewish representatives from the liquidated Reichsvertretung or the Jewish Communities, enjoying a certain respect and authority, in most cases had the complete trust of their members. On the one hand, they were known to the Gestapo, and disliked by them as local symbolic figures for the Jewish community; on the other, as a rule they possessed the qualities and abilities that were now in demand: they were able to organize the work required and to induce the voluntary and nonvoluntary members of the Reichsvereinigung to answer to and obey their calls involving donations or levies, new measures of coercion, or, later on, orders for deportation.

In 1938/1939 at the latest, each head of a district branch or Jewish Community, like the board members or RV senior officials in Berlin, had grappled with the difficult question: was it more meaningful in the interest of their members and their own safety to emigrate, or to stick it out and stay on? Many had suffered the humiliation of mistreatment and arrest during the November 1938 pogrom. Those left "unscathed" had experienced their powerlessness to help others. Younger family members had often already emigrated; those remaining or their wives were pressing to leave Germany. Many made the decision to emigrate. One was Alfred Neumeyer. Formerly state supreme court counselor in Munich, he had in 1920 founded the Association of Jewish Communities in Bavaria, and later played a key role in building up the Reichsvertretung der deutschen Juden. He had actually decided to remain with his Community, but at the last minute he chose instead to leave. Neumeyer had assessed his possibilities realistically, and had arranged a successor.[6] Leo Baeck and Otto Hirsch accompanied him personally in February 1941 to the train to see him off. From Lisbon, he proceeded to join his son in Argentina:

I had a great struggle with my conscience: am I being unfaithful to my Community, concerned as I am about the welfare of every single person there? Up to then, I had not shunned any danger, and was closely bound up with the Community come what may. I concluded that it was senseless for me to stay on. In the deportation that was certain to come [this was now after the deportations of Jews from Stettin and Baden/Palatinate], given my age and remaining strength, I could no longer serve as a leader.[7]

No one resented that the seventy-four-year-old Neumeyer no longer wished to risk deportation. The RV board and Berlin Jewish Community said farewell in a letter where they stated: "It was your fate to construct, and to dissolve what had been built up. What the fate of generations means one after the next is in your case united in the exertions of one man."[8]

His colleagues remaining behind struggled under a workload of at least fifty-four hours a week. Their salary was equivalent to that of a high school teacher, and later was reduced, although still somewhat higher than what a primary school teacher earned. Due to the increased restrictions on ration coupons for Jews, this salary was actually of little use anyhow. Heads of the smaller offices worked in most cases on a volunteer basis, unpaid.[9]

There were also a number of women among the leadership personnel in the medium-sized and smaller branch offices. In this virtually homogeneous "man's world," their presence was noticeable both to Jews and the regime's agencies of persecution. Their salaries were less than those of their male colleagues in the larger offices, and they had probably been selected for their jobs because there were no men with equivalent professional qualifications available in the specific area: among these female executives were Dina Schüften, who ran the Erfurt bureau of the Leipzig district branch, Minnie Ascher in Hanover, Rosi Karfiol in the Bielefeld bureau,[10] the young lawyer Erna Maas[11] from Hesse, and Hildegard Böhme, who was active in Brandenburg-Pomerania but based in Berlin.[12] However, after the reorganization of the district branches, Böhme was dismissed as director and was then hired on as a staff worker in the RV archive.[13]

The district branch heads were only authorized to employee their senior staff and specialists subject to prior approval by the Berlin central office of the Reichsvereinigung.[14] In addition, the Berlin RV auditors Ludwig Merzbach and department head Lilienthal and his successor Levy oversaw the finances of all regional offices, especially their accounting procedures.[15] Later on, the RSHA ordered the "concentration of all financial responsibility,"[16] and instructed that accounts of the smaller Jewish bureaus be maintained by the largest office in the respective district. The account holders now were permitted to make deposits at any time, but withdrawals could be done only with the prior approval of the RV central office.[17]

The following example illustrates just how limited the possibilities of the RV were for making decisions on organizational work and personnel in order to implement the imposed orders and instructions, especially regarding deportation of the Jews. The Berlin central office always endeavored to dispatch experienced administrative personnel and well-qualified organizers to those district branch offices where the local administrative heads appeared to be overwhelmed by the burden of work. In the interest of orderly administration and a transparent process, they took on the time-consuming task of obtaining the necessary authorizations and approvals from all participating authorities. Thus, for example, they sent the former Centralverein staff lawyer in Königsberg, Max Angerthal, now working for the RV central office,[18] to Karlsruhe; for this they had obtained approval from the RSHA and the local Gestapo, which initially had declined to give authorization. Angerthal was to support the work of the branch office head in Karlsruhe, Karl Eisemann, of whom more will be mentioned below. Angerthal arrived in late 1941. He was instructed to assist in settling the property matters involved in the liquidation of the district branch Baden/Palatinate and in preparations for the deportation of the Jews there.[19] Since in March 1942 he himself was on the deportation list in Berlin, while still busy organizing preparations for deportation of the remaining Jews in Baden/Palatinate and the subsequent merger of the corresponding branch offices, it was in his own very personal interest to stay as long as possible at his newly assigned post. He projected his work to continue until July 1942. But the Karlsruhe Gestapo intervened, although its reasons for this step cannot be determined from the available documentation. It believed that the existing Jewish personnel there was quite sufficient for handling necessary work in Karlsruhe, and recommended that the RV should utilize Angerthal's services where these were actually needed. In order to accelerate this, it came to an agreement directly with the Königsberg Gestapo. Angerthal was ordered to report to the Gestapo there. The hands of the Berlin RV central office were thus largely tied, even though Lilienthal and Eppstein believed that Eisemann "could not cope with matters on his own" and the situation "would turn terrible."[20] The RSHA, although quite interested in an "orderly" settlement of matters, avoided revoking decisions by local Gestapo offices. Why the Gestapo in this case intervened so vehemently cannot now be determined. The reasons appear to have been less in regard to Angerthal's person or qualifications, and hinged more on Gestapo suspicions about the efforts of the Jewish organization to achieve an orderly settlement. Ultimately, from the Gestapo's view, it simply was a matter of finally getting rid of the local Jews, and it considered any greater expenditure of time and energy as unnecessary. Perhaps it also hoped to render Eisemann and his staff more readily compliant without any "watchdogs" around; and/or it might have harbored some hope that it would not have to be so conscientious in reporting the assets of the deportees to the regional finance office.

The Tasks

Mitigating the Plight, Dissemination of Prohibitions, and Social Disciplining

Insofar as the condition of the roads permitted as the war intensified, the representatives of the district branches traveled regularly to meetings in Berlin.[21] Later communication was by telephone; after that, mainly by written correspondence. These meetings assisted the representatives of the district branches in exchanging information, receiving instructions about new measures, and discussion and agreement on their implementation. The central office developed unified processes for organizing procedures from the input gathered at these sessions. The Gestapo or RSHA also had interests of their own bound up with a number of these meetings. Thus, the Hamburg functionary Max Plaut described a meeting of the regional heads where all participants, on orders from the Gestapo, had been required, somewhat like schoolchildren, to write and hand in an essay on the distributing of food. In any event, Plaut suspected that the Berlin Gestapo was looking for ideas about how they could most effectively regulate the sale of food to Jews without according them the rights of normal purchasers.[22] From his testimonials, it becomes clear that Plaut himself sighed a breath of relief when he was able to return to his familiar surroundings in Hamburg. For the district branch heads, visits to Berlin were always journeys into the unknown, because the Berlin Gestapo often carried out house raids and inspections in the Jewish organization, searching or arresting all present, claiming that they had come to work late or were lazy. Probably Plaut was not the only representative who felt safer in his home community, with all its problems and headaches, than in the German capital.

Since the Reichsvereinigung had taken over all Jewish institutions and the real estate of the liquidated Jewish foundations and trusts, it was now the responsibility of the district branches to provide for education and professional training, health care, and care for the needy. According to its own data, in 1941 for example, the RV was still operating seventy-four schools across the German Reich. In the wake of the large-scale nationwide deportations, that figure plummeted: in June 1942, there were only thirty-nine such schools, and all these were closed at the end of that month.[23]

In order to alleviate poverty, the district branches requested permission to carry out collections for the Jewish Winter Relief. They then assisted the needy from money contributed in their own territory of competence. In 1941/1942, an average of 20 percent of the Jewish population benefited from this initiative. Those figures were higher in Baden-Palatinate (around 25 percent), Beuthen, Königsberg, Saxony-Thuringia, Hesse (each around 30 percent), Silesia (around 35 percent), and East Prussia (approximately 50 percent). Support payments in Berlin, Dresden, Cologne, Munich, and Westphalia were clearly less, where "only" 10–15 percent of the Jews received benefits.[24] Especially where earlier deportations had decimated the Jewish Communities, such assistance was indispensable; in Berlin and other larger localities, where Jews deployed in forced labor were receiving minimum wages, Jewish families had less need of supplementary handouts for housing, food, and clothing.

Between 1933 and 1938, Jewish religion had experienced a visible upsurge: returning to Judaism provided those in the midst of mounting social exclusion and decline a modicum of spiritual support and stability, and concrete aid through material welfare by the Jewish community.

Synagogues were now packed to the rafters, and not only on the High Holidays. Within the Reichsvertretung, the Jewish Communities had determined expenses for religious matters themselves. But now, as branches of the Reichsvereinigung, they had to obtain authorization for these funds from the RSHA. It pressed first for reductions in these expenses and then prohibited them completely. This process is reflected, for example, in the budgeting for religious expenses in the "Jewish Religious Association," as the Hamburg Jewish Community was forced to rename itself. In 1942, like all larger Communities, it was absorbed into the responsible RV district branch. In 1939, the Religious Association in Hamburg spent around 174,000 RM, in 1940 74,000, and in 1941 approximately 63,000 RM. Beginning with the summer of 1941, only private donations were available. It was no longer permitted to pay rabbis, prayer leaders, and cantors for ritual tasks. At best, such religious personnel could be employed for another fully remunerated job in the district branch, and then perform religious duties on a volunteer basis. In addition, the participants in religious services financed the services themselves by selling tickets for seats at the synagogue or through other contributions. It was only possible to continue operating the *mikvot* (ritual baths) using private means. The only religious item possible to designate as part of the budget was cemetery maintenance.[25] This was certainly not a concession to religious regulations; rather, it sprang directly from the authorities' fear (especially during wartime) of the danger of a possible epidemic arising from neglect of burial grounds or from cemeteries damaged by bombing raids.

Jews were able to learn about times and places for services in their city by notices put up in the Jewish Communities and announcements in the paper *Jüdisches Nachrichtenblatt*. In Hamburg, after demolition of the large synagogue in 1939, there was a hall available for religious services in the Jewish Community Center and a smaller synagogue; this small space was to serve a total of some ten thousand Jews. In early 1942, only two rooms were available, one in a residential home and the other in a boy's orphanage. However, the Hamburg Jews utilized an additional synagogue: the district branch head Max Plaut had originally established this with official authorization as a storeroom facility, and it was used until it went up in flames during a bombing raid in the summer of 1943. Attendance at religious services proved to be a double-edged sword: although it strengthened faith and bolstered a sense of cohesion, it was often fraught with danger, since such gatherings attracted the attention of the SS, Gestapo, police, or Hitler Youth: to Jews it seemed at times like running the gauntlet to enter or leave the synagogue, most particularly after the law on wearing the "yellow star" had been introduced. In the smaller localities, there were generally no longer any official religious services; instead, services took place secretly, in offices, apartments, or cemetery buildings, such as funeral halls.

The members of the Reichsvereinigung learned of new general regulations via the *Jüdisches Nachrichtenblatt,* but were informed about locally initiated ordinances and prohibitions only through circular letters or notices put up in the branch offices of the RV—if the municipal leaders or local party organs did not publish these in town in a bid to publicly demonstrate their staunch anti-Semitism.

For example, the Munich Jewish Community, a branch of the RV, enumerated the multitude of ordinances, regulations, and prohibitions in a leaflet and warned its members: "Should doubts arise, please seek out oral information immediately from the Jewish Community!"[26]

In many cities and towns, the mayors or *Gauleiters* banned Jews from entering the inner city or areas near to local sights. Like the Berlin Jewish Community, the district branches were also supposed to announce bans on entry for Jews to specific areas, a so-called *Judenbann*. To mention just two examples from urban public space other than the capital: in Munich, public parks such as the English Garden, the Botanical Garden, the Nymphenburg castle grounds, the Court Garden, Maximilian Park, and the Hellabrunn Zoo were off-limits to Jews. In Dresden, they were banned from entering the Brühl's Terrace, the Königsufer along the Elbe River, and other public parks, and were also prohibited from using boats on the river.[27]

Like the RV central office, the district branches also were responsible for guaranteeing "appropriate"—i.e., inconspicuous, submissive—behavior on the part of their members, and the observance of all orders and prohibitions. Thus, the Magdeburg district branch wrote to its members: "To cover over or fail to wear and display the Jewish star will be severely punished ... After Community members have repeatedly been informed about the regulations, no person will be able to assert in self-defense that he was unaware of the regulations."[28] Here it was still a matter of calling on Jews as individuals to obey the rules and regulations; but many calls suggested implicitly or explicitly that individual "misconduct" could not only harm the reputation of the Jews as a community, but could also become a pretext for drastic collective punishment. For example, the Munich Jewish Community admonished its members:

Now more than before, the visible marking of the Jews demands totally inconspicuous behavior in public places. In particular, it is important to observe the following: 1. Do not stop on the street! 2. Walk alone or at the most in groups of two. 3. Stop smoking in public! 4. Shop only at designated stores and only during the prescribed times for shopping! The behavior of each individual must be guided by the greatest sense of responsibility for oneself and the Jewish community.[29]

The Nuremberg Jewish Community issued an almost similar information sheet, which concluded: "Keep in mind that now you're being watched, every tiny aspect of your behavior is under scrutiny, even when you think you're not being observed!"[30] On 14 October 1941, a general prohibition was issued for Jews on using municipal transport in Munich, the revered "capital of the [Nazi] movement," since Jews in Munich had allegedly indulged in reckless behavior on a streetcar there: "We therefore repeat once more our appeal, in order to stress the seriousness of our situation. Should the authority find reason once again to intervene, further severe measures can be expected, and these will have a very deleterious impact on the existence of our community in Munich." The Jewish Community also consistently called upon its members to report Jews to the Community who had violated regulations. However, it insisted that the person reporting such violations should give his or her name, so as to avoid promoting a culture of anonymous informing.[31]

The district branches had to distribute the "yellow stars" to their members from September 1941 on, and beginning the following spring, *Judensterne*, on white paper, were ordered to be affixed to the front door and apartment doors of "full Jews." The RV branch offices distributed some fifty thousand such stars. This new stigmatization served to attract the attention of *Volksgenossen* and party members to Jews living in their residential neighborhood, who often then vented their anti-Semitism in violence. If the Jews there were not physically attacked, as the social worker Fanny David reported from Hamburg, the "stars" were clearly targeted: the *Judensterne* marking the apartments were often torn down again and again by persons unknown, or were defaced, rendered unrecognizable, and had to be replaced.[32]

Judenhäuser *and Barracks Settlements*
Right from the start of their work, the district branches had to grapple at various levels with the cancellation of leases and forced rehousing of their members. According to the Law on Rentals to Jews, "Aryan" landlords cancelled the leases of their Jewish tenants, and the Reichsvereinigung had to establish residential buildings to house the old, the sick, the handicapped, etc., as well as so-called "Jews' houses." The district branches were saddled with the task of relocating Jews into specified neighborhoods, to ready mass quarters and make them inhabitable, or to vacate buildings. The reasons for this varied, but in most cases, the rationale cited was the general housing shortage for "Aryans," a deficiency the regime was eager

to remedy. When the Allied bombing raids were stepped up, the authorities argued that those who had been bombed out had to be rehoused. The initiators in the regime and the Nazi Party operated on the "self-evident" premise that Jewish property was in legal reality "people's property." It was therefore in the public domain, and could thus be occupied and utilized by the RV district branches (generally on behalf of the government housing offices) regardless of any private contracts that had been concluded, and would later be placed at the disposal of the municipalities or Nazi organizations for their own purposes.

A total of thirty-eight residential and labor camps came into existence across the Reich.[33] In most cases, the RV was involved in establishing and financing these camps, but only rarely did it have a concrete say in actually designing and shaping them.

In Königsberg, beginning already in January 1939, Jews were relocated into *Judenhäuser*, apartment blocks where often several families were forced to share a single apartment.[34] Elsewhere, in most instances, such decrees from the mayors, district offices, and *Gau* directorates were not issued until a year or so later. The RSHA itself adhered to a policy line of increased occupancy density in Jewish living space, as it stressed in the spring of 1941 on the occasion of plans for barracks to house Jews in Aachen.[35] Yet as a rule, it did not act to block the plans of other offices to relocate Jews outside localities or at their periphery; rather, it adopted such plans as its own once they had already been launched. The reason for this lay in rivalry: before the start of the mass deportations, the RSHA was still vying with the *Gau* directorates over who would play the vanguard role in policy regarding the Jews. In such cases, the RSHA permitted the district branch heads who had sought help from the RV central office to at best point out alternatives where "Jews' apartments" (*Judenwohnungen*) or *Judenhäuser* could be set up—for example, when the Brandenburg Jews were to be relocated and moved to garden allotment areas (*Lauben*).[36] The extant correspondence indicates that the RSHA was not always necessarily apprised of the plans being developed by regional authorities. Sometimes the RSHA even sent the RV in advance to gather information, as, for example, in Schwerte, when it wished to learn whether the Dortmund Gestapo was planning a barracks settlement for the local Jews. It informed the Jewish functionaries beforehand that "an investment of RV funds to establish barracks should be avoided."[37] The local Jews had to move into the barracks arranged by the city as emergency housing, families with several members had to live in one single room for the whole family, but funds from the Reichsvereinigung were indeed not used.[38]

At the beginning of 1940, the Jews in Allenstein (East Prussia) were ordered to relocate into several buildings owned by the municipality. The physician Heinrich Wolffheim, head of the Jewish Community and appointed "Gestapo representative" in November 1940, reported on the daily harassment. This entailed apartment searches, for example, and a whole slew of prohibitions issued in Allenstein earlier than elsewhere in the German Reich.[39]

The head of the district branch office in Aussig in the annexed Sudetenland, Adolf Glässner, was actually notified that "his" Jews were to be concentrated in a barracks settlement. But then, coming as a total surprise, the SS Security Service (SD) informed him that the Jews and his district office were to be relocated to a castle (Schloss Hauenstein) in Schönwald, a remote locality in the Erzgebirge, some thirty kilometers from Aussig.[40] Among the Jews were many elderly and sick persons who required special care, as well as forced laborers. For the workers, this relocation necessitated traveling extremely long distances to their workplaces. This also involved huge expenses for the district branch and the Reichsvereinigung. But the SD rejected these objections by Glässner out of hand, stating baldly: "The Reichsvereinigung has enough money." Glässner quickly informed the central office in detail, because he suspected that the relocation of the Aussig Jews was intended as a forerunner, soon to be followed by many similar operations, and he warned Eppstein at the RV in Berlin: "You can well imagine what that will portend for the RV."[41] In the castle, more or less everything that a larger number of individuals would require was lacking, from telephone and electricity lines to toilets.[42] Immense pressure was put on Glässner to sign the contract immediately.[43] He was unable to prevent the "resettlement" of a portion of his members into the assembly camp quarters, nor could he stop their later deportation from there.[44]

In the small Silesian town of Peiskretscham (near Breslau), the Jewish population had some experience with suffering. In January 1940, the district branch head Kochmann had managed, with the help of the RV, to obtain a revocation of a directive by the police ordering all Jews to wear armbands with a "yellow star." But already that same year, Jews were instructed to mark their front doors with a star, and as individuals they were exposed to substantial harassment.[45] At the end of 1941, the mayor demanded that the Jews should move into a mortuary. Finally, the district branch head obtained permission to allow them to stay in the houses of other Jews, at least until they were able to move into the reserve assembly camps of the Breslau Jews.[46]

Of the twelve thousand Jews in Silesia, nine thousand lived in Breslau. The *Gau* directorate there was the main authority forcing the Jews to relocate into assembly camps outside the city. In July 1941, Jewish living space was confiscated; some of the Jews affected were forced to move to the former nursing home of Zoar in Tormersdorf near Görlitz, while others relocated to the former Reich labor service camp near Rybnik (Riebnig) in the vicinity of Brieg and the monastery Grüssau.[47] There were catastrophic hygienic conditions in all three assembly camps. The result was widespread illness; space was extremely cramped, and strict camp regulations minimized contact with the outside world.[48] The extreme brutality in dealing with inmates in the nearby "labor (education) camp" of Hundsfeld contributed to intimidating the remaining Breslau Jews. In Hundsfeld, internees were trampled to death after sacks were put on their heads and they were knocked unconscious by powerful water jets.[49] When they were scheduled for deportation in 1942, only a portion of the resettled Jews returned to Breslau; other transports were organized directly from Grüssau.[50]

Elsewhere, for example, in Cologne, the district branch had to put up funding (in advance) for mass collection accommodations. In May 1941, Jews living "to the right side of the Rhine" had already been forced to leave their homes and move into *Judenhäuser*.[51] In August 1941, the head of the Cologne Jewish Community was informed that 5,500 Cologne Jews (2,000 of them forced laborers) were in future to be housed in Fort V (400 persons) in Cologne-Müngersdorf and in a barracks camp to be constructed 500 meters from the fort. This operation was to include all Jews in Cologne except for those in nursing homes and homes for the aged. But an inspection of the premises of the fort, built in 1874 and long a military prison, revealed that without extensive remodeling it was not suitable for accommodating of hundreds of persons as residents: the plaster was peeling off the damp walls, most of the flooring had been torn up and removed, and there was only a single latrine with six seats and several water faucets. The designers of the new barracks camp had not planned for sewer plumbing, washrooms, toilets, or heating in the barracks. They had neglected to consider the necessity for large kitchens and a laundry to service the basic daily needs of hundreds of residents, and it was still necessary to clarify food provision and storage. There were no rooms available for camp administration offices or classrooms for the 430 schoolchildren, a day care center for 130 younger children, a sick bay, workshops, or consultation rooms for doctors. The only structures planned were 12 frame structures of 30 by 8 square meters plus 24 more of 26.55 by 8.14 square meters, constructed to house 100 persons each. Not even one normal-sized bed per person could be placed in these cramped quarters. More narrow cots were not available to civilians, since they were needed for the Wehrmacht. Moreover, two experts from the Reichsvereinigung concluded after an on-the-spot inspection that the barracks could at the most accommodate 1,700 Jews, not 5,000 or more, as envisioned. The planners were aware that the projected type of construction would result in very cold flooring, and because of a lack of toilets, a small number of latrines, and open sewage, there was the danger that sickness could spread quickly.[52] Nonetheless, the RV was ordered to make two partial payments of 200,000 RM each based on the 800,000 RM calculated as the final cost[53] and provide additional funds for "improvements in construction." The relocation to the fort, barracks camp, and old age home was ordered in January 1942, and now the Cologne municipality demanded further money for the expansion of the barracks camp. The Reichsvereinigung requested the municipality to submit this claim for funds directly to the RSHA.[54] It thus utilized one of the few possibilities here to refuse this new unreasonable demand, but without being saddled with the liability for the consequences. The RSHA agreed with the Cologne mayor that the municipality would reimburse the costs, presumably from the rent revenue from the camp.[55] The camp was created, but not with the level of occupancy originally planned.

Eviction and relocation into *Judenhäuser* was often an extremely brutal affair, as exemplified in Hanover, where in September 1941 the Jews affected were forced to move out and relocate into facilities owned by the Jewish Community within the short span of thirty-six hours.[56] A report sent to the RV central office described the situation: the Jews were housed in a gymnasium, crouched on their beds crowded close together, and also ate their meals on their beds. Three toilets were shared by 134 persons. In another building packed with 125 Jews who had been evicted, several were forced to sleep together in a single bed, while others were living in the kitchen. The inspector noted that there were cockroaches, and a dilapidated half-timbered building was infested by rats. His colleague from Berlin added that there was a danger of a decline in morality and the outbreak of fire.[57] But the situation worsened: as a next step in 1942, the 1,600 Hanover Jews, including the aged, the sick, and children, crowded together in 96 houses, were now herded into just 15 houses, where basement air raid shelters and attics also had to serve as living space. Even the approved minimum of 3 square meters per person was lacking, and the sick and frail could not be accommodated in separate quarters from the others. Then the municipal housing office demanded that the "Aryan" wives in "nonprivileged" mixed marriages also move in. In their own mutual interest, those Jews temporarily assigned responsibility for the *Judenhäuser* tried to convince them not to make this move.[58]

Preparatory Arrangements for the Deportations

The district branches were also ordered to do extensive preparatory work for the deportations: they had to gather statistical data, prepare lists of the items that their members had to hand over before deportation, etc.[59]

Their tasks in this preparatory work did not differ from those of the central RV office.

The Jewish functionaries were almost always pulled into preparation of the deportation lists: in a number of localities, they were ordered to extract a certain group from their card files, according to age or profession; sometimes they had to bring along complete membership lists, from which the Gestapo then made a selection. For a time, the Gestapo specified by name who was to be included in a transport and who would be exempted. It relied on the work of the Jewish leaders, but frequently checked this carefully for security purposes. The Dresden Gestapo *Judenreferent* Henry Schmidt was not alone in regarding the families of "his" Jewish representatives, Kurt Hirschel and Adolf Kahlenberg,[60] as captive hostages when the two were ordered to make a preselection of persons to be deported.[61]

The district branches had to report who among their members had household pets, surrender these animals into the hands of the local animal protection society, and then send a report on this to the RV central office in Berlin. They also had to assist in finalizing thousands of home purchase contracts for the deportees to Theresienstadt, sell their real estate, and report to the central office on every stage of this process.[62] In the meantime, Jews were now allowed only to submit petitions to the authorities via the RV district branch offices, which vetted them first and then if approved passed these requests on.[63] However, since it was only permitted to forward petitions if a time extension had been applied for or a Jewish "legal consultant" submitted an application for his client (thus accepting liability himself), the district branches were principally concerned with explaining to their members what was prohibited. In 1942, no Jew was permitted any longer to request exemption from some measure, or to file an objection against some order. Obedience was demanded: it was necessary to comply with the instructions of the authorities or to request time extensions so as to fulfill these orders. The "information officer" in each respective district branch office had to inform the RV central office about his or her decision.[64] "Legal consultants" were allowed to pass on petitions they had examined and deemed suitable. Sometimes these petitions involved extending the deadline for tax payment or sale of some Jewish-owned real estate or similar matters. Shortly thereafter, the RSHA spelled out restrictions even more clearly: the only option open to the Jewish offices was to declare that a petition by a Jew was inadmissible. If they considered it proper, they themselves were first required to apply for a permit from the "supervisory authority" in order to clear the way for the procedure of filing a petition. In practice, this often had serious consequences for the Jews involved, as in the case of a Jew from Dresden, who had been arrested and placed in "protective custody." He was living in a mixed marriage, and the Gestapo now sought to convince his wife that the "Aryan" spouses in such mixed marriages would soon be declared to be Jews, and that she could avoid this by divorce. She wrote: "I pray each and every day for him to find it in his heart to forgive me for this! I can't help it! What millions were unable to halt cannot be something expected of me." The hearing took place in the absence of the prisoner. He submitted an appeal via his "legal consultant," which the RV rejected.[65] He was not allowed to appeal the divorce decision. Probably because of this appeal devoid of prior authorization, he was transferred directly from the police jail to Auschwitz; otherwise, he would most likely have been sent to Theresienstadt.

Jews who did not take this path through the district branch office and directly submitted their petition to the RSHA or the actual recipient were threatened with "Gestapo measures."[66] Such measures also posed a threat to the heads and staff of the inspection offices of the district branches of the RV if they acted in violation of the regulations.

A Troubled Relationship:
The District Branches and the RV Central Office

As already alluded to in chapter 2, the functionaries in the Reichsvereinigung sought to counter National Socialist arbitrary actions and tyranny by creating an architecture of orderly, transparent administration. It had to be clearly spelled out who was responsible for each sphere of activity. The results of discussions with the RSHA were to be written down in memos, which were then passed on to members of the board, department heads, and subordinate staff, insofar as the matter at hand concerned them. In the memos, the Jewish representatives used the euphemisms "interview" or "discussion" to designate the often humiliating procedures of these summons by the supervisory authority. In this way, they gave them the patina of everyday consultations in the orderly administration of a large organization. Proper minutes of board meetings contained the items on the agenda and the results of internal discussion and deliberation. Financial planning was to be logical and clearly set out. Initially it had been projected for several years in advance, but soon was drafted for ever-shorter periods of time. Actual financial decisions and procedures had to be accessible to audit and inspection, and also had to be regularly reviewed. Areas of competence and official organizational channels were clearly specified. And if the regime sent powerful, even destructive shock waves through this system by means of its checks, punitive operations, arrests, and deportation orders, it was considered crucial to act immediately: at least a minimum of order had to be quickly restored, bolstered by a reorganization plan for the administration.

The district branches and Jewish Communities were an integral component to the total system of the Reichsvereinigung. For that reason, the functionaries around Eppstein and Hirsch in the RV central office tried right from the start to prevent district branch heads from developing too much autonomy and "going it alone," while at the same time utilizing their regional contacts and competencies for the organization as a whole. They obligated the district branch heads to maintain transparency, especially regarding finances. For their part, they sought to distribute funds for emigration, welfare, education, and personal staff equitably. Their auditors oversaw the work of the district branches extensively, instituting frequent checks. It is likely that not many audit reports were as detailed as that of the Hamburg Jewish Community for 1940/1941, which was worked on for almost two years and reached a length of ninety-two pages, but it is a good example of how the ongoing destruction of the Jewish community was manifested in an audit report. After the first four large-scale deportations, and more than thirty-one hundred of the approximately seventy-five hundred Jews in Hamburg had forcibly "migrated" from the city, "large changes in personnel" arose, that is, the Community and district branch were forced to fire staff, who then in most cases were also deported. The liquidation of all educational and training institutions also occurred in the vortex of this period under audit. In the foreground, the report's focus is the painstaking enumeration of income and expenses that were not quite properly recorded in the account books. But behind these facts it describes in an administrative, formal language the end of efforts for self-assertion. Moreover, the district branch had far fewer Jews on its membership lists than it had reported to the Berlin central card file. In these times of large-scale deportations, with some individuals given temporary deferment and others taken as substitutes, oversight was difficult, and thus the "inventory" of Jews in October 1941 differed by 1,667 persons from the statistical count in the card file in Berlin.[67]

On the other hand, the district branches often felt restricted in their own latitude for action as a result of centralization. For example, the head of the Düsseldorf branch office complained that quite substantial revenue had resulted from the levy imposed on emigrants, but since the money had to be transferred to a special account of the Reichsvereinigung, actually "only with great effort" was it possible to obtain funds for emigration, education, and welfare for the Düsseldorf Jews.[68] A similar criticism came from the Jews in Nuremberg, who—given their especially dire and oppressive situation in Julius Streicher's own *Gau* (see below)—reasoned that they should be allowed to claim special assistance for financing emigration.[69]

As a rule, conflicts flared when heads of district branches or external offices circumvented the central office or failed to send a report, in this way violating the principles of proper, orderly administration. Thus, for example, the Braunschweig functionary Max Guhrauer was removed by the RV central office because he had maintained an illicit account.[70] After the outbreak of the war, lifts containing the household goods of Jewish emigrants were not sent to their owners abroad. Guhrauer had obtained an official permit to remove "textiles" from the lifts, but he had sold their entire contents and deposited the proceeds in a special account for social welfare. The Gestapo learned of this and confiscated the account, forcing Guhrauer to pay for the loss of the contents of these lifts from his own pocket. It is important to note that he had not misappropriated goods or money for his own personal use, but rather obtained funds in this way to assist RV members in distress. He had even deposited the funds in an account, not some clandestine cash box, and this now became for him catastrophic. The Reichsvereinigung dismissed him and appointed a successor, Hannah Pohly,[71] but she soon received orders to report for deportation. Since with her departure the last suitable person to head the branch office had been "migrated," two months later the RV central office had to reappoint Max Guhrauer.[72] To set aside illicit funds for special expenses was an option that suggested itself and was often practiced. For example, Max Plaut maintained an illegal slush fund, black money whose existence the auditor Ludwig Merzbach was quite aware of, and which the central office sometimes resorted to.[73] In contrast with Guhrauer, Plaut enjoyed substantial trust within the organization, and had never made his "black cash" a secret, although unlike his colleagues, Eppstein was certainly not informed about Plaut's "black cash." In any event, Guhrauer proved to have a bit of luck on his side in the whole affair: he was not taken into "protective custody" and was permitted to continue to run his office until its liquidation.

Gestapo offices often intervened in conflicts between the RV central office and the district branches. Or, more precisely, these conflicts initially arose as a product of Gestapo activities and frequently then devolved into a matter ridden with complications. One imbroglio involved the head of the Westphalia district branch in Bielefeld, Max Ostwald: he had dismissed the senior coworker in the Bielefeld Jewish Community, Adolf Stern, after its liquidation.[74] The reason was ostensibly false information that Stern had given a member before his deportation who wished to donate valuable ritual objects and other items to the district branch office. Stern had informed the man that this donation could be handled without a complicated official authorization. On the basis of this "malfeasance," Ostwald obtained permission from the central office to remove Stern from his post. This was compounded by a second accusation, namely, that Stern was cooperating closely with the Gestapo and was jealously guarding his preparatory assistance in deportations from the eyes of his colleagues. Staff workers in the central office secretly questioned Stern's former colleagues about this. However, the Gestapo in Dortmund-Hörde, in whose area the deportations were scheduled, had ordered Stern to maintain silence vis-à-vis his superiors. The "supervisory" Gestapo branch in Bielefeld was likewise not prepared to accept Stern's firing by the RV. It threatened Ostwald that if he did not revoke the dismissal, he would atone for it.

As always in such cases, the RV central office did not want to acquiesce in and tolerate an infraction of official duties or circumvention of official channels. So it urged the RSHA to support Stern's dismissal. The RV suggested that Ostwald should explain to the local Gestapo, in a disguised form, that Stern's redundancy was the "customary mode of dismissal from a post in the context of reorganization."[75] Stern should, they recommended, immediately halt his cooperation with the Gestapo, and Ostwald should take over contacts there himself. An auditor from the RV central office who inspected the Bielefeld district branch then learned that Stern had been working with another person. A Jewish functionary in Dortmund had feared that his branch office would be closed as an independent bureau after the large-scale deportations, and would be incorporated into the Bielefeld district branch. He and Stern had apparently tried to "eliminate" the government district of Arnsberg as a separate administrative entity and have it incorporated within the district branch of Dortmund. So here two Jewish functionaries who were mainly involved in deportation activity had acted to save their skins, based on their realization that this activity ultimately would lead to their own dismissal and deportation at the end of the road, when there were no longer any other Jews to deport. They tried at least to gain some postponement of the end of their work. Although their attempt proved abortive, the close cooperation of Stern with the Gestapo was at least "rewarded" in a small way: he was allowed to remain on, subject to certain conditions. But the conflict had shattered the relation between Stern and Ostwald, and several conversations between the auditor Ehrlich from the Berlin central office and the two men proved necessary in order to reestablish a tolerable working atmosphere. Yet one major upshot of this conflict was that Ehrlich (at least according to his own statements) was able to convince the Gestapo office chief that in future, instructions to Jewish subordinates "must not be allowed to undermine the authority of the head of the district branch."[76]

In this conflict, only on the surface was the matter at issue purportedly false "official information" provided by a Jewish functionary. Ultimately, leading regional Jewish representatives were fighting for their lives, which depended on how large their district was, and how long they would be allowed to administer it. In an effort not to be "removed" themselves, they cooperated with the stronger side, the Gestapo, rather than their own central office. Presumably, the Gestapo had its own interests, or the Gestapo head just found some small pleasure in playing havoc with the hierarchy in the Jewish organization. In any event, by imposing an obligation of secrecy on Stern vis-à-vis his superior, the Gestapo "violated" all customary rules of orderly administration. Of course, as part of the "fighting administration" of the regime, the Gestapo in any case felt no obligation toward that administration. However, striking from today's perspective is that the internal conflict did not arise mainly because of the intrigues or connivance of the Jewish functionaries with the Gestapo, but rather was sparked by some supposed "misconduct" by an administrator: the false "official information" passed on. From the perspective of the RV central office, the intrigues of Stern and his Dortmund colleague were of less importance (at least as the extant files suggest) than the violation of official channels. And efforts were focused on inducing the Gestapo to give Jewish functionaries the possibility to strictly adhere to these channels. In another case, a ranking official of the district branch Baden/Palatinate in Karlsruhe, Karl Eisemann, was instructed by the RV central office in January 1942 to close the subordinate administrative bureau in Ludwigshafen. The neighboring administrative office in Mannheim was to take over a portion of its work. When Eisemann went to collect the files from the office in Ludwigshafen, the Gestapo office in Neustadt intervened. It still needed this administrative office in order to implement planned deportations, and the head of the Ludwigshafen office, Lothar Pinkus, had the reputation of being particularly skilled at organizing transports. The upshot of this intervention was that the liquidation of the Ludwigshafen office was briefly postponed until March 1942.[77]

The responsible functionary in the RV central office, Arthur Lilienthal, had explained that this shutdown was in line with general cost-saving measures. But from internal correspondence, it is clear that the central office considered Pinkus unsuitable as a district branch director, and thus had two goals: to downsize personnel and economize while also firing a senior staff member they considered incompetent for the job. The central office accused him of two instances of "misconduct" in office: First, he had arranged the sale of real estate on his own and only reported this to Berlin after the sale had been completed. Second, he had failed to obtain permission through channels for taking a two-week vacation. Infuriated when he learned that his office was to be shut down, Pinkus contacted Paul Eppstein privately, complaining that after eight years working in the service of Jewish organizations, he was now to be dismissed with two weeks notice! He threatened to take legal measures and demanded that his administrative office and own position be maintained until the end of June. He stated that after June, he had good prospects for a "well-paid job." On a note of reconciliation, Pinkus added that he would, however, continue to work on a volunteer basis for the Reichsvereinigung.

It is clear from the correspondence how much the Jewish officials tried to present these events as normal administrative procedure. An official standard channel had not been adhered to, and superiors had noted this; a local branch was to be closed on instructions from above, and the distribution of its work to other offices was organized according to objective criteria. It was not until the Gestapo had intervened that this was brought to a halt. Up until this point, the Jewish functionaries corresponded as if they were not working under strict conditions imposed by the Nazi regime, precisely at a juncture when the regime was embarking on the mass murder of millions of Jews: the central office could not have revoked the shutdown of the branch office ordered by the RSHA, nor could Pinkus have made any concessions, even if the Berlin Jewish representatives had wished him to. For his part, Pinkus acted as though he were entitled to certain employee rights left over from the democratic days: a decent salary, adherence to notice periods for termination of contract, negotiations over termination pay, or the possibility of resorting to petition for added compensation. As a Jew, he was unable in mid-1942 to find any freely chosen, well-paying job; rather, he would have been classified for forced labor deployment or deportation. In his letter, Pinkus did not stress that his work was indispensable for the Jewish community. In view of the fact that he had been mainly involved in preparing deportations for the Gestapo, that claim would have smacked of cynicism. So he proceeded to argue based on his purported rights as an employee. Thus, the Jews involved strove to maintain an architecture of illusion: a world in which rational arguments could be presented, and reference could be made to obligatory administrative channels and procedures. In that illusory world, people could be reprimanded, point to service merit, or accept social responsibility. Given the coercion and quandaries the Jews involved in administration repeatedly found themselves in with property transfer and sale, and the horror of ongoing mass deportations, the fact that an administrative peccadillo—a tardy report of a property sale or failure to submit application for vacation—could become a serious problem for an experienced fellow coworker on the job points to just how frantically the Jewish functionaries were clinging to the illusion of orderly bureaucratic behavior. They hoped they could put a break of sorts on the increasingly threatening dynamic of persecution by adhering strictly to Prussian bureaucracy.

However, by writing angry notes of warning to Eppstein, Pinkus was able to force him to own up and finally speak frankly: the closing had indeed been ordered by the RSHA and Pinkus could not appeal to a labor court, but rather had to enter conscript labor immediately. "Otherwise the Reichsvereinigung central office will be obliged to submit a report via the responsible office of the Gestapo."[78] Eppstein, who was responsible to the RSHA for implementation of personnel cuts and closings, now was threatening his subordinate with reporting him to the Gestapo: this would lead to "protective custody" arrest, maltreatment, torture, and/or imminent deportation, as both sides of this altercation were well aware.

Eisemann, whom the Berlin office did not consider an especially capable coworker, now took over for Pinkus, and requested that the closing of the branch office be postponed. Nonetheless, the RV central office stuck to the decision to liquidate the bureau. As a concession, it suggested that Eisemann would be allowed to employ Pinkus as an unpaid volunteer (impossible in any case given his dire situation; he needed a salary), if he were given responsibility for only individual tasks and not an entire sphere of work. Perhaps what they had in mind here was the organizing of the transports, which the Gestapo had ordered.

Although the Jewish functionaries tried hard within their seemingly ordered world of administration to search for solutions to conflicts, they remained isolated in this endeavor. There simply was no counterpart or bureau in the Nazi state apparatus, the RSHA, or the Gestapo that adhered to regulations enacted or promises made. Likewise, in this case, the Gestapo that had so vehemently insisted on Pinkus continuing at his job took him into "protective custody" two weeks later and arranged his deportation (and this without Eppstein's having reported him).[79]

The District Branches and the Deportations

As has already become clear from the internal conflicts, the district branches were forced to take on an extensive, labor-intensive role in the organizing of the transports, although they were always left with relatively little influence on the process. Where the Jewish administration had not been involved during the initial large-scale deportations, the Gestapo offices soon fell back on the Jewish organizers for assistance.[80]

Yet what seemed simple as described when read in the organizational plans came initially as a shock to the coworkers involved. It quickly then devolved into a depressing recurrent routine. Günter Singer from the Breslau Jewish Community later said the first deportation came "like a bolt from the blue." Together with other helpers, he was ordered to equip the designated collection point, the Schiesswerder Hall, with wooden beds and sacks of straw. They still had "no idea whatsoever what that was all intended for."[81] In the late morning, the Jews to be deported were marched in large groups from the police precinct stations, where they had been ordered to report before going to the assembly camp.[82] Their presence on the street was by no means inconspicuous. The Gestapo also assembled the later deportation lists based on the card files of the Jewish Community, and the liaison Martin Pollack[83] was then ordered to inform those on the list.[84] The Jewish Community evidently was not brought into matters involving the settlement of deportee property, and was also not permitted to arrange medical assistance. Guards in uniform secured the camp from the outside, and Jewish marshals were ordered to prevent Jews from leaving the hall.[85] There were numerous suicides in the assembly camp, and the Jewish assistants had to take care of burying the corpses.[86] When possible, the Breslau Jewish Community later tried to find out what had happened to the deportees. Thus, an encoded message was received from a deportee sent to Izbica, stating that on 15/16 September 1942 in Sobibor "all the oaks had been felled, as well as all trees. Only ten oaks were left standing." This communicated to the recipients stark news: the Breslau Jews had all been murdered, except for ten.[87] The head of the Gestapo's *Judenreferat* read out death notices from the camps (probably for Jewish "prisoners in protective custody") to Pollack, who then informed the relatives if they were still living in Breslau.[88]

If the heads of the district branches set up assembly camps locally, they usually were familiar with the place chosen and were able to equip it for the purpose. But if the Jews from their area of responsibility were gathered together at some more central collection point in another city before departure of a transport, contact with them was often lost already inside Germany. The respective district branch head faced huge difficulties in gathering any information about the deportees from his area. In April 1942, Alfred Marx in Stuttgart, where Jews from the Saar-Palatinate were being concentrated, contacted Eisemann at his district branch office in Karlsruhe. He asked Eisemann whether he was aware of anything regarding the fate of his fellow Jews from Saarbrücken; he also wished to know whether there was a responsible office for the Jews from Trier. Some coworkers from the branch office in Karlsruhe brought articles and equipment for "their" Jews to the Stuttgart assembly camp, but they were denied permission to enter the camp grounds.[89]

The district branch heads also had to take care of funds for financing the transports (see chapter 2). The Württemberg Jewish Community instructed its members to pay a sum of 57.65 RM per person, and in order to compensate for a lack of sufficient funds, those a bit more wealthy were instructed to transfer up to 300 RM to the "special account W" ("W" for *Wanderung*, migration) of the Reichsvereinigung. They were informed that for this purpose, they were even permitted to transfer money from their closed account, funds they normally could not access for their own needs.[90]

However, there were repeated occasions when the deportation lists for the first large-scale transports of one thousand persons each also contained the names of Jewish functionaries, as in the case of the Cologne Jewish leaders Alfred Kramer and Kurt Wolff.[91] Then the Reichsvereinigung was immediately forced to look for a successor to take over the oppressive tasks of the designated deportee, sometimes, in the case of these functionaries from Cologne, against the successor's will.[92] Sometimes intervention by the central office to halt the deportations of its district branch heads or coworkers proved successful, as in the case of Ernst Krombach, Ernst Blumenberg, and Josef Eltzbacher from Düsseldorf and Essen. They were initially deferred from deportation because they were considered indispensable personnel,[93] at least for the next six months, during which most of their membership was deported.

As a rule, the district branches had to inform their members about an imminent transport. Although they could not avoid this task, they implemented it in a variety of different ways. The Rhineland district branch in Cologne thus sent out this message: "On behalf of the Cologne Gestapo, we wish to inform you that you must get ready and prepare yourself … for a migration transport. You will be informed of the place and time to report by the responsible district chief executive."[94] Instructions followed regarding declaration of assets, regulations for baggage, money, and valuables, as well as the order to hand in typewriters, bicycles, binoculars, and telescopes, etc., to the RV district branch office. In addition, the draft of a letter to the bank was included, which was to be used

in connection with the donation that the Reichsvereinigung expects from you on the occasion of your migration. There is general authorization from the supervisory authority that at least 25 percent of liquid assets are permitted to be donated to the Rhineland District Branch of the Reichsvereinigung der Juden in Deutschland … There is thus no limit on the maximum amount of these donations.[95]

After this unmistakably clear call to donate larger amounts, the district branch warned: "We expect that every transport participant will adhere carefully to the previously mentioned guidelines. It serves no purpose to submit applications for deferment because they cannot be considered. Failure to appear at the specified time will lead to Gestapo measures against the offender."[96] Those summoned to report for transport were able to receive clothing if needed: "we have instructed liaison personnel to assist transport participants in every way and to provide them support, just as we will do everything within our power to assist."[97] So the district branch passed on the Gestapo instructions in a relatively unembellished form, but explicitly referred to the agency that had issued these instructions. That candor may have been upsetting to those called to report, but they did not remain in the dark about the situation and the fact that they could not elude transport if so ordered.

By contrast, over and beyond the smooth organization of the transport, the Westphalia district branch office endeavored to provide members slated for deportation with psychological assistance. "In strict confidentiality," Max Ostwald, Adolf Stern, and Karl Heumann wrote to the circle of Jewish helpers:

> We have been assigned difficult tasks. We are responsible to the authority for their correct and timely implementation. In the interest of our members affected by these measures, it is necessary to work quickly and precisely. Our liaison personnel are instructed to dedicate themselves fully to the success and implementation of the tasks assigned them. For that reason, you are spared evacuation for the time being. ... We hope that you will not let us down in any way. What we demand of you is necessary; the deadlines have been set by the supervisory authority. Everything must go smoothly. Otherwise there could be unpleasant complications that no one would want to assume responsibility for.[98]

By no means did the authors treat the looming deportation as an everyday event; instead, they spoke clearly about the gravity of their "difficult tasks." They pointed to the threat for all Jews—functionaries, helpers, deportees—if they did not perform as expected, since everything had to "go smoothly." But they also appeared to understand that service by volunteers in this procedure was not easy to deal with emotionally. Most certainly, it was not to be taken for granted. There was always a danger that, being in the vicinity of a transport under way, a person who was just assisting might also be seized on the spot and deported. That is why they sought to allay the fears of staff by ensuring them that those assisting were *temporarily* protected from deportation. They were also quite aware of the physical and psychological burden suffered by those scheduled to be deported. "The care of those persons affected must begin immediately. In addition, a special helper is to be assigned to every family affected. His role should be to reduce the amount of work involved and provide psychological and spiritual counseling." The functionaries even arranged for the deportees to receive a typhus vaccination, and prepared an extensive instruction sheet with suggestions regarding hygiene and medical matters. They managed to obtain permission to get a sack of straw for each person to sleep on, the charge for which would be "billed to each individual." In the "Guidelines for Assistance to Jews Being Evacuated,"[99] they advised: "Introduce yourself immediately to the family assigned to you as a helper of the District Branch Westphalia. This should make it clear to the family that the community is concerned about their welfare."

The helpers were to check whether the deportees had correctly packed the permitted items in their baggage and to report what they were lacking, to take care of trips to government offices to pay outstanding bills, etc., and to ensure that regulations were adhered to. The authors warned the helpers: "You are responsible for ensuring that the family under your care has completed its preparations on time, and that it has all the necessities that are permitted to be taken along," and to "[d]evote all your free time to this task and care for everything as if it were for your own family."[100] At the same time, the heads of the district branches and their coworkers were obligated to secrecy vis-à-vis the RV members, and any infraction was subject to possible punishment by incarceration in a concentration camp. The district branch directors understood that some of the members had "the mistaken perception that nothing had been done to alter their fate, and some even believe that we were the ones who assigned them to the transport."[101]

Brief Digression: Preparations for the Deportations by the Gestapo

Even if the RV district branches took over extensive tasks, these nonetheless represented only a small fraction of the total complex of deportation: the "evacuation of the Jews" from the cities in the *Altreich* was prepared down to the smallest detail by the individual responsible Gestapo offices. Not only were the areas of competency spelled out; the personnel required, participation by other institutions and localities, and steps in implementation were also delineated. Soon also spelled out was the preparatory assistance the Jewish leadership was expected to provide, in addition to informing the Jews affected. Most relevant documents were destroyed in February/March 1945 with the other files of the Gestapo. Nonetheless, individual statements or extant documentation shed light on some of the procedures involved.

Thus, the Gestapo office chiefs were informed about the proceedings by the RSHA in official meetings and briefings.[102] For preparation of the concrete "operations," sixty to seventy "junior officials," generally staff consultants or heads of the *Judenreferate* from the entire area of the *Altreich*, were ordered to Berlin and briefed by Eichmann.[103] He stated, for example, that problems had cropped up in connection with the deportations from the Rhineland; these were to be avoided in future by a set of guidelines regarding what group of individuals were to be deported. A key word sent by telegram would inform the Gestapo offices that a transport was to be assembled. Since the first of these was to depart in three to four weeks, the Gestapo offices could already begin with preparing lists of all Jews fit for work under the age of sixty-five and their family members. The Gestapo offices were able to make use of the district branches of the Reichsvereinigung and the Jewish Communities that had not yet been dissolved in assembling these lists.

The organizational plan in the Gestapo area of competence for Nuremberg-Fürth is also extant. The ten-page document initially spelled out those responsible for the Gestapo, and then named the heads of the "evacuation groups" I–IV. These were responsible for the Jews of Nuremberg, Central Franconia with Fürth, Lower Franconia with Würzburg, and Upper Franconia with Bayreuth, Bamberg, and Coburg. These persons had to procure mobile equipment and furnishings for an office, and to arrange necessary food for the SS personnel involved, vehicles, etc. One official was in charge of negotiations with the Reichsbahn. For the deportation of one thousand Jews, twenty detective officers (Kripo personnel) and fifteen Gestapo men were required, along with fifty-five SS men. Two days before they were to proceed to the assembly camp, the Kripo and Gestapo or the Reichsvereinigung informed the Jews affected that they were to be "resettled." They informed them of their "evacuation numbers" and announced that their assets and property had been confiscated, effective from two weeks retroactive. They had to prepare a corresponding list of assets and bring along sixty RM for travel expenses. Their apartment should be left in such a condition that it could be sealed by the police. If at all possible, the same officials should then proceed two days later to collect the Jews from their homes and transport them on trucks under guard to the assembly camps that had been readied. Jewish work contingents were responsible for handling the baggage. The camp itself was to be rendered a closed area and guarded at its perimeter; two patrols were to circulate constantly to keep inmates under surveillance. No unauthorized person was allowed to enter the camp, that is, neither visitors nor representatives of agencies that were not involved. In the first room, the suitcase of the individual was to be checked and then reclosed, and "the Jew should not be allowed further access."[104] In the second room, the valuables and transport costs of the foreign participants were collected; the third room was for body search, with males and females carefully separated.[105] In the fourth room, the bailiff was to inform the person that his or her assets had been confiscated; their passport was then stamped "evacuated." Only then were the Jews allowed in to mix with the others in the camp as *Eingeschleuste* (literally "infiltrates"), strictly separated from the Jews "not yet processed." Regulations on blackouts for the camp had to be strictly adhered to. In the event of an air raid, Jewish laborers were to dig trenches for the SS, while if an alarm siren was sounded, the Jews had to remain in their accommodations. Two days after their arrival, the Jews were to be loaded onto the railroad cars in groups according to their "evacuation numbers."

Jews who had "any doubts" and questions were instructed to turn solely to the Jewish Community for clarification. The Community had to appoint aid marshals, rendering them identifiable by armbands, and to put together a work detail to transport baggage. It was to collect money to cover transport costs in advance, provide food for the camp inmates, and if necessary provide equipment for settlement in the East.

The later transports to Theresienstadt were organized along similar lines, but the deportees were generally taken directly from their homes to the trains. Bedridden Jews were to be transported in closed furniture trucks in order "to allow the public as little sight of them as possible."[106]

The transports did not differ in their general organization and aspect, but rather in details. For example, sometimes the Gestapo transferred the task of informing the deportees to the district branch. The deportees were not taken into custody everywhere, but were on occasion simply ordered to report to the assembly camp, to which they proceeded on their own. Not every assembly camp was under strict guard; often there was just a regular police officer on patrol. And the permitted quantity of baggage and the amount of money a deportee was allowed to take along varied according to the "generosity" (and intentions) of the Gestapo.

The Jewish deportees and the district branches of the RV had to finance their "resettlement" themselves (see chapter 2). The RSHA feared—and correctly so, as it soon turned out—that the local Gestapo offices and their staff regarded the transports as a welcome opportunity for self-enrichment through cash extorted from the deportees, in the certain knowledge that any witnesses involved would disappear forever "in the East." For that reason, the RSHA pressured the RV and its district branches and external bureaus to handle all monetary transactions via the "special account W."

The Gestapo generally prepared its officers for the deportation with instructions along these or similar lines:

> I expect that you will carry out this order with the necessary severity, correctness and care.... The Jews will attempt by requests or threats to soften you or will become refractory. You must not allow yourself to be influenced by this or be hindered in any way in the completion of your duties.[107]

A Comparative Look at the District Branches

The polycratic power structures in the National Socialist state, the competition between the party, the RSHA/Gestapo, national and regional authorities, and organizations and institutions also determined, both directly and indirectly, the possibilities and latitude for action available to the Jewish functionaries. Whether the Gestapo offices joined hands with the party or Reich authorities or competed with them, whether the Gestapo sought to recruit them for an operation or vice versa—all this had a direct impact on the process of persecution and deportation locally. And this in turn influenced the possibilities for action on the part of the Jewish representatives, in any case limited, and the perception they had of this process, at the time and in retrospect.

On the spot, there was a locally evolved, complex architecture of persecution with a multitude of participating institutions. The most important actors in this structure were the NSDAP (especially the *Gau* directorates) and the Gestapo, flanked by numerous other national and regional institutions. They all had a powerful ideological and material interest in the district branches of the Reichsvereinigung, which for its part was centrally oriented to its own Berlin main office. The RV central office in turn was subordinate to the RSHA.

This section explores and compares the factors that impacted the possibilities for action and room for maneuvering by the Jewish representatives between 1941 and 1943 in the regional fabric of power, as exemplified in the larger, medium-sized, and smaller district branches. What were these possibilities, what latitude existed? What strategies among the district branch directors for dealing with the Gestapo emerge from the source materials, and what was the relationship between the RV branch offices and the Berlin central office? Were the heads and coworkers of the district branches and Jewish Communities able to feel more "secure" prior to a transport than the board members and department heads in the Reichsvereinigung main office in Berlin? What were relations between the regional Jewish functionaries and their membership? In retrospect, how did the district branch directors who survived view the climate of persecution in their own city? And how did the ordinary members see these events?

We can identify three "models" that developed, with a multitude of overlappings in their concrete configuration:

1. If the government offices cooperated with those in the party within the framework of persecution, the process of persecution intensified, thickened, and radicalized. This will be exemplified by looking at events in Frankfurt am Main and Munich. Under such circumstances, the latitude for maneuvering by the Jewish functionaries tended to be reduced virtually to nil.
2. If open conflicts flared as a result of divergent interests in this fabric of competing powers, with some luck the Jewish representatives

found an open ear on the part of one of the parties to the conflict, because the encroachments of the other party endangered their monopoly on the persecution of the Jews. However, that "bulwark" function, as one Jewish representative characterized this with some exaggeration, always came to an abrupt end when operations were initiated by one's own organization of persecution. In the brutalized anti-Semitic climate, such operations then were somewhat more radicalized than elsewhere. That will be exemplified here in looking at developments in Nuremberg.

3. In a few cases, the Jewish representatives managed to establish "reliable" relations with the Gestapo, including, to a certain degree, relations of trust. The upshot was that the process of persecution and deportation then unfolded without particular excesses of violence or openly visible brutality. Indeed, in individual instances some relief and easing of restrictions were possible; this even extended to being saved from seizure. That will be explored below by looking at the example of Hamburg, with its large Jewish Community and Northwest Germany RV district branch, and the example of the small external branch office in Mainz, whose director skillfully exploited the differences between the Gestapo offices in Frankfurt am Main and Darmstadt, which alternately were responsible for Mainz.

Nonetheless, despite all the differences in the conditions the district branches were operating under, all nonprotected "full Jews" were ultimately deported, aside from a few exceptions due to protection from high-ranking officials. The RSHA also dictated the sequencing in which deportation was to unfold from the cities and districts, the respective dates for transport departures, and the number of deportees. Conditionally, it was possible for the district branches to have some influence on the number of Jewish deportees with a criminal record who were included as "prisoners in protective custody" in large-scale transports, or sent in individual or small-scale transports to extermination camps. As a rule, they came from the circle of the still protected forced laborers and Jews in mixed marriages. If the constellation was favorable, what the Jewish representatives were still able to influence was the "psychological environment" in which the Jews lived before their final days or weeks preceding transport.

As earlier described earlier, Hitler presumably authorized the beginning of the deportations of the Jews from the *Altreich* in September 1941, a move a number of *Gauleiters* had already long been pressing for. Europe was now to be "combed through" to seek out and remove Jews from West to East, with a main focus on the Reich territory and the Protectorate. In October 1941, after the first large-scale transports from Vienna, Prague,

Luxembourg/Trier, and Berlin, Jews were also deported from Frankfurt am Main, Cologne, Hamburg, and Düsseldorf. In November, further forced "migrations" followed from these cities as well as from Bremen, Munich, Breslau, and Nuremberg. In December, there were "evacuations" again from these cities as well as Stuttgart, Kassel, Münster/Osnabrück/Bielefeld, and Hanover.[108] In 1942, deportation trains were then rolling from across the entire *Altreich*, Vienna, and Prague; transports headed to Riga, Izbica, Piaski, Theresienstadt, Warsaw, Auschwitz, Minsk, Majdanek/Sobibor, Zamosc, Krasnystaw, Wolawa, Ujazdow, and Maly Trostinez. In 1943, transports followed to Auschwitz and Theresienstadt; these included inmates from nursing homes, employees of the Reichsvereinigung, Jews from dissolved mixed marriages, and, in increasing numbers, Jewish "prisoners in protective custody."[109]

I will examine the respective *particular* constellations in the cities under focus here—not the sequences of events, which tended to unfold in a quite similar manner everywhere—exploring in this context the possibilities and latitude for action by the Jewish representatives.

Frankfurt am Main: The System of Organized Arbitrary Action

In the *Gau* Hesse-Nassau, to which Frankfurt belonged, the *Gauleiter* Jakob Sprenger pressed for rendering his area "Jew-free" as soon as possible.[110] To achieve this goal, he maintained intensive contact with Oswald Poche, head of the Gestapo there from 1941 to 1943. He often summoned him to his office, giving Poche detailed instructions. Annoyed, the RSHA finally replaced Poche and told his successor, Reinhard Breder, according to Breder's postwar testimony, that his predecessor had permitted himself to fall too much under the influence of the Nazi Party.[111] The Gestapo had allowed itself to become the willing tool of the *Gauleiter*, had followed his direction, and had in addition interpreted RSHA orders to the benefit of the *Gauleiter*. That was the case in particular when the mass deportations in the autumn of 1942 had reached a point of near completion, when interest increasingly turned to the circles of individuals who had previously enjoyed protection. For example, the guidelines on deportees specified that combat veterans should be exempted. Nonetheless, in Frankfurt they were included in the transports.[112] Jewish armaments workers who were actually deferred likewise received deportation orders.[113] Intentional massive criminalization of previously protected Jews further increased the ranks of the deportees, because the "prisoners in protective custody" were transported directly to Auschwitz, along with large-scale transports to other destinations, such as Majdanek. In 1949, the state prosecutor, after interrogation of witnesses and working through extant documentation, stated:

The slogan of the Gauleiter—to render his Gau and thus also its capital Frankfurt "Jew-free" as soon as possible—had also been adopted by [Gestapo chief] Poche, who … issued the directive that in addition to the general evacuations ordered by Berlin, at least a further 100 Jews (spouses in mixed marriages and mixed race *Mischlinge* of the 1st degree) should be arrested and deported. To achieve this goal more quickly, … around the end of 1942/early 1943, Sprenger had informed not only all local heads of offices of his plan, but also the plant managers of those factories where Jews … were deployed as forced laborers.[114]

The arbitrariness of action was carefully organized here. Thus, after receiving this instruction, the heads of the various offices and the plant managers where Jewish conscript workers were deployed denounced to the police all Frankfurt Jews who had supposedly been found guilty of some offense. The accusations covered a range of infractions: the Jews had failed to use their ordered Jewish name, they had not worn the "yellow star," they had been caught smoking in the street, their food ration cards had not been properly issued, or they had applied for an allocation of charcoal that was not granted to them after changes in the general regulations in Frankfurt.[115] The Gestapo *Judenreferat* itself had a practice of summoning Jews for "inquiries." There was always some pretext for possible arrest (for example, their ID was in such a mint condition that the Gestapo personnel suspected the individuals summoned for questioning had not always had it on their person).[116] In this manner, it is believed a total of some fourteen hundred Jews were reported to the police for violations.[117]

The summons to these "inquiries" had to be delivered to the person involved by the Jewish Community or the Reichsvereinigung district branch.[118] The "passion for the hunt" (as the later Jewish intermediary Max Cahn termed it) was directed mainly against Jews who had been temporarily protected as a result of their mixed marriages.[119] Frankfurt was one of the few Gestapo offices, along with Vienna and Berlin, that worked with a network of fifteen to twenty Jewish informers who reported infractions to the Gestapo.[120] After the war, the *Judenreferent* Heinrich Baab even accused the RV representatives of having provided certain services as informers in order to exonerate themselves.[121] Proceedings before Jewish courts of honor were believed to have refuted that charge,[122] but investigations in a de-Nazification trial before a German lay court (*Spruchkammerverfahren*) confirmed this suspicion.[123]

The Gestapo office in Frankfurt am Main went far beyond the instructions it received from superiors in Berlin: it did not punish so-called violations by warnings or incarceration in labor camps, but rather, as the RSHA itself then criticized, "a penalty of concentration camp was considered in connection with every minor violation by a Jew."[124] The RSHA followed the respective requests of the Gestapo chief, but questioned the excessive application of protective custody as a means of punishment.

In Frankfurt am Main, Jews were under the control of the fanatic anti-Semite Ernst Holland, "Gestapo representative for Jewish welfare." The RV district branch had to pay his salary. He occupied rooms in the building of Jewish welfare services and later at Hermesweg 5/7, where there was an apartment block for Jews, one of the assembly camps, and the office of the Reichsvereinigung.[125] He thus watched over the Jewish functionaries and those interned there around the clock. Witnesses report on telephone calls between him and the Gestapo *Judenreferent*, in which he remarked: "If we were in Berlin and had to solve the Jewish Question, things would go faster."[126] Or: "The 'Jewish prisoner in protective custody' no. 399 has just died."[127]

The lawyer Julius Blau, who served for almost four decades as head of the Frankfurt Jewish Community, died in February 1939. From February 1939 to September 1940, there were a series of replacements, each lasting but a few months in office: Aron Freimann, Felix Meyer, and the physician Ludwig Ascher. From August 1941 to May 1942, Otto Simon-Wolfskehl held the post, and from May to August 1942 he was succeeded by Alfred Weil. The names of Ascher and Simon-Wolfskehl were already in the first list of deportees for transport to Lódz, and Weil was deported to Theresienstadt.[128] Other leading staff members, such as Georg Goldstein, were also detained for a time under various pretexts.[129] Thus, from the beginning of 1939, there was no longer a leadership echelon that might have been able to guide the Frankfurt Jews with continuity through the dark times of heaviest repression. None of the Jewish representatives of the Jewish Community (which on 6 November 1942 was absorbed into the RV district branch Hesse-Nassau) remained in office for even a single year. As a result, there was no time here for regular relations to develop with the heads of the *Judenreferate* as they had in other localities, no matter how lopsided those relations may have been elsewhere. When the Jewish Community was merged into the district branch, there were still 235 staff employees at work in the Community, who were now mostly fired; in addition, the 11 employees of the district branch, with the exception of its new head Louis Lerner, were deported. The administration was to operate in future with a staff of 40, including a cleaning lady.[130] Lerner was allowed to stay at his post another eight months, and was deported in June 1943 to Theresienstadt.

Lerner, previously the office manager of the Jewish Community, was named district branch director by the Gestapo, against the wishes of the Berlin RV main office. That office had wanted to suspend him from his duties as office manager a year earlier due to certain financial irregularities, but now had to accept his "promotion" ordered by the "supervisory authority."[131] Lerner evidently possessed neither the authority nor the personality to halt the organized arbitrary actions via official or nonofficial means, or even to arrange some easing of restrictions for the "prisoners in protective custody." When his successor asked him, "Why don't you do anything when people are arrested without any reason?" Lerner responded: "I'm totally powerless."[132] Lerner was unable to exploit the rivalry in Frankfurt between *Gauleiter* Jakob Sprenger and the mayor, Friedrich Krebs, both men of the "old guard of fighters" in the Nazi movement.[133] Instead, the impact of rivalries here led to a "cumulative radicalization."[134]

The powerlessness of the Jewish functionaries was also evident in connection with the deportation transports from Frankfurt. When rumors began to circulate about the first deportation, the Gestapo ordered that these rumors be squelched by contrary statements read out in religious services. Two days later, the operation so denied was indeed carried out. The RV was not as yet involved. The Gestapo was assisted by the police and some seven hundred party members (SA, SS, and "political leaders" of the NSDAP), who collected the deportees in the early dawn hours. The Jews were ordered to pack their baggage under the supervision of these party members, who then immediately sealed the suitcases. They were brought to the Wholesale Market Hall, the designated collection point, where they were kept under degrading, inhumane conditions; some Jews were maltreated, and there were even cases of death.[135] The procedure was changed after the first deportation operation, because the Nazi Party "political leaders" had sought to personally enrich themselves in a striking and shameless manner.[136] In subsequent deportation transports, "only" Gestapo personnel participated, along with forty to fifty police criminal investigators, finance office officials, and employees of the Food Agency.[137] The RV district branch informed the deportees twenty-four hours beforehand that they would be collected. If a deportation was imminent, the RV was ordered to remove from their card file the names of all those in the circle of persons to be "evacuated."[138] The Gestapo put together the deportation list from this pool of names.[139]

When the district branch was liquidated in June 1943, Louis Lerner and other functionaries assumed they could, as promised, travel to Switzerland and safety.[140] But the Gestapo chief ordered them deported to Theresienstadt, because "it's not necessary to keep your word of honor to a Jew."[141] The Gestapo representative Ernst Holland, the *Judenreferent*, and his superior accompanied the transport. Lerner was deported on to Auschwitz on 29 October 1944, where he was murdered.

In Frankfurt, Max Cahn, one of the few Jewish *Konsulenten* still permitted to work in Frankfurt and living in a mixed marriage, was appointed as intermediary in July 1943 and served until February 1944. He consciously kept his distance from the Gestapo, communicating mainly in writing and by messenger with the Gestapo office. His slogan was "do nothing we don't have to do." When he was ordered to make a list of all *Mischlinge*, he tried to warn them, "so that they could leave Frankfurt or go into hiding somewhere while there was still time. However, most were ultimately discovered and registered."[142] Like Lerner, Cahn likewise had no influence. He did not even learn that the Gestapo had occupied a nursing home and deported its residents.[143] As an experienced lawyer, he utilized the chance to free himself from the dangerous post when the Gestapo ordered him to transfer funds of the Reichsvereinigung to Frankfurt accounts that the Gestapo had access to. He notified the Berlin central office, which then reported this to the RSHA. This blatant attempt by the Frankfurt Gestapo to take funds from the RSHA provided him with a basis to leave his office without any punishment.[144] His successor, Karl Oppenheimer, who remained on the job for roughly a year, endeavored to develop a strategy of building trust with the Gestapo. As Cahn acknowledged, this approach actually did result in an easing of restrictions in the case of some individuals, but it also demanded gestures of subservience from Oppenheimer, which Cahn was not prepared to engage in. Thus, Oppenheimer added to the last deportation order, presumably under pressure from the Gestapo: "This order should not be viewed like one of the earlier evacuations. It should be preserved carefully and presented at your destination if necessary as documentation to show you are in labor deployment."[145] Many of those addressed, like Cahn, did not obey this order.

In 1933, there were some 30,000 Jews in Frankfurt am Main. Before the deportations began, they still numbered 10,592. More than 10,600 were deported from or through Frankfurt; fewer than 600 survived to see liberation, most thanks to their mixed marriage.[146] The leading Jewish representatives in Frankfurt from 1941 to 1943 were deported and murdered; the only two to survive were the intermediaries under the shield of a mixed marriage, Cahn and Oppenheimer. The Jewish representatives had no chance against the interplay of the *Gau* directorate and the Gestapo; they were even unable to utilize occasional rivalries.

Munich: Hatred of Jews in the Gau of Nazi Tradition

The total area of Bavaria was divided into three *Gau* districts: Franconia, Bavaria, and the Bavarian Ostmark. They were under the control of the *Gauleiters* Julius Streicher, Adolf Wagner, Hans Schemm, succeeded after his death in 1935 by Fritz Wächtler, respectively. Streicher and Wagner were two extremely radical anti-Semites. In 1933, there were some forty-two thousand Jews living in Bavaria; approximately two-thirds of these lived in the larger cities (see table 2).

Table 2. Jews in Bavaria, 1933

Munich	9,005
Nuremberg	7,502
Würzburg	2,145
Fürth	1,990
Augsburg	1,030
Bamberg	812
Aschaffenburg	591
Regensburg	427[147]

On the basis of repressive measures beginning early on, an extraordinarily large proportion of Jews left Bavaria in the first waves of flight and emigration. In 1939, there were still some 14,300 Jews in the province, a number that fell by more than 30 percent to 9,835 on 1 August 1941.[148] During the large-scale deportations, Bamberg was the collection point for Jews from the Bavarian Ostmark, a *Gau* covering Upper Franconia and the Upper Palatinate.[149] Nuremberg was the central collection point for Franconia, and Munich served as collection depot for transports from Swabia, Upper Bavaria, and Lower Bavaria.[150]

In 1933, just under 95 percent of all Jews in southern Bavaria lived in Munich, the "capital of the Nazi movement," and of these about one-fourth were Jews from Eastern Europe.[151] At 1.3 percent, the average percentage of Jews in Munich was not any greater than in other cities in the Reich. Yet the top echelon of the Nazi leadership in Munich took an early "special interest" in the local Jews. The new police chief, Heinrich Himmler, head of the Political Police, Reinhard Heydrich, and *Gauleiter* Adolf Wagner all sought to wreak havoc here among the Jews, and even the Munich mayor, Karl Fiehler, was one of the longtime senior stalwarts of the Nazi Party. Issuing radical ordinances locally, Wagner and Fiehler anticipated some later national anti-Jewish legislation, and also substantially tightened measures introduced by Berlin for the entire Reich.[152]

When the Reichsvereinigung was created in 1939, the Munich Jewish Community continued to operate as a branch of the RV, while a new Bavaria district branch administered the affairs of the Jews in Upper Bavaria. In mid-1942, the Munich Jewish Community was incorporated into the Bavaria RV district branch, headed by Theodor Koronczyk.[153] Apparently there was little enthusiasm in Munich for belonging to the RV: this eliminated the relative autonomy of the provincial associations of Jewish Communities in southern Germany, and they were suspicious that their Prussian counterpart associations would be very pleased with this change.[154] For their part, the Jewish Community members found the emigration levy they were required to pay to the RV an oppressive burden, because it substantially reduced their available private funds for preparing their emigration. Only as the incoming revenue of the Community gradually dried up did awareness grow that the funds of the RV were also in part directly benefiting the Bavarian Jewish institutions.[155]

An SD official had been appointed as Gestapo contact for the Jewish Community, and he oversaw all operations and work schedules at the Community. He took this task seriously, and suggested that the Community chairman Alfred Neumeyer should, given his advanced age, take a longer break at noon. At regular intervals, he also requested a kind of special bonus for his efforts. Neumeyer deducted these amounts ("we were at his mercy, and I agreed"[156]) from a personal fund for which he did not have to present any account.[157]

As mentioned, the Munich Jewish Community was directed from 1920 until early 1941 by Alfred Neumeyer. Julius Hechinger, a trained lawyer like Neumeyer, was in charge of financial matters. Neumeyer felt that given the trying times, this leadership duo was precisely what was needed. He characterized his chief associate as follows:

> Hechinger was a man of great energy and breadth of vision. He was adept at approaching the authorities tactfully, cautiously and yet resolutely in dealing with the difficult and sensitive matters entrusted to him. He had great empathy with the persons persecuted for political reasons [i.e., the Jews], was inventive in finding the means to assist them, and did not shrink back from any danger. On a personal level, he was not easy-going. Ambition and a certain recklessness brought him into conflict with the heads of the other departments and even with the rabbinate. Arrogant and domineering, strict in collecting tax revenues, he was the best hated man in the Community. I was criticized for supposedly giving him too much latitude. But the extraordinary times called for extraordinary men. The Gestapo admired him for his practical and flexible manner. And he enjoyed the particular trust of the supervisory official, with whom he knew how to get along and to whom he always had a ready reply in verbal self-defense. In so doing, he maintained my authority vis-à-vis the supervisory official by regularly obtaining my decision in important questions, and was always respectful in dealing with me. ... I dealt directly with the highest offices, in particular the ministries. ... On the whole, his activity benefited the Jewish community and rescued quite a few from torment and destruction.[158]

Neumeyer thus relied on an assertive financial expert, which naturally alienated some of the members and provoked internal Jewish conflicts. Hechinger's dutiful performance on the job was appreciated by Lilienthal (in the RV central office) and the Gestapo. Initially, it was also valued by the "supervisory official" mentioned, namely, Hans Wegner, head of the "Aryanization office." But Hechinger's manner led to "stormy scenes" at the Jewish Community office, with Jews affected.[159]

The "Aryanization office" had been set up on 28 September 1939, directed by Wegner as Wagner's representative and in addition trustee for the "de-Judification of the real estate sector."[160] As head of a Nazi Party office immediately responsible to the *Gau* directorate, Wegner had far more power at his disposal than Ernst Holland, the Frankfurt "representative of the Gestapo dealing with Jewish social welfare," or the above-mentioned SD official appointed as the Gestapo contact for the Munich Jewish Community. With a staff of some twenty employees, Wegner's "Aryanization office" was quick in fulfilling its original assigned task, namely, the takeover and/or liquidation of Jewish enterprises. Already by the end of 1939, there were but twenty-nine such enterprises still in existence, out of an original total of some twenty-two hundred.[161] The "forcible de-Judification of the real estate market," which was not yet operational across the entire German Reich,[162] made rapid advances in Munich, and was largely completed in 1940/1941.[163]

Far from surrendering his role as a pacesetter in Jewish persecution, *Hauptsturmführer* Wegner, always under orders from the *Gauleiter*, now took over in particular the task of resettling the Munich Jews, the administration and utilization of the remaining real estate owned by Jews, the administration of forced labor, and the supervision of anti-Jewish measures, as well as taking a hand in the organizing of the deportation transports.[164] The "Aryanization office" also kept a detailed "card file on Jews," which contained photos, data on assets, bank accounts, and places of work.[165] The Gestapo had its own card file, which it had confiscated from the Munich Jewish Community during the November 1938 pogrom. Jewish Community staff had to prepare a new file of this type for their administration.[166]

The *Gau* directorate, followed by the municipality, regarded persecution of the Jews as its most fundamental task. Both worked hand in hand with the Gestapo, but the "Aryanization office" under the *Gau* directorate was clearly the most active institution. However, others were encouraged for a time to become active, given the prevailing general climate. Thus, for example, a bank demanded the immediate vacating of a property owned by the Jewish Community that it had supposedly acquired. The bank did not retreat until a government official, at Neumeyer's instigation, pointed out that this procedure was illegal.[167]

The largely harmonious synergy of the institutions for persecution characteristically stamped the climate in Munich, where national measures were tightened and exacerbated by a distinctive perfidious imagination and a headlong rush to implementation. Two examples are instructive: in Hamburg, for example, two centrally located "Jewish shops" had taken over the task of supplying food and groceries to the Jewish population. The Nazi Party also raked in a good profit from this, and the Jews affected bemoaned the high prices and dubbed the stores "stargazer stands" because of the long times the "wearers of the yellow star" had to wait in line to be served. In Munich, over and beyond this ordinary chicanery, there evidently were specific directives ordering that Jews from the south side of the city could only go shopping on the north side, and vice versa. This led not only to extended waiting periods but also to "shoppers' marches."[168] The Munich Jewish Community had to distribute the food ration cards itself. If Jews tried to shop at stores other than the ones designated, that was immediately punished by "cuts for the Jewish community as a whole."[169] In Munich, the principle of collective punishment, of making the entire Jewish community liable for the "infractions" of individuals, was taken to exceptional lengths.

Nonetheless, the social welfare department of the Jewish Community took steps to have parcels sent through illegal channels to the Jews deported from Stettin, Baden, and the Palatinate. The former social worker Else Behrend-Rosenfeld wrote that the Munich Jews were admirable in the way they adjusted to the situation, reacting with composure to the impossible demands made on them—this even though they were denied what elsewhere provided for a bit of diversion in their oppressive everyday lives and kept alive the memory of a life in dignity, with access to culture. Significantly, in Munich and elsewhere throughout southern Germany, after the November pogrom even the activities of the Kulturbund were banned.[170]

When Neumeyer left Munich in 1941, he thought his succession was in good hands: in a far-sighted manner, and evidently to Hechinger's chagrin, who had expected that he would have sole responsibility,[171] Neumeyer appointed the engineer Karl Stahl and Julius Hechinger together as a team to head the Jewish Community. Stahl had long chaired the Munich branch of the League of Jewish Combat Veterans (Bund jüdischer Frontsoldaten), was president of the Munich B'nai B'rith lodge, and also active in several institutions of the Community.[172] These two men, along with the representative of the Jews from Eastern Europe, senior district court judge Joseph Schäler,[173] the engineer Fritz Sänger,[174] and a gentleman named Weiss, who emigrated in the summer of 1941, formed the new board of the Community. One of its first assignments, ordered by the Berlin main office, was a substantial downsizing of personnel in the Jewish administration. This "reorganization" involved 1,700 employees in Berlin, 120 staff members in the RV main office, and a total of 73 employees in Munich.[175]

The new board found itself in the increasingly dangerous situation of being caught on the horns of an administrative dilemma: while their own central office required regular reports on all sorts of things, on orders from their "supervisory authority," the persecution authorities in Munich forbade them to do this. That was in order to prevent precise information on the interpretation of anti-Jewish measures in Munich from making its way to Berlin. For example, the Jewish Community was asked to submit a report on the use of public transport.[176] But Wegner prohibited sending out such information. He considered it "superfluous" to inform the RV in Berlin about the details of matters in Munich. In "the interest of saving paperwork and time," he thought that only as few reports as absolutely necessary should be written. This would mean less work for the Jewish Community in Munich and would also facilitate making a "substantial number of Jews" in the central office available for other tasks, so they could be "engaged in a more productive activity" in the RV.[177] Karl Stahl circumvented the conflict by informing Eppstein "privately" about why the Munich report was delayed, seeking at the same time to cast off the "odium of having disobeyed an order."[178]

One of the most serious problems for the old and new Jewish Community leadership was the rehousing of the Jewish population on orders from the *Gauleiter* Adolf Wagner, to whom housing was directly subordinate. "The measures were more oppressive than those of the Gestapo and other party offices."[179] There were plans for a barracks camp in Milbertshofen, at Knorrstrasse 148. The *Gauleiter* had taken this initiative in close agreement with the municipal administration and the Gestapo,[180] as the Jewish Community reported to the RV main office, which then informed the RSHA. The latter was displeased and demanded that the Munich office should contact them directly, not via the Reichsvereinigung in Berlin.[181]

The camp was established in the spring of 1941. The RSHA had evidently not declared that it agreed to advance government subsidies in this case, as it had in other instances. Instead, Wegner shifted most costs to the Munich Jews,[182] and the "Aryanization office" extorted "voluntary donations" from individual Jews for construction of the camp, amounting to more than half a million RM, "many times the cost of construction."[183]

The Jews forcibly interned in the camp had to pay a daily fee for accommodations. The barracks had a capacity for 1,100 persons, but were often overcrowded, for example, as a collection point for a deportation transport numbering 1,376 persons.[184] The "Jews' settlement" was not a concentration camp, but was a primitive, cramped, closed living area, which no one could leave except with a special permit.[185] Its residents had to expect constant checks by the Gestapo and employees of the "Aryanization office."

Likewise, in 1941, a section of the Convent of the Merciful Sisters was declared a "Home for Jews, Berg am Laim." Its capacity was 350 individuals (beds for 163 men and 160 women) and was to charge 1 RM rent per day per person. Jews were allowed to take along only the "barest necessities," and the Jewish Community had to appoint a camp director. It had also to cover the additional expenses,[186] which it calculated as 7,000 RM for the period prior to full occupancy and 10,000–12,000 RM at full occupancy. The residents were crowded in, with 6–16 persons per room, and some had to sleep in double bunk beds and store their belongings in military lockers in the hall. The rental charge of 30 RM for locker and floor space was more than three times the customary rate under normal circumstances.[187] After the Community (via the RV) requested the RSHA to intervene, rent was reduced to 50 pfennigs per person per day.[188] The Jewish Community called on its members for contributions in the case of both facilities, not only during construction but also for support, in order for sickrooms, first aid stations, and kitchens to be set up and the clothing storeroom to be stocked.[189] Else Behrend-Rosenfeld, appointed economic manager in Berg am Laim, provided a revealing picture of life in the convent facility. The former schoolteacher Alb and the merchants Ernst Heilbronner and Abel were appointed to head camp management.[190] Despite the cramped quarters, overcrowding, and long distances to the center of town, life together with the nuns here made accommodation of the residents much easier, and the Jews were also able to profit from gardening and fruit cultivation.

In August 1941, there were still some 3,200 Jews in Munich.[191] Of these, 300 were relocated two weeks later to the "Jewish settlement Milbertshofen." In October 1941, the population there was already 450, with 300 living in the convent in Berg am Laim.[192] The residents of the barracks camp were allowed only to take along the barest necessities. The Jewish Community appointed Hugo Railing as camp director, succeeded by Curt Mezger.[193] The representative of the *Gauleiter* stressed that it had been possible to achieve a better and more durable system of control and surveillance of the Jews by means of these "communal settlements," and the Munich area had been "cleansed of Jews" (*entjudet*) quickly and thoroughly.[194] For the Community, Hechinger was the Jewish official responsible for the camp. Camp residents later recalled him as the "Jewish liaison man of the Gestapo," in the words of the (then) young Werner Grube,[195] or as "evil incarnate," in the words of Charlotte Knobloch. As an adult, she later revised that childhood memory by adding: "Although he only did what the Nazis forced him to do."[196]

Many Munich Jews saw only one side of Hechinger: his ostensible position of power, his direct access to the "supervisory authorities," and his "privileges." They were unaware of the permanent danger that threatened him by dint of his position, particularly when he had to deal with the "Aryanization office." Only a few people, such as his coworker Theodor Koronczyk, had any picture of these perils. Hechinger repeatedly told him that if he should not return by a specified time, Koronczyk should inform the Gestapo "in order to have him released."[197] But such an attempt would probably have proved abortive, because the *Gau* directorate and the Gestapo always formed a united front in their dealings with the Jews in Munich. Hechinger was unable to deal with the *Judenreferent* of the Gestapo with any less fear than with the "Aryanization representative" and their respective coworkers. There were no rivalries he might have been able to make use of. As it later turned out, it was actually the Gestapo that handed him over to the "Aryanization office." Hechinger was caught between Scylla and Charybdis.

On 7 November 1941, the Jewish Community informed the participants of the first deportation transport train, in the so-called brown letters sent out to them, that "pursuant to an order of the Gestapo," they were not permitted to leave their homes after 11 November, but should ready themselves for transport and should take along all their three-piece mattresses.[198] In the barracks camp, a marshal distributed a "package of evacuation orders." On 8 November, Karl Stahl briefed the leading staff members and social workers, imposing on them the obligation of strictest secrecy.[199]

How were the lists for deportation put together? The postwar testimony on this differs: Koronczyk reported that Hechinger had to bring lists to the Gestapo and then mark the names as instructed by the Gestapo.[200] According to other testimony, a commission consisting of Stahl, Hechinger, and the *Krankenbehandler* Julius Spanier put the lists together, according to the guidelines the Gestapo *Judenreferat* had received from the RSHA and communicated to them. Still other testimony states that a group of eight or nine from the board of the Jewish Community prepared the lists.[201] In addition to the instructions from the RSHA and the Gestapo, Wegner evidently had specific Jews he wanted to get rid of put on the deportation list.[202] Until around the spring of 1942, physical examinations for fitness for deportation transport were carried out under the direction of Spanier.[203]

Theodor Koronczyk handled preparatory tasks for transport; he was a stateless former businessman who had then worked as a gymnastics teacher, and was no longer allowed to leave Germany. Initially he had been in charge of the card file in the Jewish Community and had then taken over direction of the tax office, where he assisted Hechinger's work.[204] In connection with the first large-scale deportation, which originally was scheduled to depart for Riga, he had to arrange procurement of food provisions and tools for the purported "settlement in the East."[205] The deportees were brought by bus to the Milbertshofen barracks camp, where they slept on straw awaiting departure. Self-satisfied, Wegner later testified that "no one had to sleep on the bare floor."[206] Checks on baggage and body checks were also carried out in Milbertshofen. The camp was guarded by the SS prior to the transport, and patrols monitored the grounds. The Jews were forced to march at 4:00 AM in pouring rain, guarded by a company of SS, to the Milbertshofen freight station.[207] The train left Munich on 20 November 1941 and was rerouted to Kovno, where the Munich Jews (together with Jews from Berlin, Frankfurt, Vienna, and Breslau, a total of five thousand persons) were shot shortly after arrival.[208] Thus, no news was received from them in Munich.

The next large-scale transport on 3/4 April 1942 went to Piaski. Board member Fritz Sänger,[209] camp director Railing, their family members, and the troika managing the facility at Berg am Laim were on the list of deportees. At the last minute, Else Behrend-Rosenfeld, also on the list, was deferred.[210] Three months later news was received in Munich from Piaski: the deportees reported that the Jews from Stettin were no longer there, they spoke of forced labor deployment, deaths, hunger and cold, indescribable filth, and the misery among the many elderly deportees. But then the messages stopped.[211]

Julius Hechinger was also to be included in the deportation to Piaski, probably on special orders from the *Gauleiter*. Stahl evidently tried to prevent the deportation of Hechinger and the other staff workers by requesting the RV in Berlin to intercede. He was successful only in the case of Else Behrend-Rosenfeld, who now was "promoted" to director of the facility in Berg am Laim. Hechinger, however, warned by a telephone call from the Jewish camp director Railing,[212] went into hiding for a few days until the transport had left. He then reported at the office of the Jewish Community. With Hechinger's agreement, Stahl then informed the Gestapo, and they took Hechinger into custody for one or two weeks. The Gestapo accused him of having broken the seal on his own room, and then handed him over to the "Aryanization office."[213]

Schrott, one of the staff there, took him in a "pitiable condition" to the Milbertshofen barracks camp that evening. The SS man ordered the Jewish marshals to hang Hechinger on the spot. He assured them in advance that they would not be punished for this. He was relying on Hechinger's unpopularity among his fellow Jews in general and the young marshals in particular. Hechinger's privileges in being able as a leading functionary to use taxis for travel in Munich, and trains and even planes for journeys to the Reichsvereinigung central office in Berlin, had spawned aversion toward him, and his uncompromising actions against his own people had also awakened aggressive anger among the Jews.[214] In addition, many young men charged that his reports had led to them being classified as *Geltungsjuden* instead of first-degree *Mischlinge*, and as a result they were forced to live in the camp.[215] Nonetheless, they refused to lay a hand on Hechinger. Schrott then locked Hechinger up in a shed and tossed some rope inside, a hint that Hechinger should take his own life. The next day, Mugler, another staff member from the "Aryanization office," appeared. He ordered Hechinger to be assigned to the most strenuous manual labor. In the morning and evening, he also had to perform an endurance run around the camp grounds. Mugler instructed that after the run, the Jewish marshals were to hose him down with powerful jets of water.[216]

Although these marshals left Hechinger in peace when no official from the "Aryanization office" was present, they had to carry out their orders when they were on hand. Once he was commanded to crawl beneath a very low cart, and he scraped his back bloody; another time the persecutors from the "Aryanization office" ordered him to dig his own grave, and they told him to kill himself. When he didn't obey, Wegner and Mugler beat him up. As the Jewish eyewitnesses later recalled, "blood was pouring from his eyes, nose and mouth. His lips were totally ripped open. His face had swollen into a shapeless mass. His clothing had been torn almost completely from his body. His body was covered with spots and welts." But this was still not enough: Wegner ordered that Hechinger had to clean the latrines, with only his bare hands and feet, and they were to continue to be used as he worked. Hechinger was "soon completely covered with feces. He was standing … up to his belly in shit," one of the Jewish marshals later reported.[217] Hechinger confided in this marshal that Wegner and Mugler wanted to get him out of the way because he knew too much about them. Koronczyk tried in the meantime to get some help via Eppstein in Berlin, but Eppstein reportedly declined, probably influenced by his own bitter experiences with "punitive transports in Berlin," saying little could be done.[218]

On 13 July 1942, Hechinger was included in a so-called punitive transport of fifty persons. Although several days prior to that and afterward transports to Theresienstadt had also left Munich, Hechinger was not accorded the "pleasure" of internment in the "preferred camp." He and other "asocials," some of them "in shackles," were, according to what their contemporaries surmised at the time, sent to Warsaw. But in actuality they were probably transported to Auschwitz and murdered there.[219]

According to many testimonies by eyewitnesses, the staff of the "Aryanization office" and Gestapo personnel abused and mistreated the Jews, and shamelessly enriched themselves in the process. Their abuse was aimed not only at high-ranking staff like Hechinger, but anyone who goaded their curiosity, such as a young Jew of Polish family background, Sabine Preiß. Her head was shaven, she was marked by a large "P" painted in oil on her head; to the amusement of the men, she was stripped half naked, then hosed down and beaten with a rubber truncheon. Like Hechinger before her, she was forced to spend a night in the mortuary. The young woman collapsed under these sadistic-sexual torments. After a further open session of torture at the "Aryanization office," she tried to take her own life.[220]

After the duo direction of Hechinger/Stahl had been dissolved, Stahl continued to head the district branch alone, appointing Koronczyk to handle imminent preparations for deportation. There was no longer any need for a commission to assemble the transports; "selection" was no longer an option.[221] In June 1942, the deportation to Theresienstadt of "almost all patients" and personnel at the Jewish Hospital Munich was imminent. It seemed questionable whether the still sixteen hundred or so Jews in Munich would be able to receive medical care in the future. In the Milbertshofen camp, there were only ten sick beds for five hundred persons; in Berg am Laim there were but twelve beds for Jews with minor ailments. Julius Spanier, director of the Jewish Hospital, wrote in vain to Stahl that with the evacuation and shutdown of the hospital, the eight hundred Jews still living in Munich would lose any chance for medical care. He noted that there were no longer any operating rooms or surgeons.[222] Spanier hoped in future that Jews might be accepted and treated for at least one day in the public hospital.[223]

Spanier himself was on the list for the next transport; he was assigned transport head and survived.[224] He later stressed: "[P]eople here could definitely not know that the transports were heading for gassing.... One day before my departure, the Reichsvereinigung phoned from Berlin and said we should be happy to go to Theresienstadt, it was a more or less tolerable ghetto."[225]

Basic medical care for Jews was no longer guaranteed, and there was likewise not enough room for the elderly, especially since Stahl had been forced to sell several plots of land to the Lebensborn.[226] Only the Milbertshofen camp had room, but it was hardly suitable for the elderly, and with rent of sixteen RM per resident, it was more than twice what the Reichsvereinigung could "allow."[227] Nonetheless, ultimately the RV had to pay that rate.

In July 1942, Karl Stahl and his wife Luise were deported; he too suspected this was due to personal intervention by Wegner, as he told friends.[228] As an RV staff worker, he was sent to the "preferential camp"

Theresienstadt and was active there in the Council of Elders, until he and his wife were deported and murdered in Auschwitz.[229]

The announcements that transports to Theresienstadt were now being regularly assembled led to suicides, especially among the elderly and sick in Berg am Laim,[230] where the mood turned ever darker. Else Behrend-Rosenfeld rejected the idea of fleeing: "[A]s long as I'm in charge here, I can't leave."[231]

In Munich, Theodor Koronczyk was now promoted to district branch head with a monthly salary of 450 RM.[232] He stated later that he had had no choice: "Either you can accept the job or not; if not, then you're put in a concentration camp until you've wised up and learned your lesson."[233] Koronczyk learned quickly. Apparently, Stahl had put together the first list of deportees for Theresienstadt; Koronczyk prepared the subsequent lists according to Gestapo dictates.[234]

The Jewish settlement in Milbertshofen was liquidated on 19 August 1942. The remaining residents were relocated to the home in Berg am Laim.[235] When Else Behrend-Rosenfeld learned that the camp director in Milbertshofen was to take over the facility, she felt free to plan her own escape and survival. She returned once more to the convent in August 1942 to prepare an assembly camp for the scheduled deportation. The Jewish home in Berg am Laim had now taken over this function from Milbertshofen. The Jews affected gathered there for transport; the Gestapo officials came to the home to carry out checks on baggage and body checks on deportees. But first, they arranged lounge chairs and a keg of beer in the convent garden for themselves, enjoyed the summer afternoon and evening, and joked and flirted with the women who had accompanied them. They then commenced with their real "work" shortly before midnight.[236] Behrend-Rosenfeld now set about implementing her own plan: she went into hiding and fled in April 1944 to Switzerland.

The deportations continued. Initially there were transports of 50 persons each to Theresienstadt, and on 13 March 1943, 219 were sent to Auschwitz. After that, Berg am Laim, the second large residential facility for Jews, was liquidated. Once again, the Reichsvereinigung had to cover the costs, paying rent subsidies and relocation aid to the last Jewish residents, an amount approved by the central office as so-called supplementary expenses.[237] The Gestapo had promised the camp director Mezger, in a mixed marriage, that he would be discharged and allowed to return home after the closing of the office. Instead, he was arrested and deported.[238]

Beginning in October 1942, the Nuremberg Jewish Community was treated as a part of the RV district branch in Munich and its personnel was cut to three workers.[239] The administrative office in Augsburg subordinate to Munich was dissolved in March 1943. At the Munich office at Lindwurmstrasse 125, there were the offices of the RV district branch Bavaria and the "administrative office" Munich (i.e., the former Munich Jewish Community), communal accommodations, and apartments, in particular for the personnel of the district branch and administrative office,[240] which at any time could also be checked and monitored, even in employees' private living quarters. Koronczyk retained his post beyond the time of the official liquidation of the RV district branch and its transformation into an organization for those in mixed marriages, and was now serving as intermediary of the RV. He himself met the precondition by dint of his own mixed marriage. It was not 10 June 1943 (liquidation of the Reichsvereinigung), as in the rest of the Reich, but a day in February 1944 that constituted the caesura in Munich: the Gestapo informed Koronczyk that the district branch was now to be closed, and "reputable" office staff would be sent to Theresienstadt.[241] Koronczyk was quick to assure the Gestapo that all employees were "reputable." He himself was now working as a volunteer, always under pressure to satisfy the demands of the Gestapo (the "Aryanization office" had been dissolved in 1943, its personnel transferred) and those of the Jews whom he was obliged to represent and care for. His strategy to behave vis-à-vis his fellow Jews like a forceful Nazi, that is, to shout and bellow, threaten people with severe consequences, and blame specific Jews for offenses was, as later examination indicated, never a truly decisive factor in the severe, sometimes deadly consequences that the Jews suffered. Yet in the minds of the Jews affected or their relatives, his behavior awakened the impression that he was the person responsible. Thus, among other accusations, it was reported that he had arrested a Jewish woman who had gone into hiding, and then handed her over to the Gestapo.[242] Another woman accused him of having refused to recognize her medical certificate, and the result was that she and her three children were deported.[243] Yet Koronczyk thought it was to his merit that of 450 Jews, only 50 had been deported to Theresienstadt.[244] Several of the *Geltungsjuden* mentioned above went into hiding shortly before the end of the war, were betrayed (by persons unknown), and arrested by the Gestapo in the presence of Koronczyk. Not only contemporary Jewish witnesses, but even some later historians term him a "Jewish Nazi agent" or "Jewish Gestapo informer."[245] The reason: Koronczyk embodied a problematic personal balancing act, a walk on the wire between an anticipatory obedience, silence toward his fellow Jews, involuntary support for the Gestapo operations, and voluntary participation in some that he could not have prevented. Perhaps he was coerced, perhaps he simply wished to be on hand, to be informed, in order if possible to do something later on for the Jews affected. In retrospect, and probably already at the time Koronczyk was in office, coercion and willingness can hardly be distinguished from one other in such a way that incontrovertible "truths" can be established. Koronczyk evidently tried to create the impression whenever Gestapo men or staff of the "Aryanization office" were on hand that he was completely following their instructions. He also warned Jews not to violate prohibitions and threatened them in advance with serious consequences. In the probably correct assessment of one survivor, the physician Schwarz, Koronczyk was not the "right man for the job. He was afraid of the Gestapo. Koronczyk became smaller and smaller, he ducked his head more and more. He was threatened with concentration camp, even in my presence. I'm sure he wasn't malicious in dealing with the people. ... He almost no longer dared to say anything. He made every effort to help his fellow Jews ... The people also became very resistant to him."[246] In retrospect, "legal consultant" Siegfried Neuland thought that unlike Stahl, Koronczyk did not have the right personality for the job and was not well suited to the challenge, in the dark years of 1942/1943, of tending to the needs of the Jews on the one hand, while on the other having the Gestapo and Wegner behind or against you.[247] However, the "right" personalities had already been deported. What other option did Koronczyk have but to attempt, with the possibilities for action personally available to him, to survive the final years—and in the process, despite all his own anxieties, to try to achieve something for the majority of the remaining members?

US troops liberated the last remaining Munich Jews. On 1 April 1945, there were still some four hundred Jews there, living in mixed marriages. One hundred and sixty deportees returned from Theresienstadt.[248]

The distinctive feature of the situation of persecution in Munich was that since 1933, fanatic anti-Semites had been agitating in all the institutions involved. They enjoyed the backing of the highest echelons in the Nazi Party or indeed themselves belonged to them. They outdid one another in promoting anti-Jewish measures. The Reichsvereinigung main office in Berlin also did not succeed in putting a stop to initiatives in Munich via the RSHA; after all, Himmler himself had been among the early Nazi activists in the birthplace and "capital of the movement." Koronczyk had no chance of finding even temporary support from any institution; he stood alone. Thus, after the war, the former persecutors who had returned were able to deny their actions in court or distort the facts unhampered. They stated that the Jews had prepared the deportation lists, the Jews had considered Hechinger an informer (while the *Gauleiter* had not tolerated any informers), the Jews had turned over those who had tried to flee to the Gestapo. More than in other places, the Jewish representatives, especially the last man in the job, had lent the persecutors in Munich a face and a voice, and in the eyes of the victims there, they came to be held responsible for the actions of the perpetrators.

Nuremberg: Uninhibited Hordes

Since the NSDAP's victory at the polls in 1930, the Jews in the "city of the *Reichsparteitage*" were already suffering from agitation by *Gauleiter* Julius Streicher and the excesses of his rabid Nazi Party comrades. Innumerable incidents described in the literature are testimony to the brutality with which the NSDAP took action against the Jews here, always associated with an unbridled urge for self-enrichment.[249] This resulted in an earlier wave of emigration by Nuremberg Jews, more extensive in comparison with other areas of the Reich.[250] Like the *Gauleiters* Sprenger and Wagner, Julius Streicher also wished to render his *Gau* "Jew-free" as soon as possible, but he took such rapid and radical initiative that Göring and Himmler felt it necessary to intervene. They sensed that Streicher was encroaching on their sphere of power. During the November 1938 pogrom, this power struggle between the party (Streicher) and SS (here personified by police head and Gestapo chief Benno Martin) escalated. The NSDAP had acquired possession of Jewish homes, businesses, and real estate by the threat of violence or engaging in its brutal use. This created a corruption scandal evident across the entire Reich; Göring intervened, ending the scandal by sidelining Streicher. However, nominally he remained at his post as *Gauleiter*.[251] Benno Martin, "Himmler's man in Nuremberg,"[252] the local representative of the SS, had ordered the Centralverein to gather together documentation from Jews who had been robbed and cheated in connection with this corruption, and had used this in the internal party struggle against Streicher.[253] The open power struggle between the *Gauleiter* and Martin in Nuremberg in 1939/1940 was useful to the Jews in that it proved possible, with the Gestapo's aid, to avoid the effects of the worst encroachments by the Nazi Party. This point was summed up by Centralverein chairman Walter Berlin after the war:

> However, while almost everywhere else in the other districts, the Gestapo was the main agent of arbitrary rule and the oppression of the Jews, and almost everywhere, it was impossible for the Jews even to find a sympathetic ear at the Gestapo, in Nuremberg the situation differed. There was ... a peculiar feature: here the Jews were listened to, and to a certain extent found protection both with the police chief and the Gestapo. And that was also true later on, as gradually most of the other authorities were no longer willing to listen and turned away.[254]

The CV chair even described the Gestapo as "one of the few bulwarks standing between them [the Jews] and naked brute force."[255] Walter Berlin emigrated in 1939 to London and Streicher lost his party office in 1940, but a similar constellation remained operative until 1945. The later chairman of the Jewish Community, Bernhard Kolb,[256] could turn to Christian Wösch, head of the *Judenreferat* in the Nuremberg Gestapo, in connection with orders from and encroachments by the *Gau* directorate. It was possible to negotiate with Wösch, and his office was the only authority able then to also implement the result.[257] The extent to which, even in the late 1930s, the social class background could determine the relation of persecutors to the persecuted becomes clear from the transcript of the court proceedings against Benno Martin: according to his own statements, Martin had a "very close relationship" with the Centralverein chairman, and accepted him as interlocutor and a partner in negotiations. Both were trained lawyers, both stemmed from the upper middle class. Martin refused to even receive Berlin's successor Kolb, a staff member in the state pension office who had been dismissed from his post there. Wösch, who regularly gave Kolb instructions, summed the matter up: "Berlin was a man of substance, while Kolb came from the lower class."[258]

Kolb had indeed worked as an employee of the Jewish Community before the Gestapo appointed him to serve as liaison;[259] Albert Fechheimer, owner of a wholesale iron company, headed the Jewish Community[260] until his arrest in the spring of 1942. Leo Katzenberger and Julius Nürnberger were also on the board.[261] In May 1942, Katzenberger was convicted of alleged "racial defilement" (*Rassenschande*) in a show trial, sentenced to death, and executed on 3 June 1942.[262] After a short transition period during which Adolf Krämer chaired the Community, Bernhard Kolb took over the helm on 10 June 1942, to remain exactly one year in office, until the association's liquidation.[263]

Before the November pogrom, the Nuremberg Jews already felt they had been let down by the Reichvereinigung main office. Given the extreme situation in Nuremberg,[264] they had requested more support for emigrants, but in vain. The main office did not take the special circumstances there into account until Otto Hirsch came face to face with it. He formed a direct personal impression of the situation during a visit to the city.[265] But even then the RV central office was unable to accomplish much more than the Nuremberg Jews themselves: that is, utilize conflicts between their persecutors and appeal to the RSHA as an office of arbitration.

Several examples can serve to give an impression of how the *Gau* directorate and other institutions of persecution operated in Nuremberg:

- In the summer of 1941, the *Gau* directorate had plans to incarcerate the Nuremberg Jews in external forced labor camps, as had been undertaken already in other German cities.[266] Families were to be torn apart and the sexes would be separated. The Gestapo stepped in and prevented implementation of the plan.[267]

- When the order to wear the "yellow star" was introduced, the Nazi Party called on every party member to monitor the Jews in Nuremberg and report even the most minor infractions. According to Kolb, however, the Gestapo ignored the reports received if the Jewish representative contested the facts.[268]
- When the district chief of the NSDAP in Nuremberg sought to compel the Jewish Community to sell its overcrowded home for the aged to the Deutscher Siedlerbund and to relocate residents within fourteen days to an unsuitable, decrepit building in the forest, the RSHA intervened and prevented the initialing of the contract.[269] Otherwise, these elderly Jews, a number of whom had been in any case separated from their families as a result of deportations, would have been forced to live sleeping in cramped bunk beds, in rooms with little heat, far from any medical attention.

It is clear from these and other examples that the Gestapo warded off encroachments by the NSDAP that endangered an "orderly resettlement of the Jews," although the term "bulwark" probably is exaggerated and hardly appropriate. Discourse about a "bulwark" becomes totally absurd if we consider the behavior of the Gestapo during the deportations. On 18 October 1941, the Gestapo informed Community secretary Bernhard Kolb that 1,000 members of the Jewish Community in Nuremberg were to be deported.[270] This plan would have included all able-bodied members of the Community under the age of 65. Kolb was able to negotiate with the Gestapo and managed to lower the number to 500 (actually 512), but at a heavy price: the other 500 were assigned to transports from the surrounding cities.[271] The Gestapo took the addresses from the card file;[272] Kolb undertook steps to ensure that families remained together and that some Community employees were given a deferment. But his colleague in Fürth refused to participate in this procedure, and evidently was not penalized for that refusal. The Gestapo there organized the transport on its own; however, no changes by the Jewish Community were allowed.[273]

The Nuremberg Jews were brought to a barracks assembly camp located on the Nazi Party Congress Grounds (*Reichsparteitagsgelände*) outside Nuremberg. The sacks of straw had been removed from the facility, so that the deportees were forced to sleep on the bare floor. Apparently there was no Jewish camp directorship, no medical service unit, and no Jewish marshals on hand. An instruction sheet from the Jewish Community ends with the statement: "We hope that it will be possible for the Nuremberg Jewish Community to maintain contact with those evacuated. Since a visit to the camp is prohibited by police order, we bid our departing members a cordial and hearty farewell."[274] A special commission of the Gestapo, SS, and uniformed police cordoned off the camp grounds. SS personnel took charge of the Jews arrested by the Gestapo for deportation, harassing and abusing them. They looted their possessions, and brutally extracted gold fillings from their teeth.[275] Despite the good character references the Jewish representatives provided for the Gestapo officials after the war, the Gestapo men were scarcely less brutal than the Nazi Party members and SS detachments: one Gestapo man ordered the camp inmates to carry chairs while running double time around a table; another directive instructed that they work out in "early morning sports." On orders from the RSHA, the first two deportation "operations" were captured on film. When a banker quite known in the city tried to elude the camera, he was beat up, his teeth were knocked out, and he was then dragged off and locked up in an outhouse toilet, where an official hung a sign: "Bankhaus Kohn closed." The film then showed him in close-up leaving the outhouse, visibly injured. The Gestapo deputy chief personally wrote the texts inserted in the film. After the deportation transport with the Jews departed, the Gestapo organized a boozing party in the assembly camp. The officials, their secretaries, and cleaning women, who had assisted during the physical body searches on the deportees, enjoyed the food looted from the deportees; liquor was provided in abundance by the local innkeeper. They arranged a raffle with prizes, comprising items taken from the baggage of the Jews, danced the polonaise accompanied on the accordion, and in the late evening watched a premier showing of "their" film.[276]

In a later deportation operation, Kolb was told to inform the deportees that they could take along two hundred RM for this transport. This was a devious trick: it allowed the Gestapo personnel to garner substantial extra income, since they collected and pocketed the money immediately after the deportees arrived in the assembly camp. In his memoirs, Kolb makes a distinction between deportation events in Bamberg and Nuremberg, stating that procedures in Bamberg were much more brutal. Kolb had to participate in organizing the transport of the Bamberg Jews, who were assembled for departure in the garden of the Weisse Taube inn. If deportation preparations were in Nuremberg, Kolb was given a "free hand in implementation," so that the participants were generally spared "maltreatment or chicanery." But in Bamberg there was a quite "different atmosphere," Kolb noted, because "they didn't want to leave any surviving witnesses."[277] In the first Bamberg deportation, the Gestapo wished to demonstrate the "untrammeled spirit of Nazism." Kolb was maltreated; they forced him to strip naked and confiscated the money he had brought along for the transport. Afterward they raided and searched the office of the district branch, where they chanced upon a letter from the Jewish

Community chair Albert Fechheimer to his predecessor Rosenzweig, who had emigrated to Switzerland. In the letter, Fechheimer spoke about a "race between power and time." Fechheimer was immediately arrested. Kolb managed to have him included in a Theresienstadt transport as an elderly man suffering from "senility." The then seventy-seven-year-old lived to survive the war.[278] In contrast with the Bamberg Gestapo, Kolb states that the Nuremberg Gestapo protected him. He was even promoted, advancing from "Gestapo liaison" to chairman of the Jewish Community. When the order was issued at the end of 1942 to relocate the remaining Jews in Nuremberg to Fürth, this was a bid to proclaim the city of the *Reichsparteitage* finally "Jew-free"; the only Jews allowed to remain in Nuremberg were those in mixed marriages and Berhard Kolb.[279] Kolb stayed at his position until the liquidation of the Reichsvereinigung. On 10 June 1943, Gestapo men stormed the Community office, where the Jews were in the midst of holding religious services for the Shavuot holiday (Jewish Pentecost). They proclaimed that the Reichsvereinigung was dissolved, and confiscated the remaining Community property and the residual library, which had been repeatedly looted since 1933; Kolb was taken into custody. The Gestapo also ordered him to provide a list of the available assets. Actually, they had promised him earlier, on the basis of his "position of trust over many years," that before deportation he would not be taken into police custody, but the order for his detention now came "from Berlin."[280] He was incarcerated along with the executive director of the Fürth RV auxiliary branch, Julius Früh. In any event, the Gestapo did keep their second promise, namely, that Kolb would be deported together with his family.[281] As a Jewish functionary, he was sent to Theresienstadt, where he soon was appointed *Zimmerältester* (room monitor).[282]

Among the inexplicable events was the fact that the Nuremberg Jews, despite the general prohibition introduced in the Reich in September 1942 on Jews conducting religious services, were allowed—with the agreement of the local Gestapo—to hold "regular full weekly religious services Friday evening and Saturday morning and on holidays" in the Community office and also in the assembly camp.[283]

After Kolb's deportation, the Gestapo appointed the former lawyer Julius Nürnberger as intermediary and he remained in that function until the war's end.[284] Once again, the Gestapo was "accommodating": for example, it allowed Nürnberger to take over the card file and Community files and to keep them at his home.[285] Nonetheless, these documents were destroyed in an Allied bombing raid.

Of the more than 10,000 Jews in Nuremberg in 1930, there were still 1,835 in the city in October 1941. Of these, 1,656 were deported. At the war's end, there were still approximately 50 Jews in mixed marriages in

Nuremberg, and 65 persons returned from concentration camps.[286] Three leading representatives of Nuremberg Jewry during the years 1941–1945 survived: two in Theresienstadt, one in his hometown. When the Nuremberg Jewish Community reconstituted itself in December 1945, it elected Julius Nürnberger as chairman.[287] Kolb emigrated in 1947 to the United States.

After the war, the special relationship with the Gestapo continued: Kolb and Nürnberger exonerated "their" respective *Judenreferent* in court, and the former CV chairman Berlin testified to clear the police president Benno Martin of blame. Yet members of a Jewish forced labor detail stated precisely the opposite in describing the behavior of the subordinate Gestapo men and their superiors.[288] Nonetheless, the character references of the Jewish functionaries helped to gain the release of Martin, the self-styled "adversary of Streicher," and his Gestapo officials.

Mainz: "Reliable" Relations?

Unlike Nuremberg and Frankfurt, which were *Gau* capital cities, with the main office of the *Gauleiter* and the regional Gestapo headquarters, the town of Mainz lay "downwind," so to speak, more in the province. *Gauleiter* Sprenger was on the other side of the Rhine, and the Jews in Mainz had "only" one NSDAP district chief to contend with.[289] The Gestapo branch office in Mainz, subordinate to the Gestapo office in Darmstadt, served as the "supervisory authority" of the Jewish Community and the RV district branch bureau in Mainz. While in Frankfurt and Darmstadt hundreds of Jews became victims of organized arbitrary rule as they were accused of offenses against regulations for Jews and were thus criminalized, another constellation crystallized in Mainz. The former government councilor in the district administration, the lawyer Michel Oppenheim, longtime liaison of the Jewish Community with the Gestapo, and from April 1941 head of the Mainz RV district branch,[290] created a relation of trust with the chief of the *Judenreferat* and his few coworkers. How did this come about? A close relative of the first *Judenreferent* in Mainz had been a legal colleague of Oppenheim's, and had given Oppenheim a good reference. So did his predecessor as liaison, Rabbi Levi (who had emigrated).[291] Initially, the relationship was based on that. The officials active there later continued the close bond of cooperation, which appeared useful to both sides.

Until October 1941, Oppenheim had explored in vain every possible option for emigration: in August 1939, he tried to emigrate to Great Britain, but despite a permit for entry, this proved abortive before the war began. Then he hoped to emigrate to Santo Domingo in the Dominican

Republic, and in June 1941 he had obtained the security clearance for this, but Washington's entry into the war in December of that year foiled his plan.[292]

Although he had not remained in Mainz voluntarily, Oppenheim felt more free as a Jewish representative than his colleagues elsewhere. This was because (a) he lived in a "privileged" mixed marriage and was thus protected from forced migration, and (b) his activity for the Reichsvereinigung was on a volunteer basis. He was not even a member of the RV.[293] In any real conflict with the Gestapo, these facts would have been unimportant; nonetheless, they evidently gave him the feeling that he had some latitude in dealing with the Gestapo and the Berlin RV central office, room for maneuvering that he could make positive use of for the Jewish Community members, and also in connection with decisions about his own situation.

Since 1940, the Gestapo external office in Mainz had registered the local Jews using data from the questionnaires of the supplementary survey to the general census. The Reichsvereinigung also put together lists. In Oppenheim's recollection, the basis for the deportation lists was a body of more than 430 Gestapo and RV documents.[294] Oppenheim suspected what function his lists of names was to serve. Nonetheless, he assumed that these lists gave the Gestapo "no new material. The Reichsvereinigung was ... assigned to prepare these only for reasons of convenience. All lists of this kind could have been prepared just as well by the Gestapo."[295] However, he took strong exception to the suspicion of an RV member that he had a hand in preparing the lists for arrest.[296] Here quite clearly lay the boundary for cooperation. Twice he refused assignments from the Gestapo: once when he was asked to put together a "list of *Mischlinge*," and on another occasion when he was requested to prepare a list of mixed marriages for the last deportation in February 1945. He argued that "lists of *Mischlinge*" were not part of the obligations of the Reichsvereinigung, and in the case of mixed marriages, he did not wish to pronounce the inevitable "death sentence" on those persons he placed on the list. Both refusals were accepted and led to no negative consequences.[297]

The deportations in Mainz unfolded as the RSHA had dictated. The board members Moritz Fried and Siegfried Kugelmann were already in the first deportation list.[298] Prior to the first large-scale operation, a curfew was imposed during the night before on the Jews to be deported. In the morning, the Gestapo informed them they had three hours to pack and leave their homes; they were ordered to wear a cardboard sign with their name and number dangling from their neck.[299] The gym hall in a school was used as an assembly camp. The report of a Jewish volunteer noted: "At the entrance to the gym was a pedestal on which a machine gun was mounted as a threat, pointed at the people inside the athletics hall. The ammunition belt was locked in place, the machine gun was loaded and in ready to fire position, a police guard unit stood in readiness behind."[300] Oppenheim makes no mention of this; instead, he describes how the Jewish Community fed the deportees from large pots of stew, cooked at the Jewish Hospital with a special food allocation from the municipal administration, authorized by the Gestapo.[301] The sick were also deported. The Jews were sent from Mainz to an assembly camp in Darmstadt, which was hermetically cordoned off by the SS. After this operation, Oppenheim was called to account by the Gestapo for several suicides that had occurred; this suggests that information about the imminent transport had been leaked.[302] In actual fact, Oppenheim had probably not been the source of any prior warning. In later transports, the Jewish Community provided Jewish marshals for helping with baggage transport and provision of food for the deportees. More than 3,240 Jews were deported from the area of Rhine-Hesse, principally in March and September 1942. Among them were some 1,300 Jews from Mainz. After that, only 60 mixed-marriage couples were still living there, and they were ordered to relocate to Darmstadt.[303] The district branch office was also moved there.[304] In March 1943, the head of the Mainz Jewish Community, Fritz Löwensberg, was deported, and Oppenheim was named as his successor.[305] Now the district branch was permitted to return to Mainz.

Oppenheim stated after the war that the Gestapo in Mainz had been "more lenient"[306] than elsewhere in its methods and actions. The constant direct communication had, he argued, provided a channel for important information. There had been no arrests without some reason; Jews who could present medical documents had been released. Postal correspondence with the Gurs camp had not been punished by arrest. For relocations inside the city, sufficient time had been approved. As a rule, Jews were likewise not subjected to beating. If a Jew from Mainz was reported to the police, Oppenheim had to deliver the Gestapo summons to him, which contained no stated grounds for the summons. As a first step, Oppenheim succeeded in arranging that the person so summoned was given some idea of what it pertained to. In a second step, he obtained approval to confront these Jews himself with their alleged "infractions," and give them a proper warning. He evidently did not realize the problem lurking in such a procedure: namely, that he now became the authority for deciding on their "crimes" in lieu of the Gestapo, and had thus at least partially adopted their system of evaluation.[307] Oppenheim later testified that the Mainz Gestapo had not used violent tactics of beating. He did not think cases such as when a Gestapo officer knocked the eyeglasses of a Jew to the ground were unjust, since in this instance, the Jewish man involved had lied both to him and to the Gestapo. However, according to Oppen-heim, the *Judenreferat* naturally was obliged to pursue the complaints to the NSDAP and arrest those accused. He noted that if the Nazi Party laid a claim to apartments, Jews had to vacate these within a short deadline. In his view, the most dangerous enemies of the Mainz Jews were in the district directorate of the party and the Security Service.[308]

When the district branches Hesse and Hesse-Nassau were merged, Op-penheim rejected the idea of any further attempts at centralization. He argued that he was not only responsible to the Frankfurt Gestapo, but was repeatedly obligated to provide the Gestapo offices in Darmstadt and Mainz with information as well. He wished to have his own independent correspondence with the RV central office in Berlin and did not want to have his personnel reduced to zero by staff cuts.[309] He was shrewd in utilizing the rivalry between the head of the Darmstadt Gestapo and the Frankfurt Gestapo chief. The latter was prohibited from demanding Op-penheim to dismiss staff. Oppenheim inveighed against instructions com-ing from the larger district branch office in Frankfurt and the Berlin main office, and their arrogant tone:

> Previously I did not believe I was in such a subordinate relation to the central office, since as you know, I volunteered my services and have dem-onstrated that I devote all my energy to the work of the R.V. ... but it is totally unacceptable, should I now have to work thinking not only that I lack any support from the central office, but that I will even be faced with difficulties and dangers.[310]

He noted that the difficult situation in Berlin was quite clear to him, yet formulations like "and we are obliged to reserve the right to further measures" contained an express threat. In a letter to Lerner in April 1943, he commented: "But what measures does the writer think he can threaten us with? I should hope not! I'd like to have this point clarified."[311]

Oppenheim evaluated the positive relationship between his district branch and the Gestapo in Mainz in terms of the comparative realities in the large nearby cities.[312] He had had a vivid experience of the differ-ences in treatment when on a number of occasions he had to deal with the Darmstadt Gestapo official Dengler regarding Jewish "prisoners in protective custody."[313] Nonetheless, his memos indicate that he was al-ways mindful of the power relations in Mainz as well: "Following this, the undersigned was warned never to try to submit anything for the newly ap-pointed official to sign that the official, if precisely apprised of the matter, could not be permitted to sign."[314]

He was actually able with some justification to point to substantial dif-ferences, and his latitude for action was far greater than that of Kolb in

Nuremberg or even Lerner in Frankfurt. Yet seen through a comparative prism, the gravity of the actual situation in Mainz appears downplayed, its seriousness understated. That is clear if we consider the above-cited report by a Jewish volunteer regarding the machine gun mounted in the assembly camp, ready to fire.

A main factor contributing to Oppenheim's positive memories in retrospect may have been that precisely toward the war's end, the level of cooperation of the Residual RV with the two responsible officials in the *Judenreferat* intensified: they had informed him already around Christmas 1944 that the Jewish spouses in "privileged" mixed marriages were still going to be deported. But they advised him not to note down all names, "the fewer the better."[315] Oppenheim, who as mentioned did not want to pass a death sentence on anyone by entering his or her name on a list, now agreed with the two officials to delete the names of some of these ninety Jews from the list, to obtain medical certificates for others, and to personally warn the rest.[316] In order to allow him time for this, one of the Gestapo officials intercepted the deportation order and delayed its delivery by one night. In this way, it proved possible to protect the Mainz Jews who could be reached from inclusion in the Frankfurt transport.

However, the Darmstadt Gestapo now issued the order to instruct auxiliary personnel to arrest these Jews, shoot them in the ruins of destroyed buildings, and bury their remains there. Quick-witted, Oppenheim's allied Gestapo officer acted: he reserved to himself exclusive responsibility for carrying out this execution operation. It was a race against time. Two weeks before the Allies captured Mainz (22 March 1945), information on the delayed delivery of the order was leaked. One of the two Gestapo officials feigned sickness, and then fled from the hospital to safety. The other stuck it out in the office until shortly before the German surrender. He was able to arrange to leave his post by an official pretext. Aided by a massive air raid on Mainz, he also managed to destroy a number of papers inconspicuously. Thus, the odd situation arose that from 20 or 22 March on, Oppenheim, head of the district branch, hid both officials from the Mainz *Judenreferat* at his home until there was no longer any danger.[317]

In September 1940, there had been 1,356 Jews still resident in Mainz. In May 1943, that number had plummeted to 205, and at the war's end, there were some 60 Jews in Mainz living in mixed marriages.[318]

The district branch director in Mainz did not have to contend with a local *Gau* directorate, and he was able to utilize the rivalry between the two responsible Gestapo offices. In addition, Oppenheim had obtained permission to exercise in part their function for monitoring and punishment, and evidently performed this task to the satisfaction of the responsible officials at the Gestapo. This was the basis for the "reliable" relations, which then also proved a great advantage for the remaining Jews in mixed marriages.

Hamburg: "Easier Going" than Elsewhere?

Max Plaut, functioning as the sole responsible head in Hamburg, was in charge of the Jewish Community and the Northwest Germany district branch of the Reichsvereinigung,[319] whose business office was likewise located in the Hamburg bureau of the Jewish Community. He used the concept of "a kind of relationship of trust" to characterize the nexus of interaction between his office and the *Judenreferat* within the Hamburg Gestapo. What was the relationship between the Jews in Hamburg and the ruling powers? In contrast with the smaller city of Mainz, there was a major Gestapo office here. In addition, Hamburg was a separate Nazi *Gau*; the city had offices of a Reich governor (*Reichsstatthalter*) and a *Gauleiter*, Karl Kaufmann, who had sworn to achieve an early and total removal of the Jews from his territory of control. In September 1941, he had appealed to Hitler, evidently with some success, to expel the Jews from Hamburg. Already in early October 1941, he had tried on his own (although in vain) to send four larger transports of Jews to the *General-gouvernement*. However, he had to bide his time until the general onset of the deportations.[320]

In Hamburg, as everywhere else, a broad spectrum of institutions were involved in the deportation process, their actions coordinated. The situation in Hamburg was characterized by what appeared externally to be for the most part a smooth and conflict-free process of expulsion and deportation of the Jews, which only rarely attracted public attention. In 1933 and 1938, the streets were rocked by open anti-Semitic violence. Otherwise, that violence in Hamburg was generally behind closed doors. Documentation reflects this: there are no extant contemporary photos of deportation collection points or transports in Hamburg, nor have any been uncovered of house searches or the accompanying deployment of police.[321] One reason why the events of deportation had no public visibility in Hamburg may be that the Gestapo chief there from 1940 to the summer of 1942, Heinrich Seetzen, who had formal responsibility for the deportation of Hamburg Jewry, was in fact not in town. He was actually stationed on the Eastern warfront from July 1941, where as commander of Special Commando 10a in *Einsatzgruppe* D in the SD Section Central Russia, and later commander of *Einsatzgruppe* B, he oversaw extensive killing operations. In his absence, launching the "resettlement" of the Hamburg Jews was the responsibility of the Higher Police and SS Leader (HPSSF) Rudolf Querner, working together with the *Gauleiter* Karl Kaufmann.[322] From the summer of 1942 until 1944, Josef Kreuzer headed the Hamburg Gestapo office. Although he was officially responsible for eight deportation transports from the city, his name in Hamburg remained largely unknown. Apparently, neither Seetzen and Kreuzer nor Querner and Kaufmann had any interest in leaving their personal stamp of approval on the events of deportation. They left their organization and implementation largely to Claus Göttsche, *Judenreferent* in the Gestapo. It was Göttsche who ordered the Jewish Community and district branch of the Reichsvereinigung to assist in preparatory work for the transports.

While the Jewish Community was responsible for the so-called *Glaubensjuden* (Jews by religion, i.e., members of a Jewish Community) in Greater Hamburg until it was integrated in November 1942 into the RV, the territory of competence of the RV district branch Northwest Germany encompassed Schleswig-Holstein, Oldenburg, Bremen, the government districts Stade and Lüneburg, and Mecklenburg. Later, after the district branch Hanover-Kassel was dissolved, it also encompassed Braunschweig-province and Hildesheim.[323] Hanover was left only with an administrative office for the RV.

Plaut, a trained lawyer and economist, since 1933 the syndic of the Hamburg Jewish Community, was one of the few German-Jewish functionaries who headed a Jewish Community in a continuous fashion, albeit in a range of different functions, from 1938 to 1943. He was the only Jewish representative allowed to leave Germany legally after the liquidation of the Reichsvereinigung in June 1943, and relocated to Palestine.

To stress once more: in Hamburg, not one less Jew was deported than was ordered by the RSHA. In September 1941, some seventy-five hundred Jews still remained from the just under twenty thousand formerly living in Hamburg (and the districts incorporated in 1937). At the war's end, seven to eight hundred Jews were left in the city, spouses in mixed marriages.

Nonetheless, despite these massive deportations, Plaut and his deputy Leo Lippmann, who took his own life in 1943, and his associate Berthold Simonsohn, survivor of several concentration camps, concurred in their assessment: the situation in Hamburg was "one step up from conditions in Berlin," or "more just, more lenient" than elsewhere, "comparatively tolerable, indeed in comparison with other towns (such as Hanover, Kassel, Berlin), humane."[324]

How can that difference be explained? This was due primarily to the way the Hamburg district branch operated: Plaut and his associates always sought to anticipate what problems might arise in connection with the new measures ordered by the authorities. They tried to present solutions that, on the one hand, were in the interest of the Jews, and on the other appeared suited to satisfy the Gestapo and reduce their burden of work. "For example, you could tell them: if you carry out this and that, you won't have the success you want. It would be much smarter to do it differently."[325] Over the course of several years, this led to the development of the "relationship of trust" Plaut referred to. In his words: the Gestapo officials worked "objectively, correctly," and acknowledged the similar quality of work of the district branch.[326] Plaut commented later that it had been "possible to talk" with some of the officials; they were ready to listen.[327]

As here indicated, the contribution of the Jewish functionaries went far beyond the correct implementation of orders, and Plaut considered himself successful in being able to deal with the Gestapo. In his view, the smooth cooperation was also due to the circumstance that as a former *Freikorps* (German Free Corps) fighter on the political right after WWI, he was better able than his predecessor Nathan Max Nathan or his deputy Leo Lippmann to adapt to the "methods of the political ethnic struggle [*Volkstumskampf*]" employed by the National Socialists, and could deal on a different basis with the Gestapo officials. The previous syndic of the Hamburg Jewish Community, Nathan Max Nathan, had, according to Plaut, been too emphatic in his insistence on principles of constitutional law. Plaut noted that Leo Lippmann, a former senate secretary and *Staatsrat* (state councilor) in Hamburg, had in Plaut's view been too arrogant in his dealings with Gestapo men.[328] Not yet aged twenty, Plaut had in 1921 joined the *Manfred Killinger Verband*, a right-wing paramilitary assault company. Manfred Freiherr von Killinger was a *Freikorps* (Free Corps) leader and later rose to a high-ranking position in the National Socialist SA. Together with the Free Corps, of which Hamburg's later *Gauleiter* Karl Kaufmann had been a member, Plaut had participated in the May 1921 storming of the Annaberg, the greatest battle in the Silesian Uprisings, part of paramilitary actions in "self-defense of Upper Silesia." For his valor, he was awarded the Silesian Order of the Eagle First Class.

Plaut utilized the available latitude for action and maneuvering in an offensive manner, particularly before the beginning of deportations. He thus himself suggested to the Gestapo that relocation by Jews into Hamburg should be subject to an "entry tax" of five thousand RM, which was then used to finance emigration by poorer Jews. In the children's transports, he helped smuggle additional children out of Germany. This was bitterly criticized by Käte Rosenheim, who organized these transports. He bought food on the black market and paid for it with illicit funds. Offering bribes, he obtained visas, passports, baptismal certificates, or certificates confirming agricultural experience in order to facilitate emigration. He undertook some of these illegal activities with the assent of the Gestapo.[329] Plaut regarded the "emigrant levy," which the Reichsvereinigung later imposed throughout the *Altreich* in order to finance emigration by Jews with fewer means, as his own invention. On behalf of the Reichsvereinigung, Plaut took steps to assist with the assets left behind by the Stettin Jews and was aware of the catastrophic living conditions in the Lublin district.[330] When in 1940 vague plans became known intending to "resettle" the approximately one thousand Jews of East Frisia, Plaut immediately ensured the authorities that he could take care of this at lesser expense than the Gestapo, and he relocated the Jews within the span of three weeks to Berlin, Hamburg, and Hanover. Otherwise, they would, like the Stettin Jews, have been deported and transported to the *Generalgouvernement*.[331]

The onset of the systematic deportations (with the concomitant prohibition on emigration) abruptly reduced Plaut's latitude for action. He rejected the demand by the Gestapo to put together deportation lists, as he later emphasized. However, the Gestapo took on this task only at the beginning; later on, the employees of the district branch had nonetheless to assemble these lists under supervision.[332] The card file of the district branch was also used by the other involved offices and agencies.[333] The Gestapo rarely appeared in the offices of the district branch. Rather, Plaut had to go to the *Judenreferat* for meetings and to receive new instructions himself, sometimes on a daily basis. Occasionally he obtained information and was able to warn individual Jews, who due to some infraction of rules or "misconduct" had come to the notice of the officials. Some information was channeled on by Plaut to the Reichsvereinigung central office in Berlin: for example, when the war began, Göttsche informed him about anti-Jewish measures being drafted, and Plaut was able to pass this information on.

Plaut had a broad interpretation of his own area of competence. For example, he also tried to provide care for the fifty Polish Jews incarcerated in Hamburg with the outbreak of the war; this assistance extended over and beyond his actual sphere of activity (and here he differed from his colleagues in Berlin).[334] He and his coworkers followed the path of these Polish Jews through various concentration camps and ghettos, for as long as possible, by means of transfers of money that the recipients had to sign for at every place they were brought to. When the mentally ill Jews were deported, Plaut obtained Göttsche's permission to inquire about the conditions at their destination, and he learned that there was no nursing home for them there.[335] He thus quickly suspected, and correctly so, that these mental patients had been sent to a concentration camp and murdered, even if the bills for their maintenance addressed to the district branch indicated the individuals had still been alive a number of months after deportation. He and his staff also tried to track deportees via money transfers, whose receipt and payment had to be signed for by the recipient. This was not without gaps, but nonetheless worked fairly well over extended periods of time.[336] Plaut evidently was also successful in several cases in arranging for elderly "prisoners in protective custody," so-called *Schutzhäftlinge*, to be transferred from the Fuhlsbüttel concentration camp to the home for the elderly operated by the Jewish Community, and then included in a "regular" deportation. Plaut and his staff also transferred money to such prisoners arrested for various alleged "crimes," who had been sent individually and in small group transports to various camps.[337] In this manner, a fairly realistic picture emerged in the Hamburg district branch office of the pathways taken by the deportees and the dangers lurking at their destinations.

Plaut did not get along as well with the local Gestapo *Judenreferenten* in other areas of his assigned territory of competence, such as East Frisia, Kiel, or Hanover, as he did with Göttsche in Hamburg, but he knew how to be resolute and carry matters through. Once, when he wanted to inspect the assembly camp of the former Jewish Horticultural School Ahlem/Hanover, the local Gestapo sought to prevent this, prevailing on Herskowitz, the Jewish liaison there, for assistance. Plaut resisted, and in effect warned them of consequences: "So I said ... well, can I report this to Berlin? He asked: to whom in Berlin? I said, it'll go to the RSHA via the Reichsvereinigung. After all, I have to submit a report on my inspection."[338] Like the Jewish functionaries elsewhere, he made argumentative use of the supervisory function entrusted to the RSHA in order to protect himself against arbitrary attempts to hinder him in the fulfillment of his duties.

When, with the deportation of Paul Eppstein, Leo Baeck, and other functionaries from the Berlin main office in early 1943, it appeared that the RSHA would probably soon liquidate the Reichsvereinigung as a whole, Plaut began to contemplate how he might salvage the effective capacity of his organization. He had already worked out a plan in the event of his departure from the organization, and from March 1943, in an anticipatory move, he began to employ Jews in mixed marriages, who were still protected from deportation, on the RV district branch staff.[339] It was clear to him and others that the dismissed coworkers who were not protected would be deported, although these employees, like the Hamburg staff members before, were sent to the "preferential camp" of Theresienstadt. In Plaut's eyes, "most Jews were no longer weighed down by anxieties, by that juncture [10 June 1943, official liquidation of the RV] they had already come to terms with their fate."[340]

During his tenure, Plaut did not make reference to his past in the German Free Corps only when dealing with the Gestapo. Since he enjoyed a monopoly of information regarding the orders and intentions of the Gestapo, "he commandeered like a sergeant major" within the Jewish community. He "eliminated" "senseless" political struggles between the various groups,[341] and no one risked letting things deteriorate to a point where Plaut had to notify the Gestapo due to insubordination.[342]

Plaut maintained close personal and collegial relations with the RV board and the department heads in the Berlin central office, and these relations were continued by his successors. Thus, he arranged to send food parcels to the functionaries confined in Theresienstadt, and at the war's end, his successors attempted to assist the survivors there.[343]

When the last thirty salaried coworkers of the Hamburg district branch boarded the train to Theresienstadt along with more than seventy other Jews, the entire *Judenreferat* of the Hamburg Gestapo accompanied then to the train station.[344] On the platform, the persecutors remained behind, and so did Max Plaut. The chronicler and Theresienstadt survivor Käthe Starke noted the open questions in her memoirs: "Would those waiting behind him at a distance, would this man Göttsche now keep his promise? Would Max Plaut later be allowed to go to safety in one piece together with his mother?"[345] Göttsche's promise to Plaut that he would be permitted to leave Germany was no secret among the staff of the district branch, and evidently none envied him this preferential treatment. Göttsche actually did keep his word: Plaut went via the internment camp Laufen/Upper Bavaria (January 1944) to Vittel in France (summer 1944)[346] and then on to Vienna, where there was an exchange involving German expatriates. He then was permitted to journey on by train through Turkey to Palestine.[347] Plaut bade formal farewell to the remaining "Jewish men and women in Hamburg" in a circular letter, where with evident pride he stressed that "Providence" had bestowed "much success" upon his work:

> Jewish men and women in Hamburg! I wish on this occasion, the hour of my departure from Hamburg, to convey my sincere greetings and heartfelt wishes to all the members of our community! For over two decades, I have enjoyed the privilege of working actively for the Jews of Hamburg in the Jewish public sphere. With our patriarch Jacob, I can say of my work: "Thus I was: in the day the drought consumed me, and the frost by night; and my sleep fled from mine eyes." If Providence has bestowed upon my work so much success, this was largely due to the fact that my coworkers stood by my side, untiringly, indefatigable, and there was always a large circle of people prepared to assist in the work. My most noble task was always to aid the many poor and weak among us. With pride I can avow that down to the present day, whenever the call went out to the Jews of Hamburg, they always responded with hearts full of joy and generosity! And now in this hour of my departure, I wish again to appeal to you: always be mindful of all

those who need our help! Give the same trust to my successors in office and my coworkers that you have granted to me, and donate as much as you are able to the relief funds I have established! It is important for us all to fulfill our responsibility to history! None are permitted to exclude themselves! Each must do his part to contribute to alleviating distress and preserving life! I leave you with my most fervent wishes for a happy peace, speedily in our days! You can rest assured that wherever Providence may carry me, my thoughts are always with you, and my work shall be dedicated to the welfare of our community![348]

A similar letter composed in the summer of 1941 might perhaps have been possible to evaluate as Plaut's wish to adhere to a conventional ritual of farewell. But in January 1944, the letter had to seem somewhat grotesque, since Plaut's fervent good wishes no longer reached the majority of "his" Jewish Community members: they had long since been deported to ghettos and camps, except for those protected by mixed marriages.

In his later reports, he described the comparatively comfortable internment in Vittel as his "time in camp," which is not directly false, but is also not quite true. He thus suggests that he himself was a concentration camp inmate, at least temporarily.

Before his departure, Plaut chalked up another success: his designated successor, the physician Martin Heinrich Corten, accompanied the transport mentioned with the last coworkers to Theresienstadt. There he was taken into custody (against the prior agreement) and forced to remain in the camp. Plaut contacted the Hamburg Gestapo, and with its help Corten was released. He then took over, as planned, the reins of the Residual Reichsvereinigung in Hamburg, catering mainly to the needs of the Jews in mixed marriages.[349]

However, the successes Plaut achieved with the Gestapo did not lead to a situation where he (and Lippmann) could really have a sense of security. House searches, harassment, chicanery, and tricks were a constant threat to the atmosphere of "good understanding," although the Jewish representatives were not exposed to direct physical violence.[350] This notwithstanding, behind closed doors, other members of the Jewish Community or the RV district branch were indeed badly mistreated again and again, either at Gestapo headquarters or in the *Judenreferat,* and some died of their injuries. A number were severely abused and later died in the KolaFu jail, the notorious police prison in Fuhlsbüttel.[351] In their everyday work, the officers proved to be open to bribes, were corrupt, and stole valuables from the opened shipping containers in the Hamburg port or in the apartments of the Jews.[352] Processing procedures in the deportations, which Plaut characterized as "comparatively tolerable," and "indeed in comparison with other towns (such as Hanover, Kassel, Berlin), humane," were described by other survivors differently. While Plaut conceded there were occasional "ugly lapses,"[353] Martin Starke, an employee of the district branch who was present during house searches and had to assist in the deportation collection points, testified after the war to more than thirty cases of maltreatment by Gestapo personnel that he had personally witnessed. These were mainly attempts at extorting confessions from people or to punish elderly Jews who had not obeyed orders quickly enough. He stated that women and men had been subjected to beatings in the air raid shelter of the Moorweide deportation collection center (a former masonic lodge) for violation of baggage regulations.[354]

Göttsche had generally instructed his subordinates to treat Jews with strict severity but not to maltreat them. However, he neither prevented nor punished any acts of brutality.[355] Plaut, who had carefully studied his interlocutor, included this behavior in his calculations. If he wished to intervene on behalf of someone who had been mistreated, he postponed his complaint until a later point in time. In this way, Göttsche was not placed in the conflictual situation of having to follow and perhaps act on the arguments put forward by a Jew if a subordinate of his, for example, had just engaged in some misconduct. Plaut described the *Judenreferent* Claus Göttsche as a staunch National Socialist, "straightforward and consistent," who displayed some characteristics of a "seasoned old administrator," and thus had been a "relatively tolerable partner in negotiations." "Göttsche never committed himself to support for terror or arbitrary measures or allowed himself to be carried away by such actions, although some of his subordinates did."[356] On the other hand, he never punished such behavior, because in Göttsche's view, his coworker was always in the right. Thus, the most favorable reaction that Plaut could achieve with a complaint was, "I don't want to know anything about it" (in any case, Plaut anticipated that in advance). That is why Plaut always let some time pass before he took up the cause of a Jew, where penalties might be expected.[357] Plaut never tried to bribe the head of the *Judenreferat*, but he did make use of the services of a corruptible government employee in order to obtain some easing of regulations from subordinate Gestapo personnel in return for cash. Plaut assessed his own actions, noting that he had never made any suggestions to Göttsche whose acceptance Göttsche might perhaps have later regretted.

> I never tried to kid or deceive him or obtain something where later on afterwards, I would have been forced to hear: if it doesn't work out, I wouldn't be the only one held to account, but others as well. Because if I had caused him any suffering, then possibly all Jews would have had to suffer as a result. And that is why I was often very open in dealings with him.[358]

Plaut was very well aware of the unchangeable external ensemble of rules and regulations in the process of persecution, and for that reason concentrated all the more on the personal relations he himself could influence: "Since the Jewish administrative offices with time became so to speak the extended arm of the Gestapo, the decisive thing was to establish a personal connection with the key Gestapo people so as then to be able to negotiate skillfully, and as far as possible achieve the best obtainable result."[359] He correctly believed he had the ability "to be able to adapt" to his interlocutors and "feel where someone could reach them and get them to listen."[360] In the period from the summer of 1943 to the war's end, the physician Martin Heinrich Corten took over Plaut's position as liaison for the Residual Reichsvereinigung in Hamburg. The lawyer Max Heinemann was chief executive heading the office.[361] After the heavy air bombardment of Hamburg in late July and early August 1943, initially the residual organization had one main concern: to become a functioning body again, that is, to reorganize the card file, to ferret out the compulsory members who had fled, and to put the Jewish Hospital back in efficient working order. There are no indications that during this period, the relationship with the Gestapo changed in any significant way, especially since Plaut (now without an office) continued to remain active down to his departure.

Like the Jewish representatives before them, the intermediaries could not feel personally that they were completely safe. To be sure, their volunteer activity protected them from deportation and conscript labor. But they were expecting that the Residual Reichsvereinigung would also soon be liquidated after those "with Jewish kin," the so-called *jüdisch Versippte*, were forced into conscript slave labor in the Organisation Todt (OT) in the autumn of 1944. Totally under the impress of the contemporary Nazi propaganda machine, the representatives suspected that "this apparatus is incompatible with mobilization for total war."[362] It did not devolve to that point. In the event, the district branch Northwest Germany was ordered to organize a larger transport to Theresienstadt with spouses in mixed marriages, but Corten and Heinemann negotiated with the Gestapo and arranged that doctors' certificates would be recognized and the persons granted deferment from deportation on medical grounds, a final proof of the "relationship of trust."

In the meantime, Plaut had reached a safe haven in Palestine.[363] He was soon inundated there by inquiries from relatives of Hamburg deportees, to which he responded in detail and with dedication, as his posthumous papers prove. But he did not stop there. Perhaps his own rescue had distorted his view of the actual realities, or maybe he hoped to make the impossible a reality with the help of the British mandatory power. In keeping with the example of his own exchange as part of a prisoner swap, he requested dozens of immigrant certificates for Jews incarcerated in Theresienstadt and other camps. He asked family members to supply him with the corresponding personal data (and reimburse him for expenses); he drafted form letters and spread illusory enthusiasm among the Palestine immigrants about the possible rescue of their relatives. His hope was that the British government would assist with the exchange. In doing so, perhaps he only distracted people from the fact that he was free, rescued in effect with the agreement of the Gestapo while the forced members of the Jewish organizations were not. In any case, it is clear that Plaut had come to identify himself so strongly with his role as a functionary and the associated prominence this distinction brought within the Jewish community that he did not wish to give up that position. Rather, he seemingly continued on in the same role without a break in his new home. He did not acknowledge his actual powerlessness, instead perpetuating it in replays in all his testimony in the postwar period. In 1950 he returned to Germany from Israel, in 1965 moving back to Hamburg (see chapter 5). His reports were included as documentation in the Eichmann trial, they were placed in archives; he gave interviews and corresponded with historians. Each document describes the oppressive situation of the Hamburg Jewry, and both implicitly and quite explicitly heralds the achievements of Max Plaut. He was a man who looked back with great pride on what he had accomplished, convinced to have prevented even worse events by his engagement and dedication. In actuality, he had been able by his exertions to promote emigration, which in Hamburg was initially below the Reich average, and after the November pogrom then rose above it. And on the whole, he had succeeded in contributing to an atmosphere that surviving Jews later also characterized as having been better than elsewhere. Yet he had not been able to save a single soul from deportation other than himself.[364]

Concluding Thoughts on the Different District Branches

The historian and Theresienstadt survivor H. G. Adler concluded that the deportations reflected the "entanglement … of the Jewish offices with the Gestapo," which "long before the beginning of the general deportations had become a routine, so that when it began, especially in the German province, even the thought of an energetic active resistance could not surface. This was because the leading officials were already totally paralyzed in their power of decision, and basically for a long time no longer knew what they were doing."[365] For that reason, Adler did not critically confront the particular given fabric of persecution: he did not inquire into the overlapping aims of the institutions involved in ideological questions, nor the differences, rivalries, and conflicts over political dominance and material loot, the jumble of competencies and their impact on the situation of the Jews. In my view, Adler's conclusion is too narrow, because the Jewish functionaries certainly sought, often over many years, to take action in the framework of the possibilities that the respective structure of persecution offered them.

A comparison is revealing: after 1941, the RV representatives had only quite minimal latitude for maneuvering in influencing the process of deportation in two situations: either (a) when they could find interlocutors within an existing rivalry between institutions or an open power struggle or (b) when they were able to establish a "relationship of trust" with participating organs of persecution. The cumulative radicalization of the institutions of persecution was able to exert an exacerbating impact on the situation of persecution, as in Frankfurt am Main and Munich, or was in part retarding in its impact, as in Nuremberg, if one actor was able to moderate the other. It certainly made a difference whether "only" ideological motives were central in the situation of persecution or whether other factors emerged in the foreground during this process. Thus, the files on events in Nuremberg and Munich point to a total lack of inhibition on the part of the perpetrators, who were able to indulge unhindered in sadistic group violence. This evidently spread like wildfire from the NSDAP to all other institutions of persecution. Neither the membership nor the leadership of the Reichsvereinigung were protected from the concomitant rituals of humiliation. The situation of persecution that thus arose in the assembly camp can be viewed as a kind of anticipatory "preview" of the concentration camp. Conspicuous here in particular is the maltreatment, abuse, and humiliation of Hechinger. The boozing parties of the Gestapo in Nuremberg and Munich at the deportation collection point have a kind of symbolic character: the perpetrators celebrate their victory over defenseless victims. To avoid misunderstandings here, let me add that such elements were also repeatedly manifest in other regions as well, in individual operations (as during the first deportation in Frankfurt am Main), related to actions by certain individuals (such as the Frankfurt *Judenreferent* Baab), and in operations involving arresting Jews for alleged "criminal acts" of various kinds, violating Nazi regulations. But these did not uniformly permeate and shape the atmosphere of the situation of persecution as a whole.

Thanks to a "relationship of trust," several district branch directors, such as in Mainz or Hamburg, were able to achieve partial easing of restrictions or deferments, and obtain useful information. If they reported about this after the war, however, their reports create the misleading impression that things were generally more lenient or better in their sphere of influence, or in any event not quite as bad as elsewhere. The fact is that the orders of the RSHA were obeyed everywhere. It is true that the (compulsory) members of the RV did not need to fear daily open violence, and perhaps the number of additional Jews arrested for alleged "criminal acts" could be reduced, but nowhere were the set numbers for deportation transports not met. "Trust" also simply meant to accept the logic of persecution and the interests of its institution, and to an extent to internalize that logic in part as your own. Almost all Jewish functionaries testified after the war to the relatively good level of cooperation with "their *Judenreferent*," even where in general open brute force had prevailed.[366] Thus, their reports and statements in postwar investigations or court trials must always also be viewed as serving to justify their own actions.

The directors of the district branches were fundamentally responsible to the Gestapo, but the Gestapo often appointed liaison persons, so-called *Vertrauensmänner* who directly worked with and assisted the Gestapo. If the chairmen of the Jewish Community or the district branch directors were deported at an early point (i.e., before the formal liquidation of the Reichsvereinigung) or accused of criminal offenses and taken into custody, the Gestapo then appointed these liaison men, such as Lerner, Koronczyk, or Kolb, as their successors. This occurred mainly in the course of 1942. Before the start of the mass transports and the first two waves of deportation, the responsible Gestapo officials had still appreciated seasoned personalities who enjoyed recognition and authority in the Jewish community and whom the members were wont to follow. But from 1942 on, such men were no longer needed by the Gestapo. In demand now were compliant successors, to some extent experienced in organizational matters, who, working rapidly and smoothly, were to assist in rendering the respective area "Jew-free."

If district branch directors who seemed to be the suitable persons for the job in the eyes of their respective Gestapo office were spouses in a mixed marriage, and performed their duties to the Gestapo's satisfaction, they were often allowed to stay on the job until 1945, as in the case of Koronczyk or Oppenheim. They initially headed a district branch and then remained active as liaison personnel in the Residual Reichsvereinigung. The "full Jews" among the functionaries who were unmarried or wed to Jewish women were deported, if they had not already been the victim of a "punitive operation" between the autumn of 1941 and the spring of 1943, or included in a transport to Theresienstadt. The Gestapo did not keep more extensive promises for satisfactory performance on the job, such as possible relocation to Switzerland or the like. Max Plaut represents the sole exception to this rule.

The documentation examined indicates that most local representatives of the RV felt that their Berlin main office was an additional organ of control over them along with the Gestapo. The more the deportations thinned the ranks of the functionaries, who as a rule had known each other before 1941 and had maintained mutual contacts, the more difficult communication with the central office became. Direct face-to-face discussion on decisions or even by telephone became increasingly more impossible. Thus, it is evident that the district branch directors soon came to expect little or no assistance from Berlin. Rather, they anticipated bureaucratic delays, demands for work that could not be met, and orders to cut staff (i.e., in effect death sentences for those dismissed, who then were regularly deported). This was because the central office had to consult with the RSHA and reach agreement on all matters it was dealing with pertaining to the districts. As described earlier, special difficulties could always arise for the district branches if they entered into direct agreements with their local Gestapo or if their orders contradicted those of the RSHA. Then, conflict with their central RV office was inevitable. In everything they did in an attempt to improve the local situation, they were always subject to double supervision, its exigencies and its constraints.

Strategies for Dealing with the Authorities

In looking at the strategies adopted by the leading Jewish functionaries described and others in dealing with the National Socialist authorities, we can roughly identify three different modes of behavior:

1. Some, like Lerner, Kolb, or Koronczyk, followed all orders and instructions to the letter, fearful and at times even envisioning in advance a directive not yet imposed.
2. Others, thinking through matters themselves and even surmising likely future developments, sought in implementing the measures ordered to offer "solutions" that provided some relief and easing of restrictions for the Jews affected, while relieving the Gestapo of some of the burden of bureaucratic work. Exemplary here were Plaut or Oppenheim.
3. A small number went one step further, overstepping their competence, and thus endangering themselves. For example, a leading staff member in the Frankfurt district branch, the former merchant Karl Wolf, sent a warning to Jews via his daughters about an imminent "evacuation." Both his daughters were Mischlinge of the first degree, so-called half Jews. If the Jews forewarned had no options to flee, they hid their valuables with "Aryans." The official responsible at the Gestapo noted: "As punishment for his breach of trust vis-à-vis

the state police, Wolf was incarcerated in the Buchenwald concentration camp, and his two daughters were sent to Auschwitz."[367] As *Mischlinge* of the first degree, the Wolf daughters would not have been subject to deportation, but since they had committed punishable crimes, they were deported from prison to Auschwitz.

A number of Jewish representatives behaved like "staff sergeants" in order to instill respect for their authority among members and to maintain the impression of their dutiful compliance in the eyes of the Gestapo; they shouted and threatened to report members to the Gestapo or even have them punished by incarceration in a concentration camp. They thus adapted their behavior to the authoritarian comportment of their persecutors in order to not be considered too "soft," or sought in this way to nip any resistance to the measures in the bud. Recalcitrant Jews posed problems for them, and their own health and life were always at stake, since ultimately they also could be included at any time in a deportation. Men like Plaut, Oppenheim, or the district branch director in Düsseldorf, Rudolf Braunschweig, had no doubts about themselves and the success of their work within the limits imposed on them from above. At least this is the recurrent message in their personal testimonials and remembrances. Probably all that impacted on their demeanor, since they did not expect attacks or punishments in every situation: these men believed they enjoyed more latitude. Although their actions were strictly legal—and how else could they act under the given prevailing power relations?—they did not shun from certain small deviations. They presented themselves as being more flexible, versatile, agile, and imaginative than their cowed and anxious, overwhelmed colleagues, who—fearful of deviating from the measures ordered—tended to go to excess in fulfilling them. It is known that three of the functionaries—Plaut, Blankenstein in Düsseldorf (see chapter 4), and Karl Eisemann—had in their younger years been members of the *Freikorps*. At least in Blankenstein's case, that did not aid him in his dealings with the Gestapo,[368] while Plaut regarded his (quasi-)military experience—which many NSDAP members, SS men, and Gestapo personnel had also had as former soldiers or members of paramilitary units on the political right—as the foundation of an uncomplicated mutual understanding.

Almost all Jewish functionaries adhered to the order of secrecy. As a rule, they did not make public their orders in the circle of their fellow workers, nor did they reveal these to the Jewish compulsory members affected. There are some rare instances where we know that district branch directors warned the Jews affected before an imminent transport, as in the case of Rudolf Braunschweig (Düsseldorf), who was in a "nonprivileged" mixed marriage (see chapter 4). However, his deputy Willy (Denny) Katzenberg, under the same pressure, committed suicide.[369] On the contrary, many Jews holding office, such as Lerner or Koronczyk, tried instead to take particular measures to prevent Jews from fleeing. Koronczyk sometimes allowed other persons from the remaining Jewish community a glance into his strife-torn personal situation, as evident from postwar investigations. However, he did not attempt to shirk his responsibility and place it on the shoulders of others, as his predecessors had been wont to do. Rather, he revealed some of his fears and anxieties, which gained him some modicum of sympathy, but did not bolster trust in his abilities as a person in a leadership position.

It remains striking that only very few of the regional representatives of the Reichsvereinigung refused the office that many others would not have been willing to accept voluntarily. As among the leading functionaries in the Berlin central office, it was rare for district branch directors to evade responsibility by disappearing into hiding. As a rule, they stuck to their post and fulfilled what was demanded of them until they were "resettled" to the Theresienstadt "preferential camp." If their deportation was imminent and unavoidable, some leading functionaries chose suicide instead, such as Leo Lippmann in Hamburg or Siegfried Falk from Düsseldorf, to name but two. Lippmann felt he had done his best for the Jewish Community and was no longer prepared to venture into the unknown.[370]

Three attempts to escape by going into hiding were uncovered during the course of research. They shed some light on the strategies of Jewish functionaries in dealing with their office and its demands:

- The financial expert Hechinger in Munich performed his appointed tasks, but evidently irked the "Aryanization representative" because he always had the interests of the Jewish community in mind. He had made no prior preparations for disappearance when he went into hiding. He presumably was certain that interventions by the Berlin central office with the RSHA would make it possible for him to stay on in Munich, because those in power would recognize that he was indispensable for dealing with the legal questions involved in property settlement. He thus handed himself in to the Gestapo, only to learn that he had made a drastic error of judgment. Despite his former acknowledged contributions, the persecutors chose to take revenge for his attempted escape, punishing this offense by deporting him to Auschwitz.
- Rudolf Braunschweig headed the Jewish Community in Düsseldorf and Krefeld from 1941 to 1943 after his predecessor, the banker Siegfried Falk, had committed suicide on 5 December 1941 after receiv-

ing a deportation order.[371] Rudolf Braunschweig was versatile, and the two years he spent in office were probably a bit of good fortune for the members of the Jewish Community. He was not only conscientious on the job but also dared to warn individual Jews, to smuggle news out of the assembly camp, to intervene in cases of arrest, etc.[372] When his tenure in office concluded, he fled, and was not seized until almost a year later, located in March 1944 in Vienna (described in detail in chapter 4).[373] Witness testimony indicates how persistent and stubborn the Gestapo was in hunting Braunschweig down. It was not prepared to accept the successful flight of even one district branch director. Rudolf Braunschweig was deported to Auschwitz and survived. After the war, he did not exonerate his persecutors, testifying on the contrary that "in no other city were manhunts for Jews so severe."[374]

• The third example involved the district branch director Karl Eisemann in Karlsruhe, who lived in a mixed marriage there. It will illustrate a problem also concerning some intermediaries, and the discussion thus anticipates some aspects explored in chapter 4 in depth. Eisemann managed over several years to ward off the closing of his branch, which was in "liquidation," and continued to head it from June 1943 to 1945. It was not until he was ordered to implement the deportation of the Jews living in still extant mixed marriages, an order that also affected him directly, that he decided to go into hiding for the final weeks of the war. Before that, he had arranged his succession, requesting in writing to the central office of the Residual RV that Hermann Hauser from Mannheim be appointed his successor.[375] His behavior closely resembled that of Jewish functionaries who fulfilled their self-imposed or compulsory "duty" right down to the end; yet at the same time, he acted like his (compulsory) members, who in these final weeks of the war attempted to escape the grip of forced deportation.

These three examples illustrate that even the few heads of Jewish Communities or district branches who tried to save their own skin by going into hiding persisted at their post until the persecutors had made it impossible for them to carry out their duties.

The Fate of the District Branch Directors

Even if every individual Jewish functionary defined his or her latitude for action differently and sought to develop their own strategies for dealing with the imposed constraints, tables 3 and 4 show that the fate of the Jewish representatives who directed district branch offices of the Reichsvereinigung or Jewish Communities between 1941 and 1943 was as a rule the same: except for a few, they were all murdered.

As was made clear above, leading Jewish functionaries were already included in the first large-scale deportations, while others were seized in the course of 1942 and put in "punitive transports."

The two lists reproduced below contain the names of twenty-nine heads of district branches and Jewish Communities who served in office from 1940 to 1942. Eighteen were deported to Theresienstadt, nine of these already in 1942, nine more when the Reichsvereinigung was dissolved in 1943. Seven of them died in the Theresienstadt ghetto; eleven were transported in the framework of the Theresienstadt autumn transports to Auschwitz and murdered there. Three branch directors were sent directly to Auschwitz in 1943.

One was accused of a crime ("racial defilement") in 1942, convicted, and executed; another was deported to an unknown destination. I was unable to ascertain the fate of two of the functionaries. Another, the Leipzig lawyer Fritz Grunsfeld, survived and was liberated in Theresienstadt. Three branch heads were not deported: one was still able to emigrate in 1941, another survived in a mixed marriage (hidden during the final weeks of the war), and a third (Max Plaut) was allowed to leave Germany legally.

Thus, the final chapter in the trying labors of the Jewish functionaries ended as a rule with one option: death. Since most were granted the privilege of the Theresienstadt ghetto, some already in 1942, they lived somewhat longer than the compulsory members of their district branches and Jewish Communities, who were transported to the ghettos "in the East" with the first large-scale deportations. Nonetheless, the chances of survival for the Jewish functionaries were not any greater than those of the members of the RV and the Jewish Communities, deported earlier and to other destinations. The predominant majority of the Jewish representatives who had managed to stay alive in Theresienstadt until October 1944 were on the lists for the direct autumn transports to the Auschwitz death camp.

Liquidation of the District Branches

Parallel with the deportation transports, the RSHA ordered the stepwise reduction of the Reichsvereinigung. In January 1943, there was a total staff of 1,077 individuals still working in the RV district branch offices across the Reich.[376] Now the RSHA stepped up the tempo once again, ordering the RV to cut jobs and eliminate superfluous and subordinate staffing. In March, the district branches reported that implementation was complete: from Königsberg and Allenstein, Hesse, Central Germany, Westphalia, the Hanover-Kassel administrative office, and many other localities.[377]

The orders mentioned in chapter 2 to deport the last protected members, staff workers, and leading functionaries also included the district branches and their directors. A number of reports by survivors mention that Gestapo men, such as Hamburg *Judenreferat* officials, escorted these last larger transports to the railway station. However, most of the district branch directors were held in custody until their transport and were then sent on to Theresienstadt. Thus, for example, the remaining Jewish representatives in Breslau spent days in detention in the Breslau Community Center until 16 June 1943: they were then escorted under guard by men armed with machine guns to the train for Theresienstadt.[378]

At this juncture, a new directive arrived in the now more or less orphaned offices of the branches regarding the further existence of the organization. The Finance Ministry issued an order that the Reichsvereinigung was to continue to exist: its assets would be administered by the regional finance director but would remain the property of the organization. It was also to continue to operate the still existing hospitals, homes for the aged, and the like.[379]

Interim Summary

The heads of the Jewish Communities, but also other Jewish functionaries as well, had decided not to leave Germany, generally based on a keen sense of responsibility for their fellow Jews. Some also feared they would not be able to practice their profession abroad; others believed they were too old to begin a new life elsewhere. None had expected the excessive demands that now were imposed on them. With the onset of the mass deportations, the district branches had to accomplish tasks identical to or similar to those of the Berlin central office, or to work assisting that office. They were stripped of their autonomy regarding the hiring of personnel and finances, and in everything they undertook, they were subordinate to the surveillance and control of their central office and the local Gestapo. Once deportations began, the options for social welfare were also changed in their sphere of competence, while assistance in preparing the deportations loomed ever larger as a central task. At the same time, they were responsible for their members (and "full Jewish" nonmembers, such as those in mixed marriages and foreigners) and for ensuring adherence

Table 3. District Branch Directors (male and female), 1940/1941[380] and 1942[381]

District Branch	Name	Subsequent Fate
Königsberg	Leo Altmann	24/25 August 1942, Theresienstadt; 28 October 1944, murdered in Auschwitz
Pomerania, Stolp	Emil Gottschalk	16 June 1943, Theresienstadt; 19 October 1944, murdered in Auschwitz
Brandenburg-Schneidemühl	Dr. Hildegard Böhme	17 May 1943, Auschwitz; murdered there
Lower Silesia (Breslau)	Marie Thilo	16 June 1943, Theresienstadt; died there 29 May 1944
Upper Silesia (Gleiwitz)	Arthur Adolf Kochmann	27 December 1943, Auschwitz; murdered there
Leipzig	Dr. Fritz Grunsfeld	June 1943, deported to Theresienstadt; survived
Bremen	Carl Katz	24 July 1942, Thereienstadt, survived; chair, Jewish Community, died 1972
Northwest Germany (Hamburg)	Dr. Max Plaut	July 1944, exchanged to Palestine
Hanover	Minnie Ascher	23 July 1942, Theresienstadt; 12 October 1944, deported to Auschwitz, murdered there
Hanover	Max Schleisner	17 March 1943, Theresienstadt; died there 8 July 1943
Bielefeld	Dr. Max Ostwald	31 July 1942, Theresienstadt; died there 7 September 1943
Hesse-Nassau, Frankfurt am Main	Erna Maas	Emigrated, 19 May 1941[382]
Hesse-Nassau, Frankfurt am Main	Georg Goldstein	1943, Auschwitz; murdered there
Kassel	Siegmund Jäckel	7 September 1942, Theresienstadt; died there 24 February 1943
Cologne	Ernst Peiser	18 June 1943, Theresienstadt; 28 October 1944, Auschwitz
Palatinate, Ludwigshafen	Lothar Pinkus	Deported 1942, unknown destination, murdered
Baden, Karlsruhe	Karl Eisemann	Mixed marriage, intermediary until February 1945, in hiding at the war's end
Bavaria, Munich	Karl Stahl	17 June 1942, Theresienstadt; died 12 October 1944
Hesse, Mainz	Fritz Löwensberg	10 February 1943, Theresienstadt; died there 25 February 1944
Sudetengau, Aussig	Adolf Glaessner[383]	11 June 1943, Theresienstadt; 28 October 1944, Auschwitz

Table 4. Heads of Jewish Communities, 1942 (in part identical to district branch directors)

Community	Name	Subsequent Fate
Beuthen	Viktor Frey	Unknown
Breslau	Georg Kohn	20 November 1942, Theresienstadt; died there 18 April 1944
Dortmund	Willy Meier	28 June 1943, Theresienstadt; deported 16 October 1944 to Auschwitz and murdered there, 31 October 1944
Dresden	Kurt Hirschel	21 June 1943, Theresienstadt; 28 October 1944, Auschwitz
Essen	Max Hirschland	21 July 1942, Theresienstadt; died there 9 June 1944
Frankfurt am Main	Alfred Weil	18 August 1942, Theresienstadt; 28 October 1944, Auschwitz
Hamburg	Max Plaut	See above
Hanover	Max Schlei(s)sner	See above
Cologne	Julius Bier	2 October 1942, Theresienstadt; 19 October 1944, Auschwitz
Königsberg-East Prussia	Leo Altmann	See above
Leipzig	Paul Michael	Unknown
Mainz	Fritz Löwensberg	See above
Munich	Karl Stahl	See above
Nuremberg	Leo Katzenberger	Convicted ("racial defilement/parasite on the people" [Rassenschande/Volksschädling]), executed 3 June 1942
Württemberg (Stuttgart)	Ernst Moos	17 June 1943, Theresienstadt; 28 October 1944, Auschwitz

to all orders and prohibitions. Their relationship with the Berlin central office was marked by two features: their strong dependence on this office and their own attempts to retain a residue of autonomy, while the central office strove to curtail that autonomy as much as possible. Official instructions and formal procedural channels determined communication, especially in cases of conflict, which at first glance resembled "normal" office misconduct, but upon closer scrutiny showed a different face: namely, that those involved were fighting for their professional existence and thus their individual right to live, under threat should their office be closed, especially in the course of 1942. Although district branch directors and members increasingly found themselves in the same situation, the gulf between them deepened in parallel with the deportations as they progressed. Consequently, the Jewish functionaries often tried to bolster their authority in the eyes of their members while gaining the good will of the Gestapo by adapting their behavior to that of the Gestapo. The preponderant majority of functionaries obeyed their orders to the letter, and likewise demanded this from their members. Yet others took action: they made suggestions (preventive as much as possible), anticipated what the Gestapo was thinking and what orders might come, and tried to shape their implementation in such a way as to obtain a certain modicum of relief and easing in restrictions for the Jews affected. A small number of representatives overstepped their instructions for the benefit of the deportees, endangering themselves. An analysis of deportation dates indicated that a large proportion of the district branch directors were deported already in 1942, most to Theresienstadt, and in 1943, their successors and colleagues followed them there. Only a very small number of functionaries from the district branches survived the deportations. In this their fate did not differ from that of their superiors in the Berlin central office and of their members.

Notes

1. See Wolf Gruner, "Die NS-Verfolgung und die Kommunen: Zur wechselseitigen Dynamik von zentraler und lokaler Politik 1933–1941," *Vierteljahrshefte für Zeitgeschichte* 48 (2000): 75–126.
2. Ibid., 115–16.
3. Else B. Rosenfeld, "Leben und Sterben der Münchener Gemeinde 1938–1942," in *Von Juden in München: Ein Gedenkbuch*, ed. Hans Lamm (Munich, 1958), 356.
4. Raul Hilberg, *The Destruction of the European Jews*, vol. 2 (New York, 1985), 456.
5. BArch, R 8150/50, diagram Reichsvereinigung der Juden in Deutschland (central office), staff appointment scheme, 1 September 1942, pag. 300.
6. YV, 033/99, Alfred Neumeyer, "Tätigkeit als Gemeindevorsitzender" [activity as head of Community], p. 240; see also Alfred Neumeyer, Alexander Karl Neumeyer, and Imanuel Noy-Meir, *"Wir wollen den Fluch in Segen verwandeln": Drei Generationen der jüdischen Familie Neumeyer: Eine autobiografische Trilogie* (Berlin, 2007); excerpts also in Monika Richarz, ed., *Jüdisches Leben in Deutschland*, vol. 3 (Stuttgart, 1982), 358–66. Alfred Neumeyer's identical text "Tätigkeit" is entitled "Erinnerungen" in both publications. It can be accessed in full at the Leo Baeck Institute, LBI Memoir Collection (283M) online: http://tinyurl.com/bqotl6s (accessed 2 August 2012).
7. YV, 033/99, Alfred Neumeyer, "Tätigkeit als Gemeindevorsitzender," p. 236.
8. Ibid., p. 240.
9. StaHH, 522-1, Jüdische Gemeinden, section 1993, folder 27.
10. LBI, NY, AR 221, folder B 30/3/7 Ms. RB, circular letter 841 to all district branches, 18 September 1939, pp. 1–3.

11. Erna Maas, born 1910, lawyer, state supreme court Celle, lived in a protective mixed marriage; see BArch, R 1509, Volkszählung [census]. She emigrated 19 May 1941 to New York via Lisbon, information from Hess. HStA (GZ 6.1.2.550-(0000)), 1 December 2009.

12. Minnie Ascher was deported on 23 July 1942 to Theresienstadt and transported on 12 October 1944 to Auschwitz, where she was murdered; see www.holocaust .cz/de/victims/PERSON.ITI.262926 (accessed 2 August 2012). Hildegard Böhme was deported from Berlin to Auschwitz on 17 May 1943, where she was murdered; see www.bundesarchiv.de/gedenkbuch/index.html.en (accessed 9 August 2012); see also Maierhof, "Central Organizations."

13. BArch, R 8150/1/2, minutes No. 23, board meeting, 29 October 1942, p. 2.

14. LBI, NY, AR 221, folder B 30/3/7 Ms. RB, circular letter 841 to all district branches, 18 September 1939, p. 4.

15. LBI, NY, AR 7183, Max Kreutzberger, box 7, folder 9, MM reels 129, Interview Max Kreutzberger with Max Plaut, 14 June 1960, p. 11.

16. BArch, R 8150/45, memo, No. 19, 8 March 1941, p. 3, pag. 47.

17. BArch, R 8150/45, memo, No. 27, 17 March 1941, p. 3, pag. 24.

18. On Angerthal, see BArch, R 8150/46, memo, F 65, consultation in RSHA, 30 March 1942, pp. 4–5, pag. 26, point 3e; see also Stefanie Schüler-Springorum, *Die jüdische Minderheit in Königsberg/Preußen 1871–1945* (Göttingen, 1996), 322, 336, 346.

19. ZAGJD, B 1/19, No. 164, letter RVJD to Eisemann, 5 September 1941; Eisemann to Gestapo office Karlsruhe, 8 September 1941 and 20 September 1941.

20. BArch, R 8150/1/2, Internal letter RVJD Selten to Eppstein, 4 February 1942, pag. 142; BArch, R 8150/1/2, letter RVJD to RSHA, 31 March 1942, pag. 130; BArch, R 8150/1/2, letter RVJD Eppstein to district branch East Prussia, 2 April 1942, pag. 140; BArch, R 8150/1/2, letter RVJD Eppstein to Angerthal, 17 April 1942, pag. 137; BArch, R 8150/1/2, letter RVJD Karlsruhe to central office, 20 April 1942, pag. 136; BArch, R 8150/1/2, letter Angerthal to Eppstein, 25 April 1942, pag. 135; BArch, R 8150/1/2, letter district branch Karlsruhe to RVJD Eppstein, 29 April 1942, pag. 132; BArch, R 8150/1/2, memo Lilienthal to Eppstein, 29 April 1942, pag. 134; BArch, R 8150/1/2, letter district branch Karlsruhe to RVJD Eppstein, 5 May 1942, pag. 131. Angerthal evidently had to return to Königsberg. He was deported in 1943 to Auschwitz and murdered there; see www.bundesarchiv.de/gedenkbuch/index.html .en (accessed 2 August 2012); see also Yad Vashem, Central Database of Shoah Victims' Names, http://goo.gl/053od (accessed 2 August 2012).

21. LBI, NY, AR 7183, Max Kreutzberger, box 7, folder 9, MM reels 129, Interview Max Kreutzberger with Max Plaut, 14 June 1960, p. 1.

22. Ibid.

23. BArch, R 8150/7, report on Jewish school system, sent to the RSHA with letter, 17 June 1942, list of teachers, pp. 1–7; BArch, R 8150/7, letter to district branches and Jewish Communities on the liquidation of the Jewish school system, 20 June 1942.

24. BArch, R 1501/127713, report on Jewish Winter Relief 1938/1940, appendix 3, pag. 403.

25. StaHH, 522-1, Jüdische Gemeinden, section 1993, folder 27, letter RVJD to district branches and Jewish Communities, 21 May 1941.

26. State Archive (hereafter Sta) Munich, 1 Js Gen. 67 ff./49, Stanw.29.499/3, leaflet (1 March 1942), pag. 391.

27. See Beate Meyer, "Der 'Eichmann von Dresden': 'Justizielle Bewältigung' von NS-Verbrechen in der DDR am Beispiel des Verfahrens gegen Henry Schmidt," in

Deutsche, Juden, Völkermord: Der Holocaust als Geschichte und Gegenwart, ed. Jürgen Matthäus and Klaus-Michael Mallmann (Darmstadt, 2006), 277.

28. LBI, NY, AR 6559, circular letter, district branch Saxony-Thuringia of the RVJD, administrative office Magdeburg, 31 October 1941, p. 1.

29. LBI, NY, AR 143, Munich, Jewish Community Collection, A 11/5, announcement, n.d.

30. See Arndt Müller, *Geschichte der Juden in Nürnberg 1146–1945* (Nuremberg, 1968), 276.

31. The same prohibition issued in Hanover was revoked after the district branch there complained to the RSHA via the RV central office; see CJA, 2 B 1/4, memo No. 10, 19 September 1941, point 4.

32. BArch, R 8150/19, letter Fanny David to RVJD, 18 May 1942; BArch, R 8150/19, listing RVJD, 15 April 1942, Identifying markers for apartments.

33. See Gruner, *Geschlossener Arbeitseinsatz*, 250. Gruner terms this a "third camp network," which he differentiates from the forced labor camps and the retraining camps run by the RV.

34. See Schüler-Springorum, *Jüdische Minderheit*, 353–54.

35. BArch, R 8150/45, memo, No. 30, 21 March 1941, pag. 12.

36. BArch, R 8150/45, memo, No. 34, 26 March.1941, pag. 7. *Judenwohnungen* were assigned in localities where there were but a small number of Jews.

37. BArch, R 8150/46, memo, F 56, 2 March 1942, p. 3, pag. 58.

38. BArch, R 8150/46, memo, F 65, 30 March 1942, p. 5, pag. 26; see Alfred Hintz, *"Ohne Meldung unbekannt verzogen": Schwerte unter der NS-Herrschaft* (Norderstedt, 2008), 81ff.

39. LBI, JMB, MM 83, Dr. med. Heinrich Wolffheim, Allenstein 1933–1943 (written spring 1947), now published by Christa Ahleit, "Allenstein 1933–1943: Die Erinnerungen des Arztes Heinrich Wolffheim von 1947," in *NS-Gewaltherrschaft: Beiträge zur historischen Forschung und juristischen Aufarbeitung*, ed. Alfred Gottwaldt, Norbert Kampe, and Peter Klein (Berlin, 2005), 172–86.

40. For details, see Jörg Osterloh, *Nationalsozialistische Judenverfolgung im Reichsgau Sudentenland 1938–1945* (Munich, 2006), 491–92.

41. BArch, R 8150/112, letter Glässner (to Eppstein), 2 September 1941, pag. 38–40, here p. 2.

42. BArch, R 8150/112, supplement to letter Glässner (to Eppstein), 5 September 1941.

43. BArch, R 8150/112, memo Glässner, 5 September 1941.

44. The transports from the Hauenstein castle and individual biographies have been reconstructed by Tomas Fedorovici; see Tomas Fedorovici, "Die Gemeinde Schönwald und ihre unfreiwilligen Einwohner," *Theresienstaedter Studien und Dokumente* (2001): 269–86.

45. See Julia Cartarius, "Jewish Persecution in Western Upper Silesia 1933–1943," MA thesis, University College London, 2003, 22–23, 27–28.

46. BArch, R 8150/46, memo, F 26, 11 November 1941, p. 6; see also Cartarius, "Jewish Persecution," 33–34.

47. BArch, R 8150/112, memo Eppstein, 24 July 1941, pag. 161; on this, see Moshe Ayalon, "Jewish Alltagsgeschichte on the Eve of the Holocaust: Jewish Life in Breslau," *LBI Yearbook* 41, no. 1 (1996): 338–39; Alfred Konieczny, "The Transit Camp for Breslau Jews at Riebnig in Lower Silesia (1941–1943)," *Yad Vashem Studies* 25 (1996): 317–42; see also Hessisches Hauptstaatsarchiv (hereafter Hess. HStA), 461/30983/29, 5 Js 192/62, bill of indictment by the chief prosecutor Bielefeld, 24 March 1966, pp. 8–9.

48. See Andreas Reinke, *Judentum und Wohlfahrtspflege in Deutschland: Das jüdische Krankenhaus in Breslau 1726–1944* (Hanover, 1999), 282ff.

49. Hess. HStA, 461/30983/29, 5 Js 192/62, bill of indictment by the chief prosecutor Bielefeld, 24 March 1966, p. 9; see also Karol Jonca, "Deportations of German Jews from Breslau 1941–1944 as Described in Eyewitness Testimonies," *Yad Vashem Studies* 25 (1996): 275–316.

50. State Archive North Rhine-Westphalia (Landesarchiv Nordrhein-Westfalen, until 2008: Staatsarchiv, hereafter LA NRW) Münster, Verfahren 45 Js 29/78 StA Dortmund (Dr. Gerke et al.), HA, Vol. II, Interrogation Günter Singer, 28 February 1963, p. 8, pag. 71.

51. See Britta Bopf, *"Arisierung" in Köln: Die wirtschaftliche Existenzvernichtung der Juden 1933–1945* (Cologne, 2004), 280ff.; on the collection quarters in the fort and barracks, see p. 284.

52. BArch, R 8150/113, letter Cologne Jewish Community to RVJD, 28 April 1941, pag. 308; BArch, R 8150/113, letter Cologne Jewish Community to Gestapo Cologne, 15 August 1941, pag. 298; BArch, R 8150/113, letter Jewish Community Cologne to RVJD, 15 August 1941, pag. 297; BArch, R 8150/113, letter RVJD to Cologne mayor, 15 August 1941, pag. 296; BArch, R 8150/113, letter Jewish Community Cologne to RVJD, 28 August 1941, pag. 309; BArch, R 8150/113, memo, 8 September 1941, pag. 294–95; BArch, R 8150/113, expert opinion RVJD Lustig and Jacoby, 6 September 1941, pag. 284–88.

53. BArch, R 8150/127/1, letter RVJD to RSHA, 11 November 1941, pag. 90.

54. BArch, R 8150/46, memo, F 39, 9 January 1942, p. 13, pag. 125, no. 14.

55. BArch, R 8150/46, memo, F 65, 30 March 1942, notification that four hundred thousand RM were being transferred back into the Reichsvereinigung account.

56. YV, 033/83 (E/83), Hans Block, according to a letter by Paul Spiegel in April 1946 to emigrated friends (inter alia, H.B.).

57. BArch, R 8150/113, letter Schleissner to Gestapo Hanover, 9 September 1941, pag. 190–91; BArch, R 8150/113, copy of memo, 2 September 1941, pag. 194; BArch, R 8150/113, travel report, 7 September 1941, pag. 196; BArch, R 8150/113, supplementary report by Auerbach, 12 September 1942, pag. 197.

58. Historian Marlies Buchholz made a study of the time of suffering of the Hanover Jews in the *Judenhäuser*, which were repeatedly subjected to house searches and checks. There is also research on the later conversion of the Jewish Horticulture School Ahlem into a deportation collection point; see Marlies Buchholz, *Die hannoverschen Judenhäuser: Zur Situation der Juden in der Zeit der Ghettoisierung und Verfolgung 1941 bis 1945* (Hildesheim, 1987); see also Hans-Dieter Schmid, *Ahlem: die Geschichte einer jüdischen Gartenbauschule und ihres Einflusses auf Gartenbau und Landschaftsarchitektur in Deutschland und Israel* (Bremen, 2008). Ruth Herskovits-Gutmann, then still a young teenager, describes the life of the Hanover Jews concentrated in Ahlem; see Ruth Herskovits-Gutmann, *Auswanderung vorläufig nicht möglich: die Geschichte der Familie Herskovits* (Göttingen, 2002).

59. CJA, 2 1/4, memo no. 21, 8 November 1941, enclosure circular letter of the RVJD, 13 November 1941, pp. 1–4; CJA, 2 1/4, memo, 12 November 1941, point 2; CJA, 2 1/4, memo, no. K 31, 13 January 1942, p. 2, point III.

60. Adolf Kahlenberg, deported on 21 June 1943 to Theresienstadt, and to Auschwitz on 16 October 1944, where he was murdered; see www.bundesarchiv.de/gedenkbuch/index.html.en (accessed 2 August 2012).

61. BStU, ZUV 74, EV, Vol. 13, Interrogation Henry Schmidt, 11 November 1986, p. 2. On Dresden, see Marcus Gryglewski, "Zur Geschichte der nationalsozialistischen Ju-

denverfolgung in Dresden 1933–1945," in *Die Erinnerung hat ein Gesicht: Fotografien und Dokumente zur nationalsozialistischen Judenverfolgung in Dresden 1933–1945*, ed. Norbert Haase, Stefi Jersch-Wenzel, and Hermann Simon (Leipzig, 1998), 129.

62. BArch, R 8150/9, internal letter, Königsberger an Lustig, 3 September 1943, pag. 164; BArch, R 8150/9, "Number of the unfinished H-contracts according to district branches," pag. 191. At this relatively late juncture, there were still nine thousand ongoing "procedures" still awaiting conclusion.

63. See *Jüdisches Nachrichtenblatt*, 13 February 1942.

64. BArch, R 8150/14, letter RVJD Lilienthal to district branch Westphalia, 15 April 1942, pag. 312.

65. BArch, R 8150/44, letter wife Hilde to husband Egon, 23 April 1943, pag. 140.

66. BArch, R 8150/39, copy extract from letter RVJD to "Legal Consultant" Fliess, pag. 3, pag. 2ff.; BArch, R 8150/39, list "petitions to authorities," 10 March 1943, pag. 9.

67. StaHH, 522-1 Jüdische Gemeinden, section 1993, folder 29, audit report, submitted on 30 August 1942.

68. YV, 01/150, WL P. IIe, Louis Elkan, "Die Synagogengemeinde Düsseldorf nach dem Pogrom," written September 1956, p. 2.

69. YV, 02/551, WL P. IIe. no. 765, Bernhard Kolb, "Die Juden in Nürnberg: Tausendjährige Geschichte einer Judengemeinde von ihren Anfängen bis zum Einmarsch der amerikanischen Truppen am 20. April 1945," Nuremberg 1946, p. 59; YV, 02/53, WL P. III No. 41, Else Dormitzer, "Experiences in Nuremberg, Holland, Theresienstadt," p. 1.

70. BArch, R 8150/46, memo, F 55, 26 February 1942, pag. 61; Max Guhrauer was deported in 1943 to Theresienstadt, where he died on 4 June 1943; see www.bundesar chiv.de/gedenkbuch/index.html.en (accessed 2 August 2012).

71. Hannah Pohly was deported in 1942 to Warsaw, and declared dead after the war; see www.bundesarchiv.de/gedenkbuch/index.html.en (accessed 2 August 2012).

72. BArch, R 8150/51, report Lilienthal to RSHA, 25 February 1942, pag. 265; 12 March 1942, pag. 261; 9 May 1942, pag. 259; BArch, R 8150/51, internal memo RVJD Sprinz to Lilienthal, 25 April 1942, pag. 260.

73. LBI, NY, AR 7183, Max Kreutzberger, box 7, folder 9, MM reels 129, Interview Max Kreutzberger with Max Plaut, 14 June 1960, p. 11.

74. For all information on this case (except quotes), see BArch, R 8150/55, letter Eppstein to Stern, 18 February 1942, pag. 106; BArch, R 8150/55, memo RVJD Lilienthal, 21 April 1942, pag. 313; BArch, R 8150/55, letter Max Ostwald to RVJD, 3 March 1942; BArch, R 8150/55, memo: re organizational matters, n.d., pag. 323; BArch, R 8150/46, memo, F 57, 5 March 1942, p. 3, pag. 54.

75. BArch, R 8150/51, letter Max Ostwald to RVJD, 3 March 1942, pag. 103.

76. BArch, R 8150/55, letter Kurt Ehrlich to RVJD Lilienthal, 5 May 1942, pag. 319.

77. On this and all subsequent data regarding the "Pinkus case" (aside from any quoted words or passages), see BArch, R 8150/55, memo on phone call Eisemann, Selten, 30 December 1941; BArch, R 8150/55, letter RVJD Lilienthal to district branch Karlsruhe, 11 January 1942; BArch, R 8150/55, letter Pinkus to Eppstein, 17 March 1942, pag. 19; BArch, R 8150/55, letter Eisemann to RVJD, 19 March 1942; BArch, R 8150/55, letter RVJD Lilienthal to district branch Baden/Palatinate, 28 March 1942, pag. 22; BArch, R 8150/55, letter district branch Baden/Palatinate, Karlsruhe Eisemann to RVJD, 16 April 1942, pag. 23.

78. BArch, R 8150/55, letter Eppstein to Pinkus, 20 March 1942, pag. 20.

79. Lothar Pinkus was transported in 1942 to an unknown deportation destination and murdered there, date of death unknown; see www.bundesarchiv.de/gedenkbuch/ index.html.en (accessed 2 August 2012).

80. CJA, 2 B 1/4, memo, K 31, 13 January 1942, Eppstein: "after initial important differences, now there are only differences due to local matters."

81. LA NRW Münster, 5 Js 192/62, Interrogation Günter Singer, 28 February 1963, pp. 5–6, pag. 69–70.

82. LA NRW Münster, 5 Js 192/62, Interrogation Hans-Werner Abraham, 16 December 1963, p. 2, pag. 365–66.

83. Martin Pollack was deported from Breslau to Theresienstadt on 16 June 1943, and transported to Auschwitz on 28 October 1944, where he was murdered; see www .bundesarchiv.de/gedenkbuch/index.html.en (accessed 2 August 2012).

84. LA NRW Münster, 45 Js 29/78, Interrogation Rudolf Zuckel (Gestapo), 9 September 1965, p. 3, pag. 335.

85. LA NRW Münster, 5 Js 192/62, Interrogation Gertrud Epstein, 12 February 1964, pp. 2–3, pag. 302–3; LA NRW Münster, 5 Js 192/62, Interrogation Herbert Sander, 21 January 1964, p. 2, pag. 272.

86. LA NRW Münster, 5 Js 192/62, Interrogation Albert Hadda, 12 February 1963, pp. 4–5, pag. 16–17.

87. LA NRW Münster, 45 Js 29/78, Interrogation Louis Grünberger, 31 October 1967, p. 4, pag. 209.

88. LA NRW Münster, 45 Js 29/78, Interrogation Rudolf Zuckel (Gestapo), 9 September 1965, pp. 6–7, pag. 338–39.

89. ZAGJD, B 1/19, No. 333, letter Marx, Württemberg Jewish Community, Stuttgart to district branch Ludwigshafen, 9 April 1942; ZAGJD, B 1/19, No. 333, letter Alfred Marx, Stuttgart to Karl Eisemann, Karlsruhe, 24 April 1942; ZAGJD, B 1/19, No. 333, letter Eisemann to Moos, 30 April 1942.

90. ZAGJD, B 1/19, No. 333, circular letter, Württemberg Jewish Community to members, 17 November 1941.

91. BArch, R 8150/46, memo, F 21, 29 November 1941, p. 4.

92. BArch, R 8150/46, memo, F 22, 1 November 1941, p. 3, pag. 169.

93. BArch, R 8150/46, memo, F 70, 20 April 1942, p. 5, pag. 3; the deportation of all three from Düsseldorf to Izbica was thus postponed from October/November 1941 to 22 April 1942, but none survived; see www.bundesarchiv.de/gedenkbuch/index .html.en (accessed 2 August 2012).

94. Rhineland district branch, Cologne, Ernst Peiser, instruction sheet and notice of deportation, 6 June 1942; see "Von denen, die blieben, überlebte keiner," www.floerken .eu (accessed 2 August 2012); reproduced in full in Dieter Corbach, 6.oo Uhr ab Messe Köln-Deutz: Deportationen 1938–1945 (Cologne, 1994), 29–30. The district chief administrator here (Landrat) refers to the top official of the local government district.

95. Corbach, 6.oo Uhr ab Messe Köln-Deutz, p. 2.

96. Ibid.

97. Ibid. The Stuttgart Jewish Community also named the Gestapo as source of the orders and stated that "any attempt to resist evacuation … is useless and … can lead to serious consequences for those involved"; USHMM, RG-14.053M, Jewish Community Stuttgart, 2003.11, reel 1, letter, Jewish Community to deportees, 19 November 1941.

98. District branch Westphalia, those assigned for the district of Minden, Adolf I. Stern, Karl I. Heumann, Dr. I. Max Ostwald, n.d., facsimile copy (in private papers); see www.kfkronenberg.com/reich.htm (accessed 2 August 2012). The initial "I" is for "Israel," the compulsory additional name.

99. Ibid.

100. Ibid.

101. ZAGJD, B 1/19, No. 333, letter Eisemann to Reis, Pforzheim.

102. LAB, B Rep. 058, 1 Js 9/65 P gr No. 2 (box 54), Interrogation Walter Albath, 12 July 1968, p. 5.

103. Sta Nürnberg, Staatsanwaltschaft, 3070/V, case against Theodor Grafenberger et al., KLs 230/48, transcript, meeting 7 March 1949, pp. 69–70; Sta München, Stanw. 29.499/1, Interrogation Johann Peuffer, 30 December 1949, 3rd p. (n. p.).

104. LAB, B Rep. 058, 1 Js 9/64 (box 80), supplement 98, "Instructions for organizing implementation of the evacuation of the Jews on 29 November 1941 (Nuremberg/ Fürth)," pp. 7–8; all other information is also from this document.

105. In performing body checks on women, secretaries, cleaning women, or on occasion local wet nurses were utilized; see, for example, the sections on specific cities in this chapter; see also USHMM, RG-14.053M, Jewish Community of Stuttgart, reel 1, 2003.11, Instructions, municipal chief inspector Hechingen, 27 November 1941.

106. LAB, B Rep. 058, 1 Js 9/64 (box 80), supplement 98, "Instructions for organizing implementation of the evacuation of the Jews on 10 September 1942," p. 5.

107. Hess. HSta Wiesbaden, 461/30983/26, Gestapo office [Staatspolizeiliche Leitstelle] Frankfurt (Poche), Instructions for officers deployed, n.d., p. 1.

108. See Gottwald and Schulle, "Judendeportationen," 444–45.

109. Ibid., 445–61.

110. On Sprenger, see Stephanie Zibell, *Jakob Sprenger (1884–1945): NS-Gauleiter und Reichsstatthalter in Hessen* (Darmstadt, 1999), 338ff. However, the author excludes Sprenger's operations designed to make his *Gau* "Jew-free."

111. Hess. HStA Wiesbaden, 461/30983, Proceedings against Reinhard Breder et al., Interrogation Grosse, 13 March 1950, pag. 85ff., obverse.

112. Ibid.; on deportation of the workers in the armaments industry, see also Monica Kingreen, "'Die Aktion zur kalten Erledigung der Mischehen'—die reichsweit singuläre Verschleppung und Ermordung jüdischer Mischehepartner im NSDAP-Gau Hessen-Nassau 1942/43," in Gottwaldt, Kampe, and Klein, *NS-Gewaltherrschaft*, 188–89.

113. See Monica Kingreen, "Gewaltsam verschleppt aus Frankfurt: Die Deportationen der Juden in den Jahren 1941–1945," in *"Nach der Kristallnacht": Jüdisches Leben und antijüdische Politik in Frankfurt am Main 1938–1945*, ed. Monica Kingreen (Frankfurt am Main and New York, 1999), 360.

114. Hess. HStA Wiesbaden, 461/37048/1, Proceedings against Heinrich Baab, bill of indictment, 29 November 1949, p. 9, pag. 1297.

115. Although Jews were discriminated against in allotment of charcoal in any case, the *Gau* directorate ordered that Jews would be supplied with fuel only after all those "of German blood" had received their allotments; according to witness testimony, the upshot was that Jews received nothing. Those who had applied for an allotment before the Germans had got their charcoal were reported to the Gestapo: Hess. HStA Wiesbaden, 461/37048/1, Proceedings against Heinrich Baab, pag. 441a; Hess. HStA Wiesbaden, 461/37048/1, Interrogation Heinrich Böscher, 20 March 1950, pp. 17–18, pag. 1640–41. An easing of restrictions and regulations did not come until March 1943, after the "unprotected" Jews had already been deported.

116. Hess. HStA Wiesbaden, 461/37048/1, Interrogation Heinrich Böscher, 20 March 1950, pag. 98.

117. Ibid., pag. 4441a. This estimate is probably too high.

118. Hess. HStA Wiesbaden, 461/37048/1, Interrogation Fritz Goldschmidt, 1 November 1948, pp. 2–3, pag. 465.

119. Hess. HStA Wiesbaden, 461/37048/1, Interrogation Max L. Cahn, 10 March 1950, p. 12; see also *Frankfurter Neue Presse*, 11 March 1950; see also Monica Kingreen,

"Verfolgung und Rettung in Frankfurt am Main und der Rhein-Main-Region," in Kosmala and Schoppmann, *Solidarität,* 176ff.

120. Hess. HStA Wiesbaden, 461/30983, Proceedings against Reinhard Breder et al., Interrogation Baab, 8 March 1950, pag. 49–50; and from 17 February 1965, pag. 160; Hess. HStA Wiesbaden, 461/30983, Proceedings against Reinhard Breder et al., Interrogation Grosse, 13 March 1949, pag. 93. While Grosse denied this, Baab stated that there had been a card file of "information people"; see Hess. HStA Wiesbaden, 461/30983, Proceedings against Reinhard Breder et al., Interrogation Heinrich Baab, 17 February 1965, pag. 160. The Gestapo informer repeatedly mentioned in testimony, Wolff, was upon request from the Frankfurt Gestapo hired on by the district branch Hesse-Nassau in addition to their actual personnel needs; the RSHA was basically opposed to this, but accepted the decision; see CJA, 2 B 1/2, memo 141, p. 5; see also Volker Eichler, "Das 'Judenreferat' der Frankfurter Gestapo," in Kingreen, *Kristallnacht,* 249–50; Adolf Diamant, *Die Gestapo Frankfurt a.M.* (Frankfurt am Main, 1988).

121. Hess. HStA Wiesbaden, 461/37048/1, Proceedings against Heinrich Baab, Interrogation Baab, 22 March 1950, p. 2, pag. 1646. On Heinrich Baab, see Edward Crankshaw, *Gestapo: Instrument of Tyranny* (New York, 1956); on the Baab trial, see also Kay Boyle, *The Smoking Mountain: Stories of Postwar Germany* (New York, 1951), 1–78; Kay Boyle, "The People with Names," *The New Yorker,* 9 September 1950, 37.

122. The Frankfurt Jewish Community reacted to Baab's accusations with a declaration published on 7 April 1950 in the *Jüdisches Gemeindeblatt/Allgemeine Wochenzeitung;* it stated that since 1945, all the accusations had been carefully investigated and the few guilty persons had been held to account, but the investigations had in the main discovered that the accusations were unfounded. However, I found no references to these investigations in the files, which have in the meantime been deposited in Heidelberg in the Central Archive for Research on the History of the Jews in Germany.

123. Hess. HStA Wiesbaden, 461/37048/1, Proceedings against Heinrich Baab, Interrogation Friedrich Witzler, 25 October 1948.

124. Hess. HStA Wiesbaden, 461/30983, Proceedings against Reinhard Breder et al., Interrogation Grosse, 13 March 1950, pag. 85, obverse.

125. On Holland, see Lutz Becht, "'die Wohlfahrtseinrichtungen sind aufgelöst worden …': Vom 'städtischen Beauftragten bei der Jüdischen Wohlfahrtspflege' zum 'Beauftragten der Geheimen Staatspolizei …' 1938–1943," in Kingreen, *Kristallnacht,* 211– 36; Charlotte Opfermann, "'Im Hermesweg': Zur Tätigkeit in der Bezirksstelle der Reichsvereinigung in Frankfurt am Main von November 1942 bis Juni 1943—ein Zeitzeugenbericht," in Kingreen, *Kristallnacht,* 403–14; see also BArch, R 8150/51, report Kurt Levy to RVJD, 12 November 1942; BArch, R 8150/51, letter Hanna Karminski to RSHA, 2 November 1942.

126. Hess. HStA Wiesbaden, 461/37048/1, Proceedings against Heinrich Baab, 461/ 37048/1, Interrogation Frieda Rudert, 10 March 1950, p. 13, pag. 1376.

127. Hess. HStA Wiesbaden, 461/37048/1, Interrogation Siegfried Katz, 16 November 1948, p. 2, pag. 529–30; in view of the intentional action by the Gestapo, the estimate by the public prosecutor of 1,400 "prisoners in protective custody" is perhaps too high, but the figure mentioned by Volker Eichler, "at least 200," seems too low; see Volker Eichler, "'Judenreferat,'" 250–51.

128. Ludwig Ascher, deported 19 October 1941 to Lódz, date of death 24 May 1942; Otto Simon-Wolfskehl, deported 19 October 1941 to Lódz, date of death 14 July

1942; Alfred Weil, deported 18 August 1942 to Theresienstadt, date of death 28 October 1944 in Auschwitz; Louis Lerner, deported 16 June 1943 to Theresienstadt, and on 28 October 1944 to Auschwitz, declared dead; for all, see www.bundesarchiv .de/gedenkbuch/index.html.en (accessed 2 August 2012). See also Gudrun Maierhof, "Selbsthilfe nach dem Pogrom: Die Jüdische Gemeinde in Frankfurt am Mai 1938 bis 1942," in Kingreen, *Kristallnacht*, 157–86.

129. BArch, R 8150/51, letter Georg Goldstein to RVJD Levy, 21 November 1943, pag. 182.

130. BArch, R 8150/51, Bericht RVJD Levy, 28 September 1942, pag. 204.

131. BArch, R 8150/51, letter RVJD to board, Frankfurt Jewish Community, 6 September 1941, report RVJD, 22 August 1941.

132. Hess. HStA Wiesbaden, 461/37048/1, Proceedings against Heinrich Baab, Interrogation Karl Oppenheimer, 10 March 1950, p. 5, pag. 1572.

133. See Zibell, *Jakob Sprenger*, 338ff.; Gruner, *Öffentliche Wohlfahrt*, 32; see also Horst Mazerath, "Oberbürgermeister im Dritten Reich," in *Der "Führerstaat": Mythos und Realität: Studien zur Struktur und Politik des Dritten Reiches*, ed. Gerhard Hirschfeld and Lothar Kettenacker (Stuttgart, 1981), 228–54; on Krebs and Sprenger, 246, 250.

134. See Monica Kingreen, "Raubzüge einer Stadtverwaltung: Frankfurt am Main und die Aneignung 'jüdischen Besitzes,'" in "Bürokratien: Initiative und Effizienz," ed. Wolf Gruner and Armin Nolzen, special issue, *Beiträge zur Geschichte des Nationalsozialismus* 17 (2001): 17–50.

135. In contrast with the Cologne Jews, who were informed about the transport five days before, orders for the Frankfurt Jews came unannounced; see Kingreen, "Gewaltsam verschleppt," 358ff. The massive *Grossmarkthalle* in Frankfurt was the largest single building in the city at the time.

136. Ibid. The "political leaders" in the NSDAP were the leaders of the various functional offices in the party, an elite group with special prerogatives.

137. Volker Eichler points out that the *Judenreferat* in the Frankfurt Gestapo participated in the ten deportations at a more subordinate level: it was too small and personnel there was too limited to take over the major proportion of work and a leadership role; see Eichler, "'Judenreferat,'" 246–47.

138. Hess. HStA Wiesbaden, Proceedings against Reinhard Breder et al., 461/30983/19, report on investigation, p. 27, pag. 166.

139. For a different description, see Eichler, "'Judenreferat,'" 244.

140. Hess. HStA Wiesbaden, 461/37048/1, Proceedings against Heinrich Baab, Interrogation Karl Oppenheimer, 10 March 1950, p. 7, pag. 1573.

141. Hess. HStA Wiesbaden, 461/30983, letter Baab to state prosecutor, 11 May 1949, pag. 49–50.

142. Private posthumous papers Max Cahn, untitled description (covering the years 1935–1945), p. 3.

143. Hess. HStA Wiesbaden, 461/30983/7, Interrogation Max Cahn, 10 March 1950, p. 14.

144. WL, P. III.e.No.456, Max Cahn, Surviving in Frankfurt a. M., 20 November 1955, pp. 2–3.

145. Order for "labor deployment," reproduced in *Dokumente zur Geschichte der Frankfurter Juden*, ed. Kommission zur Erforschung der Geschichte der Frankfurter Juden (Frankfurt am Main, 1963), pp. 531–32.

146. We still have no precise figures; for the numbers given here, see Gutman, *Enzyklopädie des Holocaust*, 481; Kingreen, "Gewaltsam verschleppt," 390.

147. Figures from Falk Wiesemann, "Judenverfolgung und nichtjüdische Bevölkerung 1933–1944," in *Bayern in der NS-Zeit: Soziale Lage und politisches Verhalten der Bevölkerung im Spiegel vertraulicher Berichte*, ed. Martin Broszat, Elke Fröhlich, and Falk Wiesemann (Munich and Vienna, 1977), 428.

148. See ibid., 413.

149. See Ophir and Wiesemann, *Die jüdischen Gemeinden*, 121.

150. See Broszat et al., *Judenverfolgung*, 431.

151. See Peter Hanke, *Zur Geschichte der Juden in München zwischen 1933 und 1945* (Munich, 1967), 169.

152. On the early introduction or tightening of individual measures, especially from 1933 to 1938, see the section on anti-Jewish policy in Hamburg and Munich from a comparative perspective in Frank Bajohr, *"Aryanisation" in Hamburg: The Economic Exclusion of Jews and the Confiscation of Their Property in Nazi Germany* (Oxford, 2002), 84–88; see also Doris Seidel, "Die jüdische Gemeinde Münchens 1933–1945," in *München arisiert: Entrechtung und Enteignung der Juden in der NS-Zeit*, ed. Angelika Baumann and Andreas Heusler (Munich, 2004), 34.

153. See also letter Bruno Finkelscherer to Alfred Neumeyer, 30 November 1942, reproduced in Lamm, *Juden in München*, 361ff.

154. YV, 033/99, Alfred Neumeyer, "Tätigkeit als Gemeindevorsitzender," p. 227.

155. Ibid., p. 226.

156. Ibid., p. 219.

157. Ibid.

158. Ibid., p. 225.

159. Ibid., p. 226.

160. *Entjudung des Grundstückmarktes.* See Hans Wegner, "Tätigkeits- und Abschlussbericht zum 30. Juni 1943" (Activity and Final Report), reproduced in Stadtarchiv München, ed., *"… verzogen, unbekannt wohin": Die erste Deportation von Münchner Juden im November 1941* (Zurich and Munich, 2000), document 22 (n.p.), "Tätigkeitsbericht," p. 1.

161. Gerd Modert, "Motor der Verfolgung—Zur Rolle der NSDAP bei der Entrechtung und Ausplünderung der Münchner Juden," in Baumann and Heusler, *München*, 167.

162. See Wolf Gruner, "Die Grundstücke der 'Reichsfeinde,'" in *"Arisierung" im Nationalsozialismus: Volksgemeinschaft, Raub und Gedächtnis*, ed. Irmtrud Wojak and Peter Hayes (Frankfurt am Main and New York, 2000), 128ff.

163. Wegner, "Tätigkeits- und Abschlussbericht," Table, p. 5; for Bavaria as a whole, see also doc. 2858, Bericht Bayerisches Staatsministerium für Wirtschaft, 27 March 1939, in Kulka and Jäckel, *The Jews*, 447–48.

164. See Modert, "Motor," 167.

165. Wegner, "Tätigkeits- und Abschlussbericht," p. 26.

166. Sta München, Spruchkammer, box 487, Georg Gassner, testimony Theodor Koronczyk, 14 August 1947.

167. YV, 033/99, Alfred Neumeyer, "Tätigkeit als Gemeindevorsitzender," p. 217.

168. Hanke, *Juden in München*, 274; see also Else R. Behrend-Rosenfeld, *Ich stand nicht allein: Erlebnisse einer Jüdin in Deutschland 1933–1944*, 3rd ed. (Cologne, 1979), 73–74; see also Ophir and Wiesemann, *Die jüdischen Gemeinden*, 53. "Stargazer stand" is a free rendering by the translator of the German *Sternwarte* (literally, observatory), playing on the German words *warten* (wait) and *Warte* (lookout, observatory).

169. YV, 033/99, Alfred Neumeyer, "Tätigkeit als Gemeindevorsitzender," p. 222.

170. See Volker Dahm, "Kulturelles und geistiges Leben," in *Die Juden in Deutschland 1933–1945: Leben unter nationalsozialistischer Herrschaft*, ed. Wolfgang Benz (Mu-

nich, 1988), 234; Ophir and Wiesemann, *Die jüdischen Gemeinden*, 54; Behrend-Rosenfeld, *Ich stand nicht allein*, 74. The author Behrend-Rosenfeld, who otherwise has a sharp memory, sometimes is mistaken in her spelling of certain personal names (e.g., Hellinger instead of Hechinger, etc.).

171. YV, 033/99, Alfred Neumeyer, "Tätigkeit als Gemeindevorsitzender," p. 240.

172. See Ophir and Wiesemann, *Die jüdischen Gemeinden*, 57.

173. Joseph Schäler was deported in 1943 to Auschwitz and murdered there on 17 March 1943; see www.bundesarchiv.de/gedenkbuch/index.html.en (accessed 1 August 2012).

174. Fritz Sänger was deported on 3/4 April 1942 to Piaski and murdered; see www.bundesarchiv.de/gedenkbuch/index.html.en (accessed 1 August 2012).

175. Letter, Karl Stahl to Alfred Neumeyer, 20 April 1941, reproduced in Lamm, *Juden in München*, 360–61.

176. BArch, R 8150/19, letter RVJD to RSHA, 2 May 1942, pag. 59.

177. BArch, R 8150/19, letter, representative of the Gauleiter for Aryanization to Jewish Community Munich, 24 April 1942, pag. 60.

178. BArch, R 8150/19, letter Stahl to Eppstein, 22 April 1942, pag. 65.

179. YV, 033/99, Alfred Neumeyer, "Tätigkeit als Gemeindevorsitzender," p. 221.

180. A detailed new study is Maximilian Strnad, *Zwischenstation "Judensiedlung": Verfolgung und Deportation der jüdischen Münchner 1941–1945* (Munich, 2011). I am grateful to Maximilian Strnad for references and his kind willingness to provide me with research findings before their publication.

181. BArch, R 8150/45, memo, No. 14, 8 March 1941, p. 3, pag. 47.

182. Declaration re: camp establishment, Munich, Knorrstr. 148, reproduced in Stadtarchiv München, "… *verzogen, unbekannt wohin*," document 2 (n.p.).

183. "Aufruf an alle Haushaltungsvorstände zur Weitergabe an sämtliche Wohnungsinsassen" [Call to all heads of households, to be passed on to all apartment residents], 30 September 1941, reproduced in *Verdunkeltes München: Geschichtswettbewerb 1985/86: Die nationalsozialistische Gewaltherrschaft, ihr Ende und ihre Folgen*, ed. Landeshauptstadt München (Lesebücher zur Geschichte des Münchner Alltags) (Munich, 1987), 24.

184. Wegner, "Tätigkeits- und Abschlussbericht," p. 18. Strnad assumes eleven or twelve hundred persons before the large-scale deportations; see Strnad, *Zwischenstation "Judensiedlung*," 64.

185. All data from Stadtarchiv München, ed., *Biographisches Gedenkbuch der Münchner Juden 1933–1945*, vol. 2, (Munich, 2007), 863–64, 866–67.

186. BArch, R 8150/114, letter, representative of Gauleiter to Jewish Community, Hechinger, 1 August 1941, pag. 124; BArch, R 8150/114, letter Jewish Community Stahl to RVJD, 3 August 1941, pag. 113–14.

187. BArch, R 8150/114, internal memo, Auerbach after consultation with Hechinger, 13 August 1941, pag. 125.

188. Behrend-Rosenfeld, *Ich stand nicht allein*, 117; see also http://goo.gl/bFnWG (accessed 30 June 2012).

189. LBI, NY, AR 143, Munich, Jewish Community Coll., A 11/5, call, 30 September 1941.

190. Behrend-Rosenfeld, *Ich stand nicht allein*, 105–6.

191. There were a total of 3,197 Jews in Munich: 424 in nursing homes (residents plus personnel), 48 in Berg am Laim, 53 in the labor camp Lohof, 1,498 in "Jews' houses," 891 in "Aryan" houses, 255 in "Aryan" boarding houses, 28 housed temporarily in

boarding houses, plus some 100 individuals outside Munich under arrest or in retraining facilities. Of this total, 371 were in mixed marriages, and 172 Jews were at this point "evicted [*entmietet*] and not yet rehoused"; BArch, R 8150/114, memo Hechinger, 13 August 1941, pag. 126.

192. Seidel, "Jüdische Gemeinde," 51. On the basis of lists for food provision, Strnad assumes the number was smaller: according to his data, in the two camps in October 1941 the total was somewhere between 157 and 245 persons; see Strnad, *Zwischenstation "Judensiedlung,"* 62ff.

193. BArch, R 8150/114, letter, representative of Gauleiter, Wegner to Jewish Community, 1 September 1941, pag. 110; Hugo Railing (in the literature also spelled Reiling), deported 3/4 April 1942 to Piaski; Curt Mezger, murdered in March 1945 in the auxiliary camp Ebensee of the Mauthausen concentration camp; see www.bundesarchiv.de/gedenkbuch/index.html.en (accessed 1 August 2012 and 25 November 2012).

194. Wegner, "Tätigkeits- und Abschlussbericht," p. 16.

195. Quoted in Landeshauptstadt München, *Lesebuch,* 37.

196. Quoted in Seidel, "Jüdische Gemeinde," 44. On Charlotte Knobloch, see http://goo.gl/8iptj (accessed 4 August 2012).

197. Sta München, Stanw. 29.499/1-3, 1 Js 67 ff./49, Interrogation Theodor Koronczyk (n.d.), p. 3 (obverse).

198. Letter, Jewish Community re: evacuation, 7 November 1941, reproduced in Stadtarchiv München, *"... verzogen, unbekannt wohin,"* document 8, n.p. The "brown letters" (*braune Briefe*) was a colloquial expression used among Munich Jews for the letters (in a brown envelope) announcing their deportation, and also containing the necessary predeportation questionnaire for completion. Jews in Berlin called them the "lists."

199. Behrend-Rosenfeld, *Ich stand nicht allein,* 119–20.

200. Sta München, Stanw. 29.499/1-3, 1 a Js 641/49, Interrogation Theodor Koronczyk (n.d.), p. 1, pag. 9.

201. Sta München, Stanw. 29.499/1-3, 1 Js 67 ff./49, Interrogation Theodor Koronczyk, 26 September 1950, n.p., p. 2; Sta München, Spruchkammer, box 939, Theodor Koronczyk, witness Dr. Schwarz, p. 24, pag. 45. After the war, *Judenreferent* Pfeuffer accused Julius Hechinger of having been the active person in all this: he selected the deportees according to the criterion of "which Jews could most easily cope with the rigors of evacuation"; see Sta München, Stanw. 29.499/1-3, 1 a Js 641/49, Interrogation Pfeuffer, 30 December 1949, p. 3, pag. 70.

202. Sta München, Stanw. 29.499/1-3, 3 Js 67 ff./49, Interrogation Heinz Meier, 16 August 1950, n.p., p. 2.

203. See Hanke, *Juden in München,* 290. Julius Spanier was a pediatrician, he headed the Jewish Hospital in Munich (Israelitisches Schwestern- und Krankenheim), was deported to Theresienstadt and survived; see Linda Lucia Damskis, *Zerrissene Biographien. Jüdische Ärzte zwischen nationalsozialistischer Verfolgung, Emigration und Wiedergutmachung* (Munich 2009), 149–158; Adler, *Theresienstadt,* 816.

204. Sta München, Spruchkammer, box 939, Theodor Koronczyk, letter RA Pfister to Jewish Community Munich, 8 November 1945, with biographical data for Koronczyk.

205. Sta München, Stanw. 29.499/1-3, 1 a Js 641/49, Interrogation Theodor Koronczyk, n.d., p. 1, pag. 9.

206. Sta München, Stanw. 29.499/1-3, 1 a Js 641/49, Interrogation Hans Wegner, 17 January 1950, n.p., p. 3, pag. 102.

207. Sta München, Stanw. 29.499/1-3, 1 a Js 641/49, letter, Senate President Alfred Hartmann, Chief public prosecutor Munich I to Public prosecutor Weiss, 12 January 1950, p. 2, data obverse.

208. See Wolfgang Scheffler, "Massenmord in Kowno," 83–87; on the first large-scale deportation from Munich (containing some errors in facts corrected only by later research), see Andreas Heusler, "Fahrt in den Tod: Der Mord an den Münchner Juden in Kaunas (Litauen) am 25. November 1941," in Stadtarchiv München, "... verzogen, unbekannt wohin," 13–24.

209. The survivor Arnold Hindels later reported that Sänger represented the Munich transport in the Jewish Council in Piaski. He stated that the engineer Hindels, who had been director in Munich of the craft training program for young Jews, had succeeded in locating funds in the ghetto to renovate the deteriorating bathing and delousing facilities there. He was then brought (reportedly in May) to Sawin, a transit labor camp southwest of the extermination camp Sobibor, for land reclamation work. There all trace of him vanishes; see Arnold Hindls, Einer kehrte zurück: Bericht eines Deportierten (Stuttgart, 1965), 25–26. The Munich deportee Jakob Liebschuetz wrote in mid-April 1942 that Sänger had requested him to serve in a work detail of sixty men; USHMM, RG-02.212; Acc. 1996.A.0551, Jakob Liebschuetz, Piaski, to Victor Bollag, 13 April 1942.

210. See Behrend-Rosenfeld, Ich stand nicht allein, 131ff.

211. USHMM, RG-02.212; Acc. 1996.A.0551, Jakob Liebschuetz, Piaski, to Victor Bollag, 13 April 1942; Sta München, Stanw. 29.499/1-3, 1 a Js 641/49, letter Senate President, Chief public prosecutor Munich I to Public prosecutor Weiss, 12 January 1950, p. 3, obverse.

212. Sta München, Stanw. 29.499/1-3, 1 Js 67 ff./49, Interrogation Siegfried Neuland, n.d., p. 1.

213. Sta München, Stanw. 29.499/1-3, 1 a Js 641/49, Interrogation Theodor Koronczyk, p. 1, obverse; p. 2, pag. 859.

214. Ibid., p. 2, obverse; p. 3, pag. 860.

215. Sta München, Stanw. 29.499/1-3, 1 a Js 641/49, Interrogation Franz Mugler, 15 December 1950, pag. 284. Mugler from the "Aryanization office" took pleasure in expatiating on the actually existing internal Jewish conflicts, blaming the Jews for punitive actions, etc. He stated that the "Aryanization office" had always sought to establish justice. Koronczyk testified that Hechinger had been ordered to present the Gestapo with the registry where the Geltungsjuden were listed; Sta München, Stanw. 29.499/1-3, 1 a Js 641/49, Interrogation Theodor Koronczyk, 30 January 1951, n.p., pag. 3.

216. Sta München, Stanw. 29.499/1-3, 1 a Js 641/49, Interrogation Kurt Kahn, 21 August 1950, p. 3.

217. Ibid., pp. 4ff.; confirmed by Sta München, Stanw. 29.499/1-3, 1 a Js 641/49, Interrogation Siegfried Bauer, 25 August 1950, p. 2; Sta München, Stanw. 29.499/1-3, 1 a Js 641/49, Interrogation Dietrich Lisberger, 5 September 1950, p. 3.

218. Sta München, Stanw. 29.499/1-3, 1 a Js 641/49, Interrogation Theodor Koronczyk v. 3o January 1951, pp. 2–3, pag. 313.

219. Sta München, Stanw. 29.499/1-3, 1 a Js 641/49, Interrogation Theodor Koronczyk, 26 September 1950, p. 1; see Strnad, Zwischenstation "Judensiedlung," 131ff.

220. Sta München, Stanw. 29.499/1-3, Interrogation Dietrich Lisberger, 5 September 1950, p. 3; the Memorial Book in the Federal Archive has no data on a Sabine Preiß.

221. Sta München, Spruchkammer, box 939, Theodor Koronczyk, witness Dr. Schwarz, p. 24 pag. 45; Koronczyk himself testified, without giving details, that the commission

had been dissolved in 1943 and in accordance with his suggestion, the coworkers had been sent to Theresienstadt; ibid., p. 25, pag. 46.

222. BArch, R 8150/114, letter, Jewish Community Stahl to representative of Gauleiter Wegner, 1 June 1942, pag. 95.

223. BArch, R 8150/114, letter, Kupfer/Spanier to Jewish Community, 31 May 1942, pag. 96.

224. BArch, R 8150/114, letter Jewish Community Stahl to Balzer, physicians' house, 1 June 1942, pag. 97; see also Sta München, Stanw. 29.499/1-3, 1 Js 67 ff./49, Interrogation Julius Spanier, 10 October 1950, pp. 1–2.

225. Sta München, Spruchkammer, box 939, Theodor Koronczyk, minutes of the public meeting, 29/30 October 1947, p. 17, pag. 42.

226. BArch, R 8150/114, Jewish Community Stahl to RVJD, 1 April 1942, pag. 102. The Lebensborn (Spring of Life) was a program set up by Heinrich Himmler to provide maternity homes and assistance to the wives of SS men; it also assisted unmarried "Aryan" mothers and ran some orphanages.

227. BArch, R 8150/114, internal memo, Cohn to RSHA and Eppstein, 24 February 1942, pag. 106.

228. Sta München, Stanw. 29.499/1-3, 1 Js 67 ff./49, Interrogation Theodor Koronczyk, 26 September 1950, p. 2, obverse; Sta München, Stanw. 29.499/1-3, 1 Js 67 ff./49, Interrogation Siegfried Neuland (n.d.), p. 2.

229. They were deported to Theresienstadt on 17 June 1942 and transported on 12 October 1944 to the Auschwitz extermination camp, where they perished; see www.bundesarchiv.de/gedenkbuch/index.html.en (accessed 1 August 2012).

230. Behrend-Rosenfeld, Ich stand nicht allein, 165ff.

231. Ibid., pp. 168–69.

232. Sta München, Spruchkammer, box 939, Theodor Koronczyk, Interrogation, 25 April 1947, p. 4, pag. 16.

233. Sta München, Spruchkammer, box 939, minutes, public meeting, 29/30 October 1947, p. 2, pag. 33.

234. Ibid., p. 3, pag. 34.

235. Wegner, "Abschluss- und Tätigkeitsbericht," p. 20.

236. Behrend-Rosenfeld, Ich stand nicht allein, 175ff.

237. BArch, R 8150/67, explanations on the April 1943 final calculations, pag. 71.

238. Sta München, Stanw. 29.499/1-3, 1 Js 67 ff./49, Interrogation Almuth Mezger, 5 September 1950, pp. 1–2.

239. BArch, R 8150/51, letter RVJD to district court Nuremberg, 7 October 1942, pag. 167.

240. BArch, R 8150/51, report RVJD Fabian, 3 March 1943, pag. 166.

241. Sta München, Stanw. 29.499/1-3, 1 a Js 641/49, Interrogation Theodor Koronczyk, n.d., p. 1, n. pag., n.d.

242. Sta München, Stanw. 29.499/1-3, 1 a Js 641/49, Interrogation Erna Lauchner, 2 October 1950, p. 1.

243. Sta München, Stanw. 29.499/1-3, 1 a Js 641/49, Interrogation Clementine Grube, 25 October 1950, p. 6, minutes of interrogation, several interrogations of witnesses.

244. Sta München, Spruchkammer, box 939, Theodor Koronczyk, public meeting, 29/30 October 1947, p. 3, pag. 34; in fact, in February 1945, Jews deported from Munich, including the Augsburg Jews, numbered as follows: fourteen (14 February), fifty-two (22 February), and thirty-one (23 February); see Gottwaldt and Schulle, "Judendeportationen," 467.

245. On the first concept, see Kurt Grosmann, "Zeugnisse menschlicher Tapferkeit im Dritten Reich," in Lamm, *Juden in München*, 346; on the second, "Jewish Gestapo informer," see Erich Kasberger, "Hans Wegner und Theodor Koronczyk—zwei Pole des Täterspektrums," in *Rechte Karrieren in München: Von der Weimarer Zeit bis in die Nachkriegsgeschichte*, ed. Marita Krauss (Munich, 2010), 230. Kasberger defines Koronczyk as someone "moving across the border between victim and perpetrator," who survived thanks to his collaboration with the Gestapo. However, Kasberger does not illuminate any further the individual "offenses" Koronczyk is accused of, and in addition confounds his activity with that of Hechinger (e.g., in the use of planes, deportations).

246. Sta München, Spruchkammer, box 939, Theodor Koronczyk, witness Dr. Schwarz, p. 24, pag. 45.

247. Sta München, Spruchkammer, box 939, Theodor Koronczyk, witness Neuland, p. 25, pag. 46; on Neuland, see http://goo.gl/rN9xf (accessed 4 August 2012).

248. Seidel, "Jüdische Gemeinde," 53.

249. See, e.g., Bajohr, *Parvenüs*, 71, 113–14, 180, 229; Peter Hüttenberger, *Die Gauleiter: Studie zum Wandel des Machtgefüges in der NSDAP* (Stuttgart, 1969), 201ff.; Ophir and Wiesemann, *Die jüdischen Gemeinden*, 212–13.

250. YV, 02/551, Bernhard Kolb, "Die Juden in Nürnberg: Tausendjährige Geschichte einer Judengemeinde von ihren Anfängen bis zum Einmarsch der Amerikanischen Truppen am 20 April 1945," Nuremberg 1946, p. 58.

251. See, inter alia, Bajohr, *Parvenüs*, 108ff.; Hüttenberger, *Gauleiter*, 218–19.

252. See Utho Grieser, *Himmlers Mann in Nürnberg: Der Fall Benno Martin: Eine Studie zur Struktur des Dritten Reiches in der "Stadt der Reichsparteitage"* (Nuremberg, 1974); see also Edith Raim, "Strafverfahren wegen der Deportation der Juden aus Unter- und Mittelfranken nach 1945," in *Wege in die Vernichtung: Die Deportation der Juden aus Mainfranken 1941–1943*, ed. Generaldirektion der staatlichen Archive Bayerns (Munich, 2003), 182ff.

253. Staatsarchiv (Sta) Nürnberg, Staatsanwaltschaften bei der LG Nürnberg-Fürth, No. 3070/II, transcript of affidavit, Walter Berlin, 27 August 1947 (character reference).

254. Ibid., pp. 4–5.

255. Ibid., p. 5.

256. On Kolb, see Adler, *Theresienstadt*, 763–64.

257. Sta Nürnberg, Staatsanwaltschaften bei dem LG Nürnberg-Fürth, 3070/I, copy of affidavit by Bernhard Kolb, 18 June 1946.

258. LA Berlin, B Rep 058, 1 Js/9/65, box 77, Beistück 68II, KS 6/51 (Kls 230/48), Sta Nürnberg-Fürth, case against Grafenberger et al., transcript main proceedings, 9 March 1949, p. 74.

259. See Leibl Rosenberg, *Spuren und Fragmente: Jüdische Bücher, jüdische Schicksale in Nürnberg* (Nuremberg, 2000), 144–45.

260. Ibid., 142–43.

261. Ibid., 96–97, 144.

262. Ophir and Wiesemann, *Die jüdischen Gemeinden*, 215; see also Christiane Kohl, *Der Jude und das Mädchen: Eine verbotene Freundschaft in Nazideutschland* (Hamburg, 1997).

263. See Müller, *Juden in Nürnberg*, 270.

264. YV, 02/551, WL P. IIe. No. 765, Kolb, "Die Juden in Nürnberg," p. 58. Kolb reports here that the still relatively opulent Nuremberg Jewish Community had wished to cover the total expenses for its emigrants, and the Berlin RV central office was solely to arrange for space on steamships, but this was rejected.

265. YV, 02/53, Else Dormitzer, "Experiences in Nuremberg, Holland, Theresienstadt," p. 1.

266. See Gruner, *Öffentliche Wohlfahrt,* 275–76.

267. Sta Nürnberg, Staatsanwaltschaften bei dem LG Nürnberg-Fürth, 3070/I, transcript of affidavit by Bernhard Kolb, 18 June 1946; see also YV, 02/551, WL P. IIe. No.765, Kolb, "Die Juden in Nürnberg," p. 60.

268. YV, 02/551, WL P. IIe. No.765, Kolb, "Die Juden in Nürnberg," p. 59.

269. BArch, R 8150, correspondence between district branch Bavaria and RVJD Berlin, various letters regarding the sale, pag. 179–94. The Deutscher Siedlerbund (League of German Settlers) was a housing association and under the supervision of the Nazi Party.

270. YV, 02/551, WL P. IIe. No. 765, Kolb, "Die Juden in Nürnberg," p. 60; Sta Nürnberg, Staatsanwaltschaften bei dem LG Nürnberg-Fürth, 3070/V, transcript of proceedings, 7 March 1949, p. 70; see also Müller, *Juden in Nürnberg,* 280–95.

271. YV, 02/551, WL P. IIe. No. 765, Kolb, "Die Juden in Nürnberg," pp. 60–61; regarding religious services, see YV, 02/387, Bernhard Kolb, "Deportation from Nuremberg."

272. Sta Nürnberg, Staatsanwaltschaften bei dem LG Nürnberg-Fürth, 3070/XV, Interrogation Lydia Finkler, 5 August 1948.

273. On the Fürth Jewish Community, 1939–1945, see ZAGJD, B 8 Fürth (*Mitteilungsblatt*), Israelitische Kultusgemeinde Fürth, September 1995, pp. 25–34.

274. ZAGJD, B 1/19, No. 333, Mitteilungen Nr. 20/41 der Israelitischen Kultusgemeinde Nürnberg, 23 November 1941; there also an instruction sheet, dated 23 November 1941, regarding what had to be taken care of prior to transport, and baggage particulars; ZAGJD, B 1/19, No. 333, call for equipping Minsk ghetto, 13 November 1941.

275. Sta Nürnberg, Staatsanwaltschaften bei dem LG Nürnberg-Fürth, 3070/II, investigation report, state prosecutor's office, n.d., p. 11, pag. 11.

276. LAB, B Rep 058, 1 Js 9/65, box 77, Beistücke II, Staatsanwaltschaft Nürnberg-Fürth, transcript of main proceedings, 9 March 1949, pp. 37–40, 96.

277. YV, 02/387a, letter Bernhard Kolb to Yad Vashem, Baruch Z. Ophir, 1 September 1960, p. 1.

278. Sta Nürnberg, Staatsanwaltschaften bei dem LG Nürnberg-Fürth, 3070/VII, Interrogation Fichtner, 9 August 1948; Sta Nürnberg, Staatsanwaltschaften bei dem LG Nürnberg-Fürth, 3070/VII, letter Kolb to district court, 26 April 1949, pag. 677ff.; YV, 02/551, WL P. IIe. No. 765, Kolb, "Die Juden in Nürnberg," p. 68; YV, 02/387a, letter Kolb to Ophir, 1 September 1960, pp. 1–3; see also Institut Theresienstädter Initiative, *Theresienstädter Gedenkbuch,* 320.

279. Ophir and Wiesemann, *Die jüdischen Gemeinden,* 215-16.

280. YV, 02/387, WL P. III Theresienstadt no. 520, Kolb, diary fragment, 1943, p. 1.

281. Ibid., p. 2.

282. YV, 02/387, Kolb, "Deportation," p. 5.

283. Ibid., p. 1.

284. Sta Nürnberg, Staatsanwaltschaften bei dem LG Nürnberg-Fürth, 3070/I, letter Julius Nürnberger to investigating judge, 6 August 1948, pag. 303.

285. YV, 02/387, Kolb, "Deportation," p. 2.

286. On the figures, see Herbert Lehnert, *Juden in Nürnberg,* ed. Stadt Nürnberg (Nuremberg, 1993), 52; Müller, *Juden in Nürnberg,* 295; Ophir and Wiesemann, *Die jüdischen Gemeinden,* 203, 215–16.

287. Ophir and Wiesemann, *Die jüdischen Gemeinden,* 217; see also http://goo.gl/ljOzl (accessed 3 July 2012), with a photo of twenty-nine survivors at the former *Judenhaus* on

Wielandstr. 6 in the summer of 1945, including Kolb, Fechheimer, and Nürnberger, on p. 12.

288. See, for example, the interrogations of Paul Baruch, Ernst Dingfelder, Albert Ehrhardt, and Leopold Friedländer, who were members of forced labor details; Sta Nürnberg, Staatsanwaltschaften bei dem LG Nürnberg-Fürth, 3070/V.

289. On deportations from Mainz and the smaller towns and localities nearby, see Michael Brodhaecker, *Menschen zwischen Hoffnung und Verzweiflung: Der Alltag jüdischer Mitmenschen in Rheinhessen, Mainz und Worms während des "Dritten Reiches"* (Mainz, 1999), 389–408. I am grateful to Monica Kingreen for calling my attention to the posthumous papers of Oppenheim.

290. Municipal Archive Mainz, posthumous papers Oppenheim, 51/19, Oppenheim, "Über meine Tätigkeit als Verbindungsmann zwischen der Reichsvereinigung der Juden in Deutschland, Bezirksstelle Hessen in Mainz und der Geheimen Staatspolizei," pp. 1–2, 5.

291. Ibid., p. 2.

292. Municipal Archive Mainz, posthumous papers Oppenheim, 51/19, various letters re: emigration. His son was able to emigrate to the United States.

293. Municipal Archive Mainz, posthumous papers Oppenheim, 51/16, letter Oppenheim to Mainz Jewish Community, 29 July 1942.

294. Municipal Archive Mainz, posthumous papers Oppenheim, 51/19, Oppenheim, "Über meine Tätigkeit," pp. 6–7.

295. Ibid., pp. 13–14.

296. Municipal Archive Mainz, posthumous papers Oppenheim, 52/27, letter Oppenheim to unknown addressee, 11 May 1943.

297. Municipal Archive Mainz, posthumous papers Oppenheim, 51/19, Oppenheim, "Über meine Tätigkeit," pp. 14–15.

298. Municipal Archive Mainz, posthumous papers Oppenheim, 51/16; this is clear from the transcript of the board meeting of the Mainz Jewish Community, 1 July 1942. Both were deported on 25 March 1942 to Piaski. Kugelmann was murdered in Majdanek; see www.bundesarchiv.de/gedenkbuch/index.html.en (accessed 4 August 2012).

299. Document reproduced in Brodhaecker, *Menschen*, 392.

300. LBI, JMB, II 11, Helmut Grünfeld, "Erinnerungen eines Davongekommenen," written 1 September 1988, p. 6.

301. Municipal Archive Mainz, posthumous papers Oppenheim, 51/19, Oppenheim, "Über meine Tätigkeit," p. 7.

302. Municipal Archive Mainz, posthumous papers Oppenheim, 49/3, memo, No. 136, 27 March 1942, point 6.

303. Municipal Archive Mainz, posthumous papers Oppenheim, 51/19, Oppenheim, "Über meine Tätigkeit," p. 7.

304. Municipal Archive Mainz, posthumous papers Oppenheim, 52/25 district branch Hesse/Hesse-Nassau of RVJD, administrative office Hesse, 4 December 1942.

305. Fritz Löwensberg was deported to Theresienstadt in February 1942 and died there on 25 February 1944; see www.bundesarchiv.de/gedenkbuch/index.html.en (accessed 4 August 2012). On Oppenheim's appointment, see Municipal Archive Mainz, posthumous papers Oppenheim, 51/19, Oppenheim, "Über meine Tätigkeit," pp. 8–9.

306. Municipal Archive Mainz, posthumous papers Oppenheim, 51/19, Oppenheim, "Über meine Tätigkeit," pp. 3–4.

307. Ibid., p. 13.

308. Ibid., p. 12.

309. Municipal Archive Mainz, posthumous papers Oppenheim, 22, regarding the merger of district branches Hesse and Hesse-Nassau; Municipal Archive Mainz, posthumous papers Oppenheim, 22, letter RVJD district branch Hesse/Hesse-Nassau to RVJD Berlin, 19 February 1943.

310. Municipal Archive Mainz, posthumous papers Oppenheim, 22, letter Oppenheim to Lerner, 28 April 1943; see also Municipal Archive Mainz, posthumous papers Oppenheim, 52/29, letter Oppenheim to Levy, 3 May 1943; see also Municipal Archive Mainz, posthumous papers Oppenheim, 51/19, Oppenheim, "Über meine Tätigkeit," p. 9; on Georg Albert Dengler and his own initiatives against Jews, see the judgment against him, reproduced in *Justiz und NS-Verbrechen: Sammlung deutscher Strafurteile wegen nationalsozialistischer Tötungsverbrechen 1945–1966*, vol. 22, ed. C. F. Rüter and Dick W. De Mildt (Amsterdam, 1981), 658–82.

311. Municipal Archive Mainz, posthumous papers Oppenheim, letter Oppenheim to Lerner 28 April 1943, p. 2.

312. Municipal Archive Mainz, posthumous papers Oppenheim, letter Oppenheim to C.I.C., 20 June 1945, p. 2–3.

313. Ibid., p. 6.

314. Municipal Archive Mainz, posthumous papers Oppenheim, 49/3, memo No. 136, 27 March 1942, point 2.

315. Municipal Archive Mainz, posthumous papers Oppenheim, 51/19, Oppenheim, "Über meine Tätigkeit," p. 15; see also Municipal Archive Mainz, posthumous papers Oppenheim, letter Oppenheim to C.I.C., 20 June 1945, pp. 5ff.

316. Municipal Archive Mainz, posthumous papers Oppenheim, letter Oppenheim to C.I.C., 20 June 1945, pp. 5ff.; Municipal Archive Mainz, posthumous papers Oppenheim, 50/II, affidavit re: Meta Schulz, 28 September 1955; Municipal Archive Mainz, posthumous papers Oppenheim, letter Oppenheim to military government Mainz, n.d., p. 3; Municipal Archive Mainz, posthumous papers Oppenheim, 46, Oppenheim, "Bericht über die Gründe, durch die verhindert wurde, dass die auch für den Bereich der Stapo-Außendienststelle Mainz im Februar 1945 angeordnete zwangsweise Evakuierung der letzten Juden zur Durchführung kam" [Report on the reasons why the forced evacuation of the last Jews also ordered for the area of the Gestapo external office Mainz in February 1945 was not implemented], p. 1.

317. Municipal Archive Mainz, posthumous papers Oppenheim, 51/19, Oppenheim, "Über meine Tätigkeit," pp. 1–4; see also Municipal Archive Mainz, posthumous papers Oppenheim, letter Oppenheim to C.I.C., 20 June 1945, p. 7. Mainz was captured by American troops under General Patton on 22 March 1945.

318. Figures are found in Municipal Archive Mainz, posthumous papers Oppenheim, 49/9, 49/1, letter Oppenheim to C.I.C., 20 June 1945, p. 5. It is difficult to ascertain the precise figures for deportation, because along with the Mainz Jews, the Jews from nearby cities were also deported, and all of these were then included in larger transports.

319. See also Beate Meyer, "Max Plaut," in *Hamburgische Biographie: Personenlexikon*, vol. 1, ed. Franklin Kopitzsch and Dirk Brietzke (Hamburg, 2001), 238–39; Beate Meyer, "Gestörte Beziehungen: Die Kommunikation zwischen Repräsentanten und (Zwangs)Mitgliedern der Reichsvereinigung der Juden in Deutschland nach der Befreiung," in *Aus den Quellen: Festschrift für Ina Lorenz zum 65. Geburtstag*, ed. Andreas Brämer, Stefanie Schüler-Springorum, and Michael Studemund-Halevy (Hamburg, 2005), 374ff.

320. With reference to Witte, see Frank Bajohr, "'… dann bitte keine Gefühlsduseleien': Die Hamburger und die Deportationen," in *Die Deportation der Hamburger Juden*

1941–1945, ed. Research Center for Contemporary History and Institute for the History of the German Jews (Hamburg, 2002), 13–15.

321. See Linde Apel, ed., *In den Tod geschickt: Die Deportationen von Juden, Roma und Sinti aus Hamburg 1940 bis 1945* (Berlin, 2009), 248.

322. Bajohr, "Keine Gefühlsduseleien," 14ff.; on Seetzen, see http://goo.gl/42f8z (accessed 10 July 2012).

323. BArch, R 8150/37, List District Branches Reichsvereinigung, n.d., probably late 1942, pag. 106; BArch, R 8150/51, report RVJD Levy to RSHA, 29 December 1942, report Lilienthal to RSHA, 1 June 1942, pag. 255.

324. Max Plaut, "Die Deportationsmaßnahmen der Geheimen Staatspolizei in Hamburg," in *Die jüdischen Opfer des Nationalsozialismus in Hamburg*, ed. Hamburg State Archive (Hamburg, 1965), xi; see Leo Lippmann, *Mein Leben und meine amtliche Tätigkeit: Erinnerungen und ein Beitrag zur Finanzgeschichte Hamburgs* (Hamburg, 1964), 640–41.

325. LBI, NY, AR 7183, Max Kreutzberger, box 7, folder 9, MM reels 129, Interview Kreutzberger/Plaut, 14 June 1960, p. 5.

326. IGdJ, 14-001.2, interview Christel Riecke with Max Plaut, conducted 1973, "Die Jüdische Gemeinde in Hamburg 1933–1943," cassette 1, p. 2, transcript, p. 2; LBI, NY, AR 7183, Max Kreutzberger, box 7, folder 9, interview Lowenthal with Plaut, p. 2.

327. IGdJ, 14-001.2, interview Riecke/Plaut, cassette 1, p. 1, transcript, p. 2.

328. IGdJ, 14-001.2, interview Riecke/Plaut, cassette 1, p. 1, transcript, p. 10.

329. FZH, persecution of the Jews/reports, transcript Schottelius, 25 January 1954, pp. 6–7.

330. YV, 01/53, Max Plaut, "Die Juden in Deutschland von 1939 bis 1941," p. 6; see also chapter 1, "A Jewish Reservation in Lublin."

331. YV, 01/53, Max Plaut, "Die Juden in Deutschland von 1939 bis 1941," pp. 4–5; on the East Frisian Jews, see chapter 1, "A Jewish Reservation in Lublin."

332. See Beate Meyer, "Die Arbeit des Jüdischen Religionsverbandes zur Zeit der Deportationen," in *Die Verfolgung und Ermordung der Hamburger Juden: Geschichte, Zeugnis, Erinnerung*, ed. Beate Meyer (Göttingen and Hamburg, 2006), 45–52.

333. See Leo Lippmann, "*… dass ich wie ein guter Deutscher empfinde und handele*": *Zur Geschichte der Deutsch-Israelitischen Gemeinde in Hamburg in der Zeit vom Herbst 1935 bis zum Ende 1942* (Hamburg, 1993), 90.

334. See Jürgen Sieleman, "Die Deportation aus Hamburg und Schleswig-Holstein am 6. Dez 1941, Hamburg," in Scheffler and Schulle, *Buch der Erinnerung*, 2:599. One thousand of these Polish Jews had already been deported in 1938.

335. YV, 01/53, Max Plaut, "Die Juden in Deutschland 1941–1943," p. 20; see chapter 1.

336. A report by Plaut also contains a list of the target group for the first transport, whose guidelines are no longer extant: Jews from the parts of the *Altreich* belonging to Germany until 1918, all naturalized Eastern European Jews, all stateless Jews, and all those unpopular with the Gestapo, along with their families and relatives by blood or marriage, could volunteer for the transport; see Plaut, "Deportationsmaßnahmen," xi.

337. StaHH, 522-1 Jüdische Gemeinden, section 1993, folder 22 op.

338. LBI, NY, AR 7183, Max Kreutzberger, box 7, folder 9, MM reels 129, Interview Kreutzberger/Plaut, 14 June 1960, p. 15.

339. BArch, R 8150/51, letter Plaut to RVJD main office, 12 March 1943.

340. LBI, NY, AR 7183, Max Kreutzberger, box 7, folder 9, MM reels 129, interview Kreutzberger/Plaut, 14 June 1960, p. 2. "By that juncture" refers to the date of the official liquidation of the Reichsvereinigung, 10 June 1943.

341. Ibid., p. 3.
342. IGdJ, 14-001.2, interview Riecke/Plaut, cassette 1, p. 2, transcript, p. 14.
343. See postcards with expressions of gratitude from the Jewish functionaries assisted, StaHH, reproduced in facsimile in Meyer, "'Altersghetto,'" 125–51.
344. Käthe Starke, *Der Führer schenkt den Juden eine Stadt: Bilder, Impressionen, Reportagen, Dokumente* (Berlin, 1975), 23. Käthe Starke-Goldschmidt (1905–1990) was deported to Theresienstadt; she survived and managed to bring the *Theresienstadt-Konvolut*, a unique typewritten bundle of ninety-two biographies of prominent prisoners, and other materials (drawings, watercolors) to safety after liberation; see Altonaer Museum, *Das Theresienstadt-Konvolut*, ed. Axel Feuss (Hamburg, 2002).
345. Starke, *Der Führer*, 26.
346. According to "Verschubliste" [list of shuntings], 3 May 1944, USHMM/ITS, 2.1.1.1, Central Name Index, Plaut, Form 10, 11 February 1948, folder 739, doc. 70005659.
347. On relocation from Laufen, see Naftali Oppenheim, *The Chosen People: The Story of the "222 Transport" from Bergen-Belsen to Palestine* (London and Portland, 1996), 75, 192.
348. StaHH, 522-1, Jüdische Gemeinden, section 1993, folder 39, Abschiedbrief [farewell letter] Plaut, 24 January 1944. The biblical quote is from Genesis 31:40; see Jewish Publication Society, *The Holy Scriptures*.
349. See report (author probably Corten), in Ina Lorenz, "Die dunklen und die schweren Jahre (1933–1945)," in *150 Jahre Israelitisches Krankenhaus Hamburg*, ed. Israelitisches Krankenhaus Hamburg (Hamburg, 1997), 83.
350. On this, see Meyer, "Gestörte Beziehungen," 366–77.
351. See, for example, Astrid Louven, "'Die Belmonte-Brüder sind tot'—Die Familie Belmonte," in Sybille Baumbach, Susanne Lohmeyer, Astrid Louven, Beate Meyer, Sielke Salomon, and Dagmar Wienrich, *"Wo Wurzeln waren …": Juden in Hamburg-Eimsbüttel 1933–1945*, ed. Galerie Morgenland (Hamburg, 1993), 142–46. "KolaFu" was an abbreviation for Konzentrationslager Fuhlsbüttel.
352. FZH, persecution of Jews/reports, interview Schottelius/Plaut, 11 July 1953, p. 2.
353. Plaut, "Deportationsmaßnahmen," xiii.
354. StaHH, 213-11, Strafsachen 6669/64, Hermann Kühn, Verf. 14 Js 829/48. Hermann Kühn was one of Göttsche's most notorious henchmen, known among Hamburg Jews as the "bloodhound" for his brutality; see www1.uni-hamburg.de/rz3a035//kuehn.html (accessed 5 July 2012). On Martin Starke, an Auschwitz survivor, and his later wife Käthe Goldschmidt, see http://tinyurl.com/79rf5vx (accessed 5 June 2012).
355. FZH, persecution of Jews/reports, interview Schottelius/Plaut, 11 July 1953, p. 7.
356. Ibid., pp. 1–2.
357. IGdJ, 14-001.2, Interview Riecke/Plaut, cassette 1, p. 2, transcript, p. 9.
358. LBI, NY, AR 7183, Max Kreutzberger, box 7, folder 9, MM reels 129, Interview Kreutzberger/Plaut, 14 June 1960, p. 2.
359. YV, 01/53, Plaut, "Die Juden in Deutschland von 1933–1941," p. 10.
360. LBI, NY, AR 7183, Max Kreutzberger, box 7, folder 9, MM reels 129, Interview Kreutzberger/Plaut, 14 June 1960, p. 17.
361. On Corten and Heinemann, see Institut für die Geschichte der deutschen Juden, ed., *Das Jüdische Hamburg: Ein historisches Nachschlagewerk* (Göttingen, 2006), 50–51, 111.
362. StaHH, 522-2, Jüdische Gemeinden, 61, letter Bruck to Berkowitz, Hanover, 26 September 1944, enclosure, letter Bruck to Corten, 25 October 1944.
363. Oppenheim, *Chosen People*, 103; for the list where Plaut, his mother, and an acquaintance are included, see ibid., 192.

364. See Beate Meyer, "Max Plaut," in *Institut für die Geschichte der deutschen Juden 2003–2008*, ed. Institut für die Geschichte der deutschen Juden (Hamburg, 2009), 54.

365. Adler, *Der verwaltete Mensch*, 354–55.

366. Aside from those mentioned, one example was the liaison for Bielefeld, Louis Sternberg, who gave "good marks" to Peters, his *Judensachbearbeiter* (special consultant for Jews), emphasizing his "humane attitude"; Hess. HStA Wiesbaden, 461/30983, according to Oberstaatsanwalt Bielefeld, memo, 25 March 1965, pp. 11–12. It later turned out that Sternberg had confirmed Peters' "humane attitude," but Peters had removed Sternberg's paragraphs on the brutality of the deportation; ZAGJD, Heidelberg, *Jüdisches Gemeindeblatt/Allgemeine Wochenzeitung*, shelf no. 296.05, 7 October 1949, p. 10. Louis Elkan from Düsseldorf testified that the Gestapo and the Jewish Community there had made the work mutually easier, expressing the concept of a "good amicable arrangement" (*gutes Einvernehmen*); YV, 01/150, WL P. II e, Louis Elkan, "Die Synagogengemeinde Düsseldorf nach dem Pogrom," written September 1956, p. 3.

367. Institute for Municipal History, Frankfurt am Main, Chroniken S 5/184, Nr. 54/1963, "Erinnerungen des Heinrich Baab ehem: SS-Untersturmführer und Kriminalsekretär an die Zeit 1937–1945 in Frankfurt a. M." [Memoirs of former SS-Untersturmführer Heinrich Baab, 1937–1945, Frankfurt], ms, p. 25.

368. NRW HStA Düsseldorf, Gestapo, RW 58 Nr. 3429, Interrogation Blankenstein by Gestapo, 22 September 1941, pag. 6.

369. Barbara Suchy, "'Schreckenstein' in Lenne? Über Zwangsarbeit von 'Mischehe': Juden aus Düsseldorf in der Endphase des Zweiten Weltkrieges—Ein Fallbeispiel," in *Zwangsarbeit: Für Industrie und Rüstung im Hils 1943–1945*, vol. 4, ed. Detlef Creydt (Holzminden, 2001), 280.

370. LBI, NY, AR 7094, Plaut, letter, Max Plaut to spouse and B. Lippmann, 18 December 1944.

371. See Ingo Köhler, *Die "Arisierung" der Privatbanken im Dritten Reich: Verdrängung, Ausschaltung und die Frage der Wiedergutmachung* (Munich, 2005), 258.

372. See Holger Berschel, *Bürokratie und Terror: Das Judenreferat der Gestapo Düsseldorf 1935–1945* (Essen, 2001), 161–62; Herbert Schmidt, *Der Elendsweg der Düsseldorfer Juden: Chronologie des Schreckens 1933–1945* (Düsseldorf, 2005), 157, 217, 271.

373. NRW HStA Düsseldorf, Außenstelle Schloss Kalkum, Gerichte Rep. 372 Nr. 83 (Waldbillig), Interrogation "Stadtverordneter" Rudolf Braunschweig, 19 September 1947, pag. 22; NRW HStA Düsseldorf, Außenstelle Schloss Kalkum, Gerichte Rep. 372 Nr. 83 (Waldbillig), letter Kurt Frank (from detention) to his wife, 20 April 1944; NRW HStA Düsseldorf, Außenstelle Schloss Kalkum, Gerichte Rep. 372 Nr. 83 (Waldbillig) NRW HStA Düsseldorf, Außenstelle Schloss Kalkum, Gerichte Rep. 372 Nr. 83 (Waldbillig), Interrogation widow Spier, 16 October 1947, pag. 25; NRW HStA Düsseldorf, Außenstelle Schloss Kalkum, Gerichte Rep. 372 Nr. 83 (Waldbillig), Interrogation Bernt Engelmann, 5 November 1948, pag. 372.

374. NRW HStA Düsseldorf, Gerichte 372/86 Ermittlungen gegen Pütz [Investigation against Pütz], Interrogation Rudolf Braunschweig, 5 July 1947, pag. 27, obverse.

375. BArch, R 8150/36, memo RVJD central office Kleemann, 24 February 1945.

376. BArch, R 8150/53, Statistische Übersicht (Statistical Overview), 1–31 January 1943.

377. BArch, R 8150/51, letter district branch Brandenburg-East Prussia to RVJD, 15 March 1943, pag. 169; BArch, R 8150/51, report Fabian re Hesse/Hesse-Nassau, 19 March 1943, pag. 179; BArch, R 8150/51, report Fabian re Central Germany, 22 March 1943, pag. 220; BArch, R 8150/51, report Fabian re Westphalia, 22 March

1943, pag. 221; BArch, R 8150/53, div. announcements of changes in the district branches.

378. NRW Sta Münster, 5 Js 192/62, Interrogation Siegmund Emanuel Hadda, 22 October 1964, pp. 2–3, pag. 663–64.

379. StaHH 522-1, Jüdische Gemeinden section 1993, folder 36, letter Plaut, n.d.

380. My own list, based on: BArch, R 8150/64, Personalaufstellung zum Etat (Bezirksstellen), Anhang zum Voranschlag des Etats der Reichsvereinigung der Juden in Deutschland für das erste Halbjahr 1941 [Personnel list for budget district branches, first half year 1941], with cover letter, 6 December 1940, pag. 56–61. The lists are incomplete; they provide in the main a momentary snapshot and do not include the changes among the Jewish representatives. The fate of those not mentioned here can be found in comments in the footnotes on individuals in this chapter. I do not include individual documentation for data in the column "subsequent fate."

381. BArch, R 8150/50, list of 24 May 1942, pag. 7ff.

382. Erna Maas, born 14 January 1910, emigrated 19 May 1941 to New York via Lisbon, information from Hess. HStA (GZ 6.1.2.550-(0000)), 1 December 2009.

383. According to the Institut Theresienstädter Initiative database. Information thanks to Anna Hájková.

Chapter 4

THE RESIDUAL REICHSVEREINIGUNG

The successor organization to the officially dissolved Reichsvereinigung, the Residual or New Reichsvereinigung (Rest-Reichsvereinigung), took up its work in June 1943. It addressed the needs of the nondeported members of the old RV who lived in mixed marriages, as well as the other Jews in such marriages who had not been members of the previous organization. The new Jewish functionaries, termed *Vertrauensmänner* or intermediaries, had to cope with a similar burden of work as their predecessors, but now were in smaller offices with reduced personnel, and had to grapple with this under the grueling conditions of the intensified air war and the limitations imposed by the "total war" that Goebbels had proclaimed in February 1943. On the other hand, the mounting chaos caused by the war also generated possibilities for eluding some of the constraints of constant control or refusing certain assigned tasks.

The Last Compulsory Members: Jews in Mixed Marriages

This rump Reichsvereinigung was focused in the main on regulating the affairs of the Jews in mixed marriages. In National Socialism, the concept of mixed marriage did not designate, as in the Weimar Republic, a marriage between spouses of different religions, but rather a union in which the marriage partners were from "different races."

Before 1933, some 35,000 Jews had lived in mixed marriages defined in this way in the German Reich. Many of these families left Germany in the first two emigration waves in 1933 and 1935, especially if they had children. The 1935 Nuremberg legislation prohibited new mixed marriages. Their number thus sank in 1939/1940 to 20,454; in December 1942, the statisticians counted 16,760 such marriages, virtually unchanged in April 1943 at 16,658. In September 1944, that figure had shrunk by a quarter to only 12,487 mixed marriages across the Reich.[1]

In December 1938, mixed marriages were subdivided into "privileged" and "nonprivileged."[2] The category of "privileged" mixed marriages included those with a Jewish wife married to a non-Jewish husband, irrespective of whether the marriage was childless or had non-Jewish children. Couples with a Jewish husband and non-Jewish wife and children raised as non-Jews were also able to apply for the preferred status of "privileged marriage," which (temporarily) protected persons from deportation, as long as the marriage was in existence. In many localities, an additional requirement was that the children also had to be living within the German Reich, that is, in some regions in Germany, the category of "privileged" could not be applied to a mixed marriage if the children had emigrated. If a "privileged" mixed marriage had been ended by divorce or death of a spouse, but minor children still lived with the Jewish mother, she could expect that she would not be deported before the youngest child had reached the age of eighteen (the age was reduced to sixteen years toward the war's end, and in some places fourteen years).

However, if the children of such a mixed union were members of a Jewish Community, they were classified under the category of *Geltungsjuden* (persons considered as Jews). They offered no protection for their Jewish parent. The *Geltungsjuden* were themselves deported beginning in 1943, and if they were married to a non-Jewish partner, their marriage was treated as a mixed marriage and also subclassified into "privileged" and "nonprivileged."

A mixed marriage was classified as "nonprivileged" if the husband was Jewish and the marriage childless or, as mentioned, if there were children from the union who had been raised as Jews. Until 1943/1944, Jews in "privileged" and "nonprivileged" marriages had, with some delay, suffered under most of the anti-Jewish measures also applied to other "full Jews." However, the Jewish partners in "privileged" mixed marriages were exempted from the obligation to wear the "yellow star," unless they worked in a Jewish organization. Then they were required to wear the star during their working hours.

A number of National Socialist officials and others sought to convince the non-Jewish partners in mixed marriages that the wisest decision was to divorce: this ensemble of persons trying to persuade them included Gestapo personnel, Nazi Party local and district heads, their civilian and military superiors, and private individuals as well, such as landlords, employers, neighbors, sometimes even relatives. To bolster this, National Socialist marriage law offered new options for a simplified divorce in the case of "racial mixed marriages."[3] The greater majority of non-Jewish marriage partners chose not to use this option, but somewhere between 10 and 25 percent divorced.

Jews in "privileged" mixed marriages only had to belong to the Reichsvereinigung if they had been members of a Jewish Community before 1939. Baptized Jews or Jews from such marriages who had left their Jewish Community and called themselves "dissidents" were not obligated to be RV members. Although the Reichsvereinigung was the principal source of information regarding orders and prohibitions, a certain proportion of Jews in mixed marriages kept their distance from the organization where feasible and for as long as possible. This notwithstanding, the Reichsvereinigung also had to include nonmembers in its card file and report on their affairs.

At least from the time of the Wannsee Conference in January 1942 and the follow-up conferences in 1942/1943, the couples in mixed marriages lived under a cloud of constant fear. At these conferences, along with the "Final Solution" of the European "Jewish Question," the fate of the Jews in mixed marriages in the German Reich (and the fate of "racially" hybrid Mischlinge) had been deliberated on, although (fortunately) no agreement could be reached.[4] One possibility envisioned including the Jewish spouses in the policy of annihilation, and in individual cases deciding between deportation or, with an eye to the relatives "with German blood," assignment to an "old age ghetto." Another idea considered compulsory divorce as the general rule to be imposed, and if the couples should adamantly refuse, both spouses would be sent to a ghetto. However, a decision on the future of mixed marriages was postponed until after the end of the war. The Jews affected remained uninformed about the details in these deliberations, but they were able to read the mounting dangers they faced, ominously reflected in the intensification of policies against those in mixed marriages and Mischlinge. Among such measures were the relocation of persons in "nonprivileged" mixed marriages into Judenhäuser, mass arrests in the course of the "Factory Operation" (February 1943), and the increasing number of Jews in mixed marriages who were accused of "criminal offenses" of various kinds, such as violations of anti-Jewish regulations like the wearing of the "yellow star." The latter were then often not included in a deportation transport, but rather from the autumn of 1942 were sent to Auschwitz, primarily as "prisoners in protective custody," so-called Schutzhäftlinge.

After nearly all the nonprotected Jews had been deported by the summer of 1943, with a small number of exceptions, the Jews in mixed marriages were the last group of "full Jews" still living in the German Reich, aside from those Jews with foreign nationality whom the National Socialist state, out of consideration for its allies, still protected or wished possibly to utilize in a future exchange. The Nazi state now turned its attention to these remaining *Volljuden*.

Structure and Tasks of the Residual Reichsvereinigung

Like its predecessor organization, the New or Residual Reichsvereinigung was subordinate to the RSHA.[5] Only those living in a mixed marriage could become functionaries in the new organization. The central office remained in Berlin and was subordinate there, like the previous RV, to the Berlin Gestapo as well.

The assets of the predecessor organization were transferred to the Residual RV, but were administered by the regional finance office in each *Gau*. Hospitals, nursing homes, and other institutions still in existence remained under the aegis of the new Jewish organization.[6] Later, the RSHA specified that the Residual Reichsvereinigung should not take over any outstanding debts of the liquidated predecessor, and the regional finance president was designated responsible for their settlement.[7]

The main bureau of the new organization was relocated to the administrative building of the Jewish Hospital on Iranische Strasse, where the hospital's new director, the former senior councilor and senior medical officer, Dr. Dr. Walter Lustig, had been in office since 1942. Lustig had been a board member of the Reichsvereinigung since 1941 as head of the medical department, and was very familiar with the organization.[8] After other members of the board were subsequently deported, he remained the only one left. Lustig lived in a "nonprivileged" mixed marriage. His accomplishments lay principally in the realm of medicine. He was not considered an authority within the Jewish community, nor was he qualified by past experience for handling general Jewish administration or even taking care of the religious needs of the remaining Jews. But no one was looking now for such qualifications, and the RSHA did not expect that he would perform like Otto Hirsch, Paul Eppstein, or even Leo Baeck as their successor. Rather, his assigned task was to direct the residual organization, attending minimally to the needs of the Jews in mixed marriages, assisted by a small band of volunteer intermediaries and other minimal personnel in the central office.[9] The rump organization had taken over the central store of materials from its predecessor, including a stash of 1,296,000 "yellow stars."[10] Yet these "yellow stars" had become largely superfluous after the conclusion of the large-scale deportations from cities across the Reich.

In Berlin, where the Jewish Community had shrunk into a mere administrative office inside the rump Reichsvereinigung, two principal institutions had to be kept in operation: the Jewish Hospital and the permanently equipped central assembly camp. The camp was housed in a former home for the elderly on Grosse Hamburger Strasse, and in the spring of 1944 was relocated to a section of the Jewish Hospital on Schulstrasse. Both the comprehensive organization of the Residual RV and the Jewish Hospital were directly subordinate to the RSHA. Adolf Eichmann had appointed his subordinate Fritz Woehrn to supervise the hospital, which Woehrn generally monitored by personal inspections.

The central office of the Residual Reichsvereinigung consisted of several departments, as outlined in table 5.[11]

Table 5. Structure of the Residual RV, Central Office

Director: Lustig

Dept. I: Central office

General matters, personal data	Kleemann
Finances	Rischowsky
Audit	Wolffsky
Statistics	Radlauer

Dept. II: Medical matters — Lustig

Hospital, home for the infirm, physicians, medical care	Lustig
Children's ward (orphaned children)	Friedländer

Dept. III: Welfare

Legal matters	Königsberger
Social welfare for youth, economic welfare, clothing storeroom	Friedländer
Petitions, applications office, burials	Wolffsky
Inheritance, guardianship, professional and trade associations	Baruch
Legal consultants, administration of assets	Abrahamsohn
Home purchase contracts	Bandmann

In July 1943, Lustig reported to his "superior authority" that the Berlin main office still had a staff of 196 Jews. The largest contingent was working in the assembly camp (52 persons), where deportees now often waited for an extended period until a transport was assembled, and not, as in the past, just 1–2 days. Forty employees dealt with "final legal processing," that is, they administered "Aryanizations," "home purchase contracts," and the like. In addition, the Residual RV employed a number of cleaning women and 150 men working as Jewish forced laborers in special work details for the RSHA, mainly deployed to clear rubble after bombing raids. The intermediaries had been required to order some of these forced laborers to relocate to Berlin from the outlying provinces, coming from Mannheim, Hamburg, Frankfurt am Main, Pforzheim, Baden-Baden, Aussig, Munich, and other localities.[12] There were also 17 highly qualified Jewish university graduates among these special workers, who under the direction of the German language specialist and classical philologist Ernst Grumach formed the "Grumach Group." Its task was to sift through the huge amount of looted Hebraica and Judaica—confiscated books, periodicals, and manuscripts from all over occupied Europe—for the central library of the RSHA on Eisenacher Strasse. Fifteen Jewish conscript laborers deployed at the Reich Genealogical Research Office (Reichssippenamt) were assigned to handle investigations on proof of "racial" descent. All these employees were working directly for their persecutors, but their formal employer was the Residual RV, and they were on its payroll.[13] Thus, the official personnel in the Berlin central office totaled 352 persons (including the forced laborers for the RSHA). In the subsequent period, this number shrank, in a slow but constant decline.[14]

The intermediaries now took up their posts outside Berlin in various localities. A list of employees of the Residual RV from 1944 includes the names of 41 persons (40 men and 1 woman) working as such or as contact personnel subordinate to these *Vertrauensmänner*.[15] In their offices and institutions, they employed a total of 109 staff members throughout the Reich. Thus, the "employer" Reichsvereinigung, with a former staff of several thousand, had in the meantime shriveled to a relatively small administrative body employing a total of 453 persons.[16] The areas of competence dealt with also shrank: the intermediaries had the task of maintaining contact with the central office, and seeing to the social welfare and medical needs of the Jews in the *Altreich* and the *Sudetengau*. The structure of the rump organization became more centralized than before, oriented to the Berlin main office. This was especially true of finances, but extended to each and every activity, which the Berlin central office had to authorize in advance after consultation with the RSHA, or could also choose to block. Thus, after inquiring at the RSHA, Lustig issued a directive that medical care for Jews should be provided locally by the licensed Jewish *Krankenbehandler*, but patients had to apply beforehand via the intermediary for a "welfare slip." This slip was both the permit for treatment and also required for the later payment made to the Jewish "practitioners for the sick," as the doctors were termed. He stipulated that Jews living in areas where there were no longer any hospitals or possibilities for accommodating patients in need of care should be relocated to Berlin. Here too, the intermediaries likewise had to apply for a permit first.[17] The "tasks of economic welfare" included one-time and periodic payments for support to needy Jews. The entitlement for such payments and their amount had likewise to be applied for in Berlin, and after authorization payment was to be paid out directly from there to the recipient. The district branches still maintained clothing storerooms available in order to provide their members with shoes, clothing for forced labor deployment, or after damage from air raids, after the intermediaries had submitted corresponding official applications for this.[18] But this regional scheme of provision was slated to be abolished, and the members were provided with the most necessary articles of daily use from Berlin directly.

The tasks of the intermediaries also included presentation to the Berlin central office for authorization of all dispositions of "their" Jews regarding their movable property and all their petitions to agencies. The offices likewise had to prepare two-thirds of the total of around two thousand still current final transactions regarding home purchase contracts.[19] In addition, the intermediaries, like their predecessors, were required to regularly submit statistical data on the Jews living in their respective district. The lists now involved:

- Jews who had "no Aryan kin" (whose number had dropped close to zero after the deportations in June 1943),
- Jews "with Aryan kin," living in "nonprivileged" and "privileged" mixed marriages,
- Jews from dissolved mixed marriages,
- Jews who were foreign nationals,
- and finally, the Geltungsjuden.[20]

It was not clearly regulated whether the Schutzhäftlinge should be included here.[21] A form in triplicate had to filled out once for each Jew. Subsequently, any changes in the personal relations in mixed marriages were recorded there: this involved in particular divorce, the death of the "non-Aryan" spouse, change of address, sickness, etc. If a son categorized as Mischling of the first degree was serving by special permission in the Wehrmacht and was killed in action, that was recorded, as was a relocation into a Judenhaus or arrest and internment in "protective custody." Thus, both via the Berlin central office and through the card files of the intermediaries, it was possible to monitor locally whether "protection" through the shield of a mixed marriage was still operative for a given individual or no longer valid. Such cases had to be reported to the Gestapo, which then ordered deportation to Theresienstadt, unless there were other mitigating circumstances. The intermediary had to organize such deportations. They themselves were protected (temporarily) from deportation by special ID cards.[22]

Among official duties not mentioned was the obligation to pass on reports on the death of Jewish *Schutzhäftlinge* in detention, which the "supervisory authority" sent to the intermediaries.[23]

In turn, the intermediaries appointed, where deemed necessary, subordinate contact personnel; these appointments had to be confirmed by the Berlin central office.[24] These contact persons worked as outpost personnel of the Residual RV, so to speak, active in areas where an appreciable although not large number of Jews lived in mixed marriages. The intermediaries were only allowed to hire a very small number of personnel for their sphere of administration, and this solely with prior approval from the Berlin main office.[25] They themselves were appointed on a volunteer basis, which for those who had an income as "legal consultants" or "practitioners for the sick" was no great problem. Others without regular income found that such an arrangement of unpaid work was virtually impossible. Consequently, until 1945, the central office repeatedly approved applications for remuneration from the budget of the Residual RV. For example, the Leipzig intermediary Heinrich Dziubas, the Cologne intermediary Heinrich Kounen, and the Hanover intermediary Siegfried Karle received small monetary benefits.[26]

A list from 1944, in table 6, provides an overview of the geographical and numerical distribution of the Jews whose affairs the intermediaries were obliged to regulate.[27]

Table 6. Regional Distribution of Jews (1 July 1944)

Aussig	387	Karlsruhe/Palatinate, Saar territory	687
Berlin	5,978	Kassel	113
Braunschweig	47	Koblenz	66
Bremen	177	Königsberg/Allenstein	173
Breslau	695	Leipzig	304
Chemnitz	116	Magdeburg	185
Cologne	763	Main-Franconia	62
Darmstadt	213	Middle Franconia	175
Dortmund	334	Munich/Augsburg and Swabia	525
Dresden	227	Nuremberg	264
Düsseldorf	616	Oppeln Silesia	72
Eger	112	Paderborn/Münster, Westphalia	163
Erfurt	173	Regensburg	31
Frankfurt am Main	428	Rostock	66
Frankfurt an der Oder	143	Stolp/Pomerania	42
Gleiwitz/Beuthen	112	Stuttgart	322
Halle	92	Tilsit	31
Hamburg	878	Trier	25
Hanover	285	Upper Franconia, Gau Bayreuth	27
		Grand total	**15,109**

Now as before, most Jews lived in Berlin, just under 40 percent, followed by Hamburg at 5.8 percent, Cologne with 5 percent, and Breslau and Düsseldorf.

In the first few months after his appointment, Lustig ordered the intermediaries to travel regularly to Berlin, where their tasks were discussed in detail.[28] Martin Heinrich Corten, a physician in Hamburg, noted, along with general instructions received, that his special area of competence, the Jewish Hospital in Hamburg, was permitted to continue in operation. He was instructed that his office should do the bulk of preparatory work on the home purchase contracts for Theresienstadt, so that they could then be finalized in Berlin. In conclusion, he complained that seven of the forced laborers dispatched from Hamburg to Berlin on orders from the RSHA were not suitable for the work demanded.[29] While Corten accepted the order that the infirm would have to be transferred to Berlin, evidently a directive for the entire Reich, several other intermediaries successfully opposed this order, such as Alfred Marx in Stuttgart. Marx wrote that "his" elderly Jews in mixed marriages preferred to waive any and all "benefits" accruing from the home purchase contracts they had concluded, so as not to be transported to Berlin and perhaps elsewhere from there. The Stuttgart Gestapo ruled that they could remain in Stuttgart.[30]

Given the deteriorating war situation, it became increasingly difficult to arrange meetings with the intermediaries. In addition, after several months, the main routines had probably become standard operating procedure in the Berlin main office and the bureaus of the intermediaries' personnel. Earlier on, there had been conflicts over these procedural questions, such as the amount of time that should be allotted for handling processing of the home purchase contracts.[31] Looming behind such seemingly everyday points of contention, not articulated but always in the air, was the question of life and death. If, for example, there was discussion about when a focal area of work would be classified as superfluous and terminated, implicit was also the fatal consequence: deportation of the staff members dealing with this area. So employees repeatedly asked themselves the existential question: how would it be possible to prolong their activity, and for how long? By 1943/1944, transfers to other departments, as had still been possible in 1941/1942, were no longer permitted.

Director Dr. Dr. Walter Lustig

Even decades after the war's end, mention of the name Walter Lustig, director of the Residual Reichsvereinigung, still sparks strong aversion among Jewish survivors. Accusations, never fully examined before a court of law, have persisted down into the present: that he conducted surgical

operations even though he had only been an administrator before the Gestapo enthroned him as RV director. That he abused women sexually, and
if they resisted, he had them placed on the deportation lists. That he put
the sick on transport lists, and was in general a veritable henchman and
drinking companion of the Gestapo. Historian Rivka Elkin arrived at a
more differentiated assessment of Lustig, namely, that the contradictions
inherent in Nazi policy on the Jews were also mirrored in the persona of
the man. In her view, he possessed good qualities of leadership, coupled
with a resolute determination to implement orders from the authorities,
and superb abilities as a "medical administrator." In addition, he maintained important connections. Unclear for Elkin, however, are the moral
criteria underpinning his actions.[32] However, that question is not only relevant for assessing Walter Lustig. It is far more valid to raise it in regard to
those responsible for the mass murder: the perpetrators, their accomplices
and supporters, and the multitude of bystanders.

What do we know about Walter Lustig?

He was born 10 August 1891 in Ratibor/Upper Silesia, the son of a
merchant. Walter attended elementary school and high school there,
took his A-level exams (*Abitur*) in 1910, and went on to study medicine
in Breslau; he received his medical doctorate and license to practice in
1915, and obtained a second doctorate in 1916 in the field of physical an-
thropology. He earned his academic laurels while serving as a field doctor
in the military, stationed in Breslau during WWI.[33]

As a physician, he had five years of clinical training, "specializing in
surgery."[34] In Breslau he worked as a senior doctor in the municipal hospital. In 1920, he became a demonstrator teaching practical anatomy at the
Anatomical Institute, University of Bonn; in 1921, he was licensed as a
district doctor and exercised this function in state service in several towns
in the Rhineland and in Stade. It is believed that in this period, Lustig
participated with colleagues in the suppression and defeat of the Spartacist uprising in Berlin in 1919, and he probably was also a member of a
Freikorps unit. In 1923, he was appointed a state medical councilor (*Me-
dizinalrat*), and relocated in 1927 to Berlin, where he initially worked as
a "medical assistant" attached to the Berlin Police Presidium, and rapidly
progressed up the ladder. He also pursued a private practice. That same
year, he married the non-Jewish pediatrician Annemarie Preuß, whom
he had known for many years. In 1929, he was appointed senior state
councilor (*Oberregierungsrat*) and senior medical councilor (*Obermedizinalrat*).[35] In the meantime, he had developed ties with the Social Democrats, and according to a relative was even a member of the SPD.[36]

As a medical department head at the Police Presidium in Berlin, he
was director of state medical administration in Berlin, "which included

… supervision of all hospitals, pharmacies, drugstores, medical personnel, social institutions, training of nurses, masseurs, disinfector personnel, lab and X-ray assistants, etc." In addition, he served on other diverse committees.[37] According to his own count, Lustig published seventy-two scientific papers and twelve books. The book known as "Der kleine Lustig" (The Little Lustig), entitled *Leitfaden der gerichtlichen Medizin einschl. der gerichtlichen Psychiatrie* (Berlin 1926), even became the standard work for administrators in the field of health at the time. Lustig's career path progressed on a steep upward curve until the National Socialists took power. His extensive list of publications and his curriculum vitae reflect a man of enormous diligence and single-minded determination to succeed in a career in the state medical system. Lustig and his wife lived in a large apartment on Eisenacher Strasse with elegant contemporary furnishings, "couches bound in leather, a study and large dining room." They also owned a car.[38]

The career of *Obermedizinalrat* Lustig came to a sudden end in 1933, when in October he was dismissed from his high-ranking post based on the Law for the Restoration of the Professional Civil Service.[39] Since Lustig was not recognized as a WWI combat veteran because he had served as a military doctor on the home front in Breslau, he was left with only a pension of five hundred RM monthly (comparatively large),[40] along with income from his private medical practice. He was allowed to continue that practice until 1938. It was not until the age of forty-three that he felt forced by circumstance to become more closely connected with the Jewish community: in 1934, he began his activity at the Berlin Jewish Community. There he rose in stature, as far as that was possible under the coercive conditions of National Socialist rule. In 1939, he was not only director of the health administration of the Community but also a board member of the Jewish Hospital, director of training for nurses, and head of the residence home for nurses. In addition, he was teaching anatomy, physiology, school hygiene, social hygiene, and pathology at the Jewish Teachers College. In 1939, he also took over direction of medical welfare provision in the Reichsvereinigung. After the former director emigrated, he became head in 1940 of the Jewish Community medical department, and as such was also on the Community board. When the large-scale deportations commenced in October 1941, he headed the Examination Department for Transport Complaints in the Jewish Hospital Berlin. This department dealt with claims by Jews notified of imminent deportation stating that they were not physically fit for deportation (see chapter 2). Lustig took his exam findings and those of his colleagues very seriously, evidently obtaining deferments from deportation on medical grounds in a number of cases. However, in 1942 the guidelines were changed, rendered more strict, and deferments became virtually impossible. Shortly after that the examination department was shut down.[41] Lustig was then appointed director of the Jewish Hospital. Contemporaneous witnesses stress his good relations with the Gestapo, his great gifts as an administrator, and his skill as a negotiator.[42] Nonetheless, the anti-Jewish legislation also applied to him, and his status in a "nonprivileged" mixed marriage did not protect him from restrictions: he was not permitted to drive his car or that of his wife, had to pay a high "levy on Jewish assets," his bank account was blocked, and like other Jews who still possessed such "luxury" items, he had to hand over to the authorities his "mink coat with otter collar," his men's gold jewelry, his set of skis, and his radio.[43]

Reports by patients and colleagues indicate that Lustig was meticulous in adherence to Gestapo orders, but in March 1943 he also acted (successfully) to prevent the Berlin Gestapo from shutting down the Jewish Hospital and deporting all patients and medical staff.[44]

When the leading functionaries of the now dissolved Reichsvereinigung and the Berlin Jewish Community were deported to Theresienstadt in June 1943, Lustig was spared. He was unable to save his father, who was deported in 1942 from Ratibor to the "old age ghetto" at Theresienstadt.[45] Lustig's wife Annemarie was transferred in the summer of 1943 to Traunstein in southeastern Bavaria, where she had been dispatched as an assistant physician to the state hospital. From that point on until after the end of the war, she lived outside Berlin. Such an extended separation generally endangered the Jewish spouse in a "nonprivileged" mixed marriage, even if there had been no divorce. It is not known to what extent Lustig sensed he was in danger because of this. Perhaps he thought that in his capacity as director of the Residual Reichsvereinigung he was protected, an office he took over in June 1943 simultaneously with the directorship of the Jewish Hospital. In addition, it is quite possible that Lustig knew Fritz Woehrn personally from his time at the Police Presidium in Berlin and trusted in his protection; *SS-Hauptsturmführer* Woehrn was responsible for monitoring the Jewish Hospital for the RSHA. At least, it is known that both had worked at the Presidium in the period 1927–1930.[46] When the Berlin District Court later summed up the testimony on Lustig in the Woehrn trial in 1971, the following picture emerged:

> Dr. Dr. Lustig was a scintillating personality. He was versatile and very skilled at negotiation, but also arrogant and egotistic. For his fellow Jews in the Jewish Hospital and later likewise for the staff of the *Reichsvereinigung der Juden in Deutschland*, he was to a certain extent "lord over life and death." He was able to place on the deportation lists whomever he wished to, and he also did just that.[47]

Yet by no means did Walter Lustig himself put together the deportation lists. Rather, he was the implementing agent for orders from the RSHA. However, he did have the power to report fellow coworkers, members, or inmates in the assembly camp for inclusion in a transport if these persons were found to have committed some "offense." His "superior" Fritz Woehrn successfully exonerated himself in court after the war by claiming that Lustig had enjoyed close ties to Eichmann's deputy, SS-*Sturmbann-führer* Rolf Günther, in the RSHA.

Jewish witnesses such as Lustig's coworkers in the Residual Reichsvereinigung, Siegbert Kleemann and his secretary Hilde Kahan, testified at the Woehrn trial that Lustig was generally anti-Semitic in his views: he tended to shout at Jews, often insulting them, and they were afraid of him. He would threaten Jews for the slightest matter. Thus, his secretary once asked whether some typing work could be left until the following day; reportedly, Lustig replied: "If you want to go to Lublin, just go ahead and leave the work until tomorrow."[48]

Several of the hospital staff and the Residual RV were accused during inspections by Woehrn, in Lustig's presence, of minor "offenses," such as not properly wearing a "yellow star," which, despite their nature as small violations of standing regulations, led to "arrest in protective custody" and subsequent death.[49] There is no existing evidence that Lustig sought in these cases to intervene on behalf of the accused. On his "credit side," there were some fifty "full Jews" and *Geltungsjuden* whom he saved, and who as indispensable staff workers in the hospital and Residual RV were able to survive. However, less urgently needed staff workers were then designated to replace them on the deportation lists, if the extent of staff reduction had been specified by the RSHA in advance, and a number of women granted a deferment, at least according to rumor, had to pay for their life with sexual favors. Lustig is said to have been particularly active in assisting the children housed in the *Kinderunterkunft* at the hospital (see chapter 2). In contrast with that, there are credible statements that Lustig recommended that individuals who had tried to flee should be deported; he rescued friends and acquaintances from deportation more than others, and withheld important information from the inmates of the camp and hospital complex.

This almost cost the prisoners in the *Lazarett* (field hospital) at the war's end their life: on 19 April 1945, a day prior to the flight from Berlin of the RSHA staff, a dispute arose in RSHA headquarters about whether the Jewish prisoners at the hospital should be shot or not. It was not Lustig, with all his connections to the Gestapo, who prevented a massacre, but rather his administrative director Selmar Neumann, together with a non-Jewish secretary. Neumann, who had heard about the dispute, instructed the secretary to pass on by phone a purported order to allow the Jews to live. When the Red Army occupied the building, they found 370 patients and up to 1,000 residents, 93 children (whose identity as "Jews" or not, so-called cases for clarification, had not yet been decided), and 76 prisoners in the police station on the hospital grounds.[50] The survival of the Jewish inmates was once again in the balance when the Soviet soldiers arrested them as suspicious persons who claimed they were Jewish prisoners, and brought them to Weissensee, since the Soviet soldiers mistakenly assumed there were no Jewish survivors left in Germany. The Jews appointed liaison men who enlightened "the Russians" about their actual origin and fate. The Russian troops believed them, gave them food, and transported them back to the assembly camp.[51] "It was there," one person involved later narrated, "that I saw Dr. Lustig for the last time.... The hatred for him because of how he had behaved—among other things, he had not explained to the Russians that we were Jews, and had only sought to protect himself—was very strong."[52] He suspected that Lustig had little more time to live, and he was right. Lustig was later arrested by the Soviets troops and executed (see the section "The War Is Over" in this chapter).

Origin and Motivation of the Intermediaries

As was shown, the director of the Residual RV, Walter Lustig, was no "outsider." Rather, he had worked for years inside the Berlin Jewish Community and the Reichsvereinigung before he was appointed director of the rump organization in 1943.

There was a similar configuration regarding the intermediaries: virtually all had worked with or inside the Reichsvereinigung in some capacity. Several district branch directors, like Michel Oppenheim (Mainz), Theodor Koronczyk (Munich), Alfred Marx (Stuttgart), and Karl Eisemann (Karlsruhe), who were in mixed marriages, were taken on in June 1943 as liaison officers working on a volunteer basis, but the majority of the new intermediaries were newly appointed. Since all other groups of university graduates had been included between 1941 and 1943 in the deportations, the new Jewish functionaries were largely trained lawyers who were still allowed to practice and represent Jewish clients as so-called *Konsulenten* (legal counselors), along with a smaller number of physicians treating Jewish patients as *Krankenbehandler*. Only a tiny minority had been working in other professions, such as in teaching or business.

An indeterminable number of the intermediaries had been baptized; some were second-generation Christians with a converted parent. Judaism as a religion was not familiar to some, while others had been practicing Jews. All had lost their jobs as a result of Nazi racial legislation and had to consider themselves fortunate to have been given permission at the end of the 1930s to work for Jewish patients or legal clients, and, later on, to avoid deportation because they were shielded by their mixed marriage. Little is known about their political orientation before 1933: extant information points to conservative, German-national, or national-liberal (Ernst Neumark) political views, aside from a small number of exceptions (Walter Lustig and Fritz Rosenbaum had ties to the Social Democrats).[53]

In this they probably did not differ from other lawyers and doctors before 1933. Three intermediaries (Lustig, Eisemann, Blankenstein) had, as mentioned, belonged to the *Freikorps*. Martin Heinrich Corten, who before locating to Hamburg had lived in Berlin, had even joined the NS-DAP on 1 May 1933, and had then resigned from the party on 18 May, "because his grandfather was a Jew."[54]

Through their previous professional activities, the *Vertrauensmänner* had worked closely together with the RV, but for the most part, aside from the medical doctors on staff in Jewish hospitals, had not been part of this organization. Yet they were quite familiar with operating procedures in larger institutions, and were used to representing clients or treating patients. Their professional and social abilities generally were of benefit both to them and the compulsory members of the Residual RV. Nonetheless, the Jews for whom they were responsible considered them, more than the district branch directors, to be compliant and convenient henchmen of the Gestapo.

As a rule, they had not pressed for this office, but rather had accepted it out of necessity, if internment in a concentration camp had been threatened should they refuse to serve.[55] Martin Heinrich Corten later reported that he suffered a great deal "under the burden of the decisions placed on his shoulders," especially because he had been forced to decide about "whom can I save, who must die?"[56] As a rule, they could not rid themselves of this office. Only in the case of Max Cahn in Frankfurt am Main is it known, as mentioned in chapter 3, that he endeavored, shrewdly and with determination, to arrange to be relieved of his post as soon as possible, without any penalty. An opportunity arose, and he exploited it: the Frankfurt Gestapo had ordered him to deposit RV funds into Frankfurt accounts in violation of the regulations, and thus in effect to withhold funds from the RSHA. He reported this to the Berlin RV main office, and managed in this way to be relieved of his duties. Cahn later commented:

> I noticed a number of times that it was still possible to deal with the Gestapo men ... if you stayed very cool, had precise knowledge of the laws and ordinances, and displayed no fear of them. Whoever thought he had to accommodate to these men, undertake things together with them that were

crooked, became putty in their hands: he was an uncomfortable accessory, and they deported him very quickly, because he knew about such secrets. Unfortunately, that's what happened with my successor, after I'd managed to be released from this office.[57]

Others who were appointed intermediaries accepted the job and their concomitant responsibilities and attempted to make the best of it, such as Erich Schlesinger in Gleiwitz. The former lawyer was now responsible for the 112 Gleiwitz Jews in mixed marriages. Like "his" Jews, he continued to be deployed in forced labor and worked part-time and as a volunteer as intermediary: "Along with my job ten hours a day down at the sewage plant, I had to take care of these matters as well. I dealt with the Jewish cemeteries … When a member of the Community was buried, I made sure the ritual regulations were adhered to … and also spoke a eulogy at graveside. At the time I was Community chairman, *shammes*, *hazzan*, and rabbi all rolled into one."[58]

The list in table 7 of personnel from the Residual Reichsvereinigung, with supplementary data on their later fate (as far as can be determined), provides some picture of which intermediaries survived the Nazi period, and who became a victim of Nazi persecution and the war.

Table 7. Intermediaries (**Vertrauensmänner**) of the Reichsvereinigung der Juden in Deutschland[59]

Place of residence	Name, profession	Subsequent Fate
Aussig/Sudetenland	Glässner, Arnold[60]	Unknown
Braunschweig	Mosberg, Karl	20 February 1945, Theresienstadt, survived; died 1962 in Braunschweig
Bremen	Bruck, Karl	Survived, five months internment after the war
Breslau, Lower Silesia	Ludnowsky, Erwin	Died 10/12 February 1945 on death march from Gross Rosen concentration camp to Buchenwald
Chemnitz	Lipp, Dr. Adolf, physician	Final weeks of the war in hiding, survived; died 17 June 1966 in Karl-Marx-Stadt (Chemnitz)
Cologne-Müngersdorf, barracks camp	Feldheim, Dr. Hans Salomon, physician	Suicide (together with daughter Annelise), 28 September 1944
Darmstadt, Hesse with Upper Hesse, Rhine Hesse, Giessen, and Offenbach	Wagner, Irma, physician	Survived, died 2003

(continued)

Table 7. continued

Place of residence	Name, profession	Subsequent Fate
Dortmund	Rosenbaum, Max, lawyer	Labor camp, 1944 Theresienstadt, survived; after 1945 board member, Dortmund Jewish Community
Dresden, Beuthen	Neumark, Dr. Ernst, lawyer	Survived; died 28 October 1948 in the Sachsenhausen internment camp
Düsseldorf	Spier, Waldemar	1944, Auschwitz; died there 2 March 1945
Eger/Karlsbad	Glück, Oswald, lawyer	Unknown
Erfurt/Weimar	Cars, Max, merchant	2 February 1945, Theresienstadt, survived; died in Erfurt in 1961
Frankfurt am Main	Cahn, Max, lawyer	Survived
Frankfurt an der Oder	Broh, Martin	Survived, fled in 1951 to the West
Gleiwitz/Kattowitz, Hindenburg	Schlesinger, Erich, lawyer	Survived
Halle/Merseburg	Hesse, Richard	14 February 1945, Theresienstadt; survived, internment in Buchenwald, Waldheim, and Bautzen until July 1954; suicide 1984
Hamburg	Corten, Dr. Martin, physician	Survived
Hanover	Karle, Siegfried	Survived
Karlsruhe/Saarbrücken	Eisemann, Karl, lawyer	Survived, died 1982
Kassel	Speyer, Max	Unknown
Kiel	Guttmann, Erich	Arrested 26 March 1944; died 6 February 1945 in Mauthausen concentration camp
Kleinmachnow/Potsdam	Rosenbaum, Fritz	Survived; mayor of Kleinmachnow; sentenced in a show trial in the GDR on 11 February 1953 to six years in prison
Koblenz	Pollack, Semi	Probably survived, died 1957 in Koblenz
Königsberg	Weinberg, Hans	Survived, shot by Soviet troops
Leipzig	Dobbriner, Walter, lawyer	Survived, fled in 1953 from the GDR
Luxembourg	Grünberg, Dr. Eugen, physician, German emigrant	Unknown
Magdeburg	Levy, Herbert	Survived

(continued)

Place of residence	Name, profession	Subsequent Fate
Munich, Upper Bavaria, and Augsburg-Swabia	Koronczyk, Theodor, teacher	Survived; after the war underwent conviction/internment; later rehabilitated
Nuremberg, West Middle Franconia, Upper Franconia, and Main Franconia	Nürnberger, Dr. Julius, lawyer	Survived
Oppeln	Traube, Alfred	Unknown
Paderborn	Sternberg, Louis	Survived; chairman of the Paderborn Jewish Community 1946–1958
Regensburg	Hermann, Ernst	Unknown
Rostock/Schwerin	Josephy, Richard	Died 11 April 1944 during an air raid
Schneidemühl	Jacoby, Gotthilf	Unknown
Stettin	Cahn, Siegfried (Samuel)	Unknown
Stolp/Pomerania, Köslin	Sabatzky, Kurt	Unknown
Stuttgart, Württemberg, and Hohenzollern	Marx, Alfred, lawyer`	14 February 1945, Theresienstadt; survived, died in Stuttgart in 1988
Tilsit	Gintz, Franz	Unknown
Trier	Frank, Gustav	Unknown
Troppau	Glücksmann, Leo	Unknown
Frankfurt an der Oder (deputy liaison officer, district branch)	Falkenberg, Josef, lawyer	Survived; practiced law after the war in Berlin

Work under the Conditions of the Bombing Raids

On 10 June 1943, the British and American allies instructed their air force commands to undertake a combined bombing offensive, a campaign of precision daytime bombing raids on industrial sites and nighttime saturation bombing runs over large population centers in Germany.[61] The air war, whose role since 1940 had increased in importance, had already taken on a new ferocity with the British raid of one thousand bombers on Cologne on 30/31 May 1942, and in 1943 the Americans had mounted air raids on the Ruhr area, Regensburg, and Schweinfurt. But in the second half of 1943, there were heavy attacks day and night, and large areas of Hamburg were devastated by several waves of aerial bombardment. This intensity was continued into 1944, despite the fact that the Allies had gained air supremacy. Again and again, the main destination of the bomber squadrons was the capital of Berlin. In February 1945, they destroyed Dresden, and in April 1945 large parts of Kassel, Braunschweig, Würzburg, Darmstadt, Pforzheim, and Nuremberg, to name but a few cities heavily hit. The air war was a threat to all residents in the cities, whether they belonged to the majority population or a persecuted minority. The bombs rained death on thousands, maimed many others, transformed residential areas into vast fields of rubble, destroyed transport and communication routes, interrupted provision of water and electricity, and much more. The aerial bombardments dictated living conditions on the ground, including those of the Jews, and impacted the concrete daily work of their new rump organization, the Residual Reichsvereinigung.

In any event, in view of the huge supply difficulties and the infrastructure devastated by the war, for Jewish functionaries to continue on with the previous strategy of attempting to utilize administrative regulations as a kind of protective shield would not have been possible under these conditions. It would probably have proven a failure simply because of trivial workaday deficiencies, such as a lack of pencils and paper. Moreover, the new Jewish functionaries no longer regarded the time-honored Prussian tradition of administration that the old RV had adhered to as a possible bulwark against an ever-escalating and more radical Jewish policy. On the contrary, the administrative structures now served the Nazi regime solely as an instrument to control the Jewish functionaries down to the smallest detail, contracting their meager latitude for action. Of this the *Vertrauensmänner* were well aware. At the same time, they had to grapple with new exigencies, such as the devastating impact of the air war. These were challenges they could never have mastered even if well equipped and with extensive competencies. I will illustrate this exemplified in the situation in Hamburg: along with the numerous practical problems they confronted, one can see a secret strategy of the intermediaries emerging. They sought to utilize the wartime chaos in order to break free in part from the procedural apparatus of their own organization. In Hamburg, like in other areas, they tried by means of delays, noncompliance with orders, and independent decisions of their own to win the race with time to the end of the war, and in the process to survive. At best, their ally in this endeavor was their intermediary in a nearby town—not Walter Lustig in the Berlin main office.

The rump Reichsvereinigung in Hamburg, under Martin Heinrich Corten and his executive officer Max Heinemann, had just started its work when the British and US air force launched the "Operation Gomorrah" raid, bombarding the city from 24 July to 3 August 1943: the attacks costs the lives of 35,000 Hamburg residents in the "fire storm" they caused, 125,000 were injured, and 255,000 apartments and homes were destroyed. Some 900,000 persons fled the city in panic.[62] Jews were more exposed to the ravages of aerial bombardment than other residents, because they were not permitted entry into most of the air raid shelters reserved for "Aryans."[63] Naturally, Jewish institutions such as the hospital were destroyed in the bombardment. Max Plaut, then in Hamburg waiting to leave Germany, noted in October 1943:

> On 25 July 1943, the card file indicated there were 1,257 Jews in Hamburg. Of these, some 600 Jews were bombed out as a result of the terror attacks on the city. On 23 October 1943, there are still 900 Jews present in Hamburg according to the card file. This figure also includes some 200 Jews who were temporarily outside Hamburg and have returned for forced labor deployment. All the Jews in these figures are in mixed marriages.[64]

The Residual Reichsvereinigung had to search the devastated city for possible emergency accommodations for the Jews who had been bombed out, and at the same time was constrained to obey orders to vacate undamaged living space for "Aryans"; that is, they were instructed to increase the occupancy of "Jewish living space."[65] These were orders from the Gestapo and the municipal housing office. Despite the chaotic situation, exact regulations had to be adhered to: mixed marriages with a Jewish husband were only allowed to share space with similar couples. Jewish women in mixed marriages who were divorced or widowed could only share quarters with couples in mixed marriages where the wife was Jewish, etc. In September and October 1943, the Gestapo twice demanded the vacating of two hundred rooms, as a rule each housing several persons. The upshot was that more than half the Jews remaining in Hamburg had to be relocated to new accommodations. If the Jews affected refused to obey the orders of the Residual RV and move to a crowded *Judenhaus* or a private home, conflicts arose between the RV and its members. The Jewish functionaries often threatened to call in the Gestapo.[66] Couples where the "Aryan" husband was the family breadwinner, the tenant of record, or the house owner were particularly resistant to being relocated by the Jewish functionaries and their rehousing schemes. They also did not comprehend why the Jewish spouse in such marriages should have to pay dues to the Jewish organization, especially since before 1933, the Hamburg Jewish Community had specifically barred Jewish women from membership if they married a non-Jew.

Given the cramped living conditions in the overcrowded *Judenhäuser*, repeated disputes and arguments flared about matters of everyday behavior, supposed rights, limitations, respect of privacy, and its lack. Here too the Jewish functionaries had to search for solutions or arbitrate in disputes. At the same time, they were busy trying to turn their beleaguered office into a functioning operation once again, and most especially to restore the all-important destroyed card file. They tried to get those who had fled the city to the surrounding countryside to return to town, and to provide for adequate food and water. They also sought to determine the whereabouts of persons who had taken the opportunity to flee or go into hiding in the chaos of the air raids.[67] Scarcely any Jew in Hamburg had attempted to elude the first large-scale deportations by fleeing into hiding, but in the summer of 1943, rumors were circulating, in particular among mixed marriages who had contact with soldiers or employees in the civil administrations: stories made the rounds about the murder of Jews in the occupied Eastern territories. In searching for those who had disappeared, the RV staff painstakingly checked all known residential addresses. In September and October 1943, they recorded brief notations on individuals: "moved, address unknown," "residence totally destroyed," "closed area," or "whereabouts unknown." Then they put together a list for the Gestapo of those missing. In the case of some, they provided more detailed commentary:

> [W]as not present in her apartment. Mrs. A. K., the proprietor of the boarding house, stated that for many weeks, Mrs. V. had only been staying temporarily in the apartment, coming for one or two days. She said she didn't know now where Mrs. V. was. Her daughter Lieselotte, believed to be working for a lawyer, has also recently only rarely spent the night at her mother's place. Mrs. K. likewise does not know her whereabouts. The daughter gave the following emergency address on the air raid protection list: Dr. A. P. … The result of a phone call to X.—whose address Mrs. K. provided me, because he is said to somehow be a friend of Miss V.—was the information that Mr. X. is at the moment on military duty, and Mrs. X. could tell me nothing about the whereabouts of Mrs. V. or her daughter.[68]

The Gestapo handled inquiries regarding Community employees who were missing, in many cases, unfortunately, with success in locating them. Yet some who had fled were not discovered, most of these females aged fifty to fifty-five.

Meanwhile, the RV central office sent several reminders about the statistical data that had to be regularly submitted.[69] However, in February 1944, the office of the Hamburg intermediary was still at work on restoration of the card file. It tried to establish with certainty what members or nonmembers had perished in the bombing raids and who had fled. Corten was unable to provide exact figures. He wrote Berlin that he needed two more months, and if the central office insisted on his supplying the requested statistical data, he would have to interrupt restoration work on the card file.[70] It was not until March 1944 that he was able to report completion of the restored card file, while a large number of Hamburg

Jews still remained unaccounted for.[71] He now gave the updated figure: there were 887 Jews registered in Hamburg.[72]

However, the statistical reports and financial statements from Hamburg continued to annoy officials in the Berlin main office. Again and again, their reports arrived very late or not at all. In part this was because the Hamburg office delayed submission in order to retain at least a portion of financial autonomy, and in part the delays were because distribution of the mail was slow, since railway links had been badly damaged. The Residual RV in Hamburg now began to shift to a practice of no longer transferring revenue to Berlin, as per instruction, but rather, unauthorized, retaining this income for its own "replenishment fund" (*Auffüllkasse*), a kind of internal reserve set aside to cover expenses for which reimbursement from Berlin was too time-consuming, or for which there was perhaps no concrete chance for reimbursement in any event. That angered director Walter Lustig, who complained that the Hamburg office was refusing to implement the central accounting system as instructed.[73]

There were similar situations elsewhere. Thus, in December 1943 the Bremen office was unable to submit a financial statement due to air raid damage. Its director, Karl Bruck, even had to request Berlin for a copy of a commentary on the Nuremberg Laws in order to review and interpret the anti-Jewish legislation,[74] since even the basic printed resources for his work had been lost and could not be replaced in another way. Karl Eisemann in Karlsruhe reported that he had been carrying his statistical materials in a briefcase, but had a small mishap: after an air raid, he had stopped on the way to assist with extinguishing the blaze and clearing rubble in three different spots; and in the excitement, he had lost his briefcase.[75] In the summer of 1944 in Aachen, all statistical paperwork and the entire card file were destroyed in a bombing raid.[76] In Cologne, with the help of the Gestapo card file on Jews, the intermediary Hans Salomon Feldheim was able, albeit in makeshift fashion, to reconstruct the data on the Jews in the municipal district, but not the surrounding environs of Cologne. Everything the RV in Berlin wanted to know over and beyond the addresses of individuals was data hard to come by, especially since the offices and agencies had given Feldheim no information. Feldheim threw up his hands in dismay: "All this is leading to incalculable delays. That is compounded by another difficulty: a quite substantial number of Jews have disappeared, forwarding address unknown. On top of that, there is an ongoing operation to merge living quarters, and this will mean that most addresses in Cologne will be changed."[77]

Since the card files had been destroyed almost everywhere (or reports at least suggested this), in the summer of 1944 the rump RV central office decided, like its predecessor organization in 1942, to conduct a fresh survey, distributing questionnaires to regain an overall picture of the number of its (compulsory) members and their living conditions. But these questionnaires were also lost in the chaos wrought by the intensifying air war or were simply ignored. Samuel Cahn, intermediary in Stettin, admitted to the Berlin central office half a year after distributing the questionnaires that the survey had failed: most of "his" Jews had not even bothered to complete them. He wrote that he did not have the necessary statistical data, particularly since his entire correspondence had been destroyed in the bombing raids.[78] So Cahn requested the Berlin RV to send him the data available there. But as chance would have it, at that same time in March 1944, one wing of the building in Berlin where the RV registry was kept had been destroyed in an air raid. So now the RV central office was itself in urgent need of statistical reports and personal data on the Jews throughout the Reich.[79] Their reciprocal requests for data crossed in the mail. Thus an odd situation arose: the offices both in Berlin and Stettin simultaneously requested precise data one from the other. Cahn: "Naturally, I couldn't assume, after we'd just informed you that our own registry had been destroyed in a bombing raid, that now you expected us to help reconstruct your registry."[80]

In the meantime, the tasks of the intermediaries now also involved personally delivering letters to their members containing the most recent Gestapo orders. Furthermore, like the district branch directors before them, they or their few coworkers had to check and vet all petitions that members wanted to submit to the authorities. Or, as in the case of Ernst Neumark in Dresden, they were required to report regularly to the *Judenreferent* on the prevailing mood among the Jews or provide data on specific individuals.[81]

Of course, not only buildings, registries, or the mail delivery system became victims of the air war and its unrelenting fury. The human cost was high, including Jewish functionaries, such as the intermediary Richard Josephy in Rostock. The former attorney lost his life in a bombing raid. As a Jew, he had been denied shelter in an air raid bunker.[82]

Intermediaries in Conflict with the Central Office

The relations of individual *Vertrauensmänner* with the Berlin central office progressively deteriorated. This was due not just to the ravaged infrastructure and lines of communication, but also to new measures of regimentation designed to advance centralization of the organization as a whole. In the eyes of the Jewish functionaries affected, these new regulations were a constricting nuisance, hindering their local work on the ground. Often they were unable to fulfill their obligation to provide reports, nor did they wish to surrender their last modicum of autonomy in matters of finance to the central office. On the other hand, they deplored the perceived lack of support from Berlin for their work. Another common complaint was their total lack of information about what was actually happening regarding the persecution of persons in mixed marriages across the Reich. To remedy this, the intermediaries who knew and trusted each other personally, and were in correspondence, attempted to help one another and pass on news items and information about their ongoing "war of words," as Karl Bruck phrased it, with the Berlin main office. For example, after the massive bombing raids on Hamburg in July and early August 1943, Bruck in Bremen sent out a call in his administrative area for donations of clothing to assist the Hamburg Jews.[83] Arnold Glässner from Aussig asked Corten "privately" whether the rumor (heard by a friend of his) was correct "that Jews from the Birkenau labor camp are supposedly now at work in Hamburg and are under the responsibility of the Reichsvereinigung." Corten confirmed that groups of Jewish conscript laborers were indeed in Hamburg, but denied they were under RV responsibility, stressing there was not even any contact with them.[84]

In late July 1944, it was not the Hamburg bureau, responsible for Bremen, but rather Bruck in Bremen who informed the Hamburg RV office that his territory of competence had been extended: it now included Osnabrück, with twenty-five Jews in mixed marriages and sixty-five *Mischlinge*.[85] He then asked the rhetorical question:

What's actually going on with your contact with Berlin? Myself, I'm not at all satisfied with these gentlemen, and at the moment we have a dispute with them regarding four dozen pencils I obtained. They say I should send two dozen on to Berlin since they assume that two dozen pencils are quite enough for my activity as *Vertrauensmann*. The tone Berlin is adopting irritates me to the point of insubordination.[86]

Office chief Heinemann in Hamburg, a lawyer in a mixed marriage, replied it was a shame

that we never even see each other so as to have a chance to discuss our shared interests. That holds especially when it comes to the chapter "Berlin"! Unfortunately, our experience with them is completely the same as yours. In general, Berlin doesn't worry about us at all ... That's reached the point where we've now sent an urgent report to Berlin, requesting that they place at least 2,000 RM at our disposal in an emergency for those suffering injury or damage from air raids ... On the other hand, when it comes to the hospital, Berlin is making a lot of difficulties for us. They do this in a petty and bureaucratic way, without any real understanding, and their tone at times is downright annoying. It would be too much now to go into any detail.[87]

After air raids had destroyed the authorized shops for Jews in his district, intermediary Alfred Marx in Stuttgart asked his colleagues in Cologne, Stettin, Frankfurt am Main, Munich, Kassel, and Darmstadt how the distribution of food ration cards and food sales were being handled in their area. He probably hoped, with reference to their practice, to be able to submit a proposal to his "superior" authority in Stuttgart that could help "his" Jews. Their answers also indicate that practices certainly differed from place to place: in Stettin, mixed marriages were permitted, with their specially marked ration cards, to buy supplies in any shop. But in Munich, they were under orders to shop only at one designated store, and their ration cards were always stamped with "J." By contrast, after aerial attacks in Mannheim, so-called air raid ration cards valid for one week were issued, without any special stamp for Jews.[88] It is not known whether Marx was able to improve the situation for the Jews affected in his native Stuttgart.

In the meantime, the Jews in mixed marriages had other worries to contend with: since 1939/1940, such Jewish spouses had been deployed in conscript labor. Beginning in the spring of 1944, and intensified in the autumn, their children older than seventeen years, *Mischlinge* of the first degree, and their non-Jewish spouses (classified as "persons with Jewish kin") were ordered to participate in forced labor in the Organisation Todt. Now the Gestapo offices also took steps to include the intermediaries in such orders for conscript labor. Bruck had learned about this development from his colleague in Hanover and informed the office in Hamburg:

Some of our colleagues, *Vertrauensmänner* in Westphalia, have now been ordered to report for forced labor. I can readily understand this development, based as it is on reasons of mobilization for "total war," and would not be surprised if such orders are soon issued for the other intermediaries. You will recall that the activity of intermediaries since 10 June 1943 is purportedly on a volunteer basis. But since the work load of the liaison personnel is only slightly less than that of the former administrative heads or district branch directors, the respective Gestapo offices probably refrained in the past from deploying intermediaries as forced laborers. We will have to wait and see how such conscript labor deployment of intermediaries will impact on their activity, which in significant measure they perform in the interest of the gentlemen experts on staff in the Gestapo offices, and to reduce their work burden. But I can well imagine that for the sake of the Reich, the entire organization of the Reichsvereinigung will soon be liquidated—since to my mind, this apparatus cannot be brought into line with mobilization for total war. If we wish to be frank, we have to admit that we waste a lot of our time on senseless activity. But I don't consider myself authorized to interfere in orders from the supervisory authority. Let's wait and see what time has in store for us.[89]

On the one hand, surprising in this letter is the disrespectful candor with which Bruck openly stated that the Residual Reichsvereinigung was reducing the burden of work of the Gestapo; on the other, striking is his explicit recognition that the statistical work his own organization was doing was largely meaningless, what he termed *Stroh dreschen* or "getting nowhere fast." He appeared neither to fear nor regret a possible disbandment of the rump RV: this is all the more astounding since his own personal fate was closely tied to the organization. However, the letter also makes clear just how much Bruck (and most certainly other colleagues as well) regarded the supposed demands and exigencies of the time, the mobilization for "total war," as the primary yardstick for his reflections. In the autumn of 1944, the war's end loomed on the horizon, but the changes he saw unfolding in the uncertain weeks or months to come could certainly have lethal consequences for him and "his" Jews.

In addition, the *Vertrauensmänner* were unable to simply restrict themselves to locally implementing the instructions or prohibitions coming from the Berlin central office. On the contrary, they were repeatedly confronted with problems for which there were no instructions, and where it did not seem opportune to inquire in Berlin about what to do. In such situations, they had to act on their own initiative. Thus, when the SS summarily shot exhausted prisoners unable to continue on the death march from Auschwitz to the Blechhammer camp in January 1945 in the territory of the Gleiwitz intermediary Erich Schlesinger, Schlesinger arranged to bury the dead in a mass grave in the Jewish cemetery in Gleiwitz. He is also believed to have helped hide two Auschwitz prisoners who had escaped, thus directly endangering his own life.[90]

Lethal Office

As evident from table 7, most of the *Vertrauensmänner* (and the one female intermediary, Irma Wagner) survived the war, a proportion of them in the Theresienstadt ghetto. Yet for some, their office and exposed position cost them their lives.

In Düsseldorf, two RV functionaries were immediately affected. After the disbanding of the RV district office there, the Gestapo appointed the lawyer Kurt Frank to head the rump organization branch office. His predecessor, the businessman Rudolf Braunschweig, had, as mentioned, headed up the administrative office until 1943. When it was shut down, Braunschweig expected possible deportation, even perhaps to Auschwitz, since the Gestapo had "uncovered" supposedly embezzled items in his office. He decided to feign suicide, drafting a bogus farewell letter, and then went into hiding.[91] Bernt Engelmann, who later became a very well-known writer and controversial journalist after the war, a *Mischling* of the first degree and member of a resistance group in the Third Reich, provided Braunschweig with false identity papers.[92]

The *Judenreferat* of the Düsseldorf Gestapo, in particular the "Jewish expert" Georg Pütz and his associate Hermann Waldbillig, who succeeded him in the post, left no stone unturned in trying to locate Braunschweig, especially since the prize of promotion awaited them if they could track him down and smash the resistance group or document forgery ring involved.

Initially, they arrested the ailing Kurt Frank.[93] Threatening him with deportation to Auschwitz, and using other perfidious deceptions (including the assurance that "nothing would happen to Rudi" if located), they extracted a confession from him stating that he knew where Braunschweig was. Then they proceeded to incite the wife of Frank's quickly appointed successor, Waldemar Spier, against Frank.[94] They also arrested Bernt Engelmann, manhandling him in captivity.[95] Finally, they had extorted enough information to locate Braunschweig, arresting him in a Vienna boarding house on 5 March 1944.[96] But they did not leave matters at that. They accused Spier of complicity, along with Braunschweig's brother Otto and his wife Luise, as well as his acquaintance Ernst Dienemann. Frank, Rudolf and Otto Braunschweig, Spier, and Dienemann were deported to Auschwitz.[97] Dienemann's file bore the lethal notation *Sonderbehandlung* (special treatment), a euphemism for liquidation, and he apparently was murdered immediately. Frank died on 24 February 1945, barely a month after Auschwitz was liberated by the Red Army; Spier perished shortly later, dying of "famine fever," a form of typhus, on 2 March 1945.[98] Rudolf and Otto Braunschweig survived.[99] When Rudolf Braunschweig returned to Düsseldorf, he had gone through the harrowing experience of almost seven months in Auschwitz and three months in "Russian protective custody," as he later wrote.[100] Bernt Engelmann, charged with *Judenbegünstigung* (aiding and abetting Jews), survived his imprisonment in the Flossenbürg and Dachau concentration camps.

But back to the events in Düsseldorf in 1944: after Spier's deportation, Ernst Blankenstein, a Jew in a mixed marriage, was appointed intermediary.[101] Blankenstein, a businessman, was a baptized Protestant and married to a Roman Catholic; he had served in WWI and then joined the *Freikorps* in Düsseldorf and fought against the revolutionaries in the "Spartacist uprising" in January 1919. In the Weimar Republic, his political views were conservative German-national. After the National Socialists came to power, Blankenstein successfully was able to conceal his Jewish family background for a number of years. He kept his distance from his mother and his three unmarried siblings, who all wore the "yellow star." He worked in a senior position as syndic in private business and had a large apartment.[102] He did not come to the Gestapo's attention until October 1941. He was not a member of the RV and wished to "have absolutely nothing to do with Judaism."[103] After discovery of his line of descent as a "full Jew," he lost his job, was forced to move to a *Judenhaus*, and was deployed as a conscript laborer in a cemetery. In April/May 1944, "his protest notwithstanding," he was selected for the post of *Vertrauens-mann*.[104] His letter to the central office shows just how unprepared he was to be hurled unexpectedly into the job.[105] The Gestapo gave him Spier's files; he was unaware of just how complete they were, and at that point was unable to ask the "prisoner in protective custody" Spier himself. He continued his work as a forced laborer and was obliged to receive new orders and instructions every other day in the Gestapo office. His work as intermediary mainly entailed informing Jews in mixed marriages that their apartments had been confiscated and that they were now ordered to relocate into *Judenwohnungen*.

A new operation was launched in September 1944 to cleanse the Rhineland and Westphalia of all Jews. In contrast with the remainder of the Reich, in the autumn of 1944, all Jews in mixed marriages, *Mischlinge*, and "persons with Jewish kin" (the *jüdisch Versippte*, i.e., "Aryan" husbands married to Jewish women) were to be resettled. In Düsseldorf, some 50 percent of those slated to be deported fled. Nonetheless, 120 women were transported to Thuringia, and an equal number of men to Lenne-Vorwohlde in Lower Saxony, a camp for forced laborers.[106] Those unfit for labor were sent to the Berlin assembly camp on Schulstrasse, where they were soon joined by some 300 more Jews from the Rhineland.[107] Shortly after the arrival of the "full Jews" at the Lenne camp, they were followed in October 1944 by *Mischlinge* of the first degree and *jüdisch Versippte* from Düsseldorf, Bremen, and the Palatinate. The Gestapo appointed Blankenstein, who was also a prisoner there, the intermediary for the approximately 555 camp inmates.[108] His fellow prisoners soon dubbed him *Schreckenstein* (Horrorstone) because of his strict regime of discipline in the camp.

Some non-Jewish wives and relatives had followed their husbands and located a place to live in the vicinity. If the camp inmates did not have to work on the weekend, they met them outside the camp, reunions where some did not wear their "yellow star." Blankenstein called them to account for this infraction of regulations and threatened penalties. His fellow prisoners also accused him of contributing to a greater differentiation between "privileged" and "nonprivileged" Jews in the camp through his reports. But more than anything else, he always behaved in the camp like a staunch National Socialist: he often shouted at his subordinates, searched sleeping quarters, confiscated radio sets that inmates had pieced together themselves, insulted Jews, and spread a "climate of panic" with his loud whistle. He later justified his actions by stating that in this way, he relieved the Gestapo of any reason for stepping in themselves. Blankenstein, like others, was deported from the Lenne camp to Theresienstadt on 25 February 1945, and survived the short period of internment there.[109]

Erwin Ludnowsky in Breslau died while serving as intermediary. His non-Jewish wife testified after the war that her husband had been forced in mid-1943 by the Gestapo to take on the post of intermediary in the Residual Reichsvereinigung. He was ordered to report on a daily basis to the head of the Jewish Department, the *Judenreferat,* and bring along the papers for the Jewish men still remaining in Breslau. On 27 January 1945, without any prior warning, the Gestapo ordered him along with forty of "his" Jews to trudge off on a three-day march to the Gross-Rosen concentration camp. As a result of this unaccustomed physical exertion under harsh conditions of extreme winter cold, Ludnowsky's feet developed extreme swelling. For that reason, he was unable to continue the march heading toward the Buchenwald concentration camp ten days later and remained in the Gross-Rosen field hospital. He died there on 10 or 12 February.[110] Erich Guttmann, intermediary in Kiel, was arrested on 26 March 1944; he was held in the police jail there until transfer to another jail at Drachensee. He was then sent on to the Mauthausen concentration camp, where he died.[111]

For Hans Salomon Feldheim, his tenure as *Vertrauensmann* for the Cologne Jews also proved lethal. The widower, who called himself a dissident, lived with his daughter Annelise in Cologne; a second daughter had fled in 1939 to the Netherlands and survived the war there. His letters to his emigrated daughter and a small number of extant documents from the RV main office are graphic testimony to his activities and views. After he began the job, he wrote in a (still) light-hearted tone in August 1943:

> Since I took on this job, I have a catastrophically huge load of work to grapple with, in both internal [office work] and external service. This for example includes negotiating with the authorities. In the consultation hours, I deal more with providing legal advice than medical matters. An experienced fellow remarked to me that now I play the role of a small-town mayor, a man who has to be master of all trades. Operating according to the motto "Whom the Lord has given an office, from him He takes (!) the power of reason," I have fond hopes and even sense that my task here, cer-

tainly not easy, will be crowned with success, to the satisfaction of one and all. And so here I sit, sweating in contentment.[112]

The medical doctor, who went about his new job with evident élan and a sizable portion of self-protective irony, should have known better what he had gotten into: already from the onset of the large-scale deportations, he had been confronted in his practice with desperate Jews who, even where their medical condition did not warrant it, requested medical certificates from him attesting that they were not fit to travel. In a letter years before in 1941 to his daughter, commenting in a distanced tone of critique, he had characterized this behavior on the part of his patients as "unpleasant."[113] The office of *Vertrauensmann* now catapulted him into a space much closer to such events: his administrative office was the employer for Jews who had been granted a temporary deferment from deportation because of their activity for the Residual RV, and who hoped to avoid deportation completely. Directly subordinate to him were the Müngersdorf camp marshals, who oversaw or and regulated the forced residents confined in the camp. And now he was even obliged to make direct preparations for the deportations (for which there had long since been no further deferments on medical grounds). In addition, the regulations of his central office in Berlin constricted his latitude for action, since Berlin only provided funding applied for in advance (and that only in restricted amounts). This was the case even if, for example, the Gestapo demanded that he prepare and equip a deportation immediately, without prior notice or the chance to file for money in advance. Feldheim, like all his other colleagues, was thus caught in the middle.

Given these exigencies, he sought to solve his financial problems by borrowing from different sources to finance the transports to Theresienstadt.[114] To pay necessary coworkers for the assembly camp or for the transports, he covered these costs in advance from his own private funds.[115] After he had created in effect such financial faits accomplis, he then applied for reimbursement of the expenses incurred.

His office was located directly in the Müngersdorf barracks camp settlement. Working in that environment was an added burden for him, because he considered his marshals there to be "extremely disgusting."[116] Moreover, quite a few residents did not wish to obey his orders or those of his staff. Soon he was reporting about brawls: his helpers had not been able to handle some "ruffians," so he had found it necessary to "intervene." He twice was hurt in ensuing scuffles, but then decided to restrain himself, because "my office did not allow me to return like for like, since after all, my aim had to be to keep things peaceful." In closing, he commented wryly that he always managed to "come out on top" in such confrontations.[117] A short time later he complained that his burden of tasks was growing ever greater, but was no longer any pleasure for him. Now he was only fulfilling his duty "to the utmost":

> Even those who have been assigned to me as coworkers at the office are, aside from one person, people I'd get rid of if I had a free hand. These gentlemen, and some have been on the job a long time, now simply cannot accept that I've been put in as boss right under their noses. They put up resistance, and this had to be broken in an extended running battle with one another. ... This is hard on the nerves, it drains energy better spent serving the tasks at hand. Despite this, the machinery is functioning pretty well, and now I've reached a point where I can assume that soon I'll be completely in control of the situation.[118]

Feldheim, evidently against his own natural disposition, practiced what he termed ironically in a letter to his daughter "tolerance in his old age," now serving in a "new and difficult office, where I have to negotiate and speak nicely instead ... of using a sledgehammer," as had been his wont in his more undiplomatic and direct younger days.[119] This comment clearly referred not to his negotiations with the authorities or the Gestapo, but rather to his Jewish coworkers and his clients in the barracks camp. He apparently could negotiate better with "Aryans," while he found repulsive the desperate attempts by Jews to obtain advantages by resorting to circuitous routes or intrigue. However, this certainly did not mean that he was unfeeling on the job, unmoved by evident distress and hardship. On the contrary, among his duties was also care for needy Jews and those who had been arrested and taken into "protective custody." In view of their material and psychological misery, the doctor felt compelled to act. He himself, despite all anti-Semitic measures, was in fact still relatively well-to-do financially. So he decided to support five Jews from his district confined in the Buchenwald camp, providing each an allowance of 7.50 RM monthly. In requesting reimbursement, he gave a detailed rationale for this action to the Berlin central office. He argued in particular that the mere existence of such an external benefit, irrespective of the amount, already served as a source of welcome "mental support" for the detainees. What he left unmentioned was that these prisoners always had to expect that they might suddenly be deported to an extermination camp. News from back home always signaled the presence of interest in those who had disappeared behind the fences. It gave them the hope that should they be deported elsewhere, someone would inquire about their situation. But the RV central office remained unimpressed: it refused to reimburse these funds. Feldheim stubbornly persisted and received a second rejection of his request for reimbursement. When he then made an advance payment to cover the moving costs for a Jewish woman, and the expenses for medicine for another, actions he likewise had no authorization for, he fell out of favor with the central office, and was reprimanded and warned.[120] Physically at a great remove from the needy Jews under its aegis of care, and always mindful of the scant total budget and its constraints, the RV central office regarded such expenses as unjustified outlay, especially if not approved in advance and their amount adjusted to the authorized payments by other intermediaries. However, Feldheim for his part was evidently not accustomed to obtaining permission from third parties for decisions he deemed necessary, and he probably did not want to be drawn into a "war of words" over trivialities. Thus, to the evident chagrin of his Jewish superiors, he also went so far as to purchase an accounts book, on his own and without prior authorization, after the one sent by the central office was lost in the mail.

Evidently he was unable to solve his problems either with the central office or with his employees. So he appeared distinctly relieved when at the end of November 1943, he was ordered to relocate the RV office from the Müngersdorf camp into his own apartment: "I've had to fire the coworkers, which will mean being stuck with all kinds of extra work for me. But it's a great advantage in itself not to have to go out every day to Müngersdorf." He wrote his daughter that he was happy to be rid of these employees. It becomes clear from his correspondence that his activity had long since ceased to give him any real "satisfaction," but after all, he reflected, "not every office and assignment a person has to deal with can be ranked among life's little pleasures."[121]

His work load increased again in early 1944 when, along with hours at his doctor's office and work in a what Feldheim called a "mini-hospital" that he and his colleagues had set up, he was ordered to deal with "substantial procedures for settlement" of various outstanding matters for the RV.[122] In the summer of 1944, pressures in his situation mounted. The central office ordered him to quickly restore the card file that had been destroyed in an air raid,[123] and he did so as far as he was possible, but refused to complete other tasks Berlin had demanded of him: "I don't think I'll be able in the near future to submit useful statistical data."[124] Two months later, the Berlin central office received alarming news: Feldheim had gone missing and had supposedly taken with him the petty cash box containing around one thousand RM.[125] The location of the money remained unexplained. Feldheim and his daughter Annelise had gone into hiding because deportations of the Rhineland Jews had been announced, and in September were indeed implemented. They sought refuge with a friend, but soon were in great danger of being reported to the police, and so left their hideaway. On 28 September 1944, father and daughter took a lethal overdose of the sedative Veronal in a park in Cologne.[126] In a farewell letter in late August 1944, Hans Salomon Feldheim explained this decision to his life partner:

> Despicable swine have threatened our noble hosts in anonymous letters, and so we have to leave here so as to prevent even greater misfortune. We were always free persons, and wish to remain so to our last living breath. For that reason, we will not expose ourselves to any treatment at the hands of the despots.[127]

At this point, the Rhenish and Westphalian Jews had already been deported. Their hope that the Americans would march into Cologne before that had proved illusory.

The Residual RV now appointed Heinrich Kounen as new intermediary to replace Feldheim. Kounen had worked for a time for the Cologne Jewish Community in connection with burials. He survived his short time in office. In contrast with Hans Salomon Feldheim, he was paid for his services,[128] and the Berlin central office allotted him two thousand RM in advance for attending to the needs of the Cologne Jews. Now there were hardly any Jews left in the city, except for some illegal Jews and eight persons behind bars, including "Dr. Rosen, the former chairman in Aachen, who in September had fled here from the camp, and who was apprehended approximately three weeks ago."[129] In September 1944, the barracks in Müngersdorf had served once more (and for the last time) as an assembly camp for the deportation of those in mixed marriages,[130] and were not supposed to be utilized any further in the future. Nonetheless, due to a lack of living space, twenty-six Jews moved into the barracks there, soon followed by others. Kounen had to procure food and charcoal for the inmates and their guards. Given the temperature outside, which had dropped to −14°C in late December 1944, residents and guards struggled with the extreme cold in the barracks in the dead of winter. However, it was far more difficult for Jews to obtain fuel.[131] For that reason, Kounen—with whom the Berlin central office had been far more accommodating than with Feldheim—found it unavoidable to act: he chose to violate regulations, and he retained a portion of the money collected from the new residents to use for buying charcoal, etc. (if necessary on the black market). (It is likely that, like the inmates in the Berlin assembly camp, these Jews had to pay the high rent of 250 RM per month for accommodation in the camp.) Kounen, who himself lived in the Müngersdorf camp, fled shortly before the end of the war, and survived his tenure as intermediary in hiding.[132]

Vertrauensmänner, the Gestapo, and Jews in the Final Phase of the War

The intermediaries of the Residual Reichsvereinigung found themselves personally in the same situation as those whose needs they now had to care for: they themselves had to fear possible relocation or resettlement at any time. Many examples clearly show that the former protection offered by a mixed marriage had shriveled to a point of ever-greater fragility. In order to initiate the deportation of a Jewish spouse in a mixed marriage, the Gestapo not only utilized cases of death and divorce, but often also resorted to separation due to the wartime conditions or various "offenses" against regulations. Nor did it exempt from possible transport the functionaries whom it had itself appointed. Consequently, the intermediaries shared the danger of arrest and deportation with their members, but the gulf between them remained: any entry in writing by an intermediary on a member regarding assets, medical condition, social benefits, change in address, or family situation could have negative consequences for those affected and their families. In short, the Jews came to mistrust their functionaries: they distributed the orders from the Gestapo, and thus represented a potential threat. On the other hand, there was no other contact person to consult for any questions and concerns that arose.

Meanwhile, the Gestapo had disbanded its own *Judenreferate* after the conclusion of the large-scale deportations, and integrated the area formerly covered by the "Jewish experts" into other departments. These units dealt principally with the persecution of foreign forced laborers or spies. However, individual officials continued to remain responsible for "Jewish affairs." Consequently, the demands for statistical data and detailed information on the Jews remained operative and were in fact expanded, when an additional order, for example, finally instructed intermediaries to put together a card file on *Mischlinge*. Despite the changes within the Gestapo structure, the *Vertrauensmänner* were under orders to continue to report to the Gestapo office every day or two to receive new instructions. Some, such as Michel Oppenheim in Mainz or Hans Salomon Feldheim in Cologne, described "their" contact official as neutral or even cooperative (a description certainly embellished given the predominant racist hierarchy). By contrast, other Jewish functionaries such as Theodor Koronczyk were forced during discussions to stand in the corner, facing the wall, and some had to repeatedly endure the verbal or physical fury and abuse of their persecutors when they appeared to report. Victor Klemperer, known later for his diary, who had various dealings with the Dresden intermediary Neumark and his associate, the Jewish physician Katz, sketched humiliating scenes from their everyday round of life.[133] The "Jewish expert" in Dresden, Henry Schmidt, would start punching the intermediaries to vent his "pent-up aggression."[134] Yet Klemperer described these final two Dresden functionaries with evident contempt:

> Each hides behind the other, calls the other prevaricator and jellyfish, lays the responsibility and the decision on the other. Basically one cannot hold it against them, because both are powerless and tremble before the Gestapo, which can destroy them at any moment and under any pretext.[135]

After the Jews from dissolved mixed marriages had been deported in 1943/1944, between January and the end of March 1945 the Gestapo ordered transports from across Germany to Theresienstadt. Officially, these transports were described as "forced labor deployment abroad." For example, at the beginning of 1945, Ernst Neumark was ordered to deport the Jews still living in mixed marriages in Dresden. He instructed Klemperer and another assistant to deliver the written order personally to those affected. Due to the massive bombing raid on Dresden in February 1945, the transport never departed. Neumark himself was bombed out and went into hiding until the Red Army arrived.[136]

The gamble by Michel Oppenheim earlier described to rescue the Jews in Mainz with the aid of the local Gestapo was doubtless unique. But some *Vertrauensmänner* also tried to spare "their" Jews deportation and also to avoid transport themselves. Adolf Lipp in Chemnitz, whose card file had just gone up in flames,[137] was ordered to organize a transport scheduled to leave on 10 March 1945. He reassured the deportees that they had no need to worry; he was going to go into hiding and take the list of the designated deportees along with him.[138] After the war, Theodor Koronczyk in Munich considered it to his merit that he removed some 450 Munich Jews from deportation transport lists, based on diverse grounds. In Hamburg, only 198 of the 276 originally ordered to report boarded the train for Theresienstadt: Martin Heinrich Corten had managed to have 32 individuals exempted on medical grounds and 19 deferred. Another 21 did not show up for the transport, with no reason given.[139] However, the transport left for Bohemia with a total of 294 Jews, including 81 Jews from Bremen and 15 Jews from Schleswig-Holstein.[140] In Düsseldorf, of 700 Jews ordered to assemble for deportation, only 200 appeared. The Gestapo then proceeded to the addresses of those missing but found no one. The deportation commenced with but four of the original ten reserved carriages.[141] The intermediaries, in some cases already assigned to planned transports, in others temporarily deferred (as in the case of Karl Bruck in Bremen, who was granted a four-week reprieve[142]), now knew definitely that they were slated to be deported along with their members. This would come to pass, if not immediately, then in the near future.

In the large-scale deportations during the fall and winter of 1941, the Jews ordered to report for "resettlement" and (compulsory) "migration" had been compelled, almost without exception, to obey the order. Deferments on medical grounds, work critical to the war effort, or to keep families together protected people from deportation only for a short time. They generally received a second deportation order a few weeks or months later. But the Jews slated to be deported between January and March 1945 found themselves in a totally different situation: the Allies were nearing the German heartland, Auschwitz had been liberated, and a looming German defeat was evident to all. In addition, ordinary German *Volksgenossen* and Gestapo officers sought to acquire some insurance for themselves for what would come after defeat: they no longer were so avid in executing orders, and instead tried to gain some credit with the persecuted that might later prove useful. Thus, doctors (including some who were not Jewish) issued certificates certifying that individual Jews were "unfit for labor" or seriously ill, thus in effect counteracting the order for "forced labor deployment abroad." Moreover, non-Jewish spouses, "Aryan" relatives, and friends of Jews in mixed marriages encouraged them to take the risk of eluding deportation by going into hiding for several days or weeks—instead of reporting for deportation to an uncertain fate. Others, such as the former *Vertrauensmann* Cahn in Frankfurt am Main, received certificates stating that they were indispensable personnel on the "home front." Supposedly, his services as a legal "consultant" were now urgently needed by the director of the district court and finance office. Nonetheless, Cahn was prudently cautious; for safety's sake, he decided to spend the final weeks of the war, not registered, in the home of friends.[143]

The approximately twenty-one hundred Jews who nevertheless were deported from the area of competence of the Residual RV to Theresienstadt[144] generally managed to survive the short span of their internment there until the ghetto was liberated by Soviet troops on 8 May 1945.

The War Is Over: Liberation and/or a Horrible End?

There is a traditional saying in German, "Lieber ein Ende mit Schrecken als ein Schrecken ohne Ende" (Better a horrible end than horror without end). This maxim is also applicable here. The German Jews who had not been deported experienced liberation in the ruins of their hometowns, and in labor and assembly camps. They, like the intermediaries of the rump Reichsvereinigung, generally greeted the arrival of Allied troops in the western areas of the former *Altreich* with feelings of great relief and joy, since the fear of arrest and deportation was now a specter of the past.

The arrival of the victors generated less rejoicing in the Soviet-occupied part of Berlin.

The Soviet soldiers falsely assumed there were no Jewish survivors on German soil, and whoever claimed to be a Jew was either a liar or a former member of the SS or Gestapo. Consequently, many a liberated Jew had to fear anew for his or her life in the initial days of the occupation. They had to try to prove that they were actually of Jewish origin and had been persecuted. Jewish-Soviet officers asked Jews to recite the traditional formula "Shema Yisrael" or checked whether they could speak or understand Yiddish. A danger at least as great arose for Jews who had exercised some function in the Reichsvereinigung. These dangers now came from Jewish survivors or the relatives of the murdered, who sought to alert the Soviets to persons they believed had been informers or collaborators, hoping the occupiers might punish them for their crimes.

One prominent early victim of such accusations was Walter Lustig. As mentioned, he had survived the war's end and initially remained at his post as director of the Jewish Hospital, where now emergency accommodations and a transit camp had been set up for Jews emerging from hiding or returning from internment in some camp.[145] In addition, Lustig had made himself available to the district of Wedding to assist as a government doctor and head of the Public Health Office in reconstructing the health care system.[146] Lustig applied to the Soviets to recognize the Reichsvereinigung as the sole legitimate organization to represent the interests of the surviving Jews, and also sent a corresponding letter on 6 June 1945 to the Berlin lord mayor, threatening immediate measures. When there was discussion on dissolving all National Socialist organizations, he announced the renaming of the Reichsvereinigung as "Jewish Community Berlin," because its work now related to the entire area of metropolitan greater Berlin.[147] He himself wished to be appointed as its highest-ranking official, and stated that his staff associates during the previous two years should be placed in slots two through twelve on the list of functionaries. As though he were already director of the Community or association, he demanded better food, exemption for Jews from work in clearing rubble, preferential allotment of clothing and footwear, and the like.[148] A declaration of loyalty to Stalin by Hirschfeld, his medical colleague at the hospital, concluded his petition: "The few surviving Jews of Berlin are grateful from the bottom of their hearts to you, distinguished Marshal, for their liberation by the glorious Red Army from the horrors of Nazi rule."[149] Lustig evidently was relying now as before on decisions from above. He was uninterested in efforts and movements from below. Other survivors and returnees from concentration camps had already established Jewish Communities in several parts of the city, and a central

Jewish Community had also been founded once again.[150] Nonetheless, Lustig adamantly insisted on his claim to sole representation. Of course, he knew that his (borrowed) power had vanished,[151] but he evidently was not worried that personal accusations by former compulsory RV members could prove potentially disastrous for him. However, survivors from the assembly camp accused him of collaboration, and the Soviet authorities then arrested Lustig at the end of June 1945. His comrades Siegbert Kleemann and others tried immediately to arrange his release. They argued that Lustig had been appointed by the Berlin Jewish Community to direct health services, and had not been put in that post by the Gestapo. They noted that during the time of the large-scale deportations, Lustig had not been an RV board member, but rather had been occupied with medical examinations in order that the seriously ill, old, and infirm could receive a deferment from deportation. Finally, they stressed that ensuring the continued operation of the hospital had been his accomplishment, and he had been able there to rescue Jewish prisoners; these had then survived until liberation. Thus, they argued, contrary to the allegations, that Lustig had "done everything possible in the interests of the Jews."[152] Their intervention proved unsuccessful. In December 1945, Lustig was put to death in the Rummelsburg prison in Berlin as a Nazi collaborator.[153] Lustig's Berlin associates continued to insist for a time that they should be recognized as the legal successors to the Jewish *Gemeinden* that had been dissolved during the Nazi period. They demanded entitlement to speak for and represent the Jewish survivors, but they were unable to stem developments: other, new, or reestablished organizations now claimed the right to represent German Jews, and were granted that by the new Allied authorities.

In other parts of Germany as well, the heads of the Residual Reichsvereinigung clung to their role as spokespersons for the Jews. In Hamburg, for example, Max Heinemann, the last executive director of the office and close associate of intermediary Martin Heinrich Corten, approached the occupying authorities as a potential interlocutor, based on the Hilfsgemeinschaft der Juden und Halbjuden (Union of Jews and Half Jews) that he had established in May 1945.[154] This association was then merged into the reestablished Hamburg Jewish Community, while Heinemann himself emigrated to the United States.

Most of the small number of concentration camp survivors among the Jewish functionaries from the RV main office and the Berlin Jewish Community left Germany as quickly as they could. Baeck went to Great Britain, taking British citizenship in 1950; Hans-Erich Fabian, who had participated in the reestablishment of the Berlin Jewish Community, later became a US citizen. Moritz and Hildegard Henschel emigrated to Palestine, where Moritz Henschel died in 1947. Only a few, such as Martha Mosse or Berthold Simonsohn, remained on in Germany.[155]

It was a different situation with surviving functionaries of the Residual Reichsvereinigung. Those who had stayed at their posts until liberation considered it self-evident to utilize the still existing structures of their organization, now without Gestapo supervision, in order to pass on information, alleviate the most severe hardship, and adhere to their position as spokespersons of the Jews, in order to negotiate with the occupation authorities, the JOINT, or other relief associations and distribute their aid. They believed their skills were urgently needed and insisted on continuing to be active. In addition, they were very happy to have survived. In short, from their point of view, they had worked down to the final day and under constant personal danger for the good of the Jews in mixed marriages, and expected some recognition for these contributions. Corten commented in his yet unpracticed English: "I am proud of having could save the life at least of these people from being slaughtered."[156] However, their former compulsory members, and in particular the returnees from concentration camps and the Jews who had survived in hiding, worked energetically to put a stop to that. They suspected the Jewish functionaries of having made common cause with the Gestapo, and accused them of concrete responsibility for having deported their family members or of complicity in implementing other measures of persecution. Moreover, they did not wish to see any continuation of an organization they regarded as suspect and that was also secular. Instead, they reestablished the Jewish Communities that had been dissolved during the Nazi period. Directors were to be elected in the Communities who would again provide for religious and social concerns, and regain the confiscated assets of the former Communities. The Allies shared this viewpoint. The first prohibition of the Reichsvereinigung was issued in Berlin: on 12 July 1945, the director of police (*Polizeipräsident*) in greater Berlin disbanded the organization by decree.[157] On 20 September 1945, the Allied Control Commission then ordered the revocation of all National Socialist legislation, including the Law on Reich Citizenship (*Reichsbürgergesetz*), a key law on whose specific basis the Reichsvereinigung had been created by the National Socialist state.[158] The RV was thus formally classified as a "Nazi organization" and dissolved.

Interim Summary

Between 1943 and 1945, Walter Lustig, director of the Residual Reichsvereinigung, and the *Vertrauensmänner* subordinate to him in the regional offices attended to the needs of the "full Jews" in mixed marriages. They labored in administrative offices whose number and personnel had been significantly reduced. The structure of the rump organization was characterized by a thrust for substantially increased centralization. However, the impact of that centralization tended to be offset and vitiated by the massive destruction of infrastructure and communication paths during the war. The intermediaries utilized disrupted postal routes and telephone lines in order to make decisions on their own authority, choosing not to pass on funds to the central office, etc., as far as this was possible. Under the fury of the mounting air war and its unrelenting bombardments, card files went up in flames, and Jews fled from the devastated areas. Consequently, the Residual RV sought in the spring of 1944 to update their registry by conducting a primary survey. The intermediaries (forty males and one woman) had generally worked as lawyers or medical doctors for or together with the former Reichsvereinigung; however, they had seldom served in its administrative structure. Most had not wished to be appointed liaison officers, but only very few could refuse that office without having to fear personal repercussions. Although they were generally suspected by RV members to be serving as veritable henchmen of the Gestapo, the source materials do not support that view. Rather, documentation substantiates the huge efforts most of the last Jewish functionaries made in providing for the needs of the "prisoners in protective custody" and their families, and in generally achieving small improvements, such as betterment of food rations. Some paid for their liaison function with their lives. On the other hand, their job also entailed organizing the deportation of Jews from dissolved mixed marriages, which in turn could also result in the death of deportees, and in 1945, they had to order the Jews from still existing mixed marriages into "forced labor deployment abroad" and deportation to Theresienstadt. A number of intermediaries and many of the Jews to be deported refused to obey this final command.

After the war's end, most of the directors of the still extant offices of the residual RV wished to continue their activity. However, incomprehensible to many of them, they were removed from office by their earlier clientele or the Allied occupying powers; the rump Reichsvereinigung was dissolved and its last director arrested and executed. As a look at later developments shows, the private and professional life of other *Vertrauensmänner* was burdened and bedeviled in the postwar period by their former office.

Notes

1. On definitions and figures for *Mischlinge, Geltungsjuden,* and mixed marriages, see Meyer, *"Jüdische Mischlinge,"* 25, 30ff., 101ff. If the Protectorate Bohemia and Mora-

via were included, the figures would cover an additional two to three thousand more couples.

2. BArch, R 18, 343-345, Secret express letter, Field Marshal Göring, Deputy for the Four-Year Plan, to Reich interior minister, 28 December 1938.

3. See Beate Meyer, "The Mixed Marriage—a Guarantee of Survival or a Reflection of German Society during the Nazi Regime?," in *Probing the Depths of German Antisemitism: German Society and the Persecution of the Jews, 1933–1941*, ed. David Bankier (New York, 1999), 54–77.

4. On the Wannsee conference and subsequent deliberations, see Kurt Pätzold and Erika Schwarz, *Tagesordnung: Judenmord: Die Wannsee-Konferenz am 30. Januar 1942* (Berlin, 1992); Mark Roseman, *The Wannsee Conference and the Final Solution: A Reconsideration* (New York, 2002); Cornelia Essner, *Die "Nürnberger Gesetze" oder die Verwaltung des Rassenwahns 1933–1945* (Paderborn, 2002).

5. StaHH, 522-1, Jüdische Gemeinden, section 1993, folder 16, file report Corten (with cover letter, 15 September 1943 to Lustig), point 3.

6. StaHH, 522-1, Jüdische Gemeinden, section 1993, folder 36, memo Plaut, September 1943.

7. BArch, R 8150/9, internal submission Wolffsky to Lustig, 4 January 1944, pag. 138.

8. On Lustig, see Daniel S. Nadav and Manfred Stürzbecher, "Walter Lustig," 221–26; see also Elkin, *Jüdisches Krankenhaus*; Meyer, "Fine Line," 339–45 (including photograph); Daniel B. Silver, *Refuge in Hell: How Berlin's Jewish Hospital Outlasted the Nazis* (New York, 2003); see also Rivka Elkin, "The Survival of the Jewish Hospital in Berlin 1938–1945," *Leo Baeck Institute Year Book* 38, no. 1 (1993): 157–92; Daniel Nadav, *Medicine and Nazism* (Jerusalem, 2010), 41–52.

9. On the persecution of those in mixed marriages and their various strategies of dealing with this from 1933 to 1945, see Meyer, *"Jüdische Mischlinge,"* 24–95.

10. BArch, R 8150/9, order, 10 August 1943, pag. 271.

11. BArch, R 8150/10, list, probably July 1943, pag. 6, 10.

12. BArch, R 8150/9, directive, 22 January 1944, pag. 217, 239.

13. BArch, R 8150/9, directive, 22 January 1944, lists, pag. 669–70. On the Grumach Group, see Dov Schidorsky, "Confiscation of Libraries and Assignments to Forced Labor: Two Documents of the Holocaust," *Libraries & Culture* 33, no. 4 (1998): 347–88, http://goo.gl/2F5mD (accessed 20 May 2013).

14. BArch, R 8150/1.3./50/7, report, number of employees, 10 July 1943; CJA, folder dossier (Jewish Community Berlin, prior to 8 May 1945, system of remuneration, etc.), reports, number of employees, October and November 1943; for March and April 1944, 325/321 persons are reported (administration and social welfare 42/43, health 140/142, special tasks 85/84, migration 51/45, final legal processing 7/7); BArch, R 8150/9 Aufstellung Mitarbeiterstand [list of persons on staff], pag. 288, 289.

15. BArch, R 8150/14, list of intermediaries of the RVJD according to district and alphabetically, n.d., pag. 337, 338.

16. CJA, folder: Allgemeines/Vertrauensmänner [General matters/ intermediaries], letter RVJD to professional association, 21 October 1943.

17. CJA, folder: Allgemeines/Vertrauensmänner, circular letter, no. 2, 9 July 1943, p. 1. The intermediaries passed on these instructions, such as Adolf Lipp (Chemnitz) on 21 July 1943; I am grateful to Jürgen Nitsche for kindly calling Lipp's circular letter no. 1 to my attention.

18. CJA, folder: Allgemeines/Vertrauensmänner, circular letter, no. 2, p. 2.

19. BArch, R 8150/9, Liste, 31 October 1943, pag. 191.

20. CJA, folder: Allgemeines/Vertrauensmänner, circular letter, no. 2, 9 July 1943, p. 3; BArch, R 8150/33 and BArch, R 8150/36, div. reports and lists by name.

21. LBI, NY, MF 456, letter Wagner to RVJD, 18 May 1944.
22. StaHH, 522-1, Jüdische Gemeinden, section 1993, folder 16, dossier Corten (with letter by him to Lustig, 15 September 1943), point 2.
23. For example, see diverse reports from the Auschwitz concentration camp on who had died of "cardiac insufficiency," "pleuro-pneumonia" (inflammation of the lungs and pleurisy), or "cardiac muscle deficiency"; StaHH, 522-1 Jüdische Gemeinden, section 1993, folder 38.
24. Such as the intermediary in Osnabrück (under competence of Bremen); BArch, R 8150/9, excerpt from memo no. 23, submissions to RSHA, 13 November 1944, pag. 15.
25. Such as Breslau; see BArch, R 8150/9, letter RVJD Berlin, Kleemann, to Erwin Ludnowsky, 18 November 1943, pag. 279.
26. BArch, R 8150/9, directive, 18 March 1944, pag. 143; BArch, R 8150/123/1, internal letter, Kleemann, 8 February 1944, pag. 84, 524; BArch, R 8150/123/1, directive, 25 August 1944, pag. 399.
27. BArch, R 8150/123/1, list, 1 July 1944, pag. 56; data lacking for Jägerndorf and Stettin.
28. StaHH, 522-1, Jüdische Gemeinden, section 1993, folder 16, File report on the negotiations in Berlin on 20/21 August 1943 in Berlin [Aktenbericht über die Verhandlungen in Berlin]; StaHH, 522-1, Jüdische Gemeinden, section 1993, folder 38, File report Corten, 17 September 1943 on negotiations, 14/15 September 1943.
29. StaHH, 522-1, Jüdische Gemeinden, section 1993, folder 38, File report Corten, 17 September 1943 on negotiations, 14/15 September 1943, points I 5, III 4; StaHH, 522-1, Jüdische Gemeinden, section 1993, folder 38, Corten, 17 September 1943, File report on negotiations in Berlin, 14/15 September 1943, point 4.
30. BArch, R 8150/731, letter Marx to RVJD, 7 October 1943, pag. 21; BArch, R 8150/731, letter Marx to RVJD, 29 October 1943, pag. 8.
31. BArch, R 8150/9, internal submission Königsberger to Lustig, 3 November 1943, pag. 183.
32. Elkin, *Jüdisches Krankenhaus*, 71; see also Elkin, "Survival"; Silver, *Refuge*, 25ff.
33. The following comments on Lustig and his biography are largely based, unless otherwise noted, on the thoroughly researched article by Nadav and Stürzbecher, "Walter Lustig," and my essay, Meyer, "Fine Line," 339–40; see also Elkin, *Jüdisches Krankenhaus*; Elkin, "Survival."
34. In private possession, Lebenslauf Walter Lustig [Walter Lustig c.v.], n.d. (probably 1939).
35. For data on Lustig's professional career, see *Volkswohlfahrt. Amtsblatt und Halbmonatsschrift des Preußischen Ministeriums für Volkswohlfahrt*, vol. 1 (1920 [April–Dec.]), with *Ministerialblatt für Medizinalangelegenheiten*, vol. 20 (Berlin, 1920 [Jan.–March]), *Volkswohlfahrt*, No. 17, 1 Dec. 1920, 390; *Volkswohlfahrt. Amtsblatt und Halbmonatsschrift des Preußischen Ministeriums für Volkswohlfahrt*, vol. 2 (Berlin, 1921), No. 3, 1 Feb. 1921, 50; *Volkswohlfahrt. Amtsblatt und Halbmonatsschrift des Preußischen Ministeriums für Volkswohlfahrt*, vol. 4 (Berlin, 1923), No. 18, 15 Sept. 1923, 425; for a recommendation of Lustig's book, see *Volkswohlfahrt. Amtsblatt und Halbmonatsschrift des Preußischen Ministeriums für Volkswohlfahrt*, vol. 6 (Berlin, 1925), 479; *Volkswohlfahrt. Amtsblatt des Preußischen Ministeriums für Volkswohlfahrt*, vol. 8 (Berlin, 1927), No. 5, 1 March 1927, 181; ibid., vol. 9 (Berlin, 1928), No. 12, 15 June 1928, 643; ibid., vol. 10, (Berlin, 1929), No. 19, 1 October 1929, 821. I am grateful to the late Thomas Jersch for pointing out these references and other documentation.
36. Since the membership lists have been lost, this cannot be checked; information by telephone from the Archive of Social Democracy, Peter Gohle, 10 February 2010.

37. In private possession, "Lebenslauf Walter Lustig," n.d. (probably 1939), p. 2.
38. In private possession, interview with Gila K.-Lustig, 10 May 2000, transcript, p. 10; see also Meyer, Simon, and Schütz, *Jews*, 339ff., 361n165.
39. *Ministerial-Blatt für die Preußische innere Verwaltung*, Teil II Ausg. A, ed. Prussian Interior Ministry 1933, No. 53, 20 December 1933, Persönliche Angelegenheiten: Auf Grund des § 3 in den Ruhestand versetzt: ObReguMedRat Dr. Lustig in Berlin [Personal matters: Retired subject to para. 3: ObReguMedRat Dr. Lustig in Berlin].
40. LAB, Pr BR Rep. 042, Kap. 60 Ti 21b/L7 Nachweisung zur Anweisung der Versorgungsbezüge, 11 January 1934 [Certificate re payment of pension benefits].
41. Elkin, *Jüdisches Krankenhaus*, 46.
42. Ibid., 55; Silver, *Refuge*, 28.
43. OFD Berlin (files stored today in the Potsdam Main State Archive), 8 WGA 2176.50, notification on Jewish assets levy, 3 January 1939; Entschädigungsamt Düsseldorf, ZK 14012, application from Annemarie Lustig.
44. See chapter 2; see also Elkin, *Jüdisches Krankenhaus*, 49ff.; Silver, *Refuge*, 140ff.
45. CJA, 2 B1/5, memo, 10 December 1942.
46. LAB, Rep 057-01, Generalstaatsanwaltschaft bei dem Kammergericht/Arbeitsgruppe RSHA, Urteil gegen Fritz Woehrn [State prosecutor's office, Court of Appeal, Working group RSHA, verdict against Fritz Woehrn], 6 April 1971, KS 1/69, p. 4; see also Silver, *Refuge*, 222.
47. LAB, Rep 057-01, Generalstaatsanwaltschaft bei dem Kammergericht/Arbeitsgruppe RSHA, Urteil gegen Fritz Woehrn, 6 April 1971, KS 1/69, p. 32.
48. Quoted from the verdict, p. 33.
49. Proven in the eyes of the court by the cases of Ruth Ellen Wagner, Kurt Bukofzer, and doorman Löwenthal; see verdict against Woehrn, pp. 24–31; see also Meyer, "Fine Line," 334–35; for the fate of Ruth Wagner and Kurt Bukofzer, see Silver, *Refuge*, 159–63.
50. Meyer, "Fine Line," 338–39.
51. Bezirksregierung Düsseldorf, Entschädigungsamt, Dr. Annemarie Lustig, ZK 14012, transcript of interrogation under oath, F.H. before District Court Krefeld, 31 March 1953; on the liberation of the hospital, see also Silver, *Refuge*, 1–4, 198–99. Silver begins his book, as the Soviet troops discover the Jewish Hospital, with the lines: "'You are Jews? Not possible,' the Russian soldier said in his own language and then in broken German: '*Nichts Juden. Juden kaputt.*' 'You can't be Jews. The Jews are all dead.'"
52. Bezirksregierung Düsseldorf, Entschädigungsamt, Dr. Annemarie Lustig, ZK 14012, transcript of interrogation under oath, F.H. before District Court Krefeld, 31 March 1953.
53. Die Bundesbeauftragte für die Unterlagen des Staatssicherheitsdienstes der Deutschen Demokratischen Republik (hereafter BStU [Federal Commissioner for the Stasi Archives, German Democratic Republic]), MfS Ast I c 1/74, examination of the conviction of former members of the SPD, 11 July 1956, pag. 213. It is evident from the report that Rosenbaum was a member of the USPD from 1918, and then joined the SPD until 1933.
54. BArch, NSDAP-Zentralkartei [NSDAP central card file], membership card Corten (card no. 2639677). His wife was excluded from the party in 1934; letter, NSDAP-Kreisgericht Berlin I to Ortsgruppe Lietzensee, 25 May 1933.
55. State Archive Munich, Spruchkammer, box 939, Theodor Koronczyk, minutes of the public meeting, 29/30 October 1947, p. 2, pag. 33.
56. As Corten stated, according to his attorney, reproduced in *Hamburger Abendblatt*,

28 November 1950, "marriage should be a long conversation." Corten had his wife committed to a psychiatric asylum after the war; see chapter 5, "In the Wake."

57. WL, WL P III e No. 456, p. 3; interview with Peter Cahn; LBY NY, AR 333, address at funeral of Max L. Cahn, 19 October 1967.

58. YV, 02/8, Erich Schlesinger, History of the Jewish Community Gleiwitz, 31.1.1933-24.1.1945, p. 9 (same text also YV, 033/71). A *shammes* is a synagogue sexton or caretaker; a *hazzan* is a cantor.

59. BArch, R 8150/14, Vertrauensmänner (n.d.), pag. 337, addenda, p. 2; list (n.d.), BArch, R 8150/14, Vertrauensmänner (n.d.), pag. 342; BArch, R 8150/32 Liste VM (n.p.). The data in the right-hand column are based on research on the Internet, the research literature, inquiries to colleagues, perusal of the Federal Archive, and other archives not individually mentioned here.

60. See the list of the district branch directors: according to that list, the district branch director in Aussig, who was deported and murdered, has this family name; this person is possibly a relative of his.

61. Horst Boog, Gerhard Krebs, and Detlef Vogel, *Das Deutsche Reich und der Zweite Weltkrieg*, vol. 7, *Das Deutsche Reich in der Defensive. Strategischer Luftkrieg in Europa, Krieg im Westen und in Ostasien 1943–1944/45* (Stuttgart and Munich, 2001), 8; see also Richard Overy, *Why the Allies Won* (New York, 1996), esp. 118ff.

62. Figures based on Frank Bajohr, "Gauleiter in Hamburg: Zur Person und Tätigkeit Karl Kaufmanns (1900–1969)," *Vierteljahrshefte für Zeitgeschichte* 43 (1995): 293. On the effects of the air raids, see also Ursula Büttner, *"Gomorrha": Hamburg im Bombenkrieg* (Hamburg, 1993); see also the documentary "Operation Gomorrha—Hamburg im Feuersturm 1943," Spiegel TV 2003, http://goo.gl/dBVNC (accessed 13 July 2012).

63. See Dietmar Süss, "Der Kampf um die 'Moral' im Bunker: Deutschland, Großbritannien und der Luftkrieg," in *Volksgemeinschaft: Neue Forschungen zur Gesellschaft des Nationalsozialismus*, ed. Frank Bajohr and Michael Wildt (Frankfurt am Main, 2009), 131–32; Hamburg Jews reported in interviews that they had only been permitted entry into the tower bunker (*Hochbunker*) in the main Jewish residential area of Grindel; otherwise, they had to rely on basements or entrance halls on the ground floor of apartment blocks.

64. StaHH, 522-1, Jüdische Gemeinden, section 1993, folder 36, memo Max Plaut, 25 October 1943.

65. StaHH, 522-1, Jüdische Gemeinden, section 1993, folder 36, letter Gestapo to Corten, 22 September 1943.

66. See Meyer, *"Jüdische Mischlinge,"* 54.

67. For detailed analysis on this, see Beate Meyer, "'A conto Zukunft'—Hilfe und Rettung für untergetauchte Hamburger Juden," *Zeitschrift des Vereins für Hamburgische Geschichte* 88 (2002): 217ff.

68. StaHH, 522-1, Jüdische Gemeinden, section 1993, folder 36, memo re E.V., born 4 April 1898 in Hamburg, investigation by I. Goldstein, 25 January 1944. Identities left anonymous by the author.

69. StaHH, 522-1, Jüdische Gemeinden, section 1993, folder 16, file report, proceedings in Berlin, 20/21 August 1943.

70. StaHH, 522-1, Jüdische Gemeinden, section 1993, folder 16, letter Corten to RVJD Berlin, 17 February 1944.

71. StaHH, 522-1, Jüdische Gemeinden, section 1993, folder 16, letter Corten to RVJD, 21 March 1944.

72. Ibid.

73. BArch, R 8150/124/1, letter VM Hamburg, Heinemann to RVJD, 23 January 1945, pag. 80.
74. BArch, R 8150/124/1, letter VM Bremen, Bruck to RVJD, 24 December 1943, pag. 62.
75. BArch, R 8150/36, letter Karlsruhe, Eisemann to RVJD, 2 October 1944.
76. BArch, R 8150/36, letter VM Aachen, Feldmann to RVJD, 18 August 1944.
77. Ibid.
78. BArch, R 8150/36, letter Cahn to RVJD, ? January 1945.
79. BArch, R 8150/36, letter RVJD, Radlauer to district branches, here Erich Guttmann, Kiel, 18 April 1944, pag. 29.
80. BArch, R 8150/36, letter, RVJD Radlauer to VM Stettin, 24 June 1944.
81. BStU, ZUV 74, EV, vol. 13, Interrogation Henry Schmidt, 15 August 1986, p. 3.
82. Frank Schröder, *160 jüdische Persönlichkeiten aus Mecklenburg-Vorpommern* (Rostock, 2003), 91. I am grateful to Bernd Kasten for this reference.
83. StaHH, 522-2, Jüdische Gemeinden, No. 98, letter Bruck to RVJD Hamburg, 27 August 1943; on Karl Bruck, see Günther Rohdenburg, "Die Beteiligung der Juden an den Deportationen—das Problem der 'Helfershelfer,'" in *"… sind Sie für den geschlossenen Arbeitseinsatz vorgesehen …": "Judendeportationen" von Bremerinnen und Bremern während der Zeit der nationalsozialistischen Gewaltherrschaft*, ed. State Archive Bremen and Günther Rodenburg (Bremen, 2006), 155.
84. StaHH, 522-2, Jüdische Gemeinden, No. 61, letter Glässner to Corten, 16 August 1944, letter Corten to Glässner, 22 August 1944.
85. StaHH, 522-2, Jüdische Gemeinden, No. 61, letter Bruck to Heinemann, 31 July 1944.
86. Ibid.
87. StaHH, 522-2, Jüdische Gemeinden, No. 61, letter Heinemann to Bruck, 2 August 1944.
88. USHMM, RG-14.053M, Jewish Community Stuttgart, 2003.11, reel 2, letter Marx to div. persons, 22 October 1944; letter Cahn to Marx, 27 October 1944; letter Koronczyk to Marx, 26 October 1944; letter Oppenheimer to Marx, 27 October 1944; letter Speier to Marx, 31 October 1944; letter Hauser to Marx, 23 October 1944.
89. StaHH, 522-2, Jüdische Gemeinden, no. 61, letter Bruck to Berkowitz, 26 September 1944, letter Corten to Bruck, 25 October 1944.
90. YV, 02/8, Erich Schlesinger, "History of the Jewish Community Gleiwitz 31.1.1933-24.1.1945," pp. 10–11.
91. NRW HStA Düsseldorf, Schloss Kalkum, Gerichte rep. 372/87, Interrogation Otto Braunschweig, 8 November 1948, pag. 205–6; this case is also described in Berschel, *Bürokratie*, 161.
92. NRW HStA Düsseldorf, Schloss Kalkum, Rep. 372/83 (Waldbillig), Interrogation Bernt Engelmann, 5 November 1948, pag. 132. On Engelmann, see http://goo.gl/W7qgQ (accessed 15 July 2012).
93. Based on Suchy, "'Schreckenstein,'" 281.
94. NRW HStA Düsseldorf, Schloss Kalkum, Gerichte rep. 372/83 (Waldbillig), Interrogation widow of Waldemar Spier, 16 October 1947, pag. 25; NRW HStA Düsseldorf, Schloss Kalkum, Gerichte rep. 372/83 (Waldbillig), letter Kurt Frank to wife, 20 April 1944.
95. See verdict in trial against Georg Pütz, reproduced in Schmidt, *Elendsweg*, 187.
96. Municipal Archive Düsseldorf, file no. XXXII 43, Reparations file Rudolf Braunschweig, duration of incarceration [Wiedergutmachungsakte].
97. Luise Braunschweig, a non-Jew, was kept for a longer time under arrest, but Rudolf Braunschweig's wife was spared incarceration on medical grounds; see NRW HStA

Düsseldorf, Schloss Kalkum, Gerichte rep.372/83 (Waldbillig), Interrogation Rudolf Braunschweig, 19 September 1947, p. 22. After the war, Waldbillig denied any responsibility. Instead, he accused Frank of having revealed the boarding house in Vienna and of having denounced Bernt Engelmann, claiming that he forged the passport; NRW HStA Düsseldorf, Schloss Kalkum, Gerichte rep.372/83 (Waldbillig), Interrogation Hermann Waldbillig, 30 September 1948, pag. 84.

98. According to statements by his widow, reproduced in Schmidt, *Elendsweg*, 266–67.

99. NRW HStA Düsseldorf, Schloss Kalkum, Gerichte rep. 372/87, Interrogation Otto Braunschweig, 8 November 1948, pag. 205–6.

100. Municipal Archive Düsseldorf, file no. XXXII 43, Reparations file Rudolf Braunschweig, duration of incarceration.

101. BArch, R 8150/9, memo, no. 21, submissions to RSHA in the period 20 April–17 May 1944; unless noted otherwise, see, on Blankenstein, Barbara Suchy's meticulous description and sensitive interpretation: Suchy, "'Schreckenstein.'"

102. NRW HStA Düsseldorf, Gestapo, RW 58 Nr. 3429, Interrogation Blankenstein by Gestapo, 22 September 1941, pag. 4ff.

103. Ibid., pag. 6.

104. NRW HStA Düsseldorf, Gestapo, RW 58 Nr. 3429, Interrogation Blankenstein, 16 December 1948, pag. 67.

105. LBI, NY, MF 456, letter Blankenstein to RVJD, 7 May 1944.

106. NRW HStA Düsseldorf, Schloss Kalkum, Gerichte rep. 372/89, addendum to minutes, Ernst Blankenstein, 16 December 1948, pag. 47–49.

107. Suchy, "'Schreckenstein,'" 285; see also Sigrid Lekebusch, *Not und Verfolgung der Christen jüdischer Herkunft im Rheinland* (Cologne, 1995), 127ff.

108. Suchy, "'Schreckenstein,'" 285.

109. *Theresienstädter Gedenkbuch*, 477.

110. NRW Staatsarchiv Münster, 45 Js 29/78, folder 11, Interrogation Grethe Ludnowsky, 8 December 1964, pp. 1–2, pag. 35-36. The site www.bundesarchiv.de/gedenkbuch/index.html.en assumes "deportation to unknown destination."

111. I am grateful to Bettina Goldberg for this information (email correspondence, 31 March 2010).

112. Archive National Socialist Documentation Center, City of Cologne, papers Dr. Feldheim, letter Feldheim to his daughter, 1 August 1943. I would like to thank Barbara Becker-Jakli for her information and the sources she called to my attention, and Ms. Göttling-Jacoby for her efforts in searching down materials. [Trans.: Feldheim plays here on the German proverb "Wem der liebe Gott ein Amt gibt, dem gibt er auch den Verstand" (roughly equivalent to "skill comes with office"), reversing it by saying God "takes away" the necessary understanding ("dem nimmt er auch den Verstand").]

113. Letter Feldheim to his daughter, 1 December 1941, reproduced in Barbara Becker-Jakli, *Das jüdische Krankenhaus in Köln* (Cologne, 2004), 326.

114. BArch, R 8150/123/2, letter Feldheim to RVJD, 28 October 1943, pag. 102.

115. BArch, R 8150/9, internal memo, RVJD Wolffsky to the pay office on premises, 10 March 1944.

116. Archive National Socialist Documentation Center, City of Cologne, papers Dr. Feldheim, letter Feldheim to his daughter, 22 August 1943.

117. Archive National Socialist Documentation Center, City of Cologne, papers Dr. Feldheim, letter Feldheim to his "granny," 6 September 1943.

118. Archive National Socialist Documentation Center, City of Cologne, papers Dr. Feldheim, letter Feldheim to his daughter, 19 September 1943.

119. Archive National Socialist Documentation Center, City of Cologne, papers Dr. Feldheim, letter Feldheim to his daughter, 24 October 1943. Feldheim was the ripe "old age" of fifty-five at the time.

120. BArch, R 8150/720, letter Feldheim to RVJD, 17 December 1943, pag. 12; BArch, R 8150/720, RVJD to Feldheim, 20 January 1944, pag. 8; BArch, R 8150/720, internal letter RVJD, 10 March 1944, pag. 6; BArch, R 8150/720, letter Feldheim to RVJD, 16 May 1944, pag. 5.

121. Archive National Socialist Documentation Center, City of Cologne, papers Dr. Feldheim, letter Feldheim to his daughter, 30 November 1943.

122. Archive National Socialist Documentation Center, City of Cologne, papers Dr. Feldheim, letter Feldheim to his daughter, 8 January 1944.

123. BArch, R 8150/36, letter district office Aachen, Feldmann to RVJD, 18 August 1944.

124. Ibid.

125. BArch, R 8150/124/4, internal letter RVJD Wolfsky, 28 October 1944, pag. 265.

126. See www.bundesarchiv.de/gedenkbuch/index.html.en (accessed 16 July 2012); BArch, R 8150/731, letter Marx to RVJD, 7 October 1943; Becker-Jakli, Jüdisches Krankenhaus, 353, 394.

127. Farewell letter, Hans Salomon Feldheim, 27 August 1944, reproduced in Becker-Jakli, Jüdisches Krankenhaus, 354.

128. BArch,R 8150/9, order, 18 March 1944, pag. 524.

129. BArch,R 8150/36, letter, district central office Cologne, barracks camp to RVJD, 20 January 1945.

130. See Lekebusch, Not, 128–29.

131. BArch, R 8150/124/4, letter Kounen to RVJD, 31 December 1944, pag. 260.

132. Becker-Jakli, Jüdisches Krankenhaus, 484.

133. Klemperer noted: "Katz and Neumark, responsible to the Gestapo and its slaves, are in the most difficult position, cannot do right by anyone, and the Jews are all incredibly overwrought and embittered"; see Victor Klemperer, I Will Bear Witness: A Diary of the Nazi Years 1942–1945 (New York, 2001), 314; see also pp. 278, 297–98, 313.

134. See Beate Meyer, "'Eichmann von Dresden,'" 278.

135. Klemperer, Diary, 327.

136. BStU, ZUV 74, EV, Vol. 13, Interrogation Neumark, 9 August 1946; BStU, ZUV 74, EV, Vol. 5.

137. Jürgen Nitsche and Ruth Röcher, Juden in Chemnitz: Die Geschichte der Gemeinde und ihrer Mitglieder (Dresden, 2002), 156.

138. Caris-Petra Heidel and Jürgen Nitsche, "Adolf Lipp (1894–1966)," in Eine Dokumentation von Verfolgung, Vertreibung, Ermordung, ed. Caris-Petra Heidel (Frankfurt am Main, 2005), 374–77.

139. StaHH, 522-1, Jüdische Gemeinden, section 1993, folder 19, List of transport participants; see also Ina Lorenz, "Das Leben der Hamburger Juden im Zeichen der 'Endlösung' (1942–1945)," in Die Verdrängung und Vernichtung der Juden unter dem Nationalsozialismus, ed. Arno Herzig and Ina Lorenz (Hamburg, 1992), 238.

140. LBI, NY, MF 456, letter intermediary Bremen, Bruck, to RVJD, 16 February 1945.

141. NRW HStA Düsseldorf, Schloss Kalkum, Gerichte Rep. 372/83 (Waldbillig), Interrogation Waldbillig, 21 September 1948, pag. 77ff.

142. LBI, NY, MF 456, letter Bruck, Bremen to RVJD, 16 February 1945.

143. Private posthumous papers Cahn, Frankfurt/Main, deportation order, letter, Cahn to district court president, 7 February 1945; Private posthumous papers Cahn, Frankfurt/Main, letter, district court president to Cahn, 8 February 1945; Private

posthumous papers Cahn, Frankfurt/Main, curriculum vitae Max L. Cahn; report "Surviving in Frankfurt a. M." (WL P. III.e.No. 456), p. 4. See also http://goo .gl/fGYDP (accessed 16 May 2013).

144. See Gottwaldt and Schulle, "Judendeportationen," 466–67 (without Vienna, Salzburg).

145. Ulrike Offenberg, "Die Jüdische Gemeinde zu Berlin 1945–1953," in *Leben im Land der Täter: Juden im Nachkriegsdeutschland (1945–1952)*, ed. Julius H. Schoeps (Berlin, 2001), 134.

146. Nadav and Stürzbecher, "Walter Lustig," 226.

147. See Ulrike Offenberg, *Seid vorsichtig gegen die Machthaber: Die jüdischen Gemeinden in der SBZ und der DDR 1945–1990* (Berlin, 1998), 16.

148. LAB, Rep. 20, Nr. 4616-4617, letter Walter Lustig, 15 June 1945, attachment, pp. 1–3.

149. LAB, Rep. 20, Nr. 4616-4617, telegram Dr. Hirschfeld to Stalin.

150. Offenberg, "Jüdische Gemeinde," 135–36; see report, Siegmund Weltlinger, 16 November 1945, "Wiederaufbau der Jüdischen Gemeinde in Berlin," reproduced as Doc. 13 in *"Ich habe es nie bereut, ein deutscher Jude zu sein !" Erinnerungen an Siegmund Weltlinger (1886–1974)*, ed. Geschichtswerkstatt am Friedrichsgymnasium Kassel (Kassel, 1997), 33. In the summer of 1945, the Berlin Jewish Community and the newly established organizations in the Berlin districts were apparently competing with one another; see Hermann Simon, "Die Jüdische Gemeinde Nordwest: Eine Episode aus der Zeit des Neubeginns jüdischen Lebens in Berlin nach 1945," in *Aufbau nach dem Untergang: Deutsch-jüdische Geschichte nach 1945*, ed. Andreas Nachama and Julius H. Schoeps (Berlin, 1992), 274–84.

151. Thus, Lustig's niece described in interview that she asked Lustig whether he could help to assist a friend, and he replied: "That's finished now"; see private papers, interview by Beate Meyer with G.K.-Lustig, June 2000, transcript, p. 5.

152. Bezirksregierung Düsseldorf, Entschädigungsamt [Düsseldorf Compensation Office], Dr. Annemarie Lustig, ZK. 14012, witness testimony Siegbert Kleemann, 16 March 1957, pag. M 70, petition, n.d., pag. M 71–72.

153. Offenberg, "Jüdische Gemeinde," 136; see also Nielsen, "Siegmund Weltlinger," 8–9.

154. See Ina S. Lorenz, *Gehen oder Bleiben: Neuanfang der Jüdischen Gemeinde in Hamburg nach 1945* (Hamburg, 2002), 13–14; see also the full English translation online, *To Leave or To Stay*, n.p., http://goo.gl/VXD9U (accessed 16 July 2012).

155. Simonsohn established the Zentralwohlfahrtsstelle der Juden in Deutschland (Central Welfare Bureau of Jews in Germany) in postwar Germany and reorganized Jewish social welfare work in theory and practice; see Wilma Aden-Grossmann, *Berthold Simonsohn: Biographie des jüdischen Sozialpädagogen und Juristen (1912–1978)* (Frankfurt am Main and New York, 2007).

156. University of Oxford, Bodleian Library, letter, Corten to the Society for the Protection of Learning and Sciences, 3 February 1949. I am grateful to Anna von Villiez and Thorsten Noack for pointing out this source.

157. LAB, Rep. 20, Nr. 4616-4617, Announcement, Berlin Jewish Community, 12 July 1945.

158. "Kontrollratsgesetz Nr. 1 betreffend die Aufhebung von NS-Recht," 20 September 1945, Art. I, 1 (Control Council Law No. 1 [20 September 1945]); see http://goo .gl/TXlel (accessed 7 August 2012).

Chapter 5

IN THE WAKE

The "Strategy of Cooperation" as an Incriminating Burden

Proceedings Before a Court of Honor and Employment Bans in Berlin

Within the ramified architecture of the Reichsvereinigung and all its institutions, Jewish personnel—at every post, from top management down to building janitor—were under orders to implement the instructions of the RSHA and the Gestapo. By contrast, on the other side of the divide, the few persecutors actually visible were at best the "Jewish experts" or camp directors. Given that skewing in perception, the Jews often associated all the suffering they or their relatives were exposed to with the names and faces of the Jewish functionaries, the district branch directors, the trustees in the assembly camp, or the collectors who came to take them to the transports. There was a special hatred for the Jewish "snatchers," *Greifer*, the Jewish spies and informers assigned to ferret out their fellow Jews who had gone into hiding and then report their whereabouts to the Gestapo. However, the Reichsvereinigung itself had never had anything to do with these informers, except that they were housed (generally in more privileged conditions) in the assembly camps.[1] In the bid to reestablish the Jewish Communities, the climate of social intercourse and interaction was poisoned by accusations, mistrust, allegations, or concrete knowledge of past behavior, especially regarding the activity of the RV personnel, denunciations to the authorities, or their past privileges.

In agreement with the municipality in Berlin (and its Main Committee on "Victims of Fascism"), the large Berlin Jewish Community decided after the war to set up special courts of honor, so-called *Ehrengerichte*, to deal with these questions. These courts were to determine "whether and to what extent a member of the Berlin Jewish Community had, by dishonorable or shameful behavior, inflicted harm on the Jews," that is, had transgressed against the Jewish "community as a whole." In particular, the courts were obliged to clarify accusations that had "arisen based on the work during the Nazi regime of those accused."[2] In practice, in the main the proceedings involved lower-ranking coworkers or their spouses.

A court of honor consisted of five persons; of these, the chair and two associate judges had to provide proof of their qualification to sit as judges. The chairpersons were appointed for temporary tenure by the assembly of representatives of the Jewish Community. Chairpersons and associate judges rotated according to a complicated procedure. The body could summon witnesses, and the accused were allowed to be represented by an attorney.[3] Proceedings were closed to the public. However, verdicts in such proceedings could be made public in the Jewish press subsequent to a corresponding resolution by the court of honor.[4] The court of honor was not empowered to hand down sentences of imprisonment or similar punishments, but its decision could affect membership in or benefits from the Jewish Community.

The courts of honor sought to apply constitutional principles of law and endeavored to do proper justice given the complexity of the circumstances. Thus, for example, they conceded that defendants at the age of seventeen or eighteen had been too young or inexperienced to comprehend that the actions by which they had sought to prevent their own deportation had harmed other Jews.[5] Sometimes the court ruled that accusations were not proven, and thus determined there had been no "serious guilt," but on occasion decided there had been "complicity."[6] Or they ruled, for example, that the behavior by a superior toward his subordinates had been "improper" and was to be "condemned."[7] In that case, the Jewish Community then had to decide what should be done with the accused as a penalty. In a small number of cases, the court of honor recommended that the Jewish Community should for a time suspend payment of social welfare benefits to the person accused.[8]

In another case, involving Martha Raphael, the court reached a quite differentiated judgment. The stenographer Raphael, employed at the Jewish Community, had been responsible beginning in 1942 for the card file in the assembly camps on Grosse Hamburger Strasse and Schulstrasse. In

1947, due to many accusations against her, she had requested a court proceeding to clear her name. After examination, the court of honor ruled that she had carried out her activity in the camp because her Jewish superiors considered it necessary to comply with the Gestapo's express desire to work for them. For the Jewish employees constrained to obey instructions under this duress, it created a serious conflict between their sense of identity as Jews and the work area they had been assigned. It required considerable strength of Jewish character to accomplish this unpleasant and compromising double task to work hard and correctly but not to damage other Jews by this.[9] In this complex and time-consuming proceeding, the court had interrogated nineteen witnesses. In its verdict, it ruled that Martha Raphael had performed her job with great zeal, without considering that "ultimately this inevitably would prove harmful to her fellow Jews." The judges noted, however, that "at times she had placed her assigned tasks over and above her own Jewish conscience."[10] Given the desperate situation of the applicants, her tone in dealing with them had been inappropriate. However, for their part, those individuals had "overestimated" the power of Raphael's position, regarding her as a "partner in negotiations," although she had not possessed any such authority.

Proceedings of this kind in the Berlin Jewish Community and in Frankfurt am Main continued until the end of the 1950s. A trial could be initiated after submission of a complaint by a Community member or based on a charge brought against oneself.

Former members of the Berlin Jewish Community who had been convicted after the war by Soviet military tribunals and courts in the GDR and then later returned to West Berlin had to face an additional legal challenge there: proceedings before a court of honor if continuing accusations were raised against them. This was the case, for example, with Max Reschke, the Jewish director of the two assembly camps in Berlin (see chapter 2) where Martha Raphael had also worked. After five years of internment in Buchenwald (Soviet Special Camp 2), the former school principal was sentenced to twenty-five years imprisonment during the Waldheim trials and was released in 1955. Then, in 1956, Reschke had to face trial before a court of honor in West Berlin. However, this court conceded that during his nonvoluntary activity as assembly camp director, he had "given no cause for complaints from a general human or purely Jewish viewpoint, but rather had endeavored to ease the situation of the camp inmates."[11]

At best, the court of honor procedure could serve to clear à person's name. But that was not always successful; a number of proceedings ended with no result and those accused suffered for the rest of their life from ill will and hostility. Martha Mosse, the former head of the accommodation advice office in the Berlin Jewish Community, became a veritable symbol of this strategy by Jewish functionaries to cooperate with the Gestapo, perceived to have been so disastrous. After her liberation from Theresienstadt, relatives of deportees accused her of complicity in assembling the deportation lists.[12] Mosse, born in Berlin in 1884, was a self-willed, cool, and assertive woman. Raised in a wealthy family, daughter of a well-known lawyer, she began studying law at the age of thirty-two despite her lack of a high school certificate. Mosse graduated with a law diploma, entered the civil service, and was promoted in 1926 as the first female assistant police commissioner (*Polizeirätin*) in Prussia. In 1933, she was dismissed from the civil service because of her Jewish origins, and began work from the autumn of 1934 in the Berlin Jewish Community, where she organized fund-raising drives and headed a consultation office, until she took charge of the accommodations advice center and later became involved in preparations for deportation.[13] She apparently lived without any problem with her non-Jewish female life companion. Mosse was a gifted administrator and demanded Prussian discipline of her coworkers. She implemented Gestapo orders but intervened if the Gestapo did not heed the guidelines.[14] She informed people in writing about her successes, but did not mention her own personal effort to have achieved them, giving the impression that deferment from deportation had been a decision of the "authority," namely, the Gestapo.[15] In Theresienstadt, Mosse worked until the end of 1944 as investigative judge in the criminal investigation department, then in the court of Jewish autonomous administration. In May 1945, she took charge of the registration and administration office.[16] Martha Mosse survived, returning to live with her life companion in Berlin. In the autumn of 1945, she entered the women's penal system as legal counsel,[17] even though suffering at the time from the medical consequences of her internment.[18] The authorities granted her recognition as a "victim of fascism." Nonetheless, after six months she was dismissed from her post on orders from the Soviet occupying authority. The reason for dismissal: Jews who had lived in hiding or in mixed marriages had accused her of being an "accomplice of the Gestapo." The same problem occurred when from the fall of 1946 on she worked for the US military government preparing files from German ministries for the Nuremberg trials.[19] On top of this, Mosse experienced personal harassment: she was cursed on the street and attacked in letters. The newspaper *Jüdischer Anzeiger* publicly sought witnesses to testify against her.[20] A trial in a court of honor in the Jewish Community was instituted to clarify matters, but although it went on from 1946 to 1948, it ended inconclusively. Mosse had submitted twenty testimonials exonerating her.[21] She would have liked to emigrate to the United States, but her non-Jewish life companion was unable to obtain a visa. Mosse was then at least professionally rehabilitated: she was employed once again by the West Berlin police in August 1948, where she worked until 1953. Martha Mosse was praised for professional knowledge, correct behavior, and a strong sense of duty in every letter of reference on her work before, during, and after the Nazi period. She characterized herself as "withdrawn and uncommunicative" and saw her postwar experiences as "very depressing."[22] Her critics described her as "too little feminine, too little warmth."[23] Unlike her murdered female colleagues in the RV, she had never been active in typically "female" areas of work in the organization; thanks to her father, she had enjoyed a certain protection and thus survived. Since she was living in Berlin and a potential target for critique because of her lesbian lifestyle, she attracted the rage of the Jewish survivors, demonized as "too little feminine" or "cold as ice." Mosse had distanced herself from the role of victim and had always demonstrated her probity as a person of action. She had worked to ensure that the few norms the Nazi rulers recognized were utilized for the benefit of the Jews, and that solid norms of life together were maintained in Theresienstadt. But she herself had violated the accepted norms of conventional sexuality.

From 1941 to 1943, she had shared the view with her Jewish superiors that in connection with deportations, correct and orderly operating procedures were imperative, utilizing the latitude that had been conceded. This, she believed, was on the whole of greater benefit to the Jews than bribes or individual attempts to rescue people, tactics that ultimately always proved to be at the expense of the weaker in the Community. After the war, the survivors accused her of espousing this view, which had in fact been shared by the other German-Jewish functionaries. She became a veritable scapegoat for the strategy of cooperation. Only Paul Eppstein among the leading male functionaries had been similarly attacked, in his case posthumously by H. G. Adler. But since Eppstein had been murdered, he was no longer alive to become a visible target for dispute and altercations. Other male survivors such as Baeck, Fabian, or Weltlinger were attacked on occasion for their former behavior, but these accusations did not result in such serious personal and professional disadvantage as in the case of Martha Mosse. This despite the fact that Baeck had after all directed the main organization, Fabian had been in charge of finances, and Weltlinger had been centrally involved with home purchase contracts. But now these former leading functionaries, who were not under critical fire and whose word was not doubted, spoke out to exonerate Mosse in the eyes of the Jewish public.[24] Martha suffered from what she regarded as unjust treatment until her death on 2 September 1977 at the age of ninety-three.[25]

Under Suspicion: Former Jewish Functionaries in the Western Occupation Zones and the Early Federal Republic

In the US occupation zone and its exclaves in northern Germany, Bre-men, and Bremerhaven,[26] the counter intelligence corps (CIC) inves-tigated persons accused of crimes against humanity, such as Gestapo officials, Nazi officials, and Jews accused of collaboration.

When the American troops occupied Munich, the former RV district branch director, Theodor Koronczyk, and the former marshal in the bar-racks camp, Kurt Kahn, conducted a house search of an especially corrupt Gestapo official with the support of the CIC.[27] But such joint actions soon came to an abrupt end, because although Koronczyk himself was con-vinced that he had been self-sacrificing in service to the Munich Jews, and personally felt innocent of any wrongdoing, in the eyes of the relatives of the deportees—and especially concentration camp survivors—Koronczyk deserved no merit. As mentioned, in their eyes he was nothing but a trai-tor. The CIC explored various accusations against Koronczyk. Auschwitz and Buchenwald survivor Philipp Auerbach, state commissioner for per-sons persecuted on racist, political, and religious grounds (and a short time later himself the victim of criminal prosecution with anti-Semitic connota-tions[28]), commented laconically that the former intermediary belonged "before the district court as a main culprit and informer ... , though it should also be kept in mind that as a Jew, Koronczyk will have to pay more heavily for his crime."[29] In Auerbach's eyes: "they set up a Jewish Gestapo, called the Reichsvereinigung der Juden in Deutschland."[30] At this point, Koronczyk had already been interrogated ten times,[31] and he was now taken into custody. He denied all allegations: no, he had not prepared any deportation lists; rather, the names had been given to him. He had only "dealt harshly" with some Jews because he had not wanted to endanger others. And he had not been on friendly terms with the Gestapo.[32] He requested understanding for his situation: "I had to take certain things into consideration. I have a family."[33] The few Jews who were able to have a brief look into Koronczyk's situation confirmed that he was threatened with possible concentration camp internment. But even their statements tended to incriminate him. Thus, the physician Schwarz testified that Ko-ronczyk had had to assemble the transports.

> That was a difficult assignment for him, but after he had taken on this ugly position, he had to do it. He probably could have resigned from the job. I don't think the Gestapo would have forced him to stay on. If they would not have let him leave, then perhaps it was because he was very docile and submissive ... because he was alone and had to handle things on his own.

I never heard that at any time from 1942 to 1944, K. ever approached any one of us with a request for help.[34]

In contrast to that, Koronczyk's lawyer, as a Jewish survivor well acquainted with the situation, testified that he most certainly had been approached by Koronczyk for advice.[35] Yet Koronczyk had also openly threatened RV members: "If I catch a Jew not wearing the star, I'll report him directly to the Gestapo."[36]

In a first trial, Koronczyk was sentenced to ten years in labor camp, confiscation of all assets, and a ban on professional practice for a period of fifteen years.[37] In a second suit, he was sentenced to three years in the Dachau labor camp, with credit for previous time behind bars. Although he regarded this conviction as unjust, he accommodated to the conditions of internment at Dachau. The head of the camp praised him for his great skill, industriousness, conscientiousness, and reliability; based on his comportment, he was accorded a special position of trust.[38] On 15 November 1948, the Court of Cassation issued an order halting the proceedings against him. Koronczyk died on 25 November 1956.[39]

His persecutor, Hans Wegner, was incarcerated in May 1945. There were several proceedings against him between 1949 and 1955, and some ended with conviction,[40] but he was released in 1952.[41] Investigations of Johannes Pfeuffer and other Gestapo officers were also conducted after the war. Koronczyk gave statements in all of these proceedings. He exonerated the head of the Jewish Department, the *Judenreferat,* who had enjoyed summoning Koronczyk to his office and forcing him to stand in the corner with his face to the wall. In a strikingly cool and unemotional letter, he wrote that Pfeuffer had executed the instructions of his superiors correctly, in a way that there were no "further consequences."[42] He stated that Pfeuffer and his colleagues had always dealt with him in a "strictly objective" manner.[43] The proceedings against Pfeuffer in 1948, 1950, and 1952/1953 were ultimately discontinued.[44]

The many statements by Jewish and non-Jewish witnesses in the postwar proceedings and investigations point to one key aspect in particular: in Munich, the institutions in Munich involved with the persecution of the Jews had managed, more than almost anywhere else, to lay a veil of obscurity over the entire complex of who had been responsible. This veil obscured conditions in the Milbertshofen camp, Jews deported "in addition" to others, Hechinger's maltreatment and punitive deportation, and most especially the assembling of the deportation lists and the seizure and arrest of Jews who had gone into hiding. Who bore responsibility? In statements by the perpetrators and the survivors who testified, and in testimony by Theodor Koronczyk as intermediary, fact and fiction intermix in the attribution of guilt. Efforts to exculpate and accusations blend here into a tangled web where responsibility for events was ultimately always found to lie not with the Germans but with the Jews, those murdered as well as the survivors.

Catapulted into the limelight of the media for quite different reasons, other former Jewish functionaries also discovered that their earlier office quickly became a topic of discussion, casting them in a questionable light. This was Martin Heinrich Corten's experience. The doctor had headed the Jewish Hospital in Hamburg until 1946, but was then dismissed and even banned from entry to the hospital. The reason he gave for seeking an emigrant visa to Great Britain in 1949 was that he had encountered certain problems in Hamburg dealing with Orthodox and Zionist Jews.[45] It was his urgent wish, the now sixty-year-old Corten wrote, to leave the continent and join an expedition as a physician, pathologist, or photographer. But he was denied a new beginning abroad. He continued to practice as a general physician in Hamburg until 1956.[46] Corten had good reason to wish to flee Hamburg. In 1950, he found himself in the headlines not only of the papers in Hamburg but in the broader supraregional press and magazines. What had he done? With the assistance of Hans Bürger-Prinz, a psychiatrist and the head of a clinic, he had had his wife committed to a psychiatric ward from February 1947 to August 1948. She had supposedly shown certain symptoms of mental illness, and doctors had given various diagnoses for her condition. But at the same time, there was another probably very important element in this story: Corten wished to live with his girlfriend, thirty years his junior. After her release, his wife sued Martin Corten for unlawful deprivation of liberty. Initially, all this had absolutely nothing to do with his earlier work as an intermediary in the Reichsvereinigung, and otherwise would have provided material for a brief scandal story soon forgotten, swept aside by other sensational new tales in the media. But in the trial and coverage in the press, new questions now arose: how had Corten been able to survive as a Jew, why had he not worn a compulsory "yellow star" (he did not have to as a Jew living in a "privileged" mixed marriage)? Why had he been removed from his position as head of the Jewish Hospital in 1946? These were all questions that implicitly suggested that Corten had collaborated in some way with the Gestapo. When a Jewish woman deported to Theresienstadt accused him of having done nothing to prevent her deportation, the openly articulated or tacit link between "Jewish" and "guilty" soon permeated most of the stories on Corten circulating in the press. But despite the extent to which the trial brought by his wife had catered to the public's lust for sensationalism, fueling anti-Jewish resentment, and had helped to spark a broad discussion about the role of psychiatry, the charges against Corten proved insupportable, and he was acquitted. Corten left Hamburg in 1958 and moved to Munich, where he died in November 1962.[47]

"Gestapo Collaborators": Former Jewish Functionaries in the Soviet Occupation Zone and the GDR

As a rule, the former intermediaries who remained in the Soviet occupation zone after 1945, the later GDR, or who returned there after internment, found it even more difficult than their colleagues in the Western zones to begin their normal lives again. Some, though not all, discovered they were entangled in a new vortex of persecution. Two men who apparently had no serious problems were the Chemnitz physician Adolf Lipp and Max Cars in Erfurt. The dermatologist Lipp stayed on in his hometown and offered his services to the new municipal administration to help deal with the concerns of the Jews in Chemnitz. He was one of the founding members of the local branch of the Association of those Persecuted by the Nazi Regime (Vereinigung der Verfolgten des Naziregimes, VVN). In 1947, he obtained permission to practice again, headed an outpatient clinic, made contributions in combating venereal diseases, and in 1961 was honored by being appointed a government medical consultant or *Sanitätsrat*.[48] However, his health suffered from the effects of the Nazi period, and he had to interrupt his professional work several times, finally halting his work as a doctor in 1963. The Ministry for State Security (Stasi) in the GDR identified him in its file as a "half Jew" who had not only been a member of the VVN and since 1950 a member of the Free Federation of German Trade Unions (Freier Deutscher Gewerkschaftsbund), but also had a "positive view" of the GDR. However, State Security was not entirely satisfied with Lipp, because the new "social organizations" had not had contact with him, and he lived quite withdrawn from society.[49] Lipp died on 16 June 1966.[50]

In Erfurt, Max Cars was apparently similarly inconspicuous; there are no problems noted in the files pertaining to him. While other Jewish functionaries were fleeing the GDR in the early 1950s, he moved up the ranks in the Association of Jewish Communities there.[51]

Those who came to the attention of the Soviet Military Administration in Germany (Sowjetische Militäradministration in Deutschland, SMAD) in the initial postwar years fared less well. Between 1945 and 1955, its military tribunals (sprung from the structure of the courts-martial of the Red Army) convicted some 40,000 Germans in the Soviet Zone and later GDR, including 3,140 sentenced for war crimes and crimes of violence. This sphere of offenses also generally included crimes the former intermediaries of the RV ("Nazi or Gestapo collaborators") were charged with. The punishment in a third of these verdicts was ten or twenty-five years imprisonment, and 7.8 percent received the death penalty (Walter Lustig and Hans Weinberg were executed; it is uncertain whether there was any preceding trial).[52] As a rule, persons who brought denunciations called the SMAD's attention to these former intermediaries.[53] Survivors, Jews returning from camps, or other Germans accused these men of "collaboration"; many of them had but vague knowledge of actual earlier events. Some who brought accusations wished to avenge family members and see the "guilty" punished, while others acted for a very selfish motive: namely, to get accessories who knew about their own actions before 1945 out of the way.

Ernst Neumark in Dresden became the victim of such a denunciation. Victor Klemperer met him again after the war, when the lawyer Neumark was a member of a committee preparing the new constitution.[54] Calamity loomed in the air as a result of a new wave of anti-Semitism that had swept across the Soviet zone.[55] Neumark felt under attack because of his work in the ensemble of legal experts; Klemperer's suspicion was more that there had been a targeted accusation stemming from Jewish circles against the former intermediary. On 26 July 1946, Neumark was arrested[56] and accused of having worked for a "fascist organization," the Gestapo. As witnesses for the prosecution, a building contractor who had employed Jewish forced laborers and had been a member of the NSDAP since 1931 testified, along with the husband of a Jewish woman whose request Neumark (acting on behalf of the Gestapo) had rejected. From the transcripts of interrogation of the Operational Sector of the People's Commissariat of the Interior of the USSR for the Province of Saxony, it emerges that Neumark ultimately was given responsibility for all deportations of Jews from Dresden, and that, probably under massive pressure, he also confessed to this charge:

> My tasks included the registration of the entire Jewish population resident in Dresden, the passing on of all information and data on the Jews of interest to the Gestapo, and I participated in the assembling of the transports of Jews of the Gestapo to the Riga and Auschwitz concentration camps and the confiscation of the property of the Jews deported.[57]

In response to the question of whether he saw himself as "directly or indirectly, a participant in the arrests of Jews carried out by the Gestapo," he answered: "Yes, I passed on the lists to them that they demanded of me, I also gave them the information they desired on the persons of interest to the Gestapo."[58] But he qualified his statement by saying that he had known nothing about the purpose of this information he had passed on. In actual fact, Neumark had had nothing whatsoever to do with the deportations to Riga or Auschwitz. They had taken place long before his tenure in office, and he had been left in uncertainty about the transports to Theresienstadt. It is clear from the questions of the Soviet official heading the interrogation that the investigators were not at all familiar with the complex structures of a Jewish compulsory organization for which the Gestapo functioned as "supervisory authority." Klemperer describes how ignorant even Jewish emigrants who had returned home, such as the state prosecutor involved in the investigations of Neumark, were of the tenuous tightrope walk between representation of Jewish interests and collaboration that the Jewish representatives faced during the Nazi period. And how the other survivors were anxiously seeking cover, since they feared any new light shed might incriminate them as well.[59] The prosecution accused Neumark of crimes against humanity, a charge also applicable to those who had acted under duress. It was argued that Neumark should have refused to implement the deportation orders; perhaps then the Gestapo would have overlooked one or another Jew. In September 1946, Klemperer noted that Neumark had been sent to an unknown internment camp. Now only his closest relatives dared to inquire about his fate.[60] Neumark was sentenced in 1946 to ten years of internment in a camp, but was not transferred to a Soviet forced labor camp. Rather, he remained in the special camp in Bautzen, until sent for internment on 18 June 1948 to the special camp in Sachsenhausen.[61] The camp diary there recorded him as a "Gestapo informer."[62] The fear now spread among the other Jewish survivors who had been on the Reichsvereinigung staff that they might be associated in some way with Neumark.[63] Neumark died on 28 October 1948 in the former Sachsenhausen concentration camp.

His colleague Richard Hesse experienced similar persecution after the war: a lawyer, licensed to practice since 1926, Hesse had worked during the Nazi years for the emigration office of the Halle Jewish Community, until it was shut down. He then was deployed in forced labor in the Jewish cemetery until January 1945, irrespective of his concomitant appointment as intermediary for Halle and Merseburg. In February 1945, he was deported to Theresienstadt together with the approximately one hundred Jews in mixed marriages in his district. After liberation he returned to Halle, working successfully in the Reconstruction Initiative that dealt with integrating refugees and persons who had been persecuted, and he joined the Liberal-Democratic Party.[64] On 16 January 1946, he was arrested by the SMAD and sent to the special camp in Buchenwald. He remained interned there until 14 February 1950. In 1950, the Soviet occupying power wanted to dissolve these internment facilities and transferred some thirty-five hundred inmates to Waldheim, where the GDR justice system took over the prisoners: around thirty-three hundred persons were convicted of war crimes and National Socialist crimes in summary proceedings; in more than thirteen hundred cases they were charged with crimes against humanity. The conclusion of the procedures was, as in Richard Hesse's case, more or less preprogrammed: the at times absurd "investigation findings" of the SMAD were contained in sealed "official documents," whose probative force as evidence was not allowed to be questioned or checked in the new trials. Hesse had been accused in 1946 of having been a paid Gestapo agent and of having some one hundred Jews "on his conscience," that is, of having caused their death.[65] Yet the Soviet prosecutors had distorted the actual facts to the point that they were unrecognizable: as with all German Jews whose assets were five thousand RM or more, Hesse's account had been placed under a security order. Like all others affected by this measure, who nonetheless had to cover their living expenses from their blocked account, Hesse was also permitted to report his current regular outlay. After the finance officials had checked the application and in most instances reduced the total amount, the applicants were then given access to the authorized monthly amount. In Hesse's case, this was one hundred and eighty RM (with assets in the blocked account of seventy thousand RM).

The SMAD summarily decided that this money was based on regular payment for services as an informer. Like all intermediaries, Hesse had been required to regularly pass on statistics on "his" Jews and any reports of changes. Without examining what had become of the Jews in mixed marriages (a large number of whom were still living in the vicinity of Halle), the Soviet military tribunal accused Hesse of having sent these persons to their doom and bearing responsibility for their death.

In the Waldheim trials initiated in 1950, these accusations were included as proven and part of the charges. In the eyes of the court, the fact that Hesse had been transported to Theresienstadt did not contradict this charge, because part of the perfidy of the Nazi system was that it had also persecuted collaborators. It was to no avail that Jews remaining in the GDR had exonerated Hesse: Julius Meyer, for example, president of the Provincial Association of Jewish Communities in the GDR, had testified that although most of the RV functionaries had worked in line with Gestapo wishes, Hesse was one of those exceptions who had always had the interests of his "Jewish fellow citizens" in mind.[66] Fritz Grunsfeld, former district branch director in Leipzig, supported that statement, and another witness reported under interrogation to the People's Police that Hesse had in addition worked unusually hard to help assist persecuted Polish Jews when they had been arrested at the beginning of the war.[67] Furthermore, Hesse's old comrades were able to clarify the origin of these allegations: a Jewish accuser, who unlike Hesse had actually worked as a Gestapo informer, had wanted to get him out of the way as a someone who "knew" about the former informer's work. But that individual was no longer alive.[68]

The court had no interest in any of these statements. It sentenced Hesse, aged fifty-four, to eighteen years imprisonment, because in the face of the Nazi regime's will for destruction, he had only been able to survive as a "henchman and lackey" of the Gestapo.[69] The court reasoned that this is why he had selfishly directed his activity against his fellow Jews. It evidently did not occur to the judges how macabre the routine final sentence of their verdict appears in light of Hesse's fate: they confiscated his assets for the benefit of the state.

In the subsequent period, Hesse asked his attorney to submit an appeal, because only the sealed "official document" had been used, and exonerating evidence had not been admitted. But these grounds for appeal were rejected, because "to doubt the correctness of the content of the official document implies mistrust in our former occupying power, which in no way does proper justice to the behavior of our Soviet friends."[70] Thus, Hesse continued his confinement in Waldheim with the prospect of release in 1968, until an amnesty of ten years for those incarcerated made release for him appear possible already in 1954. However, he was initially transferred to Bautzen in March 1954. His wife was not allowed to visit Hesse until 1952; a visit to her husband had been denied her for many years.[71] All the internment facilities where Hesse was imprisoned gave him good marks for his work and comportment as a prisoner, but complained that his attitude to the GDR was, in their words, "not transparent."[72] Finally, he was granted release in the summer of 1954, paroled with the explanation: "Upon examination of the file, it was determined that despite a large number of positive statements by witnesses, that material was not sufficiently taken into account in the proceedings."[73]

Hesse and his wife remained in the GDR. When the Halle district administrative office in the Stasi was asked in 1974 to report on the place of residence and activities of all those who had been convicted by Soviet military courts, it reported that Richard Hesse, a pensioner, was living in Halle. No connections or activities endangering state security had been identified.[74] In 1984, Hesse committed suicide.

The lawyer Fritz Grunsfeld had been deported to Theresienstadt in 1943; he survived and returned to his native Leipzig. He began his legal clerkship there, but was taken into custody by the SMAD from 14 January to 9 April 1946 for unknown reasons, and then released. After his assessor exams, he worked as a lawyer and notary public. In the summer of 1946, he published an extended article in *Aufbau* on the persecution and murder of the Leipzig Jews,[75] and was active in promoting Jewish restitution interests. Grunsfeld lived together with his unmarried sister, who worked at his law office. He belonged to the antifascist VVN, but was otherwise considered a "decidedly non-political person."[76] Apparently, other Jewish survivors suspected Grunsfeld of dishonest attitudes or actions due to his earlier activity as RV district branch director. For that reason, he acted to have proceedings against himself instituted to clear his name. But the trial came to no result and was dismissed. In the proceedings, Grunsfeld was given support by the chairman of the Leipzig Jewish Community. He himself was on the Community board and worked as head of its legal department.[77] When after the Slansky trials in Prague the GDR leadership decided to proceed against Jews who purportedly were working together with organizations in the West, he and others came to the attention of the state security agencies for one simple reason: they had received and distributed funds from the JOINT.[78] On 1 February 1954, he and his sister fled to West Berlin, two Jews among the approximately nine hundred who left the GDR during this period. Grunsfeld and his sister went to Düsseldorf, where Grunsfeld later served as a judge in the district courts and the Higher Regional Court. He passed away on 22 June 1991 in Düsseldorf.[79]

Two other former RV intermediaries came to the attention of state security organs of the GDR. However, they were accused not on the basis of their earlier activity in the RV. Rather, the allegations were that they had caused damage to the GDR by working on behalf of the class enemy: Martin Broh from Frankfurt an der Oder, who after the war had been appointed for a short time as deputy mayor of his hometown, was alleged to have sold food on the black market. He fled to the West before proceedings could be instituted against him.[80]

Fritz Rosenbaum, former intermediary for Kleinmachnow/Potsdam, had carefully concealed his previous RV work in all questionnaires. Instead, in answer to the question about ties to a "resistance group," he responded: "In circles of friends for the entire duration of the Hitler regime."[81] The auditor and merchant Rosenbaum immediately volunteered in 1945 for activities to rebuild the local community.[82] A member of the VVN and recognized as a victim of fascism, he had, however, one "blemish," which he believed would provide him with an element of honor in the "workers' and peasants' state." Like his father, he had been a member of the SPD before 1933 and had rejoined the party after 1945. After the forced union of the SPD and KPD (German Communist Party) in 1946, creating the Socialist Unity Party of Germany (SED), he joined that party.

In 1950, he was temporarily appointed mayor of Kleinmachnow, and later served in the town council. At the end of 1952, the People's Police arrested him, because during his tenure in office, supposedly or actually, a real estate agent had enriched himself by illegally allocating apartments; it was alleged that Rosenbaum had abetted this, accepted it, or at least done nothing to stop it. An additional charge was that he had traveled to West Berlin and exchanged thirty marks of East German money for ten DM, and then purchased coffee, cigarettes, and Western "inflammatory periodicals," such as the *Stern* weekly magazine.[83] The reason for the subsequent show trial in Potsdam in the House of Culture of the Railroad Workers was probably less the alleged "black marketing" of apartments and more the controversial protest signed by two thousand residents of Kleinmachnow against the closing of the Düppel border crossing into Zehlendorf in West Berlin,[84] where Rosenbaum's car had also reportedly been seen by a number of witnesses for the prosecution.

Together with eight others, including a Jew who had returned from Shanghai, Rosenbaum was accused of "acts of sabotage ... directed against the economic measures of the German Democratic Republic," and this concomitant with "crimes of speculation."[85] The main defendant was sentenced to ten years in prison; Rosenbaum was given six years behind bars, five years of suspended civil rights, and the confiscation of his assets.[86] At this point he was in the prison hospital in Potsdam. This was followed by his expulsion from the VVN and annulment of his status as a victim of Nazi persecution (*Verfolgter des Naziregimes*, VdN),[87] and probably his ouster from the SED. The Jewish background of the two Jews among the defendants was not stressed in the trial.[88] Fritz Rosenbaum continued behind bars in Potsdam, and on 15 April 1954 he was transferred to the prison in Waldheim, but was not brought once more before a court there. Repeated attempts to have his imprisonment changed to a suspended sentence, and petitions of clemency by his wife, proved abortive. Ultimately, these were rejected by the director of the prison, who attested that Rosenheim had adjusted well to the routine at the penal institution and obeyed orders, but accused him of failing to show "how he was planning to atone for his crime," and stated that he had "made no progress in the process of reeducation."[89] In the meantime, Rosenbaum was suffering from tuberculosis, and his wife had a heart ailment. She had left the GDR immediately after her husband's arrest and lived with relatives in West Berlin, purportedly for economic reasons (the assets of the couple had after all been confiscated), but she declared her intent to return immediately if her husband should be released.[90]

Finally, in July 1956 the prison agreed that Rosenbaum had demonstrated a positive change, opening the path to parole. Probably the reason behind this was less any change in Rosenbaum's behavior, as the prison director had stressed, and more rather an instruction from the Ministry for State Security. The Stasi had reviewed convictions of past SPD members and ordered that Rosenbaum be immediately paroled.[91] In November 1958, the GDR suspended the last months of Rosenbaum's sentence and he was released.[92]

Aftermath

The Conflict Surrounding Recha Freier's Let the Children Come

Controversy over the activities of the RV continued into the 1960s. These disputes arose everywhere that emigrants and camp survivors were now living: in Israel, Great Britain, the United States, and the Federal Republic of Germany, where Jewish Communities had been refounded and a new organization the Central Council of the German Jews (Zentralrat der Juden in Deutschland) had been created. Part of this discussion involved assessments and statements in various publications and by scholars; on the other hand, the postwar organizations of the German Jews also had to articulate their position on the history of their predecessors. Almost unnoticed outside of Israel, Recha Freier (see chapter 1) published a book in Hebrew in Tel Aviv in 1953 on the early years of the Youth Aliyah. In the late 1950s, she was preparing an English translation to be issued by the respected publisher Weidenfeld and Nelson, entitled *Let the Children Come: The Early History of Youth Aliyah.* This plan brought the surviving German-Jewish functionaries and Leo Baeck's daughter, Ruth Berlak, onto the scene. In a concentrated joint effort by various postwar organizations, statements by individuals, and if necessary legal steps, they were intent on preventing Freier from disseminating her allegations in the book against the Reichsvereinigung in general and Baeck in particular in the English-speaking world. Should all their efforts prove fruitless, they wanted to convince an "influential family"—evidently the financial backers of the publishing house—to try to persuade the prestigious publisher to not bring out the book.[93]

Indeed, Recha Freier had made quite a number of accusations in the book, as was evident in a draft translation of the text into English then circulating among her adversaries. Freier claimed that Leo Baeck had refused to even receive the wives of the Poles incarcerated in 1939 (by contrast, the source documentation only shows that the wives had asked Heinrich Stahl, as chair of the Berlin Jewish Community, to assist). She stated that the Reichsvereinigung had in all seriousness referred repeatedly to the Gestapo as its "supervisory authority" (which is correct, but the RV was of course ordered to do so). She alleged that the RV had distanced itself vis-à-vis the Gestapo from the way Heinrich Stahl was handling his finances, and that the result was his dismissal (there is no evidence for this). Indeed, Freier wrote that the RV had then even stated that it opposed Stahl being allowed to leave Germany (in fact, his emigration was forbidden by the RSHA).[94] In this latter charge, she thus explicitly accused the decision-making echelon in the Reichsvereinigung of complicity and guilt in Stahl's death. In addition, she charged that the German-Jewish organization had prevented the Polish Jews—for whom Freier had obtained certificates for Palestine—from being released from detention, and the RV was thus also complicit in and responsible for their later death in concentration camps.[95] Finally, she alleged that the Reichsvereinigung had distanced itself from her personally, thus placing her in danger. Most evidently, the temporal remove from past events had not prompted Freier in retrospect to thoroughly rethink the tragic situation faced by the German-Jewish functionaries under the Nazi regime, and to look for guilt and responsibility on the side of the perpetrators. On the contrary, her old feelings and resentment had apparently grown even stronger over the years. She was enraged for not having found support among her fellow Jews, whose surviving representatives, now as before, were standing together united against her, and who had seemingly no regrets about their earlier attitudes toward her. She still sensed her desperation over her own former powerlessness and all the umbrage and insults she had been forced to endure, her anger over her dismissal as responsible head of the Youth Aliyah, and the wish, sprung from this, to be able to consider someone she personally knew (namely, the Jewish chairman Baeck) liable for her distress. Thus, regardless of the fact that the conflict had been waged between her and Eppstein, she added new accusations to Baeck's purported list of sins, refusing to give more thought to the difficult situation the German-Jewish functionaries had then found themselves in.

Moreover, those whom Freier accused of these transgressions (Baeck himself was no longer alive) did not think it was necessary to revise their positions now, seen from a new temporal vantage. Instead of looking again at the events of 1939–1941 in retrospect, among themselves or even with Freier, they closed ranks immediately, and once more formed a tight, united front. Salomon Adler-Rudel, in the meantime now head of the Leo Baeck Institute in Jerusalem, intervened in November 1959 in London at the publishing house because of the Freier manuscript. He informed Robert Weltsch at the Leo Baeck Institute in London that unfortunately he had not yet been able to achieve anything with the intended publishers. In terms of the substance of the arguments, Adler-Rudel agreed with the opponents of Freier, but in Israel he felt he had to take Freier's good standing there into consideration, especially since many of those she had saved lived in the country. Simultaneous with knowledge about the upcoming English edition of Freier's book, he had received confidential notification that Kurt Ball-Kaduri had submitted an essay on the same topic (in Hebrew) to the then new journal, *Yad Vashem Studies*. The editors there could "not easily reject" the text by Ball-Kaduri, but could at least pass it on to Ernst Simon for peer review and corresponding corrections. Thus, the danger of a broader discussion of the failure to rescue the Polish Jews in Germany in 1939 was at least temporarily averted, although that could flare up again with the publication in English of Freier's book.

Norbert Wollheim and Hans-Erich Fabian now issued statements in New York in which they refuted in detail Freier's assertions, in particular as far as Stahl's departure from his office as Berlin Jewish Community chair was concerned.[96] Baeck's daughter Ruth Berlak hired a lawyer,[97] and the American Federation of Jews from Central Europe wrote to the publishers.[98] Hans Reichmann protested in the name of the Council of Jews from Germany, a group of former surviving members of the Reichsvereinigung board. The publisher initially did not respond to these letters,[99] and the critics were buoyed by the hope that their joint efforts had indeed prevented publication of the book.[100] In actuality, however, Weidenfeld had "only" asked Freier to tone down certain passages. Then he answered his critical correspondents by stating that in his opinion, the vague statements remaining in the incriminating chapters, such as that Leo Baeck had been director of the Reichsvereinigung (which was uncontested), did not damage his reputation.[101] Freier's critics did not agree. For them, as Franz Meyer wrote, Freier was and remained a "spiteful shrew" and "pathological liar."[102] They continued to think the book was "despicable," a "slanderous smear," and tried once more, although in vain, to have the entire chapter on Freier's struggle to rescue the incarcerated Polish Jews in 1939 dropped.[103] However, their intervention was only able to postpone the book's publication until 1961; it could not prevent its appearance. And in the end, the book did not damage Leo Baeck's reputation.

Those taking action here, German-Jewish emigrants and concentration camp survivors, reacted with relative speed and in solidarity if they thought that German-Jewish history between 1933 and 1945 was being presented in an inappropriate or even slanderous way in postwar accounts, as the historian Jürgen Matthäus has shown.[104] Thus, they critiqued Raul Hilberg's *Destruction of the European Jews* in 1961, and in 1963 rejected Hannah Arendt's attacks on Leo Baeck and the German-Jewish leaders in her book *Eichmann in Jerusalem*.[105] However, if they tried to come to a unanimous view on how the situation of the German Jews and their functionaries during the Nazi period was to be evaluated historically, and how its history was to be written, their common ground soon crumbled away.[106] Looking at the years 1933 to 1938, they were barely able to reach some consensus on the work of the Reich Representation, and they were sharply divided when it came to the Reich Association: Adler-Rudel's approach of seeing the work of the RV totally "from the perspective of a tendency for rescue" of the Jews patently ignored the "very peculiar things" that Max Kreutzberger, head of the Leo Baeck Institute in New York, had come across during his search for materials.[107] It was still too early for a suitable treatment of the "dark aspects." Consequently, there was no comprehensive account by anyone from the generation of the survivors.

Surviving Functionaries in Jewish Organizations

In February 1964, the topic "Reichsvereinigung" caught the attention of the Central Council of the Jews in Germany (Zentralrat der Juden in Deutschland).[108] The organization, founded in 1950, had left clarification of corresponding accusations regarding the past to the Jewish Communities and the local courts. For the sake of preserving the internal peace, the Central Council had avoided dealing with these questions. But in the face of continuing protest letters from Community members, the Zentralrat board of directors now saw itself compelled to find a new position on the explosive issue: should former Jewish representatives of the RV and "concentration camp police" be allowed to have a prominent position in the German-Jewish community in the 1960s? Those in consultation agreed that officials who had served in the Reich Representation until 1938 could not be blamed for actions in their tenure of office, but those who had served in the RV were considered per se to be under suspicion. Not yet nineteen years after the war's end, the board of directors decided:

> In the view of the board of directors of the Central Council of the Jews in Germany, individuals who in the period of National Socialism, supported or participated in measures of persecution, even if under compulsion, cannot—as a matter of basic principle—be allowed to hold any leading or representative position in the Jewish community.[109]

If a Jewish Community decided to back a person so accused, its entire executive board was to be pressured to resign. This resolution was not intended for publication. The Central Council wished if at all possible to avoid any open discussion of this in the media. So the board of directors appointed a five-person commission from its own ranks to examine corresponding accusations in future should they arise. The commission had no further powers. Carl Katz from Bremen abstained in the vote on the resolution—for good reason, since some of the accusations pertained to him personally.

Until 1942, Carl Katz had headed the Bremen administrative office, under the Northwest Germany district branch in Hamburg of the Reichsvereinigung. Katz was deported with his family via Hanover to Theresien-stadt, arriving there on 24 July 1942.[110] They survived and Katz returned to Bremen, establishing the new Jewish Community in Bremen on 6 August 1945. He would head this Community until his death in 1972.[111] In the years 1945 to 1950, the CIC had already been investigating him, but apparently without any concrete result, so that the Senator for Political Liberation in Bremen had declined to institute proceedings against him.[112] Now the Central Council commission members questioned his previous associates, and obtained contradictory character references about Katz.[113] Max Plaut in particular put forward serious accusations: he stated that Katz had "constantly" been at the Gestapo (later he corrected that to "often"), and that some persons in Bremen had been deported contrary to the RSHA guidelines. He alleged that Katz had set up an illicit account and gained financial advantage for himself through this account, and stressed that Katz's predecessor Joseph Platzer suspected that Katz had been centrally instrumental in his deportation.[114] Plaut apparently did not realize that these very same charges could also have been made against him: all district branch directors had been required to appear frequently at the Gestapo. According to a confidential RSHA decree, everywhere in the Reich a certain percentage of officially deferred Jews were nonetheless to be deported. Moreover, after the war, Plaut had specifically boasted about his illicit account that he had used for purchasing food and other necessities. As witnesses confirmed, Katz had made use of this "black" money for purchasing food, tools, heaters, etc., for the large-scale transport to Minsk and food for the transports to Theresienstadt.[115] Furthermore, it is doubtful that Katz had been so keen on obtaining the dangerous post of district branch director that he had denounced his predecessor Platzer to the authorities.

Katz defended himself before the commission regarding the charge of having been too "friendly" with the Gestapo: yes, he had had a beer with the Gestapo officials, but that was only once, in an attempt to keep them from searching baggage on the eve of a deportation to Theresienstadt. The "Jewish expert" in the *Judenreferat*, now called as a witness, denied he had played cards with Katz, but admitted he had used the familiar pronoun *Du* with Katz as a friendly form of address.[116] That actually reflected a note-worthy degree of personal closeness, which might have become dangerous for both men if the "Jewish expert" had addressed Katz in this reciprocal way in the presence of his Gestapo colleagues. In any case, it is probably doubtful that such a close personal relation between the two men would have resulted in any concrete positive effects for the RV members. None-theless, Katz was able to rebut all other accusations, especially since the Bremen savings bank was able to provide data on all transactions of the illegal account "Carl Katz honorary endowment." This showed that in 1941/1942, the account had maintained a balance ranging between two thousand and just under ten thousand RM. On his deportation, Katz had transferred the balance to his successor Karl Bruck, for whom the account likewise was to prove useful in his capacity as intermediary, and after the war Bruck had passed on the account to the reestablished Jewish Community. At the end of their investigations, despite their initial resolution and its wording, the commission members did not challenge Katz's position as chairman of the Bremen Jewish Community.

However, Katz and Plaut now continued their altercation over behavior, guilt, and responsibility outside the organization. These formerly close friends and companions were now deeply divided associates: Katz had been subordinate to Plaut in the RV administration, had welcomed him to Bremen in 1950, and had granted him power of attorney in his firm. Plaut joined the Bremen Jewish Community and was appointed to its board, which Katz headed, in 1952.[117] Plaut even organized a commemorative Festschrift volume to mark Katz's sixtieth birthday.[118]

The dispute ended up in court and Katz and Plaut brought third parties into the case proceedings: the Jewish Community, the Society for Brotherhood, Jewish witnesses, and others. This created a regional Jewish public sphere marked by heated argument. Clarification on matters of substance was not reached. Katz's successor Bruck, now once again a Protestant and distant from Jewish organizations, was astonished that two men who had worked together so closely in difficult times could now be at such loggerheads and quarrel in this bitter way.[119] The conflict ended in 1963 with Plaut's exclusion from the Bremen Jewish Community due to "behavior unworthy of a Community member."[120] Plaut moved back to Hamburg.[121] In December 1967, the chief public prosecutor discontinued and closed the case.[122]

Even more than two decades after the war's end, the aftereffects of the "strategy of cooperation" still perturbed former functionaries, compulsory RV members, and other "Jews" the organization had administered. Internment, incarceration, cases before courts of honor on the basis of accusations by others or efforts to have one's own name cleared, and employment bans in Berlin (West and East) and West Germany made the new beginning, quite different from what they had imagined, very difficult for those affected. In East Germany, their situation was more severe: renewed spying on individuals and denunciations to the police, the consequence of which could be trial before a Soviet military tribunal and internment in a special camp, resulting in death for some. For those who survived this period, accusations and internment led in any case to additional lost years in their troubled lives. In the early 1950s, former Jewish functionaries who had not been brought before a military tribunal and other Jews fled from the GDR, a number with sufficient time remaining to construct a new professional life in the Federal Republic.

The baptized Christians among the former RV intermediaries breathed a sigh of relief after the war, cast off the Jewish identity the regime had imposed on them, and returned to their Christian faith or their former secular lives. Even those who during the Nazi period had defined themselves as Jews and had participated in the reestablishment of the Jewish Communities now rarely remained active at their helm. Many emigrated in the initial postwar years. Most who remained in Germany concentrated principally on their professional lives as lawyers or doctors, or became active, for example, in professional associations. They harbored the hope that the office they had involuntarily accepted under Nazism would slowly be forgotten. In most cases, that hope was realized. To be sure, a vague general air of suspicion about collaboration with the Gestapo persisted as an invisible cloud of doubt among surviving Jews. But a segment of the non-Jewish majority of society was also wont to regard the persecution and murder of the Jews as an affair primarily between the SS and the Jews, one that they had nothing to do with. This suspicion was repeatedly revived whenever former Jewish functionaries became the focus of public attention, or when two individuals who knew (too) much about one another were transformed into bitterly feuding adversaries.

Notes

1. On dealing with the "snatchers" after the war, see Doris Tausendfreund, *Erzwungener Verrat: Jüdische "Greifer" im Dienst der Gestapo 1943–1945* (Berlin, 2006), 259–75.
2. The extant judgments, numbering approximately one hundred, can be found in the posthumous papers of Siegmund Weltlinger, former "Commissioner for Ecclesiastical Affairs," in LAB, Rep. 020, Nos. 4860-5861, Jüdische Gemeinde (n.d.), Ehrengerichts- und Verfahrensordnung [Code of Procedure for Courts of Honor]; see also YV, 02/403, Rabbi Max Eschelbacher, Berlin 1949, pp. 10–11. In individual cases, copies of judgments in proceedings before courts of honor can be found appended in court files. Documentation on court of honor proceedings has to date not been found in the files of the Jewish Community. This means that the total number of actual proceedings cannot be precisely determined, nor do we have adequate knowledge on proceedings in detail and the consequences for those affected.
3. LAB, Rep. 020, Nos. 4860-5861, Jüdische Gemeinde (n.d.), Ehrengerichts- und Verfahrensordnung, p. 2.
4. Ibid., p. 3.
5. LAB, Rep. 020, Nos. 4860-5861, Jüdische Gemeinde (n.d.), Urteil Ehrengerichtssache [judgment in case before court of honor] I.R. v. 8 October 1946, p. 1; LAB, Rep.

020, Nos. 4860-5861, Jüdische Gemeinde (n.d.), Urteil Ehrengerichtssache, S.G., 6 January 1948, p. 2.

6. LAB, Rep. 020, Nos. 4860-5861, Jüdische Gemeinde (n.d.), Urteil Ehrengerichtssache, M.G., 20 August 1947, p. 1.

7. LAB, Rep. 020, Nos. 4860-5861, Jüdische Gemeinde (n.d.), Urteil Ehrengerichtssache, W.T., 30 September 1946, p. 1.

8. LAB, Rep. 020, Nos. 4860-5861, Jüdische Gemeinde (n.d.), Urteil Ehrengerichtssache, I.R., 8 October 1946, p. 1. The Jewish Community had also proceeded in this way in the previously mentioned case; LAB, Rep. 020, Nos. 4860-5861, Jüdische Gemeinde (n.d.), Urteil Ehrengerichtssache, W.T., pp. 1–2.

9. LAB, Rep. 020, Nos. 4860-5861, Jüdische Gemeinde (n.d.), Urteil Ehrengerichtssache, Entscheidung Ehrengericht Martha Raphael [verdict, court of honor, M. Raphael], 7 May 1947, p. 2.

10. Ibid., pp. 5–6.

11. Sitzung des Ehrengerichts der Jüdischen Gemeinde zu Berlin, 5 April 1956, StA LG Berlin, 3 P (K) Ks 1/71, addendum 73, fol. 92; on Reschke's activity, see Akim Jah, "Vom Altenheim," 176–219.

12. On the following, see the biography of Martha Mosse in Kraus, *Familie Mosse*, 570–95; Maierhof, *Selbstbehauptung*, 270–77; Reinicke, "Erster 'Polizeirat,'" 297–304; diverse (in part overlapping) biographical texts by Martha Mosse in the State Archive Berlin, Yad Vashem, and LBI, New York.

13. LAB, B Rep. 235-07, Martha Mosse, "Erinnerungen," pp. 1–5; see Willems, *Der entsiedelte Jude*, 186.

14. YV, 02/769, "'Umsiedlung' der Berliner Juden," report by Martha Mosse, recorded 23/24 July 1958 by Wolfgang Scheffler, pp. 4–5.

15. On Mosse's options and limits for intervention, see LBI, NY, AR 7183 (Max Kreutzberger), box 7, folder 6, MM reels 121, report Kleemann, 12 June 1947, pp. 1–2.

16. Compensation Office [Entschädigungsamt] Berlin, file Mosse 11659, certificate from autonomous administration of the former Theresienstadt-city concentration camp, 3 July 1945 (Jiri Vogel).

17. LAB, B Rep. 235-07, MF 4170-4171, Martha Mosse, "Erinnerungen," p. 5.

18. Entschädigungsamt Berlin, file Mosse 11659, decision 57976, 5 July 1956.

19. Entschädigungsamt Berlin, file Mosse 11659, Arbeitsbuch-Ersatzkarte [work record book, replacement card], 3 July 1946; c.v., 23 February 1949, pag. 4.

20. Entschädigungsamt Berlin, file Mosse 11659, obit.

21. LBI, NY, AR 7183 (Max Kreutzberger), box 7, folder 6, MM reels 121.

22. LAB, B Rep 235-07, MF 4170-4171, Martha Mosse, "Erinnerungen," p. 5.

23. LBI, JMB, MM 111 (Max Kreutzberger), report Alexander Gutfeld, letter to Hanns (Reissner?), 20 August 1967.

24. LBI, NY, MF 4170-4171, character reference by Leo Baeck for Martha Mosse, 28 February 1947; YV, 01/192, Siegmund Weltlinger, "Tätigkeit für die Jüdische Gemeinde in Berlin in den Jahren 1939–1943" [Activity for the Berlin Jewish Comm. 1939–1943], 28 May 1957, p. 3; LBI, NY, AR 7183 (Max Kreutzberger), box 7, folder 6, MM reels 121, Siegmund Weltlinger, 17 November 1945; LBI, NY, AR 7183 (Max Kreutzberger), box 7, folder 6, MM reels 121, Siegbert Kleemann, 12 June 1947.

25. LAB, B Rep. 235-07, Martha Mosse, Traueranzeige [death notice]; her nephews wrote the obituary: "hers was a life only of goodness and courage."

26. On the structure of US occupation in Bremen and Bavaria in the early postwar years, see Andreas Röpcke, "Office of Military Goverment for Bremen," in OMGUS-*Handbuch: Die amerikanische Militärregierung in Deutschland 1945–1949*, ed. Chris-

toph Weisz (Munich, 1994), 649ff.; Reinhard Heydenreuther, "Office of Military Government for Bavaria," in Weisz, *OMGUS-Handbuch*, 143–315.

27. Sta München, Stanw. 29.499/1-3, 1 Js 67 ff./49, Interrogation Theodor Koronczyk, 26 September 1950, p. 2, obverse.
28. See Wolfgang Kraushaar, "'Die Auerbach-Affäre,'" in Schoeps, *Leben*, 208–18.
29. Sta München, Spruchkammer, box 939, Theodor Koronczyk, Auerbach to Prosecutor General, 6 March 1947, pag. 19.
30. Sta München, Spruchkammer, box 939, Theodor Koronczyk, minutes, public session, 29/30 October 1947, p. 4, pag. 34.
31. Sta München, Spruchkammer, box 939, Theodor Koronczyk, memo, pag. 14.
32. Sta München, Spruchkammer, box 939, Theodor Koronczyk, Interrogation Koronczyk, 25 April 1947, p. 3, pag. 16.
33. Ibid.
34. Sta München, Spruchkammer, box 939, Theodor Koronczyk, minutes of the public session, 29/30 October 1947, Interrogation of witness Dr. Schwarz, p. 25, pag. 46.
35. Sta München, Spruchkammer, box 939, Theodor Koronczyk, Interrogation Siegfried Neuland, pp. 26–27, pag. 47–48.
36. Ibid., p. 5, pag. 35; other witnesses gave similar testimony, p. 6, pag. 36.
37. Sta München, Spruchkammer, box 939, Theodor Koronczyk, div. letters, pag. 54–60.
38. Sta München, Spruchkammer, box 939, Theodor Koronczyk, Koronczyk, work reference Koronczyk, 14 September 1948.
39. Sta München, Spruchkammer, box 939, Theodor Koronczyk, results of the session, 12 April 1948, pag. 106–7; for date of death see Kasberger, "Hans Wegner," 244.
40. The District Court Munich I sentenced him on 12 July 1949 to two years imprisonment based on sixteen bodily injuries he had inflicted in office (1 KMs 9-11/49), and on 14 December 1954, acquitted him of the charge of unlawful detention while in office in concurrence with extortion (3 KLs 2/54) due to the deportation of Julius Hechinger. See the verdict in *Justiz und NS-Verbrechen*, 13: 13.
41. Modert, "Motor," 175.
42. Sta München, Spruchkammer, box 1316, Johannes Pfeuffer, letter Theodor Koronczyk, 23 October 1948.
43. Sta München, Stanw. 29.499/1-3, 1 Js 67 ff./49, Interrogation Theodor Koronczyk, 26 September 1950, p. 2, n. pag.
44. Sta München, Spruchkammer, box 1316, Johannes Pfeuffer, letter lawyer Weiler, 29 January 1953, judgment Main Chamber Munich, 23 January 1953, Az H/1595/49.
45. University of Oxford, Bodleian Library, MS SPSL file Martin Heinrich Corten, letter, Corten to Society for the Protection of Learning and Science, 3 February 1949.
46. Data from Reparations Office, Hamburg (now in StaHH), file Corten, 18891222; see Beate Meyer, "Corten, Martin Heinrich," in *Das Jüdische Hamburg: Ein historisches Nachschlagewerk*, ed. Institut für die Geschichte der deutschen Juden (Göttingen, 2006), 50–51; http://goo.gl/EKba5 (accessed 20 May 2013); see also Anna von Villiez, *Mit aller Kraft verdrängt: Entrechtung und Verfolgung "nicht arischer" Ärzte in Hamburg 1933 bis 1945* (Hamburg, 2009), 247.
47. For all data not referenced elsewhere, see Thorsten Noack, "Über Kaninchen und Giftschlangen: Psychiatrie und Öffentlichkeit in der frühen Bundesrepublik Deutschland," in *"Moderne" Anstaltspsychiatrie im 19. und 20. Jahrhundert—Legitimation und Kritik*, ed. Heiner Fangerau and Karin Nolte (Stuttgart, 2006), 311–40. I am grateful to Thorsten Noack and Anna von Villiez for their assistance in locating source materials on Corten.

48. All data from Heidel and Nitsche, "Adolf Lipp," 374–77.
49. BStU, C AP 1806/68, Ermittlungsbericht [investigative report], p. 2 pag. 7. The file was destroyed in 1989 by the security ministry.
50. Nitsche and Röcher, *Juden in Chemnitz*, 112.
51. See Karin Hartewig, *Zurückgekehrt: Die Geschichte der jüdischen Kommunisten in der DDR* (Cologne, 2000), 388.
52. See Horst Möller and Alexandr O. Tschubarjan, eds., *SMAD-Handbuch: Die Sowjetische Militäradministration in Deutschland 1945–1949* (Munich, 2009), 603–5; see also Natalja Jeske and Ute Schmidt, "Zur Verfolgung von Kriegs- und NS-Verbrechen durch sowjetische Militärtribunale in der SBZ," in *Sowjetische Militärtribunale*, vol. 2, *Die Verurteilung deutscher Zivilisten 1945–1955*, ed. Andreas Hilger, Mike Schmeitzner, and Ute Schmidt (Cologne, Weimar, and Vienna, 2003), 158–59.
53. This is similar to reasons mentioned by Bettina Greiner as grounds for the internment of other prisoners in Soviet special camps; see Bettina Greiner, *Verdrängter Terror: Geschichte und Wahrnehmung sowjetischer Speziallager in Deutschland* (Hamburg, 2010), 143–44.
54. Victor Klemperer, *The Diaries of Victor Klemperer, 1945–1959, The Lesser Evil*, vol. 2, trans. Martin Chalmers (London, 2004), 346; on Neumark as intermediary, see Klemperer, *I Will Bear Witness*, 278, 297–98, 313–14.
55. Klemperer, *Lesser Evil*, 59, 65, 75.
56. Ibid., 138.
57. BStU, ZUV 74, EV Vol. 16, Interrogation Ernst Neumark, 23 July 1946, p. 2; in the interrogation on 8 October 1946, he retracted this statement and insisted on "not guilty," BStU, ZUV 74, EV Vol. 16, Interrogation Ernst Neumark, fol. 000112.
58. BStU, ZUV 74, EV Vol. 16, Interrogation Ernst Neumark, fol. 000112.
59. Klemperer, *Lesser Evil*, 138, 140.
60. Ibid., 144, 149, 156, 209.
61. I am grateful to Cornelia Liebold of the Bautzen Memorial for this information; on the Sachsenhausen camp, see www.stiftung-bg.de/gums/en/index.htm (accessed 20 July 2012). On this in general, see Jeske and Schmidt, "Verfolgung"; Natalja Jeske and Jörg Morré, "Die Inhaftierung von Tribunalverurteilten in der SBZ," in Hilger, Schmeitzner, and Schmidt, *Verurteilung deutscher Zivilisten*, 651–52.
62. I wish to thank Ines Reich of the Sachsenhausen Memorial and Museum for this information and a copy of the camp diary.
63. Klemperer, *Lesser Evil*, 316. A year later he learned that Neumark ("the mysterious case—I can't blame neither him nor the Russians") had died of tuberculosis in the Bautzen camp; see ibid., 346.
64. BStU, MfS XII/RF/97, Interrogation Richard Hesse, 19 May 1950, personal data, membership card Liberal Democratic Party Germany (LDPD), 22 August 1945, pag. 3, 4, 6, 115, 126.
65. BStU, MfS XII/RF/97, bill of indictment Richard Hesse, 3 July 1950, BStU pag. 11; based on investigations by the NKVD, 16 January 1945.
66. BStU, MfS XII/RF/97, BStU pag. 58; Deutsche Volkspolizei, Interrogation Julius Meyer, 24 June 1950, pag. 73–74.
67. BStU, MfS XII/RF/97, Interrogation Fritz Grunsfeld, 24 June 1950, pag. 110–11; BStU, MfS XII/RF/97, Interrogation Salo Looser, 24 June 1950, pag. 104.
68. BStU, MfS XII/RF/97, BStU, MfS XII/RF/97, Ermittlungsbericht, 26 August 1950, pag. 63–65.
69. BStU, MfS XII/RF/97, judgment, Chemnitz district court, pag. 16–19.

70. BStU, MfS XII/RF/97, state prosecutor's office, 14 July 1950, pag. 28; BStU, MfS XII/RF/97, resolution, 14 July 1950, pag. 30.

71. BStU, Außenstelle Halle/MfS BV Halle, MfS XII/RF/189, letter wife, 12 May 1952, pag. 31; BStU, Außenstelle Halle/MfS BV Halle, MfS XII/RF/189, visitor's pass, 29 May 1952, pag. 32.

72. BStU, Außenstelle Halle/MfS BV Halle, judgment Bautzen prison, 4 May 1954, pag. 41.

73. BStU, Außenstelle Halle/MfS BV Halle, resolution, 11 June 1954, pag. 42, certificate of release, 14 July 1954, pag. 43.

74. BStU, Außenstelle Halle/MfS BV Halle, MfS XII/RF/189. The district administrative office in Halle was ordered to check 199 persons in their area who had been tried and convicted by a Soviet military tribunal. Of these, 54 were sill living there. In the corresponding list, pag. 2 (n.d.), the name of Richard Hesse, pensioner, appears pag. 7.

75. USHMM, RG-14.053M, Jewish Community of Leipzig, reel 14, copy MS of article for *Aufbau*, 26 July 1946.

76. BStU, MfS Zentralarchiv, Allg. P. 172/64, Ermittlungsbericht, 1 April 1954, pag. 4.

77. See Steffen Held, *Zwischen Tradition und Vermächtnis: Die israelitische Religionsgemeinde zu Leipzig nach 1945* (Hamburg, 1995), 17.

78. Ibid., 40–41.

79. See also Adolf Diamant, *Chronik der Juden in Leipzig: Aufstieg, Vernichtung und Neuanfang* (Chemnitz and Leipzig, 1993), 707–8, 715; Offenberg, *Seid vorsichtig*, 51, 86–87.

80. BStU, Allge. P. 1429/60, memo, 7 August 1951, pag. 25. It was not possible to check whether the indirectly reproduced statement by Broh that his wife was sent to Siberia is correct.

81. Landeshauptarchiv Potsdam, TA Rep 333 Nr. 1142, application for membership, VVN, questionnaire, 3 November 1945; Landeshauptarchiv Potsdam, TA Rep 203, MdJ, PA 44 (R/10337), personnel questionnaire, 2 December 1950, c.v., 2 December 1950.

82. Landeshauptarchiv Potsdam, TA Rep 203, MdJ, PA 44 (R/10337), c.v., pag. 2.

83. Generalstaatsanwaltschaft [Public prosecutor's office] Brandenburg/Havel, II Re 9/52, Vol. I, Interrogation Fritz Rosenbaum, 5 December 1952, pp. 1–2.

84. See DeutschlandRadio Berlin, "Schlag gegen Spekulanten und Saboteure," broadcast 6 February 2003, www.dradio.de/dlr/sendungen/merkmal/145599/ (accessed 20 July 2012); Falco Werkentin, "'Schädlinge und Saboteure aus Kleinmachnow vor Gericht'—Die Hintergründe eines Schauprozesses im Februar 1953," http://goo.gl/lU3L8 (accessed 20 July 2012).

85. Generalstaatsanwaltschaft Brandenburg/Havel, II Re 9/52, (Ss I/3 45/53 OstA, II Ks 78/53), Vol. II, bill of indictment, p. 2, pag. 363.

86. Generalstaatsanwaltschaft Brandenburg/Havel, II Re 9/52, (Ss I/3 45/53 OstA, II Ks 78/53), Vol. II, verdict, 11 February 1953, pag. 442–43, 446–47, 464–65.

87. Landeshauptarchiv Potsdam, TA Rep 333 Nr. 1142, VVN-Beschlussprotokoll [minutes of resolution on VVN], 2 January 1953, pag. 111; Landeshauptarchiv Potsdam, VdN 1456, Rep 401, Beschluss R/284, 2 May 1953, letter, council of the municipality Kleinmachnow to council district Potsdam, 20 May 1953. The status of VdN was associated with a (partial) pension and other advantages.

88. According to the literal wording of an "internal party report," it stated: "The district state prosecutor ... was very clever in destroying the arguments of the defense, which

in particular in regard to the defendants Rosenbaum and Pikarski (former victims of racist persecution), sought to reduce the sentence by referring to the great suffering that the defendants had experienced during the Nazi period." See DeutschlandRadio Berlin, "Schlag gegen Spekulanten und Saboteure," broadcast, February 2003.

89. Generalstaatsanwaltschaft Brandenburg/Havel, II Re 9/52, Vol. III, report on conduct, 6 March 1956.

90. Generalstaatsanwaltschaft Brandenburg/Havel, II Re 9/52, Vol. III, clemency appeal G. Rosenbaum, 15 December 1954.

91. BStU, MfS Ast I c 1/74, letter deputy senior state prosecutor to state prosecutor Potsdam district, 4 September 1956, pag. 189, 206ff., 213.

92. Generalstaatsanwaltschaft Brandenburg/Havel, II Re 9/52, hand file I, resolution, 10 November 1958.

93. LBI, Jerusalem, 364, Recha Freier, letter (n.s.) to Alexander, 22 September 1959. The book in the original Hebrew version was entitled *Yesharesh: Al yosodei Aliyat ha-Noar ve-shnoteha ha-rishonot* [To uproot: On the founding of Youth Aliyah and its first years] (Tel Aviv, 1953).

94. LBI, Jerusalem, 364, Recha Freier, Excerpts from Recha Freier's Book "Let the Children come. Chapter ten 1939-1941. The Last Youth Aliyah Group from Central Europe," pp. 1–2.

95. Ibid., p. 2.

96. LBI, Jerusalem, 364, Recha Freier, declaration by Fabian and Wollheim, December 1959.

97. LBI, Jerusalem, 364, Recha Freier, letter Berlak to Adler-Rudel, 21 March 1961.

98. LBI, Jerusalem, 364, Recha Freier, letter American Federation of Jews from Central Europe, Alexander to Reichmann, 29 September 1959.

99. LBI, Jerusalem, 364, Recha Freier, letter Reichmann to Adler-Rudel, 23 March 1961.

100. LBI, Jerusalem, 364, Recha Freier, memo Adler-Rudel to Moses, Gerlin, Tramer and Michaelis, 1 April 1960.

101. LBI, Jerusalem, 364, Recha Freier, letter Weidenfeld to div. persons, 12 April 1961.

102. LBI, Jerusalem, 364, Recha Freier, letter Franz Meyer (Meier) to Adler-Rudel, 22 November 1959.

103. LBI, Jerusalem, 364, Recha Freier, letter Adler-Rudel to Berlak, 16 March 1961.

104. See Jürgen Matthäus, "Between Fragmented Memory and 'Real History'—The LBI's Perception of Jewish Self-Defense against Nazi Antisemitism, 1955–1970," in *Preserving the Legacy of German Jewry: A History of the Leo Baeck Institute, 1955–2005*, ed. Christhard Hoffmann (Tübingen, 2005), 375–407.

105. Ibid., 391–99.

106. See also Moshe Zimmermann, *Die deutschen Juden in der Geschichte der Shoah: Keine Exklave!* (Tübingen, 2002), 27–28.

107. Matthäus, "Fragmented Memory," 401ff.

108. State Archive Bremen, 4,89/3-751 Vol. I, criminal case Dr. Max Plaut, minutes on the meeting of the executive of the Zentralrat der Juden in Deutschland, 23 February 1964, in the Düsseldorf Jewish Community.

109. Ibid., p. 6, pag. 168.

110. Information from Anna Hájková, 23 February 2010.

111. See www.gemeinden.judentum.de/bremen/index.htm (accessed 20 July 2012).

112. In the course of the slander suit that Katz had initiated in 1966 against Max Plaut, the chief public prosecutor requested the CIC files from the National Archives in Washington, but he had no success, since they could no longer be located. State

Archive Bremen, 4,89/3-751 Vol. I, criminal case Dr. Max Plaut; State Archive Bremen, 4,89/3-1118, bill of indictment against Plaut, p. 11, pag. 108.

113. State Archive Bremen, 4,89/3-751 Vol. I, criminal case Dr. Max Plaut, letter van Dam to Fritz Manasse, 6 April 1964, p. 2, pag. 10.

114. Joseph Platzer, born 19 December 1882, was deported to Minsk via Hamburg on 18 November 1941, and died there on 28 July 1942; see www.bundesarchiv.de/gedenk buch/index.html.en (accessed 21 July 2012).

115. State Archive Bremen, 4,89/3-751 Vol. I, criminal case Dr. Max Plaut, Interrogation Helmut Schmidt, 2 March 1966, p. 2, pag. 73.

116. State Archive Bremen, 4,89/3-751 Vol. I, criminal case Dr. Max Plaut, Interrogation Friedrich Linnemann, 25 March 1966, pag. 96. In this period and these circumstances, the open reciprocal use of familiar *Du* in the presence of others would have signaled quite a close friendship.

117. State Archive Bremen, 4,89/3-751 Vol. I, criminal case Dr. Max Plaut, complaint Plaut against Jewish Community, p. 3, pag. 24.

118. Israelitische Gemeinde Bremen, ed., *Festschrift zum 60. Geburtstag von Carl Katz: 14.9.1959, gewidmet von der israelitischen Gemeinde Bremen* (Bremen, 1959). Plaut introduced the volume with a letter of appreciation that he had sent to Katz on 16 July 1942, prior to the latter's scheduled deportation. There he stressed his qualities as head of the Bremen Jewish Community, his commitment to religion, and his social engagement; letter Max Plaut to Karl [sic] Katz, 16 July 1942, reproduced in Bremen, *Festschrift,* n.p.

119. State Archive Bremen, 4,89/3-751 Vol. I, Interrogation Karl Bruck, 15 April 1966, p. 3, pag. 117.

120. State Archive Bremen, 4,89/3-751 Vol. I, Interrogation Karl Bruck, complaint, p. 3, pag. 4.

121. State Archive Bremen, 4,89/3-751 Vol. I, Interrogation Karl Bruck, memo, chief public prosecutor, 20 January 1966, pag. 43.

122. State Archive Bremen, 4,89/3-1119, criminal case Dr. Max Plaut, decision chief public prosecutor, 11 December 1967, n.p.

CONCLUSION

On the one hand, the establishment of the Reichsvereinigung der Juden in Deutschland, legally formalized in the 10th Ordinance on the Reich Citizenship Law on 4 July 1939, was in the immediate vital interest of the German Jews. Since before the November 1938 pogrom, they no longer possessed an operational nationwide organization. However, the National Socialist state—in which the Security Service and later the RSHA had taken over the leading role in Jewish policy—also needed a Jewish interlocutor, a contact counterpart in order to implement its measures of oppression. Initially those measures were defined under the rubric of mass emigration, education, and social welfare, precisely the task areas that those Jewish functionaries who had chosen to remain in Germany felt was their responsibility. But in the years 1939–1941, they found themselves confronted with a welter of ever new and more burdensome problems in a situation where, on the one hand, they wished to care for the needs of their now disproportionately elderly membership, while, on the other, they continued to seek possibilities for the remaining Jews to emigrate. Once the war broke out, if not even before, an orderly emigration was no longer possible, and social welfare was reduced by ever new and more stringent regulations, compounded by funding cuts and finance restrictions. In addition, a uniform approach was rendered more difficult by internal conflict among the leading Jewish functionaries about whether the strict legalistic approach would best be abandoned. Eppstein, Hirsch, and others still looked to a long-term perspective for emigration, even after the external circumstances had long since altered. They did not wish to aid and abet the Gestapo in their desire to send Jews in special ships on an uncertain journey into the unknown. But they feared that after mass arrests, if they then made the few remaining options for emigration available to the Jews incarcerated in order to get them released from the concentration camps, this would serve to confirm the Gestapo in its efforts to promote "forced emigration," and it would continue now emboldened down this path. They also believed that they would anger and alienate the destination countries if they were to send former camp prisoners rather than the requested qualified emigrants those countries desired. With the war's outbreak in September 1939, the imminent end loomed for individual emigration and illegal emigration to Palestine, while attempts by the Jewish functionaries to find options for group emigration largely proved a failure. At the same time, the Nazi regime shifted from a policy of forced emigration to one of a "territorial solution" for the "Jewish problem" it had itself created. The Jewish representatives recognized the genocidal implications of the "plans for reservations" discussed in 1940, to the extent that they were indeed at all privy to the fanciful plans being discussed.

Yet they secretly hoped, now as before, to be able to participate in shaping some conception for a Jewish settlement area—this in order to secure the survival of the community, even if at a low level of material living conditions. However, the surprising deportations from Stettin/Schneidemühl, Baden, and the Palatinate, coming in anticipation of the plans afoot to settle Jews in the Lublin district or on the island of Madagascar, and the further radicalizing of anti-Jewish policy, brought home to them a realization of their own basic powerlessness. The functionaries of the RV were kept in the dark about regime intentions; they were not included in the operations themselves, nor were they permitted to do anything for the deportees at their destination. They encountered a similar impotence in the broad sphere of social welfare, an area that had been instrumental in their decision to stay on in Germany. Moreover, in 1939/1940 they came to realize that their own personal situation was endangered, because the German Reich had turned into a perilous trap, one from which those who had voluntarily remained could no longer escape. They themselves were now captives. The regime issued a stark warning to them with the arrests of Eppstein, Hirsch, and Seligsohn, which soon cost the latter two their lives.

Caught up in this vortex of a chaotic and ever more violent process, the German-Jewish representatives accepted the "offer" from their oppressors to participate from October 1941 in preparations for the mass deportations. They hoped, by continuing with the strategy of cooperation, at least now to be informed about what was happening and to be able to play a role in shaping these events. They attempted to carry out the tasks they were assigned in a manner so as to spare the Jews affected the greatest hardships during collection for transport or when brought to the deportation assembly camps. Yet their limited options for possible intervention and their small "successes" were short-lived: for example, the Nazi state accepted for only one year the policy of allowing medical examinations for deportees, where Jewish doctors could cite medical grounds to request an exemption or deferment from deportation. If the Gestapo itself violated the deportation guidelines laid down by the RSHA, Jewish functionaries were (sometimes) able to successfully intervene on a person's behalf. Yet in both such instances, others had to be selected to replace those exempted or deferred. When the Jewish functionaries learned that the Theresienstadt ghetto was to take on the function of a "ghetto for the elderly" and a "preferential camp" (*Vorzugslager*) for the German Jews, they attributed that to their own efforts to ensure that the age demographic of the remaining German Jews was taken into proper account.

Preparatory work for the transports was intensified in the RV from the winter of 1941 on, while in the course of 1942, the possibilities for social welfare work and the provision of education for children and vocational training largely evaporated or totally vanished.

In the autumn of 1941, there had as yet been no policy decision on the indiscriminate mass murder of the German and European Jews. The policy was that the Jews would be sent on to the ghettos "for the winter months." When the German-Jewish functionaries agreed to perform their role in the deportation machinery—in their eyes, to take steps helping to ensure a process as smooth as possible, orderly and "humane"—they provided the regime with an unsigned "offer" of cooperation that bound up the interests of the National Socialist state with those of the Jews. They agreed to provide assistance (as mentioned, they were at this point unable to foresee the lethal consequences), accepting in the dark bargain that they would lose a portion of the individuals they bore responsibility for. But they assumed that they would in this way be able to tend to the religious, welfare, or educational needs of those remaining. They hoped that for the deportees, they might perhaps be able from afar to relieve some of their hardship, and at the very least remain in contact with them. In addition, employment with the Reichsvereinigung would guarantee protection for several thousand staff workers across the Reich, a significant number of whom were not physically fit for heavy forced labor in the armaments industry.

However, in 1942, the protective function that employment with the RV had provided for Jews in 1941 shifted ominously to the very opposite. Jews working there could be seized at any time, hauled off, and included in an imminent transport, as a penalty for some supposed infraction or as a stopgap replacement for someone else.

Initially, the representatives may have thought that although deportation to the East entailed a harsh fate, they would be able as co-organizers to intervene in particular cases of hardship and mitigate conditions. The assumption that this was a "partial evacuation" soon turned out to be illusory, replaced by a new deception: namely, that they would be able (at least minimally) to take social concerns into account by means of transports for the aged to the "ghetto for the elderly" in Theresienstadt.

In the following period, the Jewish representatives preserved the rule of strict secrecy that the Gestapo and the RSHA had imposed on them, maintaining the fiction of "evacuation," even though some from their own ranks were deported. However, the strategy of cooperation also implied that any (compulsory) member who opposed the thinking and actions of the representatives individually and sought to escape deportation by going into hiding endangered this unsigned agreement with the oppressors in the eyes of the Jewish representatives.

Despite all efforts, the possibilities of the RV to exert any influence on events remained very limited. In addition, between the autumn of 1941 and the end of 1942, every single task area designed to guarantee a smooth process and minimally acceptable conditions for the members before or during deportation was transformed. Precisely through the effective cooperation of the functionaries, these task areas were refashioned into a sophisticated instrument of coercion and control in the oppressors' hands. It made it easier for the Gestapo to locate the last remaining Jews in Germany, to plunder their assets, and to transport them out of the Reich. That was true even in the sphere of social welfare. The nursing homes became traps, ensnaring their residents and staff workers. Even in their function as employer, the RV functionaries were soon no longer able to shield their employees from transport. In short, with the onset of the mass deportations, a gulf appeared between the functionaries, their staff associates, and the Jews summoned for deportation, and it widened over the course of 1942/1943. In the meantime, the Nazi regime declared that the Reichsvereinigung, its functionaries, and its staff workers bore collective liability for all "the Jews" to obey their orders.

The hopes the Jewish representatives had placed in their strategy of cooperation were dashed, because the RSHA did not adhere either to general rules or to concrete pledges or promises made. It believed to have no obligation whatsoever toward the Jewish organization or its functionaries. In the course of 1942, new horrific reports were received on a daily basis in the Berlin main office of the RV, while all hopes for even minimal concessions had vanished. This was especially true once it became clear with the onset of mass transports to Theresienstadt that all German Jews were to be deported, most "to the East," the others to the "preferential camp." In addition, rumors and information about the mass murder of the Jews began to spread inside the *Altreich*.

From the autumn of 1941, the Jewish functionaries attempted to decelerate the dynamics of Nazi Jewish policy by seeking to press the persecutors to adhere to a predictable style of Prussian administrative behavior, to which they themselves felt some bureaucratic obligation. The highly ramified architecture of the RV and its administrative apparatus—with its numerous departments, task areas, and associated institutions, its fixed spheres of responsibility and official channels of operation (and the temporal rules governing administrative operations, laying down the necessary time frames until all levels had been passed through)—was structurally based in large part on state administration and procedures. When Eppstein was summoned to the RSHA, his "supervisory authority," he regularly prepared reports on these meetings, noting down the orders given, his proposals on how the RV could implement them, and the rejection or authorization of these proposals. The total text was sent on to the RSHA and the RV executive board, and individual passages were forwarded as memos to the responsible department heads or specialists who were obliged to implement the orders. It is evident that the RV functionaries wished to capture on paper, in specific and exacting particular, all those events involving the deportations in the broadest sense—this so that they could then be handled in a transparent and comprehensible, uniform manner, independent of specific individuals. Michael Wildt has termed the RSHA, with its specific structure, as a "new type of uniquely National Socialist institution,"[1] an agency that in substance was not bound to any set rules. Alternately, its leading officials organized the persecution and deportation of the Jews in the *Altreich* and murder operations on the "killing fields" in the East, for example, as leaders of *Einsatzgruppen*. Over and against Heydrich's "fighting administration" (*kämpfende Verwaltung*), the Jewish functionaries sought to maintain an "old-style administration." They viewed this as a kind of bulwark counterposed to the corruption, looting, arbitrary will, and inhumanity that swirled in the maelstrom around them. Even in Theresienstadt, they constructed once more a final supradimensional administration. However, an orderly functioning administration does not exclude mass murder per se. It represented a hapless attempt by its administrators to prevent what Dan Diner has termed the *Zivilisationsbruch* ("rupture of civilization").[2] And that rupture ultimately cost almost all the Jewish leaders their lives.

What did the German-Jewish functionaries know about the mass murder? Some board members, ranking staff, or those in leading positions in the district branches had extensive, detailed information, but after liberation, the few remaining survivors were unanimous in asserting credibly that they had had no knowledge of the general mass murder of the Jews. They were aware of individual events, rumors, perhaps also knew about some mass shootings. But the "rupture in civilization" was for them unimaginable as a comprehensive event. Moreover, neither in their circles nor among non-Jews was there any contemporary concept that could have been applied to encompass the singular enormity of the events today designated as the Holocaust or Shoah. In addition, it was fully in keeping with their general attitude and working approach to concentrate on pressing practical tasks at hand and to try to act as effectively as possible—simply for the sake of preserving the organization, and at the same time in the best interests of their members—instead of surmising the worst. They maintained that approach even within the confines of Theresienstadt. Yet even if we assume that in 1942, when German Jews were being deported on to the extermination camps, they might have been able to piece together the fragments of news from the ghettos and camps into the mosaic of a comprehensive picture of mass annihilation, one thing is clear: that process would have been unstoppable. The Jewish functionaries would not have been able to step aside from it: that would have meant only the more rapid and brutal deportation of the elderly, the weak, and the infirm, and their own immediate death.

A large proportion of the German Jews lived in the capital of Berlin, where the institutions of persecution and the main office of the RV were also located. The historian and Theresienstadt survivor H. G. Adler wrote that for the district branch directors in the *Altreich,* their entanglement with the Gestapo had become so routine that even the thought of a bold and vigorous resistance could not occur to them. Nonetheless, it makes sense, as a comparison of the events of persecution in several different cities points to, to analyze the respective regional conditions that prevailed on the ground. The Jewish functionaries outside Berlin certainly tried to exploit the possibilities offered to them by their respective fabrics of persecution. However, they were always only able to have some influence on the events of deportation if they found counterparts and interlocutors within the context of an open ongoing struggle over power, or if they were successful in utilizing rivalries between institutions or creating a "relationship of trust" with participating institutions of persecution. If, by contrast, these institutions were working together in local harmony, in most instances this generally led to an intensification of the persecution, and the Jewish functionaries got nowhere with their efforts. The instructions from the RSHA regarding place, time, and extent of the deportations were carried out everywhere, but sometimes the Jewish representatives were able to influence the psychological environment and the number of Jewish "prisoners in protective custody" who were deported.

The German-Jewish functionaries who had not been deported already in 1942 were sent to Theresienstadt, as the RSHA had announced. More extensive promises made by Gestapo offices to individual district branch directors were generally not kept, and the only functionary allowed to depart abroad was Max Plaut in Hamburg.

The extant source materials from the everyday work routine of the RV indicate that most of the district branch directors felt their main office in Berlin was an additional organ of control over them alongside the Gestapo. They apparently expected little assistance from their central office; on the contrary, they anticipated bureaucratic delays, demands for completing tasks that were impossible to meet, and orders to cut staff (i.e., death sentences for those dismissed, who were regularly deported). This was because the central office had to consult with the RSHA and reach an agreement on all the district affairs it was dealing with. The district offices always encountered difficulties if they had entered separately into agreements with the local Gestapo; this inevitably brought them into conflict with the RV main office in Berlin. If the Gestapo issued orders that contradicted those from the RV central office or the RSHA, then they were compelled to ask these offices in Berlin to take action so as to be able to avert implementation of such orders. As a rule this, to say the least, did not serve to improve the local situation. The district branches were always subject to double control.

They were obligated to carry out identical or similar assistance as their colleagues in Berlin in preparing the deportations, and in the course of this process they lost their autonomy in hiring staff and determining the budget. They too were strictly obligated by the (self-)imposed norms of administration. Service regulations and standard operating channels determined communication, especially in conflicts that often only at second glance reveal the underlying basic existential situation: namely, that those involved in the district branch offices, especially during the course of 1942, were fighting for their professional existence—and thus for their very right to life as individuals—if an order had come to downsize or close their office. The gap between the functionaries and their members also deepened in the district branches. For that reason, the Jewish functionaries often tried to bolster their authority with members (and simultaneously garner the favor of the Gestapo) by adapting their own behavior to that of the Gestapo: they did this by implementing orders to the letter and obligating their members, in a strict fashion, to do the same. Other representatives were adept at submitting proposals to the Gestapo that anticipated their orders in terms of content, and then went about structuring the implementation of these in such a way that they could arrange some modicum of relief or mitigation for the Jews affected. Only a small number dared to warn their members, because by doing so they risked endangering themselves, their fellow workers, and their family members.

As is evident from deportation data, a large proportion of the district branch directors were deported already in 1942, most to Theresienstadt as an ostensible "reward" for their service. In 1943, their successors and colleagues soon followed them. Thus, with minor temporal differences, functionaries, coworkers, and RV members in Berlin and elsewhere across the *Altreich* were scheduled for deportation. Like their superiors in the Berlin main office, only a very small number of representatives from the district branches survived the Nazi period.

After the official dissolving of the Reichsvereinigung, from June 1943 to May 1945, a new category of representatives in the rump Reichsvereinigung, the so-called *Vertrauensmänner* or intermediaries, living in mixed marriages, were appointed to regulate the affairs of the remaining "full Jews" and *Geltungsjuden* in the *Altreich*. The intermediaries, in the main lawyers or medical doctors, took over direction of the administrative offices, which had been heavily reduced in size and staff. The Residual Reichsvereinigung was more centralized than its predecessor. However, the destruction of infrastructure caused by the mounting air war tended to create free spaces that the intermediaries could utilize to make their own independent decisions. A certain chaos on the ground intensified: offices of the rump RV went up in flames during air raids, destroying documents, files, and member card files; Jews fled from the areas ravaged by the aerial bombardments, rendering their former addresses invalid. As a rule, the intermediaries had not pressed for the administrator's office they had been assigned, but were unable to refuse such an appointment. Despite their reputation of having been henchmen of the Gestapo, the source materials suggest a different picture: on the contrary, they endeavored to provide for the needs of the "prisoners in protective custody" and their families, to arrange small improvements in food provisions, and to protect their coworkers from deportation. But among their assigned tasks was the deportation of Jews from dissolved mixed marriages and, from early 1945, the deportation of Jews from still existing mixed marriages. Some refused to implement this final order. The preponderant majority of these last Jewish representatives survived the war. In the immediate postwar period, they sought to continue their organizational activity for the remaining Jewish community, but encountered resistance everywhere. Their former clientele, relatives of those murdered, and Jews returning from the concentration camps pressed the Allied occupiers to strip these former representatives of their office, and this was quickly done. In September 1945, the Residual Reichsvereinigung was dissolved, deemed from its birth a National Socialist organization.

The German-Jewish functionaries themselves believed they had worked entirely on the behalf of the interests of their membership. Yet in the eyes of the surviving former compulsory members, the persecution of the Jews also bore the indelible physiognomy of the Jewish functionaries and their coworkers. With the exception of the work of Leo Baeck, whose pastoral commitment to the German-Jewish community was repeatedly praised by survivors, and Otto Hirsch, murdered in June 1941 before the onset of mass deportations, the tragic efforts of the functionaries were little valued. On the contrary, what was perceived as the perfidious inclusion of the German-Jewish functionaries in the process of preparing deportations generated lasting mistrust within the Jewish postwar community in Germany, which in any case was under heavy pressure to justify why it was settling down permanently once more in the land of the perpetrators. Some of the surviving German-Jewish functionaries who had not immediately left the country, and some of their subordinate coworkers, accounted for their actions in trials before courts of honor, in some cases stretching on for years. They sought to provide answers about whether, how, and to what extent the strategy of cooperation (which had been decided by the top echelon of the organization, but was binding for all staff workers, under penalty of death) had led to a dilemma: where thoroughness on the job, fulfillment of their duty, and zeal for their work had eventuated in life-threatening dangers for their members. Former members of the Reichsvereinigung, not Gestapo or RSHA officials, answered for their alleged actions in court in the early postwar period. Meanwhile, in the territory of the Soviet occupation zone, the surviving Jewish functionaries disappeared from sight, often for years on end, sent as "Gestapo agents" to internment in special camps, and a number did not survive this ordeal. Even in the 1960s, the Central Council of the Jews in Germany admonished by resolution that no former functionary of the Reichsvereinigung would be permitted to serve in a leadership function in a postwar Jewish Community in the Federal Republic of Germany, and created a special commission to monitor this.

In the introduction to this volume, I explored the question of whether the leaders and ranking staff of the Reichsvereinigung would have had any alternative to the strategy of cooperation. Had there been other better, more promising pathways than the one they proceeded to follow? Should they have communicated their knowledge about the transports to their members and affected nonmembers? German Jews had no available paths open to flee to neighboring countries, and safe places of flight no longer existed within the country. Would it have been possible to create a public sphere of protest abroad as an option for eventual rescue, and/or to organize public protests inside the country? It is unlikely that that approach would have achieved any success given the heavily censored press and the readiness of the National Socialist regime to engage in violence. It pursued attempts to flee and even the smallest protest actions with unrelenting fury. This was compounded by multiple factors: the reluctance on the part of the potential destination countries to accept emigrants in 1938, the closed borders after the outbreak of the war, and the fact that the first reports about the mass murder of the Jews in the East did not lead the Allies to direct their military assets in a concerted effort to bomb the routes leading to the death camps.

Notes

1. See Wildt, *Uncompromising Generation*, 19.
2. Diner, "The Limits of Reason," in *Beyond the Conceivable*, 104.

BIBLIOGRAPHY

Archival Materials Cited

American Joint Distribution Commitee (JDC): 33/44, 632; 33/44, 642; 658; 678.

Archiv Centrum Judaicum (CJA): 2 B 1/1; 2 B1/2; 2 B 1/3; 2 B ¼; 2 B 1/5; Sammlung Ausstellung Juden in Berlin 1938–1945; Ordner: Allgemeines/Vertrauensmänner, Z 1997/47; I 75a Be 2.

Brandenburgisches Landeshauptarchiv, Potsdam: TA Rep 333 Nr. 1142; Rep 203, MdJ, PA 44 (R/10337); VdN 1456, Rep 401.

Bundesarchiv (BArch): R 18, R 58, R 8150, R 1501/1; R 2301/2073/2; R 1509; Z 42 IV/4959; NSDAP-Zentralkartei.

Die Bundesbeauftragte für die Unterlagen des Staatssicherheitsdienstes der ehemaligen Deutschen Demokratischen Republik (BStU): BStU C AP 1806/68; ZUV 74, EV Bd. 16; MfS XII/RF/97; BStU, Außenstelle Halle/MfS BV Halle, MfS XII/RF/189; MfS Zentralarchiv, Allg. P. 172/64; Allge. P. 1429/60, BStU, MfS Ast I c 1/74.

Central Archives for the History of the Jewish People, Jerusalem: D/Be 4/329A.

Central Zionist Archives, Jerusalem: Zionist Organisation of America 1918–1976, Bericht ueber die politische Lage in Deutschland, dem Protektorat Boehmen-Maehren, der Slowakai und Polen.

Entschädigungsamt Berlin: 253555.

Entschädigungsamt Düsseldorf: ZK 14012.

Forschungsstelle für Zeitgeschichte (FZH): Judenverfolgung/Berichte.

Generalstaatsanwaltschaft, Brandenburg/Havel: II Re 9/52.

Hessisches Hauptstaatsarchiv (Hess. HstA), Wiesbaden: 461/30983; 461/37048/1.

Institut für die Geschichte der deutschen Juden, Archiv (IGdJ), Hamburg: 14.001.1; 14.001.2; 14.001.3.

Institut für Stadtgeschichte, Frankfurt am Main: S 5/184-185, S3/A 170, 54/1963.

Institut Theresienstädter Initiative, Prag: Matriken, Nationalarchiv Prag/ITI, Todesfallanzeige Heinrich Stahl; Terezín Digital Resource Centre.

ITS Arolsen: 1.2.4.1.

Landesarchiv Berlin (LAB): B Rep 58, 1 Js 9/65; 1 Js 5/65; B Rep. 235-07, MF 4170-4171; B Rep. 057-01; Rep. 20, Nr. 4860-4861; B Rep 057-01, 1 Ks 1/69; Pr BR Rep. 042, Kap. 60 Ti 21b/L7; Rep. 20, Nr. 4616-4617.

Landesarchiv Nordrhein-Westfalen (LA NRW) Münster (until 2008: Staatsarchiv Münster): 45 Js 29/78; 5 Js 192/62; 45 Js 29/78 (StA Dortmund).

Leo Baeck Institut, Außenstelle Berlin (LBI JMB): MF 8; MF 546, MM 131, MM 83, ME 863, MF 456.

Leo Baeck Institute, Jerusalem: 111, 643, 554, 555, 556, 427, 207, 364.

Leo Baeck Institute, New York (LBI NY): AR 221; AR 7171; AR 25033, AR 1619; AR 2038, AR 1249; AR 7183; AR 7094; AR 6559; AR 143; AR 333.

Nordrhein-Westfälisches Hauptstaatsarchiv (NRW HStA), Düsseldorf: RW 58 Nr. 3429.

NRW HStA Düsseldorf, Außenstelle Schloss Kalkum: Rep. 231 Nr. 512-521; Rep. 372/82-892.

NS-Dokumentationszentrum der Stadt Köln, Archiv: Bestand Dr. Feldheim.

Potsdamer Hauptstaatsarchiv: OFD Berlin, 8 WGA 2176.50.

Sächsisches Hauptstaatsarchiv Dresden, Leipzig: 12916 Nr. 2331-2337.

Schocken, Archive Family in Schocken Library, Jerusalem: file 921/141/761.

Staatsarchiv Bremen: 4,89/3-751 Bd. I, 4,89/3-1118; 4,89/3-1119.

Staatsarchiv Hamburg (StaHH): 522-1; 522-2, 58; Strafsachen 6669/64; (jetzt StaHH, 351-11, 18891222).

Staatsarchiv (Sta) München: 1 Js 67ff./49, 1 a Js 641/49; Stanw. 29.499/1-3; Spruchkammer, Karton 487; Karton 939, Karton 1316.

Staatsarchiv (Sta) Nürnberg: 3070/I- XV.

Stadtarchiv Düsseldorf: XXXII 43.

Stadtarchiv Mainz: Posthumous papers Oppenheim.

Stadtarchiv Mannheim: Posthumous papers Eppstein.

Státnú ústredni archiv, Prague: URP-109, 109-4-985.

Státnú ústredni archiv v Praze (State Central Archive, Prague): Z-845-1, 213-11.

United States Holocaust Memorial Museum (USHMM): Acc. 2008.189.1; RG-14.035M, (2001.150); 2010.200; ITS; RG-14.053M, 2003.11; RG-02.212; Acc. 1996.A.0551.

Yad Vashem: Testimonies: 01/6, 01/13; 01/15; 01/161, 01/150; 01/156; 01/18; 01/192; 01/197; 01/199; 01/200; 01/204; 01/212; 01/215; 01/216; 01/220; 01/226; 01/227; 01/232; 01/241; 01/243; 01/245; 01/256; 01/26; 01/263; 01/267; 01/28; 01/285; 01/286; 01/294; 01/320; 01/4; 01/5; 01/50; 01/51; 01/53;01/150; 01/61; 01/65; 02/1063; 02/241; 02/244; 02/283; 02/30; 02/340; 02/373; 02/387; 02/387a; 02/403; 02/411; 02/421; 02/443; 02/53; 02/546; 02/551; 02/560; 02/74; 02/769; 02/772; 02/8; 03/3455; 033/102; 033/69; 033/71; 033/76; 033/83 (E/83); 033/85; 033/988; 033/99; 033/998; 1151/92. Andere: E/210 (129/56). P1,YV, Tr3-1129, T/142, Bo6-1129.

Wiener Library, London: WLL, P. III.c.No. 622, WL P III e No. 456.

Zentralarchiv zur Erforschung der Geschichte der Juden in Deutschland (ZAGJD), Heidelberg: B. 1/19, Nr. 164, 243, 312, 333 446; B 8, 296.05.

Zentrale Stelle der Landesjustizverwaltungen, Ludwigsburg (Außenstelle Bundesarchiv): Dokumentation "Judendeportationen aus dem Reichsgebiet."

Other Sources

Aufbau
Berliner Allgemeine
Contemporary Jewish Record
Frankfurter Neue Presse
Hamburger Abendblatt
Die Jüdische Allgemeine

Das Jüdische Nachrichtenblatt
Jewish Telegraphic Agency
Reichsgesetzblatt
Yedioth Hayom
Volkswohlfahrt. Amtsblatt und Halbmonatsschrift des Preußischen Ministeriums für Volkswohl-fahrt, vol. 1, 1920 (April–Dec.), with *Ministerialblatt für Medizinalangelegenheiten*, vol. 20 (Jan.–March), *Volkswohlfahrt*, No. 17, 1 Dec. 1920, Berlin 1920
Volkswohlfahrt. Amtsblatt und Halbmonatsschrift des Preußischen Ministeriums für Volkswohl-fahrt, vol. 2, No. 3, 1 Feb. 1921, Berlin 1921; vol. 4., No. 18, 15 September 1923, Berlin 1923; vol. 6, Berlin 1925
Volkswohlfahrt. Amtsblatt des Preußischen Ministeriums für Volkswohlfahrt, vol. 8, No. 5, 1 March 1927, Berlin 1927; vol. 9, No. 12, 15 June 1928, Berlin 1928 ; vol. 10, No. 19, 1 October 1929, Berlin 1929
Ministerial-Blatt für die Preußische innere Verwaltung, Teil II Ausg. A, published by Preußisches Ministerium des Innern 1933, No. 53, 20 December 1933

Websites Cited

http://goo.gl/TXlel (Allied Control Council, laws)
http://www.holocaust.cz/de/victims/PERSON.ITI.262926 (Minnie Ascher)
http://goo.gl/bFnWG (Else Behrend-Rosenfeld)
http://www.gemeinden.judentum.de/bremen/index.htm (Bremen Jewish Community)
http://goo.gl/fGYDP (Max Cahn)
http://goo.gl/EKba5 (Martin Heinrich Corten)
http://goo.gl/jrp79 (Margarete Draeger)
http://goo.gl/W7qgQ (Bernt Engelmann)
http://www.bundesarchiv.de/gedenkbuch/index.html.en (Gedenkbuch, BArch)
http://goo.gl/2F5mD (Grumach group)
http://goo.gl/vW4cZ (Wolf Gruner, H-Net)
http://archive.org/details/edmundhadra (Edmund Hadra)
http://utoronto.academia.edu/AnnaHajkova (Anna Hajkova)
http://goo.gl/dBVNC (video, "Operation Gomorrha," Hamburg 1943)
http://www.bendorf-geschichte.de/bdf-0155.htm (Jacoby'sche Heil- und Pflegeanstalt)
http://goo.gl/zzkeo (JTA, deportations)
http://goo.gl/gqmPw (JTA, Madagascar)
http://goo.gl/I8GXX (JTA, Madagascar)
http://goo.gl/ZF8rB (JTA, Madagascar)
http://goo.gl/zzZJg (JTA, Madagascar)
http://goo.gl/7b2wd (Jewish Women, A Comprehensive Historical Encyclopedia)
http://goo.gl/lU3L8 (Kleinmachnow)
http://www.dradio.de/dlr/sendungen/merkmal/145599/ (Kleinmachnow)
http://goo.gl/8iptj (Charlotte Knobloch)
http://www1.uni-hamburg.de/rz3a035//kuehn.html (Hermann Kühn)
http://tinyurl.com/bqotl6s (LBI Memoir Collection)
http://goo.gl/mQEHP (Madagascar Plan, Brechtken)
http://goo.gl/rN9xf (Fritz Neuland)
http://tinyurl.com/bqotl6s (Alfred Neumeyer)
http://goo.gl/ljOzl (Nuremberg, Jewish topography)

http://goo.gl/gauhT (Ernst Peiser)
http://www.kfkronenberg.com/reich.htm (RV, texts in English)
http://www.stiftung-bg.de/gums/en/index.htm (Sachsenhausen Museum)
http://goo.gl/LZbVs (Hermann Samter letters)
http://goo.gl/42f8z (Heinrich Seetzen)
http://goo.gl/lO6cQ (video interviews, Shanghai Jews)
http://tinyurl.com/79rf5vx (Martin Starke)
http://www.ghwk.de/2006-neu/stettin.jpg (Gestapo decree, Stettin)
http://makarovainit.com/first.htm (lectures, Theresienstadt)
http://www.floerken.eu (Troisdorfer Juden)
http://goo.gl/053od (Yad Vashem database of victims)

Literature and Printed Sources

Adam, Uwe Dietrich. *Judenpolitik im Dritten Reich.* Düsseldorf, 1972; Königstein im Taunus, 1979.

Adelsberger, Lucie. *Auschwitz: Ein Tatsachenbericht.* Berlin, 1960.

Aden-Grossmann, Wilma, and Berthold Simonsohn. *Biographie des jüdischen Sozialpädagogen und Juristen (1912–1978).* Frankfurt am Main, 2007.

Adler, H. G. *Die verheimlichte Wahrheit: Theresienstädter Dokumente.* Tübingen, 1958.

———. *Theresienstadt 1941–45.* 2nd ed. Tübingen, 1960.

———. *Der verwaltete Mensch: Studien zur Deportation der Juden aus Deutschland.* Tübingen, 1974.

Adler-Rudel, S. *Ostjuden in Deutschland 1880–1940.* Tübingen, 1959.

———. *Jüdische Selbsthilfe unter dem Naziregime 1933–1939.* Tübingen, 1974.

Ahleit, Christa. "Allenstein 1933–1943: Die Erinnerungen des Arztes Heinrich Wolffheim von 1947." In *NS-Gewaltherrschaft: Beiträge zur historischen Forschung und juristischen Aufarbeitung,* edited by Alfred Gottwaldt, Norbert Kampe, and Peter Klein, 172–86. Berlin, 2005.

Altman, Avraham, and Irene Eber. "Flight to Shanghai, 1938–1940: The Larger Setting." *Yad Vashem Studies* 28 (2000): 51–86.

Altonaer Museum. *Das Theresienstadt-Konvolut.* Edited by Axel Feuss (Hamburg, 2002).

Anderl, Gabriele, and Dirk Rupnow. *Die Zentralstelle für jüdische Auswanderung als Beraubungsinstitution.* Vienna, 2004.

Angrick, Andrej, and Peter Klein. *The "Final Solution" in Riga: Exploitation and Annihilation, 1941–1944.* New York, 2009.

Apel, Linde, ed. *In den Tod geschickt: Die Deportationen von Juden, Roma und Sinti aus Hamburg 1940 bis 1945.* Berlin, 2009.

Arendt, Hannah. *Eichmann in Jerusalem: A Report on the Banality of Evil.* New York, 1977.

Ayalon, Moshe. "Jewish Alltagsgeschichte on the Eve of the Holocaust: Jewish Life in Breslau." *LBI Yearbook* 41, no. 1 (1996): 323–45.

———. "'Gegenwaertige Situation': Report on the Living Conditions of the Jews in Germany. A Document and Commentary." *LBI Yearbook* 43 (1998): 271–85.

Ayass, Wolfgang. "'Ein Gebot der nationalsozialistischen Arbeitsdisziplin': Die Aktion 'Arbeitsscheu Reich.'" *Beiträge zur nationalsozialistischen Gesundheit- und Sozialpolitik* 6 (1988): 43–74.

———. *"Asoziale" im Nationalsozialismus.* Stuttgart, 1995.

Backhaus, Fritz. "'Ein Experiment des Willens zum Bösen'—Überleben in Theresienstadt." In *Leo Baeck: 1873–1956: Aus dem Stamme von Rabbiner*, edited by Georg Heuberger and Fritz Backhaus, 111–28. Frankfurt am Main, 2001.

Backhaus, Fritz, and Martin Liepach. "Ein Schatten im Leben des hoch angesehenen Rabbiners: Über die Rolle Leo Baecks im Nationalsozialismus: Neue Funde, Spurensuche und ungeklärte Fragen (Dokumentation)." *Frankfurter Rundschau*, 1 October 2001.

———. "Leo Baecks Manuskript über die 'Rechtsstellung der Juden in Europa': Neue Funde und ungeklärte Fragen." *Zeitschrift für Geschichtswissenschaft* 1 (2002): 55–70.

Baeck, Leo. "A People Stands Before Its God." In *We Survived: Fourteen Histories of the Hidden and Hunted in Nazi Germany*, 2nd rev. ed., edited by Erich H. Boehm, 284–98. Boulder, CO, 2003.

Bajohr, Frank. "Gauleiter in Hamburg: Zur Person und Tätigkeit Karl Kaufmanns (1900–1969)." *Vierteljahrshefte für Zeitgeschichte* 43 (1995): 267–95.

———. *Parvenüs und Profiteure in der NS-Zeit*. Frankfurt am Main, 2001.

———. "'… dann bitte keine Gefühlsduseleien': Die Hamburger und die Deportationen." In *Die Deportation der Hamburger Juden 1941–1945*, edited by Research Center for Contemporary History and Institute for the History of the German Jews, 13–29. Hamburg, 2002.

———. *"Aryanisation" in Hamburg: The Economic Exclusion of Jews and the Confiscation of Their Property in Nazi Germany*. Oxford, 2002.

———. "Vom antijüdischen Konsens zum schlechten Gewissen: Die deutsche Gesellschaft und die Judenverfolgung 1933–1945." In *Der Holocaust als offenes Geheimnis: Die Deutschen, die NS-Führung und die Alliierten*, edited by Frank Bajohr and Dieter Pohl, 15–79. Munich, 2006.

Bajohr, Frank, and Dieter Pohl. *Der Holocaust als offenes Geheimnis: Die Deutschen, die NS-Führung und die Alliierten*. Munich, 2006.

Baker, Leonard. *Hirt der Verfolgten: Leo Baeck im Dritten Reich*. Stuttgart, 1982.

Ball-Kaduri, Kurt Jakob. *Vor der Katastrophe: Juden in Deutschland 1934–1939*. Tel Aviv, 1967.

Barkai, Avraham. *From Boycott to Annihilation: The Economic Struggle of German Jews, 1933–1943*. Translated by William Templer. Hanover, NH, 1989.

———. "The Fateful Year 1938: The Continuation and Acceleration of Plunder." In *November 1938: From "Reichskristallnacht" to Genocide*, edited by Walter H. Pehle, translated by William Templer, 95–122. New York, 1991.

———. *Hoffnung und Untergang: Studien zur deutsch-jüdischen Geschichte des 19. und 20. Jahrhunderts*. Hamburg, 1998.

———. "Von Berlin nach Theresienstadt: Zur politischen Biographie Leo Baecks 1933–1945." In *Hoffnung und Untergang: Studien zur deutsch-jüdischen Geschichte des 19. und 20. Jahrhunderts*, edited by Avraham Barkai, 141–66. Hamburg, 1998.

Bauer, Yehuda. *American Jewry and the Holocaust: The American Jewish Joint Distribution Committee, 1939–1945*. Detroit, 1981.

———. *Jews for Sale? Nazi-Jewish Negotiations, 1933–1945*. New Haven, CT, 1994.

Baumann, Angelika, and Andreas Heusler, eds. *München arisiert: Entrechtung und Enteignung der Juden in der NS-Zeit*. Munich, 2004.

Becht, Lutz. "'die Wohlfahrtseinrichtungen sind aufgelöst worden …': vom 'städtischen Beauftragten bei der Jüdischen Wohlfahrtspflege' zum 'Beauftragten der Geheimen Staatspolizei …' 1938–1943." In *"Nach der Kristallnacht": Jüdisches Leben und antijüdische Politik in Frankfurt am Main 1938–1945*, edited by Monica Kingreen, 211–36. Frankfurt am Main and New York, 1999.

Becker-Jakli, Barbara. *Das jüdische Krankenhaus in Köln*. Cologne, 2004.

Behrend-Rosenfeld, Else. "Leben und Sterben der Münchener Gemeinde 1938–1942." In *Von Juden in München: Ein Gedenkbuch*, edited by Hans Lamm, 354–59. Munich, 1958.

———. *Ich stand nicht allein: Erlebnisse einer Jüdin in Deutschland 1933–1944*, 3rd ed. Cologne, 1979. First published as Elsbeth Rosenfeld. *Verfemt und verfolgt: Erlebnisse einer Jüdin in Nazi-Deutschland 1933–1944*. Zurich, 1945.

Behrend-Rosenfeld, Else, and Gertrud Luckner, ed. *Lebenszeichen aus Piaski: Briefe Deportierter aus dem Distrikt Lublin 1940–1943*. Munich, 1968.

Benz, Wolfgang, ed. *Die Juden in Deutschland 1933–1945*. Munich, 1988.

———. *The Holocaust*. Translated by Jane Sydemham-Kwiet. New York, 1999.

Bierman, John T. *Odyssey*. New York, 1984.

Berschel, Holger. *Bürokratie und Terror: Das Judenreferat der Gestapo Düsseldorf 1933–1945*. Essen, 2001.

Boas, Jacob. "German-Jewish Internal Politics under Hitler 1933–1938." *LBI Yearbook 29* (1984): 3–25.

Boehm, Erich H., ed. *We Survived: Fourteen Histories of the Hidden and Hunted in Nazi Germany*. 2nd rev. ed. Boulder, CO, 2003. First edition published 1949 in New Haven, CT.

Boog, Horst, Gerhard Krebs, and Detlef Vogel. *Das Deutsche Reich und der Zweite Weltkrieg*. Vol. 7, *Das Deutsche Reich in der Defensive: Strategischer Luftkrieg in Europa, Krieg im Westen und in Ostasien 1943–1944/45*. Stuttgart and Munich, 2001.

Bopf, Britta. *"Arisierung" in Köln: Die wirtschaftliche Existenzvernichtung der Juden 1933–1945*. Cologne, 2004.

Borinski, Anneliese-Ora. *Erinnerungen 1940–1943*. Nördlingen, 1970.

Boyle, Kay. "The People with Names." *The New Yorker*, 9 September 1950, 37.

———. *The Smoking Mountain: Stories of Postwar Germany*. New York, 1951.

Brechtken, Magnus. *"Madagaskar für die Juden": Antisemitische Idee und politische Praxis 1885–1945*. Munich, 1997.

Breitman, Richard. *Official Secrets: What the Nazis Planned, What the British and Americans Knew*. New York, 1998.

Brodhaecker, Michael. *Menschen zwischen Hoffnung und Verzweiflung: Der Alltag jüdischer Mitmenschen in Rheinhessen, Mainz und Worms während des "Dritten Reiches."* Mainz, 1999.

Broszat, Martin, Elke Fröhlich, and Falk Wiesemann, eds. *Bayern in der NS-Zeit: Soziale Lage und politisches Verhalten der Bevölkerung im Spiegel vertraulicher Berichte*. Munich and Vienna, 1977.

Browning, Christopher. "Nazi Resettlement Policy and the Search for a Solution to the Jewish Question, 1939–1941." In Christopher Browning, *The Path to Genocide: Essays on Launching the Final Solution*, 3–27. Cambridge, 1995.

———. *The Origins of the "Final Solution": The Evolution of Nazi Jewish Policy, September 1939–March 1942*. Lincoln, NE, and Jerusalem, 2004.

Buchholz, Marlies. *Die hannoverschen Judenhäuser: Zur Situation der Juden in der Zeit der Ghettoisierung und Verfolgung 1941 bis 1941*. Hildesheim, 1987.

Burger, Reiner. *Von Goebbels Gnaden: "Jüdisches Nachrichtenblatt" (1938–1943)*. Münster, Hamburg, and London, 2001.

Büttner, Ursula, ed. *Die Deutschen und die Judenverfolgung im Dritten Reich*. Hamburg, 1992.

———. *"Gomorrha": Hamburg im Bombenkrieg*. Hamburg, 1993.

Cartarius, Julia. "Jewish Persecution in Western Upper Silesia 1933–1943." MA thesis, University College London, 2003.

Cesarani, David. *Adolf Eichmann: His Life and Crimes*. London, 2004.

Cohn, Willy. *Kein Recht, nirgends: Tagebuch vom Untergang des Breslauer Judentums 1933–1941*. 2 vols. Cologne, Weimar, and Vienna, 2006.

Corbach, Dieter. *6.oo Uhr ab Messe Köln-Deutz: Deportationen 1938–1945*. Cologne, 1994.

Crankshaw, Edward. *Gestapo: Instrument of Tyranny*. New York, 1956.

Dahm, Volker. "Kulturelles und geistiges Leben." In *Die Juden in Deutschland 1933–1945: Leben unter nationalsozialistischer Herrschaft*, edited by Wolfgang Benz, 75–267. Munich, 1988.

Damskis, Linda Lucia. *Zerrissene Biographien. Jüdische Ärzte zwischen nationalsozialistischer Verfolgung, Emigration und Wiedergutmachung*. Munich, 2009.

Dettmer, Klaus. "Die Deportationen aus Berlin." In *Buch der Erinnerung: Die ins Baltikum deportierten deutschen, österreichischen und tschechoslowakischen Juden*, vol. 1, edited by Wolfgang Scheffler and Diana Schulle, 191–97. Munich, 2003.

Deutschkron, Inge. *Ich trug den gelben Stern*. Cologne, 1978.

Diamant, Adolf. *Chronik der Juden in Leipzig: Aufstieg, Vernichtung und Neuanfang*. Chemnitz and Leipzig, 1993.

———. *Die Gestapo Frankfurt a.M.* Frankfurt am Main, 1988.

Dieckmann, Christoph, and Babette Quinkert, "Einleitung." In "Im Ghetto, 1939–1945: Neue Forschungen zu Alltag und Umfeld," edited by Christoph Dieckmann and Babette Quinkert, special issue, *Beiträge zur Geschichte des Nationalsozialismus* 25 (2009): 9–29.

Dietz, Edith. *Den Nazis entronnen: Die Flucht eines jüdischen Mädchens in die Schweiz: Autobiographischer Bericht 1933–1942*. Frankfurt am Main, 1990.

Diner, Dan. "The Limits of Reason: Max Horkheimer on Anti-Semitism and Extermination." In *Beyond the Conceivable: Studies on Germany, Nazism and the Holocaust*, 97–116. Berkeley, 2000. http://goo.gl/IKm1Q (accessed 1 August 2012).

———. "Beyond the Conceivable: The Judenrat as Borderline Experience." In *Beyond the Conceivable: Studies on Germany, Nazism and the Holocaust*, 117–29. Berkeley, 2000. http://goo.gl/IKm1Q (accessed 1 August 2012).

———. "Historical Understanding and Counterrationality: The Judenrat as Epistemological Vantage." In *Beyond the Conceivable: Studies on Germany, Nazism and the Holocaust*, 130–37. Berkeley, 2000. http://goo.gl/IKm1Q (acccessed 1 August 2012).

Dirks, Christian. "Sad Experiences in the Hell of Nazi Germany: The Scheurenberg Family." In *Jews in Nazi Berlin: From Kristallnacht to Liberation*, edited by Beate Meyer, Hermann Simon, and Chana Schütz, translated by Caroline Gay and Miranda Robbins, 214–25. Chicago, 2009.

———. "Snatchers: The Berlin Gestapo's Jewish Informants." In *Jews in Nazi Berlin: From Kristallnacht to Liberation*, edited by Beate Meyer, Hermann Simon, and Chana Schütz, translated by Caroline Gay and Miranda Robbins, 248–74. Chicago, 2009.

———. "The *Juni-Aktion* (June Operation) in Berlin." In *Jews in Nazi Berlin: From Kristallnacht to Liberation*, edited by Beate Meyer, Hermann Simon, and Chana Schütz, translated by Caroline Gay and Miranda Robbins, 22–35. Chicago, 2009.

Döscher, Hans-Jürgen. *"Reichskristallnacht": Die November-Pogrome 1938*. Frankfurt am Main and Berlin, 1988.

Düwell, Kurt. *Die Rheingebiete in der Judenpolitik des Nationalsozialismus vor 1942: Beitrag zu einer vergleichenden zeitgeschichtlichen Landeskunde*. Bonn, 1968.

Dwork, Deborah. *Children with a Star: Jewish Youth in Nazi Europe*. New Haven, CT, 1993.

Edvardson, Cordelia. *Burned Child Seeks the Fire*. Translated by Joel Agee. New York, 1997.

Ehrlich, Ernst Ludwig. "Erinnerungen an Leo Baeck." In *Leo Baeck 1873–1956: Aus dem Stamme von Rabbinern*, edited by Georg Heuberger and Fritz Backhaus, 188–91. Frankfurt am Main, 2001.

Eichler, Volker. "Das 'Judenreferat' der Frankfurter Gestapo." In *"Nach der Kristallnacht": Jüdisches Leben und antijüdische Politik in Frankfurt am Main 1938–1945*, edited by Monica Kingreen, 237–58. Frankfurt am Main and New York, 1999.

Elkin, Rivka. *Das Jüdische Krankenhaus in Berlin zwischen 1938 und 1945*. Berlin, 1993.

———. "The Survival of the Jewish Hospital in Berlin 1938–1945," *Leo Baeck Institute Year Book* 38, no. 1 (1993): 157–92.

———. "Kinder zur Aufbewahrung im Jüdischen Krankenhaus zu Berlin in den Jahren 1943–1945." *Tel Aviver Jahrbuch für deutsche Geschichte* 23 (1994): 247–74.

———. "Some Remarks in the Wake of My Book The Heart Beats On." In *Aspects of Jewish Welfare in Nazi Germany*, edited by Guy Miron, Jacob Borut, and Rivka Elkin, 47–55. Search and Research: Lectures and Papers, 7.Yad Vashem. Jerusalem, 2006.

Essner, Cornelia. *Die "Nürnberger Gesetze" oder die Verwaltung des Rassenwahns 1933–1945*. Paderborn, 2002.

Fabian, Hans Erich. "Die letzte Etappe." In *Festschrift zum 80. Geburtstag von Leo Baeck am 23. Mai 1953*, edited by Council for the Protection of the Rights and Interests of Jews from Germany, 85–97. London, 1953.

———. "Zur Entstehung der 'Reichsvereinigung der Juden in Deutschland.'" In *Gegenwart im Rückblick: Festgabe für die Jüdische Gemeinde zu Berlin 25 Jahre nach dem Neubeginn*, edited by Herbert A. Strauss and Kurt R. Grossmann, 165–79. Heidelberg, 1970.

Feder, Richard. *Jüdische Tragödie—letzter Akt. Theresienstadt 1941–1945: Bericht eines Rabbiners*. Potsdam, 2004.

Fedorovici, Tomas. "Die Gemeinde Schönwald und ihre unfreiwilligen Einwohner." *Theresienstädter Sudien und Dokumente* 8 (2001): 269–86.

Freier, Recha. *Let the Children Come*. London, 1961.

Friedlander, Albert H. *Leo Baeck: Leben und Lehre*. Stuttgart, 1973.

Friedlander, Henry. *The Origins of Nazi Genocide: From Euthanasia to the Final Solution*. Chapel Hill, NC, 1997.

Friedländer, Saul. *The Years of Extermination: Nazi Germany and the Jews 1939–1945*. New York, 2007.

Friedman, Philipp. "The Lublin Reservation and the Madagascar Plan: Two Aspects of Nazi Jewish Policy during the Second World War." *YIVO Annual of Jewish Social Science* 8 (1953): 151–77.

Friedmann, Tuviah. *Die verantwortlichen SS.Führer für die Durchführung der Endlösung der Judenfrage in Europa*. Haifa, 1993.

Fröhlich, Elke, ed. *Die Tagebücher von Joseph Goebbels*. Munich, 1996.

Generaldirektion der staatlichen Archive Bayerns, ed. *Wege in die Vernichtung: Die Deportation der Juden aus Mainfranken 1941–1943*. Munich, 2003.

Gerlach, Christian. "Die Wannsee-Konferenz, das Schicksal der deutschen Juden und Hitlers politische Grundsatzentscheidung, alle Juden Europas zu ermorden." *WerkstattGeschichte* 18 (1997): 7–44.

Geschichtswerkstatt am Friedrichsgymnasium Kassel. *"… Ich habe es nie bereut, ein deutscher Jude zu sein!" Erinnerungen an Siegmund Weltlinger (1886–1974)*. Kassel, 1997.

Gottwaldt, Alfred, Norbert Kampe, and Peter Klein, eds. *NS-Gewaltherrschaft: Beiträge zur historischen Forschung und juristischen Aufarbeitung*. Berlin, 2005.

Gottwaldt, Alfred, and Diana Schulle. *Die "Judendeportationen" aus dem Deutschen Reich 1941–1945*. Wiesbaden, 2005.

Grabower, Rolf. "Tagesberichte." In *Wenn im Amte, arbeite, wenn entlassen, verbirg dich— Prof. Dr. jur. Dr. phil. Rolf Grabower in Zeugnissen aus der Finanzgeschichtlichen Sammlung der Bundesfinanzakademie, ein Lesebuch und Materialband*, edited by Werner Nigbur and Bundesfinanzakademie im Bundesministerium der Finanzen. Brühl, 2010.

Greiner, Bettina. *Verdrängter Terror: Geschichte und Wahrnehmung sowjetischer Speziallager in Deutschland.* Hamburg, 2010.

Grieser, Utho. *Himmlers Mann in Nürnberg: Der Fall Benno Martin: Eine Studie zur Struktur des Dritten Reiches in der "Stadt der Reichsparteitage."* Nuremberg, 1974.

Grossmann, Kurt. "Zeugnisse menschlicher Tapferkeit im Dritten Reich." In *Von Juden in München: Ein Gedenkbuch*, edited by Hans Lamm. Munich, 1958.

Grüber, Heinrich. "An der Stechbahn: Erlebnisse und Berichte aus dem Büro Grüber in den Jahren der Verfolgung." In *Bevollmächtigt zum Brückenbau: Heinrich Grüber: Judenfreund und Trümmerprobst: Erinnerungen, Predigten, Berichte, Briefe*, edited by Jörg Hildebrandt, 41–75. Leipzig 1991.

Gruner, Wolf. "Terra Incognita? Die Lager für den 'jüdischen Arbeitseinsatz' (1938–1943) und die deutsche Bevölkerung." In *Die Deutschen und die Judenverfolgung im Dritten Reich*, edited by Ursula Büttner, 131–60. Hamburg, 1992.

———. "Die Reichshauptstadt Berlin und die Verfolgung der Berliner Juden 1933–1945." In *Jüdische Geschichte in Berlin*, edited by Reinhard Rürup, 229–66. Berlin, 1995.

———. *Der Geschlossene Arbeitseinsatz deutscher Juden: Zur Zwangsarbeit als Element der Verfolgung 1938–1943.* Berlin, 1997.

———. "Poverty and Persecution: The Reichsvereinigung, the Jewish Population, and Anti-Jewish Policy in the Nazi State, 1939–1945." *Yad Vashem Studies* 27 (1999): 23–60.

———. "Die Grundstücke der 'Reichsfeinde.'" In *"Arisierung" im Nationalsozialismus: Volksgemeinschaft, Raub und Gedächtnis*, edited by Irmtrud Wojak and Peter Hayes, 125–56. Frankfurt am Main and New York, 2000.

———. "Die NS-Verfolgung und die Kommunen: Zur wechselseitigen Dynamik von zentraler und lokaler Politik 1933–1941." *Vierteljahrshefte für Zeitgeschichte* 48 (2000): 75–126.

———. *Öffentliche Wohlfahrt und Judenverfolgung: Wechselwirkung lokaler und zentraler Politik im NS-Staat (1933–1942).* Munich, 2002.

———. "The Factory Action and the Events at the Rosenstrasse in Berlin: Facts and Fictions about 27 February 1943—Sixty Years Later." *Central European History* 36, no. 2 (2003): 179–208.

———. "Von der Kollektivausweisung zur Deportation der Juden aus Deutschland (1938–1943)." In *"Die Deportation der Juden aus Deutschland: Pläne-Praxis-Reaktionen,"* edited by Birthe Kundrus and Beate Meyer, special issue, *Beiträge zur Geschichte des Nationalsozialismus* 20 (2004): 21–62.

———. *Widerstand in der Rosenstraße: Die Fabrik-Aktion und die Verfolgung der "Mischehen" 1943.* Frankfurt am Main, 2005.

Gryglewski, Marcus. "Zur Geschichte der nationalsozialistischen Judenverfolgung in Dresden 1933–1945." In *Die Erinnerung hat ein Gesicht: Fotografien und Dokumente zur nationalsozialistischen Judenverfolgung in Dresden 1933–1945*, edited by Norbert Haase, Stefi Jersch-Wenzel, and Hermann Simon, 87–150. Leipzig, 1998.

Gutman, Israel, ed. *Enzyklopädie des Holocaust: Die Verfolgung und Ermordung der europäischen Juden.* Vol. 2. 2nd ed. Munich and Zurich, 1998.

Haase, Norbert, Stefi Jersch-Wenzel, and Hermann Simon, eds. *Die Erinnerung hat ein Gesicht: Fotografien und Dokumente zur nationalsozialistsicehn Judenverfolgung in Dresden 1933–1945.* Leipzig, 1998.

Hanke, Peter. *Zur Geschichte der Juden in München zwischen 1933 und 1945*. Munich, 1967.

Harris, Bonnie M. "Refugee Rescue in the Philippines, 1937–1941." In *"Wer bleibt, opfert seine Jahre, vielleicht sein Leben": Deutsche Juden 1938–1941*, edited by Susanne Heim, Beate Meyer, and Francis R. Nicosia, 265–80. Göttingen, 2010.

Hartewig, Karin. *Zurückgekehrt: Die Geschichte der jüdischen Kommunisten in der DDR*. Cologne, 2000.

Hartung-von Doetinchem, Dagmar, and Rolf Winau, eds. *Zerstörte Fortschritte: Das Jüdische Krankenhaus in Berlin (1756-1861-1914-1989)*. Berlin, 1989.

Heidel, Caris-Petra, and Jürgen Nitsche. "Adolf Lipp (1894–1966)." In *Eine Dokumentation von Verfolgung, Vertreibung, Ermordung*, edited by Caris-Petra Heidel, 374–77. Frankfurt am Main, 2005.

Heim, Susanne, and Hans Ulrich Dillmann. *Jüdische Emigranten in der Dominikanischen Republik*. Berlin, 2009.

Heim, Susanne, Beate Meyer, and Francis R. Nicosia, eds. *"Wer bleibt, opfert seine Jahre, vielleicht sein Leben": Deutsche Juden 1938–1941*. Göttingen, 2010.

Held, Steffen. *Zwischen Tradition und Vermächtnis: Die israelitische Religionsgemeinde zu Leipzig nach 1945*. Hamburg, 1995.

Henschel, Hildegard. "Aus der Arbeit der Jüdischen Gemeinde Berlin während der Jahre 1941–1943: Gemeindearbeit und Evakuierung von Berlin (16. Oktober 1941–16. Juni 1943)." *Zeitschrift für die Geschichte des Judentums* 9, nos. 1/2 (1972): 34–52.

Hering, Sabine, ed. *Jüdische Wohlfahrt im Spiegel von Biographien*. Frankfurt am Main, 2006.

Herskovits-Gutmann, Ruth. *Auswanderung vorläufig nicht möglich: Die Geschichte der Familie Herskovits*. Göttingen, 2002.

Herzig, Arno, and Ina Lorenz, eds. *Die Verdrängung und Vernichtung der Juden unter dem Nationalsozialismus*. Hamburg, 1992.

Heuberger, Georg, and Fritz Backhaus, eds. *Leo Baeck: 1873–1956: Aus dem Stamme von Rabbinern*. Frankfurt am Main, 2001.

Heusler, Andreas. "Fahrt in den Tod: Der Mord an den Münchner Juden in Kaunas (Litauen) am 25. November 1941." In *Die erste Deportation von Münchner Juden im November 1941*, edited by Stadtarchiv München, 13–24. Zurich and Munich, 2000.

Hilberg, Raul. The *Destruction of the European Jews*. Rev. ed. 3 vols. New York, 1985.

———. *Perpetrators, Victims, Bystanders: The Jewish Catastrophe, 1933–1945*. New York, 1992.

Hildesheimer, Esriel. *Jüdische Selbstverwaltung unter dem NS-Regime*. Tübingen, 1994.

Hindls, Arnold. *Einer kehrte zurück: Bericht eines Deportierten*. Stuttgart, 1965.

Hintz, Alfred. *"Ohne Meldung unbekannt verzogen": Schwerte unter der NS-Herrschaft*. Norderstedt, 2008.

Hoffmann, Christhard, ed. *Preserving the Legacy of German Jewry: A History of the Leo Baeck Institute, 1955–2005*. Tübingen, 2005.

Holzer, Charlotte. "Bericht über die 'Herbert-Baum-Gruppe.'" In *Erinnerungen deutsch-jüdischer Frauen, 1900–1990*, edited by Andreas Lixl, 333–36. Leipzig, 1992.

Hüttenberger, Peter. *Die Gauleiter: Studie zum Wandel des Machtgefüges in der NSDAP*. Stuttgart, 1969.

Institut für die Geschichte der deutschen Juden, ed. *Das jüdische Hamburg: Ein historisches Nachschlagewerk*. Göttingen, 2006. www.dasjuedischehamburg.de/ (accessed 1 August 2012).

Israelitische Gemeinde Bremen, ed. *Festschrift zum 60. Geburtstag von Carl Katz: 14.9.1959*. Bremen, 1959.

Jah, Akim. "Vom Altenheim zum Sammellager: Die Große Hamburger Straße 26, die Deportation der Berliner Juden und das Personal der Stapoleitstelle Berlin." *Theresienstädter Studien und Dokumente* 14 (2007): 176–219.

Jansen, Hans. *Der Madagaskar-Plan: Die beabsichtigte Deportation der europäischen Juden nach Madagaskar.* Munich, 1997.

Jersch-Wenzel, Stefi, ed. *Juden und Armut in Mittel- und Osteuropa.* Cologne, Weimar, and Vienna, 2000.

Jeske, Natalja, and Ute Schmidt. "Zur Verfolgung von Kriegs- und NS-Verbrechen durch sowjetische Militärtribunale in der SBZ." In *Sowjetische Militärtribunale,* vol. 2, *Die Verurteilung deutscher Zivilisten 1945–1955,* edited by Andreas Hilger, Mike Schmeitzner, and Ute Schmidt, 155–92. Cologne, Weimar, and Vienna, 2003.

Jewish Publication Society of America. *The Holy Scriptures According to the Masoretic Text: A New Translation* (Philadelphia, 1917 [5677]). http://goo.gl/2eEmL (accessed 4 June 2012).

Jonca, Karol. "Deportations of German Jews from Breslau 1941–1944 as Described in Eyewittness Testimonies." *Yad Vashem Studies* 25 (1996): 275–316.

Jung, Ulla. "'Ich werde mich wehren': Werner Jacobowitz, ein Überlebender des Auerbach'schen Waisenhauses, Schönhauser Allee 162." In *Leben mit der Erinnerung: Jüdische Geschichte am Prenzlauer Berg,* edited by Kulturamt Prenzlauer Berg, 49–56. Berlin, 1997.

Kaplan, Marion. *Dominican Haven: The Jewish Refugee Settlement in Sozua, 1940-1945.* New York, 2008.

Kárný, Miroslav. "Die Theresienstädter Herbsttransporte 1944." *Theresienstädter Studien und Dokumente* 2 (1995): 7–37.

———. "Jakob Edelsteins letzte Briefe." *Theresienstädter Studien und Dokumente* 4 (1997): 216–29.

———. "Theresienstadt 1941–1945." In *Theresienstädter Gedenkbuch: Die Opfer der Judentransporte aus Deutschland nach Theresienstadt 1942–1945,* edited by Institut Theresienstädter Initiative, 15–44. Prague, 2000.

Kasberger, Erich. "Hans Wegner und Theodor Koronczyk—zwei Pole des Täterspektrums." In *Rechte Karrieren in München: Von der Weimarer Zeit bis in die Nachkriegsgeschichte,* edited by Marita Krauss, 230–44. Munich, 2010.

Kaul, Karl Friedrich. *Nazi-Mordaktion T 4: Ein Bericht über die erste industriemäßig durchgeführte Mordaktion des Naziregimes.* Berlin, 1973.

Kingreen, Monica. "Gewaltsam verschleppt aus Frankfurt: Die Deportationen der Juden in den Jahren 1941–1945." In *"Nach der Kristallnacht": Jüdisches Leben und antijüdische Politik in Frankfurt am Main 1938–1945,* 357–402. Frankfurt am Main and New York, 1999.

———. *"Nach der Kristallnacht": Jüdisches Leben und antijüdische Politik in Frankfurt am Main 1938–1945.* Frankfurt am Main and New York, 1999.

———. "Raubzüge einer Stadtverwaltung: Frankfurt am Main und die Aneignung 'jüdischen Besitzes.'" In "Bürokratien, Initiative und Effizienz," edited by Wolf Gruner and Armin Nolzen, special issue, *Beiträge zur Geschichte des Nationalsozialismus* 17 (2001): 17–50.

———. "Verfolgung und Rettung in Frankfurt am Main und der Rhein-Main-Region." In *Solidarität und Hilfe für Juden während der NS-Zeit,* edited by Beate Kosmala and Claudia Schoppmann, 167–90. Berlin, 2002.

———. "'Die Aktion zur kalten Erledigung der Mischehen'—die reichsweit singuläre Verschleppung und Ermordung jüdischer Mischehepartner im NSDAP-Gau Hessen-

Nassau 1942/43." In *NS-Gewaltherrschaft, Beiträge zur historischen Forschung und juristischen Aufarbeitung*, edited by Alfred Gottwaldt, Norbert Kampe, and Peter Klein, 187–201. Berlin, 2005.

Klee, Ernst. *"Euthanasie" im NS-Staat: Die "Vernichtung lebensunwerten Lebens."* Frankfurt am Main, 2004.

Klein, Peter. *Die "Ghettoverwaltung Litzmannstadt" 1940 bis 1944: Eine Dienststelle im Spannungsfeld von Kommunalbürokratie und staatlicher Verfolgungspolitik.* Hamburg, 2009.

Klemperer, Victor. *I Will Bear Witness: 1942–1945. A Diary of the Nazi Years.* Translated by Martin Chalmers. New York, 2001.

———. *The Diaries of Victor Klemperer, 1945–1959, The Lesser Evil.* Translated by Martin Chalmers. London, 2004.

Kohl, Christiane. *Der Jude und das Mädchen: Eine verbotene Freundschaft in Nazideutschland.* Hamburg, 1997.

Köhler, Ingo. *Die "Arisierung" der Privatbanken im Dritten Reich: Verdrängung, Ausschaltung und die Frage der Wiedergutmachung.* Munich, 2005.

Kommission zur Erforschung der Geschichte der Frankfurter Juden, ed. *Dokumente zur Geschichte der Frankfurter Juden.* Frankfurt am Main, 1963.

Konieczny, Alfred. "The Transit Camp for Breslau Jews at Riebnig in Lower Silesia (1941–1943)." *Yad Vashem Studies* 25 (1996): 317–42.

Kosmala, Beate. "Missglückte Hilfe und ihre Folgen: Die Ahndung der 'Judenbegünstigung' durch NS-Verfolgungsbehörden." In *Solidarität und Hilfe für Juden während der NS-Zeit*, vol. 5, *Überleben im Untergrund: Hilfe für Juden in Deutschland 1941–1945*, edited by Beate Kosmala and Claudia Schoppmann, 205–22. Berlin, 2002.

———. "Zwischen Ahnen und Wissen: Flucht vor der Deportation (1941–1943)." In "Die Deportation der Juden aus Deutschland: Pläne-Praxis-Reaktionen," edited by Birthe Kundrus and Beate Meyer, special issue, *Beiträge zur Geschichte des Nationalsozialismus* 20 (2004): 135–59.

Kosmala, Beate, and Claudia Schoppmann, eds. *Solidarität und Hilfe für Juden während der NS-Zeit*, vol. 5, *Überleben im Untergrund: Hilfe für Juden in Deutschland 1941–1945.* Berlin, 2002.

Kraus, Elisabeth. *Die Familie Mosse: Deutsch-jüdisches Bürgertum im 19. und 20. Jahrhundert.* Munich, 1999.

Krauss, Marita, ed. *Rechte Karrieren in München: Von der Weimarer Zeit bis in die Nachkriegsgeschichte.* Munich, 2001.

Kraushaar, Wolfgang. "Die Auerbach-Affäre." In *Leben im Land der Täter: Juden im Nachkriegsdeutschland (1945–1952)*, edited by Julius H. Schoeps, 208–18. Berlin, 2001.

Kulka, Otto D. "The Reichsvereinigung and the Fate of the German Jews, 1938/1939–1943. Continuity or Discontinuity in German-Jewish History in the Third Reich." In *Die Juden im nationalsozialistischen Deutschland*, edited by Arnold Paucker, 353–63. Tübingen, 1986.

Kulka, Otto Dov. "Singularity and its Relativization: Changing Views in German Historiography on National Socialism and the 'Final Solution.'" *Yad Vashem Studies* 19 (1988): 151–84.

———. *Deutsches Judentum unter dem Nationalsozialismus.* Vol. 1, *Dokumente zur Geschichte der Reichsvertretung der deutschen Juden 1933–1939.* Tübingen, 1997.

Kulka, Otto Dov, and Eberhard Jäckel, eds. *Die Juden in den geheimen NS-Stimmungsberichten 1933–1945.* Düsseldorf, 2004.

———. *The Jews in the Secret Nazi Reports on Popular Opinion in Germany, 1933–1945.* Translated by William Templer. New Haven, CT, 2010.

Kundrus, Birthe, and Beate Meyer, eds. "Die Deportation der Juden aus Deutschland: Pläne-Praxis-Reaktionen." Special issue, *Beiträge zur Geschichte des Nationalsozialismus* 20 (2004).

Kuwalek, Robert. "Das kurze Leben 'im Osten': Jüdische Deutsche im Distrikt Lublin aus polnisch-jüdischer Sicht." In "Die Deportation der Juden aus Deutschland: Pläne-Praxis-Reaktionen," edited by Birthe Kundrus and Beate Meyer, special issue, *Beiträge zur Geschichte des Nationalsozialismus* 20 (2004): 112–34.

Kwiet, Konrad, and Helmut Eschwege. *Selbstbehauptung und Widerstand: Deutsche Juden in Kampf um Existenz und Menschenwürde*. Hamburg, 1984.

Lamm, Hans. *Von Juden in München: Ein Gedenkbuch*. Munich, 1958.

Landeshauptstadt München, ed. *Verdunkeltes München: Geschichtswettbewerb 1985/86: Die nationalsozialistische Gewaltherrschaft, ihr Ende und ihre Folgen*. Lesebücher zur Geschichte des Münchner Alltags. Munich, 1987.

Lehnert, Herbert. *Juden in Nürnberg*. Edited by Stadt Nürnberg. Nuremberg, 1993.

Leichsenring, Jana. *Die katholische Kirche und "ihre Juden": Das "Hilfswerk beim Bischöflichen Ordinariat Berlin" 1938–1945*. Berlin, 2007.

Lekebusch, Sigrid. *Not und Verfolgung der Christen jüdischer Herkunft im Rheinland*. Cologne, 1995.

Lifton, Robert J. *The Nazi Doctors: Medical Killing and the Psychology of Genocide*. New York, 1986. www.holocaust-history.org/lifton/ (accessed 1 August 2012).

Lippmann, Leo. "*... dass ich wie ein guter Deutscher empfinde und handele": Zur Geschichte der Deutsch-Israelitischen Gemeinde in Hamburg in der Zeit vom Herbst 1935 bis zum Ende 1942*. Hamburg, 1993.

———. *Mein Leben und meine amtliche Tätigkeit: Erinnerungen und ein Beitrag zur Finanzgeschichte Hamburgs*. Hamburg, 1964.

Loewenstein, Karl. "Minsk: Im Lager der deutschen Juden." *Aus Politik und Zeitgeschichte, Beilage zur Wochenzeitung "Das Parlament"* B 45, no. 56 (1956): 705–18.

Longerich, Peter. *Holocaust; The Nazi Persecution and Murder of the Jews*. New York, 2010.

Lorenz, Ina S. *Gehen oder Bleiben: Neuanfang der Jüdischen Gemeinde in Hamburg nach 1945*. Hamburg, 2002. http://goo.gl/isE0Y (accessed 1 August 2012).

———. *To Leave or To Stay: The New Beginning of the Hamburg Jewish Community post 1945*. www1.uni-hamburg.de/rz3a035//lorenz.html (accessed 1 August 2012).

———. "Das Leben der Hamburger Juden im Zeichen der 'Endlösung' (1942–1945)." In *Die Verdrängung und Vernichtung der Juden unter dem Nationalsozialismus*, edited by Arno Herzig and Ina Lorenz, 207–48. Hamburg, 1992.

———. "Die dunklen und die schweren Jahre (1933–1945)." In *150 Jahre Israelitisches Krankenhaus Hamburg*, edited by Israelitisches Krankenhaus Hamburg, 65–86. Hamburg, 1997.

Louven, Astrid. "'Die Belmonte-Brüder sind tot'—Die Familie Belmonte." In "*Wo Wurzeln waren ...*" In Sybille Baumbach, Susanne Lohmeyer, Astrid Louven, Beate Meyer, Sielke Salomon, and Dagmar Wienrich, *Juden in Hamburg-Eimsbüttel 1933–1945*, edited by Galerie Morgenland, 141-46. Hamburg, 1993.

Ludwig, Hartmut. "'So gehe hin und tue desgleichen!' Zur Geschichte des 'Büros Pfarrer Grüber' 1938–1940." In *Bevollmächtigt zum Brückenbau: Heinrich Grüber: Judenfreund und Trümmerprobst: Erinnerungen, Predigten, Berichte, Briefe*, edited by Jörg Hildebrandt, 11–40. Leipzig, 1991.

Maier, Clemens. "Das Jüdischen Nachrichtenblatt (1938–1943): Ein jüdisches Presseerzeugnis im Kontext nationalsozialistischer Verfolgung." MA thesis, Free University Berlin, 2001.

———. "The *Jüdisches Nachrichtenblatt* 1938–43." In *Jews in Nazi Berlin: From Kristallnacht to Liberation*, edited by Beate Meyer, Hermann Simon, and Chana Schütz, translated by Caroline Gay and Miranda Robbins, 100–20. Chicago, 2009.

Maier, Dieter. *Arbeitseinsatz und Deportationen: Die Mitwirkung der Arbeitsverwaltung bei der nationalsozialistischen Judenverfolgung in den Jahren 1938–1934*. Berlin, 1994.

Maierhof, Gudrun. "Selbsthilfe nach dem Pogrom: Die Jüdische Gemeinde in Frankfurt am Main 1938 bis 1942." In *"Nach der Kristallnacht": Jüdisches Leben und antijüdische Politik in Frankfurt am Main 1938–1945*, edited by Monica Kingreen, 157–86. Frankfurt am Main and New York, 1999.

———. *Selbstbehauptung im Chaos: Frauen in der Jüdischen Selbsthilfe 1933–1943*. Frankfurt am Main, 2002.

———. "Central Organizations of Jews in Germany (1933–1943)." In *Jewish Women: A Comprehensive Historical Encyclopedia*. 2009. Jewish Women's Archive http://goo .gl/7b2wd (accessed 6 June 2012).

Maierhof, Gudrun, Chana Schütz, and Hermann Simon, eds. *Aus Kindern wurden Briefe: Die Rettung jüdischer Kinder aus Nazi-Deutschland*. Berlin, 2004.

Makarova, Elena, Sergei Makarov, and Victor Kuperman. *University Over The Abyss: The Story Behind 520 Lecturers and 2,430 Lectures in KZ Theresienstadt 1942–1944*. Jerusalem, 2004.

Matthäus, Jürgen. "'You have the right to be hopeful if you do your duty': Ten letters by Leo Baeck to Friedrich Brodnitz, 1937–1941." *LBI Yearbook* 54 (2009): 333–55.

———. "Between Fragmented Memory and 'Real History'—The LBI's Perception of Jewish Self-Defense against Nazi Antisemitism, 1955–1970." In *Preserving the Legacy of German Jewry: A History of the Leo Baeck Institute, 1955–2005*, edited by Christhard Hoffmann, 375–407. Tübingen, 2005.

Matthäus, Jürgen, and Klaus-Michael Mallmann, eds. *Deutsche, Juden, Völkermord: Der Holocaust als Geschichte und Gegenwart*. Darmstadt, 2006.

Maurer, Trude. "The Background for Kristallnacht: The Expulsion of Polish Jews." In *November 1938: From "Reichskritallnacht" to Genocide*, edited by Walter H. Pehle, translated by William Templer, 44–72. New York, 1991.

Mazerath, Horst. "Oberbürgermeister im Dritten Reich." In *Der "Führerstaat": Mythos und Realität. Studien zur Struktur und Politik des Dritten Reiches*, edited by Gerhard Hirschfeld and Lothar Kettenacker, 228–54. Stuttgart, 1981.

Meyer, Beate. *"Jüdische Mischlinge": Rassenpolitik und Verfolgungserfahrung 1933–1945*. Hamburg, 1999.

———. "The Mixed Marriage—a Guarantee of Survival or a Reflection of German Society during the Nazi Regime?" In *Probing the Depths of German Antisemitism: German Society and the Persecution of the Jews, 1933–1941*, edited by David Bankier, 54–77. New York, Oxford, and Jerusalem, 1999.

———. "Max Plaut." In *Hamburgische Biographie: Personenlexikon*, vol. 1, edited by Franklin Kopitzsch and Dirk Brietzke, 238-39. Hamburg, 2001.

———. "'A conto Zukunft'—Hilfe und Rettung für untergetauchte Hamburger Juden." *Zeitschrift des Vereins für Hamburgische Geschichte* 88 (2002): 205–33.

———. "Das unausweichliche Dilemma: Die Reichsvereinigung der Juden in Deutschland, die Deportationen und die untergetauchten Juden." In *Solidarität und Hilfe für Juden während der NS-Zeit*, vol. 5, *Überleben im Untergrund: Hilfe für Juden in Deutschland 1941–1945*, edited by Beate Kosmala and Claudia Schoppmann, 273–96. Berlin, 2002.

———. "Geschichte im Film: Judenverfolgung, Mischehen und der Protest in der Rosenstraße 1943." *Zeitschrift für Geschichtsforschung* 52 (2004): 23–36.

———. "Gestörte Beziehungen: Die Kommunikation zwischen Repräsentanten und (Zwangs)Mitgliedern der Reichsvereinigung der Juden in Deutschland nach der Befreiung." In *Aus den Quellen: Festschrift für Ina Lorenz zum 65. Geburtstag*, edited by Andreas Brämer, Stefanie Schüler-Springorum, and Michael Studemund-Halevy, 366–77. Hamburg, 2005.

———. *Die Verfolgung und Ermordung der Hamburger Juden: Geschichte, Zeugnis, Erinnerung*. Göttingen, 2006.

———. "Der 'Eichmann von Dresden': 'Justizielle Bewältigung' von NS-Verbrechen in der DDR am Beispiel des Verfahrens gegen Henry Schmidt." In *Deutsche, Juden, Völkermord: Der Holocaust als Geschichte und Gegenwart*, edited by Jürgen Matthäus and Klaus-Michael Mallmann, 273–91. Darmstadt, 2006.

———. "Die Arbeit des Jüdischen Religionsverbandes zur Zeit der Deportationen." In *Die Verfolgung und Ermordung der Hamburger Juden: Geschichte, Zeugnis, Erinnerung*, 45–52. Göttingen, 2006.

———. "'Altersghetto,' 'Vorzugslager' und Tätigkeitsfeld: Die Repräsentanten der Reichsvereinigung in Deutschland und Theresienstadt." *Theresienstädter Studien und Dokumente* 13 (2006): 125–51.

———. "Corten, Martin Heinrich." In *Das Jüdische Hamburg: Ein historisches Nachschlagewerk*, edited by Institut für die Geschichte der deutschen Juden, 50–51. Göttingen, 2006. www.dasjuedischehamburg.de/inhalt/corten-martin-heinrich (accessed 1 August 2012).

———. "Max Plaut." In *Institut für die Geschichte der deutschen Juden 2003–2008*, edited by Institut für die Geschichte der deutschen Juden, 50–55. Hamburg, 2009.

———. "The Fine Line Between Responsible Action and Collaboration; The Reichsvereinigung der Juden in Deutschland and the Jewish Community in Berlin, 1938–45." In *Jews in Nazi Berlin: From Kristallnacht to Liberation*, edited by Beate Meyer, Hermann Simon, and Chana Schütz, translated by Caroline Gay and Miranda Robbins, 310–62. Chicago, 2009.

Meyer, Beate, Hermann Simon, and Chana Schütz, eds. *Jews in Nazi Berlin: From Kristallnacht to Liberation*. Translated by Caroline Gay and Miranda Robbins. Chicago, 2009.

Meyhöfer, Rita. *Gäste in Berlin: Jüdisches Schülerleben in der Weimarer Republik und im Nationalsozialismus*. Hamburg, 1996.

Michman, Dan. "'Judenräte' und 'Judenvereinigungen' unter nationalsozialistischer Herrschaft: Aufbau und Anwendung eines verwaltungsmäßigen Konzepts." *Zeitschrift für Geschichtswissenschaft* 4 (1998): 293–304.

———. "Reevaluating the Emergence, Function, and Form of the Jewish Councils Phenomenon." In *Ghettos 1939–1945: New Research and Perspectives on Definition, Daily Life, and Survival*, edited by USHMM Center for Advanced Holocaust Studies, 67–83. Washington, 2005. http://goo.gl/moz12 (accessed 1 August 2012).

Mildt, Dick de. *In the Name of the People: Perpetrators of Genocide in the Reflection of Their Post-War Prosecution in West Germany: The "Euthanasia" and "Aktion Reinhard" Trial Cases*. Leiden, 1996.

———. ed. *Tatkomplex: NS-Euthanasie*. 2 vols. Amsterdam, 2009.

Modert, Gerd. "Motor der Verfolgung—Zur Rolle der NSDAP bei der Entrechtung und Ausplünderung der Münchner Juden." In *München arisiert: Entrechtung und Enteignung der Juden in der NS-Zeit*, edited by Angelika Baumann and Andreas Heusler, 145–75. Munich, 2004.

Möller, Horst, and Alexandr O. Tschubarjan, eds. *SMAD-Handbuch: Die Sowjetische Militäradministration in Deutschland 1945–1949*. Munich, 2009.

Mommsen, Hans, ed. "The German Resistance Movement and the Holocaust." In *On Germans and Jews under the Nazi Regime: Essays by Three Generations of Historians: A Festschrift in Honor of Otto Dov Kulka*, edited by Moshe Zimmermann, 239–58. Jerusalem, 2006.

———. "The German Resistance Movement and the Holocaust." In *On Germans and Jews under the Nazi Regime: Essays by Three Generations of Historians: A Festschrift in Honor of Otto Dov Kulka*, edited by Moshe Zimmermann, 239–58. Jerusalem, 2006.

———. "Der Wendepunkt zur "Endlösung": Die Eskalation der nationalsozialistischen Judenverfolgung." In *Zur Geschichte Deutschlands im 20. Jahrhundert: Demokratie, Diktatur, Widerstand*, 214–32. Munich, 2010.

Müller, Arndt. *Geschichte der Juden in Nürnberg 1146–1945*. Nuremberg, 1968.

Murmelstein, Benjamin. *Il Ghetto Modello di Eichmann*. Bologna, 1961.

Nadav, Daniel. *Medicine and Nazism*. Jerusalem, 2010.

Nadav, Daniel S., and Manfred Stürzbecher. "Walter Lustig." In *Zerstörte Fortschritte: Das Jüdische Krankenhaus in Berlin (1756-1861-1914-1989)*, edited by Dagmar Hartung-von Doetinchem and Rolf Winau, 221–26. Berlin, 1989.

Neue Synagoge—Centrum Judaicum, ed. *Heinrich Stahl (13. April 1868–4. November 1942)*. Berlin, 1993.

Neumeyer, Alfred, Alexander Karl Neumeyer, and Imanuel Noy-Meir. *"Wir wollen den Fluch in Segen verwandeln": Drei Generationen der jüdischen Familie Neumeyer: eine autobiografische Trilogie*. Berlin, 2007.

Nicosia, Francis R. "Revisionist Zionism in Germany (II): Georg Kareski and the Staatszionistische Organisation, 1933–1938." *LBI Yearbook* 32 (1987): 231–67.

———. *Zionism and Anti-Semitism in Nazi Germany*. New York, 2008.

Nielsen, Philipp J. "'I've never regretted being a German Jew': Siegmund Weltlinger and the Re-establishment of the Jewish Community in Berlin." *LBI Yearbook* 54 (2009): 3–24.

Nitsche, Jürgen, and Ruth Röcher. *Juden in Chemnitz: Die Geschichte der Juden und ihrer Mitglieder*. Dresden, 2002.

Noack, Thorsten. "Über Kaninchen und Giftschlangen: Psychiatrie und Öffentlichkeit in der frühen Bundesrepublik Deutschland." In *"Moderne" Anstaltspsychiatrie im 19. und 20. Jahrhundert—Legitimation und Kritik*, edited by Heiner Fangerau and Karin Nolte, 311–40. Stuttgart, 2006.

Ofer, Dalia. "Die illegale Einwanderung nach Palästina: Politische, nationale und persönliche Aspekte (1939–1941)." In "Flüchtlingspolitik und Fluchthilfe," special issue, *Beiträge zur nationalsozialistischen Gesundheits- und Sozialpolitik* 15 (1999): 9–38.

Offenberg, Ulrike. *Seid vorsichtig gegen die Machthaber: Die jüdischen Gemeinden in der SBZ und der DDR 1945–1990*. Berlin, 1998.

———. "Die Jüdische Gemeinde zu Berlin 1945–1953." In *Leben im Land der Täter: Juden im Nachkriegsdeutschland (1945–1952)*, edited by Julius H. Schoeps, 133–56. Berlin, 2001.

Opfermann, Charlotte. "'Im Hermesweg': Zur Tätigkeit in der Bezirksstelle der Reichsvereinigung in Frankfurt am Main von November 1941 bis Juni 1943—ein Zeitzeugenbericht." In *"Nach der Kristallnacht": Jüdisches Leben und antijüdische Politik in Frankfurt am Main 1938–1945*, edited by Monica Kingreen, 403–14. Frankfurt am Main and New York, 1999.

Ophir, Baruch Z., and Falk Wiesemann. *Die jüdischen Gemeinden in Bayern 1918–1945*. Munich and Vienna, 1979.

Oppenheim, Naftali. *The Chosen People: The Story of the "222 Transport" from Bergen-Belsen to Palestine*. London and Portland, 1996.

Osterloh, Jörg. *Nationalsozialistische Judenverfolgung im Reichsgau Sudentenland 1938–1945*. Munich, 2006.

Overy, Richard. *Why the Allies Won*. New York, 1996.

Pätzold, Kurt, and Erika Schwarz. *Tagesordnung: Judenmord. Die Wannsee-Konferenz am 30. Januar 1942*. Berlin, 1992.

Paucker, Arnold. *Deutsche Juden im Kampf um Recht und Freiheit*. Teetz, 2004.

Pehle, Walter H. *November 1938: From "Reichskristallnacht" to Genocide*. Translated by William Templer. New York, 1991.

Plaut, Max. "Die Deportationsmaßnahmen der Geheimen Staatspolizei in Hamburg." In *Die jüdischen Opfer des Nationalsozialismus in Hamburg*, edited by Hamburg State Archive, xi–xiii. Hamburg, 1965.

Plum, Günter. "Deutsche Juden oder Juden in Deutschland?" *Die Juden in Deutschland 1933–1945*, edited by Wolfgang Benz, 35–74. Munich, 1988.

Pohl, Dieter. *Von der "Judenpolitik" zum Judenmord: Der Distrikt Lublin des Generalgouvernements 1939–1941*. Münchner Studien zur neueren und neuesten Geschichte 3. Frankfurt am Main, 1993.

———. "Die Deportation von Juden aus dem Deutschen Reich 1941–1943." In *Wege in die Vernichtung: Die Deportation der Juden aus Mainfranken 1941–1943: Begleitband zur Ausstellung des Staatsarchivs Würzburg*, edited by Generaldirektion der staatlichen Archive Bayerns, 57–72. Munich, 2003.

———. "Das NS-Regime und das internationale Bekanntwerden seiner Verbrechen." In *Der Holocaust als offenes Geheimnis: Die Deutschen, die NS-Führung und die Alliierten*, edited by Frank Bajohr and Dieter Pohl, 81–129. Munich, 2006.

Rabinovici, Doron. *Eichmann's Jews: The Jewish Administration of Holocaust Vienna, 1938–1945*. Translated by Nick Somers. Cambridge, 2011.

Raim, Edith. "Strafverfahren wegen der Deportation der Juden aus Unter- und Mittelfranken nach 1945." In *Wege in die Vernichtung: Die Deportation der Juden aus Mainfranken 1941–1943: Begleitband zur Ausstellung des Staatsarchivs Würzburg*, edited by Generaldirektion der staatlichen Archive Bayerns, 178–92. Munich, 2003.

Reichmann, Eva, ed., *Worte des Gedenkens für Leo Baeck*. Heidelberg, 1959.

Reichmann, Hans. *Deutscher Bürger und verfolgter Jude: Novemberpogrom und KZ Sachsenhausen 1937 bis 1939*. Munich, 1998.

Reinharz, Jehuda. "Ideology and Structure in German Zionism, 1882–1933." In *Essential Papers on Zionism*, edited by Jehuda Reinharz and Anita Shapira, 268–97. New York, 1996.

Reinicke, Peter. "Erster 'Polizeirat' in Preußen und Arbeit in der jüdischen Gemeinde unter Aufsicht der Gestapo. Martha Mosse (1884–1977)." In *Jüdische Wohlfahrt im Spiegel von Biographien*, edited by Sabine Hering, 297–304. Frankfurt am Main, 2006.

Reinke, Andreas. *Judentum und Wohlfahrtspflege in Deutschland: Das jüdische Krankenhaus in Breslau 1726–1944*. Hanover, 1999.

Reyer, Herbert. "Die Vertreibung der Juden aus Ostfriesland und Oldenburg im Frühjahr 1940." In *Collectanea Frisica: Beiträge zur historischen Landeskunde Ostfrieslands: Walter Deeters zum 65. Geburtstag*, edited by Hajo van Lengen, 363–90. Abhandlungen und Vorträge zu Geschichte Ostfrieslands 74. Aurich, 1995.

Richarz, Monika, ed. *Jüdisches Leben in Deutschland*. Vol. 3. Stuttgart, 1982.

Riesenburger, Martin. *Das Licht verlöschte nicht. Ein Zeugnis aus der Nacht des Faschismus*. Berlin, 1960.

Rohdenburg, Günther. "Die Beteiligung der Juden an den Deportationen—das Problem der 'Helfershelfer.'" In *"… sind Sie für den geschlossenen Arbeitseinsatz vorgesehen …": "Judendeportationen" von Bremerinnen und Bremern während der Zeit der nationalsoziali-*

stischen Gewaltherrschaft, edited by Günther Rohdenburg and State Archive Bremen, 151–58. Bremen, 2006.

Röpcke, Andreas. "Office of Military Goverment for Bremen, und Reinhard Heydenreuther, Office of Military Goverment for Bavaria." In *OMGUS-Handbuch: Die amerikanische Militärregierung in Deutschland 1945–1949*, edited by Christoph Weisz, 597–670. Munich, 1994.

Roseman, Mark. *The Wannsee Conference and the Final Solution: A Reconsideration.* New York, 2002.

Rosenberg, Leibl. *Spuren und Fragmente: Jüdische Bücher, jüdische Schicksale in Nürnberg.* Nuremberg, 2000.

Rosenfeld, Else B. *See* Behrend-Rosenfeld, Else

Rothkirchen, Livia. "Die Repräsentanten der Theresienstädter Selbstverwaltung." *Theresienstädter Studien und Dokumente* 3 (1996): 114–26.

Rupnow, Dirk. "'Zur Förderung und beschleunigten Regelung der Auswanderung …': Die Zentralstelle für jüdische Auswanderung Wien." In *Ausgeschlossen und entrechtet: Raub und Rückgabe: Österreich von 1938 bis heute*, edited by Verena Pawlowsky and Harald Wendelin, 13–31. Vienna, 2006.

Rürup, Reinhard, ed. *Jüdische Geschichte in Berlin.* Berlin, 1995.

Rüter, Christiaan F. and Dick W. de Mildt, eds. *Justiz und NS-Verbrechen: Sammlung deutscher Strafurteile wegen nationalsozialistischer Tötungsverbrechen 1945–1966.* Vols. 13 and 22. Amsterdam, 1975, 1981.

Safrian, Hans. *Eichmann's Men.* Translated by U. Stargardt. Cambridge, 2010.

Salinger, Eliyahu Kutti. *"Nächstes Jahr im Kibbuz": Die jüdisch-chaluzische Jugendbewegung in Deutschland zwischen 1933 und 1943.* Paderborn, 1998.

Samter, Hermann. *"Worte können das ja kaum verständlich machen": Briefe 1939–1942*, edited by Daniel Fraenkel. Göttingen, 2009.

———. "Letters of Hermann Samter from Berlin." Shoah Resource Center, Yad Vashem. http://goo.gl/LZbVs (accessed 1 August 2012).

Scheer, Regina. "Eine Treppe ins Nichts: Josepha Gutmann, Kinderheim Greifswalder Str. 138/9." In *Leben mit der Erinnerung: Jüdische Geschichte am Prenzlauer Berg*, edited by Kulturamt Prenzlauer Berg, 102. Berlin, 1997.

———. *Im Schatten der Sterne: Eine jüdische Widerstandsgruppe.* Berlin, 2004.

Scheffler, Wolfgang. "Das Schicksal der in die baltischen Staaten deportierten deutschen, österreichischen und tschechoslowakischen Juden 1941–1956." In *Buch der Erinnerung: Die ins Baltikum deportierten deutschen, österreichischen und tschechoslowakischen Juden*, vol. 1, edited by Wolfgang Scheffler and Diana Schulle, 83–87. Munich, 2003.

———. "Massenmord in Kowno." In *Buch der Erinnerung: Die ins Baltikum deportierten deutschen, österreichischen und tschechoslowakischen Juden*, vol. 1, edited by Wolfgang Scheffler and Diana Schulle, 1–43. Munich, 2003.

———. "Der Brandanschlag im Berliner Lustgarten im Mai 1942 und seine Folgen: Eine quellenkritische Betrachtung." In *Berlin in Geschichte und Gegenwart: Jahrbuch des Landesarchivs Berlin 1984*, edited by Hans J. Reichard, 91–118. Berlin, 1984.

Scheffler, Wolfgang, and Diana Schulle. *Buch der Erinnerung: Die ins Baltikum deportierten deutschen, österreichischen und tschechoslowakischen Juden.* Vols. 1–2. Munich, 2003.

Schidorsky, Dov. "Confiscation of Libraries and Assignments to Forced Labor: Two Documents of the Holocaust." *Libraries & Culture* 33, no. 4 (1998): 347–88. http://tinyurl.com/72ezojd (accessed 1 August 2012).

Schmid, Hans-Dieter. *Ahlem: die Geschichte einer jüdischen Gartenbauschule und ihres Einflusses auf Gartenbau und Landschaftsarchitektur in Deutschland und Israel.* Bremen, 2008.

Schmidt, Herbert. *Der Elendsweg der Düsseldorfer Juden: Chronologie des Schreckens 1933–1945*. Düsseldorf, 2005.

Schoenberner, Mira, and Gerhard Schoenberner. *Zeugen sagen aus: Berichte und Dokumente über die Judenverfolgung im "Dritten Reich."* Berlin, 1998.

Schoeps, Julius H., ed. *Leben im Land der Täter: Juden im Nachkriegsdeutschland (1945–1952)*. Berlin, 2001.

Schröder, Frank. *160 jüdische Persönlichkeiten aus Mecklenburg-Vorpommern*. Rostock, 2003.

Schüler-Springorum, Stefanie. *Die jüdische Minderheit in Königsberg/Preußen 1871–1945*. Göttingen, 1996.

———. "Fear and Misery in the Third Reich: From the Files of the Collective Guardianship Office of the Berlin Jewish Community." *Yad Vashem Studies* 27 (1999): 61–103. Available at Shoah Resource Center, Yad Vashem, http://goo.gl/2qAfX (accessed 1 August 2012).

Segev, Tom. *The Seventh Million: The Israelis and the Holocaust*. New York, 1994.

Seidel, Doris. "Die jüdische Gemeinde Münchens 1933–1945." In *München arisiert: Entrechtung und Enteignung der Juden in der NS-Zeit*, edited by Angelika Baumann and Andreas Heusler, 31–53. Munich, 2004.

Sieleman, Jürgen. "Die Deportation aus Hamburg und Schleswig-Holstein am 6. Dez 1941, Hamburg." In *Buch der Erinnerung: Die ins Baltikum deportierten deutschen, österreichischen und tschechoslowakischen Juden*, vol. 2, edited by Wolfgang Scheffler and Diana Schulle, 599–626. Munich, 2003.

Silver, Daniel B. *Refuge in Hell: How Berlin's Jewish Hospital Outlasted the Nazis*. New York, 2003.

Simon, Ernst. *Aufbau im Untergang: Jüdische Erwachsenenbildung im nationalsozialistischen Deutschland als geistiger Widerstand*. Tübingen, 1959.

Simon, Hermann. "Die Jüdische Gemeinde Nordwest: Eine Episode aus der Zeit des Neubeginns jüdischen Lebens in Berlin nach 1945." In *Aufbau nach dem Untergang: Deutsch-jüdische Geschichte nach 1945*, edited by Andreas Nachama and Julius H. Schoeps, 274–84. Berlin, 1992.

———. "Bislang unbekannte Quellen zur Entstehungsgeschichte des Werkes 'Die Entwicklung der Rechtsstellung der Juden in Europa, vornehmlich in Deutschland.'" In *Leo Baeck. 1873–1956: Aus dem Stamme von Rabbinern*, edited by Georg Heuberger and Fritz Backhaus, 103–10. Frankfurt am Main, 2001.

Simonsohn, Berthold. "Gedenkblatt für Paul Eppstein." *Jüdische Sozialarbeit* 4, nos. 3/4 (1959).

Stadtarchiv München, ed. *"… verzogen, unbekannt wohin": Die erste Deportation von Münchner Juden im November 1941*. Zurich and Munich, 2000.

———. *Biographisches Gedenkbuch der Münchner Juden 1933–1945*. Vol. 2. Munich, 2007.

Starke, Käthe. *Der Führer schenkt den Juden eine Stadt: Bilder, Impressionen, Reportagen, Dokumente*. Berlin, 1975.

State of Israel, Ministry of Justice. *The Trial of Adolf Eichmann: Record of Proceedings in the District Court of Jerusalem*. Vol. 2. Jerusalem, 1992.

Stecklina, Gerd. "'Was wir am Mitmenschen tun, ist Gottesdienst': Leo Baeck (1873–1946)." In *Jüdische Wohlfahrt im Spiegel von Biographien*, edited by Sabine Hering, 66–73. Frankfurt am Main, 2006.

Steur, Claudia. *Theodor Dannecker: Ein Funktionär der "Endlösung."* Essen, 1997.

Strauss, Herbert A. "Jewish Emigration from Germany: Nazi Policies and Jewish Responses (II)." *LBI Yearbook* 26 (1981): 343–404.

———. In *The Eye of The Storm: Growing Up Jewish in Germany, 1918–1943*. New York, 1999.

———. "Erinnerungen an Leo Baeck." In *Leo Baeck 1873–1956: Aus dem Stamme von Rabbinern*, edited by Georg Heuberger and Fritz Backhaus, 191–94. Frankfurt am Main, 2001.

Strauss, Herbert A., and Kurt R. Grossmann, eds. *Gegenwart im Rückblick: Festgabe für die Jüdische Gemeinde zu Berlin 25 Jahre nach dem Neubeginn*. Heidelberg, 1970.

Strnad, Maxamilian. *Zwischenstation "Judensiedlung": Verfolgung und Deporttion der jüdischen Münchner 1941–1945*. Munich, 2011.

Suchy, Barbara. "Schreckenstein' in Lenne? Über Zwangsarbeit von 'Mischehe'-Juden aus Düsseldorf in der Endphase des Zweiten Weltkrieges—Ein Fallbeispiel." In *Zwangsarbeit: Für Industrie und Rüstung im Hils 1943–1945*, vol. 4, edited by Detlef Creydt, 275–93. Holzminden, 2001.

Süss, Dietmar. "Der Kampf um die 'Moral' im Bunker: Deutschland, Großbritannien und der Luftkrieg." In *Volksgemeinschaft: Neue Forschungen zur Gesellschaft des Nationalsozialismus*, edited Frank Bajohr and Michael Wildt, 124–43. Frankfurt am Main, 2009.

Süss, Winfried. *Der "Volkskörper" im Krieg: Gesundheitspolitik, Gesundheitsverhältnisse und Krankenmord im nationalsozialistischen Deutschland 1939–1945*. Munich, 2003.

Tausendfreund, Doris. *Erzwungener Verrat: Jüdische "Greifer" im Dienst der Gestapo 1943–1945*. Berlin, 2006.

Teschner, Gerhard J. *Die Deportation der badischen und saarpfälzischen Juden am 22. Oktober 1940: Vorgeschichte und Durchführung der Deportation und das weitere Schicksal der Deportierten bis zum Kriegsende im Kontext der deutschen und französischen Judenpolitik*. Frankfurt am Main, 2002.

Thomas, Gordon, and Max Morgen Witts. *Voyage of the Damned*. New York, 1974.

Trunk, Isaiah. *Judenrat: The Jewish Councils in Eastern Europe under Nazi Occupation*. New York and London, 1972.

Villiez, Anna von. *Mit aller Kraft verdrängt: Entrechtung und Verfolgung "nicht arischer" Ärzte in Hamburg 1933 bis 1945*. Hamburg, 2009.

Walk, Joseph. *Das Sonderrecht für die Juden im NS-Staat*. Heidelberg, 1996.

Wegner, Hans. "Tätigkeits- und Abschlussbericht zum 30. Juni 1943." In *"… verzogen, unbekannt wohin": Die erste Deportation von Münchner Juden im November 1941*, edited by Stadtarchiv Munich. Zurich and Munich, 2000.

Weismann, Ernest H. "Die Nachfolge-Organisationen." In *Die Wiedergutmachung nationalsozialistischen Unrechts durch die Bundesrepublik Deutschland*, vol. 2, *Das Rückerstattungsgesetz*, edited by Bundesminister der Finanzen. Munich, 1981.

Weiss, Aharon. "Jewish Leadersdhip in Occupied Poland. Postures and Attitudes." *Yad Vashem Studies* 12 (1977): 335–65.

Weiss, Yfaat. *Deutsche und polnische Juden vor dem Holocaust: Jüdische Identität zwischen Staatsbürgerschaft und Ethnizität 1933–1940*. Schriftenreihe der Vierteljahrshefte für Zeitgeschichte 81. Munich, 2000.

Weltlinger, Siegmund. *Hast Du es schon vergessen? Erlebnisbericht aus der Zeit der Verfolgung*. Edited by Berliner Gesellschaft für jüdisch-christliche Zusammenarbeit. Berlin, 1954.

Weltsch, Robert. "Aufzeichnung über eine Unterredung." In *Worte des Gedenkens für Leo Baeck*, edited by Eva Reichmann, 237–41. Heidelberg, 1959.

Wetzel, Juliane. "Auswanderung aus Deutschland." In *Die Juden in Deutschland 1933–1945: Leben unter nationalsozialistischer Herrschaft*, edited by Wolfgang Benz, 413–98. Munich, 1988.

Wietog, Jutta. *Volkszählung unter dem Nationalsozialismus: Eine Dokumentation zur Bevölkerungsstatistik im Dritten Reich*. Berlin, 2001.

Wildt, Michael, ed. *Die Judenpolitik des SD von 1935 bis 1938: Eine Dokumentation*. Munich, 1995.

———. *An Uncompromising Generation: The Nazi Leadership of the Reich Security Main Office*. Translated by Tom Lampert. Madison, WI, 2010.

Willems, Susanne. *Der entsiedelte Jude, Albert Speers Wohnungsmarktpolitik für den Berliner Hauptstadtbau*. Berlin, 2000.

Witte, Peter, Michael Wildt, Martina Voigt, Dieter Pohl, Peter Klein, Christian Gerlach, Christoph Dieckmann, and Andrej, eds. *Der Dienstkalender Heinrich Himmlers 1941/42*. Hamburg, 1999.

Wojak, Irmtrud, and Peter Hayes, eds. *"Arisierung" im Nationalsozialismus: Volksgemeinschaft, Raub und Gedächtnis*. Frankfurt am Main and New York, 2000.

Zibell, Stephanie. *Jakob Sprenger (1884–1945): NS-Gauleiter und Reichsstatthalter in Hessen*. Darmstadt, 1999.

Zimmermann, Moshe. *Die deutschen Juden in der Geschichte der Shoah: Keine Exklave!* Tübingen, 2002.

———. *Deutsche gegen Deutsche: Das Schicksal der Juden 1938–1945*. Berlin, 2008.

INDEX